WORLDVI

WORLDVIEW

The History of a Concept

DAVID K. NAUGLE

WILLIAM B. EERDMANS PUBLISHING COMPANY
GRAND RAPIDS, MICHIGAN / CAMBRIDGE, U.K.

Wm. B. Eerdmans Publishing Co.
255 Jefferson Ave. S.E., Grand Rapids, Michigan 49503 /
P.O. Box 163, Cambridge CB3 9PU U.K.

Printed in the United States of America

07 06 05 04 03 02   7 6 5 4 3 2 1

Library of Congress Cataloging-in-Publication Data

Naugle, David K.
Worldview: the history of a concept / David K. Naugle.
p.   cm.
Includes bibliographical references and index.
ISBN 0-8028-4761-7 (pbk.: alk. paper)
1. Christianity.   I. Title.

BR121.3.N38   2002
230 — dc21
2002019439

www.eerdmans.com

Dedicated to:

Deemie,
whose "worth is far above jewels"
(Proverbs 31:10)

Courtney,
who is growing up as
"a corner pillar fashioned as for a palace"
(Psalm 144:12)

Dave and Beverly Naugle,
parents of whom "the world is not worthy"
(Hebrews 11:38)

Mark Naugle,
a brother who is also "a friend who sticks closer than a brother"
(Proverbs 18:24)

Contents

CONTENTS

Contents

CONTENTS

Let me repeat once more that a man's vision is the great fact about him. Who cares for Carlyle's reasons, or Schopenhauer's, or Spencer's? A philosophy is the expression of a man's intimate character, and all definitions of the universe are but the deliberately adopted reactions of human characters upon it.

William James, *A Pluralistic Universe*

Those who have not discovered that world view is the most important thing about a man, as about the men composing a culture, should consider the train of circumstances which have with perfect logic proceeded from this. The denial of universals carries with it the denial of everything transcending experience. The denial of everything transcending experience means inevitably — though ways are found to hedge on this — the denial of truth.

Richard Weaver, *Ideas Have Consequences*

But there are some people, nevertheless — and I am one of them — who think that the most practical and important thing about a man is still his view of the universe. We think that for a landlady considering a lodger, it is important to know his income, but still more important to know his philosophy. We think that for a general about to fight an enemy, it is important to know the enemy's numbers, but still more important to know the enemy's philosophy. We think the question is not whether the theory of the cosmos affects matters, but whether, in the long run, anything else affects them.

G. K. Chesterton, *Heretics*

But this means . . . that no human conception of the cosmic process can replace God as the object of the belief in providence. Man makes such conceptions. It is inevitable that he should do so, for otherwise he would not be capable of any practical orientation and decision. It is difficult to see how to forbid this. It belongs to his very life as man to do it. Every man has some conception at least of his own life and that of his nearest fellow; a picture of his own or someone else's life-work as it has so far developed and will do so, or should or should not do so, according to his insight, understanding and judgment. His particular notion of those different determinations of creaturely being, of good and evil, right and wrong, weal and woe etc., will naturally play an important part in this. Such pictures may have a wider reference. They may be pictures of the life-process of a society, e.g., the Church, or a particular form of the Church, or a nation, or group of nations, or the whole of human history. Some standards, moral or amoral, technical, cultural, political or economic, will dominate the one who forms them, leading him to assert progress or decline, formation, reformation or deformation, and determining both his assessment of the past and his expectations, yearnings and fears for the future. And such pictures, always on the same assumptions on the part of the one who forms them, may have an even wider reference. They may embrace the whole of being known to man, perhaps as a kind of evolution, perhaps more modestly as an analysis and description of the eternal movement of all being and its laws and contingencies, possibly including or defiantly or gaily excluding the good God, who at bottom, subject to what the one who forms them thinks concerning Him, might well be able to call some place his own within this total picture. There is no objection to man making these small and great conceptions of the course of things. Indeed, there is much to be said for it. . . . Our present point is that no such conception can replace God as the object of the belief in providence.

Karl Barth, *Church Dogmatics* III/3 (§11.48.2)

Foreword

I t was just after the Second World War that I first heard the phrase "world and life view." After nearly five years in the military, a young person trying to see life and live it from a Christian perspective, I had finally made it to college. One or two of my teachers, I noticed, would draw attention to presuppositions and use the term "Christian worldview." It could not have been more timely, for the terrible conflict we had just survived — as well as barrack room debates — had revealed conflicting perspectives on life. More than half a century later, worldview disagreements continue in international affairs, culture wars, bioethics, and all the academic disciplines, and for that matter in everything we think and do. For it is the very nature of world and life views to be all-inclusive.

This was recently brought to the fore by public reactions to George Marsden's revealing study of secularization in *The Soul of the American University* and by his subsequent title, *The Outrageous Idea of Christian Scholarship*, which proposed that Christian perspectives should be acceptable in a pluralistic university. In arguing the legitimacy of Christian learning, he effectively called into question the Enlightenment myth of worldview-neutral reasoning. What Christian academics have long asserted is that biblical religion is not inimical to serious scholarship but motivates it, illumines the mind, opens new avenues for inquiry, and draws things together in a meaningful whole. All truth in the final analysis is about the ways and works of God. But the secular academy under the spell of modernity found it outrageous that a place be given to scholarship from a religious point of view: the rule of "reason alone" excludes it.

Christians are by no means alone in rejecting modernity's claims to intellectual neutrality. The postmodern mind defines itself over against the modern, and claims a place at the table for a plurality of perspectives, be they gender-based, ethnic, or whatever. But the Christian objection is more premodern than postmodern; it is basically Augustinian in that faith seeks understanding, and the wisdom of God is both the objective locus of truth and the ultimate source for all possible human knowledge. But as David Naugle points out, the language of worldviews stems from romanticist strains in nineteenth-century idealism and its heirs in the early twentieth-century *Lebensphilosophie* tradition. Yet it has gained wide acceptance in the social sciences and among Christians of various theological traditions, generating discussion of its propriety. For this reason alone, a thorough study of the worldview concept is well worthwhile.

But this volume is important for other reasons too. Some introductions to a Christian worldview talk briefly about the origin of the concept, but to my knowledge no thorough study of this sort exists in the English language. The emergence of postmodern thought makes it both timely and strategic to take stock of the similarities and differences between Christian belief and the concept of a worldview. It is important for apologetics, and for theologians who want to talk about meaning in life, and for Christian educators who need to be explicit about worldviews at work in their disciplines and in society at large, and who try to nurture worldview thinking in their students. The fact is that Western civilization has become thoroughly secularized; Christianity is regarded as largely irrelevant (or ought to be) to culture and science and learning, reduced to a private and inward affair.

David Naugle speaks to these concerns with impassioned scholarship. His philological and historical chapters encapsulate two hundred years of philosophy, and he responds at length to problems that have been raised in theology and social sciences; he goes to the heart of the issues. Here is a volume to keep.

ARTHUR F. HOLMES

Preface

Perhaps the time is right — for ecclesial, cultural, and global reasons — to explore the history of worldview as a concept and to reflect upon it theologically and philosophically. First of all, the last several decades have witnessed an explosion of interest in worldview in certain circles of the evangelical church.[1] Several writers, including Carl Henry, Francis Schaeffer, James Sire, Arthur Holmes, Brian Walsh and Richard Middleton, Albert Wolters, and Charles Colson and Nancy Pearcey have introduced many believers to worldview thinking and its importance. This wave of interest has appeared to some extent in Catholic and Orthodox contexts as well. Christians of all kinds are discovering that overt human beliefs and behaviors, as well as sociocultural phenomena, are — consciously or not — most often rooted in and expressions of some deeper, underlying principle and concept of life. Furthermore, worldview has served a hermeneutic purpose in the church by helping believers understand the cosmic dimensions and all-encompassing implications of biblical revelation. This more generous interpretation has enabled them to eschew reductionistic versions of the faith that have kept it from blooming into full flower. It has also generated salient applications for the ministry of the church, for the Christian life, for apologetics, evangelism, and mission, for education and scholarship, and for a host of other sociocultural concerns. The goals of

1. However, if one particular survey is correct, this explosion of worldview interest has affected a relatively small portion of evangelical Christians. According to a George Barna poll cited by Charles Colson in an interview in *Touchstone: A Journal of Mere Christianity* 12 (November/December 1999): 45, only 12 percent of evangelicals knew what a worldview was, only 12 percent could give an adequate definition, and only 4 percent said they needed to know anything about it. Perhaps, then, this book can serve the twofold purpose of not only providing background on this concept but of stimulating some interest in it as well.

"thinking worldviewishly," of shaping "a Christian mind," and of developing biblical perspectives on all aspects of human life seem to be the order of the day. Along these lines, the notion of worldview has spawned something of a revolution within evangelicalism (and perhaps beyond). Thus, an investigation into the background and nature of this concept appears pertinent.

Second, the presence of a multitude of alternative worldviews is a defining characteristic of contemporary culture. Ours is, indeed, a multicultural, pluralistic age. This wide range of cosmic perspectives on offer stands in some contrast to the basic intellectual unity of the classical and Christian West. Traditional thought affirmed the existence of metaphysical and moral truth and the necessity of understanding and living in the world aright. But since the Renaissance and Enlightenment, things have changed. Human beings at large have rejected any overarching ontic or epistemic authorities and set themselves up autonomously as the *acknowledged* legislators of the world (to invert a line from Percy B. Shelley). Now they claim an essentially divine prerogative to conceptualize reality and shape the nature of life as they please. It is no wonder, then, that the concept of worldview emerged to explain this burgeoning cultural phenomenon of intense religious and philosophical diversity. Even the United States Supreme Court echoes this pluralistic mind-set, arguing in *Planned Parenthood v. Casey* (1992) that each person possesses "the right to define one's own concept of existence, of meaning, of the universe, and of the mystery of human life."[2] For some time now, the result has been an ever-increasing *heteroglossolalia* in which human beings speak about the meaning and purpose of life in radically different tongues. This environment has produced human beings who are more or less "reeds shaken by the wind" (Luke 7:24). It valorizes tolerance, but this single virtue is rarely applied with consistency. In short, the postmodern public square is cognitively dissonant and morally cacophonous, bordering on chaos. Thus, if we hope to understand the cultural maelstrom in which we presently live, then we must become better acquainted with the intellectual career of a central conception that elucidates it well — namely worldview, with its emphasis on the various ways in which human beings have sought to depict reality.

Third, since the horrific events of 11 September 2001 in New York City and Washington, D.C., many thoughtful observers have championed the "clash of civilizations" thesis as one perceptive way to understand the present state of global affairs. The best known, though not the only, proponent of this perspective is the Harvard professor of political science, Samuel P. Huntington. His virtually prophetic (and controversial) argument is set forth in a celebrated article

---

2. *Planned Parenthood v. Casey,* 505 U.S. 833 (1992).

in *Foreign Affairs* (1993) and in his book *The Clash of Civilizations and the Re-making of World Order* (1996).[3] Huntington's basic point is that in the post–Cold War, geopolitical world, the most important distinctions and sources of conflict among human beings are no longer ideological, political, or economic. They are cultural. "Peoples and nations," he writes, "are attempting to answer the most basic question humans can face: Who are we? And they are answering that question in the traditional way human beings have answered it, by reference to the things that mean most to them."[4] And the things that mean the most to most people are their ancestry, language, history, values, customs, institutions, and especially religion. At the heart, then, of this current culture war — whether at a local, national, or international level — is a clash of worldviews. Sometimes the clash is more than verbal. More and more, it seems, the conflicts between competitive ways of conceptualizing human existence turn bloody. This pressing fact alone would be enough to justify an investigation into the worldview concept.

But these "collisions of consciousness," as Peter Berger calls them, which reside at the center of the current political situation, have also been a determining factor in the drama of history since time immemorial. The struggle over first principles marks the human condition. Ideas do, indeed, have consequences, as Richard Weaver has taught us. And yet there is an even deeper layer of reality to consider when reflecting upon the ideological discord that resides at the heart of the human story. From the perspective of Christian theism, a clash of worldviews also assumes a crucial role in the hidden, spiritual battle between the kingdom of God and the kingdom of Satan in which the very truth of things is at stake. Between these regimes a conflict of epic proportion rages for the minds and hearts, and thus the lives and destinies, of all men and women, all the time. Since nothing could be of greater final importance than the way human beings understand God, themselves, the cosmos, and their place in it, it is not surprising that a worldview warfare is at the heart of the conflict between the powers of good and evil. Consequently, an in-depth look at a concept that plays such a pivotal role in human affairs seems particularly worthwhile.

But even apart from these factors that make a study of worldview a timely one, the notion itself, having suffered a measure of neglect, is deserving of some overdue attention. There are, to be sure, a sizable number of fine, accessible

---

3. Samuel P. Huntington, "Clash of Civilizations?" *Foreign Affairs* 72 (Summer 1993): 22-49; *The Clash of Civilizations and the Remaking of World Order* (New York: Simon & Schuster, A Touchstone Book, 1996).

4. Huntington, *The Clash of Civilizations*, p. 21.

works on worldview *alternatives* of the religious and philosophical kind. The concept has also surfaced in a variety of discipline-specific studies. And, of course, German-speaking scholars have investigated the career of worldview — or *Weltanschauung* — quite extensively. However, no work in English has been written that amasses a substantial portion of the literature on worldview from the various disciplines — theology, philosophy, religion, the natural sciences, the social sciences, etc. — and reflects upon it in a comprehensive, systematic way. There is a considerable gap in Anglo-American scholarship in this regard. This book is designed, therefore, to reverse this present situation through an extensive, interdisciplinary study of the worldview concept. My hope is that this volume will supply what appears to be a missing chapter in the history of ideas.

Now I should perhaps clarify this book's basic thrust. It is *not* primarily an investigation of the multiple worldviews that have adorned the intellectual and cultural landscape. I will make no effort per se to discuss, except indirectly, basic worldviews such as theism, deism, naturalism, pantheism, polytheism, and so on. In other words, this book is not a study in religious or philosophic pluralism. Rather, this book *is* an historical examination of an intellectual concept. My goal is to concentrate on how worldview has been treated by a variety of thinkers, including Christians, in the course of its theoretical development. Thus, the very *idea* of worldview itself is what is chiefly on display in this work. Those looking for a discussion of alternative belief systems, including Christianity, will for the most part be disappointed and must look elsewhere.[5]

So with this fundamental purpose in mind, what is the overall design of this book and its basic points? In chapter 1, I begin by taking a look at the "wonder of worldview" in evangelical Protestantism. I suggest that the headwaters of Christian worldview thinking can be traced back to the Scottish Presbyterian theologian James Orr and to the Dutch Reformed polymath Abraham Kuyper. I highlight the contributions of these two pioneering thinkers and flesh out their ideas on this significant theme. I proceed to show how the popularity of worldview as a comprehensive approach to the faith was enhanced in the work of Gordon H. Clark, Carl F. H. Henry, Herman Dooyeweerd, and Francis A. Schaeffer. In chapter 2, I investigate the "wonder of worldview" in Roman Catholicism and Eastern Orthodoxy, including a brief examination of Karol Wojtyla's (Pope John Paul II's) vision of Christian humanism. Catholic and Orthodox interpretations of reality assume a robust sacramental and liturgical cast and as such provide a helpful complement to standard evangelical reflection on this topic.

---

5. See both appendices at the end of this volume for books on Christian and other worldviews.

Because the worldview concept has notably influenced these three major Christian traditions, I propose that there is a need to understand something about its origin and historical development. So I turn in chapter 3 to a philological history of worldview. Here the spotlight focuses upon the origin of the term "worldview" *(Weltanschauung)* in Immanuel Kant's *Critique of Judgment* (1790) and follows its rapid proliferation in Germany, Europe, and the English-speaking world. In chapters 4-6, I undertake a philosophical history of worldview in the nineteenth and twentieth centuries through a study of the insights of key Western thinkers on this notion. These include G. W. F. Hegel, Søren Kierkegaard, Wilhelm Dilthey, Friedrich Nietzsche, Edmund Husserl, Karl Jaspers, Martin Heidegger, Ludwig Wittgenstein, Donald Davidson, and the postmodernists (Jacques Derrida and Michel Foucault). In chapters 7-8, I give attention to a disciplinary history of worldview and examine the role this idea has played respectively in the natural sciences (Michael Polanyi and Thomas Kuhn) and the social sciences (psychology: Sigmund Freud and Carl Jung; sociology: Karl Mannheim, Peter Berger, Thomas Luckmann, Karl Marx, and Friedrich Engels; anthropology: Michael Kearney and Robert Redfield).

As this survey shows, worldview has enjoyed a distinguished place in the history of recent thought. However, because the term has acquired certain nuances during its intellectual pilgrimage, several Christian critics have raised concerns about its suitability as a way of expressing evangelical versions of biblical faith. So, in chapter 9, "Theological Reflections on Worldview," I attempt to set forth a Christian view of worldview. Here I highlight the sociological relativity of worldview theory itself and offer a biblical understanding of this notion that connects it with a proper view of objectivity and subjectivity as well as the doctrines of sin and spiritual warfare, grace and redemption. In this context, chapter 10 is devoted to philosophical reflections on worldview. I suggest that a worldview is best understood as a semiotic phenomenon, especially as a system of narrative signs that establishes a powerful framework within which people think (reason), interpret (hermeneutics), and know (epistemology). In chapter 11, "Concluding Reflections," I offer a critical assessment of the church's use of worldview by pointing out its dangers and benefits — philosophically, theologically, and spiritually. Lastly, in two appendices I provide summaries of additional contributions to evangelical reflection on worldview and offer a bibliography of Christian books on this topic.

Overall (but especially in chapter 9), I argue that a worldview is an inescapable function of the human heart and is central to the identity of human beings as *imago Dei*. This theme can be detected directly or indirectly throughout the work, and it is illustrated in the prologue and epilogue based on selected episodes in *The Chronicles of Narnia* by C. S. Lewis.

Throughout my Christian life, I have taken an interest in worldview in general, and a Christian or biblical worldview in particular. Three extraordinary Christian communities have nourished my thinking on this topic over the years. I became a believer at the age of seventeen while watching a televised Billy Graham Crusade in August 1970. A week or two later I began my senior year in high school and quickly became involved in the Young Life Club there. The spiritual growth I experienced during the next twelve months eventually led me to an association with the Young Life Leadership group in Fort Worth, Texas, for the better part of the decade of the 1970s. In this remarkable Christian community — where in-depth Bible study, systematic theology, and the writings of C. S. Lewis and Francis Schaeffer were standard fare — I first encountered the notion of a Christian worldview and was encouraged to think about it deeply and live it out faithfully. Those were the days!

By the time the 1980s arrived, I had earned a master of theology degree, with a major in Old Testament Hebrew and a minor in New Testament Greek. A year after graduation, I was hired by a local Bible church to share in the leadership of a campus ministry at The University of Texas at Arlington, where I also taught religion courses as an adjunct professor. Meanwhile I had enrolled in a doctoral program in biblical and systematic theology. Toward the end of that course of study, however, I experienced a significant paradigm shift from dispensational premillennialism to covenant, reformed theology. Like a scientist undergoing a scientific revolution, I began to see and live in the world differently. Exposure to thinkers in this newfound tradition began to solidify and deepen my understanding of the Christian worldview. I especially relished the discovery of the "creation, fall, redemption" schema as the outline of Scripture and as the basis of the divine economy in history. From then until now, my imagination has been captivated by this biblical vision of the world. So, when the leadership of our campus ministry fell exclusively into my hands, there was no question in my mind about what its mission would be: "Helping College Students Develop a Christian Worldview"! In this thriving community of university students, headquartered next to campus in a large, old, two-story house we called "The Cornerstone," we explored as effectively as we could what it meant to take the lordship of Christ over the whole of life seriously. Those, too, were the days!

By the time the 1990s arrived, I had earned that Th.D. But my theological paradigm shift resulted in my dismissal from the church where I had served for eight and a half years. After a season of unemployment, I was hired at Dallas Baptist University where I have had the privilege of establishing our philosophy department and directing our Pew College Society. In a community of some of the best and brightest students on campus, I have, by the grace of God, continued to encourage them in this process of biblical worldview formation. We have attempted to actualize this objective through regular course work, and also through a variety of extracurricular activities including study retreats, guest lecturers, student conferences, film nights, and so on. To the glory of God I must say that it has been a rewarding experience to see a number of students make the wonderful discovery of the creation/fall/redemption scenario and undergo a significant transformation at the root of their being and in the fruit of their lives. These now are the days!

But allow me to backtrack just a bit. Looking for something to do while unemployed and searching for a new opportunity of service, I enrolled in a Ph.D. humanities program back at UT-Arlington. It took me nine years to finish as a part-time student. But my studies finally culminated in a dissertation on the history and theory of the concept of worldview, this present book's first incarnation. So now I gladly thank all the people who have helped make both of these projects possible. First are those members of my dissertation committee who capably and graciously guided me through that arduous but rewarding process: Jan Swearingen, chair (now at Texas A&M University), Tim Mahoney, Charles Nussbaum, Tom Porter, and Harry Reeder.

I owe a significant debt of gratitude to Albert Wolters of Redeemer University College, whose essay "On the Idea of Worldview and Its Relation to Philosophy"[6] inspired the original project. Professor Wolters's article contained a very short section (less than a page) on the history of the concept of worldview and mentioned his unpublished manuscript on the same topic. He kindly sent a copy of it to me and it proved to be an invaluable resource. Thanks to him also for his courteous annual inquiries at AAR/SBL meetings on the progress of my work!

I am grateful to Jim Sire, Arthur Holmes, and Steve Garber, who read and offered many helpful comments on lengthy portions of the manuscript of the book. A very special thanks to Arthur Holmes for writing the foreword to this volume and for generous help and moral support over the years. Thanks also to Tim Mahoney for his contributions to the chapter on worldview in Catholicism and Orthodoxy. Thanks to Dr. Deborah McCollister, my colleague in the English department at Dallas Baptist University, for her careful reading of a large portion of the manuscript in search of errors of form and grammar. Thanks also to my friend Paul R. Buckley, assistant editor of the religion section of *The Dallas Morning News*, for his review of the introduction. Thanks to my student

---

6. Albert M. Wolters, "On the Idea of Worldview and Its Relation to Philosophy," in *Stained Glass: Worldviews and Social Science,* ed. Paul A. Marshall, Sander Griffioen, and Richard J. Mouw, Christian Studies Today (Lanham, Md.: University Press of America, 1989), pp. 14-25.

research assistant, Joy McCalla, who helped me gather and organize copious amounts of bibliographic material, especially early on in this endeavor. I am also grateful to the administration of Dallas Baptist University for a semester's sabbatical in the fall of 2000, without which completing this work would have been much more difficult. And I am grateful to the editors at William B. Eerdmans Publishing Company, especially Jon Pott and Jennifer Hoffman, for their consummate professionalism in working with me on this project and seeing it through to completion.

I also greatly appreciate a number of friends and colleagues who have encouraged and supported me along the way with their words and prayers: Brent Christopher, Greg Kelm, Gail Linam, Carey and Pam Moore, Rob Moore, John Plotts, Mike Rosato, Todd Still, Fred White, and Mike Williams. And to those special students, past and present, in the philosophy department and the Pew College Society at DBU — who have formed a close-knit spiritual and learning community on campus and who have asked me often about the progress of this book and seemed as eager about it as I was — to them I express my heartfelt thanks.

I thank in a most profound way my wonderful family, my wife Deemie and our dear Courtney, for all their love and support, patience and sacrifice, as I was writing this book. Also I want to express sincere gratitude to my parents, Dave and Beverly Naugle, and to my brother Mark Naugle for their unconditional love over the years and for their encouragement as I worked on this project. It is dedicated to them all.

Above all, thanks and praise be to God — Father, Son, and Holy Spirit — for answering many prayers regarding the composition of this book. May it please him in all respects, glorify his holy name, and benefit his church and world. "Now to the King eternal, immortal, invisible, the only God, be honor and glory forever and ever. Amen" (1 Tim. 1:17).

Holy Saturday   DAVID K. NAUGLE
March 30, 2002
Dallas, Texas

Uncle Andrew in C. S. Lewis's
The Magician's Nephew

At the heart of *The Magician's Nephew* is the story of the founding of Narnia. But its appearance is interpreted in two very different ways by two very different sorts of people with two very different kinds of hearts. The story runs as follows. Digory and Polly through magic rings had inadvertently brought the wicked Queen Jadis with them to London where she takes up with Digory's uncle Andrew, who is an amateur magician and occultist. The children attempt to return the witch to her homeland of Charn where she was empress. But by accident they arrive in Narnia at the very moment of its creation by Aslan, not only with the wicked queen but also with Uncle Andrew as well as a friendly London cabby and his horse, Strawberry. It was an empty world when they first arrived, very much like nothing. But then in the darkness, a Voice began to sing in the most sonorous tones imaginable. All at once the blackness overhead was ablaze with stars who joined in on the chorus, though in lesser voices. As the main Voice reached a crescendo, the sun was born, laughing for joy as it arose! In the fresh light of the young sun stood the Lion Aslan — huge, shaggy, and bright as it was singing the new world into being. As his song continued, the valley grew green, trees were born, flowers blossomed, and then, as a stretch of grassy land was bubbling up like water in a pot and swelling into humps, out came the animals great and small. For a while "there was so much cawing, cooing, crowing, braying, neighing, baying, barking, lowing, bleating, and trumpeting"[1] that they could barely here the Lion's song. Then in a solemn moment, there was a flash of fire and Aslan's fiat: "Narnia, Narnia, Narnia, awake. Love. Think. Speak. Be walking trees. Be talking beasts. Be divine waters"

---

1. C. S. Lewis, *The Magician's Nephew* (New York: Macmillan, Collier Books, 1955, 1970), p. 114. Subsequent references will be made parenthetically in the text.

(p. 116). And the creatures replied in unison: "Hail, Aslan. We hear and obey. We are awake. We love. We think. We speak. We know" (p. 117). And he said to them: "Creatures, I give you yourselves. . . . I give to you forever this land of Narnia. I give you the woods, the fruits, the rivers. I give you the stars and I give you myself" (p. 118). And after the first joke and the formation of a security council, the creation of Narnia was complete.

However, when compared to the impression this whole glorious episode made on the cabby and the children, it looked totally different from Uncle Andrew's perspective (not to mention that of Queen Jadis, for she also hated it). What was his impression of the whole episode, and why did he respond to it so differently?

When they first heard the Voice, and the stars shone, and the first light of the sun was revealed, like the cabby and the children, Uncle Andrew's mouth fell open, but not with joy like theirs. He did not like the Voice. His knees shook and his teeth chattered, and he could not run because of his fear. Still, "If he could have got away from it by creeping into a rat's hole, he would have done so" (p. 100). He agreed with the witch that they were in a terrible world, a most disagreeable place, and if he were younger, Uncle Andrew affirmed he would have tried to kill the brute of a lion with a gun. For like the witch, all he seemed to be able to think of was killing things. There was one exception, however. The only thing he valued about this magical world, where new lampposts grew out of the ground from the parts of old ones, was that it possessed commercial possibilities even greater than America. Bury bits and pieces of train engines and battleships and watch new ones grow. "They'll cost nothing," he dreamed, "and I can sell 'em at full prices in England. I shall be a millionaire" (p. 111). Nonetheless, it was that song of the Lion's that he detested more than anything else. It made him think and feel things he just did not want to think and feel. So he convinced himself completely that it was nothing but an ugly roar. But if you suppress the truth, and make yourself more stupid than you really are, you often succeed, just as Uncle Andrew did. "He soon did hear nothing but roaring in Aslan's song. Soon he couldn't have heard anything else even if he had wanted to. And when at last the Lion spoke and said, 'Narnia awake,' he didn't hear any words: he heard only a snarl. And when the Beasts spoke in answer, he heard only barkings, growlings, bayings and howlings. And when they laughed — well, you can imagine. That was worse for Uncle Andrew than anything that had happened yet. Such a horrid, bloodthirsty din of hungry and angry brutes he had never heard in his life" (p. 126).

But why did Uncle Andrew interpret the founding of Narnia by Aslan's song in such a dreadful manner? What was it about him that gave him such a different view of this enchanted world? The answer, Lewis suggests, is this: "For what you see and hear depends a good deal on where you are standing: it also depends on what sort of person you are" (p. 125).

Because of who he was and where he stood, Uncle Andrew saw everything differently and made himself unable to hear Aslan's voice. And as the Lion himself said, "If I spoke to him, he would hear only growlings and roarings. Oh Adam's sons, how cleverly you defend yourselves against all that might do you good!" (p. 171).

Chapter One

The Wonder of Worldview I:
Protestant Evangelicalism

Conceiving of Christianity as a worldview[1] has been one of the most significant developments in the recent history of the church. Whether it is understood theologically "as a theistic system exhibiting the rational coherence of
the biblical revelation," to use Carl Henry's phrase,[2] or embraced as the overall
narrative of creation, fall, and redemption, Christianity as a worldview has
risen to considerable prominence in the last one hundred and fifty years. Its
popularity is due in part to its attempt to provide a comprehensive explanation
of reality that is rooted in the Word of God. Since the onset of modernity, secu-
larizing forces in contemporary culture have been virtually irresistible and the
consequences for the church and her conception of the faith have been substantial. Christianity's comprehensive scope was soon forgotten, theistic perspectives were squeezed out of public life, and the essence of the faith was reduced
to matters of personal piety. "We have rather lost sight of the idea," bemoaned
Dorothy Sayers during the turbulent days of the Second World War, "that
Christianity is supposed to be an interpretation of the universe."[3] In this recent
setting the concept of worldview has, in a sense, come to the rescue. It offers the

---

1. The English word "worldview" is derived from the noted German term *Weltanschauung*. Both will be used interchangeably throughout this book.

2. Carl F. H. Henry, "Fortunes of the Christian World View," *Trinity Journal*, n.s., 19
(1998): 163.

3. Dorothy L. Sayers, *1937-1943: From Novelist to Playwright*, vol. 2 of *The Letters of Dorothy L. Sayers*, ed. Barbara Reynolds (New York: St. Martin's Press, 1998), p. 158. Even Friedrich
Nietzsche recognized the all-encompassing, coherent nature of the Christian faith. He writes:
"Christianity is a system, a *whole* view of things thought out together." See *Twilight of the Idols*,
in *The Portable Nietzsche*, ed. and trans. Walter Kaufmann (New York: Penguin Books, 1988),
p. 515.

church a fresh perspective on the holistic nature, cosmic dimensions, and universal applications of the faith. Plus, the explanatory power, intellectual coherence, and pragmatic effectiveness of the Christian worldview not only make it exceedingly relevant for believers personally, but also establish a solid foundation for vigorous cultural and academic engagement.

Though the word "worldview" is of relatively recent origin, such a grand, systematic vision of the faith is not. It has a distinguished genealogy, going all the way back, of course, to the Bible itself with its doctrine of a trinitarian God who is the creator and redeemer of heaven and earth and whose sovereignty rules over all. It was developed by many of the Church Fathers and medieval theologian-philosophers, Augustine and Aquinas in particular. It was deepened in biblical ways by the reformers Luther and Calvin, and by their successors among the English and American Puritans. Out of the stream of the Reformation tradition, this expansive interpretation of Christianity has reached the North American evangelical community, where it has been conceived as a worldview, and as such has had a notable impact. In this chapter we will explore the history of this impact, seeking to ascertain who in the evangelical tradition is responsible for originally conceiving of Christianity as a *Weltanschauung*, and what its influence has been.

Original Worldview Thinkers in Protestant Evangelicalism

The headwaters of the worldview tradition among evangelical Protestants can be traced to two primary sources, both of which flow from the theological wellsprings of the reformer from Geneva, John Calvin (1509-64).[4] The first is the Scottish Presbyterian theologian, apologist, minister, and educator James Orr (1844-1913). The second is the Dutch neo-Calvinist theologian and statesman Abraham Kuyper (1837-1920). Appropriating the concept from the broader intel-

---

4. Calvin himself apparently recognized that his own theological system constituted the basis for a "Christian philosophy," which may be roughly analogous to a Christian worldview. In introducing the subject matter of his *Institutes of the Christian Religion*, he informs his readers that God provides guidance to help simple people discover "the sum of what God meant to teach them in his Word." He then says this cannot be done in any better way than "to treat the chief and weightiest matters comprised in the Christian philosophy." That Calvin understood the Scriptures and his reflections upon them to constitute a comprehensive view of things seems evident. See his *Institutes of the Christian Religion*, ed. John T. McNeill, translated and indexed by Ford Lewis Battles, Library of Christian Classics, vol. 20 (Philadelphia: Westminster, 1960), p. 6. See also n. 8 on the same page for extensive references on the development of the idea of a Christian philosophy in the history of the church.

lectual milieu on the European continent in the middle to late nineteenth century, these two seminal thinkers introduced the vocabulary of worldview into the current of Reformed Christian thought. In their creative efforts they gave birth to an agenda to conceive of biblical faith as a robust, systemic vision of reality that opened up Christianity to full flower so that it could meet the challenges of the modern world head-on. A steady stream of pioneering disciples, including Gordon Clark, Carl Henry, Herman Dooyeweerd, and Francis Schaeffer, have stood in their wake, deliberately raising consciousness among thoughtful believers about the importance of a complete biblical vision of life. We begin this survey of "the wonder of worldview" within evangelicalism with an exposition of the thought of James Orr.

James Orr

According to J. I. Packer, this big, burly, polymathic professor with a pugilistic temper was a "heritage theologian" who contended for "great-tradition Christianity."[5] With this basic judgment Glen Scorgie agrees, demonstrating in his monograph on Orr that his primary theological contribution "can best be described as a call for continuity with the central tenets of evangelical orthodoxy."[6] Such was the need of his times, characterized as they were by the modernist revolution in virtually every department of life, especially in religion, philosophy, and science. During Orr's life the West was undergoing its most catastrophic cultural transition, passing through what C. S. Lewis has referred to aptly as "the un-christening of Europe," leading to the loss of the "Old European" or "Old Western Culture" and to the advent of a "post-Christian" age.[7] At

5. J. I. Packer, "On from Orr: Cultural Crisis, Rational Realism and Incarnational Ontology," in *Reclaiming the Great Tradition: Evangelicals, Catholics, and Orthodox in Dialogue*, ed. James S. Cutsinger (Downers Grove, Ill.: InterVarsity, 1997), pp. 163, 161.

6. Glen G. Scorgie, *A Call for Continuity: The Theological Contribution of James Orr* (Macon, Ga.: Mercer University Press, 1988), p. 2. To reinforce this thesis, Scorgie quotes Orr in an epigraph: "When I am asked, as I sometimes am, which of these articles of Evangelical faith I am prepared to part with at the instance of modern thought, and in the interests of a reconstructed theology, I answer, with fullest confidence: None of them." The description of Orr in the first sentence is taken from pp. 39, 57. For an abridgment of Scorgie's discussion of Orr, see his "James Orr," in *Handbook of Evangelical Theologians*, ed. Walter A. Elwell (Grand Rapids: Baker, 1993), pp. 12-25. For additional discussion on Orr, see Alan P. F. Sell, *Defending and Declaring the Faith: Some Scottish Examples, 1860-1920*, foreword by James B. Torrance (Colorado Springs: Helmers and Howard, 1987), pp. 137-71.

7. C. S. Lewis, "De Descriptione Temporum," in *Selected Literary Essays*, ed. Walter Hooper (Cambridge: At the University Press, 1969), pp. 4-5, 12.

this pivotal moment in Western Christendom, the burden which weighed heavily on Orr's mind focused upon the exhibition and defense of the Christian faith, and the strategy he chose to accomplish this task was the strategy of *Weltanschauung*. The opportunity to articulate the Christian faith as a total worldview arose when Orr was invited by the United Presbyterian Theological College in Edinburgh to present the first of the Kerr Lectures whose stated purpose was for "the promotion of the study of Scientific theology."[8] These addresses took him three years to prepare, were delivered in 1891, and were published in 1893 as *The Christian View of God and the World*.[9] This book, which established his reputation as a theologian and apologist of note, is regarded by many as his magnum opus. In it he devoted the first chapter and several corresponding endnotes to the concept of *Weltanschauung* in general, and to the idea of the Christian worldview in particular.

At the outset of chapter 1, Orr felt constrained to begin with an explanation of the unique title of his book. As one preeminently familiar with nineteenth-century German theology, he encountered the virtually omnipresent term *Weltanschauung* and its synonym *Weltansicht* in academic theology books, especially those dealing with the philosophy of religion. According to Orr, the English equivalents of these words tended to be associated with physical nature, but in German they were virtually technical terms, "denoting the widest view which the mind can take of things in the effort to grasp them together as a whole from the standpoint of some particular philosophy or theology." In Orr's opinion the Christian faith provides such a standpoint, developing its loftiest principle and view of life into "an ordered whole."[10] While defending Christian doctrines atomistically may have its place, he believed that the worldview concept enabled him to deal with Christianity in its entirety as a system. Furthermore, given the increasingly anti-Christian zeitgeist of the late nineteenth century, he perceived "that if Christianity is to be effectually defended from the attacks made upon it, it is the comprehensive method which is rapidly becoming the more urgent." Nothing less than a fresh, coherent presentation of the Christian definition of reality in all its fullness would be adequate for the times. Orr's thinking in this regard, which finds an identical echo in Abraham Kuyper a bit later, is worth detailing.

8. *Proceedings of the Synod of the United Presbyterian Church* (1887), pp. 489-90, quoted in Scorgie, *A Call for Continuity*, p. 47.

9. James Orr, *The Christian View of God and the World as Centering in the Incarnation* (Edinburgh: Andrew Eliot, 1893). This book has undergone many editions and reprints, the most recent being *The Christian View of God and the World*, foreword by Vernon C. Grounds (Grand Rapids: Kregel, 1989).

10. Orr, *The Christian View*, p. 3.

The opposition which Christianity has to encounter is no longer confined to special doctrines or to points of supposed conflict with the natural sciences, . . . but extends to the whole manner of conceiving of the world, and of man's place in it, the manner of conceiving of the entire system of things, natural and moral, of which we form a part. It is no longer an opposition of detail, but of principle. This circumstance necessitates an equal extension of the line of the defence. It is the Christian view of things in general which is attacked, and it is by an exposition and vindication of the Christian view of things as a whole that the attack can most successfully be met.[11]

This conviction generated the purpose of Orr's book. If Christianity was to be exhibited and defended in a way that engaged the contemporary mind effectively, it could not be presented in a typical piecemeal fashion. Rather, the radical shift in the metaphysical underpinnings of the West called for a new strategy, and the fashionable German conception of *Weltanschauung* provided the key. Thus, as Orr's title indicates, his goal was to present in a systematic way a *Christian View of God and the World*.

Furthermore, according to Orr, this Christian vision of reality had a focus: it was rooted in the person of Jesus Christ. This is indicated in the second part of his title: *As Centering in the Incarnation*. An entire worldview was bound up in an historic, orthodox Christology. Indeed, believing in the biblical presentation of Jesus entailed a host of additional convictions, forming an overall view of things. "He who with his whole heart believes in Jesus as the Son of God is thereby committed to much else besides. He is committed to a view of God, to a view of man, to a view of sin, to a view of Redemption, to a view of human destiny, found only in Christianity. This forms a 'Weltanschauung,' or 'Christian view of the world,' which stands in marked contrast with theories wrought out from a purely philosophical or scientific standpoint."[12]

Indeed, Orr rightly asserts that Jesus held to a particular conception of the universe, one grounded in the Old Testament, fulfilled in himself, and distinguished fully from contemporary humanistic perspectives. Biblical belief in Jesus Christ logically entailed a commitment to his *Weltanschauung*. For the Scottish theologian, then, Christianity was a christocentric worldview, a revolutionary and apologetically expedient approach to the faith necessitated by the challenges of modernity at its apex.

To contextualize his presentation of Christianity as an overall worldview,

---

11. Orr, *The Christian View*, p. 4.
12. Orr, *The Christian View*, p. 4.

Orr proceeds to investigate the history of *Weltanschauung* as a concept. Where did the idea and the word come from in the first place? To answer this question, Orr traces its origin to Immanuel Kant and his notion of a world concept, or *Weltbegriff*. This term functioned as an idea of pure reason to bring the totality of human experience into the unity of a world-whole, or *Weltganz*. In "Note A" to chapter 1, Orr continues his historical investigation, noting that though *Weltanschauung* was not common with Kant (nor with Fichte or Schelling), still his Copernican revolution in philosophy gave momentum to its use, focusing on the human mind about which the world orbited. Hegel also employed it in inquiring about the relationship of a man's religion and of philosophic knowledge to his *Weltanschauung*. From the middle part of the nineteenth century the term flourished, being used frequently to speak of alternative views of reality — theistic, atheistic, pantheistic, and so on.[13] As a result, Orr could confidently affirm in his own day that "Within the last two or three decades the word [*Weltanschauung*] has become exceedingly common in all kinds of books dealing with higher questions of religion and philosophy — so much so as to have become in a manner indispensable."[14] He then concludes his brief history by noting those works in German which have dealt with *Weltanschauung* historically and theoretically (and is surprised at the lack of attention it has received), making special mention of its role in the theology of Albrecht Ritschl.

Though the word is recent, Orr believes the reality of worldview is as old as thought itself. It is found in every historical religion and philosophy, but with varying degrees of sophistication. Crudely developed worldviews are ensconced in ancient cosmogonies and theogonies. More refined versions characterize pre-Socratic philosophies of which Lucretius's naturalism in *De rerum natura* is an example. Comte's religion of humanity is a good illustration of a contemporary *Weltanschauung* "in which knowledge and action are knit up together, and organised into a single view of life."[15]

Orr digs deeper still. What are the causes, he asks, that lead to the formation of worldviews? For him, the answer lies deep within human nature and its native capacities for thinking and acting. *Theoretically*, the human mind is not satisfied with piecemeal knowledge, but seeks integrity in its understanding of reality. Worldviews are generated by the mind's aspiration to a unified comprehension of the universe, drawing together facts, laws, generalizations, and answers to ultimate questions. Even behind the agnostic's refusal to define the

---

13. Orr presents several basic principles used in the "Classification of *Weltanschauungen*" in "Note B" of *The Christian View*, pp. 367-70.

14. Orr, *The Christian View*, p. 365.

15. Orr, *The Christian View*, p. 6.

universe there lurks a unifying theory of reality or what Orr calls "an uncon-scious metaphysic."[16] *Practically,* human beings are motivated from within to find answers to the "why, whence, and whither" questions of life. Worldviews are generated by the mind's quest for a framework to orient people to the world around them and to the ultimate issues of life. Agnostic and naturalistic re-sponses to this existential quest would culminate respectively in nihilism and the elimination of the basis for traditional moral and social responsibility. Nonetheless, according to Orr, worldviews are inescapable realities, rooted in the constitution of human beings who must think about and act in the world.[17]

Orr makes it clear that despite the late nineteenth-century empirically based aversion to metaphysics, "the tendency to the formation of world-systems, or general theories of the universe, was never more powerful" than in his day.[18] This must be due in part to the abiding characteristics of human na-ture and also to the remarkable scientific discovery of the unity which pervades the cosmos: "Everywhere, accordingly, we see a straining after a universal point of view — a grouping and grasping of things together in their unity."[19]

Yet Orr feels a tension between these philosophical reflections and the traditional view of Christianity. What does the faith have to do with such elaborate theorizing and speculative questions? He realizes it is neither a sci-entific system nor a philosophy per se (though it is in harmony with the truth contained in both). Instead it is an historical religion rooted in divine revela-tion and concerned with salvation. Despite this emphasis, Christianity's point of contact with the above issues, Orr believes, is that *it has a particular world-view of its own,* just as other religions and philosophies do. Its own interpreta-tion of reality, however, is rooted in a personal, holy, self-revealing God and a doctrine of redemption. As a *Weltanschauung,* it explains the particulars and purposes of life theistically and unites all things into an ordered whole. "It

16. See Orr's "Note C" on the idea of an "Unconscious Metaphysic," in *The Christian View,* p. 370.

17. E. J. Carnell, perhaps taking his cue from Orr, begins his study of Christian apologetics by investigating these two traits of human nature under the headings "The *Practical* Human Predicament" and "The *Theoretical* Human Predicament." Indeed, his entire defense of the faith centers on the worldview concept, examining "The Need for a Christian World-View" in part 1, "The Rise of the Christian World-View" in part 2, and "The Implications of the Christian World-View" in part 3 of his *An Introduction to Christian Apologetics: A Philosophic Defense of the Trinitarian-Theistic Faith* (1948; reprint, Grand Rapids: Eerdmans, 1981). In the preface to the first edition, he states explicitly that the purpose of his volume is to show "how Christianity is able to answer the fundamental questions of life as adequately as, if not more adequately than, any other world-view" (p. 10).

18. Orr, *The Christian View,* p. 7.

19. Orr, *The Christian View,* p. 8.

has, as every religion should and must have, its own peculiar interpretation to give to the facts of existence; its own way of looking at, and accounting for, the existing natural and moral order; its own idea of a world-aim, and of that 'one far off Divine event,' to which, through slow and painful travail, 'the whole creation moves.' As thus binding together the natural and moral worlds in their highest unity, through reference to their ultimate principle, God, it involves a 'Weltanschauung.'"[20]

A bit later Orr elaborates on the overall purpose of *The Christian View,* and in so doing explains how integral a unified worldview is to biblical religion.

> [T]here is a definite Christian view of things, which has a character, coherence, and unity of its own, and stands in sharp contrast with counter theories and speculations, and . . . this world-view has the stamp of reason and reality upon itself, and can amply justify itself at the bar both of history and of experience. I shall endeavor to show that the Christian view of things forms a logical whole which cannot be infringed on, or accepted or rejected piecemeal, but stands or falls in its integrity, and can only suffer from attempts at amalgamation or compromise with theories which rest on totally distinct bases.[21]

Orr specifies several advantages to approaching Christianity as a *Weltanschauung.* First, this strategy brings into bold relief the difference between Christianity and modern theories of the universe which are unified by a thoroughgoing antisupernaturalism.[22] Second, worldview thinking reconfigures the debate over miracles. The discussion is no longer about this or that particular miraculous event or supernatural occurrence. Rather, it is about the very essence of Christianity as a supernatural religion and about whether the universe ought to be conceived naturalistically or theistically. The debate about miracles, in other words, is ultimately a debate about underlying worldviews. Third, worldview thinking alters the approach of Christianity to opposing viewpoints. There is no need either to be surprised at or to deny outright the truth found in other philosophies and religions; it is there by divine providence. Nor does Christianity need to be modified to accommodate it. Instead, it values the genuine insights other outlooks contain, though they have been severed from their original source. The Christian *Weltanschauung* is the higher system which synthesizes and reunites all truth into a living whole with Christ supreme. Fourth

20. Orr, *The Christian View,* p. 9.

21. Orr, *The Christian View,* p. 16.

22. Orr spells out in more detail the "Antagonism of Christian and Modern Views of the World — Antisupernaturalism of the Latter" in "Note D," *The Christian View,* pp. 370-72.

and finally, a worldview perspective ties the Old and New Testaments together. Christianity is not entirely new, but is dependent upon the rich, concrete, and unique perspective of the Old Testament and carries it through to completion.[23] The biblical religion that results is distinguished from all others by its monotheism, clarity, unity, moral character, and teleology, establishing a complete view of life that cannot be explained except on the basis of divine revelation.[24] For Orr, such are the various advantages that follow from apprehending Christianity as a total worldview.

Orr's project had potential detractors, however, and they voiced two primary objections. He concludes his reflections by responding to both of them. First are those — Friedrich Schleiermacher and his followers in particular — who advocate a theology of feeling and identify religion with the conditions and affections of the heart. Consequently they rule out the cognitive element from spirituality altogether, and deny that there is any such thing as an intellectual Christian *Weltanschauung*. To this objection Orr offers a detailed response. In sum, he asserts that such a position is based upon several false presuppositions, and that it misunderstands the very nature of religion itself.[25] Orr highlights the necessary ideational component to religious life, especially in Christianity, which has distinguished itself by its doctrinal emphasis. Thus he states, "A strong, stable, religious life can be built up on no other ground than that of intelligent conviction. Christianity, therefore, addresses itself to the intelligence as well as to the heart."[26] A theology of feeling, therefore, is unsuccessful in its attempt to destroy the project of forming a cogent Christian worldview.

Second, Orr takes on a tradition in Continental theology, especially the school of Albrecht Ritschl, which does not deny the existence of a biblically based worldview but does make a strong distinction between religious and theoretic conceptions of the world. This position, which has Kantian roots, demarcates between the spiritual and scientific spheres of knowledge, and separates positive facts from personal values. On the basis of this dichotomy, any alleged Christian worldview is automatically consigned to the categories of subjectivity and practicality, and is disqualified as epistemically credible. Orr grants that religious and theoretical knowledge are not strictly the same, differences in aim, nature, and object being the most important. Still he takes on this epistemic dualism and defends a holistic view of truth and the unified operation of the

23. Orr details the "Uniqueness of the Old Testament View" in "Note F," *The Christian View*, pp. 376-78.

24. Orr, *The Christian View*, pp. 9-15.

25. Orr discusses the "Nature and Definition of Religion" in "Note H," *The Christian View*, pp. 380-85.

26. Orr, *The Christian View*, pp. 20-21.

human mind. In good Augustinian fashion he reunites faith and reason, stating that "faith cannot but seek to advance knowledge — that is, to the reflective and scientific understanding of its own content."[27] Hence he restores cognitive credibility to the process of Christian worldview construction. As he puts it, "I conclude, therefore, that it is legitimate to speak of a Christian 'Weltanschauung,' and that we are not debarred from investigating its relations to theoretic knowledge."[28]

Orr's theological contribution has been declared by some unfavorable critics, especially his academic peers, to be minimal.[29] This in itself is a questionable judgment. However, at least in one respect — that of relating *Weltanschauung* and Christianity — his contribution has been of enduring value. If for no other reason, Orr deserves credit for being one of the first English-speaking theologians to undertake this kind of project. As J. I. Packer has stated, *The Christian View* was "in fact the first attempt in Britain to articulate a full-scale Christian world and life view against modernist variants."[30] That the Christian faith may be conceived as a christocentric, self-authenticating system of biblical truth characterized by inner integrity, rational coherence, empirical verisimilitude, and existential power is one of his most distinctive contributions. In touch with the temperament of the times, Orr knew that this Christian *Weltanschauung* was engaged with modern naturalism in a cosmic spiritual and intellectual battle for the soul of the church and the Western world. Only by presenting Christianity as a comprehensive system of belief that embraced all aspects of reality would any progress be made in this all-determinative culture war. As a populist of sorts, he encouraged the people of God to recognize the grandeur of their worldview, to live faithfully in accordance with its covenantal requirements, and to proclaim it in all its fullness for the good of humanity and the glory of God. Orr was a "worldviewish" theologian, and in continuity with historic orthodoxy he has bequeathed to the evangelical community the heritage of Christianity as a comprehensive, systematic *Weltanschauung*.

27. Orr, *The Christian View*, p. 30.
28. Orr, *The Christian View*, p. 31.
29. See Scorgie, *A Call for Continuity*, p. 163; and Packer, p. 161. Some found his arguments uncompelling, his combative spirit off-putting, his antimodernist sentiments uninformed, and his literary style boring. Perhaps some of these complaints are justified, but some no doubt stem from his critics' modernist *Weltanschauung* which was deeply at odds with his own.
30. Packer, p. 165.

Gordon H. Clark and Carl F. H. Henry

Both Gordon H. Clark and Carl F. H. Henry appear to be immediate heirs of Orr's worldview legacy. As a professional philosopher writing from a Protestant evangelical point of view, Gordon Clark (1902-86) was, at the height of his powers, recognized as "perhaps the dean of those twentieth century American philosophers who have sought to develop a Christian *Weltanschauung* consistent with the Christian Scriptures."[31] Indeed, the title of one of his best-known books — *A Christian View of Men and Things* — suggests a continuity with Orr's work.[32] In the introduction Clark acknowledges the popularity of the Scottish theologian's own volume in an earlier day. More important, however, than title or acknowledgment is the fact that, like Orr before him, Clark recognized that naturalism engulfed the modern mind as a total explanation of reality. If Christianity was to meet this challenge successfully, it too must be explained and defended in comprehensive terms. A bits-and-pieces approach simply would not do. Clark explains his strategy in language that echoes Orr's exact approach.

> Christianity therefore has, or, one may even say, Christianity *is* a comprehensive view of all things; it takes the world, both material and spiritual, to be an ordered system. Consequently, if Christianity is to be defended against the objections of other philosophies, the only adequate method will be comprehensive. While it is of great importance to defend particular points of interest, these specific defenses will be insufficient. In addition to these details, there is also needed a picture of the whole into which they fit.[33]

In his book, Clark proceeds to present this big picture, analyzing the current state of the discussion in history, politics, ethics, science, religion, and epistemology and offering a Christian perspective on each. He was convinced that the most comprehensive, coherent, and meaningful philosophical system should be chosen for adherence. As he puts it, "who can deny us, since we must choose, the right to choose the more promising first principle?"[34] For Clark, Christianity was the clear, logical choice.

31. Ronald H. Nash, preface to *The Philosophy of Gordon H. Clark: A Festschrift*, ed. Ronald H. Nash (Philadelphia: Presbyterian and Reformed, 1968), p. 5. Clark also has an extended discussion on the need of a worldview and the theistic worldview in particular in the first two chapters of his *A Christian Philosophy of Education* (Grand Rapids: Eerdmans, 1946).

32. Gordon H. Clark, *A Christian View of Men and Things: An Introduction to Philosophy* (Grand Rapids: Eerdmans, 1951; reprint, Grand Rapids: Baker, 1981).

33. Clark, *A Christian View*, p. 25.

34. Clark, *A Christian View*, p. 34.

Orr's worldview tradition influenced Carl F. H. Henry (b. 1913) as well. During his student days he became enamored of comprehending and defending the faith as a total "world-life view" by reading Orr's volume.[35] In his autobiography Henry recalls that "It was James Orr's great work, *The Christian View of God and the World,* used as a Senior text in theism [at Wheaton College], that did the most to give me a cogently comprehensive view of reality and life in a Christian context."[36] Through Henry, the idea of worldview in general and of the Christian worldview in particular has been promoted widely among professional theologians and the evangelical public. "His emphasis was always on the big picture," says Kenneth Kantzer. "Above all he sought to think clearly and effectively, consistently and comprehensively, about the total Christian world and life view."[37] Thus, unsurprisingly, Henry frames the discussion in his greatest work, *God, Revelation, and Authority,* in terms of worldviews, and he has authored numerous volumes for more popular audiences that address the same theme.[38] In these works he argues for a resurgence of Christian perspectives across the whole spectrum of life to thwart the increasing paganization of contemporary culture. Even as recently as 1998 Henry defended the concept of the Christian worldview against numerous critics.[39] As the often recognized "dean" of contemporary American evangelical theologians, Henry has wielded considerable influence in promoting Christianity as a complete world and life view.

Thus the wellsprings of conceiving Christianity as a comprehensive, systematic *Weltanschauung* originated in Scotland in the life and thought of the great Presbyterian theologian James Orr. From this source the waters of worldview

---

35. Scorgie, *A Call for Continuity,* p. 156 n. 4.

36. Carl F. H. Henry, *Confessions of a Theologian: An Autobiography* (Waco, Tex.: Word, 1986), p. 75.

37. Kenneth S. Kantzer, "Carl Ferdinand Howard Henry: An Appreciation," in *God and Culture: Essays in Honor of Carl F. H. Henry,* ed. D. A. Carson and John D. Woodbridge (Grand Rapids: Eerdmans, 1993), p. 372.

38. See especially Carl F. H. Henry, *God Who Speaks and Shows: Preliminary Considerations,* vol. 1 of *God, Revelation, and Authority* (Waco, Tex.: Word, 1976). Other relevant works by Henry spotlighting the worldview theme include the following: *Remaking the Modern Mind* (Grand Rapids: Eerdmans, 1946); *The Christian Mindset in a Secular Society: Promoting Evangelical Renewal and National Righteousness* (Portland, Oreg.: Multnomah, 1984); *Christian Countermoves in a Decadent Culture* (Portland, Oreg.: Multnomah, 1986); *Toward a Recovery of Christian Belief: The Rutherford Lectures* (Wheaton, Ill.: Crossway, 1990); *Gods of This Age or God of the Ages?* (Nashville: Broadman and Holman, 1994).

39. Henry, "Fortunes," pp. 163-76. The critics to whom Henry responds in defense of the notion of worldview argue that it is a modernist construct and too rationalistic or speculative in nature, or that worldviews themselves are mythological in content or are entirely culturally conditioned. See chaps. 9 and 11 in this volume for a critical discussion of the strengths and weaknesses of the notion of worldview, and the use of this concept by Christians.

thinking have been pumped steadily into the evangelical mainstream in North America through writings of philosopher Gordon Clark and theologian Carl Henry. Meanwhile, in Orr's day a similar agenda was developing on the continent of Europe, this time by an increasingly prominent Dutch ecclesiastical and political figure, the second of two main intellectual gateways through which the idea of a Christian worldview has reached the contemporary evangelical church.

Abraham Kuyper

Described by his enemies as "an opponent of ten heads and a hundred hands" and by his friends as "a gift of God to our age,"[40] Abraham Kuyper (1837-1920) was truly a renaissance man, a veritable genius in both intellectual and practical affairs. A noted journalist, politician, educator, and theologian with Mosaic vigor, he is especially remembered as the founder of the Free University of Amsterdam in 1880 and as the prime minister of the Netherlands from 1901 to 1905. The source of this man's remarkable contributions is found in a powerful spiritual vision derived from the theology of the Protestant reformers (primarily Calvin) which centered upon the sovereignty of the biblical God over all aspects of reality, life, thought, and culture. Indeed, as he thundered in the climax to his inaugural address at the dedication of the Free University, "there is not a square inch in the whole domain of our human existence over which Christ, who is Sovereign over *all*, does not cry: 'Mine!' "[41] From this theological axiom Kuyper drew inspiration for the all-consuming goal of his life, namely, the renewal of the Dutch church and nation, expressed in these often quoted words:

> One desire has been the ruling passion of my life. One high motive has acted like a spur upon my mind and soul. And sooner than that I should seek escape from the sacred necessity that this is laid upon me, let the breath of life fail me. It is this: That in spite of all worldly opposition, God's holy ordinances shall be established again in the home, in the school and in the State for the good of the people; to carve as it were into the conscience of the nation the ordinances of the Lord, to which the Bible and Creation bear witness, until the nation pays homage again to God.[42]

40. John Hendrik De Vries, biographical note to *Lectures on Calvinism: Six Lectures Delivered at Princeton University under Auspices of the L. P. Stone Foundation*, by Abraham Kuyper (1931; reprint, Grand Rapids: Eerdmans, 1994), p. iii.

41. Abraham Kuyper, "Sphere Sovereignty," in *Abraham Kuyper: A Centennial Reader*, ed. James D. Bratt (Grand Rapids: Eerdmans, 1998), p. 488.

42. Quoted in De Vries, p. iii.

Indeed, this is the hallmark characteristic of the "Kuyperian" tradition as it has come to be known, and the concept of worldview became a tool in his hands by which he expressed this comprehensive vision of the faith. Over the course of time, Kuyper realized that both obedience and disobedience to God were closely bound up, if not identified with, a particular persuasion or pattern of life, that is, a worldview. If non-Christian worldviews characterized by idolatry and religious insubordination are worked out across the whole spectrum of life (which they are), then likewise Christianity must also be articulated in terms of a comprehensive vision of reality engendering the worship of God and submission to his will in all things.[43] Indeed, when Kuyper was at the height of his powers, he had just this opportunity — to demonstrate that his beloved Calvinism was more than just a church polity or doctrinaire religion but an all-encompassing *Weltanschauung* — when he was invited to deliver the prestigious Stone Lectures at Princeton University in 1898. These addresses and the book that resulted from them, *Lectures on Calvinism*, became a second influential source for conceiving of Christianity as a worldview among evangelical Protestants.[44]

The consensus in recent Kuyperian scholarship is that though the Dutch polymath was quite cognizant of the notion of worldview early on in his career, and even used the word occasionally, nevertheless he did not define it carefully or work it out Calvinistically until the invitation came to give the esteemed lectures at Princeton. If Peter Heslam's proposal is correct, Kuyper's reading of James Orr's recently published book *The Christian View of God and the World* might have been the turning point, underscoring the value of *Weltanschauung* in his eyes and prompting him to cast his entire lectures on Calvinism as a complete belief system.[45] Indeed, the similarities between the two thinkers on worldview are remarkable, and it appears that Kuyper drew considerably from Orr's thought on the topic.[46] The following survey of Kuyper's first Stone Lec-

43. R. D. Henderson, "How Abraham Kuyper Became a Kuyperian," *Christian Scholars Review* 22 (1992): 22, 34-35.

44. For an excellent study of Kuyper's Stone Lectures, see Peter S. Heslam, *Creating a Christian Worldview: Abraham Kuyper's Lectures on Calvinism* (Grand Rapids: Eerdmans, 1998).

45. Orr also delivered the Stone Lectures for the academic year 1903-4, an effort which resulted in the publication of *God's Image in Man, and Its Defacement, in the Light of Modern Denials* (London: Hodder and Stoughton, 1905).

46. Heslam shows that both Orr and Kuyper delivered their respective lectures, Kerr and Stone, in order to show that there is an explicit Christian *Weltanschauung*. He explains other parallels between Kuyper and Orr thusly: "Orr argued that Christianity had an independent, unified and coherent worldview derived from a central belief or principle, an argument which is virtually identical to that of Kuyper on behalf of Calvinism. Kuyper also resembles Orr in his argument that modern worldviews are expressed in a unified system of thought, that they are de-

ture, "Calvinism as a Life-System," will outline his basic thinking on the topic, marking the point from which the concept of *Weltanschauung* became a permanent fixture in his thought and writings.[47]

Kuyper begins by highlighting the common cultural and religious heritage that Europe and America share. Yet, as he points out, "the storm of Modernism has arisen with violent intensity" against their revered Christian tradition on both continents, especially in the form of the malevolent influences of the French Revolution, Darwinian evolution, and German pantheism. Like Orr before him, Kuyper sees the present cultural moment defined in both Europe and America by a life-and-death struggle between two antithetical worldviews, or as he calls them, "life systems." "Two *life systems* are wrestling with one another, in mortal combat. Modernism is bound to build a world of its own from the data of the natural man, and to construct man himself from the data of nature; while, on the other hand, all those who reverently bend the knee to Christ and worship Him as the Son of the living God, and God Himself, are bent upon saving the 'Christian Heritage.' This is *the* struggle in Europe, this is *the* struggle in America."[48]

Kuyper takes a dim view of the role of traditional apologetics in this single most important battle for the soul of the Western world. He notes that such an approach to defending the faith does not advance the Christian cause "one single step," and later in his volume refers to it as "useless," likening it to a man trying to adjust a crooked window frame when the entire building is tottering on its foundations.[49] Apologists, in other words, must occupy themselves with more fundamental and extensive matters, and this is precisely what Kuyper intends to do. Hence, as Orr proposed in his own lectures, Kuyper argues that a

---

rived from a single principle and are embodied in certain forms of life and activity, and that they are antithetical to Christianity. Kuyper's claim, likewise, that Calvinism's only defense against modernism was in the development of an equally comprehensive worldview, in which principle would be arrayed against principle — is almost indistinguishable from Orr's argument regarding Christianity." See Heslam, pp. 93-94.

47. Heslam, p. 96.

48. Kuyper, *Lectures on Calvinism*, p. 11. Kuyper takes advantage of this reference to "life system" to mention in a footnote on p. 11 Orr's "valuable lectures" contained in *The Christian View*, pointing out the difficulty of translating *Weltanschauung* into English. He notes that Orr employed the literal translation "view of the world," even though he prefers the more explicit phrase "life and world view." American colleagues convinced him, nonetheless, that the expression "life system" was an appropriate synonym with wide currency in the United States. He chose this translation for the title of his first chapter ("Calvinism as a Life-System"), though he interchanges the two expressions later in his lectures, depending upon the context and the nuance of his argument.

49. Kuyper, *Lectures on Calvinism*, pp. 11, 135-36.

piecemeal apologetic approach must be replaced with a strategy that countered an all-encompassing modernism with a comprehensive Christian *Weltanschauung.* "If the battle is to be fought with honor and with hope of victory, then *principle* must be arrayed against *principle:* then it must be felt that in Modernism the vast energy of an all embracing *life-system* assails us, then also it must be understood that we have to take our stand in a life-system of equally comprehensive and far-reaching power. And this powerful life-system is not to be invented nor formulated by ourselves, but is to be taken and applied as it presents itself in history."[50]

In his concluding lecture, "Calvinism and the Future," Kuyper reiterates this point with even greater clarity and power.

> As truly as every plant has a root, so truly does a principle hide under every manifestation of life. These principles are interconnected, and have their common root in a fundamental principle; and from the latter is developed logically and systematically the whole complex of ruling ideas and conceptions that go to make up our life and world-view. With such a coherent world and life-view, firmly resting on its principle and self-consistent in its splendid structure, Modernism now confronts Christianity; and against this deadly danger, ye, Christians, cannot successfully defend your sanctuary, but by placing in opposition to all this, *a life- and world-view of your own, founded as firmly on the base of your own principle, wrought out with the same clearness and glittering in an equally logical consistency.*[51]

For Kuyper, of course, the only expression of Christianity adequate to enter into warfare against the powers of modernity was not to be found in vague versions of Protestantism. Rather, "this manifestation of the Christian principle is given us in Calvinism," which, according to him, had developed the theology of the Reformation more consistently and fruitfully than any other tradition.[52] Consequently, there was no doubt in Kuyper's mind that the subject he would develop and present before his American audience in his Stone Lectures would be Calvinism. He was quick to clarify, however, that he was addressing it not in a sectarian, confessional, or denominational sense, but rather as a scientific name, developing its connotations not only for the church but across the whole spectrum of thought and life. Thus he presents Calvinism as a total life system (lecture 1); draws out its implications in the areas of religion, politics, science, and art (lectures 2 through 5); and suggests the kind of role it ought to play in

50. Kuyper, *Lectures on Calvinism,* pp. 11-12.
51. Kuyper, *Lectures on Calvinism,* pp. 189-90.
52. Kuyper, *Lectures on Calvinism,* p. 12.

the future of the world (lecture 6). So conceived and articulated, Calvinist Christianity could take its place alongside the other great systems of human thought, including paganism, Islamism, Romanism, and modernism, and be effective in the spiritual and intellectual warfare being waged for cultural dominance.[53]

Of course, Kuyper was anxious to justify his claim that Calvinism was far more than just a church view or religious tradition but an entire worldview. In order to do this, he offers some theoretical reflections on the nature of worldviews. He demonstrates that just like other credible systems of belief, Calvinism is capable of meeting the conditions every *Weltanschauung* must meet by providing insights into the three primary relationships that make up human existence: to God, man, and the world. Kuyper elaborates upon the Calvinist view of each of these areas, contrasts its position with those of its philosophic and religious competitors, and articulates his conclusions in this succinct summary:

> For our relation *to God:* an immediate fellowship of man with the Eternal, independently of priest or church. For the relation of man *to man:* the recognition in each person of human worth, which is his by virtue of his creation after the Divine likeness, and therefore of the equality of all men before God and his magistrate. And for our relation *to the world:* the recognition that in the whole world the curse is restrained by grace, that the life of the world is to be honored in its independence, and that we must, in every domain, discover the treasures and develop the potencies hidden by God in nature and in human life.[54]

Since worldviews must articulate cogent positions on each of these relationships, so must Calvinism. Since it does, and does so successfully, Kuyper is convinced that it can stand on its own among alternative perspectives. Thus Kuyper affirmed, as Orr also did, that Christianity was capable of "claiming for itself the glory of possessing a well-defined principle and an all-embracing life-system."[55]

53. Here is where I see Kuyper and Orr deviating in their respective purposes. On the one hand, Orr's concern was to spell out the essence of the Christian worldview *theologically,* centering his presentation on the incarnation; Kuyper on the other hand was concerned to demonstrate the implications of the Calvinist worldview *culturally,* showing the relevance of Reformed theology across the whole of life. For an expanded treatment on the cultural implications of Calvinist theology, including a discussion of Kuyper's perspective, see Henry R. Van Til, *The Calvinistic Concept of Culture* (Grand Rapids: Baker, 1959).

54. Kuyper, *Lectures on Calvinism,* p. 31.

55. Kuyper, *Lectures on Calvinism,* p. 32. Albert Wolters has pointed out that as a worldview, Calvinism is eminently comparable to Marxism in its comprehensiveness and direct

The Wonder of Worldview I: Protestant Evangelicalism

The contest between the life systems of modernity and Christianity comes to expression in all the social and cultural domains that Kuyper addresses in his lectures. However, the rivalry is particularly poignant in science, that is, in theorizing in general, or what the Germans call *Wissenschaft,* especially in the debate regarding the origin of life. He makes the point that this aspect of the culture war is not between religion and science per se, but between two competing life systems underlying the two distinctive approaches to scientific investigation. There is the worldview represented by the *normalists,* who assert that the cosmos is in its customary state as its various potentials are actualized by the mechanism of evolution (naturalism). On the other hand, there is the worldview represented by the *abnormalists,* who insist that the cosmos is in an aberrant state because a fundamental disturbance has taken place in the past which can only be remedied by a regenerating power that can restore it to its original goals (theism). So the origins debate is technically not one of religion and science at all, but between two life systems underlying the science practiced by the respective groups, each having its own unique set of motivations and assumptions.[56] As Kuyper puts it, "[T]he difference between the science of the Normalists and Abnormalists is not founded upon any differing result of investigation, but upon the undeniable difference which distinguishes the *self-consciousness* of the one from that of the other."[57]

In another place Kuyper argues that because there are basically two kinds of people, there are two kinds of science. The difference between people is established upon their relation to *palingenesis,* that is, spiritual regeneration. Regenerate people with a Christian worldview produce a roughly theistic interpretation of science, and nonregenerate people with a non-Christian worldview produce an idolatrous science. While Kuyper carefully nuances his position to avoid absurd conclusions, nonetheless he is clear that the experience of *palingenesis,* which radically alters the content of human consciousness and reshapes worldview, makes a decisive difference in the way the cosmos is interpreted and science is pursued. Kuyper summarizes his viewpoint, famously known as the "antithesis," in these words from his book on Reformed theology:

We speak none too emphatically, therefore, when we speak of two kinds of people. Both are human, but one is inwardly different from the other [be-

---

applicability to the total range of cultural phenomena and intellectual concerns. See his "Dutch Neo-Calvinism: Worldview, Philosophy and Rationality," in *Rationality in the Calvinian Tradition,* ed. Hendrick Hart, Johan Van Der Hoeven, and Nicholas Wolterstorff, Christian Studies Today (Lanham, Md.: University Press of America, 1983), p. 117.

56. Kuyper, *Lectures on Calvinism,* pp. 130-36.

57. Kuyper, *Lectures on Calvinism,* p. 138, emphasis added.

cause of *palingenesis*], and consequently feels a different content rising from his consciousness; thus they face the cosmos from different points of view, and are impelled by different impulses. And the fact that there are two kinds of *people* occasions of necessity the fact of two kinds of human *life* and *consciousness* of life, and of two kinds of *science;* for which reason the idea of the *unity of science,* taken in its absolute sense, implies the denial of the fact of palingenesis, and therefore from principle leads to the rejection of the Christian religion.[58]

The seamless robe of science, according to Kuyper, is torn asunder by the experience of spiritual regeneration which makes a homogeneous approach to the enterprise impossible. Scientific reason is not the same for all people. It depends upon whether or not the scientist has or has not been religiously renewed. There is not a neutral, scientific rationality leading to certain objective and shared conclusions. Instead, scientific theories are a function of the religious backgrounds and philosophical orientations of the scientists or theorists.[59] For these reasons, disparate worldviews, Christian and otherwise, are at the heart of science broadly conceived. More than anything else, they establish its most fundamental assumptions and account for the frequent conflicts among its philosophically and religiously diverse practitioners.

In summary, Abraham Kuyper has bequeathed to the evangelical church the legacy of the Calvinist Christian worldview. It is a rich description of the faith, zeroing in on the pillar points of creation, fall, and redemption, and is characterized by several important themes. First is the idea that God's redemptive "grace restores nature"; that is, the salvation achieved by Jesus Christ is cosmic in scope and entails the renewal of everything in creation to its original divine purpose. Second is the assertion that God is sovereign and has ordered the universe and all aspects of life within it by his law and word ("sphere sovereignties"), thereby giving each thing its particular identity, preserving the wondrous diversity of creation, and preventing the usurpation of one sphere of existence over another. Third is the wholehearted affirmation of the "cultural mandate" in the opening chapters of Genesis, demonstrating that God intends the pro-

58. Abraham Kuyper, *Principles of Sacred Theology,* trans. J. Hendrik De Vries, introduction by Benjamin B. Warfield (Grand Rapids: Baker, 1980), p. 154.

59. While such an understanding of scientific theorizing is explicitly religious, Kuyper's proposal anticipates aspects of Thomas Kuhn's postmodern paradigm thesis by seven or eight decades. See chap. 7 for details. Nicholas Wolterstorff has offered some sharp criticisms of Kuyper's concept of two people/two sciences, arguing against what he calls its "religious totalism" in his essay "On Christian Learning," in *Stained Glass: Worldviews and Social Science,* ed. Paul A. Marshall, Sander Griffioen, and Richard J. Mouw, Christian Studies Today (Lanham, Md.: University Press of America, 1989), pp. 56-80.

gressive development of the creation in history as a fundamental human occupation to God's glory and for the benefit of mankind. Finally there is the concept of the spiritual "antithesis"; namely, that the human race is divided distinctly between believers who acknowledge the redemption and kingship of Jesus Christ and unbelievers who do not, with the concomitant implications of both life orientations across the whole spectrum of human existence. Thus, a spiritually sensitive and holistic interpretation of Christianity that includes the transformation and development of all aspects of human thought and culture is at the heart of the Kuyperian vision.[60]

Two additional aspects of the preeminent Dutchman's neo-Calvinistic worldview tradition touched on earlier need to be reinforced by way of summary. First, Kuyper's approach to Christianity as a complete worldview provided him with an alternative to traditional apologetic strategies. As mentioned earlier, in his estimation the rationalist and evidentialist approach to defending individual aspects of the faith based on the assumption of the mind's ability to decide objectively regarding matters of truth was naive. It must be replaced by a method that recognizes the influence of underlying presuppositions on the mind's perception of what constitutes reason and evidence in the first place. Apologetic warfare must be conducted at the more basic level of underlying worldviews. Consequently, Kuyper emphasized the importance of presenting the faith as a complete life system or fundamental interpretative principle, for what was at stake first and foremost was the very conception and meaning of the universe. Kuyper's denigration of old school apologetics and his advocacy of a worldview approach fueled the controversy that persists even today between evidentialists and presuppositionalists.[61]

Second, to extend the previous contribution in another direction, the notion of worldview provided Kuyper with a mechanism for critiquing the scientific and scholarly enterprise, broadly conceived. Kuyper showed that human reason is not neutral in its operation, but functions under the influence of a set

---

60. Albert M. Wolters, "The Intellectual Milieu of Herman Dooyeweerd," in *The Legacy of Herman Dooyeweerd: Reflections on Critical Philosophy in the Christian Tradition*, ed. C. T. McIntire (Lanham, Md.: University Press of America, 1985), pp. 4-10.

61. See the excellent discussion illuminating this issue by George M. Marsden, *Understanding Fundamentalism and Evangelicalism* (Grand Rapids: Eerdmans, 1991), pp. 122-52. Recent contributions to this debate on apologetics include R. C. Sproul, John Gerstner, and Arthur Lindsley, *Classical Apologetics: A Rational Defense of the Christian Faith and a Critique of Presuppositional Apologetics* (Grand Rapids: Zondervan, Academie Books, 1984); Timothy R. Phillips and Dennis L. Okholm, eds., *Christian Apologetics in the Postmodern World* (Downers Grove, Ill.: InterVarsity, 1995); Steven B. Cowan, ed., *Five Views on Apologetics*, Counterpoints Series (Grand Rapids: Zondervan, 2000).

of antecedent assumptions that condition all thinking and acting. This realization led to a powerful critique of the modern ideal of scientific neutrality and objectivity. Given the recognition that all theorizing arises out of a priori faith commitments, it also encouraged Christian thinkers to undertake their academic projects on the basis of theistic beliefs with confidence. It is hard to overstate the profound impact this insight has had in engendering a renaissance in Christian scholarship across the disciplines in recent days.[62] Accordingly, George Marsden can speak in cautious terms of "The triumph — or nearly so — of what may be loosely called Kuyperian presuppositionalism in the evangelical [academic] community."[63] Thus a worldview apologetic and a presuppositional critique of theorizing constitute two additional aspects of Kuyper's *Weltanschauung* legacy.

This conception of Calvinistic Christianity subsumed under the rubric of worldview was appropriated by Kuyper's followers — the Dutch neo-Calvinists or Kuyperians — and passed down to subsequent generations. Eventually it migrated with them across the Atlantic and became a significant theme among them as an immigrant community in North America. Both Calvin College in Grand Rapids, Michigan, and the Institute for Christian Studies in Toronto, Ontario, Canada — where Kuyperian ideals and worldview thinking have flourished — were birthed out of this tradition. From this community of faith it spread into mainstream American evangelicalism, where it has had a substantial impact. Its more immediate influence, however, was registered through the second generation of Kuyperians in both theology and, in an amazingly fruitful way, in the Christian philosophy inspired by this tradition.[64] His contributions were matched by colleagues and by those following in his wake, especially theologian Herman Bavinck (1854-1921)[65] and second-

---

62. Both Alvin Plantinga and Nicholas Wolterstorff have extended this aspect of the Kuyperian tradition. In his famous address "Advice to Christian Philosophers," *Faith and Philosophy* 1 (1984): 253-71, Plantinga has advised Christian academics (philosophers in particular) to take certain biblical doctrines as assumptions in their philosophic work. Similarly, Wolterstorff, in his equally influential *Reason within the Bounds of Religion*, 2nd ed. (Grand Rapids: Eerdmans, 1984), has argued that the religious commitments of the Christian scholar ought to function as "control beliefs" in the devising and weighing of theories. The success of the Kuyperian vision in academic life has been noted in the popular press. See Alan Wolfe, "The Opening of the Evangelical Mind," *Atlantic Monthly* 286 (October 2000): 55-76.

63. George Marsden, "The State of Evangelical Christian Scholarship," *Reformed Journal* 37 (1987): 14. See also Richard J. Mouw, "Dutch Calvinist Philosophical Influences in North America," *Calvin Theological Journal* 24 (April 1989): 93-120.

64. See Mouw, "Dutch Calvinist Philosophical Influences in North America."

65. In a booklet titled *Christian Worldview (Christelijke Wereldbeschouwing)* written in 1904, Bavinck presents a version of the Christian faith that stands in the Neoplatonist tradition

generation Christian philosophers D. H. T. Vollenhoven (1892-1978)[66] and, most notably, Vollenhoven's brother-in-law, Herman Dooyeweerd (1894-1977). Among his American disciples, Cornelius Van Til (1895-1987) has been an exponent of Kuyperian presuppositionalism par excellence.[67] We must elaborate a bit about Dooyeweerd, however, who more than any other of Kuyper's intellectual descendants has developed and transmitted his vision with unique power and insight.

Herman Dooyeweerd

Professor of jurisprudence at the Free University from 1926 to 1965, Herman Dooyeweerd should probably be regarded as the most creative and influential philosopher among the neo-Calvinists in the twentieth century. Originally holding that the reformation of culture and scholarship must proceed on the basis of the Calvinist worldview, he continued and extended the Kuyperian tradition in an exhaustive way as the author of more than two hundred books and articles in the fields of law, political theory, and philosophy. His magnum opus, which is translated into English, is the voluminous *A New Critique of Theoretical Thought* (1953-58).[68]

Two stages of his thought regarding worldview are discernible. At first he

---

of Augustine and Aquinas. A few years later in 1908, when his own opportunity to present the Stone Lectures at Princeton arose, Bavinck articulated a conception of worldview similar to Kuyper's, describing it as the pretheoretical substructure to all forms of theoretical thought. In these lectures he referred to Wilhelm Dilthey's recent publications, in which he described *Weltanschauung* as the subterranean wellspring of the sciences. From Albert M. Wolters, "On the Idea of Worldview and Its Relation to Philosophy," in *Stained Glass*, p. 21.

66. D. H. T. Vollenhoven, who was professor of philosophy at the Free University from 1926 to 1963, argued that Calvinistic philosophy was not the same as world and life view, but was "the latter's scientific elaboration." See Wolters, "Idea of Worldview," p. 22.

67. As Van Til himself testifies, he always sought to work "in Kuyper's line," rejecting traditional apologetics and taking up his position in the Christian theistic system as the fundamental presupposition of his thought. As he puts it, "Calvin was right. We must not, like the Greeks and the scholastics after them, engage in vain speculations about the essence of God. We must not, like Descartes, start from man as a final point of reference in predication. We must listen to what God has told us about himself, and about ourselves, and our relation to him throught [*sic*] Christ in Scripture as our Creator-Redeemer." Van Til's comments are found in response to an article on his apologetics by Herman Dooyeweerd in E. R. Geehan, ed., *Jerusalem and Athens: Critical Discussions on the Philosophy and Apologetics of Cornelius Van Til* (Phillipsburg, N.J.: Presbyterian and Reformed, 1980), p. 92.

68. Herman Dooyeweerd, *A New Critique of Theoretical Thought*, trans. David H. Freeman, William S. Young, and H. De Jongste, 4 vols. (Jordan Station, Ont.: Paideia Press, 1984).

follows the Kuyperian line in positing life and thought as the products of an underlying *Weltanschauung*. Later on, however, he began to question whether or not all human artifacts are expressions of a deeper worldview. Instead, he came to believe that spiritual and religious factors play a more important role in determining the shape of things than abstract, intellectual constructs like worldviews. In due course Dooyeweerd rejected the romantic totalism associated with the Kuyperian model, and in doing so introduced his *new* critique of theoretical thought, which takes the following shape.[69]

The first task of Christian philosophy, according to Dooyeweerd, is to expose the *religious* condition that is determinative of all theoretical activity and cultural endeavor. For Dooyeweerd, all human endeavor stems not from worldview, but from the spiritual commitments of the heart, as Jacob Klapwijk explains:

> Dooyeweerd doesn't conclude that all philosophy and theory are necessarily preconditioned by the cultural, historical inheritance of some worldview. Instead, he concludes that the only (and necessary) precondition of philosophy and theory is the ultimate conditions and commitments of the human heart, which is fallen into sin, and is either still in that condition or reborn and restored by God's spirit. Thus, at the basis of philosophy and theory, there is no historical pluralism of worldviews but only two "religious" ground-motives in antithetical opposition. This "religious" antithesis, i.e., of man converted to God versus man averted from God, is decisive for all life and thought.[70]

According to the Enlightenment project, reason enjoys a free, independent status and can undertake its scientific projects without the stain or blemish of any conditioning factor — social, cultural, economic, religious — that might jeopardize the objectivity of its findings. Theoretical thought, on this account, is completely autonomous and unaffected. However, Dooyeweerd's argument is that this dogma of the *autonomy of theoretical thought* is a farce, not because of interference from worldviews but because of the belief content and inclination of the heart. When Dooyeweerd made the biblical discovery of the central significance of the heart as the religious root of human existence, a great transition took place in his thinking and the rule of reason was dethroned. He explains as follows: "The great turning point in my thought was marked by the discovery of the religious root of thought itself, whereby a new light was shed on the failure of all attempts, including my own, to bring about an inner syn-

69. Jacob Klapwijk, "On Worldviews and Philosophy," in *Stained Glass*, p. 51.
70. Klapwijk, p. 51.

thesis between Christian faith and a philosophy which is rooted in faith in the self-sufficiency of human reason."[71]

Because of the implications of this discovery, Dooyeweerd suggests that the thesis of the religious basis of all science introduces a philosophical revolution of greater magnitude than the one launched by Immanuel Kant.

> On the basis of this central Christian point of view I saw the need of a revolution in philosophical thought of a very radical character. Confronted with the religious root of creation, nothing less is in question than a relating of the whole temporal cosmos, in both its so-called "natural" and "spiritual" aspects, to this point of reference. In contrast to this basic Biblical conception, of what significance is a so-called "Copernican" Revolution which merely makes the "natural aspects" of temporal reality relative to a theoretical abstraction such as Kant's "transcendental subject"?[72]

Whereas Kant in his *Critique of Pure Reason* reversed the tradition of Western reason by shifting the emphasis away from the primacy of independent objects to the a priori categories of the subjective mind, Dooyeweerd shifted the emphasis away from the universal, a priori categories of the human mind to the universal affections of the human heart. Theory and practice are a product of the will, not the intellect; of the heart, not the head. In making this proposal Dooyeweerd introduced his "new critique of theoretical thought," contra Kant, on the premise that religion is supremely transcendental. Religion is no longer subsumed within the bounds of reason, but reason is subsumed within the bounds of religion, as all of life is. In Dooyeweerd's reckoning, religion trumps reason in providing the transcendental unity of apperception. Tensions and conflicts in and between theories are not due to diversity of scientific judgments or worldviews, but rather to alternative religious convictions. Theory in and of itself is helpless to adjudicate fundamental conflicts in science and philosophy. Only by means of a new religious critique of theoretical thought will intellectual disputes at least be elucidated if not solved.[73]

The condition of the heart constitutes what Dooyeweerd calls the "religious ground motive" *(grondmotief)* which determines the substance of theories and the makeup of worldviews. According to the Dutch professor, there are two fundamental religious ground motives, "two central mainsprings operative

---

71. Dooyeweerd, 1:v.

72. Dooyeweerd, 1:v.

73. Roy A. Clouser has elaborated on this theme in *The Myth of Religious Neutrality: An Essay on the Hidden Role of Religious Belief in Theories* (Notre Dame, Ind.: University of Notre Dame Press, 1991).

in the heart of human existence." One is born of the spirit of holiness, and the other of the spirit of apostasy. The ground motive of the Holy Spirit is derived from the divine Word-revelation and is the key to understanding the Bible: *"the motive of creation, fall, and redemption by Jesus Christ in the communion of the Holy Ghost."* The ground motive of apostasy leads away from the true God and culminates in idolatry: "As a religious dynamis (power), it leads the human heart in an apostate direction, and is the source of all deification of the creature. It is the source of all absolutizing of the relative seen in the theoretical attitude of thought. By virtue of its idolatrous character, its religious ground-motive can receive very diverse contents."[74]

Thus, on this basis, Dooyeweerd concludes that worldviews are not the most deeply rooted thing in the soil of the heart. Rather, religion or faith is. The religion of the heart is the cause; the philosophies and worldviews are the cognitive effect. Worldviews and philosophies stand side by side as the intellectual siblings of religious parentage. Dooyeweerd explains the similarities and differences between philosophy and "life- and world-view," and traces the origin of both to the foundational impulses that reside at the affective core of the human person.

> The genuine life- and world-view has undoubtedly a close affinity with philosophy, because it is essentially directed toward the totality of meaning of our cosmos. A life- and world-view also implies an Archimedian point. Like philosophy, it has its religious ground motive. It, as well as philosophy, requires the religious commitment of our selfhood. It has its own attitude of thought. However, it is not as such, of a *theoretical* character. Its view of totality is not *theoretical,* but rather *pre-theoretical.* It does not conceive reality in its abstracted modal aspects of meaning, but rather in typical structures of individuality which are not analyzed in a theoretical way. It is not restricted to a special category of "philosophical thinkers," but applies to everybody, the simplest included. Therefore, it is entirely wrong to see in Christian philosophy only a philosophically elaborated life- and world-view [as Kuyper would say]. To do so would be a fundamental misunderstanding of the true relationships. The Divine Word-revelation gives the Christian as little a detailed life- and world-view as a Christian philosophy, yet it gives to both simply their *direction* from the starting-point in their central basic motive [the heart]. But this direction is really a *radical* and *integral* one, determining everything. The same holds for the direction and outlook which the *apostate religious* motives give to philosophy and a life- and world-view.[75]

74. Dooyeweerd, 1:61.
75. Dooyeweerd, 1:128.

In Dooyeweerd's thinking, both worldview and philosophy share several things in common, including a mutual concern for totality, Archimedean foundations, and religious ground motives. There are also differences. Philosophies are abstract, theoretical systems devised by a select group of professional thinkers, whereas everyone universally, even the most simpleminded, has a worldview, pretheoretical in nature since it lacks systematic formulation. Dooyeweerd makes it plain that, unlike Kuyper, he does not understand Christian philosophy to be the elaboration of an underlying biblical worldview, since both philosophy and worldview are the outworkings of the religious ground motive, juxtaposed to one another as cognitive phenomena of diverse kinds that share a common root.[76] Indeed, for Dooyeweerd worldviews are not philosophic systems at all, for the latter as theoretical thought are detached from and even antithetical to life, whereas a worldview knows no such estrangement in its direct contact with life and its efflorescence. Though Christian revelation does not provide either a ready-made worldview or a developed systematic philosophy, it does give direction to both in a radical, all-determinative way. Similarly, the spirit of apostasy residing at the core of the unbelieving person gives rise to non-Christian worldviews as well. In any case, as Dooyeweerd here indicates, the content of the human heart — the single root of all thought and action — is the bottom line, the very key to existence. It is the ultimate factor in shaping one's understanding of reality, whether practically in worldview or theoretically in philosophy and science. However, since Dooyeweerd so closely identifies the ground motive of the Holy Spirit with the themes of creation, fall, and redemption — the essence of the biblical worldview — we cannot help but wonder how much of a distinction can be made between his point of view and Kuyper's. Perhaps he has put too fine a point on the matter, for it would seem that any line of demarcation between ground motives and the content of basic worldviews is razor thin.

Francis A. Schaeffer

This discussion on watershed evangelical thinkers who contributed significantly to thinking about worldview would be incomplete without acknowledging the role of Francis A. Schaeffer (1912-84). Since the middle of the twentieth century, countless believers, myself included, cut their worldview teeth on Schaeffer's writings. He affirmed what is now a commonplace, that all people have a worldview and nobody, whether ditchdigger or professional thinker, can

---

76. Dooyeweerd, 1:157-58.

live without one. Philosophy is the only unavoidable occupation.[77] Also, his rich interpretation of a Christianity that embraced the whole of life was uniquely attractive to many, and his discussion of a significant range of cultural issues from a Christian point of view was deeply refreshing after decades of evangelical obscurantism.

As an evangelist and popular Christian apologist, Schaeffer was deeply concerned about the drift of modern culture into relativism. In his understanding, autonomous man beginning with himself as his reference point and by his own intellectual resources sought to create a system of knowledge, meaning, and values that would provide a cogent interpretation of life. This represented an epistemological sea change in the West, away from divine revelation into humanistic rationalism. In due course, however, modern man realized he would not be able to create this comprehensive system of thought, and he fell below the "line of despair." In this condition the law of noncontradiction was abrogated, absolutes were denied, and pragmatic relativism was born. In the modern world nature had "eaten up" grace, and a thoroughgoing secularism had become deeply embedded in all aspects of social, cultural, and political life. In their quest for meaning and purpose, twentieth-century denizens had to resort to various contentless, "upper story" experiences (a famous Schaefferism) as an alternative to the ennui of contemporary life. Schaeffer was indeed a master in illustrating vividly these profound human yearnings and yet-futile attempts for fulfillment in areas as diverse as philosophy, art, music, popular culture, and even in theology and the church.

In this context of emptiness and despair, the Swiss missionary and founder of L'Abri Fellowship recommended the Christian worldview as the only credible answer to the deep dilemmas of modern, secular life. Schaeffer was a man of many admirable passions, as James Sire has pointed out, and one of the most important was for the comprehensive system of "true truth" set forth in the Scriptures.[78] In *Escape from Reason* Schaeffer says, "I love the biblical system as a system,"[79] and in *The God Who Is There* he explains why. "The Christian system (what is taught in the whole Bible) is a unity of thought. Christianity is not just a lot of bits and pieces — there is a beginning and an end, a whole system of truth,

---

77. Francis A. Schaeffer, *He Is There and He Is Not Silent,* in vol. 1 of *The Complete Works of Francis A. Schaeffer: A Christian Worldview,* 2nd ed. (Wheaton, Ill.: Crossway, 1982), pp. 279-80.

78. James Sire has suggested recently that five "passions" characterized Schaeffer's life: "a passion for the God who is there, a passion for truth, a compassion for people, a passion for relevant and honest communication, and a passion for Scripture." See his foreword to *The God Who Is There,* by Francis A. Schaeffer, Thirtieth Anniversary Edition (Downers Grove, Ill.: InterVarsity, 1998), pp. 15-16.

79. Francis A. Schaeffer, *Escape from Reason,* in vol. 1 of *Complete Works,* p. 221.

and this system is the only system that will stand up to all the questions that are presented to us as we face the reality of existence."[80]

As Ronald Nash has noted, "Schaeffer . . . helped people understand the importance of understanding Christianity and its competitors in terms of world views. Christianity is not simply a religion that tells human beings how they may be forgiven. It is a total world and life view. Christians need to recognize that their faith has important things to say about the whole of human life."[81] Schaeffer articulated his understanding of the biblical *Weltanschauung* in the first three books he published. The trilogy of *The God Who Is There, Escape from Reason,* and *He Is There and He Is Not Silent* formed the hub of his system, and all his other works gave expression to his conception of the Christian vision as if they were spokes.[82] Through Schaeffer an entire generation of evangelicals were (and continue to be) inducted into the notion of thinking Christianly about the whole of human existence. They have him to thank for stimulating an abiding interest in cultivating a comprehensive, systematic understanding of biblical faith with all its concomitant personal, intellectual, and cultural implications.

Conclusion and Questions

The trailblazing efforts of Scottish Presbyterian theologian James Orr along with the herculean efforts of Dutch neo-Calvinist Abraham Kuyper have stimulated a most remarkable movement within evangelicalism in conceiving of Christianity as a worldview. Under their combined influence, with assistance from Gordon Clark, Carl Henry, Herman Dooyeweerd, and Francis Schaeffer, the amount of theoretical reflection and practical concern devoted to this theme in this religious tradition is quite remarkable. As a matter of fact, in the entire history of "worldview," no single philosophic school or religious community has given more sustained attention to or taken more advantage of this concept than Protestant evangelicals.[83] The range of topics to which the notion

80. Francis A. Schaeffer, *The God Who Is There,* in vol. 1 of *Complete Works,* p. 178.

81. Ronald Nash, "The Life of the Mind and the Way of Life," in *Francis A. Schaeffer: Portraits of the Man and His Work,* ed. Lane T. Dennis (Westchester, Ill.: Crossway, 1986), p. 68.

82. The subtitle to Schaeffer's *Complete Works* is aptly designated "A Christian Worldview." Vol. 1 deals with a Christian view of philosophy and contains the three books mentioned above. Vol. 2 deals with a Christian view of the Bible as truth. Vol. 3 deals with a Christian view of spirituality. Vol. 4 deals with a Christian view of the church. Vol. 5 deals with a Christian view of the West.

83. See Appendix A for synopses of additional evangelical contributions to worldview thinking.

of worldview has been applied in the evangelical faith context is vast. Indeed, it has been related to a plethora of important areas from the practical to the pedantic, including such domains as the Christian life and mind, theology and philosophy, biblical studies, missions and evangelism, contemporary culture, and Christian higher education.[84]

This significant interest in worldview by evangelicals does raise several important questions, however — three to be specific. First, what is the definition of the word "worldview"? What do we mean precisely (if it is possible to be precise in this matter) when we employ the expression "Christian worldview"? Considerable confusion and controversy attends this question of definition, but it is important to be as clear as possible when encountering and employing this term.

Second, why has evangelicalism been particularly enamored of the idea of worldview and made such prodigious use of it in its reflections on the faith? Peter Heslam has pointed out that "worldview" belongs to the vocabulary of modernity,[85] and perhaps some kind of evangelical affinity for either the objectivism and subjectivism of this cultural mind-set accounts for the wide use of the term. Is the evangelical adaptation (or capitulation) to modern cultural trends partly responsible for its ready embrace of this concept? Or is the attraction grounded in weightier reasons, perhaps because "worldview" taps into something deeply embedded in human nature?

Third, given the background of the term with its various possible connotations, can evangelicals use it without distortion to the essence of the faith? Does its employment convey subtle nuances that make it an infelicitous choice to communicate the sum and substance of biblical Christianity? Or is it a notion that admirably conveys its true scope, content, and nature without serious defect? While we cannot answer these questions at this point, we will do well to keep them in mind as our history unfolds.[86]

---

84. See Appendix B for books on worldview in each of these areas.

85. Heslam, p. ix.

86. The questions raised in this conclusion are addressed in chaps. 9, 10, and 11 of this work.

Chapter Two

The Wonder of Worldview II:
Roman Catholicism and Eastern Orthodoxy

Protestant evangelicals would be mistaken to entertain the notion that the idea of a Christian or biblical worldview is their exclusive possession. In fact, this pattern of thinking is present in unique ways within Roman Catholicism and Eastern Orthodoxy as well. Hence we explore in this chapter how these two traditions have appropriated the notion of worldview, or themes similar to it, to communicate their respective visions of the faith.

Roman Catholicism

When compared with its extensive use among Protestant evangelicals, the idea of worldview may appear on the surface to be of little interest to Roman Catholics in general, their clergy and intelligentsia included. The word appears infrequently in Catholic literature, and according to one recent reference work, the doctrinal office at the Vatican has not "taken a position directly on the topic of a worldview."[1] Despite this dearth of explicit linguistic usage and the lack of any official ecclesiastical pronouncement, something akin to the notion of worldview suffuses Catholic thought and life. In at least one book, the author has chosen to cast his introduction to the Catholic faith in terms of worldview, and it may be entirely appropriate to refer to John Paul II as a "worldviewish" pope. A survey of this particular book and a look at what many consider to be the

---

1. *Handbook of Catholic Theology* (1995), s.v. "worldview," p. 748. Despite this fact, cognizance of this theme within Roman Catholicism is supported by its treatment in various Catholic reference works, especially *Sacramentum Mundi,* edited by Karl Rahner, S.J. (1968-70), which contains helpful articles on both "world picture" and "views of the world," vol. 6, pp. 385-90.

most important pontificate since the Council of Trent will demonstrate the centrality of what amounts to a Catholic *Weltanschauung*.[2]

Catholicism as Worldview

According to Lawrence Cunningham, in his work *The Catholic Faith: An Intro-duction*, being a Catholic is not like being a member of a political party, say a Democrat, or having involvement in some kind of social club, perhaps the Ro-tary. Instead, identifying oneself as a Catholic Christian "is, rather, a mode of being in the world and, as such, it is a certain way of looking at the world from a particular point of view. That mode of being which is called Catholic should enhance a kind of seeing which, if not totally unique, is, at the very least, char-acteristic of Catholicism."[3] Since every person is governed by a set of assump-tions that shape the meaning of life, Cunningham is anxious to spell out the foundational beliefs that determine how a Catholic views, or should view, the world. To accomplish this, he discusses four crucial themes.

The World as Gift

Like all major religions, Christianity is concerned about the question of origins. The opening chapters of the book of Genesis and their description of God's rela-tionship to the world serve as the primary source of the church's perspective on this basic issue. According to Cunningham, the doctrine of creation, which can be summarized succinctly in four points, is the foundation of the Catholic worldview. First, the world is not self-sufficient or self-explanatory, but was cre-ated by a free and generous God who is the ultimate reference point for all real-ity. Second, the Catholic view of creation eschews both pantheistic and animistic interpretations, but instead affirms a qualitative distinction between the infinite God and his finite creation. Third, God's world is a very good one, a viewpoint that stands in sharp contrast to those who condemn the material world as an ac-tual evil or as an illusion masking the reality of the divine. Fourth, the world as

2. Abraham Kuyper referred to "Romanism" as one of the "great *complexes* of human life," embodying "its life-thought in a world of conceptions and utterances entirely its own." For him "the fruits of Rome's unity of life-system" served as a model for his construction of Calvinism as a complete, life-shaping worldview. See his *Lectures on Calvinism: Six Lectures Delivered at Princeton University under Auspices of the L. P. Stone Foundation* (1931; reprint, Grand Rapids: Eerdmans, 1994), pp. 17-18.

3. Lawrence S. Cunningham, *The Catholic Faith: An Introduction* (New York: Paulist, 1987), p. 111.

the proper sphere of human activity is given to man and woman as a gift, and as such, it is to be received with gratitude and pursued as a stewardship.

Combined, these four themes have important implications, according to Cunningham. They prompt wonder and gratitude, serve as the basis for the Catholic position on natural theology, and establish the foundation for Christ's incarnation — a doctrine at the heart of Catholic theology and experience. Christians must take their stand in the world and in human history, avoiding all world-denying or life-denying attitudes and recognizing that the creation speaks of the Creator sacramentally. After all, "Catholicism is at its best when it is most openly world affirming, sacramental, iconic, and earthy."[4] Furthermore, as God's image and likeness, people stand at the zenith of creation, and on the basis of their intrinsic dignity ought to oppose all dehumanizing influences and work to make the world a better place. Contrary to the prevailing spirit of nihilism in today's culture, God's creation is filled with grace and meaning.[5]

Sin in the World

How does the Catholic worldview account for the immeasurable amounts of wickedness and suffering in the world? Apart from an answer to this question, the previous assertions about the goodness of creation seem hollow. In response, Cunningham states that "The other side of the Catholic worldview, in short, must take account of the fact of sin."[6] A distinction, however, must be made between sin as a perpetual condition and sin as a discrete act. The etiological story of the fall in Genesis 3 shows that the archetypal man and woman struggled between the poles of heteronomy and autonomy, and in succumbing to the latter they inherited a propensity toward evil called "original sin." Out of this root of corruption stem the discrete acts of evil that wreak havoc in human life. "Moral evil," therefore, says Cunningham, "is both the condition of humanity and the ineluctable fact of all human existence."[7] That this is the case can be seen in each individual life at a personal level; it is manifested in monsters of depravity in the nation and in the neighborhood; it shows up in institutions which become structurally corrupt and fail to fulfill their goals. Were it not for redemption in Christ by which this sinful state is healed, it would be easy to embrace a completely negative view of human nature. But as it is, the Catholic worldview strikes a solid balance. It succumbs to neither an excessive optimism or a hope-

---

4. Cunningham, p. 119.
5. Cunningham, pp. 111-15.
6. Cunningham, p. 115.
7. Cunningham, p. 117.

less pessimism, but embraces a realistic viewpoint grounded in the themes of a good creation, a tragic fall, and a hopeful redemption in Jesus Christ.

Christian Realism

This is the third main aspect of the Catholic worldview according to Cunningham.[8] It is a mediating position that seeks to do justice to the tensions existing between the goodness of creation as God's gift and the inescapable reality and consequences of original sin. This balanced perspective is worked out in several important areas, including attitudes toward the world, which Catholics should neither abandon nor worship; toward human beings, who are neither completely perfect nor totally depraved; toward evil, which, though very real, does not destroy meaning and purpose; toward Jesus, who is both fully God and fully man; toward being truly human, which entails both physical and spiritual dimensions; and toward the cultural environment in which believers must not only live but to which they must also contribute significantly. This realist aspect of the Catholic worldview, therefore, seeks to bring potential antitheses into actual syntheses forming an harmonious pattern of beliefs. In this sense of wholeness, its genuine catholicity is detected.

The Experience of Time

Though some may mistakenly view Christianity as an ahistorical, nonspatial religion, it is actually characterized by an emphasis on the flow of history in creation and the unique events — the mighty deeds of God — that transpire within it. For this reason the Catholic worldview stresses the importance of time: past, present, and future. The past and present are vitally connected, for the latter affords the occasion to recall the events of the former, both in biblical and church history, as a source that enriches the lives of the faithful today. "Everything that the Church does," according to Cunningham, "is saturated in the memory of the community of faith which has gone before." Such an attempt at cultivating a Christian memory creates an understanding of solidarity with the

8. Cunningham points out that his articulation of "Christian realism" is inspired by, but different from, the position of Bernard Lonergan which goes by the same name. The latter, which is explained in "The Origins of Christian Realism," in *A Second Collection*, ed. William Ryan and Bernard Terrell (Philadelphia: Westminster, 1974), pp. 239-61, concerns fundamental epistemological approaches to the world. It attempts to strike a balance between a naive realism/empiricism and an idealistic antirealism, and argues for a critical realism by which the true nature of things is conveyed not by unexamined experience or systems of ideas alone, but by judgments and beliefs which, though historically conditioned, are tethered to reality.

historic church and enables contemporary believers to sense a communion with the saints and that they are heirs of a shared New Testament faith. The church is not just a here-and-now thing, but is a vibrant spiritual reality — the organic body of Christ — existing as a single unity in space and developing through time. In the celebration of the Holy Eucharist, the past, present, and future merge as a celebration of memory, presence, and expectation: "When we eat this bread and drink this cup, we proclaim your death, Lord Jesus, until you come in glory."[9] And to be sure, awaiting the future return of Christ in glory does not entail passivity or idleness. Rather, the faithful are to be about the business of cultivating the kingdom of God in its inaugurated form, as if it were a mustard seed, until that day in which it is fully grown.

For Cunningham, then, and for many others, Catholicism is indeed a worldview, a distinctive conception of life and a veritable *habitus* or way of being in the world. It begins with creation as the gift of God, acknowledges the problem of sin, and recognizes the hope of redemption in the work of Jesus Christ. It is a realistic view of faith that brings together apparent doctrinal antinomies into a pattern of balance, consistency, and wholeness. It places special emphasis on time, remembering God's work in the past, celebrating and proclaiming the good news in the present, and anticipating the victorious return of Christ to the earth in the future.[10]

There is another feature to the Catholic *Weltanschauung*, however, that Cunningham fails to mention specifically, though it may be implied in his discussion. If we are to honor the Catholic belief in "the hierarchy of truths" which states that theological precepts "vary in their relation to the foundation of the Christian faith,"[11] then basic to the above discussion of creation, sin, realism, and time is the doctrine of the Trinity. That God is one in substance, essence, or nature, and yet subsists as three divine persons — Father, Son, and Holy Spirit — who are distinct from and yet in relation with one another is at the heart of Catholic teaching and experience. Indeed, the revealed truth of the Holy Trinity is not only the root of the church's dynamic faith, but is also central to understanding how God fulfills his perfect plan in history. It is, therefore, crucial to the Catholic worldview. The recently published *Catechism of the Catholic Church* explains the pivotal nature of this doctrine and connects it with God's redemptive purposes in history.

9. Cunningham, p. 123.

10. Richard P. McBrien, *Catholicism,* 2 vols. (Minneapolis: Winston Press, 1980), 1:135-37, presents two additional summaries of the Catholic mind, one based on various historic documents and the other culled from the *Pastoral Constitution on the Church in the Modern World* of Vatican II (1965).

11. *Catechism of the Catholic Church* (Liguori, Mo.: Liguori Publications, 1994), p. 28 (§90).

The mystery of the Most Holy Trinity is the central mystery of Christian faith and life. It is the mystery of God in himself. It is therefore the source of all the other mysteries of the faith, the light that enlightens them all. It is the most fundamental and essential teaching in the "hierarchy of the truths of faith." The whole history of salvation is identical with the history of the way and means by which the one true God, Father, Son, and Holy Spirit, reveals himself to men, "and reconciles and unites with himself those who turn away from sin."[12]

Established upon this high trinitarian foundation, the riches of Latin Christianity and the Catholic worldview come into sharper focus. There was, however, a time in which these doctrines were shrouded in mystery, communicated in a dead language, and, as in other Christian traditions, placed in eclipse by an overpowering secularity. In the last fifty years, however, they have been brought to the attention of the modern world in a most powerful way, beginning with the Second Vatican Council, and in particular through the remarkable pontificate of Pope John Paul II.

A "Worldviewish" Pope

In recommending the apologetic strategy of James Orr for imitation in postmodern times, J. I. Packer mentions the names of several prominent twentieth-century thinkers, including G. K. Chesterton, C. S. Lewis, and Francis Schaeffer, who in one sense or another assumed the Scotsman's mantle. Then he makes this almost off-the-cuff comment: "It is arguable that the present pope [John Paul II] comes close to qualifying as Orr's successor." According to Packer, what Orr and his successors, including the pope, have provided, and what is needed for Christian renewal amidst the hurricane forces of postmodernity, is nothing less than a vigorous presentation of the complete biblical picture of reality: "a flow of wide-ranging, well-focused and magisterially combative declarations of the total Christian view of things as being supremely realistic and rational."[13] Thus for Packer, the pope is in this sense a "new Orr." And not only that, but Catholic philosopher Michael Novak has compared the pontiff's ambition to clear away the contemporary cultural debris to make room

12. *Catechism*, p. 62 (§234). I am indebted to Tim Mahoney for pointing out this important aspect of the Catholic worldview.
13. J. I. Packer, "On from Orr: Cultural Crisis, Rational Realism and Incarnational Ontology," in *Reclaiming the Great Tradition: Evangelicals, Catholics, and Orthodox in Dialogue*, ed. James S. Cutsinger (Downers Grove, Ill.: InterVarsity, 1997), pp. 166-67.

for a biblical vision of life to the similar work of evangelical thinkers Carl Henry and Francis Schaeffer.[14] If these observations from both sides of the Protestant/Catholic divide are allowed to stand, then it may be safe to say that Karol Jozef Wojtyla (b. 1920) — the 246th bishop of Rome — is indeed a "worldviewish" pope. For indeed, he has sought to apply the resources of Catholic faith across the whole spectrum of life, focusing upon the dignity of the human person, and seeking to bring lasting reform within the church and transformation to human culture worldwide. He has been labeled a "Christian radical" (in the literal sense of *radix,* meaning "root") — one who believes that some things are simply *true,* and that Jesus Christ — who is the truth — is the final answer to the question that is every human life. On this foundation he has conducted "an evangelical papacy of great intellectual creativity and public impact," and as a result has become perhaps "the most consequential pope since the Reformation and Counter-Reformation in the sixteenth century."[15] What accounts for this man's extraordinary greatness and influence?

Wojtyla grew up in Poland and lived his early life in the midst of the horrors and brutality of the Nazi and Communist occupations. There he witnessed firsthand the devastating consequences of various humanistic ideologies which promised a utopian dream but delivered a cultural nightmare, stripping away the freedom and dignity of countless multitudes. In due course Wojtyla became convinced at intuitive, experiential, and philosophical levels that the fundamental crisis in the West rested squarely upon false ideas about the nature of persons. Consequently, even in the midst of the proceedings of the Second Vatican Council, Wojtyla was at work on a programmatic book that addressed this very issue. In a letter to Father Henri de Lubac, he explains the nature of his project which arose out of his deep concern for the plight of the person.

> I devote my very rare free moments to a work that is close to my heart and devoted to the metaphysical sense and mystery of the PERSON. It seems to me that the debate today is being played out on that level. The evil of our times consists in the first place in a kind of degradation, indeed in a pulverization, of the fundamental uniqueness of each human person. This evil is even much more of the metaphysical order than of the moral order.

14. Michael Novak, foreword to *Karol Wojtyla: The Thought of the Man Who Became Pope John Paul II,* by Rocco Buttiglione, trans. Paolo Guietti and Francesca Murphy (Grand Rapids: Eerdmans, 1997), p. xi.

15. These observations about the pope come from George Weigel, *Witness to Hope: The Biography of Pope John Paul II* (New York: Harper Collins, Cliff Street Books, 1999), pp. 4, 9, 10, 855.

To this disintegration planned at time by atheistic ideologies, we must oppose, rather than sterile polemics, a kind of "recapitulation" of the inviolable mystery of the person.[16]

Wojtyla was not only concerned about the devastation of those who suffered under the icy grip of the Nazi and Communist regimes, but he also recognized the disfiguring consequences upon those held in bondage to the excesses of Western individualism and selfish capitalism. Regardless of location, for Wojtyla various political and economic systems based upon secular and atheistic assumptions led to a profound betrayal of the true nature and nobility of persons. The twentieth century, despite its astonishing scientific, technological, and economic progress, was a moral and spiritual wasteland, and its impact upon humanity was nothing short of catastrophic.

What must be done? The above quotation discloses Wojtyla's deft strategy. First of all, the antidote to the present crisis is not to be found in moral sloganeering, since the question about humanity is not primarily an ethical one. Second, it is not to be found in "sterile polemics," that is, in feckless, helterskelter defenses trumpeting the value of persons. Rather, since the problem is primarily metaphysical, rooted in comprehensive atheistic ideologies, the only modus operandi capable of taking on such a pervasive and powerful interpretation of reality would be to match it with an equally exhaustive and potent philosophy, one that entailed a "'recapitulation' of the inviolable mystery of the person." In other words, Wojtyla knew, in a manner similar to Orr and Kuyper before him, that the battle for the soul of the world and its human occupants must be based upon a reconstituted metaphysics, that is, upon a fresh articulation of an overall theistic view of life that upheld the majesty of man. Thus Wojtyla's vision of a Catholic Christian humanism, as the only adequate response to the crisis of contemporary humanism, was born.

The man who became the pope based his agenda on three fundamental convictions. The first is that without exception, human beings are characterized intrinsically by a philosophical aspiration to search for the truth, and by a desire to discover the answers to the ultimate questions of life. "All men and women," the pope says in his encyclical on faith and reason (Fides et Ratio), "are in some sense philosophers and have their own philosophical conceptions with which they direct their lives."[17] Indeed, a person may even be defined as "the

---

16. Henri de Lubac, At the Service of the Church (San Francisco: Ignatius, 1993), pp. 171-72, quoted by Weigel, p. 174. Wojtyla's book on the metaphysics and mystery of the person is his major philosophical work available in English: The Acting Person (Dordrecht: D. Reidel, 1979).

17. Pope John Paul II, Fides et Ratio: On the Relationship between Faith and Reason, encyclical letter (Boston: Pauline Books and Media, 1998), p. 43.

one who seeks the truth."[18] Promoting philosophical activity of this kind — especially encouraging the Catholic faithful to draw upon the twin resources of faith and reason in order to form an overall view of life — has been an enduring trait of the pontiff's career. He is optimistic about such a project, affirming that "In Sacred Scripture are found elements, both implicit and explicit, which allow a vision of the human being and the world which has exceptional philosophical density."[19] According to the pope, then, philosophical formation is a central and inescapably human enterprise.

This leads naturally to Wojtyla's second fundamental conviction, and that is that human culture is based upon and the outgrowth of particular philosophical and religious commitments. Culture, as the term suggests — though it is often forgotten — is ultimately the product of the *cult*. How people think and what they worship determines what they make and how they live. Culture, therefore, is the engine which guides events and determines destiny. "Of all the factors that shape history," explains Richard John Neuhaus, "this Pope is convinced that culture is the most important. How people try to make sense of the world, how they define the good life, how they inculcate the moral visions by which they would live — this is the stuff of culture."[20] Culture, therefore, is the root cause of the human condition.

The pope's third basic conviction is a consequence of the previous two.

18. Pope John Paul II, *Fides et Ratio*, p. 41.

19. Pope John Paul II, *Fides et Ratio*, p. 100. In a fascinating footnote to *Fides et Ratio*, pp. 45-46 n. 28, he discloses his abiding interest in philosophical formation within the traditional Catholic framework in which faith perfects reason: "'What is man and of what use is he? What is good in him and what is evil?' (Sir. 18:8). . . . These are questions in every human heart, as the poetic genius of every time and every people has shown, posing again and again — almost as the prophetic voice of humanity — the *serious question* which makes human beings what they are. They are questions which express the urgency of finding a reason for existence, in every moment, at life's most important and decisive times as well as more ordinary times. These questions show the deep reasonableness of human existence since they summon human intelligence and will to search freely for a solution which can reveal the full meaning of life. These enquiries, therefore, are the highest expression of human nature; which is why the answer to them is the gauge of the depth of his engagement with his own existence. In particular, when *the why of things* is explored in full harmony with the search for the ultimate answer, then human reason reaches its zenith and opens to the religious impulse. The religious impulse is the highest expression of the human person, because it is the highpoint of his rational nature. It springs from the profound human aspiration for the truth and it is the basis of the human being's free and personal search for the divine." This quote may also be found in *General Audience* (19 October 1983): 1-2; *Insegnamenti* 6 (1983): 814-15.

20. Richard John Neuhaus, foreword to *Springtime of Evangelization: The Complete Texts of the Holy Father's 1998 ad Limina Addresses to the Bishops of the United States*, by Pope John Paul II (San Francisco: Ignatius, 1999), p. 14.

Given that culture is the history-shaping outcome of humanity's native philosophical and religious impulse, in order to alter human experience for the better, a radical transformation must take place at the cultural level and in the set of basic ideas that make it up. The pontiff's settled solution, therefore, to the modern problem of human pulverization is through the instrumentality of cultural change, and indeed a change in its underlying philosophy and religion as the ultimate sources from which it springs. While there may be a place for active resistance against the forces of terror, it seems that for Wojtyla such efforts deal only with the symptoms, not with the root causes of the political and social disease. Change at the most primordial level, therefore, requires a metamorphosis in ultimate meaning through words — both human and divine — that conceptualize reality and frame human existence. Hence, in taking aim at this deeper level of reality, Wojtyla seeks to displace the well-ensconced ideologies responsible for the miseries of contemporary man through the proclamation and practice of a vibrant Christian humanism grown in Catholic soil. He has offered this fresh, comprehensive vision of life as a new basis for Western culture and as the wellspring of genuine hope.

Wojtyla's vast and richly developed understanding of Christian humanism is beyond a fair description in a short space. Nevertheless, as the name suggests, it is radically christocentric, focusing upon the person and work of the incarnate Lord. Summarizing in the extreme, the essence of the pope's viewpoint is, in his own words, that "in Christ and through Christ man has acquired full awareness of his dignity, of the heights to which he is raised, of the surpassing worth of his own humanity, and of the meaning of his existence."[21] This view of the world and the dignity of human persons arising out of the mystery of the incarnate Christ is the cornerstone of the pope's Christian humanistic worldview whose implications embrace the totality of life.

It is this majestic theme which Wojtyla promoted vigorously as the archbishop of Kraków at the Second Vatican Council (1962-65), that famous *aggiornamento*, or "updating" of Catholicism to meet the challenges of the modern world.[22] It is this theme that undergirds his book on the Council, titled *Sources*

---

21. Pope John Paul II, *The Redeemer of Man: Redemptor Hominis,* encyclical letter (Boston: Pauline Books and Media, 1979), pp. 20-21. For a discussion of the pope's vision of Christian humanism, see Andrew N. Woznicki, *The Dignity of Man as a Person: Essays on the Christian Humanism of His Holiness John Paul II* (San Francisco: Society of Christ Publications, 1987).

22. See Weigel's discussion on Wojtyla's influential role at Vatican II and his pressing the issue of the nature of the human person and his promulgation of the vision of Christian humanism, pp. 145-80. The Pastoral Constitution on the Church in the Modern World, known as *Gaudium et Spes,* ratified on 7 December 1965, deals with "man's deeper questionings" and, on the basis of answers found in Jesus Christ, sets forth the church's understanding of a whole host of social and cul-

of Renewal, which is devoted to the formation of the theological consciousness and practical attitudes of Catholic believers.[23] It is this theme that has been at the center of his entire pontificate, declared boldly at its outset in the very first of his thirteen papal encyclicals bearing the title *Redemptor Hominis,* "Redeemer of Man."[24] It is the theme of his hope for a "new springtime of evangelization" designed to bring the gospel of Christ to the whole world as the true solution to the crises of contemporary life.[25] It is, finally, the theme of the pope's year of Jubilee, a great ecclesiastical renewal movement and celebration at the beginning of the third millennium in which the implications of Christian humanism are being explored in all the categories of human existence.[26]

On the basis of this revolutionary philosophy, Pope John Paul II, one of the most influential leaders in the twentieth century, has proclaimed that it is possible to enter the next thousand years of human history on a confident note, "crossing the threshold of hope."[27] For in the Christian gospel, the true story of the world is told: the existence of the trinitarian God — Father, Son, and Holy Spirit; a good and glorious creation as a divine gift; the honor and dignity of persons as the *imago Dei;* the tragedy of the fall which explains human misery; and the forgiveness of sin and the renewal of life through the incarnation and redemption of the God-man Jesus Christ. This biblically based, tradition-rich interpretation of life with its unrelenting emphasis on the dignity of the human person is the worldview orientation of the pope, a spiritually sensitive man who even in his old age arises while it is still dark in order to see the sunrise.[28]

---

tural issues, beginning with an affirmation of the dignity of the human person. See Austin P. Flannery, ed., *Documents of Vatican II,* rev. ed. (Grand Rapids: Eerdmans, 1984), pp. 903-1014.

23. See Cardinal Karol Wojtyla, *Sources of Renewal: The Implementation of the Second Vatican Council,* trans. P. S. Falla (San Francisco: Harper and Row, 1980). This work almost seems to be an exercise in the formation of a Vatican II Catholic worldview.

24. This encyclical, the content of which Wojtyla brought with him to the papacy as its governing theme, was his programmatic essay on Christian humanism.

25. Pope John Paul II, *Springtime of Evangelization.*

26. Virgil Elizondo and Jon Sobrino, eds., *2000: Reality and Hope* (Maryknoll, N.Y.: Orbis, 1999), see especially pp. 59-65. Also the Vatican website provides much information about the Jubilee Year 2000, including details about a series of ongoing conferences addressing twenty-seven vital topics from the vantage point of Christian humanism and the dignity of the person. These include gatherings of artists, craftsmen, scientists, journalists, university professors, families, sports figures, representatives from the armed forces and police, the disabled, and so on. See http://www.vatican.va/jubilee_2000/jubilee_year/novomillennio_en.htm. Accessed 16 March 2002.

27. See the pope's popular declaration of the Catholic view of life and Christian manifesto for the twenty-first century, Pope John Paul II, *Crossing the Threshold of Hope,* ed. Vittorio Messori, trans. Jenny McPhee and Martha McPhee (New York: Knopf, 1994).

28. Weigel, p. 864.

Eastern Orthodoxy

Eastern Orthodox theologian and liturgical scholar Alexander Schmemann (1921-83) has observed that despite significant dialogue between the Western and Eastern Churches, there is precious little understanding of Orthodoxy on the part of Occidental believers, especially when it comes to its underlying worldview. He writes: "In spite of the ecumenical encounter between the Christian East and the Christian West, an encounter that has lasted now for more than half a century, in spite of an officially acknowledged state of 'dialogue,' in my opinion it is still very difficult for a Western Christian fully to understand Orthodoxy, and not so much the officially formulated dogmas and doctrines of the Orthodox Church as the fundamental world view, the experience that lies beneath these formulations and constitutes their living and 'existential' context."[29]

This low cognizance on the part of provincial Westerners is not because Orthodoxy has necessarily underemphasized the worldview concept. Indeed, "Weltanschauung," says James Counelis, "is what the Orthodox theological enterprise is all about," though he rightly notes that "Orthodox theology traditionally does not speak in these terms."[30] Nevertheless, the idea is present, just as it resides tacitly in Roman Catholic discourse on the incarnation. As Schmemann notes, to be found in the debates within the Eastern Church over "the great theandric mystery," that is, the doctrine of the God-man, are "the roots and the presuppositions of a truly Christian 'humanism,' of a Christian vision of the world."[31] There are good reasons, however, why the Orthodox environment has generated a measure of reticence when it comes to the more abstract project of worldview formation.

Orthodoxy and Worldview

Christian thinkers in the West assume axiomatically the ratio-scientific nature of the theological enterprise. Beginning as early as the patristic period, it has

29. Alexander Schmemann, *Church, World, Mission* (Crestwood, N.Y.: St. Vladimir's Seminary Press, 1979), p. 25.

30. James Steve Counelis, "Relevance and the Orthodox Christian Theological Enterprise: A Symbolic Paradigm on Weltanschauung," *Greek Orthodox Theological Review* 18 (spring-fall 1973): 35. For additional discussion on this matter of an Orthodox worldview, see also John Chryssavgis, "The World as Sacrament: Insights into an Orthodox Worldview," *Pacifica* 10 (1997): 1-24.

31. Schmemann, *Church, World, Mission*, p. 48.

been pursued more or less as an academic exercise often detached from the life and worship of the church. As an analytic study, it focuses on the interpretation of biblical propositions about God and his relationship to the world and organizes them into a systematic whole. This scientifically oriented model is well ensconced in Catholic and Protestant theological consciousness.

Orthodoxy, however, views the project differently. In the seventeenth through nineteenth centuries, the appropriation of Western thought-styles for the Orthodox theological task, in particular the scholastic and the confessional methods, resulted in what has come to be known as the "Western Captivity" of the church. By pulling its roots out of patristic soil and forsaking its grounding in the mysteries of the faith and its liturgy, false forms of Orthodox theology were produced, at least temporarily.[32] In order to be faithful to its distinctive character, however, Orthodox formulations of the faith, including its worldview, must be anchored in the experience of liturgical worship. As Daniel Clendenin notes, "While Westerners tend to learn their theology from books in the library, Orthodoxy specializes in learning theology from the liturgy and worship in the sanctuary."[33] Timothy Ware, in his popular introductory volume to the Orthodox Church, explains this historic approach in depth.

> The Orthodox approach to religion is fundamentally a liturgical approach, which understands doctrine in the context of divine worship: it is no coincidence that the word "Orthodoxy" should signify alike right belief and right worship, for the two things are inseparable. It has been truly said of the Byzantines: "Dogma with them is not only an intellectual system apprehended by the clergy and expounded to the laity, but a field of vision wherein all things on earth are seen in their relation to things in heaven, first and foremost through liturgical celebration." In the words of Georges Florovsky, "Christianity is a liturgical religion. The Church is first of all a worshipping community. Worship comes first, doctrine and discipline second." Those who wish to know about Orthodoxy should not so much read books as . . . attend the Liturgy. As Philip said to Nathaniel: "Come and see" (John 1:46).[34]

---

32. Bradley Nassif, "New Dimensions in Eastern Orthodox Theology," in *New Dimensions in Evangelical Thought: Essays in Honor of Millard J. Erickson,* ed. David S. Dockery (Downers Grove, Ill.: InterVarsity, 1998), pp. 106-8.

33. Daniel B. Clendenin, ed., introduction to *Eastern Orthodox Theology: A Contemporary Reader* (Grand Rapids: Baker, 1995), pp. 7-8. See also Clendenin's exposition of Orthodoxy in *Eastern Orthodox Christianity* (Grand Rapids: Baker, 1994).

34. Timothy Ware, *The Orthodox Church* (New York: Penguin Books, 1964), p. 271.

This liturgical modus operandi has a direct impact not only on theologizing, but also on the development and understanding of an Orthodox worldview, an approach considerably distant in spirit from the more abstract, systematic Protestant reflections of Orr, Kuyper, Dooyeweerd, and even the pope. Drawing on the resources of the Eastern paradigm, Schmemann has articulated a classic statement of the Orthodox *Weltanschauung* that is derived from her liturgy and generates a sacramental perspective on life. The essential themes of this outlook are well worth summarizing.

A Sacramental Worldview

In the preface to his volume *For the Life of the World: Sacraments and Orthodoxy,* Schmemann notes that the purpose of his book, written primarily for a student audience, is "to outline . . . the 'Christian world-view,' i.e., the approach to the world and man's life in it that stems from the liturgical experience of the Orthodox Church."[35] Schmemann's goal, in fidelity to the Eastern ethos, is not to present an abstract explanation or formal analysis of Orthodox theology or its worldview, but rather to show that a sacramental way of perceiving the world and the kingdom is cultivated through the experience of the church at worship. "It is my certitude that the answer comes to us not from neat intellectual theories, but above all from that living and unbroken experience of the Church which she reveals and communicates to us in her worship, in the *leitourgia* always making her what she is: the sacrament of the world, the sacrament of the kingdom — their gift to us *in Christ*" (p. 8).[36]

So he proceeds in chapter 2 to a description of the high point of the Orthodox liturgy — the Eucharist — and details in chapter 3 how the principles of God's kingdom, freshly experienced in the Sacrament, can be deployed in the renewal of life. In chapters 4, 5, and 6 he discusses the liturgies of baptism, marriage, and healing as the basis for extending the kingdom of God into all aspects of life. He concludes the volume with an exhortation to the church in her vocation of mission to testify to the reality of the world and to be about the business of transforming it. This entire discussion, however, is placed in the context of the first chapter, in which Schmemann sketches the framework of the Orthodox worldview. In it he focuses on the priestly role of human beings in relation

35. Alexander Schmemann, *For the Life of the World: Sacraments and Orthodoxy* (Crestwood, N.Y.: St. Vladimir's Theological Seminary Press, 1973), p. 7. The parenthetical page references in the following analysis are to this text.

36. Here Schmemann uses the word "sacrament" in a general way as a virtual synonym for "revelation."

to creation, the fall, and redemption as the context of the Orthodox perception of life.[37]

Schmemann begins by focusing on the seemingly innocuous theme of food, quoting Ludwig Feuerbach, who said that "man is what he eats." By this quip the German materialist philosopher attempted to convey the idea that human beings are nothing but physical creatures, virtually the product of their diets. In point of fact, however, Schmemann says he unwittingly hit upon the most religious idea of humanity. In the biblical story of creation, man is presented first of all as a hungry being, and the whole world is set before him as his food. Second only to the command to propagate and have dominion over creation is the command to eat of the earth (Gen. 1:29). Schmemann explains this idea in these words:

> Man must eat in order to live; he must take the world into his body and transform it into himself, into flesh and blood. He is indeed that which he eats, and the whole world is presented as one all-embracing banquet table for man. And this image of the banquet remains, throughout the whole Bible, the central image of life. It is the image of life at its creation and also the image of life at its end and fulfillment: ". . . that you eat and drink at my table in my Kingdom." (p. 11)

As Schmemann explains, he begins with this seemingly secondary topic of food because he wants to answer a basic question about the nature of life itself: "Of what life do we speak," he asks, "what life do we preach, proclaim and announce when, as Christians, we confess that Christ died for the life of the world? What *life* is both motivation, and the beginning and the goal of Christian *mission?*" (pp. 11-12). Certainly Christ offers abundant *life*, but exactly what is it?

Two basic responses are typically given to this query, Schmemann asserts. First, some believe the life Christ offers is the distinctively religious and spiritual life that is associated with the church but cut off from the ordinary life of the world. Second, others believe the life Christ offers is the distinctively human and cultural life associated with the world, the renewal of which is the primary business of the church. Both are representative of the "church of the extreme," to invoke Niebuhrian categories. The first group consists of the "radicals," embody-

---

37. Chryssavgis, pp. 6-8, is in full agreement with Schmemann's threefold analysis of the Orthodox worldview. He asserts that "The essential christian vision consists of holding together three fundamental intuitions concerning creation," and then discusses the themes of the world as good, evil, and redeemed. He summarizes by saying, "When one of these is isolated or violated, the result is an unbalanced and destructive vision of the world" (p. 6).

ing a Manichean "Christ against culture" mentality, those for whom religion is the only thing. The second group involves the "culturals," exemplifying a liberal "Christ of culture" mind-set, those for whom the world is the only thing.[38]

The answers provided by these opposing groups are inadequate, according to Schmemann, for nowhere in the Bible do we find these standard dualistic categories that are so prevalent in Western (if not world) religious conscious-ness. Thus the question remains wide open regarding the nature of this *life* for which Christ died. "Whether we 'spiritualize' our life or 'secularize' our reli-gion, whether we invite men to a spiritual banquet or simply join them at the secular one, the real life of the world, for which we are told God gave his only-begotten Son, remains hopelessly beyond our religious grasp" (p. 13).

To get beyond the impasse, Schmemann proposes a third alternative to these two traditional categories: Christ did not die for the *spiritual* life or the *secular* life, but for the total *sacramental* life of the world. To explain what he means, he presents his understanding of human beings as the priests of cre-ation as it is expressed in the church's liturgy.

Humanity as Priest of Creation

Picking up with the theme mentioned earlier, the Bible begins with the person as a hungry being and the *whole* world is set before him as the provision for his need. As Schmemann points out, since the world is God's creation and food is his gift, the act of eating, typically understood as a purely natural matter, is transformed into an experience of communion with God. Consequently, the dichotomy between the secular and the sacred is thereby destroyed. In receiving and enjoying the gifts of God's creation, believers simultaneously enjoy fellow-ship with God and gain a knowledge of him. The spiritual and material worlds are intimately bound up with each other, eliminating any artificial division be-tween them. God is not opposed to the material world; the material world is not opposed to God. Since the material world is God's creation, it must be under-stood as the source and revelation of his presence and provision.

> In the Bible the food that man eats, the world of which he must partake [literally] in order to live, is given to him by God, and it is given as *commu-nion with God*. The world as man's food is not something "material" and limited to material functions, thus different from, and opposed to, the specifically "spiritual" functions by which man is related to God. All that exists is God's gift to man, and it all exists to make God known to man, to

38. H. Richard Niebuhr, *Christ and Culture* (New York: Harper and Row, 1951), pp. 116-20.

make man's life communion with God. It is divine love made food, made life for man. God *blesses* everything He creates, and, in biblical language, this means that He makes all creation the sign and means of His presence and wisdom, love and revelation: "O taste and see that the Lord is good." (p. 14)

For Schmemann, obviously, the world cannot be reduced to Feuerbachian materialism. Instead, on the basis of the creation narratives in the book of Genesis, he makes the wonderful rediscovery of the world as God's creation with all of its attendant sacramental implications. The world as creation speaks of its Creator in its deepest, essential nature. "The world, be it in its totality as cosmos, or in its life and becoming as time and history, is an *epiphany* of God, a means of His revelation, presence, and power. In other words, it not only 'posits' the idea of God as a rationally acceptable cause of its existence, but truly 'speaks' of Him and is in itself an essential means both of knowledge of God and communion with Him, and to be so is its true nature and ultimate destiny" (p. 120).

Since this is what the world is, how should people relate to it? What is the proper role of human beings in relation to creation? The answer is found in the office of priest. God has so made human beings that all the hungers of life, signified by the need for food, are to be met through the stuff of the very good world as a sign and symbol of God himself. For this gift of the world and its provisions, the appropriate response is a priestly one: to thank and bless God for it in an act of worship that fulfills the true nature of human beings. People are "thinkers" and "makers," to be sure, but more deeply they are worshipers. In gratefully receiving the gifts of the world and transforming them into life in God, people become the priests of this cosmic sacrament of creation.

> "Homo sapiens," "homo faber" . . . yes, but, first of all, "homo adorans." The first, the basic definition of man is that he is the priest. He stands in the center of the world and unifies it in his act of blessing God, of both receiving the world from God and offering it to God — and by filling the world with this eucharist, he transforms life, the one that he receives from the world, into life in God, into communion with Him. The world was created as the "matter," the material of one all-embracing eucharist, and man was created as the priest of this cosmic sacrament. (p. 15)

The Loss of Priestly Life in Sin

Given this Orthodox understanding of the sacramental nature of the creation and the human priestly role within it, how does Schmemann conceive of the fall of humanity into sin in Genesis 3? What is the meaning, and what are the consequences, of this catastrophic act? As he says, it is not surprising that the fall focuses again on the theme of food. The primeval couple ate the forbidden fruit from the tree of the knowledge of good and evil in violation of the divine commandment. The real significance of this act, however, was not that Adam and Eve simply stepped across the line and transgressed God's commandment. Rather the fall means the rejection of the world as the sign of the presence and provision of God, and a renunciation of humanity's priestly vocation. It meant that they desired the world as a thing in itself apart from its Maker. They sought to live by it and its bread *alone*. The world is no longer viewed as God's world; it is just there, not as creation, but as mere "nature." In other words, the fall of humanity in Genesis 3 means the loss of the sacramental, revelatory perspective on reality. Schmemann explains it this way:

> The fruit of that one tree, whatever else it may signify, was unlike every other fruit in the Garden: it was not offered as a gift to man. Not given, not blessed by God, it was food whose eating was condemned to be communion with itself alone, and not with God. It is the image of the world loved for itself, and eating it is the image of life understood as an end in itself. . . . Man has loved the world, but as an end in itself and not as transparent to God. He has done it so consistently that it has become something that is "in the air." It seems natural for man to experience the world as opaque, and not shot through with the presence of God. It seems natural not to live a life of thanksgiving for God's gift of a world. It seems natural not to be eucharistic. (p. 16)

Human beings were to live "eucharistically," that is, acknowledging the divine source of the world and its gifts and responding with profound gratitude. In the fall, however, humanity lost cognizance of its priestly role and the power to live with such understanding and thanksgiving. Rather, humanity's dependence upon and appropriation of the world became a "closed circuit." It refers only to itself and not to God as its point of reference, and consequently people fail to worship and give thanks.

Human beings in the condition of sin are still hungry beings. They still seek the satisfaction of their needs in what the world provides. People know they are dependent upon what lies beyond or outside of them (food, air, water, other people, etc.). But in a state of alienation from God, human loves and hungers and their fulfillment are carried out in reference to the world alone and on its own terms, with Edenic results. "For the one who thinks food in itself is the source of life, eating is communion with death." When the world is pursued autonomously, as a value in and of itself, it loses all value. In the fall, "Man lost the eucharistic life, he lost the life of life itself, the power to transform it into Life. He ceased to be the priest of the world and became its slave" (p. 17).

> In our perspective, . . . the "original" sin is not primarily that man has "disobeyed" God; the sin is that he ceased to be hungry for Him and for Him alone, ceased to see his whole life depending on the whole world as a sacrament of communion with God. The sin was not that man neglected his religious duties. The sin was that he thought of God in terms of religion, i.e., opposing Him to life. The only real fall of man is his noneucharistic life in a noneucharistic world. The fall is not that he preferred the world to God, distorted the balance between the spiritual and the material, but that he made the world material, whereas he was to have transformed it into "life in God," filled with meaning and spirit. (p. 18)

Renewal of the Priestly Life in Redemption

Schmemann conceives of "creation" as the sacrament of God's presence and blessing, and human beings as its priests, and the fall as the loss of both. How, then, does he understand redemption in Jesus Christ? As we might well expect, it has to do with the recovery of the sacramental perspective on life and the renewal of our priestly role within it. God did not leave the human race in bondage to confused longings, overtaken by countless desires and hungers for which there seems to be no final satisfaction. Human beings have fought and struggled to find the meaning of the mysterious needs and hungers within. God created human beings after his own heart and for himself. Thus, only through the light and gospel of the person of Jesus Christ is the source and satisfaction of these hungers to be found.

> In this scene of radical unfulfillment God acted decisively: into the darkness where man was groping toward Paradise, He sent light. He did so not as a rescue operation, to recover lost man: *it was rather for the completing of what He had undertaken from the beginning.* God acted so that man might understand who He really was and where his hunger had been driving him.
>
> The light God sent was his Son: the same light that had been shining unextinguished in the world's darkness all along, seen now in full brightness. (p. 18, emphasis added)

Notice in this that the ministry of Christ was not so much a rescue operation as "the completing of what He had undertaken from the beginning." What had God undertaken from the beginning? Was it not the creation of a world that served as the sign and symbol of his presence and love? Was it not in God that the gifts of his creation were to satisfy the hungers of the human heart? Were not the desperate cravings of the soul pointing to God all along? Does not the human heart long to offer thanks for the blessings of life? Does not the long history of religion point in a fragmentary way to human aspirations for God? In Christ, all religion came to an end because he is the final answer to all religious aspirations and to all human hunger. In him the true *life* that was lost by man was restored, for redemption as new creation means "that in Christ, life — life in all its totality — was returned to man, given again as sacrament and communion, made Eucharist" (pp. 20-21). In redemption, the world is restored as God's creation and human beings resume their priestly vocation. Christ died for this life of the world.

Of course, it is not surprising if the restoration to this holy form of living in Christ is celebrated, even accessed, by means of food. The benefits of this act of total self-giving on Jesus' part are received, according to Schmemann, through a sacred meal: the Holy Eucharist or Communion. The elements of bread and wine, offered up on the altar and received in remembrance of him, embody the whole range of sacramental experience. Human life is dependent upon food, upon bread and wine, upon the creation spread forth as a banquet feast. Human beings were created to be the celebrants of the cosmic eucharist and enjoy the transformation of life in God. In receiving the elements of Communion, believers realize what these elements really are, and indeed, what the entire creation actually is — the gifts of God that manifest his presence and make him known. To offer this food, this world, and this life to God is the priestly, eucharistic function of human beings and their very fulfillment. In this liturgy the true meaning of the world and the identity of persons — the sum and substance of the Orthodox worldview — is disclosed.

Conclusion

The word "worldview" is not particularly prominent in the spiritual or theological vocabulary of either Catholicism or Orthodoxy. Nonetheless, embedded in both traditions is an inner impulse to express their comprehension of Christianity as a *Weltanschauung*. Cunningham employs the concept explicitly as a means of summarizing the essentials of Catholic thought as he understands it. Nestled in the pope's program of Christian humanism is nothing less than a comprehensive Catholic interpretation of the universe centered on the incarnation of Jesus Christ and the dignity of persons. Since the spirit of Eastern Or-

thodoxy militates against theological ratiocination, formulating a propositional Orthodox worldview is a rarity. This does not mean that such an entity is
missing in this tradition, however. Its source is found in the church's liturgy,
and from this wellspring Schmemann is capable of outlining an Orthodox perception of life at its sacramental and priestly best.

Now, without minimizing the serious differences that exist between the
three great Christian traditions of evangelical Protestantism, Catholicism, and
Orthodoxy, they share much in common regarding the matter of a Christian
Weltanschauung. Each stream in the historic church has its particular strengths
and weaknesses. As the body of Christ, the better part of wisdom would suggest
that we capitalize on each other's strengths in order to shore up the weaknesses
in our own attempts to construct an authentic Christian vision of reality that
will inevitably be limited in scope and balance. If we can grant that the Holy
Spirit has been at work throughout the ages in various God-honoring traditions other than our own (as Richard Foster has shown),[39] then there would
seem to be no reason why a kind of mutual learning should not take place between us. Such an openness can help to fill in the gaps in our respective formulations of a Christian worldview. In supporting this kind of cooperation, Avery
Dulles, S.J., has recommended that the various parties involved "should pursue
an ecumenism of mutual enrichment, asking how much they can give to, and
receive from, one another. . . . What each group affirms in faith may be seen as
held in trust by them for the whole *oikoumene.*"[40]

As the first two chapters of this study have shown, there is a remarkable
common denominator among these three traditions in affirming the overall
biblical schema of creation, fall, and redemption. Protestant evangelicals, in
keeping with their emphasis on the authority and supremacy of Scripture,
have been particularly adept at setting forth the biblical meanings and cultural
implications of these three themes in a systematic fashion. The contributions
of the Catholic and Orthodox wings have been especially keen in fleshing out
the spiritual and theological significance of these same concepts in sacramental and liturgical ways. Both aspects—the biblical/cultural and the sacramen-
tal/liturgical—are *unsurprisingly* compatible and equally needed, along with
salient offerings from other traditions, if the church is to enjoy "a comprehensive, universal Christian worldview" that deepens and enriches the faith of all

---

39. Richard J. Foster, *Streams of Living Water: Celebrating the Great Traditions of Christian
Faith,* foreword by Martin Marty (New York: HarperCollinsPublishers, HarperSanFrancisco,
1998).

40. Avery Dulles, S.J., "The Unity for Which We Hope," in *Evangelicals and Catholics Together: Toward a Common Mission,* ed. Charles Colson and Richard John Neuhaus (Dallas:
Word, 1995), p. 141.

believers, and is capable of fruitfully engaging "a culture awash in nihilism and hedonism."[41]

Still, Protestant evangelicalism, more than any other Christian tradition, has deployed the idea of worldview most extensively. While it might be too much to say that it is a characteristic *of* evangelicalism, it is certainly a prominent feature *within* it, especially in the Reformed context. Given its prominence as a vehicle for communicating a comprehensive and cohesive view of biblical faith, it is important to know something about this concept's origin and role in the history of thought. This will be our task for the next six chapters.

41. Charles Colson, "The Common Cultural Task: The Culture War from a Protestant Perspective," in *Evangelicals and Catholics Together*, p. 37.

Chapter Three

A Philological History of "Worldview"

Word Studies on *Weltanschauung*

At the time of his Kerr Lectures in 1891, James Orr in *The Christian View of God and the World* could say of *Weltanschauung* that "the history of this term has yet to be written."[1] Orr was surprised by the lack of attention given to this notion which had attained academic celebrity status in the second half of the nineteenth century. As he observed, "Within the last two or three decades the word has become exceedingly common in all kinds of books dealing with the higher questions of religion and philosophy — so much so as to have become in a manner indispensable."[2] Though it was one of the favorite terms of the day, much to the dismay of Orr and others, its philological history for the most part was unexplored territory.

This is no longer the case, at least not among German-speaking scholars who have devoted themselves to the taxing disciplines of *Wortgeschichte* (history of words) and *Begriffsgeschichte* (history of concepts or ideas).[3] Much energy has been devoted to the historical investigation of the German lexicon, and this effort has provided a gold mine of information about the background and usage of crucial terms and concepts in the natural and social sciences, humani-

1. James Orr, *The Christian View of God and the World as Centering in the Incarnation* (New York: Scribner, 1887), reprinted as *The Christian View of God and the World*, with a foreword by Vernon C. Grounds (Grand Rapids: Kregel, 1989), p. 365. Despite his complaint, Orr does cite several works in German that address the history of *Weltanschauung*.

2. Orr, *The Christian View of God and the World*, p. 365.

3. Arthur O. Lovejoy has championed the study of the history of ideas as a legitimate academic discipline in the Anglo-American context. For its essential features, see chap. 1 in his *The Great Chain of Being: A Study of the History of an Idea* (Cambridge: Harvard University Press, 1964); and his *Essays in the History of Ideas* (New York: George Braziller, 1955).

ties, philosophy and theology. When *Weltanschauung* had reached its zenith in popularity in both common and academic discourse around the turn of the twentieth century, it finally began to receive noteworthy attention. That attention has continued right up to the present time.

At least seven influential studies by German scholars detailing the history of *Weltanschauung* are worthy of mention. In chronological order, one of the first studies on *Weltanschauung* is found in the context of Albert Gombert's remarks on the discipline of *Wortgeschichte* (1902 and 1907).[4] Much more prominent is the frequently cited "Euphorion-Artikel" written by Alfred Götze in 1924. This essay became the basis for a succinct examination of the term by Franz Dornseiff in 1945-46, and for the lengthy analysis of the concept in 1955 in the magisterial *German Dictionary (Deutsches Wörterbuch)*, which originated with the Brothers Grimm.[5]

A most notable doctoral dissertation titled "Worldview: Studies toward a History and Theory of the Concept" was written by Helmut G. Meier and appeared in 1967.[6] This work is perhaps the most exhaustive treatment of the history and theory of the concept of *Weltanschauung* in German available to date. Meier begins with an examination of the theoretical problems associated with the discipline of the history of ideas *(Begriffsgeschichte)*. He then proceeds to survey the current status of word history studies as they pertain to *Weltanschauung*. He not only analyzes each of the word history resources cited above, but also explores articles on *Weltanschauung* in dictionaries of philosophy in German and in various foreign languages, including English. Next is an in-depth look at the use of *Weltanschauung* in the context of German idealism and romanticism focusing on the use of the notion by Kant, Fichte, Schelling, and Hegel, among others. He then investigates the scope of the term's application by various thinkers halfway through the nineteenth century. After considering worldview as an individual and subjective outlook, Meier then discusses the relationship of *Weltanschauung* and ideology in an excursus. He proceeds to sur-

---

4. Albert Gombert, "Besprechungen von R. M. Meyer's 'Vierhundert Schlagworte,'" *Zeitschrift für deutsche Wortforschung* 3 (1902): 144-58; "Kleine Bemerkungen zur Wortgeschichte," *Zeitschrift für deutsche Wortforschung* 8 (1907): 121-40.

5. Alfred Götze, "Weltanschauung," *Euphorion: Zeitschrift für Literatur-geschichte* 25 (1924): 42-51; Franz Dornseiff, "Weltanschauung. Kurzgefasste Wortgeschichte," *Die Wandlung: Eine Monatsschrift* 1 (1945-46): 1086-88; *Deutsches Wörterbuch von Jacob Grimm und Wilhelm Grimm*, Vierzehnter Band, 1 Teil, Bearbeitet von Alfred Götze und der Arbeitsstelle des Deutschen Wörterbuches zu Berlin (Leipzig: Verlag von S. Hirzel, 1955), pp. 1530-38. The latter work also contains helpful studies of *Weltanschauulich, Weltanschauunglehre, Weltanschauungweise, Weltansicht*, and *Weltbild*.

6. Helmut G. Meier, "'Weltanschauung': Studien zu einer Geschichte und Theorie des Begriffs" (Ph.D. diss., Westfälischen Wilhelms-Universität zu Münster, 1967).

vey its use in the disciplines of philosophy and religion. His final chapter is an inquiry into the structure and function of "Weltanschauung-Philosophie," with attention given to Riehl, Gomperz, Rickert, Husserl, Dilthey, and Jaspers. This work — given its depth of analysis, its extensive notes, and its lengthy bibliography — makes an invaluable contribution to *Weltanschauung* studies.

A "guidebook" on worldviews was also published in German in 1980 which contains the very helpful essay by Werner Betz titled "Toward a History of the Word 'Weltanschauung.'"[7] In this survey the author covers much of the ground contained in the works mentioned above. In addition to the word study, this volume also examines the use of the worldview concept in political theory as well as in esoteric religion and life reform. At the end of the work is an extensive bibliography of over thirty pages compiled by Armin Mohler which demonstrates "the flood of worldview literature" in a variety of helpful categories.[8]

Finally and most recently, Andreas Meier published an article in 1997 in which he traces the birth of the term *Weltanschauung* to the nineteenth century. As the discussion to follow will indicate, however, the term was actually coined in the late eighteenth century, but certainly came into prominence in Germany and throughout Europe during the nineteenth century, as this article indicates.[9]

To these primary German works documenting the word history of *Weltanschauung* must be added two sources in English, both by the same author. Albert M. Wolters has written a very helpful unpublished manuscript titled "'Weltanschauung' in the History of Ideas: Preliminary Notes."[10] In tracing the origin of the word and intellectual history of *Weltanschauung*, Wolters draws heavily on Götze, Dornseiff, Kainz, and the *German Dictionary (Deutsches Wörterbuch)*, and focuses especially on the relationship between personal worldview and scientific philosophy.

This theme of the interface between philosophy as an academic enterprise and worldview as a personal value system is the subject of Wolters's published essay titled "On the Idea of Worldview and Its Relation to Philosophy."[11] On the basis

7. Werner Betz, "Zur Geschichte des Wortes 'Weltanschauung,'" in *Kursbuch der Weltanschauungen*, Schriften der Carl Friedrich von Siemens Stiftung (Frankfurt: Verlag Ullstein, 1980), pp. 18-28.

8. Armin Mohler, "Bibliographie," in *Kursbuch der Weltanschauungen*, pp. 401-33.

9. Andreas Meier, "Die Geburt der 'Weltanschauung' im 19. Jahrhundert," *Theologische Rundschau* 62 (1997): 414-20.

10. Albert M. Wolters, "'Weltanschauung' in the History of Ideas: Preliminary Notes" (n.d., photocopy).

11. Albert M. Wolters, "On the Idea of Worldview and Its Relation to Philosophy," in *Stained Glass: Worldviews and Social Science*, ed. Paul A. Marshall, Sander Griffioen, and Richard J. Mouw, Christian Studies Today (Lanham, Md.: University Press of America, 1989), pp. 14-25.

of various understandings of *Weltanschauung* by a number of German thinkers, Wolters devises a taxonomy of the "worldview-philosophy" relationship in which the former either "repels," "crowns," "flanks," "yields," or "equals" the latter.[12] How to relate individual worldview and professional philosophy has been of historic concern, and Wolters's model, along with his investigation into the history of the term, provides helpful points of departure for reflection on these important topics. However, outside of his work, very little if any attention has been given by English-speaking scholars to the history of *Weltanschauung* as an intellectual conception. Hopefully, this present work will be a step toward rectifying this omission.

The First Use of *Weltanschauung* in Immanuel Kant

In the dynamic "century of Goethe," says Hans-Georg Gadamer, a variety of "key concepts and words which we still use acquired their special stamp," *Weltanschauung* included.[13] During this culturally fertile period, Immanuel Kant was a towering figure, and there is virtually universal recognition that this notable Prussian philosopher coined the term *Weltanschauung* in his work *Critique of Judgment* published in 1790.[14] It comes in a quintessential Kantian paragraph that accents the power of the perception of the human mind.

> If the human mind is nonetheless to *be able even to think* the given infinite without contradiction, it must have within itself a power that is super-sensible, whose idea of the noumenon cannot be intuited but can yet be regarded as the substrate underlying what is mere appearance, namely, our

12. Wolters, "Idea of Worldview," pp. 16-17.

13. Hans-Georg Gadamer, *Truth and Method*, 2nd rev. ed., translation revised by Joel Weinsheimer and Donald G. Marshall (New York: Continuum, 1993), p. 9. In addition to "worldview," he highlights such notions as art, history, the creative, experience, genius, external world, interiority, expression, style, and symbol as central to that enduring era.

14. For example, Betz, p. 18, notes that "The word Weltanschauung appears first in 1790 in Kant in his *Critique of Judgment*." The *Deutsches Wörterbuch*, col. 1530, notes very simply that *Weltanschauung* is "first in Kant." Helmut Meier, p. 71, asserts that "The creator of the word Weltanschauung is I. Kant." M. Honecker, in his article in *Lexikon für Theologie und Kirche* (1938), s.v. "Weltanschauung," agrees with this assessment, though he adds, importantly, that *Weltanschauung* no longer retains Kant's original meaning: "Up to now, the word has first of all been directed to Kant (*Critique of Judgment*, 1790, part one, book two, section 26), though not with the meaning it has today." However, Gadamer, p. 98, makes the interesting comment that *Weltanschauung* "first appears in Hegel in the *Phenomenology of Mind* as a term for Kant's and Fichte's postulatory amplification of the basic moral experience into a moral world order." Yet, the fact that Kant's use of the term in 1790 predates Hegel's in 1807 by seventeen years would obviously falsify Gadamer's assertion.

intuition of the world [*Weltanschauung*]. For only by means of this power and its idea do we, in a pure intellectual estimation of magnitude, comprehend the infinite in the world of sense *entirely under* a concept, even though in a mathematical estimation of magnitude *by means of numerical concepts* we can never think it in its entirety.[15]

Various phrases in the context of this quotation, such as "mere appearance" and the "world of sense," suggest that for Kant the word *Weltanschauung* means simply the sense perception of the world. Wolters, for example, believes there is nothing remarkable about this first use of *Weltanschauung* in the above quote, "since it is an incidental coinage by Kant, comparable to such existing compounds as *Weltbeschauung* [world examination or inspection], *Weltbetrachtung* [world consideration or contemplation] and *Weltansicht* [world view or opinion] and moreover refers simply to an *Anschauung* of the world in the regular sense of sense perception."[16] This is Martin Heidegger's understanding of Kant's use of the term as well. He notes that Kant (as well as Goethe and Alexander von Humboldt) employed *Weltanschauung* in reference to the *mundus sensibilis;* that is, to refer to a "world-intuition in the sense of contemplation of the world given to the senses."[17] From its coinage in Kant, who apparently used the term only once and for whom it was of minor significance, it evolved rather quickly to refer to an intellectual conception of the universe from the perspective of a human knower. Kant's Copernican revolution in philosophy, with its emphasis on the knowing and willing self as the cognitive and moral center of the universe, created the conceptual space in which the notion of worldview could flourish. The term was adopted by Kant's successors and soon became well ensconced as a celebrated concept in German and European intellectual life.

The Use of *Weltanschauung* in German and Other European Languages

The term prospered in the decades following its origination, especially under the influence of a number of key thinkers mostly in the German idealist and ro-

---

15. Immanuel Kant, *Critique of Judgment: Including the First Introduction,* translated and introduction by Werner S. Pluhar, with a foreword by Mary J. Gregor (Indianapolis: Hackett, 1987), pp. 111-12, emphasis Kant's.

16. Wolters, "Weltanschauung," p. 1.

17. Martin Heidegger, *The Basic Problems of Phenomenology,* translation, introduction, and lexicon by Albert Hofstadter, Studies in Phenomenology and Existential Philosophy (Bloomington: Indiana University Press, 1982), p. 4.

mantic traditions. First of all, Kant's progressive disciple, Johann Gottlieb Fichte (1762-1814), adopted the term immediately.[18] His initial use of *Weltanschauung* came in his very first book, *An Attempt at a Critique of All Revelation* (1792), which was published only two years after the word had originally appeared in Kant's *Critique of Judgment* (1790). In this work Fichte adopts Kant's basic meaning of the term as the perception of the sensible world. In one place he refers to the principle of a "higher legislation" that harmonizes the tensions between moral freedom and natural causality, and serves as a way of perceiving the empirical world. "If we were able to take its principle as a basis for a *world view [einer Welt Anschauung]* then according to this principle one and the same effect would be cognized as fully necessary — an effect which appears to us in relation to the world of sense as *free* according to the moral law, and when attributed to the causality of reason, appears in nature as *contingent*."[19]

Fichte continues by suggesting that God is the basis for the union of both the moral and natural domains, and that their actual unity is foundational to the "worldview" of the divine. Consequently, God perceives no fundamental distinctions in the nature of things. "In him, therefore, is the union of both legislations, and that principle on which they mutually depend underlies his *world view [Welt Anschauung]*. For him, therefore, nothing is natural and nothing is supernatural, nothing is necessary and nothing is contingent, nothing is possible and nothing actual."[20]

With this new term in his academic arsenal, Fichte moved in 1794 from Königsberg to Jena, and by 1799 it had been taken up by his younger colleague Friedrich Wilhelm Joseph von Schelling (1775-1854). As Martin Heidegger points out, however, the meaning of the word changes in Schelling, who gave it its commonplace meaning as "a self-realized, productive as well as conscious way of apprehending and interpreting the universe of beings."[21] This makes good sense in light of Schelling's understanding of the purpose of philosophy. In his work titled *Philosophical Letters* (1795), he asserts that "the chief business of all philosophy consists in solving the problem of the existence of the world."[22] For

---

18. For a discussion of Fichte's doctrine of worldviews, see Hartmut Traub, "Vollendung der Lebensform: Fichte's Lehre vom seligen Leben als Theorie der Weltanschauung und des Lebensgefühls," *Fichte-Studien* 8 (1995): 161-91.

19. Johann Gottlieb Fichte, *Attempt at a Critique of All Revelation,* translated and introduction by Garrett Green (Cambridge: Cambridge University Press, 1978), p. 119, emphasis added.

20. Fichte, p. 120, emphasis added.

21. Heidegger, p. 4.

22. Friedrich Schelling, *Werke,* ed. M. Schröter, vol. 1 (Munich, 1927-28), p. 237, quoted in Frederick Copleston, S.J., *A History of Philosophy,* vol. 7, *Modern Philosophy from the Post-*

Schelling, especially in the last phase of his career, this required an answer to the existential question that Heidegger took and developed as the theme of his *Being and Time:* "Just he, man, impelled me to the final desperate question: Why is there anything at all? Why not nothing?"[23] Worldviews themselves, if only tacitly, are a response to the problem of the existence and meaning of the world, and at least sketch a subliminal answer to the ultimate question of existence. This seems to be the sense implied in Schelling's *On the Concept of Speculative Metaphysics,* written in 1799, where he discusses two options for the intellect: "The intelligence is of two kinds, either blind and unconscious or free and with productive consciousness; productive unconsciousness in a worldview, with consciousness in the creation of an ideal world."[24] Thus a *Weltanschauung* is the product of the unconscious intellect. It refers to subterranean impressions about the world conceived by an anesthetized yet functioning mind. On the other hand, the intellect that has produced an "ideal world" is fully aware of its operations and content. Thus, from its birth in Kant to its use by Schelling, the term's primary meaning shifted from the sensory to the intellectual perception of the cosmos.

From these early beginnings, *Weltanschauung* took deep root and branched out, especially among a number of prominent intellectuals such as Friedrich Schleiermacher (1799), A. W. Schlegel (1800), Novalis (1801), Jean Paul (1804), G. W. F. Hegel (1806), Joseph Görres (1807), Johann Wolfgang von Goethe (1815), and others.[25] Though German theologians, poets, and philosophers primarily made use of the term during the first two decades of the nineteenth century, by the century's midpoint it had infiltrated a number of other disciplines, including the work of the historian Ranke, the musician Wagner, the theologian Feuerbach, and the physicist Alexander von Humboldt. Alexander's brother, Wilhelm von Humboldt — the German philosopher of language — also used the word in 1836 to argue that language gives expression to a particular worldview: "The variety among languages," he argued, "is not that of sounds and signs, but a variety of world-views themselves."[26] Thus, throughout the nineteenth century, *Weltanschauung* became enormously popular, and by the 1890s Orr could say it had become "in a manner indispensable."[27] It is no

---

Kantian Idealists to Marx, Kierkegaard, and Nietzsche (New York: Doubleday, Image Books, 1994), p. 100.

23. *The Encyclopedia of Philosophy* (1967), s.v. "Schelling, Friedrich Wilhelm Joseph von."

24. Quoted in Helmut Meier, p. 327 n. 147 (translation mine).

25. Wolters, "Weltanschauung," p. 1. See also Betz, pp. 19-25, and Helmut Meier, pp. 78-107, for further discussion of the early use of *Weltanschauung* by these German thinkers.

26. Wolters, "Weltanschauung," pp. 1-2. Von Humboldt's quotation is from *Handbook of Metaphysics and Ontology* (1991), s.v. "grammar-history."

27. Orr, *The Christian View of God and the World,* p. 365.

wonder that Orr himself, as well as Abraham Kuyper, capitalized on its notoriety as a convenient and potent expression to configure their respective visions of a comprehensive Calvinist worldview. As Wolters points out, in its notable role among thinking Germans, *Weltanschauung* stood alongside "philosophy" as a companion concept. "In the course of the nineteenth century, then, the word becomes part of the standard vocabulary of the educated German. It comes to stand alongside the term 'philosophy,' which, in the words of K. Kuypers, now 'receives as its most closely related neighbor, with an identity that is hard to classify, the term worldview, especially in German usage.'"[28]

At the opening of the twentieth century, the reputation of *Weltanschauung* reached a climax. Countless books and articles employed the word in their titles. For example, Meier's dissertation bibliography contains some 2,000 German works with *Weltanschauung* in the title, many of which bear an early twentieth-century copyright date.[29] Moreover, the adjective *weltanschauungliche* was coined in 1911, and this neologism prompted a quest among philologists to discover the origin of *Weltanschauung* itself, leading ultimately to the discovery of its coinage by Kant. Evidently in the idealist and romanticist environment of nineteenth-century Germany, *Weltanschauung* was a felicitous term, even a core concept *(Herzwort)*, as Kainz called it,[30] one that expressed keenly the human aspiration to comprehend the nature of the universe. To the extent, then, that it struck a vital chord of human interest, *Weltanschauung* was apparently "an idea whose time had come."[31]

Weltanschauung captured the imaginations not only of the German intelligentsia, but of thinkers throughout Europe and beyond. The term's linguistic success is seen by how readily it was adopted by writers in other European languages either as a loanword, especially in the Romance languages, or as a calque (or copy word) in the idiom of Slavic and Germanic languages. Among the Germanic family of languages, Danish and Norwegian have *verdensanskuelse* as its equivalent, a term Wolters thinks may have been minted by Søren Kierkegaard. He used it along with *livsanskuelse* as his equally creative Danish coinage for the German *Lebensanschauung* (life view).[32] Betz, however, traces *verdensanskuelse* back to the Danish poet and philosopher Paul Møller in 1837.[33] Swedish has developed *världsåskådning*, Icelandic uses *heimsskodun*, and Dutch has employed the compound *wereldaanschouwing* or *wereldbeschouwing*, from

28. Wolters, "Weltanschauung," p. 3.
29. Helmut Meier, pp. 368-90.
30. Wolters, "Weltanschauung," p. 2.
31. Wolters, "Weltanschauung," p. 4.
32. Wolters, "Weltanschauung," p. 5.
33. Betz, p. 25.

which are derived both the Afrikaans *wêreldbeskouing* and the Frisian *wrâldskoging*.[34] In Slavic languages, Polish utilizes the word *swiatopoglad* and the Russian equivalent is *mirovozzrenie,* which was rendered formerly as "world outlook" in official Soviet translations.[35]

In the Romance languages *Weltanschauung* has made its way as a loan-word into a number of philosophical dictionaries in French and Italian. In the Italian *Enciclopedia Filosofica* (1958), L. Giusso notes the difficulty in translating it accurately, but offers this definition nonetheless: "The term, difficult to translate in Italian, signifies a vision, intuition or (more appropriately) a conception of the world."[36] The French *Dictionnaire Alphabétique et Analogique de la Langue Française* (1994) cites *Weltanschauung* as a loanword and attributes its first appearance in French to Jean Grenier in 1930. Designated as a philosophical term, it is defined as "A metaphysical view of the world regarding a conception of life."[37] Several citations of *Weltanschauung* in French philosophical dictionaries are also notable. A. Cuvillier, in the *Nouveau Vocabulaire Philosophique* (1956), suggests that it "designates a conception of the universe and of life." R. Jolivet, in his *Vocabularie de la Philosophie* (1957), translates it as a "vision of the world," "a general view of the world," "a comprehensive point of view on the world," and a "practical attitude regarding the world." P. Foulquié, in the *Dictionnaire de la langue philosophique* (1962), argues that *Weltanschauung* should be translated as "an intuitive view of the world," and defines the concept as "a whole collection of metaphysical theses regarding the conception which everyone has of life." R. Vancourt, in the same dictionary, suggests that *Weltanschauung* has to do with the "com-

---

34. Wolters, "Weltanschauung," p. 28 n. 26. Wolters also makes a correction regarding the Dutch equivalent for *Weltanschauung* as it appears in both Götze and the *Deutsches Wörterbuch* (which error is also carried over into Betz as well). He notes that the normal Dutch equivalent for *Weltanschauung* is not *wereldaanschouwing* (which was a nineteenth-century Germanism that never gained currency in Dutch), but rather *wereldbeschouwing.* Wolters also points out that this latter Dutch term actually antedates Kant's coinage of *Weltanschauung* by about seventy-five years. *Wereldbeschouwing* occurs in the title of Bernard Nieuwentijdt's book *Het regt gebruik der wereltbeschouwingen,* published in Amsterdam in 1715. He notes, nonetheless, that the Dutch word *wereldbeschouwing* gained its present meaning and stature under the influence of the German *Weltanschauung.*

35. Wolters, "Weltanschauung," p. 28 n. 28a, p. 33 n. 118. For an interesting discussion of worldview or *mirovozzrenie* from a Marxist point of view, see *Great Soviet Encyclopedia,* 3rd ed. (1977), s.v. "world view." Not surprisingly, the article states: "The material conditions of a particular society, its material being, give rise to its specific world view."

36. *Enciclopedia Filosofica* (1958), s.v. "Weltanschauung" (translation mine).

37. *Dictionnaire Alphabétique et Analogique de la Langue Française,* 2nd ed. (1994), s.v. "Weltanschauung" (translation mine).

reaction of an individual to the universe, from the point of view
ice, affection, and action."[38]

this brief survey, it seems clear that worldview was indeed an idea
with legs, migrating throughout Europe, where it found lodging in a variety of linguistic and cultural contexts. Given the term's increasing prominence, it was impossible for it to remain isolated on the Continent for long. Soon it crossed the channel to Great Britain and was exported across the Atlantic to the United States. Hence we must investigate its fortunes in the Anglo-American context as well.

Weltanschauung and "Worldview" in the English-Speaking World

Weltanschauung has been received both as a loanword and as a calque or copy word in the English language. The *Oxford English Dictionary* (1989) has an independent entry for *Weltanschauung* as a loanword which, it notes, is derived from the German *Welt*, for "world," and *Anschauung*, for "perception."[39] The *OED* defines the term as "a particular philosophy or view of life; a concept of the world held by an individual or a group," and suggests it be rendered in English as "world-view." According to the textual apparatus, *Weltanschauung* first appeared in an English context in 1868 in a letter written by William James and quoted by R. B. Perry in his book *The Thought and Character of William James* (1935): "I remember your saying . . . that the characteristic of the Greek '*Weltanschauung*' was its optimism." Other documentations of the English usage of *Weltanschauung* are carried up through 1978. Of particular interest is the 1934 citation in M. Bodkin's *Archetypal Patterns in Poetry;* she wrote that "a man's philosophy . . . is his *Weltanschauung* — the individual vision, or perspective of reality."

The *OED* treats "world-view" very briefly as a calque or copy word.[40] It is listed in the twenty-sixth subheading under the discussion of "world," where it is shown to be the English equivalent of *Weltanschauung*. Here "world-view" is defined succinctly as "contemplation of the world, view of life." The textual apparatus indicates it was first used in English in 1858 by J. Martineau in his book *Studies of Christianity,* where he refers to "The deep penetration of his [Saint

---

38. These citations of French philosophical dictionaries are from Helmut Meier, p. 60 (translations mine; assisted by Jim Nelson Black). Wolters, "Weltanschauung," p. 27 n. 24, presents additional references to French philosophical dictionaries and encyclopedias where *Weltanschauung* is defined and discussed.

39. *The Oxford English Dictionary,* 2nd ed. (1989), s.v. "Weltanschauung."

40. *The Oxford English Dictionary,* 2nd ed. (1989), s.v. "world."

Paul's] mistaken world-view." A second citation dates from 1906 in D. S. Cairns's *Christianity in the Modern World*, where he states that "Christianity, alike in its Central Gospel, and in its World-view, must come to terms with Hellenism."

Thus, within sixty-eight years of its inaugural use in Immanuel Kant's *Critique of Judgment, Weltanschauung* entered the English language in its naturalized form as "world-view." Ten years later the German word itself gained currency in Anglo-American academic discourse. Since their middle nineteenth-century beginnings, both *Weltanschauung* and "world-view" have flourished and become significant terms in the thought and vocabulary of thinking people in the English-speaking world.[41]

What is surprising, however, in light of the virtual omnipresence of *Weltanschauung* and "worldview," is how little attention has been paid to it in English encyclopedias and dictionaries of philosophy. By comparison, there is more in-depth discussion about *Weltanschauung* in social science and theological reference literature than there is in philosophy.[42] For example, there is no independent entry for either *Weltanschauung* or "worldview" in the *Encyclopedia of Philosophy* (1967), though there are brief discussions of the notion scattered throughout its eight volumes.[43] The recent *Cambridge Dictionary of Philosophy* (1995) has no specific entry for "worldview," and under *Weltanschauung* refers the reader to the article on Wilhelm Dilthey where the notion is mentioned only very briefly.[44] The *Oxford Dictionary of Philosophy* (1994) is scarcely more complete with its brief definition of *Weltanschauung* as "a general world view; an overarching philosophy."[45] The *Oxford Companion to Philosophy* (1995) adds

41. The question has arisen regarding the proper formation of the Anglicized equivalent of *Weltanschauung*. Should it be formed as a single term ("worldview") or written as two separate words ("world view"), and if as two separate words, should it employ a hyphen ("world-view")? Though the *OED* employs the hyphenated form "world-view," and though the hyphen is common in many compound words, "for some years now, the trend in spelling compound words has been away from the use of hyphens" (*The Chicago Manual of Style*, 14th ed. [Chicago: University of Chicago Press, 1993], 6.38). Since this is the case, "world-view" should perhaps be dropped in favor of the single compound or two separate, nonhyphenated words. Since *Weltanschauung* itself is an amalgam in the original German *(Welt + Anschauung)*, for the sake of accuracy in reproduction the term will be formed as a single compound English word throughout this work. The expression, nonetheless, is found frequently in both versions, and indeed, perhaps more often as two separate words.

42. For reasonably substantial articles, see *International Encyclopedia of the Social Sciences* (1968), s.v. "world view," and *Sacramentum Mundi: An Encyclopedia of Theology* (1970), s.v. "world, views of the."

43. See these articles in the *Encyclopedia of Philosophy* (1967): s.v. "political philosophy, nature of"; s.v. "Schiller, Friedrich"; s.v. "Dilthey, Wilhelm"; s.v. "Mauthner, Fritz."

44. *The Cambridge Dictionary of Philosophy* (1995), s.v. "Dilthey, Wilhelm."

45. *The Oxford Dictionary of Philosophy* (1994), s.v. "Weltanschauung."

little with its succinct definition and brief bibliography. Antony Flew's *A Dictionary of Philosophy* (1979) pays scant attention to the concept, defining it as "any general view of the Universe and man's relationship to it." He does make this important point, however, about its relationship to philosophy proper: "Usually the term is applied to a philosophy affecting the practical (as opposed to purely theoretical) attitudes and beliefs of its adherents."[46] Finally, and perhaps most surprisingly, the recent *Routledge Encyclopedia of Philosophy* (1998), despite its otherwise commendable thoroughness, offers no discussion of "worldview" or *Weltanschauung* as a concept. It merely references several examples of worldviews (e.g., Cartesian, ecological, Newtonian), and cites related concepts such as "historical consciousness" and the importance of language in worldview formation. *Weltanschauung* receives only one negligible mention.[47]

From the rather sparse attention given to *Weltanschauung* in these reference works, we could easily draw the conclusion that in Anglo-American philosophical discourse, this notion is a relatively minor one (perhaps it is, in comparison with its Continental usage). Nonetheless, the frequent use of the term by numerous thinkers across the disciplines seems incongruent with its neglect by English-speaking philosophers. This dearth of attention, however, does not diminish the role or significance that *Weltanschauung* and "worldview" have played in an Anglo-American context. Few transplanted European notions have enjoyed as much success as *Weltanschauung,* as a first cousin to "philosophy," in aptly capturing the intrinsic human aspiration to formulate a worthy view of life.

Conclusion

Since its inception in Immanuel Kant's *Critique of Judgment* in 1790, the notion of *Weltanschauung* has become one of the central intellectual conceptions in contemporary thought and culture. Though the history of the term has for the most part been neglected in the English-speaking world, scholars in the prodigious German enterprises of word history and the history of ideas have thoroughly investigated its background. Notable works by Alfred Götze and Werner Betz (among others) as well as the entry in the *German Dictionary (Deutsches Wörterbuch),* plus the comprehensive dissertation by Helmut G. Meier, have admirably charted the term's pilgrimage. Though this fascinating notion has its

---

46. *A Dictionary of Philosophy,* 2nd ed. (1979), s.v. "Weltanschauung."

47. See the index in vol. 10 of the *Routledge Encyclopedia of Philosophy* (1998), s.v. "worldview" and *"Weltanschauung."*

roots sunk deeply in German soil, its rapid transcontinental transplantation manifests the amazing fertility of the concept. A penetrating idea that felicitously expressed core human concerns had been born. No wonder, then, that within seven decades of its birth it entered Anglo-American discourse and became as fruitful across the channel and overseas as it had been on the European continent. Given its success, what is surprising is the lack of reflection devoted to the history and theory of the notion among English-speaking philosophers and scholars. A history of the concept in nineteenth- and twentieth-century philosophy and among the disciplines of the natural and social sciences should help to rectify this situation.

Chapter Four

A Philosophical History of "Worldview": The Nineteenth Century

There is more to *Weltanschauung* than its linguistic past. For an even greater degree of elucidation, especially in light of its prominent role in Christian thought, we must backtrack a bit and pick up on the role of worldview in the history of European philosophy in the nineteenth century. Therefore, in this chapter we will hit the highlights by focusing on the role of this conception in the thought of G. W. F. Hegel, Søren Kierkegaard, Wilhelm Dilthey, and Friedrich Nietzsche.

"Worldview" in G. W. F. Hegel

In an intense and extensive development, "the German mind during the short span of four decades (1780-1820) produced a wealth of systems of philosophical *Weltanschauung* . . . such as has at no other time been compressed with so narrow a space."[1] The thought and work of Georg Wilhelm Friedrich Hegel (1770-1831) certainly crowns this remarkable period of amazing intellectual achievement. Though his college diploma noted his inadequate grasp of philosophy, the fact is that Hegel "presented mankind with one of the most grandiose and impressive pictures of the Universe which are to be met with in the history of philosophy."[2] Not only does he employ the concept of *Weltanschauung* in interesting ways, but the substance of his system makes it possible to credit him not

1. Wilhelm Windelband, *A History of Philosophy,* ed. and trans. James H. Tufts, 2nd ed. (New York: Macmillan, 1901), p. 529.
2. Frederick Copleston, S.J., *A History of Philosophy,* vol. 7, *Modern Philosophy from the Post-Kantian Idealists to Marx, Kierkegaard, and Nietzsche* (New York: Doubleday, Image Books, 1994), p. 162.

only with the notion of the Absolute Spirit, but also with "the discovery of alternative conceptual frameworks."[3]

Early on Hegel showed an interest in the term *Weltanschauung*.[4] During the inaugural year of his professorship at Jena in 1801, he published his first work, titled *The Difference between Fichte's and Schelling's System of Philosophy*. This book contains his initial use of the word in a section concerned with the "relation of philosophizing to a philosophical system." In a dialectical movement, reason joins together the objective and subjective antitheses to form an infinite and substantive worldview. Hegel writes: "Reason then unites this objective totality with the opposite subjective totality to form the infinite world-intuition [*unendlichen Weltanschauung*], whose expansion has at the same time contracted into the richest and simplest identity."[5] From the beginning of his career, *Weltanschauung* served as Hegel's term of choice to convey an important idea within the framework of dialectical thought.

Hegel's use of "worldview" in the *Phenomenology of Mind* is more significant. This work, published in 1807, presents the essential parameters of his philosophical system. Its subject matter is the biography of the consciousness of the *Geist* or Spirit. In Kant's analysis of consciousness, there is one set of determining categories for all rational minds, making a single basic view of the world possible. For Hegel in the *Phenomenology*, however, there are a variety of forms of consciousness such that Jacob Loewenberg could describe the book as a treatment of "different and recurrent views of life — sensuous and intellectual, emotional and reflective, practical and theoretical, mystic and philistine, sceptical and dogmatic, empirical and speculative, conservative and radical, selfish and social, religious and secular."[6] Hegel, in systematic fashion, examines these various conscious outlooks, one of which is called "the moral view of the world," the content of which he describes in these terms:

> Starting with a specific character of this sort, there is formed and established a moral outlook on the world [*moralische Weltanschauung*] which

3. Robert C. Solomon, *Continental Philosophy Since 1750: The Rise and Fall of the Self*, A History of Western Philosophy, vol. 7 (Oxford: Oxford University Press, 1988), p. 59.

4. Helmut Reinicke cites some thirty-six notable uses of *Weltanschauung* in Hegel's collected works in the index to Georg Wilhelm Friedrich Hegel, *Werke*, vol. 21 (Frankfurt: Suhrkamp Verlag, 1979), p. 725. For a lengthy study of Hegel's use of *Weltanschauung*, see Helmut G. Meier, "'Weltanschauung': Studien zu einer Geschichte und Theorie des Begriffs" (Ph.D. diss., Westfälischen Wilhelms-Universität zu Münster, 1967), pp. 112-40.

5. G. W. F. Hegel, *The Difference between Fichte's and Schelling's System of Philosophy*, trans. H. S. Harris and Walter Cerf (Albany: State University of New York Press, 1977), p. 114.

6. Jacob Loewenberg, ed., introduction to *Hegel: Selections* (New York: Scribner, 1929), p. xviii.

consists in a process of relating the implicit aspect of morality and the explicit aspect. This relation presupposes both thorough reciprocal indifference and specific independence as between nature and moral purposes and activity; and also, on the other side, a conscious sense of duty as the sole essential fact, and of nature as entirely devoid of independence and essential significance of its own. The moral view of the world [*Die moralische Weltanschauung*], the moral attitude, consists in the development of the moments which are found present in this relation of such entirely antithetic and conflicting presuppositions.[7]

Gadamer suggests that Hegel uses *Weltanschauung* here "as a term for Kant's and Fichte's postulatory amplification of the basic moral experience [transmuted] into a moral world order."[8] It carries the force of a practical perspective on life, a conscious attitude that is permeated with the tension of moral concern and obligation. It was one of the many viewpoints that Hegel examines in this work, not as if they were formal philosophical systems, but rather as "ways of living and of looking at the universe."[9] Hegel's phenomenology entails the discrete recognition of a diversity of world models as the Absolute Spirit instantiated itself in human thought and culture on its dialectical journey through history toward eschatological self-understanding. Along the historical way, however, alternative theories of life are developed, contrasted, and synthesized. The notion of *Weltanschauung* as the cognitive offspring of the Absolute Spirit in the historical process was well suited to convey this aspect of his philosophy.

In his *Philosophy of History* Hegel suggests that worldviews are embedded in both the individual and national consciousness. Regarding the individual, each person may have a characteristic worldview as well as an idiosyncratic religious perspective. He states "that as everyone may have his particular way of viewing things generally [*Weltanschauung*], so he may have also a religion peculiar to himself."[10] Later in the book Hegel employs the term to refer to the outlook of an entire nation. After presenting a forthright interpretation of the Hindu deity (as one "degraded to vulgarity and senselessness"), he then com-

7. G. W. F. Hegel, *The Phenomenology of Mind,* translated with introduction and notes by J. B. Baillie, 2nd ed. (London: George Allen and Unwin, 1961), pp. 615-16. For additional references to the notion of a "moral worldview," see also pp. 625 and 644.

8. Hans-Georg Gadamer, *Truth and Method,* 2nd rev. ed., translation revised by Joel Weinsheimer and Donald G. Marshall (New York: Continuum, 1993), p. 98.

9. Jean Hyppolite, *Genesis and Structure of Hegel's Phenomenology of Spirit,* trans. Samuel Cherniak and John Heckman, Northwestern University Studies in Phenomenology and Existential Philosophy (Evanston, Ill.: Northwestern University Press, 1974), pp. 469-70.

10. G. W. F. Hegel, *The Philosophy of History,* trans. J. Sibree, in *The Great Books of the Western World,* vol. 46 (Chicago: Encyclopaedia Britannica, 1952), p. 193.

ments that such a theology "gives us a general idea of the Indian view of the Universe [*indischen Weltanschauung*]."[11] Again we see that *Weltanschauung* is an apt term referring to various styles of thought about the nature of existence, shared in common nationally or ethnically, and is influential on the *intellectus* of the particular individual. As Vincent McCarthy states, "For Hegel, *Weltanschauung* means the world-view of a certain nation, in a certain time: a shared view in which the poet participates. Thus a world-view is a general, shared view which one acquires automatically by participation in the times and society which one forms with one's fellows. . . . World-view, à la Hegel, is the understanding from apprehending the unfolding of Spirit in the exterior world."[12]

The relationship of *Weltanschauung* to philosophy and religion is on Hegel's mind in his *Lectures on the Philosophy of Religion*. After arguing that religion is intrinsic to human nature, he then poses a question about the relation of religion to worldview and suggests that philosophy is responsible to explain the nature of the connection. "As man, religion is essential to him, and is not a feeling foreign to his nature. Yet the essential question is the relation of religion to his general theory of the universe [*Weltanschauung*], and it is with this that philosophical knowledge connects itself, and upon which it essentially works."[13]

But first the relationship between philosophy and worldview must be clarified. As the context indicates, "forms of consciousness" and "the principles of the time," worldviews are not to be confused with philosophy per se. Yet, because of the ongoing contact, strife, and antagonism between them, their relation will have to be clarified as well. Philosophy as the chief discipline must elucidate its own nature, explain its connection with worldview, and articulate the relationship between worldviews and religion. Once this order of things is clear, then the discipline of the philosophy of religion is freed to proceed properly on its own terms. Hegel, therefore, draws concrete distinctions and explains the connection between these fundamental areas of human interest and concern, worldview among them.

While there are a few rather benign references to *Weltanschauung* in Hegel's *Lectures on the History of Philosophy,*[14] the word does yeoman's duty in

---

11. Hegel, *The Philosophy of History*, p. 221.

12. Vincent A. McCarthy, *The Phenomenology of Moods in Kierkegaard* (Boston: Martinus Nijhoff, 1978), p. 136.

13. Georg Wilhelm Friedrich Hegel, *Lectures on the Philosophy of Religion Together with a Work on the Proofs of the Existence of God*, trans. Rev. E. B. Speirs and J. Burdon Sanderson, vol. 1 (New York: Humanities Press, 1962), p. 6.

14. See Georg Wilhelm Friedrich Hegel, *Lectures on the History of Philosophy*, trans. E. S. Haldane and Frances H. Simson, 3 vols. (Lincoln: University of Nebraska Press, 1995), 1:37-38; 3:25, 166, 507.

his lectures on aesthetics.[15] Francis Schaeffer has said that an "artist makes a body of work and this body of work shows his world view."[16] This is the gist of Hegel's view as well. For example, he speaks of the development of the course of Spirit manifested concurrently in both a *Weltanschauung* and in the art which expresses it. He writes: "This development is itself a spiritual and universal one, since the sequence of definite conceptions of the world [*Weltanschauungen*], as the definite but comprehensive consciousness of nature, man, and God, gives itself artistic shape."[17] This suggests that in different historical epochs, a worldview and its expression in art will be different: "the art expressive of one world-view differs from that which expresses another: Greek art as a whole differs from Christian art as a whole. The sequence of different religions gives rise to a sequence of different art-forms."[18] Art is indeed called upon to represent "the inner essence of the content" of a given period. Hegel, at the outset of his treatment of romantic art, is constrained to clarify the contours of the romantic mind-set which "comes into consciousness in the shape of a new vision of the world [*neuen Weltanschauung*] and a new artistic form."[19] Thus for Hegel, the calling of art is to exhibit the spirit of the age. Ways of viewing the world are woven into art and revealed by it.[20]

As a worldview incarnate, art is manifested especially in epic and lyric poetry as well as in the dramatist or singer of lyrics. Regarding the epic genre, Hegel says: "Consequently the content and form of epic proper is the entire world-outlook [*gesamte Weltanschauung*] and objective manifestation of a national spirit presented in its self-objectifying shape as an actual event." Again regarding epic, Hegel asserts: "Thus viewed, the rounding off and the finished shape of the epic lies not only in the particular content of the specific action but just as much in the entirety of the world-view [*Totalität der Weltanschauung*], the objective realization of which the epic undertakes to describe." What is true of epic is also true of lyric verse. Hegel writes: "General views, the fundamental basis of an outlook on life [*einer Weltanschauung*], deeper conceptions of the decisive relations of life are therefore not excluded from lyric, and a great part of the subject matter . . . is equally within the province of this new specie of po-

15. G. W. F. Hegel, *Aesthetics: Lectures on Fine Art,* trans. T. M. Knox, 2 vols. (Oxford: At the Clarendon Press, 1975). Gadamer, p. 98, has noted the importance of *Weltanschauung* in Hegel's "admirable lectures on aesthetics."

16. Francis A. Schaeffer, *Art and the Bible,* L'Abri Pamphlets (Downers Grove, Ill.: InterVarsity, 1973), p. 37.

17. Hegel, *Aesthetics,* 1:72.

18. Hegel, *Aesthetics,* 1:72 n. 1.

19. Hegel, *Aesthetics,* 1:517.

20. Hegel, *Aesthetics,* 1:517, 603, 604; 2:613.

etry." Finally, Hegel notes that whereas the epic and lyric poets are the conduits of a larger, collective vision of reality, "the singer of lyrics expresses his own heart and his personal outlook on life [*subjektive Weltanschauung*]."[21] Thus, whether individually through the dramatist or collectively through the lyricist or writer of epic, poetry as well as other art forms are expressions of world-views, as these are instantiations of Spirit in a variety of historical moments and movements.

The notion of *Weltanschauung* is certainly on display in the writings of G. W. F. Hegel. Though he did not give sustained attention to a theory of worldview as such — a task that was eventually undertaken by Wilhelm Dilthey — nonetheless his frequent use of the term and his international prominence surely imparted to the idea an importance that it might not have enjoyed otherwise. For him worldviews are the phenomena of the Absolute Spirit in the dialectic of history. Anthropologically, they become the moods, perceptions, attitudes, and states of human consciousness as frameworks of reality. Richard Rorty is correct, therefore, when he states that "The notion of alternative conceptual frameworks has been a commonplace of our culture since Hegel."[22] They are to be distinguished from philosophy and religion, and are held individually and corporately by the body politic. Worldviews sustain an important relationship to art, which serves often as the medium by which various views of life are manifested and promoted. Because of Hegel's philosophy and use of *Weltanschauung*, we can justly say, along with Michael Ermath, that "much of German intellectual history of the modern period may be said to center upon the properties and perplexities of the notion of world-view."[23] Thus, Hegel played a significant role in the promotion of *Weltanschauung* as an incisive concept in the nineteenth-century European intellectual scene.

"Worldview" and "Lifeview" in Søren Kierkegaard

As I discussed earlier, the popular notion of *Weltanschauung* spread rapidly among Continental thinkers and migrated far from its intellectual birthplace in Germany, even making its way rather quickly to the Scandinavian region. Though the specifics are uncertain, by 1838 Søren Kierkegaard (1813-55) had heard and embraced the term, coined its Danish counterpart, and employed it

21. Hegel, *Aesthetics*, 2:1044, 1090, 1114, 1179.

22. Richard Rorty, "The World Well Lost," in *Consequences of Pragmatism: Essays: 1972-1980* (Minneapolis: University of Minnesota Press, 1982), p. 3.

23. Michael Ermath, *Wilhelm Dilthey: The Critique of Historical Reason* (Chicago: University of Chicago Press, 1978), p. 323.

in his first published work. Throughout his career "worldview" and its companion term, "lifeview," played a crucial role in his philosophic reflections and personal life. As McCarthy observes, the latter notion in particular penetrates to the depth dimension of Kierkegaard's existential thought.

> Life-view emphasizes the duty and importance of the individual to understand himself, both his "premises" and his "conclusions," his conditionality and his freedom. Each man must answer for himself about the meaning of life, and thus he cannot take his cue from the spirit of the age which will all too readily answer on his behalf. In addition, life-view, as philosophy of life, challenges established, academic philosophy which proceeds exclusively from thought. The new philosophy which Kierkegaard suggests by his emphasis on life-view and his definition of it is no longer detached thought but reflection upon the meaning of experience and then its articulation in a coherent view. Life-view is not to be the sole aspect of new philosophizing, but will instead properly take its place at the center of the search for wisdom, which philosophy once claimed to be.[24]

Given the importance of both "worldview" and "lifeview" for Kierkegaard, some technical information about his invention and use of these terms is in order. Kierkegaard's Danish copy word for *Weltanschauung* is *verdensanskuelse*, which occurs only five times in his collected works, according to the basic concordance to Kierkegaard's complete works.[25] The more important term for Kierkegaard is *livsanskuelse*, which is his equivalent of the German *Lebensanschauung*, and is translated in English as "lifeview." Kierkegaard's remarkable

24. McCarthy, pp. 136-37. This author, who is deeply enamored with Kierkegaard's use of "lifeview," points out how "references to the importance of a life-view, its nature and its function in existence, are numerous in Kierkegaard's authorship" (p. 136; see also pp. 133, 155). Other contemporary Kierkegaardologists recognize the pivotal role of the world and lifeview conception in the body of his writings. Wolters, "'Weltanschauung' in the History of Ideas: Preliminary Notes" (n.d.), photocopy, p. 5, says: "It is a central category in his thought." Michael Strawser, *Both/And: Reading Kierkegaard from Irony to Edification* (New York: Fordham University Press, 1997), p. 20, also asserts that lifeview is "an idea of great importance . . . in Kierkegaard's writings taken as a whole." Josiah Thompson, *The Lonely Labyrinth: Kierkegaard's Pseudonymous Works*, foreword by George Kimball Plochmann (Carbondale: Southern Illinois University Press, 1967), p. 71, believes that Kierkegaard's recognition of alternative lifeviews and the ability to move freely between them is, if not "the core," then at least "a fundamental theme" in his later authorship.

25. *Fundamental Polyglot Konkordans til Kierkegaards Samlede Værker* (Leiden: E. J. Brill, 1971), s.v. "verdensanskuelse." The *Index Verborum til Kierkegaards Samlede Værker* (Leiden: E. J. Brill, 1973), s.v. "verdensanskuelse," p. 1250, cites three more uses of the word plus an additional variant not cited in the *Konkordans*.

143 usages of this latter term is over twice the number of times the word "philosophy" appears in his collected works.[26] Having thus been minted by Kierkegaard, *livsanskuelse* and *verdensanskuelse* made their Danish debut in Kierkegaard's 1838 publication titled *From the Papers of One Still Living*.[27] Unquestionably, he preferred *livsanskuelse* (lifeview) over *verdensanskuelse* (worldview), since it best captured the existential character of his philosophy, though on a few occasions he uses the terms synonymously.[28] As one for whom the purpose of life was to find a truth for which one could live and die[29] (Kierkegaard's so-called Gilleleje Entry), it seems that he was searching for nothing other than a *livsanskuelse*, a deep and satisfying view of life that would enable him to become a total human self. Kierkegaard's understanding of this rich concept and his contribution to the history of worldview will be seen as we examine some selected passages in his authorship dealing with the subject.

Kierkegaard's forty-page *From the Papers of One Still Living* (1838), aptly described by one commentator as an "overgrown newspaper article,"[30] is replete with reflections on "lifeview" *(livsanskuelse)*. It is a scathing review of Hans Christian Andersen's third novel, titled *Only a Fiddler* (1837). According to Kierkegaard, a lifeview is the *conditio sine qua non* for a novel in both positive and negative ways. He explains its supreme function as a literary ballast in these words: "A life-view is really providence in the novel; it is its deeper unity, which makes the novel have a center of gravity in itself. A life-view frees it from being arbitrary or purposeless, since the purpose is immanently present everywhere in the work of art. But when such a life-view is lacking, the novel either seeks to insinuate some theory (dogmatic, doctrinaire short novels) at the expense of

26. *Fundamental Polyglot Konkordans til Kierkegaards Samlede Værker,* s.v. "livsanskuelse." The *Index Verborum til Kierkegaards Samlede Værker,* s.v. "livs-anskuelse," p. 668, notes that the *Konkordans* cites 143 references of *livsanskuelse,* and lists an additional 28 previously uncited variations of the word as well.

27. Danish linguistic authorities have apparently failed to note this earliest use of *livsanskuelse* and *verdensanskuelse* in the Kierkegaard authorship. As Wolters points out, p. 28 nn. 33 and 34, the great Danish lexical source — *Ordbog over det Danske Sprog* — indicates that the first uses of *livsanskuelse* and *verdensanskuelse* are after 1838, and that *livsanskuelse* is still considered a new compound as late as 1868, despite Kierkegaard's earlier coinage of the word.

28. See Kierkegaard's *On Authority and Revelation,* translated with an introduction and notes by Walter Lowrie, introduction to the Torchbook edition by Frederick Sontag (New York: Harper and Row, Harper Torchbooks, Cloister Library, 1966): "And after all a world-view, a life-view, is the only true condition of every literary production" (p. 4); "For he has a definite world-view and life-view . . ." (p. 7).

29. *The Journals of Kierkegaard, 1834-1854,* trans. and ed. Alexander Dru (London: Oxford University Press, 1938), pp. 15-16.

30. McCarthy, p. 140.

poetry or it makes a finite or incidental contract with the author's flesh and blood."[31]

Unfortunately, a lifeview is exactly what Andersen's novel lacked. In pointing out his deficiency, Kierkegaard describes the nature of a lifeview and mentions two possible alternatives, Stoicism and Christianity.

> Now when we say that Andersen altogether lacks a life-view *(livsanskuelse)*, then that utterance is as much founded on the foregoing as that it itself provides the foundation for the latter. A lifeview is more than a pure idea or a sum of propositions held fast in abstract neutrality; it is more than experience which as such is always atomistic, it is namely the transubstantiation of experience, it is an unshakable certainty in oneself which has been won by all [of one's] experience — either it has become familiar with all worldly relations (a mere human standpoint, e.g., Stoicism) which by doing this keeps itself out of contact with a deeper experience — or in its direction toward heaven (the religious), it has found therein what is crucial, both for its heavenly and its earthly existence, has won the true assurance "that neither death, nor life, nor angels, nor Principalities, nor Powers, nor the present, nor the future, nor the heights, nor the depths nor anything of any sort shall be able to separate us from God's love in Christ Jesus our Lord."[32]

Two things are notable about this quotation. First is the rejection of intellectualist and experientialist definitions of lifeview in favor of the rather striking description of it as a "transubstantiation of experience." A lifeview, though not to be identified with simple experience, is nevertheless achieved through experience leading to personal transfiguration and self-certainty. Secondly, this unruffled assurance and transformed state can be of two kinds, one worldly and humanistic as exemplified in Stoicism, and the other deeper and heavenly as instantiated in Christianity. What is significant is how Kierkegaard, who clearly defends the latter alternative over the former, designates both Stoicism and Christianity as lifeview options.

In this same context Kierkegaard points out that not everyone obtains a lifeview, either because of the interference of life itself or because of an unreflective preoccupation with suffering. Assuming these obstacles are overcome, however, Kierkegaard describes the basics of lifeview formation: "If now we ask how a life-view comes about, then we reply that for him who does not permit his life to fizzle out, but who tries insofar as possible to balance the individual events in life — that for him there must necessarily come a moment of unusual

---

31. Quoted in Strawser, p. 21.
32. Compiled from Wolters, pp. 6-7, and McCarthy, p. 145.

illumination about life, without his needing in any way to have understood all the possible particulars to the subsequent understanding of which he has in the meantime [come to have] the key: I say, there must come the moment when as Daub observes, life is understood backwards through the Idea."[33]

Here a lifeview is described as an "unusual illumination about life" which is granted at a *kairos* moment in one's experience. It consists not in an understanding of everything but rather supplies the key (i.e., a framework or outline) by which all things can indeed be understood. Though life moves ahead into the future, it is only understood backwards, and the possession of lifeview — the Idea — is the means to private and public enlightenment.

Thus, in Kierkegaard's first published work, he introduces the motif of lifeview. Though it is primarily a work of literary criticism, as McCarthy notes, his concern was also "with a mature, serious life-view not merely for the purpose of epic poetry but for the grasp of what is crucial for both heavenly and earthly existence."[34]

In Kierkegaard's two-volume work *Either/Or* (1843), two stages of existence, the aesthetic and the ethical, square off in pugilist fashion. In one corner is Johannes Climacus, or A, the incorrigible aesthete whose points of view are expressed in part 1 of the work. In the other corner is Judge William, or B, the representative of the ethical outlook, whose critiques of A are presented in the second part of the treatise. At its core *Either/Or* is a contest between two lifeview alternatives: between living aesthetically or ethically. As the editor/referee of these two respective volumes, Victor Eremita, points out, "A's papers contain a multiplicity of approaches to an esthetic view of life. . . . B's papers contain an ethical view of life."[35] Out of the drama of this agonistic relationship between A and B, there emerge valuable Kierkegaardian insights about "lifeview" abstractly, and "lifeviews" concretely.

At the abstract level, Judge William proclaims to Johannes Climacus that a lifeview is not only a "natural need" but is also something absolutely "essential." Like Climacus, the person who lives aesthetically has a lifeview, though he may not recognize or understand it because of his immersion in the immediacy of experience. To offset his dim-wittedness, William informs Climacus that "every human being, no matter how slightly gifted he is, however subordinate his position in life may be, has a natural need to formulate a life-view, a conception of the meaning of life and its purpose." Though an arrogant Climacus may wish to distinguish him-

33. Quoted in McCarthy, p. 144.
34. McCarthy, p. 146.
35. Søren Kierkegaard, *Either/Or,* edited and translated with introduction and notes by Howard V. Hong and Edna H. Hong, 2 vols. (Princeton: Princeton University Press, 1987), 1:13.

self from lesser aesthetes who seem to be unable to enjoy life as he does, William informs him that he has "something in common with them, and something very essential — namely, a life-view," and that what in fact does distinguish him from them is something entirely unessential.[36] A lifeview, therefore, is bound up with crucial hermeneutic and teleological questions. This search is both natural and necessary for human beings. Lifeview and human existence are inseparable.

Furthermore, William affirms that positive answers to these lifeview queries, when combined with the ingredient of the ethical, form the basis for stable human friendships. "The absolute condition for friendship," William plainly states, "is unity in a life-view." Such a foundation for friendship has distinct advantages. "If a person has that, he will not be tempted to base his friendship on obscure feelings or on indefinable sympathies. As a consequence, he will not experience those ridiculous shifts, so that one day he has a friend and the next day he does not." Furthermore, William declares, though many people possess a philosophical "system," in their formal ratiocinations the ethical component is conspicuously absent. Conversely, "the ethical element in the life-view becomes the essential point of departure for friendship, and not until friendship is looked at in this way does it gain meaning and beauty." Hence, William concludes, "Unity in a life-view is the constituting element in friendship."[37]

Kierkegaard points out elsewhere that a lifeview is not only foundational for friendship, but is also a prerequisite for parenthood and an essential component of the Christian education of children. Regarding the former matter, a child has as much right to learn of the meaning of life from his father as he does to expect milk from his mother. The possession and impartation of a lifeview is as intrinsic to the calling of fatherhood as breast-feeding is to motherhood.

> Do you not think that to be a father requires that you have reached the maturity of really having a view of life which you dare vouch for and dare commend to your child when, with the right it has in being a child and in owing you its life, it asks you about the meaning of life? Or supposing that what nature takes care of, breast milk, etc. happened to be the woman's special task to attend to — would it not be loathsome to want to be a mother, to satisfy one's desires, but not to have in readiness what the child needs? But from the father a child has the right to demand a view of life, that the father really has a view of life.[38]

36. Kierkegaard, *Either/Or*, 2:179-80.
37. Kierkegaard, *Either/Or*, 2:319-21.
38. Søren Kierkegaard, *Journals and Papers*, vol. 3, L-R, ed. and trans. Howard V. Hong and Edna H. Hong, assisted by Gregor Malantschuk (Bloomington: Indiana University Press, 1975), p. 140.

Friendship and parenthood are bound up in this matter of a lifeview. So is education. In his *Attack upon "Christendom,"* Kierkegaard bemoans the fact that in nominally Christian homes children suffer from the failure of parents to impart to them a distinctively Christian education, including a lifeview. "The education of children," he complains, "consists in formal training, in learning a few things, but one does not undertake to convey any religious and still less any Christian view of life, to talk to the child about God, still less to speak of Him in accordance with the concepts and ideas which are peculiar to Christianity."[39] For Kierkegaard, by implication, the impartation of a concept of life steeped in Christian thought was an indispensable educational requirement in families making a claim to the faith.

Either/Or also focuses on a number of concrete lifeviews that fall under the broad headings of the aesthetic and the ethical. In their sparring with one another, Judge William informs Johannes Climacus that the latter's aesthetic outlook boils down to a single proposition: one must enjoy life. Some lifeviews, in which the condition for the enjoyment of life lies *inside* the individual, focus on health, beauty, or talent.[40] Other lifeviews, in which the condition for enjoying life lies *outside* the individual, concentrate on wealth, honor, noble birth, romantic love, and so on.[41] Additionally, William seeks to persuade Climacus that the relentless pursuit of pleasure terminates ultimately in despair, sadness, or sorrow.[42] William's ultimate goal, therefore, is to convince Climacus that his own lifeview is bankrupt, and that a significant shift of paradigms from the aesthetic to the ethical is in order. "All the same, you have no life-view. You have something that resembles a view, and this gives your life a kind of composure that must not, however, be confused with a secure and revitalizing confidence in life. You have composure only by contrast with the person who is still pursuing the phantoms of enjoyment."[43]

Judge William's point is plain: there is no viable lifeview available under the category of the aesthetic. As Kierkegaard had chastised Andersen for his neglect of a lifeview in his novel, so Judge William reproaches Johannes Climacus for the same heinous omission in his own life. Only by a transition from the aesthetic to the ethical can he obtain a new viewpoint that would sustain him. The choice was his: *either* to live aesthetically *or* to live ethically.

The ethical sphere of existence, however, is only penultimate to the final

---

39. Søren Kierkegaard, *Attack upon "Christendom,"* translated, introduction, and notes by Walter Lowrie, new introduction by Howard A. Johnson (Princeton: Princeton University Press, 1968), p. 223.

40. Kierkegaard, *Either/Or*, 2:181.

41. Kierkegaard, *Either/Or*, 2:182-83.

42. Kierkegaard, *Either/Or*, 2:190, 195, 204, 232, 235.

43. Kierkegaard, *Either/Or*, 2:202.

stage of the religious. In *Stages on Life's Way* (1845),[44] a crisis in lifeview is detected in which a transition is made from the aesthetic domain all the way to the religious. The story unfolds in Quidam's diary, "Guilty?/Not Guilty?" — one of the "studies by various persons" in Kierkegaard's *Stages*. The occasion is a broken relationship. In the midst of his contemplation about the basic categories of his life, Quidam realizes that his lifeview must be renovated, and in "a moment of unusual illumination" he knew that its fundamental premise must be religious. In listening to the preacher he gains enlightenment: "The next point is that each person prepares the way of the Lord within himself. This, of course, is what ought to be spoken about, and on this point a life-view can be built." The resolution to the collapse of the aesthetic, for Quidam, as for all, is in the religious stage of existence. This thesis is also presented in another essay in *Stages* entitled "Reflections on Marriage," where "a married man" states: "The resolution is a religious view of life constructed upon ethical presuppositions, a view of life that is supposed to pave the way, so to speak, for falling in love and to secure it against any external and internal danger."[45] The religious does not replace the previous spheres of existence, but absorbs and redeems them all. Thus, in the stages along life's way, the religious lifeview is final and all-inclusive.

The contribution of *Concluding Unscientific Postscript* (1846) to Kierkegaard's theory of lifeview is relatively minor, with one exception. It has to do with an assertion of Johannes Climacus which associates lifeview with "the Greek principle," and it implicitly raises the perennial question: What is philosophy? "To understand oneself in existence was the Greek principle. However little content the doctrine of a Greek philosopher sometimes represented, the philosopher had nevertheless one advantage: he was never comical. I am well aware that if someone were nowadays to live like a Greek philosopher, existentially expressing and existentially probing the depths of what he must call his view of life, he would be regarded as a lunatic. Let it be so."[46]

The Greek principle, and its lifeview analogue, is the very antithesis of abstract thought. "While abstract thought seeks to understand the concrete abstractly, the subjective [lifeview] thinker has conversely to understand the abstract concretely."[47] The best in early Greek philosophy — exemplified for

44. Søren Kierkegaard, *Stages on Life's Way: Studies by Various Persons*, edited and translated with introduction and notes by Howard V. Hong and Edna H. Hong (Princeton: Princeton University Press, 1988).

45. Kierkegaard, *Stages on Life's Way*, p. 162.

46. Søren Kierkegaard, *Concluding Unscientific Postscript*, trans. David F. Swenson, completed after his death with introduction and notes by Walter Lowrie (Princeton: Princeton University Press, 1941), p. 315.

47. Kierkegaard, *Concluding Unscientific Postscript*, p. 315.

Kierkegaard in the historical, pre-Platonic Socrates — pursued "the 'love of wisdom' in an authentic human existence grounded in reflection and the desire to understand oneself."[48] This is precisely the burden of lifeview philosophy as well. However, just as the existentially oriented Greek philosophy had been eclipsed by the abstractions of Platonic idealism in Socrates' day, so lifeview philosophy had been thwarted by Hegelian idealism in Climacus's day. Because academic philosophy — Platonic, Hegelian, or otherwise — was so disengaged from the pathos of human existence, it had become "comic" or silly. Greek and lifeview philosophy, however, because of its profound existential encounter with the stuff of human existence, was never comic or silly, though professional philosophers or abstract thinkers in the ancient or contemporary periods may scoff at it. In Climacus's day, to live and think like a Greek philosopher in prob- ing and searching out a lifeview would be considered madness, sheer lunacy. What was Climacus's response to such ridicule? "Let it be so." What, then, is true philosophy? Climacus suggests that true philosophy is found in the "Greek principle" of the classical world, and in the "lifeview philosophy" of his own day. The serious pursuit and development of a *livsanskuelse,* in short, is the true love of wisdom, and ought to replace the comedy of abstract thought.

Through these remarkable reflections, Søren Kierkegaard introduced the concept of both worldview and lifeview in Scandinavia.[49] Preferring the more existential orientation of lifeview over the more Hegelian and abstract notion of worldview, he employed the idea as a way of referring to alternative ways of being in the world (aesthetic, ethical, religious) and as a theme that penetrates to the meaning and purpose of life itself, whether in Christian or non-Christian terms. For Kierkegaard, a lifeview is essential to literature, friendship, parent- hood, and education. The pursuit of a lifeview is at the heart of philosophy, a genuine love of wisdom that trumps the abstractions of professional thought. His reflections on this subject, however, were serendipitous, not systematic. Meanwhile, back on the Continent, a German philosopher by the name of Wil- helm Dilthey had recognized the importance of worldview as a concept and made it a crucial component of his attempt to work out an epistemology of the

48. McCarthy, p. 139.

49. Another Danish philosopher by the name of Harald Høffding, who was deeply influ- enced by Kierkegaard, devoted a significant amount of energy to reflecting upon the meaning and implications of world and life view. Known primarily for his two-volume *History of Modern Philosophy* (1894-95), Høffding published a summary of his system in 1910 at the age of sixty- seven under the Danish title *Den Menneskelige Tanke* (Human thought). This work, which has been translated into German and French, devotes some forty pages to an analysis of worldview. Høffding's theory of world and life view is also discussed in his *The Problems of Philosophy* (ET, 1905). For more on Høffding, see Wolters, pp. 9-10 nn. 41-50.

human sciences. The richness of his thought and its historical significance demand that we discuss it in some detail.

"Worldview" in Wilhelm Dilthey

Wilhelm Dilthey (1833-1911), whom José Ortega y Gasset called "the most important philosopher in the second half of the nineteenth century,"[50] is best known for his theories of the human sciences *(Geisteswissenschaften)*, his contributions to certain methodological problems in the study of history, and his creative advances in the discipline of hermeneutics. Not to be overlooked, however, is his pioneering, systematic treatment of worldviews. Like many others, Michael Ermath has recognized the unique contribution of Dilthey's reflections on worldview, and the importance of the concept in his philosophy.

> It was Dilthey who raised the problem of the world-views to a comprehensive theoretical statement. In this area he pioneered and mapped intellectual terrain which was later to be explored by students in many different disciplines. His writings provide full scale treatment of the genesis, articulation, comparison, and development of the world-views. His doctrine or "science" of the world-views *(Weltanschauunglehre;* often *Wissenschaft der Weltanschauung)*, which is frequently treated as a marginal dimension of this thought, is in reality one of its fundamental elements and requires careful analysis in its own right.[51]

Dilthey's reflections on worldview were a part of his overall attempt to formulate an objective epistemology for the human sciences, just as Immanuel Kant had done for the natural sciences. Though he was supremely concerned about scientific truth and the possibility of objective historical and cultural knowledge, his thinking was nonetheless rooted in the issues of real life and what he called "lived experience." "Every true world-view," Dilthey argued, "is

---

50. José Ortega y Gasset, *Concord and Liberty,* trans. Helene Weyl (New York: Norton, 1946), p. 131. Ortega y Gasset concludes this work with "A Chapter from the History of Ideas — Wilhelm Dilthey and the Idea of Life" (pp. 129-82). Among other things in this final section, he discusses Dilthey's theory of world visions (or worldview). Largely due to the work of Ortega y Gasset, Dilthey has become reasonably well known in the Spanish-speaking world. Evidence of this is found in a translation of Dilthey's analysis of worldviews by Eugenio Ímaz. See his *Orbas de Wilhelm Dilthey: Teoria de la Conception Del Mundo* (Mexico and Buenos Aires: Fondo de Cultura Económica, 1945).

51. Ermath, p. 324. This author also notes at the outset of his volume that "worldview" had "come into wide usage through Dilthey's own work" (p. 15).

an intuition which emerges from the standing-in-the-middle-of-life."[52] Life itself was an enigma requiring explication. Like trying to guess what a soul is like from a brief glimpse of a human face, so the cryptic countenance of life invites deeper investigation. Cosmic and personal questions are forever the preoccupation of thoughtful people who seek to understand life's secrets.

> The riddle of existence faces all ages of mankind with the same mysterious countenance; we catch sight of its features, but we must guess at the soul behind it. This riddle is always bound up organically with that of the world itself and with the question what I am supposed to do in this world, why I am in it, and how my life in it will end. Where did I come from? Why do I exist? What will become of me? This is the most general question of all questions and the one that most concerns me. The answer to this question is sought in common by the poetic genius, the prophet and the thinker.[53]

Human life is largely carried out in the interrogative mood. Questions about the origin, action, purpose, death, and especially the destiny of human beings in the world are the concern of poet, philosopher, and prophet alike. Hence Dilthey, sounding very much like an existentialist in the Kierkegaardian tradition, asserted that "to understand life as it is lived by man — that is the aim of man today."[54]

This goal to understand life was in fact perpetual, according to Dilthey, and had expressed itself in the universal metaphysical impulse to ascertain the contours of reality in absolutist terms. The rise of historical consciousness had demonstrated that these universal metaphysical systems were in fact highly conditioned and relative, and a mere function of the historical particularities and dispositions of their authors. In the final analysis, metaphysical systems, as authoritative and grandiose as they may appear, were false. The history of metaphysics was in fact the history of philosophical failure. Any attempt at a future metaphysic would share in the same fate.[55]

In place of traditional metaphysical systems that claimed universal valid-

---

52. Wilhelm Dilthey, *Gesammelte Schriften*, 8:99, quoted by Ilse N. Bulhof, *Wilhelm Dilthey: A Hermeneutic Approach to the Study of History and Culture,* Martinus Nijhoff Philosophy Library, vol. 2 (Boston: Martinus Nijhoff, 1980), p. 89.

53. Dilthey, *Gesammelte Schriften*, 8:208-9, quoted by Theodore Plantinga, *Historical Understanding in the Thought of Wilhelm Dilthey* (Toronto: University of Toronto Press, 1980), pp. 81-82.

54. Dilthey, *Gesammelte Schriften*, 8:78, quoted by Ermath, p. 17.

55. On historicism and its relation to metaphysics in Dilthey's thought, see Plantinga, pp. 122-48.

ity, Dilthey set forth his metaphilosophy of worldview. In it he proposed an analysis and comparison of basic attitudes toward life as these underlie and are expressed in poetry, religion, and metaphysics. He called this metaphilosophical enterprise a "philosophy of philosophy" *(Philosophie der Philosophie)* and a "doctrine" or "science" of worldviews *(Weltanschauunglehre)*. This innovative philosophical task, this historical investigation of worldviews, would disclose how the human mind in the context of lived experience had sought to make sense out of the mystery of the cosmos. "It is the task of the theory of worldviews," Dilthey stated, "by analyzing the historical course of religiosity, poetry, and metaphysics in opposition to relativity, systematically to present the relationship of the human mind to the riddle of the world and life."[56] The investigation of worldviews historically, according to Dilthey, avoids the absolutist error of traditional metaphysics and yet renders insights, partial though they may be, into the nature of the cosmos as these have been garnered by the ever inquisitive human mind.

Dilthey's theory of worldviews is perhaps best examined in the context of his program for the human sciences, and as it relates to his hermeneutic philosophy.[57] Nonetheless, it is intrinsically interesting and worthy of independent investigation. Dilthey's reflections on worldview are found in three primary locations in his collected works.[58] The *locus classicus* is found in the eighth volume of his *Collected Writings*, which has been translated into English.[59] This material, which justifies labeling Dilthey the "father of worldview theory," can be analyzed in four main sections.

56. Dilthey, *Gesammelte Schriften*, 5:406, quoted by Ramon J. Betanzos, trans., in his introduction to *Introduction to the Human Sciences: An Attempt to Lay a Foundation for the Study of Society and History*, by Wilhelm Dilthey (Detroit: Wayne State University Press, 1988), p. 29.

57. On the influence of Dilthey's doctrine of worldviews on his hermeneutic philosophy, see Thomas J. Young, "The Hermeneutical Significance of Dilthey's Theory of World-Views" (Ph.D. diss., Bryn Mawr College, 1985). See also Young's abridgment of his dissertation in "The Hermeneutical Significance of Dilthey's Theory of World Views," *International Philosophical Quarterly* 23 (June 1983): 125-40.

58. Dilthey's basic discussions of worldview may be found in the following locations in his *Collected Writings (Gesammelte Schriften)*: (1) "The Essence of Philosophy" (5:378-416), (2) scattered references in vol. 7, and (3) the entirety of vol. 8.

59. Wilhelm Dilthey, *Dilthey's Philosophy of Existence: Introduction to Weltanschauunglehre*, translated and introduction by William Kluback and Martin Weinbaum (New York: Bookman Associates, 1957), pp. 17-74. The same material is abridged in W. Dilthey, *Selected Writings*, edited, translated, and introduction by H. P. Rickman (New York: Cambridge University Press, 1976), pp. 133-54. The page numbers in the text are from the Bookman Associates edition.

On the Conflict of Systems

The "anarchy of philosophical systems" (p. 17), according to Dilthey, is largely responsible for the persistence of skepticism. The historically proven fact of a multitude of mutually exclusive metaphysical systems, each claiming universal validity, produces a tension of almost unbearable proportions. The history of philosophy does nothing but exacerbate this tension. The contest among Greek interpretations of the universe, the conflict between Christians and Muslims, the debates between the followers of Averroes and Aristotle, the revival of Greek and Roman thought in the Renaissance, the age of the discovery of new climates and cultures, and the reports of international travelers all served to extinguish "man's confidence in his hitherto firmly set convictions." Despite the human compulsion to fashion theoretical systems to demonstrate "how things are interrelated," the fact of the matter is, according to Dilthey, "every single one of these systems excludes the other, each one refutes the other, [and] none can prove itself fully" (pp. 17-18). This history has instilled a cynical sense of "amused curiosity" regarding the advent of any new philosophical system: Who will believe it, and how long will it last?

Even more destructive to traditional metaphysics than the recognition of the "anarchy of philosophical systems" was the implication "of the continuous unfolding of the historical awareness of man" (p. 19). Historicism has murdered metaphysics. The natural law tradition rooted in the perennial Western belief that there was "but one type of man, endowed with a particular nature," eventually fell victim to an all-encompassing doctrine of evolution as it was applied consistently to both biological and historical life. Dilthey observes that during the Enlightenment, "the old concept of the typical man was lost and transmuted into the process of evolution." When this theory of evolution was combined "with the recognition of the relativity of every historical form of life," the result was the destruction of "the belief in the absolute validity of any one philosophy which might have undertaken to interpret the world compellingly by an interrelation of concepts" (pp. 19-20). The powerful principle of historicism solved the problem of competing metaphysical models making a claim to universal validity: they were *all* the products of the fluctuating historical process. Hence, in Dilthey's estimation, metaphysics is dead. If any kind of worldview is to be achieved, the starting point for reflection must be in the light of history, on the basis of experience, and rooted in life itself. To satisfy the innate need for an understanding of human existence, Dilthey proposes his doctrine of worldviews in which he attempts to steer a middle course between a defunct metaphysical absolutism and the nihilism of historical relativism. But what are worldviews in the first place, where do they come from, and how do they arise?

Dilthey answers with his theoretical reflections on the nature of life itself and of worldviews.

Life and Worldview

If the meaning of life is to be grasped in the form of a worldview, then it must begin with the initial recognition that "the ultimate root of any world view is life itself." This "life," which Dilthey almost seems to divinize, is not the personal life of individuals, but life in its objective manifestation, life which everywhere possesses "identical traits and common features." The particulars of daily experience — a bench, a tree, a house, a garden — are "meaningful only in this objectification" (pp. 21-22). The experience of this objectified life is the beginning point of a worldview. A life world, or *Lebenswelt,* begets a worldview, or *Weltanschauung.*

Despite the fact that life is experienced differently in each individual, the immutability of human existence guarantees that "the fundamental features of life's experience [are] common to all men." For example, the destiny and corruptibility of life plus the fact of death determine "the significance and meaning of life" for everyone. Given these boundaries, a series of patterns, traditions, and habits emerge at the communal level that provide a kind of epistemic certainty, though this certainty is markedly different from the kind obtained in science with its precise methods and principles. Still, a "fixed system of relations" and a "framework of life experiences" rooted in "empirical consciousness" establish the possible horizons of meaning. Worldview formation, then, partakes of the paradox of form and freedom. The liberty of interpretation is circumscribed by the limits of reality (pp. 22-23).

The more philosophically inclined, Dilthey argues, see life in all its conditions, contradictions, and changes as an "enigma." The certainty of death, the cruelty of the natural process, a general transitoriness, plus a myriad of other factors have prompted a quest in minds past and present to penetrate these unfathomable mysteries. Worldviews, therefore, are an attempt to solve "the riddle of life" (pp. 23-24).

Out of the whirlwind of experience, human beings form attitudes toward life and the world by necessity, and eventually universal attitudes or moods are established. Though there will be some fluctuation in these attitudes at the behest of new experiences, nonetheless Dilthey believes that "in different individuals there prevail certain attitudes according to their own character" (p. 25). These various attitudes toward life — marked either by enjoyment, security, religiosity, futility, or otherwise — may be subsumed under the two larger headings of optimism and pessimism. These great "moods of life" (*Lebensstimmung*), which shape and give substance to all worldviews, are finely nuanced as well. Attitudes toward the world and the dispositions of optimism or pessimism are an expression of a person's character, and this constitutes a basic law of worldview formation.

Worldviews are not only shaped by character, but also possess an "identical structure" that reflects "an inherent psychic order" in human beings. In short, "world views tend towards uniformities in which the structure of psychological life is expressed." Since there are three structural aspects to the human mind (mind, emotion, will), there are therefore three structural aspects to a worldview. First of all, according to Dilthey's analysis, it begins with the mind's formation of a "cosmic picture," or *Weltbild*, which is a product of the "immutable laws of the phases of cognition." A world picture is a depiction of what is, a set of concepts and judgments that adequately capture "the relatedness and true being of reality." Second, on the basis of the *Weltbild* and other unchangeable laws of psychic experience, there is the formation of the "effectual value" of life. Objects, people, and other phenomena are deemed worthy or unworthy depending on their perceived value. What is deemed useful is approved, and what is considered harmful is rejected. "Thus conditions, persons, and objects assume their importance in relation to the whole of reality, and this whole itself is stamped with meaningfulness." Third is the "upper level of consciousness" consisting of the highest ideals, the greatest good, and the supreme principles for the conduct of life which imbue a *Weltanschauung* with vitality and power. "At this stage the world view becomes creative, formative, and indeed reforming." The result is "a comprehensive life plan, a highest good, the highest norms of action, an ideal of shaping one's personal life as well as that of society" (pp. 25-27). Thus for Dilthey, the metaphysical, axiological, and moral structure of a worldview is derived from the constituents of the human psyche — intellect, emotion, and will respectively. Macrocosmic visions, in their composition and content, are intrinsically reflective of the inner constitution of microcosmic human beings as they seek to illuminate the darkness of their cosmos.

Worldviews are not one but many. According to Dilthey, the multiplicity of worldviews can be explained by the simple fact that they are developed under radically different conditions by radically different kinds of people. Analogous to the vast array of animal species struggling for existence, so also "the world of man knows a growth of structures of world views and a struggle between them for power over the minds of men." This struggle, like all evolving things, is subject to the law of the survival of the fittest. Cogent, useful models of life and the world are preserved and perfected while others are eliminated.

Despite their rich diversity, worldviews retain a "structural uniformity" because of their grounding in the architecture of the human mind. Nonetheless, the varieties of cultures, the succession of historical epochs, the changes in the mindsets of nations and individuals can be explained by the fact that "there is a permanent renewal of combinations of life experience, sentiments and ideas within a given world view, prevailing in a certain period of history and its context" (pp. 27-29). In other words, worldviews can fluctuate internally, adding and subtracting ideas, values, and actions consistently or inconsistently. Dilthey points out that when these alternative conceptual schemes are subject to comparative analysis, a typology of worldviews emerges. Only appropriate historical methods will suffice in ascertaining worldview types and their variations.

Dilthey summarizes this aspect of his discussion in one main thesis. In brief, worldviews spring from the totality of human psychological existence: intellectually in the cognition of reality, affectively in the appraisal of life, and volitionally in the active performance of the will. In so exercising their native capacities over the centuries in a painstaking and arduous process, human beings have formulated their outlooks on life with one primary goal in mind: stability. The ultimate irony, however, is that "mankind has not made the slightest progress on this particular path." No winner has been declared in the contest between worldviews. Dilthey prognosticates that there never will be one, for the fact of the matter is that worldviews are "undemonstrable and indestructible" (pp. 29-30). They are largely the functions of faith, and are anchored in the dynamic, ever flowing waters of the river of *life* into which no one can ever step twice, or maybe even once. Out of the flux and dynamism of human experience, worldviews come to conscious expression religiously, poetically, and metaphysically.

Religious, Poetic, and Metaphysical Worldviews

Religionists, poets, and metaphysicians are fortunately freed from the fetters of the economic, social, legal, and political machinery of life that distorts the world pictures of those who occupy these restricted spheres of existence. In the purer regions of freedom which these cultural architects inhabit, there originate and grow "world views of worth and power" (p. 31). Though conceived in freedom, worldviews obtain a religious, poetic, or metaphysical orientation, depending upon the cast of the minds that produced them.

The Religious Worldview

According to Dilthey, the powers of the unseen, invisible world and an attempt to placate and interact with such powers constitute the original religious forms of worship and establish the fundamental category of religious life. Through the efforts of a "particular religious genius," the various aspects of religious thought and experience are consolidated, and this "concentrated religious experience" inspires a codification of religious ideas. Against this background Dilthey offers this description of the religious worldview: "From such a relationship to the invisible, there emerge the interpretation of reality, the appraisal of life and the ideal of practical conduct. All of them are contained in parabolic speech and in doctrines of faith. They rest on a whole order of life. They develop in prayer and meditation. From the outset all these world views harbor in themselves a conflict of beneficent and evil beings, of an existence according to the understanding of our senses, and of a higher world transcending the senses" (p. 34).

Dilthey isolates three main types of religious worldviews focusing on (1) "the immanence of universal reason," which suggests a kind of idealism; (2) "the spiritual All-One," which corresponds to pantheism; and (3) the "creative divine will," which has theistic implications. Dilthey points out that religious worldviews are harbingers of metaphysics, but they never blend or dissolve into this philosophical discipline. Nonetheless, he suggests that the Judeo-Christian teachings segued into the monotheistic idealism of freedom, that notions of the All-One anticipated the metaphysical pantheism of the Neoplatonists Bruno, Spinoza, and Schopenhauer, and that the original monotheism transitioned to the scholastic theology of Jewish, Arabian, and Christian thinkers, which in turn fostered the philosophies of Descartes, Wolf, and Kant (deism) and the reactionary thinkers of the nineteenth century (naturalism). The religious worldview always retains its distinctively spiritual traits which prevent its amalgamation into metaphysics, especially the traits of an unshakable epistemic confidence and a fixity upon the transcendent world. Dilthey notes that despite the fact that this otherworldly orientation was shown to be the historical product of "sacerdotal techniques" (p. 35), it nevertheless preserved strains of idealism and induced the discipline of a harsh asceticism. Thus the religious worldview, in Dilthey's estimation, was too morally rigorous and too personally restricting. The human spirit must be freed up to embrace life and the world more exuberantly. The poetic worldview is just such an example, for whereas religion is riveted on the celestial, art is deeply rooted in the terrestrial.

The Poetic Worldview

While art in its early stages was developed under the auspices of religious life, gradually in the flow of history it achieved its liberation and "the ordered life of the artist obtained its full freedom" (p. 36). The very structure of worldviews spawned by art — the naturalistic, the heroic, and the pantheistic — manifests this freedom and independence, as the history of painting and music demonstrates.

Of all the arts, Dilthey maintains in a way similar to Hegel that poetry enjoys a unique relationship to all worldviews primarily because language is its medium. In either lyric, epic, or dramatic genres, poetry expresses and represents in words "all things seen, heard, or experienced" (p. 37). Poetry serves a variety of functions. It liberates people from the burden of reality; it opens up new worlds and vistas through flights of fancy; and most importantly, it gives expression to the universal moods of life (as these are expressed in works ranging from the book of Job to Hölderlin's *Empedocles*). Poetry should never be confused with the scientific understanding of reality. Rather, poetry reveals the significance of people, events, and objects in the context of relationships, and thereby sheds light on the enigma of life. Paralleling the course of cultural development from initial creeds and habits to the daunting task of interpreting and clarifying life, poetic genres have been invented — from epic to drama to the novel — to enable a society to express itself appropriately in accordance with its stage of maturity.

Most important, however, is the fact that poetry originates in life (not in unseen realms, as religions do). Consequently, it reveals its view of life in its depiction of a certain event, thing, or person. Poetry, in other words, is the avenue of expression for poets and the poets' various views of the world. "Life makes poetry always represent new aspects," says Dilthey. "The writer shows the boundless opportunities of looking at life, of evaluating it, and of creatively shaping it anew" (p. 38).

What are some examples of these poetically portrayed views of life? According to Dilthey, the work of Stendhal and Balzac presents an interpretation of naturalism, the lines of Goethe set forth a version of vitalism, and the verses of Corneille and Schiller represent a moral outlook. Each order of life has its corresponding poetic genre, and thus each poetic genre conveys one of the great types of worldviews. Through their poetic content and genre, then, Balzac, Goethe, and Schiller, among others, must be credited with the lofty accomplishment of articulating an understanding of life (pp. 38-39).

In the final analysis, poetry — as the medium of a worldview — is a critical evangelistic conduit by which particular interpretations of *reality* are

90

spread throughout the whole of culture and promulgated among human beings. There is a progression, therefore, from religious to poetic to metaphysical
worldviews.

The Metaphysical Worldview

Out of the resources of both poetry and religion, prompted by a desire for stability and at the demand of reason, metaphysics, also supported scientifically,
makes its appearance. While religion lays the foundation and poetry provides
expression, it is "the will to acquire a universally true knowledge which gives a
unique structure to this new form of world view" (p. 40). Working within the
context of a metaphysical viewpoint, philosophers in their ordained task devise
and defend its propositions and apply them thoroughly to the most important
aspects of human society. Any historical accretions associated with their systems of thought are judged to be purely accidental and are quickly removed.
The goal, once again, is the establishment of "a single and demonstrable conceptual whole, by which one might eventually solve life's enigma in a methodi-
cal fashion" (p. 42). Still, the many deep differences between metaphysical systems are apparent, thereby generating an attempt at classification, the most
basic of which is the division between idealism and realism.

At this point Dilthey returns to the concept which makes sense of these
differences and undergirds his attempt at a science of worldviews: "it is the concept of historical consciousness." This key opens the door to understanding the
lack of metaphysical progress and the conflict between metaphysical systems.
Thus we come full circle as Dilthey writes that historicism "demonstrates how
all metaphysical effort at conceptual mastery has not moved one inch toward
the goal of a unified system. Only through historical consciousness can we
grasp that the conflict of the metaphysical systems is deeply embedded, nay
founded in life, in life's experience, and in actually assumed positions toward
life's problems." Metaphysics is in no way the product of pure thought, but
rather emerges out of the stickiness of life, and out of the personalities and perspectives of its creators. Indeed, the great metaphysicians, according to Dilthey,
"have stamped the particular constitution of their own lives on systems of conceptions which claim to have universal validity. The typical element therein is
identical with their character and is expressed in their particular order of life"
(p. 44). Dilthey mentions Spinoza, Fichte, Epicurus, and Hegel as good examples of this point. Still, the plethora of metaphysical viewpoints, born out of the
vagaries of history and human subjects, must be taxonomized. For Dilthey
there is only one method adequate to the task: descriptive history and comparison. He explains why:

If we want to arrive at a conception of types of world views, we must study history. The most important lesson we learn from history in this respect is that we comprehend how life and metaphysics are connected, that we penetrate life in order to reach the core of these systems, and that we become conscious of the interrelation of the great systems which show a typical attitude — without any regard to how we limit or classify them. The only thing that counts is that we learn to look deeper into life and to follow the great intentions of metaphysics. (p. 50)

Of course, Dilthey will need a hermeneutical standard by which the various interpretations of life may be compared and contrasted. Because of the historical relativity of any criterion subjectively selected and employed for this task, Dilthey makes the admission that his proposal "must remain quite provisional" (p. 50). Despite this liability, his undertaking provides a deeper insight into history and therefore into life itself. It leads to a threefold typology of worldviews.

Naturalism, the Idealism of Freedom, and Objective Idealism

Influenced by Goethe and others, and by the typological method fashionable around the turn of the twentieth century, Dilthey formulated his typology of worldviews in which he discerned three basic forms: naturalism, the idealism of freedom, and objective idealism. Several commentators note how this threefold typology indicates the dominance of either the body (naturalism), the mind (idealism of freedom), or the interpenetration of body and mind (objective idealism).[60] Each type represents not just a rational scheme but a total life attitude as organizing centers. Also, these types are coherent and stabilizing but not closed or static, since they vibrate by an inner dialectic that breeds revision. Consequently, Dilthey did not ossify these worldview types. He simply posited them as a means to elucidate history, as a kind of heuristic device, as provisional aids to inquiry, as a means of seeing deeper into life. All devices like this worldview typology must be perpetually open to new insights and reformulations. Nonetheless, from Dilthey's historical investigation, three *Weltanschauung* models emerged.[61]

---

60. A very similar observation was made long ago by Augustine, *De doctrina Christiana*, in *The Works of St. Augustine — a Translation for the Twenty-first Century*, vol. 11 (Hyde Park, N.Y.: New City Press, 1996), p. 109 (§1.7).

61. An interesting comparison may be made between Dilthey's typology and the three "true reality values" identified and discussed by Pitirim Sorokin in his *The Crisis of Our Age: A*

Naturalism

According to Dilthey, naturalism as a worldview is established upon the thesis that human beings are determined by nature. The experience of the natural world and the physical instincts of the human body are determinative for what the cosmos itself is like. Indeed, in this framework the aim in life is to provide for the needs of the body; all other features of human experience are subordinated to the overriding demand of sensate life. This overpowering physical experience is thereby attributed to the cosmos at large and forms the naturalistic worldview. Nature is thereby deemed to be the sum total of reality. Nothing whatsoever exists outside of nature, and even intellectual experience and human consciousness are explained by natural causes. Dilthey focuses on two fundamental aspects of naturalism in his discussion, sensationalist epistemology and mechanistic metaphysics.

First, the naturalistic theory of cognition has its basis in sensationalism. Knowledge is thus derived from physically determined cognitive processes, and along with it all values and goals are evaluated by the experience of physical pleasure or pain. Sensationalism, as "the direct philosophical expression of the naturalistic habit of soul" (p. 54), becomes the basis for epistemology, axiology, and morality in this paradigm. The result of sensationalism in cognition, however, is relativism, as Protagoras demonstrated so long ago. Over against this relativity, it was necessary for naturalism to establish cognition and a science of cognition on its own assumptions. Carneades struggled with this problem in the ancient world, as did David Hume in the eighteenth century. In the context of later-day positivism, sensationalism was detached from any metaphysical association, and was deemed to be part and parcel of the positivist method of knowing in which "the brilliant perspicuity of the sensible" world was achieved (p. 57).

Second, the metaphysics of naturalism from the atomists onward was primarily mechanistic: the world is conceived exclusively in physical terms as a law-abiding machine. Ideas, the causes of motion, and intellectual facts are all reduced to the functioning of the cosmic mechanism, which is stripped entirely of the enlivening effects once supplied by religion, myth, and poetic fiction. "Nature," in short, "lost its soul" (p. 57). The task incumbent upon mechanists

---

Social and Cultural Outlook (New York: Dutton, 1945), pp. 13-29. Sorokin's "ideational" reality value equates to Dilthey's "idealism of freedom," his "idealistic" reality value corresponds to Dilthey's "objective idealism," and his "sensate" reality value matches Dilthey's "naturalism." Sorokin's own categories have been recently revived and updated by Harold O. J. Brown in his *The Sensate Culture: Western Civilization between Chaos and Transformation* (Dallas: Word, 1996).

was to draft some model of intellectual life out of a universe consisting entirely of particles in motion. This was done in the ancient world in an admirable way by Epicurus and Lucretius, and later on by Hobbes, Feuerbach, Buechner, and Moleschott. In the eighteenth century this mechanistic metaphysic, with its thoroughgoing naturalism and rationalism, rejected every transcendental value and goal, and used its growing political power to eliminate every vestige of superstition and religion and to overthrow the tyranny of the church.

The inner dialectic that pervades naturalism arises from the conflict between the perception of nature and the self-perception of consciousness. In Dilthey's words, "Man is a slave of this course [of nature] because of his passions — a shrewdly calculating slave. However . . . he is superior to nature by the power of his mind" (p. 58). The theme of human beings as sensual slaves is worked out in the hedonistic thought of Aristippus on the basis of presuppositions supplied by Protagoras, while the advantages conferred on human beings by their minds are worked out by Democritus, Epicurus, and Lucretius (especially in his poem *De rerum natura*) in their concept of "the serenity of the mind" (p. 59). Thus the autonomous conscious mind is difficult to explain solely in terms of matter alone, and consequently the inner dialectic of naturalism inclined it toward the other paradigms. Still, the naturalistic worldview, with its rejection of all things invisible, exerted a powerful influence on "the poetical ideas, on literature, and on poetry" (p. 60).

The Idealism of Freedom

Whereas naturalism has its origin in the experience of the physical world and the human body, the idealism of freedom originates out of the verities of mind and consciousness. It is the brainchild of the great ancient Athenian philosophers. This worldview boasts an amazing company of adherents: Anaxagoras, Socrates, Plato, Aristotle, Cicero, Christian apologists and Church Fathers, Duns Scotus, Kant, Jacobi, Maine de Biran, Bergson and other French thinkers. As Dilthey's sketch makes clear, the proponents of this vision of life, which radiates around the axis of mental and spiritual consciousness, are vehemently opposed to any and every form of naturalism and pantheism.

First, this worldview is an outgrowth of the idea of the sovereign superiority of the mind, which is separate and independent from every other kind of reality. The mind is free and unaffected by any form of physical causality. The mind's freedom in relation to itself and everything else is also the basis for human community wherein persons are tied together by ethical obligations and yet maintain their inward liberty. Springing out of this matrix of ideas is the notion of the unfettered, responsible individual in relation to God or Spirit, the "absolute personal or free cause" (p. 63). The interplay between God and the world, from which the deity is clearly separated, has been conceived differently by various adherents to this outlook. Anaxagoras and Aristotle see the divine in relation to matter; Christianity focuses on a personal God who created the world *ex nihilo;* and Kant has articulated transcendence by positing God as the necessary postulate for pure practical reason.

Second, this worldview has been articulated metaphysically in a variety of ways. Attic philosophy spoke of a "formative intellect that transforms matter into the world." Plato envisioned a mind free from nature which is able to grasp transcendental realities by the power of unaffected reason. Aristotle, says Dilthey, built on the same notion in his ethics. Christianity fosters a vision of God as the Creator who rules and governs his creation providentially as a father with whom communication is possible. In German transcendental philosophy, especially in Schiller, the idealism of freedom is brought to perfection in the exaltation of the ideal world which is posited by and exists only for the will in its endless striving.

The inner dialectic of this *Weltanschauung,* for which Schiller is the poet and Carlyle the prophet and historian, expresses itself in the fact that mind or spirit is not sufficient independently since it furnishes only a tenuous basis for the real world. In Dilthey's terms, "as the metaphysical consciousness of heroic man, it [the idealism of freedom] is indestructible and will come to life again in every great active man. However, it is unable to define and scientifically demonstrate its principle in a universally valid manner" (p. 65). It is thus compelled to accommodate a resistant reality that is conveyed by empirical experience. As naturalism tends to reduce mind to natural reality, so subjective idealism tends to reduce natural reality to mind. Hence the inner dialectic emerges out of this pensive opposition in both models. An alternative view of reality that integrates or synthesizes the mental and natural realms is needed. Such is the genius of the final worldview Dilthey proposes, which he labels objective idealism, a perspective on things that has pantheistic overtones.

Objective Idealism

Objective idealism, from Dilthey's point of view, attempts to integrate naturalism and subjective idealism by viewing the mind and empirical reality as an integrated, intuited whole.[62] Aesthetics and contemplation are the generative atti-

---

62. Ermath, p. 334, says that though Dilthey is generally classed as an objective idealist for various reasons, this is not necessarily the case. He states, "If Dilthey is to be snared in his own typology, then he can be regarded as representing a combination of all three — with the major

tudes of this outlook which, in Dilthey's estimate, constitutes the major strand in traditional metaphysics. Again, the proponents of this point of view constitute a veritable philosophical and literary hall of fame: Xenocrates, Heraclitus, Parmenides, the Stoics, Giordano Bruno, Spinoza, Shaftesbury, Herder, Goethe, Schelling, Hegel, Schopenhauer, and Schleiermacher. In broad brush, these devotees of pantheism teach that the world is the unfolding of God, who has diffused himself in the cosmos in countless ways. Every object in the universe mirrors the whole of which it is a part. As a monistic system, particulars are sublimated into the whole, even though individual entities possess value and reflect the whole macrocosm. Given these well-defined parameters, the advocates of objective idealism were just as vocal in their condemnation of naturalism and the idealism of freedom as the adherents of the idealism of freedom were against naturalism and objective idealism.

Naturalism is an impression determined by the subjugation of the intellectual facts to the mechanical order of things. The idealism of freedom is established in the facts of consciousness. The predominance of the body in naturalism and the soul in the idealism of freedom are combined in a body/soul amalgam in objective idealism. Objective idealism is also established upon the structure of the life of the thinkers who created the system, combining contemplation and sensual experiences into a kind of universal sympathy. By this, the whole of reality is filled and animated with the values, activities, and ideas of the human authors of this system. The sensation of being alive is expanded and attributed to the whole universe. The structure of the soul is united with the divine coherence of all things. Goethe, in a way like no one else, expressed these worldview conceptions in poetry.

The principle of unity and coherence in objective idealism causes all the discordances of life to be reconciled into one harmonious whole. Despite the contradictions of existence, there is an innermost core of everything that is real. The dissonances lead upward like a ladder to a point from which there is an awareness of a universal connection of existence and values. In objective idealism, there is the simultaneous view of all parts in their totality where they are unified and held together in harmony.

Metaphysically speaking, objects in the universe can be perceived in two ways. One, as objects of sense in an external physical connection. Two, as objects of coherence in an internal sense as a relation between the parts of the uni-

---

constituents being objective and subjective idealism, but with a considerable dose of naturalism. But such a characterization has only limited value at best, since Dilthey the catechist of the world views is beyond any one of them. Or perhaps it is more adequate to say that his interpretative posture is one of immanent critique: he is both immanent and transcendent to them."

verse and the divine core. Thus, according to Dilthey, "this consciousness of affinity is the main metaphysical feature [of objective idealism], equally inherent in the religiosity of the Indians, Greeks, and Germans" (p. 72). Since all things are a part of the whole, contemplation and intuition are to be understood ultimately in terms of a divine activity as "a living, divine, inward complex" (p. 73). On the basis of this same principle, there results a total determinism since all parts are ordered and governed by the necessary whole.

The inner dialectic produced by this model derives from the tension created in the mind's attempt to grasp reality as an integrated whole and what it can actually grasp in particular. Despite exhortations to the contrary, the whole remains an elusive ideal. As naturalism tends to reduce mind to natural reality, and as subjective idealism tends to reduce natural reality to mind, so objective idealism binds mind and matter together into a whole which is never fully comprehended. "Ultimately," according to Dilthey, speaking rather skeptically, "nothing remains of all metaphysical systems but a condition of the soul and a world view" (p. 74).

Summary

Dilthey's simple recognition of the conflict of philosophic systems and the increasing awareness of the historical condition of humanity led to the skeptical conclusion that there is no absolute, scientific, metaphysical construct which defines the nature of reality with finality. In other words, metaphysics does not have the answer. What is available, however, are worldviews — worldviews which are rooted in the contingencies of human and historical experience and which seek to elucidate the riddle of life. Worldviews not only reflect the structure of the human soul in its intellectual, affective, and volitional aspects, but are also influenced in their formation by the optimistic or pessimistic mood of the worldviewer. Worldviews are vehicles of expression for the religious, poetic, and metaphysical impulses of humanity, and can be categorized into the three basic types of naturalism, the idealism of freedom, and objective idealism. Each allegedly is privy to some aspect of reality. None of them, however, tell the whole story. According to Dilthey, therefore, one must never mistake one's corner for the world.

In light of all this, some critics assert that Dilthey found no rescue for his culture from the grip of metaphysical and epistemological relativism. When it comes to the nature of things, there is no god's-eye point of view, no pure *theorein* in the original sense of the term, no ocular clarity devoid of historical cataracts, no pure, universal reason. As Dilthey put it, "every cognitive effort is conditioned by the relation of the knowing subject and his historical horizon to a specific group of facts which is also conditioned in scope according to a specific horizon. For every attempt at understanding, the object is there only from a specific standpoint. Therefore, it is a specifically relative way of seeing and knowing its object."[63] The concept of worldviews, therefore, generates seemingly an inescapable skepticism about truth and the ultimate nature of things. In this light, a fundamental question is posited in all its provocation and intensity: "what is the individual to do in this welter of relativities?"[64] One radical response to this dilemma is found in the thought of Friedrich Nietzsche, whose notion of perspectivism seems to carry the relativist implications of Dilthey's doctrine of worldviews to their logical conclusion.

"Worldview" and Perspectivism in Friedrich Nietzsche

Friedrich Nietzsche (1844-1900) was the apogee of trends in Western philosophy launched by Kant's Copernican revolution. The themes of the titanic self, the omnicompetent mind, thoroughgoing historicism, biological evolutionism, and radical relativism were for Nietzsche indicative of the death of the myth of God, whose existence had undergirded Western civilization for nearly two millennia. Not only was Nietzsche the one in whom these trends met, but he was also architect of a fleet of philosophical lifeboats — *Übermenschen,* Dionysianism, transvaluationism, linguisticism, aestheticism — which he deployed to rescue moderns who were threatened by the encroaching floodwaters of nihilism that were inundating the West. By virtue of his incisive understanding of the inevitable drift of Western thought and in light of his bold proposals for a new age, Nietzsche was not only the *terminus ad quem* of the nineteenth century but also the *terminus a quo* of the twentieth.

Central to Nietzsche's appraisal of his times were the related notions of *Weltanschauung* and perspectivism. The breakdown of Christianity and the eventual collapse of idealist philosophy meant the elimination of any kind of transcendent or mental category as a metaphysical reference point, leaving only nature and the ongoing historical process as the two foci for understanding the world and human life. Nineteenth-century naturalism and historicism, consequently, set the stage for Nietzsche's thought. Peter Levine believes that his en-

---

63. From *Gesammelte Schriften,* 7:233; quoted in Ermath, p. 289.

64. H. A. Hodges, *Wilhelm Dilthey: An Introduction* (New York: Howard Fertig, 1969), p. 104. For an attempt to exonerate Dilthey from the charge of relativism and skepticism, see Ermath, pp. 334-38.

counter with historical diversity as a philologist first led him to conclude "that people must be the products, results, or mere 'fluctuations' of real entities that he called cultures or *Weltanschauungen* — world-views," each of which "encompassed a consistent, homogeneous and clearly delimited set of values."[65] Not only did Nietzsche's exposure to historicism in the context of his philological studies incline him toward such strong relativism, but so also did influences from Immanuel Kant and Ralph Waldo Emerson.

With Kant, Nietzsche certainly believed in the constructive nature and activity of the human mind, only more so. Nietzsche embraced the Kantian a priori categories not by asking how the judgments they produced are possible, but by asking why they are necessary.[66] For Nietzsche the judgments were necessary not because they were true (in fact, they probably were not), but rather because they were indispensable for the preservation and survival of humanity. Conceptual schemes were a human necessity. Furthermore, Nietzsche did not believe that the specific Kantian categories were the only ones possible. His exaltation of freedom and embrace of the Dionysian imagination led him to aver that the mind's operation on the world was ceaselessly creative. According to Mary Warnock, he believed that "our contribution to, indeed our construction of, our world is a fact; but we could construct it a different way [from the Kantian one]."[67] This position, allowing for multiple cognitive pathways, plus Nietzsche's rejection of Kant's notion of a reality in itself, the *ding an sich* (which for him was worthy only "of Homeric laughter; that it appeared to be so much, indeed everything, and is actually empty, that is to say empty of significance"),[68] fostered in him a deep appreciation for the reality of multiple logics.

Another compelling force on Nietzsche's philosophical development was, perhaps surprisingly, Ralph Waldo Emerson (1803-82), whom he read assidu-

---

65. Peter Levine, *Nietzsche and the Modern Crisis of the Humanities* (Albany: State University of New York Press, 1995), p. xiii. George J. Stack, *Nietzsche: Man, Knowledge, and Will to Power* (Durango, Colo.: Hollowbrook Publishing, 1994), p. 96, points out that Nietzsche's philological studies produced in him a "sensitivity to the [historical] problems of textual interpretation [that] tended to spread to a variety of aspects of existence, to questions of truth in philosophy and science, and to the general issue of our knowledge of the world."

66. Friedrich Nietzsche, *Beyond Good and Evil*, in *Basic Writings of Friedrich Nietzsche*, translated and edited with commentaries by Walter Kaufmann (New York: Modern Library, 1968), p. 209 (§11).

67. Mary Warnock, "Nietzsche's Conception of Truth," in *Nietzsche's Imagery and Thought: A Collection of Essays*, ed. Malcolm Pasley (Berkeley: University of California Press, 1978), p. 38.

68. Friedrich Nietzsche, *Human, All Too Human: A Book for Free Spirits*, trans. R. J. Hollingdale, introduction by Erich Heller, Texts in German Philosophy, gen. ed. Charles Taylor (New York: Cambridge University Press, 1986), p. 20 (§17).

ously and sympathetically over a twenty-six-year period.[69] Emerson's essay "Experience" was particularly influential in its description of the powerful impact of subjective factors on the human exchange with the world. Our temperament, Emerson argued, deeply conditions our worldview by the way it "enters fully into the system of illusions and shuts us in a prison of glass which we cannot see."[70] Thus Emerson declared that "we do not see directly, but mediately, and that we have no means of correcting these colored and distorting lenses which we are, or of computing the amount of their errors. Perhaps these subject-lenses have a creative power."[71] Creative subjective lenses and diverse personal temperaments, plus a whole host of other conditionals, radically determine the way human beings interpret the world and operate within it. "Thus inevitably," Emerson concluded, "does the universe wear our color, and every object fall successively into the subject itself."[72]

Under these Kantian and Emersonian influences, along with the a prioris of naturalism and historicism, Nietzsche formulated his thinking about "worldview." Levine suggests that "Nietzsche did depend upon the concept of the *Weltanschauung* at an early stage in his development," and that "without it, the later stages would not have followed."[73] He employed the word often enough. A computer search of Nietzsche's complete works in German reveals fifty uses of *Weltanschauung* (two spelled with only one *u*), one use of the plural form *Weltanschauungen*, five uses of *Weltansicht* (also translated "worldview"), and twenty-four uses of *Weltbild* (world picture).[74] He seems to have defined "worldview" in a rather ordinary way as a perspective on reality and basic conception of life. He frequently associates a name, nation, religion, era, race, or metaphysic with *Weltanschauung*. For example, he can speak of the Hellenic, Dionysian, Christian, Hegelian, and mechanistic views of life.[75] A survey of the texts in which these phrases occur shows that Nietzsche did not spend much

69. Stack, pp. 97-98.

70. Ralph Waldo Emerson, "Experience," in *Selected Essays* (Chicago: People's Book Club, 1949), p. 285.

71. Emerson, p. 300.

72. Emerson, p. 303.

73. Levine, p. xv.

74. Friedrich Nietzsche database in "Past Masters in Philosophy," InteLex Corporation.

75. The following citations of Nietzsche's use of *Weltanschauung* are from his *Sämtliche Werke: Kritische Studienausgabe in 15 Bänden,* herausgegeben von Giorgio Colli und Mazzino Montinari (New York and Berlin: Walter de Gruyter, 1980): "the dionysian worldview," 1:551, 598; 15:23, 25, 26, 27; "the Christian worldview," 7:13; "worldview of the Hegelian epoch," 7:61; "in the worldview from Sophocles to Apollo," 7:67; "Hellenic worldview," 7:75; "the tragic worldview," 7:79, 118, 123, 288; "the musical worldview," 7:116; "the mystical worldview," 7:123; "a mechanistic worldview," 2:200; "metaphysical worldview," 15:102; "the Nietzschean worldview," 15:197.

time reflecting upon the nature of *Weltanschauung* per se, though a sketch of his understanding of it is possible in light of the ethos of his own philosophy.

Nietzsche believes worldviews are cultural entities which people in a given geographical location and historical context are dependent upon, subordinate to, and products of. He posits a general law that "every living thing can become healthy, strong and fruitful only within a horizon."[76] A *Weltanschauung* provides this necessary, well-defined boundary that structures the thoughts, beliefs, and behaviors of people. From the point of view of its adherents, a worldview is incontestable and provides the ultimate set of standards by which all things are measured. It supplies the criteria for all thinking and engenders a basic understanding of the true, the good, and the beautiful. Worldviews for Nietzsche tend to be incommensurable constructs that render cross-cultural communication difficult if not impossible.

According to Nietzsche, worldviews are nothing but reifications. They are the subjective creations of human knowers in formative social contexts who ascribe their outlook to nature, God, law, or some other presumed authority. But they forget that they themselves are the creators of their own model of the world. The alleged "truth" of a worldview is merely an established convention — the product of linguistic customs and habits. Nietzsche's answer to the question about the nature of truth in general would apply equally well to the question about the alleged truth claims of any worldview. When he asks, "What, then, is truth?" he responds with these provocative words: "A mobile army of metaphors, metonyms, and anthropomorphisms — in short, a sum of human relations, which have been enhanced, transposed, and embellished poetically and rhetorically, and which after long use seem firm, canonical, and obligatory to a people: truths are illusions about which one has forgotten that this is what they are; metaphors which are worn out and without sensuous power; coins which have lost their pictures and now matter only as metal, no longer as coins."[77]

---

76. Friedrich Nietzsche, *On the Advantage and Disadvantage of History for Life*, translated and introduction by Peter Preuss (Indianapolis: Hackett, 1980), p. 10 (§1). Gadamer, p. 301, describes the concept of horizon and discusses the meaning attributed to it by Nietzsche and Husserl. He writes: "The horizon is the range of vision that includes everything that can be seen from a particular vantage point. Applying this to the thinking mind, we speak of narrowness of horizon, of the possible expansion of horizon, of the opening up of new horizons, and so forth. Since Nietzsche and Husserl, the word has been used in philosophy to characterize the way in which thought is tied to its finite determinacy, and the way one's range of vision is gradually expanded."

77. Friedrich Nietzsche, "On Truth and Lie in an Extra-Moral Sense," in *The Portable Nietzsche*, ed. and trans. Walter Kaufmann (New York: Penguin Books, 1982), pp. 46-47.

In other words, out of the dynamics of a human community words are established, conceptions become fixed, and truths are institutionalized. Worldviews feign authenticity, but actually are artificial constructs necessary for human survival. As Nietzsche makes clear, "*Truth is that kind of error* without which a certain species of living [human beings] cannot exist."[78] There is no true truth, only subjective projections, linguistic customs, habituated thinking, and reified cultural models. All worldviews are ultimately fictions.

In the absence of true truth, the mandatory question for Nietzsche and his age is how to live meaningfully in the face of the metaphysical, epistemic, and moral nihilism native to *Weltanschauung* historicism. This question seems all the more intensified in light of Nietzsche's deliberations on perspectivism which are closely related to *Weltanschauung*. Like the latter, perspectivism focuses on an individual's unique interpretation of any and every possible object, including the world on the grand scale, for one's "perspective" on the "world" is presumably one's worldview, or world perspective. In Robin Small's succinct words, "perspectivism means that the world is always understood within the perspective of some point of view; all knowledge is thus an interpretation of reality in accordance with the set of assumptions that makes one perspective different from another."[79] There is, therefore, an interface between worldview and perspectivism.

A complete perspectivism is at the heart of Nietzsche's philosophy. His writings are brimming with aphorisms and declarations about the perspectival nature of all cognition and perception. For example, in *The Genealogy of Morals* Nietzsche states, "There is only a seeing from a perspective, only a 'knowing' from a perspective, and the *more* emotions we express over a thing, the *more* eyes, different eyes, we train on the same thing, the more complete will be our 'idea' of that thing, our 'objectivity.'"[80] Thoroughgoing perspectivism thus renders genuine objectivity farcical. That there is only perspectival seeing and knowing implies that "there are no facts, only interpretations."[81] For Nietzsche there are no objective personalities and therefore no objective points of view,

78. Friedrich Nietzsche, *The Will to Power,* trans. Anthony M. Ludovici, in *The Complete Works of Friedrich Nietzsche,* ed. Oscar Levy, vol. 15 (New York: Russell and Russell, 1964), p. 13 (§493).

79. Robin Small, "Nietzsche and a Platonist Idea of the Cosmos: Center Everywhere and Circumference Nowhere," *Journal of the History of Ideas* 44 (January-March 1983): 99.

80. Friedrich Nietzsche, *The Genealogy of Morals,* in *The Complete Works of Friedrich Nietzsche,* ed. Oscar Levy, vol. 13 (New York: Russell and Russell, 1964), p. 153 (§12).

81. Friedrich Nietzsche, *Nachlaß,* in *Nietzsche's Werke in Drei Bände,* ed. Karl Schlechta (Munich: Carl Hanser Verlag, 1958), p. 903, quoted in Arthur C. Danto, *Nietzsche as Philosopher* (New York: Macmillan, 1965), p. 76.

only subjective persons and person-relative points of view. Thought, therefore, is the product of visceral humanity. "It is our needs," Nietzsche says, "that *interpret the world*."[82] All hermeneutic endeavors (artistic, scientific, religious, moral) are a "symptom of a ruling instinct."[83] There are no, to use a phrase from Nietzsche in another context, "immaculate perceptions."[84] Or, as Nietzsche wrote in a letter, there are "no single beatific interpretations."[85] Thus the conclusion is that there can be no pure facts, only hundreds of interpretations, feelings, guesses, hunches, opinions, and intuitions. For "our ideas, our values, our yeas and nays, our ifs and buts, grow out of us with the necessity with which a tree bears fruit."[86]

Thus, when it comes to views of self, the world, and everything else, the human race speaks in many different tongues. This hetero-glossolalia reflects the limitless possibilities for world interpretation, what Nietzsche, in a play on religious language, called "our new 'infinite.'" "The world," he claims, "has once more become 'infinite' to us: in so far as we cannot dismiss the possibility that it contains infinite interpretations."[87] The ocean provides Nietzsche with an apt metaphor for the vast yet frightening opportunities for worldview and perspectival exploration cut off from traditional verities. "In the horizon of the infinite. — We have left the land and have embarked. We have burned our bridges behind us — indeed, we have gone farther and destroyed the land behind us. Now, little ship, look out! Beside you is the ocean. . . . Woe, when you feel homesick for the land as if it had offered more *freedom* — and there is no longer any 'land.'"[88] This journey into the landless sea is precisely what the Nietzschean doctrine of *Weltanschauung* and perspectivism is about.

82. Nietzsche, *The Will to Power*, p. 13 (§481).

83. Nietzsche, *The Will to Power*, p. 150 (§677).

84. Friedrich Nietzsche, *Thus Spoke Zarathrustra*, in *The Portable Nietzsche*, p. 233.

85. Quoted in Jean Granier, "Perspectivism and Interpretation," in *The New Nietzsche*, edited with an introduction by David B. Allison (Cambridge: MIT Press, 1985), p. 197.

86. Friedrich Nietzsche, *On the Genealogy of Morals*, trans. and ed. Walter Kaufmann (New York: Modern Library, 1968), p. 452 (§2).

87. Friedrich Nietzsche, *The Joyful Wisdom*, trans. Thomas Common, in *The Complete Works of Friedrich Nietzsche*, ed. Oscar Levy, vol. 10 (New York: Russell and Russell, 1964), p. 340 (§374).

88. Friedrich Nietzsche, *The Gay Science, with a Prelude in Rhymes and an Appendix of Songs*, translated with commentary by Walter Kaufmann (New York: Random House, Vintage Books, 1974), pp. 180-81 (§124).

Concluding Implications

In this chapter we have examined the fortunes of *Weltanschauung* in the thought of four very remarkable nineteenth-century thinkers. Whether in Hegelian idealism, Kierkegaardian existentialism, Diltheyan historicism, and Nietzschean perspectivism, the idea of worldview found a home in these diverse universes of discourse. Each raises important questions and issues pertaining to the idea of worldview from a Christian vantage point.

For Hegel, worldviews as alternative frameworks are the historically embedded, culturally significant phenomena of the Absolute Spirit, each of which finds expression aesthetically. The truth about the universe — the final worldview — awaits eschatological realization at the end of time. Would it not be more biblically correct, however, to attribute the production and influence of multiple conceptual schemes not to the philosophical fantasy of some alleged Absolute Spirit in search of itself, but rather to the rulers, the powers, the world forces of darkness, and the spiritual forces of wickedness in the heavenly places (see Eph. 6:12)? As Augustine pointed out long ago, at the heart of the historical process is a battle between the demonic spirits or powers and the Holy Spirit and their respective human adherents and agents who ultimately align themselves with either the city of man or the city of God. Interpreted in biblical terms, Hegel's philosophy of history ignites interest in understanding the historical process as spiritual warfare with the notion of competing worldviews at the center (see more on this in chap. 9). He also invites consideration of the manner in which art serves as a powerful communicative medium of diverse *intellectūs*. Since the aesthetic impulse is directed at least in part toward the expression of a particular outlook on life, how might Christian artists take their place on the stage of history and most effectively communicate a biblical vision of the world with sophistication and power? Finally, Hegel's eschatological orientation stimulates reflection on the Christian meaning of the end of history in terms of worldview. Is not the biblical eschaton designed in part to vindicate the sovereignty of God over against all competing authorities as well as to manifest the divine source, the sacramental character, and the glorious destiny of the entire cosmos in conquest of rival religious and philosophical explanations? At the end of history, the existence of God, the true nature of the universe, the identity of persons, and the purpose of life — issues which have been debated for millennia — are finally resolved.

For Kierkegaard, lifeviews are central to human existence. His valorization of the project of forming a lifeview, in particular a Christian one, seems well founded. It is a task from which no genuine believer is exempt. His exhortation to this end raises important questions, however, about the content, method, and outcome of this endeavor. How does the Christian lifeview define the meaning of life and its purpose? As an unusual illumination about life, how is a lifeview formed, and to what extent is the process dependent upon the gracious activity of a sovereign God? What personal and communal benefits accrue from the development of a lifeview grounded in Christian truth? To employ Kierkegaardian categories, how does a biblically based lifeview affect literature, friendship, parenthood, and education, among other things? Kierkegaard distinguished sharply between the profound, existential nature of a lifeview and the disinterestedness of abstract, academic thought. How does this project of lifeview formation differ from the professional disciplines of theology and philosophy? Should it even replace these enterprises, as Kierkegaard suggested? If not, how ought the relationship between life and worldview, philosophy and theology be articulated? Kierkegaard was pessimistic about justifying the Christian lifeview epistemologically. Can a biblically based outlook be defended, and if so, how? Or is it truly a "leap of faith"? Though his denigration of the value of academic theology and philosophy and his diminution of the epistemic credibility of the Christian revelation raise serious concerns, Kierkegaard's advocacy of the practical, existential task of developing a Christian lifeview ought to be well received.

In Dilthey, worldviews are historically produced perspectives on reality. His reflections force us to confront the matter of historicism along with its associated relativism. The fact that human beings, given their various cognitive capacities, are embedded in the ebb and flow of history would seem to impart to their conceptual attempts to solve the riddle of life a highly relative quality. Are all worldviews, Christianity included, sucked into this black hole? Does everything that occurs *in* history also arise *from* history? An affirmative answer to this question is necessary only if one is committed antecedently to a perspective on life that eliminates any otherworldly reality and absolutizes the historical process. Conversely, leaving the door open to a transcendent principle or person which reveals itself or who communicates from the outside or the top down makes it possible to deny that the relativism of historicism has the last word.

Nonetheless, Dilthey's reflections make it clear that the question is not *whether* history shapes human consciousness, but rather *how* and with *what* content. This would even seem to be the divine plan and intent. God has chosen to reveal himself and his works of creation and redemption to Israel and the church through that particular strand of history that is set apart or holy: *Heilsgeschichte.* Therefore, on the one hand, contact with and acceptance of this unique stream of holy history — either directly, or by means of divine revelation, or by involvement in an historical and cultural context shaped by this revelation — would be necessary for the formation of a Judeo-Christian worldview. For the chain is this: sacred or holy history shapes regular history, which shapes the formation of consciousness. On the other hand, to be separated from or rebellious toward this Judeo-Christian revelation or an historical and cultural context shaped by it means to be barred from forming a biblically based view of life. Concomitantly, it means to be confined to the relative forces of the historical process, which itself may be indicative of the judgment of God in a fallen world upon a rebellious humanity. Thus Christians may agree with Dilthey when it comes to the role played by history in shaping consciousness and forming worldviews. History is the inescapable context of cultural communication. However, they would surely reinterpret his thesis of relativism even as a sign of judgment in light of divine revelation which offers a stable point of view on the nature of reality amidst the flux and change of historical life.

For Nietzsche, God is dead, only nature exists, and history reigns. On this basis he conceived of worldviews as reified cultural constructs and idiosyncratic perspectives on life, artificial to be sure, but necessary for human survival in an ultimately chaotic, unnavigable world. The Christian community would certainly challenge Nietzsche directly regarding his hard-core atheism, thoroughgoing naturalism, and radical historicism. As alternatives they would propose a doctrine of the Holy Trinity, the thesis of a very good creation, and a view of history as the arena of divine revelation. They would be open, however, to some of his insights about reification and perspectivism. Might not a Christian's worldview contain various elements that seem to be theologically grounded but are in fact merely conventional? Upon this recognition, what changes can and should be made in what Christians believe *(credenda)* and how they behave in the world *(agenda)?* The Nietzschean theme of reification may serve as an important corrective and help believers move toward a greater degree of biblical fidelity in their basic conception of life.

Though Nietzsche was extremist in his perspectivism, his position does contain an essential insight nevertheless: all human beings see things aslant, Christians included. This is what having a worldview, biblical or otherwise, is all about. It has to do with viewing the cosmos and all things within it through a particular set of lenses or from a specific point of view. If held in balance, this position can avoid the excesses of both modernist dogmatism and postmodernist skepticism and terminate in a kind of critical realism which recognizes the role of both objectivist and subjectivist factors in the knowing process. There is a real world to be known, but we always comprehend it from our vantage point. There seems to be a biblical warrant for this epistemology. As Paul himself said, "For now we see in a mirror dimly" (see 1 Cor. 13:12). Nietzsche's perspectivism, therefore, can be appropriately modified to render an apt insight into the epistemic significance of worldviews (see chap. 10 for additional discussion). Meanwhile, we move on to consider the role of worldview in twentieth-century philosophy.

Chapter Five

A Philosophical History of "Worldview": The Twentieth Century I

Philosophical reflection on the theme of worldview seems to intensify in the twentieth century. A number of noteworthy thinkers representing diverse philosophical traditions directed their attention to the notion of *Weltanschauung* with a variety of interests and purposes in mind. Because this material is so extensive, we will divide our history of this concept during this time period into two parts. In this chapter we will survey the salient contribution of Edmund Husserl, who was determined to distinguish worldviews from scientific philosophy. Then we will look at Karl Jaspers, whose interest in worldviews was psychological in orientation. And finally we will examine the thought of Martin Heidegger, who took up some of Husserl's concerns and also wanted to explain worldviews as purely modernist constructs. In the next chapter we will continue this twentieth-century investigation with an examination of the thought of Ludwig Wittgenstein, Donald Davidson, and several postmodern thinkers. But for now, we begin with Edmund Husserl.

"Worldview" in Edmund Husserl

For Edmund Husserl (1859-1938), the relativism of historicism, which was an outgrowth of Hegel's idealist philosophy of Spirit and intrinsic to worldview philosophy, was partly responsible for the grave crises afflicting the natural and human sciences in Western culture. To the extent that European civilization itself rested upon a weakened scientific base, it was at risk and in need of reinforcement. To offset such pernicious effects, Husserl wrote a landmark article in which he defended philosophy as a rigorous science over against the relativism of worldviews. He also crafted the notion of "lifeworld" *(Lebenswelt)* to rescue modern thought from the truth-destroying forces of a seemingly omnipotent historicism. In turning our attention to these respective themes, Husserl's early twentieth-century contribution to the history of *Weltanschauung* comes to light.

Husserl's Rejection of "Worldview" and His Defense of Philosophy as a Rigorous Science

Wilhelm Dilthey's apparent relativism and skepticism was the target of Husserl's sharp criticism in his programmatic article titled "Philosophy as Rigorous Science."[1] This accusation brought these two notable thinkers into an important epistolary relationship "by means of which we are immediately placed within the great events of philosophy at the beginning of . . . [the twentieth] century."[2] Husserl's criticism prompted a written response from the "father of worldview theory" in which he vigorously proclaimed that he was "neither an intuitionist, nor a historicist, nor a skeptic."[3] He believed firmly that Husserl had concluded too much from too little. Be that as it may, Husserl's article has been viewed as "phenomenology's manifesto" in light of its defense of the scientific nature of philosophy over against various mitigating forces, especially naturalism and worldview historicism.[4] The argument of this work not only presents aspects of Husserl's phenomenological agenda, but is also a striking example of how prominent the concept of worldview had become, and how from Husserl's perspective it posed a threat to objectivist conceptions of philosophy as a scientific discipline.

According to Husserl, philosophy since its beginning has claimed to be a rigorous and exact endeavor, though history clearly reveals that it has not been

---

1. Edmund Husserl, "Philosophie als strenge Wissenschaften," *Logos* 1 (1910-11): 289-341. For the English translation, see Edmund Husserl, "Philosophy as Rigorous Science," in *Husserl: Shorter Works*, ed. Peter McCormick and Frederick A. Elliston (Notre Dame, Ind.: University of Notre Dame Press; Brighton, England: Harvester Press, 1981), pp. 185-97; the page references in the following text are to this article. A similar discussion was taken up several years later by Heinrich Rickert, "Wissenschaftliche Philosophie und Weltanschauung," *Logos* 22 (1933): 37ff.

2. Walter Biemel, "Introduction to the Dilthey-Husserl Correspondence," ed. Walter Biemel, trans. Jeffner Allen, in *Husserl: Shorter Works*, pp. 199, 201.

3. Edmund Husserl and Wilhelm Dilthey, "The Dilthey-Husserl Correspondence," in *Husserl: Shorter Works*, p. 204. Dilthey's response is dated 29 June 1911.

4. Biemel, p. 199. For further discussion on Husserl's view of scientific vis-à-vis worldview philosophy, see Michael J. Seidler, "Philosophy as a Rigorous Science: An Introduction to Husserlian Phenomenology," *Philosophy Today* 21 (1977): 306-26, and Wayne F. Buck, "Husserl's Conception of Philosophy," *Kinesis* 8 (1977): 8, 10-25.

successful in fulfilling its own alleged scientific criteria. To remedy this deficiency, he presents the phenomenological method as the solution to philosophy's ultimate vocation. The kind of exactitude that Husserl calls for is so extreme that philosophy and philosophy alone would be able to supply the
foundation for all the other sciences, natural and human. In this way Husserl
not only seeks to save philosophy from the encroachment of the various sciences as the basis of all thought, but in fact makes them entirely dependent
upon it.[5]

In order to accomplish his task, Husserl must deliver the discipline from
two menaces that were prevalent around the turn of the century: naturalism
and *Weltanschauung* philosophy. After a discussion on the substance of naturalism and a refutation of its implications upon consciousness and ideas, he turns
his attention to the issue of worldviews. According to Husserl, *Weltanschauung*
philosophy is "a result of the transformation of Hegel's metaphysical philosophy of history into a sceptical historicism" (p. 168). Just as naturalism endan-
gers the sciences with its reductionistic psychologism, so also worldview
historicism threatens to undo philosophic and other theoretical enterprises
with its lethal epistemic relativism. Hence Husserl is constrained to respond to
the peril of historicism itself, and then to describe the nature of *Weltanschauung* philosophy in order to contrast it with the robust nature of philosophy, especially as it is found in his own phenomenological method.

The first thing Husserl does in his critique of historicism per se is to set
forth its claim, quoting Dilthey, that "the formation of historical consciousness
destroys more thoroughly than does surveying the disagreement of systems a
belief in the universal validity of any of the philosophies that have undertaken
to express in a compelling manner the coherence of the world in an ensemble
of concepts" (p. 186). Husserl agrees with Dilthey regarding the impact of historical consciousness on the formation of a multitude of worldviews that come
and go regularly. The issue is whether the principle of historicism must be applied in a mitigating way to all theoretical endeavors. The history-bound sciences, like worldviews themselves, are in a constant state of flux. "Do they for
that reason lack objective validity?" The historicist would answer affirmatively,
given the indisputable fact of persistent alterations in scientific viewpoints.
This suggests they are subject to multiple historical influences and are not,
therefore, universally valid. "Does that mean," Husserl asks, "that in view of this
constant change in scientific views that we would actually have no right to
speak of sciences as objectively valid unities instead of merely as cultural for-
mations?" He concludes on this note: "It is easy to see that historicism, if con-

5. Biemel, p. 199.

sistently carried through, carries over into extreme sceptical subjectivism" (p. 186).

In a clever manner, however, Husserl demonstrates the self-defeating nature of historicism. If historicism is true, then it must be false, for the principles of historicism must also be a product of historical forces, and therefore relative. If they are relative, then they cannot be used in some absolute way to deny the objective validity of the sciences. Husserl writes, "just as historical science can advance nothing relevant against the possibility of absolute validities in general, so it can advance nothing in particular against the possibility of an absolute (i.e., scientific) metaphysics or any other philosophy" (p. 187). Furthermore on the positive side, if there are conceptions whose objective validity can be refuted by philosophical criticisms, then there must be a domain within which something can be grounded as objective. In Husserl's words, "Any correct, profoundly penetrating criticism itself provides means for advancing and ideally points to correct goals, thereby indicating an objectively valid science." On these grounds, Husserl asserts that historicism is an "epistemological mistake," but this does not negate his appreciation of the value of history in the broadest sense for the philosopher.

With this rejection of historicism now in place, Husserl moves on to his exposition and evaluation of worldview philosophy in order to compare it to his own scientific view of the discipline. Husserl notes that *Weltanschauung* philosophy is "a child of historical scepticism," yet insofar as its goal is "to satisfy as far as possible our need for thorough-going and unifying, all-embracing and all-penetrating knowledge, it looks on all particular sciences as its basis" (p. 188). However, simply because it admits scientific knowledge into its epistemic kingdom, this does not make it a bona fide scientific construct. Most worldview philosophers, Husserl notes, readily admit this and even glory in it. They rejoice to point out that worldview formation is really the only type of philosophy possible since historicism has effectively crippled a scientifically based conception of the world.

Furthermore, the motives for the formulation of worldviews disclose their nonscientific character. They have a unique teleological function to fulfill, namely, the acquisition of "wisdom." For Husserl, all experiences, education, and values — theoretic, axiological, and practical — are united together in a worldview which is synonymous with "wisdom." "With regard to particularly high levels of value," he writes, "there is the old-fashioned word 'wisdom' (wisdom of the world, wisdom of world and life), and most of all, the now-beloved expressions 'world view' and 'life view,' or simply *Weltanschauung*" (p. 189). Furthermore, the development of wisdom or *Weltanschauung*, he asserts, is not the achievement of a single, isolated person. Rather the accomplishment "belongs to the cultural community and to the time," such that reference can be made not only to the "culture and *Weltanschauung* of a determined individual but also of that of the time" (pp. 189-90). The Hegelian influence seems evident here.

The possession of this "wisdom," which is the primary value and goal of worldview thinking, is still vague and unconceptualized even in great philosophical personalities. It requires conceptual elaboration, logical development, and fusion with the content of other disciplines. When a worldview undergoes this process of intellectual refinement, it is transformed into full-fledged *Weltanschauung* philosophy which sets forth "relatively perfect" answers to the enigmas of life. Husserl explains in these words:

> Insofar, then, as the vital and hence most persuasive cultural motives of the time are not only conceptually grasped but also logically unfolded and otherwise elaborated in thought, insofar as the results thus obtained are brought, in interplay with additional institutions and insights, to scientific unification and consistent completion, there develops an extraordinary extension and elevation of the originally unconceptualized wisdom. There develops a *Weltanschauung* philosophy, which in the great systems gives relatively the most perfect answer to the riddles of life and the world, which is to say, it affords as well as possible a solution and satisfactory explanation to the theoretical, axiological, and practical inconsistencies of life that experience, wisdom, mere world and life view, can only imperfectly overcome. (p. 190)

Thus *Weltanschauung* philosophy surpasses mere *Weltanschauung* as a mature adult surpasses the immature child. Not only this, but worldview philosophy aims at an admirable goal, namely, the formation of an ideal human being characterized by ability and wisdom. Husserl elaborates on this lofty anthropological vision in these terms: "It is clear, then, how each one should strive to be as universally able a personality as possible, able in all the fundamental orientations of life, which for their part correspond to the fundamental types of possible attitudes. It is clear, too, how each should strive to be in each of these orientations as 'experienced,' as 'wise,' and hence also as much a 'lover of wisdom' as possible. According to this idea, every man who strives is necessarily a 'philosopher,' in the most original sense of the word."

A number of admirable factors make *Weltanschauung* philosophy extremely attractive and commendable. It is intimately associated with the ideals of humanity, perfect wisdom, and the desideratum of capability. It establishes itself in the collective consciousness of an epoch, and thus emits an aura of objective validity. Consequently, *Weltanschauung* philosophy is, according to Husserl, "a most significant cultural force, a point of radiation for the most worthwhile personalities of the time" (p. 190). In this manner Husserl attributes remarkable importance and value to the idea of worldview formation. Though it is not technically scientific, it is still concerned with science; though it is personal and practical, it nevertheless seeks to be rational. Nothing, it would seem, should stand in the way of recommending this form of philosophy or of striving toward it wholeheartedly.

That is, except for one thing. In regard to the idea of genuine philosophy, Husserl argues that other and higher values must be satisfied, "which is to say, those of a philosophical science." On the basis of "the high scientific culture of our time," and in light of the "mighty forces of objectified strict sciences," Husserl argues that worldview as a practical philosophy, and science as an objectively valid discipline, "have been sharply separated, and from now on they remain separated for all eternity" (p. 191).[6] In this assertion we see the modern "fact/value" dichotomy in bold relief. In the past, all historical philosophies were *Weltanschauung* philosophies comprised of an undifferentiated mixture of both wisdom and science. Worldview pragmatics and scientific reason were blended into a kind of indiscriminate philosophical alloy. However, since the advent of the "supratemporal universality of strict science," this situation has changed drastically. The clear and important distinction between finite, individualistic, temporal, and fluctuating worldviews and infinite, collective, eternal, and changeless science must now be steadfastly maintained. "Thus," Husserl concludes, "*Weltanschauung* philosophy and scientific philosophy are sharply distinguished as two ideas, related in a certain manner to each other but not to be confused" (p. 191).

Still, scientific philosophy must be regarded as a promissory note. Whereas *Weltanschauung* philosophies have been plentiful for thousands of years, no philosophy in the past or present has met the requirements of rigor-

---

6. This same fact/value dichotomy permeates the famous address delivered by Max Weber in 1918 titled "Science as a Vocation," in which he describes the nature of the professoriate in strictly scientific terms. No student, says Weber, should expect a professor in the execution of his duties to "sell him a *Weltanschauung* or a code of conduct." That is simply not the teacher's business; if he thinks it is, it should be an extracurricular activity only. "And if he feels called upon to intervene in the struggle of worldviews and party opinions, he may do so outside, in the market place, in the press, in meetings, in associations, wherever he wishes" ("Science as a Vocation," in *From Max Weber: Essays in Sociology*, translated, edited, and introduction by H. H. Gerth and C. Wright Mills [New York: Oxford University Press, 1946], p. 150). For Weber, as for Husserl, worldview philosophy and genuine science simply do not mix. See Weber's essay, pp. 129-56.

ous science. What kind of thinker, then, will or should undertake the challenge to develop scientific philosophy? According to Husserl, the decision to pursue either option is rooted primarily in the various types of human temperaments. Some people, he observes, are preeminently theoretical in nature, and are uniquely qualified for the rigorous task of the development of a scientific philosophy. Interestingly, he notes that such an inclination might be rooted in and an expression of an individual's total outlook on life. Conversely, other persons — artists, theologians, and jurists, for example — possess aesthetic and practical natures and would be more inclined to the nontheoretical and practical sphere of worldview philosophy. Nevertheless, in real life Husserl notes that the distinction between these two types of temperaments is not airtight.

The issue regarding the development of the two types of philosophies, however, must also be viewed not only in light of personal dispositions, but also in terms of what is at stake culturally, and from the perspective of the development of humanity as an eternal ideal. The question Husserl is considering here is this: How long can or should human history and culture wait for scientific philosophy to develop so as to provide a foundation to insure the objective validity and certainty of all scientific enterprises? Since these sciences are necessary for the final understanding of life and reality, can humankind afford to delay the process of establishing a solid philosophic basis for their endeavors? No, the West can wait no longer, says Husserl. The current crisis in European science and civilization demands some kind of immediate response.

However, several factors would suggest to others that the priority must still be given to the continuing development of worldviews. First of all, rigorous science offers only a partially developed system of doctrine with much still awaiting explication. Second, even strict scientists themselves perform their work under the auspices of paradigmatic intuitions *(Anschauungen)* which reveal their ultimate orientation and point of view (foreshadowings of Thomas Kuhn's postmodern philosophy of science can be seen here). Third, the explanations of strict science still leave the mysteries and riddles of life unsolved (as Lotze said, "to calculate the course of the world does not mean to understand it" [p. 193]). Finally, given the unbearable spiritual need and existential crisis of the times, the wisest course of action would be to take refuge in a perspective that explains the world and gives meaning to life. Out of deference to pressing pragmatic considerations, Husserl seems to surrender the priority of establishing philosophy as a strict science to the overwhelming need for worldview formation. "It is certain we cannot wait [for the development of a scientific philosophy]. We have to take a position, we must bestir ourselves to harmonize the disharmonies in our attitude to reality — to the reality of life, which has significance for us in which we should have significance — into a rational, even though unscientific, 'world-and-life-view.' And if the *Weltanschauung* philosopher helps us greatly in this, should we not thank him?" (p. 193).

Husserl's forthright answer to this question is an unqualified negative. No matter how powerful the previous pragmatic considerations may be, Husserl refuses adamantly to compromise. The development of philosophy as a strict science must take precedence over any dalliance with *Weltanschauung* philosophy. "For the sake of time," Husserl asserts, "we must not sacrifice eternity; in order to alleviate our need, we have no right to bequeath to our posterity need upon need as an eventually ineradicable evil." Though the present crisis has its roots in science, Husserl is convinced that only science properly conceived and executed can overcome it. His faith in the power of science is extraordinary. Hence, with evangelical passion he defends the development of a rigorous scientific philosophy as the top cultural priority, thereby demoting worldview formation to an inferior status.

> There is only one remedy for these and all similar evils: a scientific critique and in addition a radical science, rising from below, based on sure foundations, and progressing according to the most rigorous methods — the philosophical science for which we speak here. *Weltanschauungen* can engage in controversy; only science can decide, and its decision bears the stamp of eternity. And so whatever be the direction the new transformation of philosophy may take, without question it must not give up its will to be rigorous science. Rather, as theoretical science it must oppose itself to the practical aspiration toward *Weltanschauung* and quite consciously separate itself from this aspiration.

Any attempt at reconciling or harmonizing *Weltanschauung* and scientific philosophy is flatly rejected by Husserl. He believes that any blurring of the lines between them could "only lead to a softening and weakening of the scientific impulse and to promoting a specious scientific literature destitute of all intellectual honesty. There are no compromises here." In fact, worldview thinking has only one responsibility according to Husserl, and that is to disassociate itself completely from any vestige of science and step aside. "Here there is only one thing to do: *Weltanschauung* philosophy itself must in all honesty relinquish the claim to be a science, and thereby at the same time cease confusing minds and impeding the progress of scientific philosophy — which after all, is certainly contrary to its intentions" (p. 194). Assuming that this occurs, in due course philosophy will appropriate the language of science, and will also rid itself of the much-praised yet inappropriate quality of "profundity." For Husserl, profundity is a trait of wisdom or "worldview," whereas conceptual clarity, logical order, and rational forms are the marks of robust science (and modernity). His undying hope is that strong "philosophy will fight through from the level of profundity to that of scientific clarity." He believes earnestly that despite the accomplishments of his age, what it "most needs is philosophical science" (p. 195), a science consisting "of the most rigorous and, for all further philosophy, decisive cognitions" (p. 196). By this standard, *Weltanschauung* philosophy — characterized by historical relativity and oriented toward the personal and pragmatic — is forthrightly and forever excommunicated from philosophical fellowship.

For Husserl, therefore, the only solution to the crisis of the West is to be found in his notion of philosophy as a rigorous science. Of course, this rigorous scientific philosophy is identified with transcendental phenomenology, by means of which all philosophical disputes will be settled, the relativity of worldviews will be overcome, and the foundation of all the sciences will be established. Phenomenology as hard-core science will provide the absolute foundation for all human knowledge, the Archimedean point by which the world is to be moved, or perhaps more accurately, described. Husserl claims that his particular research program is a presuppositionless endeavor. By means of the phenomenological reduction known as "bracketing" or the "*epoche*," all metaphysical and scientific assumptions are set aside, the "sedimented" thought of the centuries is "held in abeyance," and the "natural outlook" that has been unconsciously assimilated must be "put out of action." This is to make an objective, phenomenological description (not interpretation) of consciousness and its intentional objects possible. As Arthur Holmes says, "Husserl wants a perennial philosophy possessing timeless validity, a rigorous descriptive science rather than an exercise in historical empathy. 'To the things themselves' becomes his cry, and by bracketing all scientific theories and worldviews he proceeds to search for universal and essential structures in the lived-world of prereflective consciousness."[7] Such was the clarion call of Edmund Husserl and his remarkable attempt to establish philosophy and the sciences on a sure and certain foundation.

Toward the end of his career, however, Husserl apparently cultivated severe doubts not only about the success of his philosophic project, but also about its conceptual possibility. Holmes suggests that his increasing recognition of the "lived-world" of the existentialists led him to acknowledge "the essentially historical character of philosophic thought."[8] Did the later-day

---

7. Arthur Holmes, "Phenomenology and the Relativity of World-Views," *Personalist* 48 (summer 1967): 335.

8. Holmes, p. 332. See also David Carr, *Interpreting Husserl: Critical and Comparative Studies* (Boston/Dordrecht: Martinus Nijhoff, 1987), pp. 217-18, who writes: "The conceptual

Husserl either give up on or modify his understanding of the absolute nature of the philosophic enterprise? A response to these questions can be found in an appendix to one of his last books and in his concept of the "lifeworld" (*Lebenswelt*).

Lebenswelt and Weltanschauung

In a curious ninth appendix of his *Crisis of European Sciences and Transcendental Phenomenology*, published just two years before his death, Husserl writes these words of apparent defeat in the battle to establish philosophy as a rigorous science: "Philosophy as science, as serious, rigorous, indeed apodictically rigorous, science — *the dream is over*."[9] The reason why "the dream" was over, according to Husserl, was because of the takeover in Europe by nonscientific *Weltanschauung* philosophy, which seemed to be the only kind of intellectual apparatus human beings were capable of constructing. Husserl writes that "a powerful and constantly growing current of philosophy which renounces scientific discipline, like the current of religious disbelief, is inundating European humanity."[10] He explains the nature of this worldview philosophical deluge which was overrunning the European continent in words worth quoting *in extensio*.

> The conviction has certainly become dominant that philosophy is a task for man as struggling for his existence [*Existenz*], man who has raised himself to autonomy in the European cultural development and sees himself as standing, thanks to the sciences, within the horizon of the infinities — and of the destinies these involve. The world-reflection of autonomous man necessarily leads to the transcendent as something which is unknowable and cannot be practically mastered. Man is capable only of arriving, by starting from his own position, from his horizons of knowledge and feeling, at certain conjectures and thereby of forming for himself certain ways of believing which, *as his world-view*, offer him a personal evidence

relativist may want to point out that Husserl himself introduced the idea of such a world-picture is [*sic*] his late work. Husserl speaks of man as a 'historical being,' and of the 'sedimented conceptuality' belonging to every consciousness. What is taken for granted . . . is not only the prejudices of the natural attitude but also those of a historical tradition."

9. Edmund Husserl, *The Crisis of European Sciences and Transcendental Phenomenology: An Introduction to Phenomenological Philosophy*, translated and introduction by David Carr, Northwestern University Studies in Phenomenology and Existential Philosophy (Evanston, Ill.: Northwestern University Press, 1970), p. 389, emphasis Husserl's.

10. Husserl, *Crisis of European Sciences*, p. 390.

for conjectures and for norms of action under the guidance of the conjecturally believed absolute. Such a posture also provides groups of men who bear within themselves a similar original direction with something like common understanding and mutual advancement.

A *world-view* is thus essentially an individual accomplishment, a sort of personal religious faith; but it is distinguished from traditional faith, that of revealed religion, through the fact that it makes no claim to an unconditioned truth binding for all men and communicable to all men: just as scientific truth about the absolute is not possible, so it is impossible to establish a *world-view* truth which is totally valid for each human being. Any such claim would mean that knowledge upon rational — i.e., scientific — grounds was possible about the absolute and its relation to man.[11]

On this basis Husserl concludes that the future of "philosophy is in danger." This set of circumstances imparted a sense of urgency to the question about the ongoing task of philosophy. According to Enzo Paci in his commentary on this appendix in *Crisis*, the specific question facing Husserl was this: "Must we, therefore, surrender to personal philosophies, to philosophies as 'world-views' or as 'subjective' philosophies, not in the sense of phenomenological subjectivity, but in the relativistic sense?"[12] The answer again seems to be in the negative, and the reason why Husserl refused to surrender is found in his notion of lifeworld *(Lebenswelt)*.

In his writings the idea of *Lebenswelt* is notoriously ambiguous.[13] As a seemingly confused, or at least complex, multilayered concept, "lifeworld" is maddening to decipher. However, one aspect of its meaning which is relatively clear can be discerned by asking this question: Can a clear and proper distinction be made between the world in and of itself and diverse conceptions of it?[14] Is there an independent world given as the object of consciousness that exists prior to any set of presuppositions and the explanations of science? Husserl answers affirmatively and designates this a priori domain as the "lifeworld," which he describes as follows: "The lifeworld is the world that is constantly pregiven, valid constantly and in advance as existing, but not valid because of some purpose of investigation, according to some universal end. Every end presupposes

---

11. Husserl, *Crisis of European Sciences*, pp. 389-90, emphasis added.

12. Enzo Paci, *The Function of the Sciences and the Meaning of Man*, translated with an introduction by Paul Piccone and James E. Hansen, Northwestern University Studies in Phenomenology and Existential Philosophy (Evanston, Ill.: Northwestern University Press, 1972), pp. 240-41.

13. John Scanlon, "The Manifold Meanings of 'Life World' in Husserl's *Crisis*," *American Catholic Philosophical Quarterly* 66 (spring 1992): 229.

14. Carr, *Interpreting Husserl*, pp. 213-15.

it; even the universal end of knowing it in scientific truth presupposes it, and in advance; and in the course of [scientific] work it presupposes it ever anew, as a world existing, in its own way [to be sure], but existing nevertheless."[15]

The lifeworld exists in its native state prior to any conceptualization.[16] The *Lebenswelt* is immediately present in intuition.[17] It exists for consciousness as its object and is structured or constituted by phenomenologically understood subjectivity. It is not a chaos, but possesses a general structure. Hence the lifeworld itself is absolute, not relative.[18] The lifeworld functions as "subsoil," and its many "prelogical validities" act as the ground for logical, theoretical truths.[19] Thus, according to Husserl, all objective scientific theories are founded upon and have reference to the lifeworld.

> Objective theory in its logical sense (taken universally: science as the totality of predicative theory, of the system of statements meant "logically" as "propositions in themselves," "truths in themselves," and in this sense logically joined) is rooted, grounded in the life-world, in the original self-evidences belonging to it. Thanks to this rootedness objective science has a constant reference of meaning to the world in which we always live, even as scientists and also in the total community of scientists — a reference, that is, to the general life-world.[20]

By appealing to the objective substrate of the *Lebenswelt*, not in realist or Kantian terms but in terms of transcendental phenomenology, Husserl is attempting to rescue philosophy as a rigorous science from the relativizing forces of *Weltanschauung* historicism.[21] As Carr says, "the life-world is *not* [an] historically relative phenomenon but the constant underlying ground of all such phenomena, the world from which the scientific interpretation takes its start and which it constantly presupposes."[22] The fact that the lifeworld is the preceding reality and objective domain of consciousness to which both worldview and science make their appeal is what enables Husserl to argue that scientific philosophy can claim an objective, universal, and timeless validity.

15. Husserl, *Crisis of European Sciences*, p. 382, brackets in original.
16. Husserl, *Crisis of European Sciences*, p. 122.
17. Husserl, *Crisis of European Sciences*, p. 134.
18. Husserl, *Crisis of European Sciences*, p. 139.
19. Husserl, *Crisis of European Sciences*, pp. 124, 141.
20. Husserl, *Crisis of European Sciences*, pp. 129-30.
21. Carr, *Interpreting Husserl*, p. 219.
22. David Carr, "Husserl's Problematic Concept of the Life-World," in *Husserl: Expositions and Appraisals*, edited and introduction by Frederick A. Elliston and Peter McCormick (Notre Dame, Ind.: University of Notre Dame Press, 1977), pp. 206-7.

In any case, what is most significant about Husserl's overall contribution to the philosophical history of worldview is the firm line of demarcation he attempted to draw between *Weltanschauung* and philosophy as a rigorous science. For Husserl historicism and a deadly naturalism constituted the chief causes of the crisis of European science and civilization. The fascinating, if not clumsy, conception of lifeworld as the shared objective reference point for all theoretical activity was his final key to overcoming the threat of relativism posed by the ever-growing popularity of *Weltanschauung* philosophy. Husserl would brook no rival to his radical scientific view of the philosophic task.

Perhaps the greatest irony associated with this herculean effort on Husserl's part to establish a presuppositionless and scientific philosophy over against the prejudices and subjective nature of worldview formation is the contention that his entire phenomenological enterprise could itself be classified as a worldview. Along with other Husserlian interpreters, Carr has noted the self-defeating nature of his attempt at a presuppositionless philosophy. He has pointed out the fact that phenomenology is historically embedded, and is an instantiation, along with all other methods and systems, of a conditioned approach to life and the world. He writes these perceptive words:

> Attempting and claiming to have set aside historically acquired prejudices which stood in the way of a phenomenological grasp of the structure of the world and world-consciousness, Husserl seems, at a deeper level, to exhibit such prejudices in his description of the lifeworld. And . . . the very motivation to overcome prejudice, historically or otherwise acquired, is itself the expression of a historical prejudice, i.e., what Gadamer calls the "prejudice against prejudices." Husserl's philosophy seems to end up in the same position as any other philosophy, according to the view of those who describe philosophy as *Weltanschauung*, or the culminating expression of a historical period's view of the world.[23]

Husserl's work, like all philosophical endeavor and human thought, takes place within historical boundaries and frames of reference. Thus, as Jan Sarna asserts, it is clear that "Husserl's postulate of presuppositionlessness is impossi-

---

23. David Carr, *Phenomenology and the Problem of History: A Study of Husserl's Transcendental Philosophy* (Evanston, Ill.: Northwestern University Press, 1974), p. 246. For other examinations and critiques of Husserl's alleged presuppositionlessness, see the following: Adrian Mirvish, "The Presuppositions of Husserl's Presuppositionless Philosophy," *Journal of the British Society for Phenomenology* 26 (May 1995): 147-70; Teresa Reed-Downing, "Husserl's Presuppositionless Philosophy," *Research in Phenomenology* (1990): 136-51; B. C. Postow, "Husserl's Failure to Establish a Presuppositionless Science," *Southern Journal of Philosophy* 14 (summer 1976): 179-88.

ble to realize and that a theory which would stand above science and above the history of man's experience — that is, a theory free from any worldview's domain — is impossible to construct."[24] Given the inescapable nature of these historico-mental paradigms within which all thinking and acting occur, a psychological investigation of them is as necessary as a philosophical explanation. Such a project was undertaken by Karl Jaspers in his *Psychology of Worldviews*, which constitutes the next important stage in the history of *Weltanschauung* in the twentieth century.

"Worldview" in Karl Jaspers

Karl Jaspers's (1883-1969) contribution to the history of this theme lies in his important early work titled *Psychology of Worldviews* (1919).[25] Jaspers's goal in this volume is to describe the various frames of reference "in which the mental life of the individual takes place and which determine the formal characteristics of his mental manifestations."[26] These frames of reference Jaspers calls *Weltanschauungen*, which in his own words represent "what is ultimate and complete in man, both *subjectively* as experience, power and conviction, and *objectively* as the formed world of objects."[27] Thus Jaspers approaches the question about worldviews from two angles. From the subjective side he discusses *Weltanschauung* under the heading of "attitudes" *(Einstellungen)*, and from the objective side he investigates the same as "world pictures" *(Weltbilder)*. Attitudes are the formal patterns and structures of mental existence by means of which the world is experienced either actively, contemplatively, rationally, aesthetically, sensualistically, ascetically, or in other ways. They are the product of innate ideas or childhood experiences and are subject to psychological analysis. World pictures, on the other hand, are "the whole of the objective mental con-

---

24. Jan W. Sarna, "On Some Presuppositions of Husserl's 'Presuppositionless' Philosophy," *Analecta Husserliana* 27 (1989): 240.

25. Karl Jaspers, *Psychologie der Weltanschauungen* (Berlin: Verlag von Julius Springer, 1919). This book has undergone six total editions in German, the most recent published in 1971. It has been translated into several other languages, including an Italian version from the third German edition: *Psicologia Delle Visioni del Mondo,* trans. Vincenzo Loriga (Rome: Astrolabia, 1950); a Spanish translation from the fourth German edition: *Psicología de las Concepciones del Mundo,* trans. Mariano Marin Casero (Madrid: Gredos, 1967); and a Japanese translation: *Sekaikan no Shinrigaku,* trans. Tadao Uemura and Toshio Madea (Tokyo: Risôsha, 1971). Unfortunately, the work has not been translated into English.

26. Ludwig B. Lefebre, "The Psychology of Karl Jaspers," in *The Philosophy of Karl Jaspers,* Library of Living Philosophers, augmented edition (La Salle, Ill.: Open Court, 1981), p. 489.

27. Quoted in Lefebre, p. 489, emphasis added.

tent an individual possesses."[28] By means of these basic attitudes, a person encounters the objective world and forms a mental picture of it. The combination of attitudes and world pictures constitutes a worldview.[29]

Some view Jaspers's volume as a Nietzschean psychological treatise in its attempt to provoke a deep dissatisfaction with one's present state of being. Similar to Nietzsche, Jaspers believes that "the first and the very last question concerning *Weltanschauung* is whether one says Yes or No to life as a whole."[30] Others view the work as "a progeny of Dilthey's psychologizing," and still others suggest affinities to Kierkegaard's various stages on life's way and his notable spheres of existence. Furthermore, Hegel's *Phenomenology of Mind* is evident in Jaspers's tome (which contains a lengthy discussion of the former volume), and it even concludes with an appendix entitled "Kant's Doctrine of Ideas."[31] Under the influence of these various thinkers, each of which in his own right has contributed to the philosophic history of *Weltanschauung*, Jaspers authored this work. Indeed, Jaspers himself acknowledges Hegel, Kierkegaard, and Nietzsche as the harbingers of his reflections in his *Psychology of Worldviews*.

> At the very moment when the question concerning the original *Weltanschauungen* arose, the magnificent tradition of the thinkers who had developed this kind of psychology, sometimes not at all under the name of psychology, came to light. Hegel's *Phenomenology of Mind*, then above all Kierkegaard, whom I had been studying since 1914, and secondly Nietzsche, struck me as revelations. They were able to make communicable a universal and at the same time quite concrete insight into every corner of the human soul and to its very deepest sources.[32]

As Jaspers himself tells the story in his philosophical autobiography, of all his early lectures on psychology, this book on the psychology of worldviews was the most important to him. This is probably because it eventually became the

---

28. Lefebre, p. 489.

29. Lefebre, pp. 489-90. On p. 488 n. 38, Lefebre notes that Jaspers's term *Weltanschauung* is somewhat ambiguous since he uses it to refer to both a "general view of life" and a "conception of the world," depending upon whether the more concrete or conceptual aspect is being emphasized. For the concrete aspect he tends to use *Weltanschauung*, and for the conceptual aspect he typically employs *Weltbild*. He also complicates matters by using *Weltanschauung* in reference to both individual attitudes and philosophical and religious systems.

30. Walter Kaufmann, "Jaspers' Relation to Nietzsche," in *The Philosophy of Karl Jaspers*, p. 414.

31. Kaufmann, pp. 411, 417. For Jaspers's discussion of Hegel and Kant, see his *Psychologie*, pp. 323-32 and 408-28 respectively.

32. Karl Jaspers, "Philosophical Autobiography," in *The Philosophy of Karl Jaspers*, p. 26.

basis of his approach to philosophy, though he did not know it at the time.[33] Jaspers's original intentions for the work were psychological, not philosophical. In its highest sense, according to Jaspers, philosophy should be prophetic and provide people with a worldview. Psychology, on the other hand, simply "understands all the possibilities of philosophic points of view by looking at them."[34] Though some have viewed his book as "a gallery of *Weltanschauungen*, from which people were free to choose," Jaspers has another explanation for it. "Actually," he says, "it is the ascertainment of all possibilities as one's own and the elucidation of the largest possible realm in which the *'existential'* decisions occur which no thought, no system, no knowledge anticipates." In Jaspers's mind, then, whereas prophetic philosophy ought to be about the business of articulating a life perspective that could even be set forth as a substitute for religion in teaching people how to live, his *Psychology of Worldviews* was written simply to elucidate the possibilities for self-reflection and to present means of personal orientation.

In retrospect, however, Jaspers realized that his native impulses had pushed him "under the cloak of psychology" toward a philosophical consideration of the totality of things. Thus, as he put it, "In my *Psychologie der Weltanschauungen* I was, naively, engaged already in philosophizing without knowing clearly as yet what I was doing."[35] In the perspicuity of hindsight, what he was doing, as he himself says, was authoring "the earliest writing in the later so-called modern Existentialism." Motivated "to bring into view the greatness of man," Jaspers explains the real thrust of his *Psychology of Worldviews* in these words:

> Decisive was the interest in man, the concern with himself on the part of the thinker, an attempted radical integrity. Present are nearly all the fundamental questions which later on occurred in lucid consciousness and in broad expansiveness: about the world, what it is for man; about the situation of man and about his ultimate situations from which there is no escape (death, suffering, chance, guilt, struggle); about time and the multidimensional nature of its meaning; about the movement of freedom in the process of creating one's self; about Existenz; about nihilism and about shells; about love, about the disclosure of the real and the true; about the way of mysticism and the way of the idea; etc. All of it, however, was so to speak, comprehended in a quick grasp, and had not been worked out systematically. The mood of the entire work was more encompassing than

33. Jaspers, "Philosophical Autobiography," p. 25.
34. Jaspers, "Philosophical Autobiography," p. 26.
35. Jaspers, "Philosophical Autobiography," p. 27.

what I succeeded in saying. This mood became the foundation of my further thinking.[36]

Turning to the work itself, we notice first that it is arranged dialectically as a triad of three main chapters, and as triads within each of the three chapters. This dialectic, however, is not Hegelian, which typically consists of the resolution of a tension between a thesis and antithesis in a synthesis. Rather, in Jaspers's dialectic the third aspect is the centerpiece and source of the other two. The third is the least objective and understandable, and from it emerge the first and second aspects, which are more concrete and comprehensible. The "first" aspect of Jaspers's discussion concerns attitudes *(Einstellungen),* and the "second" consists of world pictures *(Weltbilder).* Both attitudes and world pictures are grounded in the third and primordial source of "the life of the spirit" *(Das Leben des Geistes).*[37] In order to appreciate the cause/effect relationship of Jaspers's triadic format, in this brief overview I will work my way backwards beginning with the life of the spirit as the source of world pictures and attitudes, which, when combined, form worldviews.

In order to understand the "life of the spirit," we must understand "spirit types." And in order to understand "spirit types," we must first explore what Jaspers calls "limit," "boundary," or "ultimate" situations *(Grenzsituationen).*[38] The notion of "ultimate situations" is one of Jaspers's most important contributions in this book. It conveys the commonsense idea that human beings are always in a set of circumstances and that they cannot live apart from conflict, suffering, guilt, and death. The diverse responses that people make to these ultimate situations provide the basis for categorizing various "spirit types." The challenging realities of life cause the different types of human spirits to seek security or grounding in one way or another.[39] Hence, according to Jaspers, "to ask about the nature of spirit-types is to ask, where do men have their

---

36. Jaspers, "Philosophical Autobiography," pp. 28-29.

37. Oswald O. Schrag, *An Introduction to Existence, Existenz, and Transcendence: The Philosophy of Karl Jaspers* (Pittsburgh: Duquesne University Press, 1971), p. 99.

38. Schrag, pp. 102-3. See Jaspers, *Psychologie,* pp. 202-47. For further discussion on the concept of "ultimate situations," see Charles F. Wallraff, *Karl Jaspers: An Introduction to His Philosophy* (Princeton: Princeton University Press, 1970), pp. 141-66, and Edwin Latzel, "The Concept of 'Ultimate Situation' in Jaspers' Philosophy," in *The Philosophy of Karl Jaspers,* pp. 177-208. At the end of this latter work is a brief bibliography of other works on this theme. Jaspers deepens his reflections on this topic later in his career in his *Philosophy,* vol. 2, trans. E. B. Ashton (Chicago: University of Chicago Press, 1970), pp. 177-218.

39. Karl Jaspers, *Basic Philosophical Writings,* edited, translated, and introduction by Edith Ehrlich, Leonard H. Ehrlich, and George B. Pepper (Atlantic Highlands, N.J.: Humanities Press, 1986), p. 96.

hold?"[40] Some have their hold in skepticism and nihilism.[41] Others seek refuge in that which is limited or finite *(Begrenzten)*, in rationalisms, in authoritarianisms, and in absolute values, or in what Jaspers calls protective "shells" *(Gehause)*.[42] A third group, which includes the author himself, turns toward the "infinite" or the "unlimited" *(Der halt im Unendlichen)*.[43]

Regarding the provocative concept of "shells," Jaspers says that when "ultimate situations" are encountered, a vital process of change begins. "The conscious experience of ultimate situations, situations which previously had been covered over with the hard shells of objectively self-evident forms of life, worldviews, beliefs and ideas; and the movement of limitless reflection, of dialectic, initiate a process which ends with the dissolution of what was previously a self-evident shell." As Jaspers continues, however, he notes that human beings cannot live without shells any more than mussels can without theirs. Hence, in the process of life and in confrontation with ultimate situations, one shell is removed only to be replaced by another. "The process of living," says Jaspers, "thus includes both a dissolution and a formation of shells. Without dissolution rigidity would set in; but without shells there would be destruction."[44]

Spirit types in their confrontation with ultimate situations always are caught in the battle raging between form and chaos. Though the various spirit types attempt to bring everything together into some kind of unity or totality, such efforts are futile, and constitute what Jaspers calls the impossible "antinomial synthesis." In relation to form, chaos, and the antinomial synthesis, Jaspers identifies three spirit types: first, the chaotic person who lives on the basis of impulse, chance, and self-interest; second, the pragmatic person who focuses on functionality and efficiency; and third, the demonic person who discovers himself in the creative tensions of a fragmented life.[45]

A final feature of the life of the spirit is what he identifies as the way of the "mystic" and the way of the "idea." The way of the mystic breaks through the subject-object dichotomy to find unity and wholeness. The way of the idea dissolves this totality and perceives the world, the soul, and life itself in terms of ideas as logical regulative principles and as psychological powers.[46]

In any case, there is a cause-and-effect relationship between the life of the spirit, diverse spirit types, and world pictures. World pictures are the

---

40. Quoted in Schrag, p. 103.
41. Jaspers, *Psychologie*, pp. 252-69.
42. Jaspers, *Psychologie*, pp. 269-88.
43. Schrag, pp. 103-4; see Jaspers, *Psychologie*, pp. 289-305.
44. Quoted from Latzel, p. 185.
45. Schrag, pp. 104-5; see Jaspers, *Psychologie*, pp. 306-81.
46. Schrag, pp. 105-6; see Jaspers, *Psychologie*, pp. 387-407.

objectifications of the powers of the life of the spirit. The responses of the various spirit types to life's ultimate situations are crystallized into "objective" world conceptions. There is a kind of symbiotic relationship between life and world pictures: they more or less grow up together. Images of reality are thoroughly assimilated and become a part of the person as much as any other characteristic. They are the construct of the self, though the self may not always be aware of their influences or how they are formed. They are not necessarily chosen but are a function of life itself. "That I have chosen an idea appears only from my living with it as Socrates lived as though there were immortality. It is just this life itself . . . that is my choice."[47] World pictures and experience ebb and flow: ever changing, ever deepening, ever evolving, though a final totality is never reached.[48]

Jaspers identifies a triad of world pictures: the sensory-space, the psychical-cultural, and the metaphysical, which is the most unique and inclusive.[49] There are two types of metaphysical world pictures according to Jaspers — the mythological-demonic and the philosophical. The mythological-demonic world pictures are fabulous or chimerical in nature. Philosophical world pictures are not derived from authority or revelation, but have their origin in the absolutization of the experience of either subjectivity or objectivity. The absolutization of subjectivity engenders a kind of spiritualism or idealism, and the absolutization of objectivity produces a kind of materialism or naturalism.[50] Thus the encounter with the ultimate situations in life causes different spirit types to respond differently, and the various responses of the diverse spirit types engender a variety of world conceptions. Such is the objective aspect of *Weltanschauung*.

The subjective aspect of worldview according to Jaspers is found in "attitudes" or mental frameworks which are the subjectifications of the powers of the life of the spirit. These attitudes become the powerful sources and motivations for human action. Culminating in behavior, they can be observed psychologically and studied as universals. Jaspers again proposes a trinity of attitudes: the objective, the self-reflective, and the enthusiastic.[51] As one of several objective attitudes, the "rational" is designed to establish relations, clarity, and unity in the face of the unstable, the chaotic, and the accidental. The rational attitude is fed by perception, but can ossify and become lifeless. Because it is suffused with intuitive and aesthetic attitudes, it can never be divided, but neither can it

---

47. Quoted in Wallraff, p. 150.
48. Jaspers, *Psychologie*, pp. 123-33.
49. Jaspers, *Psychologie*, pp. 133-88.
50. Schrag, p. 102.
51. Jaspers, *Psychologie*, pp. 44-121.

comprehend the totality of things. The rational attitude can be subdivided into the scholastic and the experimental categories which provide knowledge, and a dialectic which Jaspers says sustains growth and movement.

Of the self-reflective attitudes, the most significant one is "immediacy" *(Augenblick)*. Acknowledging his dependence here on Kierkegaard's *Either/Or*, Jaspers argues that in the attitude of immediacy or the moment, the concrete present and direct reality is emphasized and time is experienced as a continuity and endless succession, as an atom of eternity. In Jaspers's words, time is "the one reality, the absolute reality in the life of the spirit. The experienced moment is the final, bloodwarm, immediate aspect of what is alive, the living present, the totality of the real, the only concrete."[52]

Both preceding attitudes are derived from and a function of the third, "enthusiasm," which is the most comprehensive and yet the least understood of the three subjective attitudes. The enthusiastic attitude is manifested in the rational and self-reflective attitudes and expresses itself in a variety of concrete forms of life: sexuality, science, the arts, and personal relations.

Worldviews for Jaspers, then, are a fusion of both the objective and subjective standpoints. In the subjective aspect they are derived from the threefold human attitudes which express themselves in the concreteness of life and in forms of behavior. In the objective aspect they are educed from a trio of world pictures which delineate some kind of image or understanding of reality. Worldviews as amalgams of attitudes and world pictures are forever fluid and mobile, changing and evolving, though they can become a shell (as in nihilism, individualism, rationalism, romanticism, skepticism, etc.) which must be regularly replaced. As protective casings, worldviews are the means by which persons protect themselves from the horrors of ultimate situations, which were the very conditions that originally prompted the various spirit types to draft certain outlooks on life and to cultivate a diversity of internal dispositions. They are entities without which human beings could not survive.[53]

Jaspers's *Psychologie der Weltanschauungen* has been described as the book that led to his "radical awakening."[54] Because of its enlightenment, this work became the foundation for his subsequent existential philosophy. From the point of its publication onward, the multiplicity of descriptions and perspectives of the world was central to his philosophic project. Through this work he

---

52. Quoted in Schrag, p. 100.

53. Elisabeth Young-Bruehl, *Freedom and Karl Jaspers' Philosophy* (New Haven: Yale University Press, 1981), p. 211. Like Jaspers, Ernest Becker has argued that the fear of death is a strong unconscious motivation for producing alternative worldviews. For a discussion, see Eugene Webb, "Ernest Becker and the Psychology of Worldviews," *Zygon* 33 (1998): 71-86.

54. Young-Bruehl, p. 211.

broke with traditional philosophy in its attempt to present an objective, universal explanation of reality. In light of his recognition of "universal relativism," he concentrated his energies on the task of philosophic communication over against any form of dogmatism, which he construed as a conversation stopper. Thus Husserl's vilification of worldview as the opponent of true scientific philosophy and Jaspers's glorification of the same as the natural human response to the encounter with limit situations must be interestingly juxtaposed. These alternative perspectives on worldviews provide a necessary context for considering the contribution of Martin Heidegger, who is up next, as the philosophic history of worldview in the twentieth century continues to unfold.

"Worldview" in Martin Heidegger

Few individuals in the Western intellectual tradition have altered the philosophical landscape as rapidly or as profoundly as Martin Heidegger (1889-1976). Under the influence of the early Greeks as well as the scholastic theological tradition, and in the wake of such seminal thinkers as Søren Kierkegaard, Friedrich Nietzsche, Karl Jaspers, and Edmund Husserl, Heidegger's philosophy — especially as set forth in his magnum opus, *Being and Time* (1927) — was concerned with the ontological question regarding the nature of being and the existential analysis of the subjectivity, historicity, and hermeneutic (or self-interpreting) nature of human Dasein. In the context of these larger concerns, Heidegger dedicated a surprising amount of time and effort to reflecting on the nature and role of *Weltanschauung* philosophy. His interest in this vital topic can perhaps be explained by the fact that his existential analysis proved to him that "something like a world-view belongs to the essential nature of the Dasein."[55]

There are three major components to Heidegger's reflections on this topic. First is his important review of Karl Jaspers's *Psychologie der Weltanschauungen*, written around 1919-20 upon his return to Freiburg University after the First World War. Second is his effort in at least three separate works to call attention, in a manner reminiscent of Husserl, to the contrast between the relativism of *Weltanschauung* and the notion that philosophy must be a rigorous scientific undertaking. Third is his significant essay titled "The Age of the World Picture," in which he argues that the notion of worldview or world picture is unique to the modern period. We begin with a look at his review of Jaspers's book.

---

55. Martin Heidegger, *The Basic Problems of Phenomenology*, translation, introduction, and lexicon by Albert Hofstadter, Studies in Phenomenology and Existential Philosophy (Bloomington: Indiana University Press, 1982), p. 10.

Review of Jaspers's Psychologie der Weltanschauungen

The treatise titled "Critical Comments on Karl Jaspers' *Psychology of World-views*"[56] was originally intended by Heidegger to appear as a review of this influential book which itself launched the movement known in Germany as existence philosophy *(Existenzphilosophie)*. A typescript edition of this critical essay was distributed as a "private communication" to Jaspers, Husserl, and Rickert in June 1921. It was not published, however, until 1972, after a copy of it was found among Jaspers's papers upon his death in 1969.[57] Shortly after it was originally sent to Jaspers, Heidegger decided not to publish the piece for reasons unknown. He only reluctantly agreed to its issuance some five decades later in a collection of critical articles on Jaspers's philosophy. The work is a most significant piece not only because it touches on matters related to worldview, but also because it contains adumbrations of many significant Heideggerian themes that appeared several years later in his celebrated *Being and Time*.[58]

The text itself can be roughly divided into four sections.[59] The first section consists of statements of appreciation and initial criticisms of Jaspers's book (pp. 70-76). The second focuses on the "phenomenon of existence" and the notion of limit situations (pp. 76-89). In the third section Heidegger strikes out on his own by setting forth his own new starting point for the analysis of the phenomenon of existence (pp. 89-94). The fourth section is a recapitulation of the initial commendations and criticisms found in the first section (pp. 94-99). An appendix offers several suggestions for improvement should Jaspers publish a revised edition (pp. 99-100).

Heidegger's critique centers on Jaspers's methodology as well as his uncritical acceptance of a variety of anthropological assumptions. In the opening section Heidegger asks, for example, whether "the choice and manner of the

56. See Martin Heidegger, "Anmerkungen zu Karl Jaspers' *Psychologie der Weltanschauungen*," in *Karl Jaspers in der Diskussion*, ed. Hans Saner (Munich: R. Piper, 1973), pp. 70-100. The review is also in Martin Heidegger, *Wegmarken*, in *Gesamtausgabe*, ed. F.-W. von Herrmann (Frankfurt: Klostermann, 1976), 9:1-44. The work has not been translated into English.

57. Theodore Kisiel, *The Genesis of Heidegger's "Being and Time"* (Berkeley: University of California Press, 1993), p. 137. Kisiel analyzes Heidegger's review of Jaspers's book on pp. 137-48.

58. David Farrell Krell, *Intimations of Mortality: Time, Truth, and Finitude in Heidegger's Thinking of Being* (University Park: Pennsylvania State University Press, 1986), pp. 11-12. Krell's material is duplicated in "Toward *Sein und Zeit*: Heidegger's Early Review of Jaspers' 'Psychologie der Weltanschauungen,'" *Journal of the British Society for Phenomenology* 6 (1975): 147-56.

59. Krell, *Intimations of Mortality*, p. 12. The page numbers in the text are to the published piece in Heidegger, "Anmerkungen zu Karl Jaspers' *Psychologie der Weltanschauungen*."

application of the methodological means genuinely correspond" to the motifs Jaspers wishes to analyze. Of course, what he wishes to diagnose is humanity's spiritual and psychic life, a philosophical psychology of worldviews defined as "the ultimate nature and totality of man, . . . his preoccupation with the whole." Heidegger also questions whether "these motifs and tendencies themselves have been grasped radically enough" to fulfill Jaspers's purposes since he naively accepts certain preunderstandings of human beings inherited from the Western ontological tradition. There is an important difference, according to Heidegger, between what human beings really are and what Jaspers assumes they are. In connection with the question of human identity — the "I am" — Heidegger believes that "what we ourselves ostensibly 'have' and 'are'" must be ascertained as a preliminary consideration, and this is precisely what is missing in Jaspers's study.[60]

Furthermore, for Jaspers the "primal phenomenon" of human life is the split between subjectivity and objectivity which constitutes the ultimate antinomy of existence. Such a split even forms the basic format of Jaspers's book: a consideration first of the *subjective* "engagements" possible for the human psyche, and secondly a discussion of the *objective* world images corresponding to these psychic engagements. According to Heidegger, lying behind this salient subject-object dichotomy is a set of influential presuppositions regarding psychic life which Jaspers accepts uncritically. As Heidegger puts it, "In the very starting-point, a preconception of the psychic articulated in a definite way, is pre-given and works its effects." This very supposition, according to Heidegger, must itself come within the compass of Jaspers's analysis. "If genuine psychology is to enable us to see 'what man is,' . . . then preconceptions concerning the ontological meaning . . . of this totality of psychic-spiritual life lie within the prerequisite and proper scope of the task. So do these preconceptions about the possible method of clarifying life as it is supposedly lived, and also those about the basic meaning of that from which something like 'possibilities' can emerge at all."[61]

The primary point is that the preconceptions of the subjectivist tradition in which Jaspers stands must be exposed by a concrete analysis of the basic character and possibilities of human existence. If "being there," or Dasein, is the canvassed object, especially its psychic life in relation to totalities, no simple psychological description of it will be adequate until its own interpretative behavior and existential character becomes an issue itself. Jaspers cannot simply describe what is there; rather, he must undertake "a radical interrogation . . .

60. Krell, *Intimations of Mortality*, pp. 12-13.
61. Krell, *Intimations of Mortality*, pp. 13-14.

which keeps itself [Dasein] in the question."[62] Until Jaspers scrutinizes these assumptions, and raises this problem of method to conscious examination, no genuine progress is possible.

Regarding the phenomenon of existence, Heidegger asserts that Jaspers's description of what he calls "limit situations" is the "strongest" aspect of his entire treatise. Of Jaspers's three limit situations that disclose the struggle of human existence (accident, death, and guilt), Heidegger is especially appreciative of his analysis of death, aspects of which eventually make their way into *Being and Time*. Still he believes there are serious shortcomings in Jaspers's discussion, and the familiar "problem of preconceptions" once again is the nemesis. Furthermore, Heidegger complains that Jaspers's reliance on the old-school metaphysics of Kant and Kierkegaard for his description of existence is inadequate. Thus he argues that a new starting point for an analysis of the phenomenon of existence is needed.[63]

In the longest section of his review of Jaspers's book, Heidegger presents his own method for an analysis of existence which he says must begin with "the full, concrete, historical, factical self." This is precisely what Jaspers failed to do because of his tacit acceptance of certain doctrines in current psychology. The remedy, according to Heidegger, in proposing his new method, "is to take the concrete self as the starting-point of the problem and to bring it to the appropriate fundamental level of phenomenological interpretation, namely, that related to our factical experience of life, in this way bringing the concrete self to 'givenness.'"[64] The balance of the presentation in this section consists of a discussion of several tasks by which this method might be implemented.

Heidegger refers to Jaspers on three separate occasions in *Being and Time*, and each reference is to his book *Psychology of Worldviews*. The third of these citations simply refers the reader to Jaspers's analysis of the "moment of vision" in amplification of Kierkegaard, who has explained the "*existentiell* phenomenon" of this theme "with the most penetration."[65] The first and second of these

---

62. Krell, *Intimations of Mortality*, pp. 14-15.

63. Krell, *Intimations of Mortality*, pp. 15-17.

64. Krell, *Intimations of Mortality*, pp. 17-22. In their personal correspondence, Jaspers recognized Heidegger's effective criticisms of his book, especially with regard to his deficiencies of method. However, he subtly points out, in *tu quoque* fashion, that Heidegger also lacks a "positive method" of his own. Jaspers writes: "Of all the reviews which I have read, yours is, in my opinion, the one which has dug most deeply to the root of my thoughts. It has in fact touched me profoundly. Nevertheless, I still miss — in the discussions of the 'I am' and the 'historical' — the positive method [of your own]." Quoted in Kisiel, *The Genesis*, p. 527 n. 5.

65. Martin Heidegger, *Being and Time*, trans. John Macquarrie and Edward Robinson (New York: Harper and Row, 1962), p. 497 n. iii.

references demonstrate that the significance of Jaspers's work for Heidegger lay not in his discussion of a "typology of worldviews," but rather in his analysis of existence, principally his notion of "limit situations." For example, Heidegger proposes a comparison of his own analysis of death as a limit situation not only with those of Wilhelm Dilthey, Rudolf Unger, Georg Simmel, but "especially" with Karl Jaspers in his book on worldviews. Thus he writes: "Jaspers takes as his clue to death the phenomenon of the 'limit situation' as he has set it forth — a phenomenon whose fundamental significance goes beyond any typology of 'attitudes' and 'world-pictures.'"[66] Furthermore, in discussing the existential "situation" of Dasein in terms of openness, authenticity, and care, Heidegger states that the task of portraying "the factical *existentiell* possibilities in their chief features and interconnections, and to interpret them according to their existential structure, falls among the tasks of a thematic existential anthropology."[67] This, he points out, is the direction taken by Jaspers in his book on worldviews. Over against its value as a treatment of various mental paradigms, Heidegger again finds the book's primary value in its existential analysis of Dasein and in its description of limit situations. He states: "Here the question of 'what is man' is raised and answered in terms of what he essentially can be.... The basic existential-ontological signification of 'limit-situations' is thus illuminated. One would entirely miss the philosophical import of his 'psychology of world-views' if one were to 'use' it simply as a reference-work for 'types of world-view.'"[68] Heidegger, therefore, while critical of Jaspers for his methods and assumptions, was nonetheless appreciative to him for his innovative analysis of the human condition, and had only a secondary regard for his work as an anatomy of worldviews.

Heidegger's Idea of Scientific Philosophy and the Problem of Worldview

The question that emerges at this juncture in the consideration of Heidegger and *Weltanschauung* is one that occupied him throughout his career: What is philosophy? Is philosophy that which specifies the meaning of life and its purpose, and gives practical advice for the conduct of it, as worldviews intend to do? Conversely, is it a robust enterprise concerned with veracity and exactitude, a discipline that sets forth clear, timeless, universal principles, as scientific phi-

66. Heidegger, *Being and Time*, p. 495 n. vi.
67. Heidegger, *Being and Time*, p. 348.
68. Heidegger, *Being and Time*, p. 496 n. xv.

losophy purposes to do? Heidegger presented his firm convictions about these questions in at least three separate publications. First, his earliest reflections are found in a lecture course titled "The Idea of Philosophy and the Problem of the Worldviews" given at Freiburg University during the "War Emergency Semester" (*Kriegsnotsemester* = KNS) held from 7 February until 11 April 1919.[69] He continued the discussion in a second installment in his volume *The Basic Problems of Phenomenology*, the contents of which originally consisted of a lecture course given at the University of Marburg in the summer of 1927.[70] Finally, he briefly investigated these issues in the eleventh section of his work *The Metaphysical Foundations of Logic*, given originally as a summer school lecture course at Marburg in 1928.[71] The reason for Heidegger's ongoing preoccupation with the question about philosophy in these three works is this: the proliferation of worldviews posed a threat to an authentic metaphysics of Dasein, and he was eager to distinguish a scientific ontology of being over against the quicksands of *Weltanschauung* philosophy. An analysis of the first two of the above-mentioned documents will demonstrate his strategy to this end.[72]

In the KNS of 1919, Heidegger devoted himself to the subject of "the idea of philosophy and the problem of worldview." In the tradition of his mentor Edmund Husserl, he here asserts as an opening salvo that philosophy and worldview are two different kinds of endeavors. The KNS course consists of his attempt to articulate "a brand new conception of philosophy . . . which would . . . place it outside of any connection with the ultimate human [worldview] questions."[73] Insofar as Heidegger defends the notion that philosophy is the

69. Martin Heidegger, "Die Idee der Philosophie und das Weltanschauungs problem," in *Zur Bestimmung der Philosophie*, in *Gesamtausgabe*, ed. Bernd Heimbüchel, vol. 56/57 (Frankfurt: Klostermann, 1987), pp. 3-117. This work is not available in English.

70. Heidegger, *The Basic Problems of Phenomenology*. For the German, see *Die Grundproblem der Phänomenologie*, in *Gesamtausgabe*, ed. F.-W. von Herrmann, vol. 24 (Frankfurt: Klostermann, 1975, 1989).

71. Martin Heidegger, *The Metaphysical Foundations of Logic*, trans. Michael Heim (Bloomington: Indiana University Press, 1984). For the German, see *Metaphysische Anfangsgründe der Logik im Ausgang von Leibniz*, in *Gesamtausgabe*, ed. Klaus Held, vol. 26 (Frankfurt: Klostermann, 1978).

72. Because of the brevity of the third text, and because it repeats many of the themes contained in the second treatise, this document will not be analyzed in this book. For a discussion of this material, however, see Robert Bernasconi, *Heidegger in Question: The Art of Existing*, Philosophy and Literary Theory (Atlantic Highlands, N.J.: Humanities Press, 1993), pp. 28-31. Others have examined Heidegger's contrast between scientific philosophy and worldview. See Ingo Farin, "Heidegger's Early Philosophy between World-View and Science," *Southwest Philosophy Review* 14 (1997): 86-94; Tom Rockmore, "Philosophy or Weltanschauung? Heidegger on Honigswald," *History of Philosophy Quarterly* 16 (1999): 97-115.

73. Quoted in Kisiel, *The Genesis*, p. 39. In addition to Kisiel's lengthy treatment of this

genuine "Ur-science," he must articulate a new configuration of this discipline in terms of its first principles, subject matter, methods, and goals. Only against a background of "the problem of worldview" will his constructive alternative make sense. He begins, therefore, with a discussion of three possible ways of associating worldview and philosophy in the first main section of this treatise.

First of all, Heidegger suggests that, historically speaking, philosophy and worldview are virtually one and the same, that "all great philosophy culminates in a worldview."[74] The time-honored task for philosophy has been the development of a final interpretation of reality and an ideal for living. It would take into consideration even those values of truth, goodness, and beauty that transcend the empirical domain in a comprehensive view of things. Therefore, all philosophy is ultimately worldview philosophy.

This direct identification, however, has been undermined by the claims of modern science, leading to a second way of conceiving of the relationship between these two domains. The modern theory of knowledge posits the human *inability* to comprehend realities and causes that lie beyond the realm of empirical experience. Only those propositions verified by strict scientific procedures count as knowledge. In the context of modern critical consciousness, therefore, scientific philosophy becomes the foundation for and culminates in a scientific worldview. In other words, to be legitimate, philosophically begotten worldviews must be scientifically conceived. Worldview and philosophy are still identified, but must rest on a scientific base.

These are not the only two possibilities according to Heidegger for expressing the philosophy/worldview relationship. A third alternative refuses to associate the two in any manner, but instead argues for their essential incompatibility and necessary separation. Indeed, according to Heidegger, both the precritical and critical traditions in philosophy culminating in worldview, whether practical or scientific, must now be acknowledged as a "catastrophe." Philosophy's task is not to construct a worldview, not even a critical or methodologically sophisticated one. Worldview is a "stranger" to philosophy, is in fact "unphilosophical" in character, and constitutes the primary obstacle to philosophy's true identity. Heidegger therefore proposes an alternative. His answer to

course here in this work (pp. 38-59), he also has summarized its contents in "Why Students of Heidegger Will Have to Read Emil Lask," in *Emil Lask and the Search for Concreteness*, ed. Deborah G. Chaffin (Athens: Ohio University Press, 1993). See also his discussion in "The Genesis of *Being and Time*," *Man and World* 25 (1992): 21-37.

74. Quoted in George Kovacs, "Philosophy as Primordial Science in Heidegger's Courses of 1919," in *Reading Heidegger from the Start: Essays in His Earliest Thought*, ed. Theodore Kisiel and John van Buren, SUNY Series in Contemporary Continental Philosophy (Albany: State University of New York Press, 1994), p. 94.

the question about the definition of philosophy is found in his own notion of the "primordial science" of phenomenology. In an "off-the-cuff" comment recorded by a student that was excluded from the official text of this lecture, Heidegger states his understanding of the true idea of philosophy in contrast to the problem of worldview.

> Phenomenology is the investigation of life in itself. Despite the appearance of a philosophy of life, it is really the opposite of a worldview. A worldview is an objectification and immobilizing of life at a certain point in the life of a culture. In contrast, phenomenology is never closed off, it is always provisional in its absolute immersion in life as such. In it no theories are in dispute, but only genuine insights versus the ungenuine. The genuine ones can be obtained only by an honest and unreserved immersion in life itself in its genuineness, and this is ultimately possible only through the genuineness of a personal life.[75]

After this introductory section in which Heidegger deconstructs the Western equation of philosophy and worldview, and given his call for a reconfiguration of philosophy, the remainder and bulk of this lecture course is devoted to elucidating the contours of primordial scientific phenomenological philosophy. His goal here is to show that this form of philosophy is wholly different in kind from that associated with *Weltanschauung*.

Some eight years later, in 1927, Heidegger remained committed to his unique vision of the philosophic task, and continued to differentiate it sharply from worldview. The source of these reflections is found in *The Basic Problems of Phenomenology*. This text is important not only because it forwards the philosophy/worldview distinction, but also because it includes a brief history of *Weltanschauung* and presents Heidegger's own definition of the term. He begins his discussion by explaining why it is necessary to refer to philosophy explicitly as "scientific philosophy." This redundancy, he says, is needed to distinguish it from worldviews and their corrupting influence. "We speak of 'scientific philosophy' principally because conceptions of philosophy prevail which not only imperil but even negate its character as science pure and simple. These conceptions of philosophy are not just contemporary but accompany the development of scientific philosophy throughout the time philosophy has existed as a science."[76]

Heidegger then explains what *Weltanschauung* philosophy is and contrasts

75. Quoted in Kisiel, *The Genesis*, p. 17.
76. Heidegger, *Basic Problems*, p. 4. The page numbers in the text in the following paragraphs are to this work.

it with its scientific counterpart. "On this view [worldview] philosophy is supposed not only, and not in the first place, to be a theoretical science, but to give practical guidance to our view of things and their interconnection and our attitudes toward them, and to regulate and direct our interpretation of existence and its meaning. Philosophy is wisdom of the world and life, or, to use an expression current nowadays, philosophy is supposed to provide a Weltanschauung, a world-view. Scientific philosophy can thus be set off against philosophy as world-view."

Since the notion of worldview has played a major role in human reflection, Heidegger feels constrained to investigate the concept, and proceeds to survey the history of the term *Weltanschauung*. He covers in very brief compass much of the material delineated in chapter 3 of this book. He notes that in Kant, Goethe, and Alexander von Humboldt, the word refers to the perception of the sensible world, or to the "world-intuition in the sense of contemplation of the world given to the senses" (p. 4). Its meaning changes in Schelling, who referred it "not to sense-observation but to intelligence, albeit to unconscious intelligence." Heidegger believes that through Schelling, *Weltanschauung* acquired its common philosophical meaning as "a self-realized, productive as well as conscious way of apprehending and interpreting the universe of beings." Furthermore, it was frequently used by a number of other prominent German thinkers to refer to "the different possible world-views which appear and take shape in fact," including the "moral world-view" (Hegel), the "poetic world-view" (Görres), the "Christian and religious world-view" (Ranke), and so on (p. 5).[77] On the basis of these observations and references to various worldview models, Heidegger also spells out how *Weltanschauung* is used in popular discourse.

> From the forms and possibilities of world-view thus enumerated it becomes clear that what is meant by this term is not only a conception of the contexture of natural things but at the same time an interpretation of the sense and purpose of the human Dasein and hence of history. A world-view always includes a view of life. A world-view grows out of an all-inclusive reflection on the world and the human Dasein, and this again happens in different ways, explicitly and consciously in individuals or by appropriating an already prevalent world-view. We grow up within such a world-view and gradually become accustomed to it. Our world-view is determined by environment — people, race, class, developmental stage of culture. Every world-view thus individually formed arises out of a natural

77. Heidegger also cites references to the democratic, the pessimistic, and the medieval worldviews. He notes Schleiermacher's observation that a worldview makes knowledge of God complete, and also mentions Bismarck's comment on the strange worldviews of clever people.

world-view, out of a range of conceptions of the world and determinations of the human Dasein which are at any particular time given more or less explicitly with each Dasein. We must distinguish the individually formed world-view or the cultural world-view from the natural world-view. (pp. 5-6)

In continuing his description of the traits of worldview, Heidegger notes that it is not just a matter of theoretical knowledge, and that it is not simply held in memory as if it were a piece of cognitive property. Instead, it is a dynamic entity shaping human affairs and providing guidance and strength, among other things.

Rather, it is a matter of a coherent conviction which determines the current affairs of life more or less expressly and directly. A world-view is related in its meaning to the particular contemporary Dasein at any given time. In this relationship to the Dasein the world-view is a guide to it and a source of strength under pressure. Whether the world-view is determined by superstitions and prejudices or is based purely on scientific knowledge and experience or even, as is usually the case, is a mixture of superstition and knowledge, prejudice and sober reason, it all comes to the same thing; nothing essential is changed.

A most important factor derived from this discussion of worldviews is that they are always rooted in real life, that is, in and from "the particular factical existence of the human being in accordance with his factical possibilities of thoughtful reflection and attitude-formation, and it arises thus for this factical Dasein. The world-view is something that in each case exists historically from, with, and for the factical Dasein" (p. 6). Worldviews, in other words, are not the products of pure thought, but are born of the dynamics of human experience.

Heidegger makes a further distinction between an unexamined, inchoate worldview (that is, a factical and historical worldview) and a philosophical *Weltanschauung* which has been worked out theoretically. An intellectually sophisticated worldview must be distinguished not only from the sciences which focus on a limited aspect of reality, but also from artistic and religious interpretations of the reality which remain largely untheoretical. Historically speaking, a philosophical worldview is not just the casual by-product of the discipline of philosophy, but is its very goal and nature. "It seems to be without question," Heidegger observes, "that philosophy has as its goal the formation of a world-view." The philosophic formation of a worldview is also understood to be a scientific task, drawing on both the content and rules of science. This task of worldview development also shapes the popular understanding of the very essence and value of philosophy as a discipline. Only insofar as a scientifically informed philosophy successfully develops a coherent *Weltanschauung* in response to the ultimate questions of life, is the enterprise considered worthwhile.

He notes that regardless of whether philosophy is pursued scientifically or not, the goal of philosophy has always been the same: the formation of a worldview. Thus any "distinction between 'scientific philosophy' and 'philosophy as world-view' vanishes. The two together constitute the essence of philosophy, so that what is really emphasized ultimately is the task of the world-view" (p. 7).

At this point, however, Heidegger reaches a turning point in his discussion, and returns to the distinction he made earlier. In a passage that is diametrically opposed to his historical analysis, Heidegger now claims rather abruptly that "the formation of a world-view cannot be the task of philosophy." Here the term "philosophy" is no longer being used as before, but in a technical manner. From this point on Heidegger labors to explain what *he means* by "philosophy" within the framework of his fundamental ontology. His conception rests on a set of assumptions quite different from those associated with the traditional perspective. Heidegger's hypothesis revolves around the relationship of philosophy to the notion of being. "The thesis that world-view formation does not belong to the task of philosophy is valid . . . ," Heidegger explains, "only on the presupposition that philosophy does not relate in a positive manner to some being qua this or that particular being, that it does not posit a being." Traditionally thinkers, in search of a worldview, have always concerned themselves with beings of various kinds as objects of consideration. Thus he asks: "What then is philosophy supposed to concern itself with if not with beings, with that which is, with the whole of what is?" (p. 10). From Heidegger's standpoint, however, the analysis of beings native to traditional philosophy is not its real province. Instead, he asserts that we can understand particular beings only if we first understand being itself in a broad, universal sense. Philosophy, strictly speaking, is the science of being as such, and therefore is prerequisite to worldview as the interpretation of beings. Consequently, Heidegger makes his case for the point of view "that being is the proper and sole theme of philosophy" (p. 11). He then reiterates that a philosophy of being must be sharply distinguished from a worldview philosophy of beings, and for this reason the latter discipline is alienated from the domain of true philosophy as Heidegger defines it.

> Philosophy is the theoretical conceptual interpretation of being, of being's structure and its possibilities. Philosophy is ontological. In contrast, a world-view is positing knowledge of beings and a positing attitude toward

beings; it is not ontological, but ontical. The formation of a world-view falls outside the range of philosophy's task, but not because philosophy is in an incomplete condition and does not yet suffice to give a unanimous and universally cogent answer to the questions pertinent to world-views; rather, the formation of a world-view falls outside the range of philosophy's tasks because philosophy in principle does not relate to beings. It is not because of a defect that philosophy renounces the task of forming a world-view but because of a distinctive priority: it deals with what every positing of beings, even the positing done by a world-view, must already *presuppose* essentially [that is, being]. (p. 12)

For Heidegger, then, the expression "worldview philosophy" is technically oxymoronic. Worldview is one thing, namely, the positing of specific things about beings. Philosophy is something else, namely, its focus on being as such. Philosophy as the science of being "must legitimate by its own [historical] resources its claim to be universal ontology" (p. 12). Hence, as different pursuits, worldview and philosophy must remain segregated. Husserl's contentions in "Philosophy as Rigorous Science," therefore, are reincarnated in these idiosyncratic Heideggerian reflections.

"The Age of the World Picture"

Presumably, Jaspers intended his arguments in the *Psychology of Worldviews* to be timelessly and universally applicable. However, the atemporal, transglobal relevance of Jaspers's descriptions about worldviews as ideas about what is ultimate and total in human beings, both subjectively and objectively, provoked a response from Martin Heidegger. His essay "The Age of the World Picture" might best be seen, in part at least, as a reaction to Jaspers's work.[78] Rather than

---

78. This lecture was originally given on 9 June 1938 under the title "The Establishing by Metaphysics of the Modern World Picture." It was delivered before the Society for Aesthetics, Natural Philosophy, and Medicine at Freiburg in Breisgau. The theme for this gathering was the establishment of the modern worldview. The fifteen appendices that accompany the piece were a part of the original lecture but were not delivered. Heidegger's text has been published several times, including the following: "Die Zeit des Weltbildes," in *Holzwege*, in *Gesamtausgabe*, ed. F.-W. von Herrmann, vol. 5 (Frankfurt: Klostermann, 1977), pp. 75-113. For English translations, see "The Age of the World Picture," in *The Question concerning Technology and Other Essays*, translated and introduction by William Lovitt (New York: Harper and Row, Harper Torchbooks, 1977), pp. 115-54 (the page references in the text are from this translation); Marjorie Green, trans., "The Age of the World View," *Boundary* 4 (1976): 341-55. The assertion that Heidegger's lecture is a "recoil" to Jaspers's work is from Krell, *Intimations of Mortality*, p. 178 n. 6.

embracing worldviews as ubiquitous phenomena rooted in the essential psychology of human Dasein, Heidegger seems convinced that worldviews or, more accurately, world pictures *(Weltbild)* are possible only when humans are conceived as subjects and the world is presented as an object for interpretation. Indeed, this subject/object dualism is the basis for Jaspers's anatomy of the mental gestalts within which people think and live. From Heidegger's point of view, not only does this dichotomizing of reality engender the production of world pictures, but it also obscures the nature of being and the identity of Dasein itself. Hence, as an apology for his overall philosophic project and in defense of his own brand of humanism, Heidegger found it necessary to explain the phenomena of world pictures as the outgrowth of a misleading metaphysic that is in fact limited in space and time to the modern age. His arguments are intriguing, and they take the following form.

Heidegger begins with a statement about the importance of metaphysics as the basis for any age's interpretation of what is and its conception of truth. There is also the need for the courage to reflect and scrutinize the metaphysical foundations which have dominion over all things and which impart to every epoch its distinctive form (pp. 115-16). Heidegger argues that there are five essential features of the modern age: science, machine technology, art as aesthetics, culture, and the loss of the gods.[79] What he wants to know is what metaphysical program, with its concomitant view of truth, has led to these five defining characteristics. His strategy is to investigate the nature of contemporary science and to ascertain what metaphysical foundation and epistemology underlie it. If he can make this discovery, he will grasp the philosophical basis of the entire modern age (pp. 116-17).

Heidegger's investigation leads him to conclude that the projection and rigor, methodology and ongoing activity of modern science transform it into a program of research (pp. 117-26). Science as research also entails the necessity of propositional representation, and the entire enterprise means the objectifica-

---

79. Heidegger (pp. 116-17) makes the interesting comment that the loss of the gods, which in his mind does not necessarily translate into gross atheism, is largely the fault of the church for reasons related to *Weltanschauung*. He writes: "The loss of the gods is a twofold process. On the one hand, the world picture is Christianized inasmuch as the cause of the world is posited as infinite, unconditional, absolute. On the other hand, Christendom transforms Christian doctrine into a world view (the Christian world view), and in that way makes itself modern and up to date. The loss of the gods is the situation of indecision regarding God and the gods. Christendom has the greatest share in bringing it about." The last of the two reasons is especially intriguing. Christianity, in an attempt to be modern by transforming itself into a worldview, has apparently violated its own nature, or forfeited something essential, and contributed to the contemporary uncertainty regarding deity. Thus it would seem as if "worldview," at least as Heidegger interprets it, is incompatible with traditional Christianity.

tion of whatever is. In Heidegger's opinion, the person responsible for the metaphysical objectification of things that makes modern science possible as a program of research is René Descartes. His metaphysical framework dominates the age all the way up through Nietzsche. Heidegger states his viewpoint in this way: "We first arrive at science as research when and only when truth has been transformed into the certainty of representation. What it is to be is for the first time defined as the objectiveness of representing, and truth is first defined as certainty of representing, in the metaphysics of Descartes. . . . The whole of modern metaphysics taken together, Nietzsche included, maintains itself within the interpretation of what it is to be and of truth that was prepared by Descartes" (p. 127).

In ascertaining the metaphysical ground for science, Heidegger has also verified the underpinnings of the entire modern age. At the center of modernity is the freedom and autonomy of humanity. "The essence of the modern age," he argues, "can be seen in the fact that man frees himself from the bonds of the Middle Ages in freeing himself to himself" (p. 127). Accompanying this liberation is the introduction of a revolutionary subjectivism and individualism which sustain a dynamic interplay with objectivism and collectivism. What is most important, however, is that in this process "the very essence of man itself changes, in that man becomes subject." This is not a superficial change; rather, a kind of Copernican revolution takes place such that humanity becomes the locus and ground of all that is. When man becomes the primary and only real subject, he "becomes that being upon which all that is, is grounded as regards the manner of its Being and its truth. Man becomes the relational center of that which is as such." Modernity is characterized therefore by the ascendancy of the human self as the all-determinative subject, a development that can been traced in the respective idealisms of Kant, Fichte, Schelling, and Hegel.

When humanity changes its conception of itself in such a radical manner so as to become the metaphysical epicenter, the understanding of the whole of things also changes. Thus Heidegger asks: "In what does this change manifest itself? What, in keeping with it, is the essence of the modern age?" (p. 128). His response is that such changes are manifested in the notion of the "world picture," which is the chief characteristic of modernity. In his discussion of the nature of the "world picture," Heidegger is clear about what he means. He states that "world picture, when understood essentially, does not mean a picture of the world but the world conceived and grasped as picture. What is, in its entirety, is now taken in such a way that it first is in being and only is in being to the extent that it is set up by man, who represents and sets [it] forth" (pp. 129-30). Thus the world as picture is the world as object, as an object of knowledge and representation, and as an object of use and disposal. Accordingly, the human self is conceived as subject, as knower and interpreter of the world as object, and as user and disposer of the world which is there to be mastered and possessed (Descartes). The conception of the world as a picture or object and the self as subject will result in its depiction as worldview, as Heidegger will explain later.

Such a relationship between humanity (subject) and the world (object) in which the latter is conceived as a picture by the former is utterly foreign to both the Christians and Greeks. It is foreign to the Christians because it changes their previous understanding of their specific rank in the order of creation as the *analogia entis* (analogous being) to God. It is foreign to the Greeks because it revises their understanding of the primacy of Being which apprehends humanity. In modern secularism, however, man has freed himself from both the intuition of Being and from his location in the divine schema as specified in Christian revelation. From this fresh autonomous vantage point as the supreme subject, modern man has sought to apprehend being rather than being apprehended by it; he has sought to dominate nature rather than being its steward. In this new context of liberation, however, humanity comes to be one thing among other things, though he has precedence over all other things. He too is part of the world, part of the world as picture, part of the world, like everything else, that must be represented, explained, and viewed. "That the world becomes picture," Heidegger says, "is one and the same event with the event of man's becoming *subiectum* in the midst of that which is" (p. 132).[80]

Thus, according to Heidegger, this recasting of human beings as subjects in the midst of that which is has several important implications. First of all, it means that human beings must not only define or explain themselves and all other things, but they must also seek to have mastery or dominion over the world as well. Thus "there begins that way of being human which means the realm of human capability as a domain given over to measuring and executing, for the purpose of gaining mastery over that which is as a whole" (p. 132). Second, it means that human beings must wrestle with the dynamics of self and society, between a subjectivism that is always teetering on the edge of a rank individualism and a communitarianism entailing responsibilities for the body politic. Learning how one ought to be a subject in society is a distinctively modern task. "Only where man is essentially already subject does there exist the possibility of his slipping into the aberration of subjectivism in the sense of individualism. But also, only where man *remains* subject does the positive strug-

---

80. C. S. Lewis treats similar themes in chapter 3 of his prophetic *The Abolition of Man* (New York: Simon and Schuster, Touchstone, 1996).

gle against individualism and for the community . . . have any meaning." Third, it means the emergence of the central event of modern history, that is, the rise and development of a humanism or anthropology. "Namely, the more extensively and the more effectually the world stands at man's disposal as conquered, and the more objectively the object appears, all the more subjectively, i.e., the more importunately, does the *subiectum* rise up, and all the more impetuously, too, do observation of and teaching about the world change into a doctrine of man, into anthropology. It is no wonder that humanism first arises where the world becomes picture."

Heidegger is clear about what he means by humanism or anthropology. It should not be conceived under the umbrella of the natural sciences or theology. Rather it is thoroughly secular in substance: "it designates that philosophical interpretation of man which explains and evaluates whatever is, in its entirety, from the standpoint of man and in relation to man." Humanity thus becomes the measure of all things, including what the world itself is and how it is viewed. Humanity stands at the center of existence and explains and evaluates the sum total of reality. Human beings become the authors of the world.

This leads directly to the fourth and final implication of human beings becoming subjects and the world becoming an object. It constitutes one of Heidegger's primary points in this essay. It is the proposition that the modern age as the age of the world picture is therefore also the age of the worldview. His argument is that the domination of the West since the Enlightenment by anthropological humanism has expressed itself primarily in approaching the cosmos in terms of worldview. Thus he writes: "The increasingly exclusive rooting of the interpretation of the world in anthropology, which has set in since the end of the eighteenth-century, finds its expression in the fact that the fundamental stance of man in relation to what is, in its entirety, is defined as a world view *(Weltanschauung)*" (p. 133). He notes that since the *Aufklärung*, the term "worldview" has become a standard part of the vocabulary, for as soon as the world became a picture, humanity approached it as an object to be viewed and interpreted. The term "worldview" is subject to misunderstanding, however. It does not simply refer to a passive contemplation of the world or a "view of life" as the term was commonly used in the nineteenth century. Rather it reveals how the world has come to be viewed as picture, and it possesses profound anthropological or humanistic implications, as Heidegger explains: "The fact that, despite this [misleading meanings], the phrase 'world view' asserts itself as the name for the position of man in the midst of all that is, is proof of how decisively the world became picture as soon as man brought his life as *subiectum* into precedence over other centers of relationship. This means: whatever is, is considered to be in being only to the degree and to the extent that it is taken into and referred back to this [human] life, i.e., is lived out, and becomes life-experience."

Thus, according to Heidegger, "the fundamental event of the modern age is the conquest of the world as picture." In his role as subject, man has conceived of the world as a picture, as an object, as a structured image which he represents and sets before himself. In this way man strives for a position from and by which he can be "that particular being who gives measure and draws up the guidelines for everything that is" (p. 134). Man, at the apex of reality, seeks to rule and dominate the cosmos, and to interpret and arrange it as he will. Insofar as this exalted position of humanity expresses itself in the formulation of worldviews, there is the potential for conflict among the most prominent among them. There ensues therefore the conflict of worldviews in the quest for cosmic domination. "Because this position [of man] secures, organizes, and articulates itself as world view, the modern relationship to that which is, is one that becomes, in its decisive unfolding, a confrontation of world views; and indeed not of random world views, but only of those that have already taken up the fundamental position of man that is most extreme, and have done so with the utmost resoluteness" (pp. 134-35).

Even the services of science are enlisted in this battle between competing worldviews, for science is a key *organon* to the establishment of the reign of the self over the earth. "For the sake of this struggle of world views and in keeping with its meaning, man brings into play his unlimited power for the calculating, planning, and molding of all things. Science as research is an absolutely necessary form of this establishing of self in the world; . . . With this struggle of world views the modern age first enters into the part of its history that is the most decisive and probably the most capable of enduring" (p. 135).

With this Heidegger closes his essay, except for a brief meditation on the nature of being for which modern man longs but which the age of the world picture has obscured. Here Heidegger's residual Thomism seems to manifest itself, for it is the very fact and presence of worldviews that pose such a problem for him and his philosophical project. He seeks a recovery of being, but the depiction of the world in objectivist terms as a picture blocks this perception. Not only do worldviews inhibit an encounter with being, but as we saw in his lecture courses, they are often confused with the nature of philosophy as a scientific discipline. To clarify this latter situation, Heidegger traces the history of worldview philosophy and carefully distinguishes between it and his alleged scientific method of fundamental ontology. Heidegger, therefore, opposes the notion of worldview on two fronts, both as method and as content.

There is an irony, however, in Heidegger's antipathy toward *Weltanschauung*. As we have seen, though Edmund Husserl defended phenomenological philosophy as a strict, presuppositionless science, many have suggested that his proposals were context-dependent and rested on significant modern assumptions. He was unable to free himself or his thought from the influence of his worldview framework. This same response applies also to the work of Martin Heidegger. Despite his strong criticisms of *Weltanschauung* philosophy and though he sought to establish a purely scientific, fundamental ontology in quest of being, it would seem that his entire project is conditioned as well not only by the early twentieth-century *Sitz im Leben,* but also by his own autobiography and worldview.

In an important article on this very topic, "Work and Weltanschauung," Jürgen Habermas investigates "the question of whether — and, if so, to what extent — . . . [Heidegger's] work itself may be affected, in its philosophical substance, by the intrusion of elements from what we Germans call '*Weltanschauung*' — an ideologically tinged worldview."[81] In this essay Habermas draws on his own account of ideology as *Weltanschauung* which he worked out in his *Theory of Communicative Action* to see "whether there was an internal connection between Heidegger's philosophy and his political perception of the world-historical situation" (p. 189). Because he believes that "no short-circuit can be set up between work and person," Habermas argues forcefully that from about 1929 on, "Heidegger's thought exhibits a *conflation* of philosophical theory with ideological motifs" (pp. 203, 191). Indeed, he is even able to speak of "the invasion of the philosophy of *Being and Time* by ideology," and that "the spirit of the times, with which our author was already imbued, shows itself in this central work" (pp. 192, 190). Judgments similar to this are echoed by others. For example, Richard Wolin notes that if the historically contingent character of *Being and Time* is demonstrated convincingly, its "ontological" pretensions would be significantly deflated. He asserts that "*Being and Time* must simultaneously be understood as a historical document — as a product of determinate historical conditions and of a specific intellectual lineage."[82] Even statements within *Being and Time* itself seem to suggest the influence of pretheoretical commitments on Heidegger's overall project. In what amounts to an admission of this fact, Heidegger asks: "But does not a definite ontic interpretation of authentic existence, a factical ideal of Da-sein, underlie our ontological interpretation of

81. Jürgen Habermas, "Work and Weltanschauung: The Heidegger Controversy from a German Perspective," in *Heidegger: A Critical Reader,* ed. Hubert L. Dreyfus and Harrison Hall (Cambridge, Mass.: Basil Blackwell, 1992), p. 186. Page references in this paragraph are to this work.

82. Richard Wolin, *The Politics of Being: The Political Thought of Martin Heidegger* (New York: Columbia University Press, 1990), p. 23. For similar comments, see Richard Rorty, "Heidegger, Contingency, and Pragmatism," in *Heidegger: A Critical Reader,* pp. 209-30.

the existence of Da-sein? Indeed." Heidegger continues by recognizing that "Philosophy will never seek to deny its 'presuppositions,' but neither may it merely admit them. It conceives them and develops them with more and more penetration, both the presuppositions themselves and that for which they are presuppositions."[83] Kisiel notes that this question and comment of Heidegger's have always perplexed commentators because they "open up the old Pandora's box of worldviews which can contaminate the very roots of a philosophy claiming to outstrip all worldviews."[84]

Like Husserl, then, Heidegger's philosophy must have failed to "outstrip" his *Weltanschauung*. Perhaps he increasingly recognized this as his career progressed. Maybe he acknowledged the need for outside assistance in solving the enigmas of life. Perchance this is why Heidegger said some ten years before his death: "Only a god can save us."[85]

Concluding Implications

This first half of the history of "worldview" in twentieth-century philosophy is very intense. And the reflections of the three thinkers surveyed in this chapter raise important questions for consideration by Christian thinkers concerned about the concept of *Weltanschauung*. On the basis of Husserl's effort to distinguish the personal and value orientation of worldviews from philosophy as a strong, factual science, we might ask two questions: (1) How ought believers relate the idea of worldview to academic philosophy and theology, and how do they relate their own Christian *Weltanschauung* to the findings of science and scholarship in general? (2) Do Christians consider the biblical worldview to be epistemically trustworthy, as genuine knowledge, or simply as a personal value system or perspective on life that lacks cognitive credibility? Also, if the interpretation of Husserl's notion of "lifeworld" as an underlying objective reality was cogent, we might also be stimulated to inquire about the nature of the connection between a Christian interpretation of reality and what is in fact really there. To what extent does a Christian take on the nature of things correspond to the true nature of God's creation, and on what basis and how?

83. Martin Heidegger, *Being and Time: A Translation of "Sein und Zeit,"* trans. Joan Stambaugh, SUNY Series in Contemporary Continental Philosophy (Albany: State University of New York Press, 1996), p. 286.

84. Kisiel, *The Genesis*, p. 430.

85. Martin Heidegger, "'Only a God Can Save Us': The Spiegel Interview (1966)," in *Heidegger: The Man and the Thinker*, ed. Thomas Sheehan (Chicago: Precedent Publishing, n.d.), p. 57. This interview may be found in *Der Spiegel* 23 (1966): 193-219.

Karl Jaspers focused his reflections on worldviews as mental frameworks in his *Psychology of Worldviews.* In this work he sought to connect the response of the human soul to the limit situations in life, to the formation of subjective life attitudes and objective world pictures. Jaspers's notions raise several inquiries: (1) How are worldviews in general psychologically significant, and what impact should the Christian outlook on life have on the mental state of believers? (2) What theoretical and practical resources does the biblical worldview offer to the person who encounters the tragedies of life? (3) How can a Christian's encounter with the horrors of existence help him or her to foster thinking and attitudes commensurate with the biblical *Weltanschauung?*

Martin Heidegger, in addition to valorizing Jaspers's notion of limit situations and distinguishing his scientific ontology from the value-laden philosophy of worldviews, also claimed that modernity was the age of the world picture. The influence of Cartesian thought posits human subjects as thinking beings who view the world as an object to be pictured. For Heidegger, this dualism obfuscated an encounter with being. His provocative ideas lead to these questions: (1) Does the notion of worldview as a modernist invention commit Christian believers to a subject/object dichotomy and a dualistic relationship with the world? (2) If so, does it foster inappropriately aggressive approaches to creation as an entity to be categorized and subjugated scientifically and technologically? (3) How has this manner of being in the world prevented believers from recognizing the sacramental character of creation, their solidarity with it, and their caring stewardship over it? (4) Have believers been co-opted by modernity in employing the vocabulary of worldview as an objectified way of relating to reality?[86]

---

86. I will offer a brief response to these questions on Heidegger in chap. 11.

Chapter Six

A Philosophical History of "Worldview":
The Twentieth Century II

There seems to be something for everyone in this philosophical history of worldview in the twentieth century. It has been analyzed in the context of Husserl's phenomenology, Jaspers's incipient existentialism, and Heidegger's fundamental ontology. And now we will take a look at its fortunes in the hands of linguistic, analytic, and postmodern philosophers. Indeed, it is well ensconced in Ludwig Wittgenstein's notions of forms of life and language games. Donald Davidson critiques the very idea of a conceptual scheme in analytic terms. And postmodern thinkers have jettisoned the category for a variety of interesting reasons. It seems to take its place at the center of some of the most significant philosophical developments in the last hundred years. We proceed, then, to spell out its role in the thought of the Austrian-born turned British philosopher Ludwig Wittgenstein.

"Worldview" and "World Picture" in Ludwig Wittgenstein

Though the concept of *Weltanschauung* was firmly rejected by Husserl and Heidegger for the respective reasons demonstrated in the previous chapter of this work, Ludwig Wittgenstein (1889-1951) can arguably be declared — at least later in his career — a life and worldview philosopher. Under the influence and impetus of several thinkers, and because of his own recognition of the conventional nature of the rules of grammar and the multiplicity of various forms of life, Wittgenstein moved, as Nicholas Gier believes, "in the direction of a full *Weltanschauungsphilosophie*."[1] However, he moved in this direction in an atypi-

---

1. Nicholas F. Gier, *Wittgenstein and Phenomenology: A Comparative Study of the Later*

cal manner.[2] Wittgenstein in no way wanted to set forth yet another metaphysical worldview or philosophical thesis about the true nature of things within the Cartesian framework. He came to reject the modern approach in which the mind of the human subject proffers fresh representations about the world as an interpreted object. Rather, Wittgenstein sought to overthrow the Enlightenment vision of the world with its demand for an absolute foundation for knowledge and life, along with its concomitant alienation of the world itself. He wished to bring an end to the age of the world picture in the "subject-object" sense as described by Heidegger. His ambition was to liberate human beings from captivity to this picture and indeed all fixed pictures, even his own previously held picture theory of language, for as he put it in another context, "a picture held us captive."[3] In this sense his aim in philosophy was "To shew the fly the way out of the fly-bottle."[4] To accomplish this exodus he endeavored to replace the old modernist scenario with its emphasis on certain foundations and accurate linguistic representations with a new "picture" — indeed, a new kind of non-Cartesian, Wittgensteinian world picture *(Weltbild)* that consists of unverifiable forms of life and nonrepresentational language games. In short, he wanted to change the way humans "see" the world. "I wanted to put this picture before your eyes, and your *acceptance* of this picture consists in your being inclined to regard a given case differently; that is, to compare it with *this* series of pictures. I have changed your *way of seeing*."[5]

In attempting to change the human way of seeing, Wittgenstein introduces a new epoch into Western thinking. Whereas Plato upheld ontology and Descartes submitted epistemology as the primary concern, Wittgenstein nominated grammar and language as the governing principles. Major paradigm shifts in Western philosophy have run roughly from the Platonic form-world of being to the Cartesian inner world of knowledge to the Wittgensteinian sayable-world of meaning. His innovation is to take meaning as the primordial

---

Wittgenstein, Husserl, Heidegger, and Merleau-Ponty, SUNY Series in Philosophy (Albany: State University of New York Press, 1981), p. 48. Gier discusses Wittgenstein's association with life-philosophy and his adoption of worldview philosophy in several places in this book (pp. 49-71, 101-2, 113). In summary he says: "Wittgenstein's radical pluralism, based as it is on the possibility of different world-views and world-pictures, definitely avoids the denigration of the 'particular case' and preserves the fullness and richness of lived experience" (p. 48).

2. Adapted from James C. Edwards, *Ethics without Philosophy: Wittgenstein and the Moral Life* (Tampa: University Presses of Florida, 1982), pp. 184-85.

3. Ludwig Wittgenstein, *Philosophical Investigations,* trans. G. E. M. Anscombe, 3rd ed. (New York: Macmillan, 1968), §115 (p. 48e).

4. Wittgenstein, *Philosophical Investigations,* §309 (p. 103e).

5. Ludwig Wittgenstein, *Zettel,* ed. G. E. M. Anscombe and G. H. von Wright, trans. G. E. M. Anscombe (Los Angeles: University of California Press, 1970), §461 (p. 82e).

category, more basic than either being or knowledge. Thus, according to Wittgenstein, whatever being and knowledge there may be, both are determined by and are a function of the grammar and language well ensconced in a form of life.[6] These themes are native to Wittgensteinian *Weltanschauung* territory, which we must now explore.

Wittgenstein and Weltanschauung

Wittgenstein rarely employed the word *Weltanschauung* (only six times altogether), and he may have been at pains to distance himself from it. In the context of his later philosophy of pluralism and relativism, the reason for this is probably because of the association of worldview with metaphysics, and its alleged embodiment of the truth about the nature of things (at least according to one understanding of the term). This interpretation of the concept seems clear in an early reference in his *Tractatus Logico-Philosophicus,* wherein he compares the recent embrace of the modern worldview of naturalism with the old-fashioned, resolute belief in the former "inviolable" and reified worldviews of theism and fatalism.

> 6. 371 The whole modern conception of the world [*Weltanschauung*] is founded on the illusion that the so-called laws of nature are the explanations of natural phenomena.

> 6. 372 Thus people today stop at the laws of nature, treating them as something inviolable, just as God and Fate were treated in ages past.[7]

Worldviews as sacrosanct reality constructs must be understood as sure and certain conceptions or ways of looking at the world. Far from superficial, they reside at a very deep level, underlying the character and culture of an entire people. Thus, when Wittgenstein argues that "humor" as a worldview or way of looking at life was wiped out in Nazi Germany, he notes that something quite profound and penetrating was lost. "Humor is not a mood but a way of looking at the world [*Weltanschauung*]. So if it is correct to say that humor was stamped out in Nazi Germany, that does not mean that people were not in good

---

6. Henry LeRoy Finch, *Wittgenstein: The Later Philosophy — an Exposition of the "Philosophical Investigations"* (Atlantic Highlands, N.J.: Humanities Press, 1977), p. 246.

7. Ludwig Wittgenstein, *Tractatus Logico-Philosophicus,* trans. D. F. Pears and B. F. McGuinness, introduction by Bertrand Russell (London: Routledge and Kegan Paul, 1961), §§6.371, 6.372 (p. 70).

spirits, or anything of that sort, but something much deeper and more important."[8]

This understanding of *Weltanschauung* as something deep and important was acquired by Wittgenstein from the thought of the German historian and life philosopher Oswald Spengler (1880-1936). Spengler states that a worldview is "a picture of the world (cosmos, universe)," a paradigm or model of reality "in which the whole of consciousness, becoming and the become, life and what is experienced" is understood.[9] This comprehensive conception of worldview as the context in which things are seen, interpreted, and connected is evident in a passage from Wittgenstein's *Remarks on Frazer's "Golden Bough."* In giving credit to Spengler for his definition, Wittgenstein asserts that a worldview as a comprehensive "perspicuous presentation" of things is "fundamental."

> "And all this points to some unknown law" is what we want to say about the material Frazer has collected. I can set out this law in an hypothesis of development . . . but I can also do it just by arranging the factual material so that we can easily pass from one part to another and have a clear view of it — showing it in a "perspicuous" way.
>
> For us the conception of a perspicuous presentation . . . is fundamental. It indicates the form in which we write of things, the way in which we see things. (A kind of *"Weltanschauung"* that seems to be typical of our time. Spengler.)
>
> This perspicuous presentation makes possible that understanding which consists just in the fact that we "see the connections." Hence the importance of finding *intermediate links.*[10]

Worldviews undoubtedly are contextual phenomena enabling people to see things and make connections. Wittgenstein, however, did not want his revised version of philosophy and language to be mistaken for one. This is most clear in a text from *Philosophical Investigations* in which he is stating that philosophical problems arise when human beings lack a clear understanding of their words. In setting forth the need for linguistic perspicuity, Wittgenstein worries that his proposal could be mistaken for a *Weltanschauung.*

> 122. A main source of our failure to understand is that we do not *command a clear view* of our words. — Our grammar is lacking in this sort of perspi-

8. Ludwig Wittgenstein, *Culture and Value*, ed. G. H. von Wright in collaboration with Heikki Nyman, trans. Peter Winch (Chicago: University of Chicago Press, 1980), p. 78e.

9. Quoted in Gier, p. 62.

10. Ludwig Wittgenstein, *Remarks on Frazer's "Golden Bough*," ed. Rush Rhees, trans. A. C. Miles, rev. Rush Rhees (Atlantic Highlands, N.J.: Humanities Press, 1979), pp. 8e-9e.

cuity. A perspicuous representation produces just that understanding which consists in "seeing connexions." Hence the importance of finding and inventing *intermediate cases.*

The concept of a perspicuous representation is of fundamental significance for us. It earmarks the form of account we give, the way we look at things. (Is this a "Weltanschauung"?)[11]

In asking the question "Is this a 'Weltanschauung'?" Wittgenstein seems to be concerned that a line of demarcation be drawn between his own approach to the world via language and meaning and the concept of a full-blown worldview. He does not want his linguisticism to be identified as a competing paradigm, or understood as one more modernist way of articulating reality. From his last published work, *On Certainty,* Wittgenstein is apparently content to label his philosophical outlook a *Weltbild* or world picture, but to call it a *Weltanschauung* is unacceptable. The reason for this, in Judith Genova's opinion, is that for Wittgenstein "a *Weltanschauung* forgets its status as *a* way of seeing and parades itself as *the* way of seeing. It takes itself too seriously, as the ultimate explanation and foundation of our convictions. In contrast, the concept of *Weltbild* completely avoids the knowledge game."[12] This is the very game that Wittgenstein sought to avoid. He recognized that his own philosophy could be interpreted as another system of thought that seeks to get the world right. Any association, however, with a worldview constructed to this end would undermine his real purpose. As Edwards states, this would mean being "seduced by a particular *Weltanschauung,* one which assumes that the response to a philosophical puzzlement must be the promulgation and defense of a philosophical thesis. And, of course, it is just that assumption that Wittgenstein so vehemently rejects, for that assumption is but a corollary of the literalization of mind and speech that lies at the root of the Cartesian conception itself."[13] What Wittgenstein is willing to acknowledge are not modernist solutions to the enigmas of life and the world — quintessentially expressed in worldviews — but rather the fact of a multiplicity of mutually exclusive world pictures, forms of life, and language games. For this reason Wittgenstein is a

---

11. Wittgenstein, *Philosophical Investigations,* §122 (p. 49e).

12. Judith Genova, *Wittgenstein: A Way of Seeing* (New York: Routledge, 1995), p. 50. For the other two uses of *Weltanschauung* in Wittgenstein's writings, see his *Notebooks, 1914-1916,* ed. G. H. von Wright and G. E. M. Anscombe, trans. G. E. M. Anscombe (New York: Harper and Row, Harper Torchbooks, 1969), 05.06; and *On Certainty,* ed. G. E. M. Anscombe and G. H. von Wright, trans. Denis Paul and G. E. M. Anscombe (New York: Harper and Row, Harper Torchbooks, 1972), §§421-22 (p. 54e).

13. James Edwards, p. 184.

central figure in the transition from modernity to postmodernity in which the struggle of worldviews over one and the same world is replaced by a variety of noncompetitive, linguistic constructions of reality. Wittgenstein thus becomes the architect of a new approach to philosophy focusing on multiple conceptual schemes, all of which are relative and none of which is privileged over another. In this way his goal is to enable people to see the world differently, not as it really is, but as it is given to them in their sociolinguistic context. This aggregate of Wittgensteinian themes is crucial to his contribution to the history of worldview.

Wittgenstein: Forms of Life (Lebensform) and Language Games (Sprachspiel)

Of course, there is a well-known and profound difference between Wittgenstein's penultimate "positivist" philosophy of language as set forth in the *Tractatus Logico-Philosophicus* and his ultimate "analytic" outlook expressed in *Philosophical Investigations*. In a remarkable act of philosophical repentance, Wittgenstein changed his mind about the nature of language and adopted an entirely different approach. These successive stages in Wittgenstein's thinking about language have been succinctly laid out by Finch in the two following propositions:

(1) language as *logical picture* depicting forms and structures of *objects* through forms and structures of *names;*
(2) language as *human activities,* integrated with *other human activities* through countless different kinds of *uses of words.*[14]

In this second statement, which encapsulates Wittgenstein's later point of view, the *other human activities* with which language itself is intimately bound up are what he calls "forms of life" *(Lebensform),* and the countless different kinds of *uses of words* associated with forms of life are what Wittgenstein denominates as "language games" *(Sprachspiel).* The respective ideas of forms of life and language games are the cardinal notions in Wittgenstein's later philosophy.[15]

The concept of "form of life," which Norman Malcomb says "one could

---

14. Finch, p. 7. Making such a sharp distinction in Wittgenstein's thought and career has been questioned recently by several interpreters of his work. See *The Cambridge Dictionary of Philosophy,* 2nd ed. (1999), s.v. "Wittgenstein, Ludwig," for a brief discussion on this matter.

15. Gordon Hunnings, *The World and Language in Wittgenstein's Philosophy* (Albany: State University of New York Press, 1988), p. 244.

hardly place too much stress on,"[16] is nevertheless a most difficult expression to comprehend. Much ink has been spilled in an attempt to ascertain its precise meaning. However, for present purposes our goal is not to enter into the mammoth discussion on the question, but rather to exposit the use of the phrase in its five appearances in *Philosophical Investigations*, and to show how closely intertwined the concept is to the notion of "language games." Then I will suggest in the next section that this interpenetration of life and language constitutes what Wittgenstein calls a *Weltbild*, or "world picture," as this concept is set forth in his final book titled *On Certainty*.

In the first reference to a form of life and language game in *Philosophical Investigations*, the two ideas are so closely related that they appear to be virtually identical. "19. It is easy to imagine a language consisting only of orders and reports in battle. — Or a language consisting only of questions and expressions for answering yes and no. And innumerable others. — And to imagine a language means to imagine a form of life."[17]

In this particular assertion, Wittgenstein envisions two distinct uses of language, the first in a military context wherein orders and reports are given, and the second in a Socratic context wherein the possible answers to questions are yes and no. Then he requests that his readers employ their imaginations to consider what form of life is implied by the use of the language of either battle or inquiry. To envision a language of orders and reports means to envision the activity of warfare, and to envision the language of yes and no means to envision the activity of interrogation. These are just two possible language games and forms of life. Wittgenstein is quite cognizant of the many different uses of language and the diversity of language games, which, as he points out, are not static but evanescent. "23. But how many kinds of sentence are there? Say assertion, question, and command? — There are *countless* kinds: countless different kinds of use of what we call 'symbols,' 'words,' 'sentences.' And this multiplicity is not something fixed, given once for all; but new types of language, new language-games, as we may say, come into existence, and others become obsolete and get forgotten. (We can get a *rough picture* of this from the changes in mathematics.)"[18]

16. Norman Malcomb, "Wittgenstein's *Philosophical Investigations*," in *Wittgenstein: The Philosophical Investigations*, ed. George Pitcher (Garden City, N.Y.: Anchor Books, 1966), p. 91.

17. Wittgenstein, *Philosophical Investigations*, §19 (p. 8e).

18. Wittgenstein, *Philosophical Investigations*, §23 (p. 11e). In this context Wittgenstein continues by suggesting that his readers "review the multiplicity of language-games in the following examples, and in others: Giving orders, and obeying them — Describing the appearance of an object, or giving its measurements — Constructing an object from a description (a drawing) — Reporting an event — Speculating about an event — Forming and testing a hypothesis

In this assertion Wittgenstein makes a very helpful comment that not only places language games within the context of forms of life, but also provides something of a definition of the latter conception. He continues: "Here the term 'language-*game*' is meant to bring into prominence the fact that the speaking of language is *part of an activity,* or of a form of life."[19] A language game is not equivalent to a form of life, but one part or aspect of it. The form of life itself ought to be understood as an "activity." With this in mind, Finch believes, and rightly so, that "forms of life are established patterns of [meaningful] action shared in by members of a group."[20]

Furthermore, this foundational form of life characterized by meaningful action is what enables a group of people to decide upon what is true and false. While such a decision may appear to be a function of the language spoken, it really relies upon the mutual affirmation of the more basic and primordial model of human existence. Wittgenstein explains in these words: "241. 'So you are saying that human agreement decides what is true and what is false?' — It is what human beings say that is true and false; and they agree in the language they use. That is not agreement in opinions but in form of life."[21]

On the surface, the epistemic task of making distinctions between truth and falsehood seems to be a matter of what human beings, by convention, agree upon. Whatever people in consensus, by means of their native tongues, say is true and false is indeed for them true and false. However, the real basis for their mutual understanding of such matters lies not just in their overt opinions or words, but in their common agreement with and commitment to a way of being in the world. The shared activities of life itself and an understanding of their meaning is the underlying basis of epistemology. Even the phenomenon of hope and its idiomatic meaning expressed in talk by those who have mastered a language is bound up in what Wittgenstein enigmatically calls "this complicated form of life." "Can only those hope who can talk? Only those who have mastered the use of a language. That is to say, the phenomena of hope are modes of this complicated form of life. (If a concept refers to a character of human handwriting, it has no application to beings that do not write.)"[22]

Hope is not the only thing meaningfully expressed by the members of a

---

— Presenting the results of an experiment in tables and diagrams — Making up a story; and reading it — Play-acting — Singing catches — Guessing riddles — Making a joke; telling it — Solving a problem in practical arithmetic — Translating from one language into another — Asking, thanking, cursing, greeting, praying" (pp. 11e-12e).

19. Wittgenstein, *Philosophical Investigations,* §23 (p. 11e), emphasis added.
20. Finch, p. 90.
21. Wittgenstein, *Philosophical Investigations,* §241 (p. 88e).
22. Wittgenstein, *Philosophical Investigations,* IIi (p. 174e).

group sharing a unique context and manner of speaking. So also, and perhaps surprisingly, is an understanding of even mathematics and color. Underlying the language games about calculations and colorations — previously assumed universals — is the reception of a given form of life.

> What has to be accepted, the given, is — so one could say — *forms of life.*
>
> Does it make sense to say that people generally agree in their judgments of colour? What would it be like for them not to? — One man would say a flower was red which another called blue, and so on. — But what right should we have to call these people's words "red" and "blue" our "colour-word"? —
>
> How would they learn to use these words? And is the language-game which they learn still such as we call the use of "names of colour"? There are evidently differences of degree here.
>
> This consideration must, however, apply to mathematics too. If there were not complete agreement, then neither would human beings be learning the technique which we learn. It would be more or less different from ours up to the point of unrecognizability.[23]

Thus, on the basis of these five citations from Wittgenstein's *Philosophical Investigations,* the conclusion to be drawn is that the conception of form of life is the *more* basic category. Not far behind it and inextricably linked to it is language game. Perhaps this is because Wittgenstein embraced life itself as the *most* basic category. After all, he was indeed a life philosopher, as mentioned above. In his unpublished text *Big Typescript* (§213), the father of ordinary language philosophy penned this aphorism: "If we surrender the reins to language and not *to life,* then the problems of philosophy arise."[24] Hence Gier surmises that for Wittgenstein, "*Lebensphilosophie* even takes precedence over *Sprachsphilosophie.*"[25] Despite this priority, language is still vitally and organically related to every form of life, and is the epiphany or manifestation of its activity and content. Life and language are the two sides of the same coin. Language-in-life and life-in-language determine what those in the context of a living sociolinguistic community deem to be the true, the good, and the beautiful. To be a member of some form of life — to participate in its activities, learn and speak its language, embrace its culture — means to make, have, and share a world. Forms of life and their respective language games embody and express the fundamental features and categories of the world, what Wittgenstein called

23. Wittgenstein, *Philosophical Investigations,* IIxi (p. 226e).
24. Quoted in Gier, p. 70.
25. Gier, p. 68.

a "world picture" (Weltbild), a critical notion he discusses in considerable depth in his final book, On Certainty.

Wittgenstein and "World Picture" (Weltbild)

Wittgenstein's primary goal in On Certainty is to undercut the Cartesian paradigm of knowledge, resting as it does upon the two primary theses of an unshakable foundation for knowledge and the conception of the person as an incarnate mind (mind/body dualism). Furthermore, insofar as G. E. Moore's famous attempt to overcome skepticism by means of his "defence of common sense" and "proof of an external world" is undertaken in a Cartesian framework, Moore's work also is the object of Wittgenstein's censure in this book. Wittgenstein, however, will not be co-opted and thus fall into the same Cartesian trap by simply offering another competing Weltanschauung for rational consideration. Rather, he wishes to critique this presupposed Cartesian model by some kind of metaphilosophic method that will engender a new way of seeing.[26] He does this largely by means of his concept of a Weltbild (world picture), which makes its only appearance in the Wittgensteinian writings in this volume (seven times total). The result is what has become known as "Wittgensteinian fideism" — an approach to the world that consists of unverifiable models of life, language, culture, and meaning. In his Investigations, Wittgenstein's pluralism, of course, consists in a plethora of epistemically unjustified forms of life and language games that provide the contexts within and by which people see and make their way in the world. This same theme is pursued in On Certainty as well. As Finch explains, the essential content of this volume focuses on taken-for-granted frameworks and "worldview facts," or what Wittgenstein himself referred to as Weltbild.

> On Certainty concerns the role of facts which serve as frameworks for world views. They might be called framework facts because in some ways they are like other facts, though in other ways they are not like other facts at all. They are facts which . . . are the basis for our thoughts, our language, our judgments, and our actions. Such world view facts (to give them still another name) include also the various strata we call common sense. They include the vast numbers of things which we take for granted and which provide the settings for all our questions and investigations, as well as for our language activities. They are facts which we do not doubt because,

26. James Edwards, pp. 168-74.

among other things, they define what *doubting* is or *what it makes sense to doubt.* They establish what is accepted or agreed-upon in ways of talking and acting.[27]

These framework or worldview/picture "facts," however, are not the positivistic or absolute facts of Wittgenstein's *Tractatus* — facts which there served as the ultimate foundation for truth about reality and action in the world. Rather, these *Weltbild* facts are doubt-proof and serve, to use Wittgenstein's own metaphors, as the "axis," "river-bed," "scaffolding," and "hinges" of a particular way of thinking and acting.[28] These reified world pictures, creating "reality" as they do, thus form for their adherents a kind of pseudometaphysics in which they live, move, and have their being.

A number of salient features of Wittgenstein's understanding of the nature of world pictures can be ascertained from a survey of the texts of *On Certainty* in which the concept is discussed. First of all, a *Weltbild*, in very basic terms, forms one's way of seeing and conceiving of the world, and understanding its fundamental character. As Wittgenstein points out, Moore had argued and knew that he had lived his life close to the earth. Wittgenstein is forced to agree with this proposition for this reason: there is nothing in his own way of picturing the world that could dispute such a claim. All people in fact live in close relationship to the earth, and Wittgenstein knows this to be the case based on his picture of the world.

> 93. The propositions presenting what Moore *"knows"* are all of such a kind that it is difficult to imagine *why* anyone should believe the contrary. E.g. the proposition that Moore has spent his whole life in close proximity to the earth. — Once more I can speak of myself here instead of speaking of Moore. What could induce me to believe the opposite? Either a memory, or having been told. — Everything that I have seen or heard gives me the conviction that no man has ever been far from the earth. Nothing in my picture of the world [*Weltbild*] speaks in favour of the opposite. (pp. 14-15e)

Along these same lines, Wittgenstein says he would be conveying his basic image of the world, particularly an understanding of its age, to a child who should ask him "whether the earth was already there before . . . [his] birth." In responding to this query by affirming his conviction that the world had existed

---

27. Finch, pp. 221-22.
28. Finch, p. 222. For Wittgenstein's metaphors, see *On Certainty*, §152 (p. 22e), §97 (p. 15e), §211 (p. 29e), §341 (p. 44e). The references in the following text are to *On Certainty*.

long before his birth, Wittgenstein believes he would have been "imparting a picture of the world [*Weltbild*] to the person who asked it." Yet he follows up with this curious statement that calls into question the assurance with which he might present his answer: "If I do answer the question with certainty," Wittgenstein wonders, "what gives me this certainty?" (§233 [pp. 30-31e]). The implication seems to be that he really lacks the confidence that nonetheless accompanied his answer to the childish question. This leads to a second important point. Not only is a *Weltbild* a foundational representation or picture of reality, but a belief in it and a reception of it is *not* the result of some verification process. Rather a world picture is simply inherited from one's context so that it serves as the presupposed backdrop, as forms of life did in the *Investigations,* for discerning what is true and false. "94. But I did not get my picture of the world [*Weltbild*] by satisfying myself of its correctness; nor do I have it because I am satisfied of its correctness. No: it is the inherited background against which I distinguish between true and false" (p. 15e).

World pictures are not examined, proven, and chosen, but rather are "swallowed down" (§143 [p. 21e]) in childhood by virtue of living in given milieus. For this reason the great chemist Lavoisier conducts his experiments according to certain propositions that he has accepted as "norms of description" rooted in a world picture which he did not create or invent but learned when he was very young. Now it serves as the unexamined presuppositions of his research.

> 167. It is clear that our empirical propositions do not all have the same status, since one can lay down such a proposition and turn it from an empirical proposition into a norm of description.
>
> Think of chemical investigations. Lavoisier makes experiments with substances in his laboratory and now he concludes that this and that takes place when there is burning. He does not say that it might happen otherwise another time. He has got hold of a definite world-picture [*Weltbild*] — not of course one that he invented: he learned it as a child. I say world-picture [*Weltbild*] and not hypothesis, because it is the matter-of-course foundation for his research and as such also goes unnoticed. (p. 24e)

Not only are Lavoisier's assumptions "unnoticed," but at the end of the day they are also "untested." The fundamental presuppositions upon which all human activity (science included) is based may be investigated for a time, but as Wittgenstein asks rhetorically: "Doesn't testing come to an end?" There is no doubt about his answer. As he puts it, "The difficulty is to realize the groundlessness of our believing" (§164 and §166 [p. 24e]). This assertion captures the quintessence of Wittgenstein's fideism. Thus a world picture serves as the untested, groundless "substratum" for all inquiry and assertions. Even basic knowledge learned in school is validated on the unsubstantiated foundation of a *Weltbild* which one cannot necessarily say is true or false. "162. In general I take as true what is found in text-books, of geography for example. Why? I say: All these facts have been confirmed a hundred times over. But how do I know that? What is my evidence for it? I have a world-picture [*Weltbild*]. Is it true or false? Above all it is the substratum of all my enquiring and asserting. The propositions describing it are not all equally subject to testing" (pp. 23-24e).

The reason why certain "facts" are accepted as true is because they are congruent with the underlying world picture, the propositions of which, in the third place, function as a kind of governing "mythology." These mythological propositions are analogous to the rules of a game, a game that may be learned practically by playing it, not by theoretical examination or study. Some of the propositions associated with a world picture mythology become fixed and serve as the "channel" or "river-bed" which guides an entire way of life, though it is sometimes difficult to distinguish between which propositions constitute the channel or riverbed and which ones are governed by it. Here is Wittgenstein's explanation:

> 95. The propositions describing this world-picture [*Weltbild*] might be part of a kind of mythology. And their role is like that of rules of a game; and the game can be learned purely practically, without learning any explicit rules.

> 96. It might be imagined that some propositions, of the form of empirical propositions, were hardened and functioned as channels for such empirical propositions as were not hardened but fluid; and that this relation altered with time, in that fluid propositions hardened, and hard ones became fluid.

> 97. The mythology may change back into a state of flux, the river-bed of thoughts may shift. But I distinguish between the movement of the waters on the river-bed and the shift of the river-bed itself; though there is not a sharp division of the one from the other. (p. 15e)

If indeed world pictures are a kind of mythology — stories with themes that may cohere one with another but do not correspond to the real world — then an attempt to explain this outlook on life would be a matter of persuasion, not scientific or philosophic argumentation in pursuit of truth. Thus, and finally, world pictures are promulgated rhetorically and are accepted in faith.

Wittgenstein imagines a situation where a rhetoric of persuasion would be deployed: "262. I can imagine a man who had grown up in quite special circumstances and been taught that the earth came into being 50 years ago, and therefore believed this. We might instruct him: the earth has long . . . etc. — We should be trying to give him our picture of the world [*Weltbild*]. This would happen through a kind of *persuasion*" (p. 34e).

Wittgenstein in the very next entry makes a statement that seems out of context. Enigmatically he writes: "263. The schoolboy *believes* his teachers and his schoolbooks" (p. 34e). Could it be that in light of the preceding entry (§262), what he is seeking to communicate here is that all "knowledge," so to speak, is a matter of persuasion-engendered belief, even the kind that is communicated in schoolbooks as deposits of information traditionally regarded as "truth"? World pictures in Wittgensteinian terms, therefore, are not to be conceived as epistemically credible constructs competing for rational adherence, but as webs of belief which must be set forth in effective terms to be received as a way of organizing reality. In the final analysis, all one can say about one's outlook on the world is that this is what we are, this is what we understand, and this is what we do, period.

Hence, four basic themes are evident in Wittgenstein's discussion of world pictures in his book *On Certainty*. First, a *Weltbild* forms one's way of seeing and conceiving of the world and its basic character. Second, a *Weltbild* is not chosen as a result of some verification process, but rather is inherited from one's context so that it serves as the assumed substratum for all thinking, acting, judging, and living. Third, the narratives constituting a world picture function as a kind of governing mythology. Finally, world pictures are promulgated rhetorically and are accepted in faith. Given these various characteristics, world pictures and forms of life with their inherent language games seem almost identical. Indeed, Genova does not shy away from this connection, saying that "the concept of a form of life . . . [is] synonymous with a *Weltbild*," and that "the latter provides a more subjective way of speaking of what the former hopes to name more objectively."[29] But if the above interpretations are correct, for Wittgenstein the notion of *Weltanschauung* itself was even a more objective construct than a *Weltbild*. Indeed, Wittgenstein rejected *Weltanschauung* as a hangover from the Cartesian era, and embraced forms of life and world pictures as the trademarks of his own analytic approach to philosophy rooted in life, language, and meaning.

The irony, of course, is that Wittgenstein, like Husserl, Heidegger, and any others who have sought to jettison the necessity of a worldview, is unable to es-

29. Genova, p. 208 n. 13.

cape some reasonably fixed position on what reality and the world is really like.[30] Indeed, Wittgenstein embraces what might be accurately called a "linguistic" *Weltanschauung* rooted in words, their use and meaning. But the irony is this: he uses language which presumably connects with reality to suggest that no use of language really connects with reality. He has used the ladder of language to climb to the roof only to deny the necessity of the ladder. But if this is so, then his own system is not simply another way of seeing, but *the* way of seeing. Despite the self-defeating nature of his proposals, his new (exclusive) way of seeing the world results in a major revisioning of the essential task of philosophy — a task which in his hands is reduced considerably in terms of its purpose and scope. From the vantage point of Wittgensteinian fideism, philosophy should never have conceived itself as a "rigorous science." Such an understanding seems hopelessly retrograde and naive, to say the least. It is better to look upon it as a form of therapy. Rather "than endlessly seeking access to reality in itself," as Conway explains, for Wittgenstein "philosophy may help us to consider ways of coping with, dealing with our human world. Philosophy may promote self-conscious, critical awareness of social conventions, practices, and world pictures whereby we learn about ourselves and other forms of life."[31] Such an approach to philosophy has not only sparked interest in ordinary language analysis, but has led to a variety of new quasi-philosophic pursuits in areas such as narratology, hermeneutics, semiotics, and rhetoric, each focusing on language and its meaning and use in the context of a form of life and language game.

Donald Davidson on "Conceptual Schemes"

In his noted critique of the very idea of a conceptual scheme and its concomitant doctrine of relativism, Donald Davidson (b. 1917), contemporary metaphysician and philosopher of mind and language, is certainly swimming against the current. Indeed, his analysis is contrary to the "mainstream of modern philosophy that began when Kant exchanged the structure of the world for the structure of the mind, continued when C. I. Lewis exchanged the structure of the mind for the structure of concepts, and that now proceeds to exchange the structure of

30. Several writers have attempt to sketch Wittgenstein's basic worldview, including K. Kollenda, "Wittgenstein's *Weltanschauung*," *Rice University Studies* 50 (1961): 23-37; J. F. Miller, "Wittgenstein's *Weltanschauung*," *Philosophical Studies* 13 (1964): 127-40; Wilhelm Baum, "Ludwig Wittgenstein's World View," *Ratio* 22 (June 1980): 64-74.

31. Gertrude D. Conway, *Wittgenstein on Foundations* (Atlantic Highlands, N.J.: Humanities Press, 1989), p. 168.

concepts for the structure of the several symbol systems of the sciences, philosophy, the arts, perception, and everyday discourse."[32] In the theistic context of medieval scholasticism, theologians and philosophers understood that the human mind was subordinate to the external and objective structure of the world as designed by God and ordered by his laws. Even in the Kantian exchange of the cosmic for the mental structure, the great Copernicus of philosophy allowed for only a single scheme of apprehending the world based on the mutually shared categories of the human mind. As Davidson himself points out, however, "once the dualism of scheme and content was made explicit, the possibility of alternative conceptual schemes was apparent."[33] Indeed, C. I. Lewis is the one who has championed this point of view in his volume *Mind and the World Order* (1929). In this text he argues that "There are, in our cognitive experience, two elements; the immediate data, such as those of sense, which are presented or given to the mind, and a form, construction, or interpretation, which represents the activity of thought."[34] Consequently, Lewis believes that the natural task of philosophy must be to ascertain those fundamental concepts by which the mind organizes experience; that is, "to reveal those categorical criteria which the mind applies to what is given to it."[35] On the basis of these lines of thought, the notion of alternative conceptual schemes comes to prominence, and along with it a commitment to conceptual relativism as well.

These arguments pertaining to conceptual schemes and relativism, which are at the heart of modern philosophy, are the very things that Davidson seeks to evaluate carefully in his provocative essay. "Schemers," as those who embrace these doctrines are often called, have employed a number of synonymous expressions for conceptual matrices, including "world version" (Goodman), "paradigm" (Kuhn), "categorical framework" (Körner), "linguistic framework" (Carnap), "ideology" (Mannheim), and "form of life" (Wittgenstein).[36] For our purposes, "worldview" and *Weltanschauung* are closely identified with conceptual schemes as well. Joseph Runzo, for example, states forthrightly that "the notion of a 'conceptual schema' is equivalent to a 'world-view.'"[37] Nicholas

---

32. Nelson Goodman, *Ways of Worldmaking* (Indianapolis: Hackett, 1978), p. x.

33. Donald Davidson, "The Myth of the Subjective," in *Relativism: Interpretation and Confrontation*, edited and introduction by Michael Krausz (Notre Dame, Ind.: University of Notre Dame Press, 1989), p. 160.

34. C. I. Lewis, *Mind and the World Order* (New York: Scribner, 1929), p. 38.

35. Lewis, p. 36.

36. Steven D. Edwards, *Relativism, Conceptual Schemes, and Categorical Frameworks*, Avebury Series in Philosophy of Science (Brookfield, Vt.: Gower, 1990), p. 120.

37. Joseph Runzo, *World Views and Perceiving God* (New York: St. Martin's Press, 1993), p. 43 n. 3a.

Rescher is of a similar opinion when he asserts that "a conceptual scheme for operation in the factual domain is always correlative with a *Weltanschauung* — a view of how things work in the world."[38] Thus, because of the kinship between "conceptual scheme" and *Weltanschauung,* Davidson's critique of the plausibility of the former entails an analysis about the very idea of the latter as well. To understand the basis of Davidson's hesitation regarding conceptual schemes, an examination of his celebrated address, "On the Very Idea of a Conceptual Scheme," is in order.[39]

Davidson's "On the Very Idea of a Conceptual Scheme"

While the arguments of the essay itself are quite difficult, Davidson's overall goal is clear. In the introduction he states that his purpose is to scout "the intelligibility of claims that different languages or conceptual schemes 'divide up' or 'cope with' reality in importantly different ways."[40] Employing a general method of interpretation frustrates the notion that different people have different intellectual equipment with which they categorize the world. *Alternative* conceptual schemes, therefore, are really nonexistent. Furthermore, and even more importantly, Davidson states that "if we reject the idea of an uninterpreted source of evidence[,] no room is left for a dualism of scheme and content" (p. xviii). Without this dualism, conceptual relativism itself is defunct as well, for it is possible only if there are both multiple schemes and something waiting there to be schematized. For Davidson this does not mean a forfeiture of an objective world prior to human interpretation of it. Rather, he wants to show simply that "language is not a screen or filter through which our knowl-

38. Nicholas Rescher, "Conceptual Schemes," in *Midwest Studies in Philosophy,* vol. 5, ed. Peter A. French, Theodore E. Uehling, Jr., and Howard K. Wettstein (Minneapolis: University of Minnesota Press, 1980), pp. 330-31.

39. This paper by Davidson was presented originally as the Presidential Address before the seventieth annual meeting of the Eastern division of the American Philosophical Association in Atlanta, Ga., 28 December 1973. It is found in *Proceedings and Addresses of the American Philosophical Association* 47 (November 1973-74): 5-20, and also in Davidson's work, *Inquiries into Truth and Interpretation* (Oxford: Clarendon, 1984), 183-98. It is also available in *Relativism: Cognitive and Moral,* edited and introduction by Jack W. Meiland and Michael Krausz (Notre Dame, Ind.: University of Notre Dame Press, 1982), pp. 66-79. Barry Stroud has presented an argument similar to Davidson's in his "Conventionalism and the Indeterminacy of Translation," in *Words and Objections: Essays on the Work of W. V. Quine,* ed. Donald Davidson and J. Hintikka (Dordrecht: Reidel, 1969), pp. 89-96.

40. Davidson, "On the Very Idea of a Conceptual Scheme," in *Inquiries into Truth and Interpretation,* p. xviii; the page references in the text are to this volume.

edge of the world must pass." Thus his point is that "no sense can be made of the idea that the conceptual resources of different languages differ dramatically." If this is indeed the case, an important (almost realist) conclusion about the world can be reached; namely, that "the general outlines of our view of the world are correct; we individually and communally may go plenty wrong, but only on condition that in most large respects we are right." Hence, when it comes to language and ontology, "we are not just making a tour of our own picture of things: what we take there to be is pretty much what there is" (p. xix). Things are conceived such that there is a basic agreement among languages and conceptual schemes regarding what is really there.[41]

Davidson begins the body of the essay itself with a description of conceptual schemes and their offspring of conceptual relativism. He defines the former notion in words that correspond very closely to the idea of worldview, highlighting their alleged incommensurability. "Conceptual schemes . . . are ways of organizing experience: they are systems of categories that give form to the data of sensation; they are points of view from which individuals, cultures, or periods survey the passing scene. There may be no translating from one scheme to another, in which case the beliefs, desires, hopes and bits of knowledge that characterize one person have no true counterparts for the subscriber to another scheme."

The cognitive implication of these truly disparate conceptual schemes is conceptual relativism, the notion, as Davidson describes it, that "reality itself is relative to a scheme: what counts as real in one system may not in another" (p. 183). This is a "heady," "exotic," and even "exciting" doctrine, or at least it would be, Davidson avers, if it were truly intelligible or coherent. However, it is not, largely because of a debilitating paradox underlying it. "The dominant metaphor of conceptual relativism, that of differing points of view, seems to betray an underlying paradox. Different points of view make sense, but only if there is a common coordinate system on which to plot them; yet the existence of a common system belies the claim of dramatic incomparability. What we need, it seems to me, is some idea of the considerations that set the limits to the conceptual contrast" (p. 184).

The common system that constitutes the paradox of conceptual relativism and sets the limits to conceptual contrast is language and its translatability. On the basis of his "method of translation," Davidson shows that just as one language may be successfully translated into another, so conceptual schemes con-

---

41. One of Davidson's interlocutors who has deployed his arguments for his own purposes is Richard Rorty in his "The World Well Lost," in *Consequences of Pragmatism: Essays: 1972-1980* (Minneapolis: University of Minnesota Press, 1982), pp. 649-65.

ceived as languages may also be subject to intertranslatability as well. If so, then the radical differences between them collapse. Like language itself, conceptual schemes contain something unmistakably similar, thus reducing if not eliminating their radical equivocity. In another place he asserts that "If by conceptual relativism we mean the idea that conceptual schemes and moral systems, or the languages associated with them, can differ massively — to the extent of being mutually unintelligible or incommensurable, or forever beyond rational resolve — then I reject conceptual relativism."[42] The reason he rejects it is because of the analogy of language and the "criteria of translation" which establish the basis for the confluence of conceptual schemes. Davidson explains in these words: "We may accept the doctrine that associates having a language with having a conceptual scheme. The relation may be supposed to be this: if conceptual schemes differ, so do languages. But speakers of different languages may share a conceptual scheme provided there is a way of translating one language into the other. Studying the criteria of translation is therefore a way of focusing on criteria of identity for conceptual schemes" (p. 184).

Hence Davidson's strategy is to "identify conceptual schemes with languages, then, or better, allowing for the possibility that more than one language may express the same scheme, sets of intertranslatable languages" (p. 185). Thus, on the one hand, if languages can be translated into each other, then so can conceptual schemes. If both languages and conceptual schemes are mutually translatable, then they are not radically alternative but similar. On the other hand, if languages are not mutually translatable, then neither are conceptual schemes. They must be entirely incommensurate. However, since it is virtually impossible to make a case for the total or even partial failure of translatability between languages, so also is it impossible to make a case for mutually exclusive conceptual schemes. If so, conceptual relativism is negated ipso facto. Hence, what Davidson does in the balance of the essay is to "consider two kinds of cases that might be expected to arise: complete, and partial, failures of translatability" (p. 185). However, since he is able to show that there are neither complete nor partial failures of linguistic translation, then the very idea of *alternative* conceptual schemes collapses of necessity.

At the heart of Davidson's critique is what he calls the "third dogma" of empiricism, the dualism of conceptual scheme and empirical content, the very distinction valorized by C. I. Lewis mentioned above. Davidson's argument is essentially an extension of W. V. O. Quine's classic essay "Two Dogmas of Empiricism."[43] The first dogma of empiricism that Quine debunks is the tradi-

---

42. Davidson, "Myth of the Subjective," pp. 159-60.

43. W. V. O. Quine, "Two Dogmas of Empiricism," in *From a Logical Point of View* (Cambridge: Harvard University Press, 1953), pp. 20-46.

tional distinction between analytic and synthetic truths, an unempirical thesis of the empiricists grounded in a metaphysical article of faith, sustained only by sociological and circular reasoning. The second dogma Quine exposes as fraudulent is what he calls "reductionism"; namely, the attempt to verify the truth of a single, independent statement by experiential means in isolation from other propositions and beliefs. Contrary to this fundamental dictum of empiricism and analytic philosophy, Quine argues that the proof or disproof of a proposition depends on an entire belief system, including assumptions about what experiences should be accepted or rejected, how experiences should be interpreted, and what their implications should be. Furthermore, these two dogmas regarding the analytic-synthetic distinction and reductionism, according to Quine, "are indeed, at root identical" since the truth of synthetic statements depends on "extra-linguistic fact" or experience as in the case of reductionism, whereas in analytic statements "the linguistic component is all that matters."[44] Despite the demise of both these dogmas of empiricism, Davidson suggests that a third has arisen like a phoenix out of the ashes to take their place, the dogma of the dualism of conceptual scheme and empirical content. This new dualism, Davidson contends, "is the foundation of an empiricism shorn of the untenable dogmas of the analytic-synthetic distinction and reductionism — shorn, that is, of the unworkable idea that we can uniquely allocate empirical content sentence by sentence" (p. 189). Of course, this dualism of scheme and content is a dualism that engenders conceptual relativism, and Davidson sets himself to the task of demonstrating the frailty of the former thesis. As he puts it, "I want to urge that this second dualism of scheme and content, of organizing system and something waiting to be organized, cannot be made intelligible and defensible. It is itself a dogma of empiricism, the third dogma" (p. 189).[45] As such, it is destined to fail like the previous two. Indeed, because of the intrinsic connection that exists between analytic truths and conceptual schemes, and synthetic truths and empirical content, the failure of the empiricists to sustain a genuine distinction between the analytic and synthetic truths likewise makes it extremely difficult to sustain a separation between conceptual scheme and empirical content. In short, if the analytic-synthetic distinction has collapsed, so the conceptual scheme–empirical content dichotomy will flounder as well. Despite the demise of the first two dogmas of empiricism, the third has somehow survived, as a number of capable scholars including Whorf, Kuhn, Feyerabend, and even Quine himself have articulated cogent defenses of the scheme-content

44. Quine, "Two Dogmas of Empiricism," p. 41.

45. For Quine's response to Davidson's proposal, see his essay "On the Very Idea of a Third Dogma," in *Theories and Things* (Cambridge: Harvard University Press, 1981), pp. 38-42.

dualism, as Davidson demonstrates (pp. 190-91). Nonetheless, he will not rest content until this third dogma concerning conceptual schemes encounters the same fate as the first two.

Davidson's move against the scheme-content distinction takes the form of an assault on the various metaphors used to describe this relationship (pp. 191-95).[46] In the first metaphor, conceptual schemes or languages are said to *organize, systematize,* or *divide up* the stream of experience, reality, the universe, the world, or nature. But according to Davidson, one cannot organize a single object unless that object contains or consists of other objects. For example, someone who organizes a closet does not organize the "closet" but the things in it. However, any two conceptual schemes or languages which organize the same items (in the world) must have a common ontology with concepts that individuate the same objects. Thus, if alternative languages organize and talk about the same entities, this allows for their intertranslatability and hence the breakdown of alternative conceptual schemes or languages. Furthermore, a background of generally successful translation provides a way to understand any translation breakdowns which must be merely local. The bottom line of Davidson's argument is this: the metaphor of languages organizing items in the world entails translatability into familiar idioms, and fails to sustain the notion of alternative conceptual schemes.

In the second metaphor, conceptual schemes and languages are said to *fit, predict, account for,* or *face* the tribunal of experience, the passing show, surface irritations, sensory promptings, sense data, or the given. Here when the move is made from talk of *organization* to talk of *fitting,* there is also the move, according to Davidson, from the referential apparatus of language to whole sentences. Sentences, rather than terms, predict, cope, deal with things, and face the tribunal of experience as a united body of propositions. However, to say that the sentences of some theory fit all the possible sensory evidence (actual, possible, present, future) seems to say little more than that the theory is true. If both theory A and theory B fit the evidence and are therefore true, and yet they belong to two different conceptual schemes or languages, then presumably translation between theories A and B would fail. Both theories would be true in their own context, but they would not be intertranslatable. Yet the concept of truth, according to Tarski's test of theories of truth, cannot be divorced from translation. Truth, in other words, entails translation. As Davidson puts it, "Since [Tarski's] Convention T embodies our best intuition as to how the concept of

---

46. This section is partially based on Robert Kraut, "The Third Dogma," in *Truth and Interpretation: Perspectives on the Philosophy of Donald Davidson,* ed. Ernest LePore (Cambridge, Mass.: Basil Blackwell, 1986), pp. 400-403.

truth is used, there does not seem to be much hope for a test that a conceptual scheme is radically different from ours if that test depends on the assumption that we can divorce the notion of truth from that of translation" (p. 195). Hence the metaphor of "fitting" either sacrifices this notion of truth as entailing translation, or it simply sets forth the routine notion that certain theories fit the evidence and are therefore true. In either case, both metaphors of *organizing* and of *fitting* suggest the possibility of translation of one language or conceptual scheme to another, and if so, the third dogma of empiricism, that of alternative conceptual schemes and empirical content, breaks down. Yet as Davidson concludes, this does not mean the loss of either the world or object truth. Rather, it reestablishes contact with both.

> In giving up dependence on the concept of an uninterpreted reality, something outside all schemes and science, we do not relinquish the notion of objective truth — quite the contrary. Given the dogma of a dualism of scheme and reality, we get conceptual relativity, and truth relative to a scheme. Without the dogma, this kind of relativity goes by the board. Of course truth of sentences remains relative to language, but that is as objective as can be. In giving up the dualism of scheme and world, we do not give up the world, but reestablish unmediated touch with the familiar objects whose antics make our sentences and opinions true or false. (p. 198)

In this final statement in his essay, Davidson alludes to his larger project, which in all likelihood motivated this present one as a subset. He seems to be after bigger game than purely and simply seeking to question the very idea of conceptual schemes. His deeper agenda of which these arguments are a part is to challenge the modernist assumption of the nature of the self and to transform the very relationship of human subjects to the cosmos. This is somewhat indicated in the above quotation, in which Davidson says his efforts are devoted to the recovery of a certain kind of "objective truth" and of "reestablishing unmediated touch" with familiar objects in the world. This would require a considerable shift in philosophical anthropology as well as a fresh understanding of the nature of human knowing.

In his essay "The Myth of the Subjective," Davidson states that the "deep mistake" of the modernist division between uninterpreted experience and an organizing conceptual scheme was "born of the essentially incoherent picture of the mind as a passive but critical spectator of an inner show."[47] This incoherent picture of the mind, of course, has its roots in Descartes, and is not only the defining feature of modernity but also the progenitor of the majority of mod-

---

47. Davidson, "Myth of the Subjective," p. 171.

ern philosophical problems, indeed, problems of greater magnitude than that of the benighted notion of conceptual schemes themselves. In something of a retraction, Davidson asserts that "Instead of saying it is the scheme-content dichotomy that has dominated and defined the problems of modern philosophy, then, one could as well say it is how the dualism of the objective and the subjective has been conceived. For these dualisms have a common origin: a concept of mind with its private states and objects." What is needed, and is indeed in the process of development, in Davidson's estimation, is "a radically revised view of the relation of mind and the world."[48] In this sense Davidson is something of a forerunner in his rejection of the pervasive modernist anthropology, and in his call for a new way of relating human subject and external object.

What Davidson is saying is a clear echo of Martin Heidegger: the modern age under the dominion of the Cartesian model of the mind and representationalism has become the age not only of the world picture but also of the conceptual scheme, though, for all practical purposes, they are one and the same thing. As J. E. Malpas keenly observes, "To some extent, the Davidsonian argument against the idea of a conceptual scheme is paralleled by Heidegger's much broader attack on what he calls the idea of the 'world picture' . . . the world conceived and grasped as picture."[49] As we have seen, for Heidegger, when the world is conceived and grasped as objective picture, the notion of *Weltanschauung* becomes prominent. Similarly for Davidson, when the world is presented as something waiting to be parsed by an organizing system, the very idea of a conceptual scheme emerges. For both Davidson and Heidegger, however, the idea of autonomous human beings standing over against an objective cosmos in an attempt to grasp its nature on the basis of the language and concepts of the subjective mind was contrary to essential human nature and the normal way of encountering and being in the world. On this score Frank Farrell has captured nicely the mutual concerns and clear analogies that obtain between Davidson and Heidegger.

> Heidegger, like Davidson, is trying to rethink the structure of subjectivity that led to the problems of modern philosophy. He rejects the picture of a subjective determining power that, from a position of independence, constructs or orders or projects its patterns upon a world of objects. Thinking is what it is only through already "belonging to" the world and through letting it manifest its character. It is only in "being toward" the world, in being situated in its surroundings, that I as thinker or experiencer have

48. Davidson, "Myth of the Subjective," p. 163.

49. J. E. Malpas, *Donald Davidson and the Mirror of Meaning: Holism, Truth, Interpretation* (Cambridge: Cambridge University Press, 1992), p. 197.

any real content to my activity; and language, rather than being the embodiment of some conceptual scheme or other, is an "openness" in which things themselves are making their appearance. We do not have to work to bring an alienated subjectivity back in touch with things, because it is by its very nature as subjectivity always in touch with them.[50]

Heidegger and Davidson both make convincing cases on similar grounds that there is something to the substance of modernist anthropology with its objectivist epistemology and autonomous orientation that has produced both the age of the world picture and the conceptual scheme. Heidegger, of course, wanted to replace the former notion with some kind of authentic, existential communion with Being, and Davidson would seek to substitute the latter construct with a generally holistic theory of knowledge and meaning. To draw upon Heidegger and Davidson and tie their arguments to present concerns, it seems possible to assert that the concept of worldview, or *Weltanschauung*, itself is a peculiarly modern product. Since this notion is primarily concerned with a fundamental understanding of the nature and operations of the world and all things in it by a subjective interpreter, it is a concept deeply rooted in the soil of modern philosophy. How have Davidson's critics responded to his suggestions?

A Response to Davidson's Critique of Conceptual Schemes

Davidson has not been without his critics, of course, and each of them in one way or another has been forced to address the issue of the viability of the scheme-content distinction.[51] Kraut makes a very interesting comparison when he observes that "The scheme-content distinction is not unlike the 'inside-outside' distinction: it's a genuine distinction hard to get along without; but it hardly commits us to the existence of a region necessarily excluded from everyone's living space."[52] Analogously, the dichotomy between conceptual scheme and empirical content is also bona fide, and in fact may be inescapable given that self-conscious, language-speaking human beings by necessity occupy a

---

50. Frank B. Farrell, *Subjectivity, Realism, and Postmodernism — the Recovery of the World* (Cambridge: Cambridge University Press, 1994), p. 133.

51. Prominent responses to Davidson include Kraut, pp. 398-416; Quine, "On the Very Idea," pp. 38-42; Rescher, pp. 323-45; Chris Swoyer, "True For," in *Relativism: Cognitive and Moral*, pp. 81-108; Alasdair MacIntyre, "Relativism, Power, and Philosophy," in *Relativism: Interpretation and Confrontation*, pp. 182-204.

52. Kraut, p. 414.

world and must make sense of it. Though scheme and content remain distinct, yet they are never separated, just like inside-outside, the two sides of the same coin, or, to change the metaphor, the two wings of a single airplane. Kraut consequently believes that the notion of a conceptual scheme with its images of slicing, organizing, and carving up the world should not be regarded as a misguided epistemological theory. The content of a conceptual scheme will indeed correspond, according to innate human proclivities, to the favored ontology of the interpreter. He states his case in these words: "The possibility of alternative conceptual schemes corresponds to the possibility of non-trivial expressive and discriminate disparities between theories. Such disparities need not entail global translation breakdowns; but they nonetheless have fairly interesting ontological consequences, consequences of the sort that schemers everywhere are trying to capture with their metaphors."[53]

Indeed, the conceptual schemes by which human beings define reality and out of which they think, live, interpret, and experience the world are, as George Lakoff and Mark Johnson demonstrate, "very much a matter of metaphor."[54] The alterity of conceptual schemes is thus exposed in the diverse content invested in these "metaphors we live by" which are exclusive to a paradigm and incapable of direct translatability.

Nicholas Rescher, in a complementary fashion, believes that Davidson has made too much of the claim that translatability into one's own language is the essential criterion of something being a language, and thus the primary indicator for the presence of a conceptual scheme. Rather, insistence should be placed only on the weaker requirement of interpretability. "There is good reason, however, to think that the whole focus on actual *translation* is misguided. The key category in this area is surely not *translation* but *interpretation*. What counts for 'their having a language' is not (necessarily) that we can literally *translate* what they say into our language but that we be able to *interpret* their sayings — to make some sort of intelligible sense of them through paraphrase, 'explanation,' or the like."[55]

Rescher argues that to insist on the translatability into one's own language as the criterion for the presence of a conceptual scheme frustrates any possibility of ascertaining how the genuine differences between schemata actually

---

53. Kraut, p. 415.

54. George Lakoff and Mark Johnson, *Metaphors We Live By* (Chicago: University of Chicago Press, 1980), p. 3. Stephen C. Pepper has described the role of "root metaphors" as an approach to worldviewing in his *World Hypotheses: A Study in Evidence* (Berkeley: University of California Press, 1970).

55. Rescher, p. 326; the page references in the text in the remainder of this section are to Rescher's article, "Conceptual Schemes."

work. As he says, "For such schemes differ precisely where and just to the extent that the resources of paraphrase and circumlocution [i.e., interpretation] become necessary" (p. 327). For him, then, conceptual schemes do indeed differ and differ radically, for "it is not just that one [scheme] says things differently but that one says altogether different things." He elaborates as follows: "What is involved with diverse schemes is a different way of conceptualizing facts — or rather *purported* facts — as to how matters stand in the world. Different conceptual schemes embody different theories, and not just different theories about 'the same things' . . . but different theories about different things. To move from one conceptual scheme to another is in some way to change the subject. It is not a quarrel about the same old issues" (p. 331).

Thus Rescher contends that alternative conceptual schemes are indeed conceptually incommensurate, that key themes, questions, and issues in one scheme are entirely unavailable in another. Hence his central thesis is that "the difference of different conceptual frameworks lies not so much in points of disagreements . . . as in points of mutual incomprehension, in their lack of mutual contact. . . . [Thus] the key to scheme-differentiation lies in the nonoverlap of theses — the fact that what can be said by one is simply outside the range of the other" (p. 333). Therefore alternative conceptual schemes are a reality, and can be identified not by way of mutual translation from one to another, as Davidson proposed, but because of mutual interpretative ability in such a way that the true differences between schemata might become fully manifest.

Conceptual schemes, it seems, along with worldviews, must be an inescapable part of the intellectual furniture of the modern world. "There is, after all, something a bit eccentric about rejecting the idea of alternative conceptual schemes — something that smacks of the unrealism of one who closes one's mind toward what people are actually saying and doing" (p. 324). And what people are thinking and doing is conceiving of conceptual schemes by which to parse the world. However, the meaning of these meaning systems has changed significantly in the recent move from the modern to the postmodern era.

"Worldview" and Postmodernity

In the premodern period, there was substantial confidence on the part of the average Westerner, the Christian in particular, to obtain a comprehensive view of the universe, its facts as well as its values, based on God and his self-revelation in the Bible. In the modern period the center of gravity shifted from God to man, from Scripture to science, from revelation to reason in the confidence that human beings, beginning with themselves and their own methods of knowing, could gain an understanding of the world, at least its facts if not its values. In the postmodern period, confidence in humanity as an objective, omnicompetent knower has been smashed, destroying any hopes of ascertaining the truth about the universe, its facts or its values. The result has been what Jean-François Lyotard has famously called an "incredulity toward meta-narratives,"[56] or to paraphrase, a disbelief that any worldview or large-scale interpretation of reality is true and ought to be believed and promulgated. What remains for the postmodern denizen is a plethora of socially and linguistically constructed meaning systems, each unprivileged, nonhegemenous, and thoroughly tolerated. To play with Heidegger's lecture title, postmodernism is an age of world *pictures*, and is characterized by "an incommensurable plurality of *ways of speech*."[57] The resultant pluralism *in extremis*, as Griffioen, Mouw, and Marshall explain, has led to the advent of a postworldview era. "Such stark pluralism can no longer be described as a *Streit der Weltanschauungen* [conflict of worldviews], for worldviews can conflict only if they compete as [rational] accounts of the same 'world.' In the extreme pluralism of . . . [postmodernity], there is no single 'world' — there are as many worlds as there are worldviews. It is possible . . . that we are now on the threshold of the end of the age of worldviews."[58]

Does the advent of postmodernism signal the death of worldviews?[59] To respond to this question, I will examine several important aspects of postmodern thought as these bring our present exploration of the philosophical history of *Weltanschauung* to a close.

Jacques Derrida's Deconstruction of Logocentrism and the Metaphysics of Presence

If worldview schemes may be associated with a language aimed at an accurate representation of reality, then they become a prime target for Jacques Derrida's (b. 1930) program of deconstruction. This undertaking aims at language (a

---

56. Jean-François Lyotard, *The Postmodern Condition: A Report on Knowledge,* trans. Geoff Bennington and Brian Massumi, foreword by Fredric Jameson, Theory and History of Literature, vol. 10 (Minneapolis: University of Minnesota Press, 1984), p. xxiv.

57. William Rowe, "Society after the Subject, Philosophy after the Worldview," in *Stained Glass: Worldviews and Social Science,* ed. Paul A. Marshall, Sander Griffioen, and Richard J. Mouw, Christian Studies Today (Lanham, Md.: University Press of America, 1989), p. 174.

58. Marshall, Griffioen, and Mouw, introduction to *Stained Glass,* p. 12.

59. Howard Snyder, "Postmodernism: The Death of Worldviews?" in his *EarthCurrents: The Struggle for the World's Soul* (Nashville: Abingdon, 1995), pp. 213-30.

realist theory of language in particular), and it casts serious doubt about the ability of language to represent reality accurately and objectively. As Walter Truett Anderson points out, deconstructionists like Derrida want to show "how difficult it is to tell the truth."[60] Thus worldviews, once deconstructed, are reduced to a self-referential system of linguistic signifiers dispossessed of any authentic metaphysical, epistemological, or moral import.

Derrida focuses his attack on a notion foundational to the Western intellectual tradition that he terms "logocentrism." As the name suggests, words *(logos)* have assumed center stage in Occidental theories of speech and writing as the reliable vehicles of meaning and truth. Words as signifiers, according to this esteemed tradition, refer to an *ad extra* reality beyond the symbolic apparatus of texts. That *ad extra* reality serves as the foundation and final point of reference for all meaning and truth through the instrumentality of language. Barring skepticism, there has been considerable confidence in the human mind to ascertain the nature of objective reality and to communicate its essence through the medium of words. In commenting on Derrida's attack on this thesis, Terry Eagleton explains how the Western mind has been perennially logocentric and has maintained a persistent search for an ultimate that would serve as the secure basis of all human thought, language, and experience.

> It has yearned for the sign which will give meaning to all others — the "transcendental signifier" — and for the anchoring, unquestionable meaning to which all our signs can be seen to point (the "transcendental signified"). A great number of candidates for this role — God, the Idea, the World Spirit, the Self, substance, matter and so on — have thrust themselves forward from time to time. Since each of these concepts hopes to found our whole system of thought and language, it must itself be beyond that system, untainted by its play of linguistic differences. It cannot be implicated in the very languages which it attempts to order and anchor.[61]

The search for a language bearing the freight of the ultimate — the "transcendental signifier" — naturally implies the existence of the ultimate itself — the "transcendental signified." Western logocentrism, in other words, is closely juxtaposed to what Derrida calls the "metaphysics of presence," that is, the

60. Walter Truett Anderson, *Reality Isn't What It Used to Be: Theatrical Politics, Ready-to-Wear Religion, Global Myths, Primitive Chic, and Other Wonders of the Postmodern World* (San Francisco: Harper and Row, 1990), p. 90.

61. Terry Eagleton, *Literary Theory* (Minneapolis: University of Minnesota Press, 1983), p. 131.

presence or actuality of something metaphysically real. As Brian Walsh and J. Richard Middleton explain it, "what is assumed to be present in our conceptual systems of truth is seen as a real *given* which exists prior to language and thought and which we have adequately grasped by our language and thought. That is, the Western intellectual tradition . . . claims to reflect and represent reality so accurately that it simply *mirrors* the way things really are."[62] This accurately represented metaphysical presence serves as the coordinating center of conceptual structures, and thereby limits philosophical play with alternative possibilities. As Derrida explains, "The function of this center was not only to orient, balance, and organize the structure . . . but above all to make sure that the organizing principle would limit what we might call the play of the structure."[63]

This entire Western metaphysical tradition — classical, medieval, and modern — with its confidence in language to mimic or imitate reality truthfully, is the very thing that Derrida seeks to overturn. In company with radical Nietzschean perspectivism, Derrida discards the doctrines of logocentrism and the metaphysics of presence. He remains unconvinced that human beings can access reality linguistically, or that knowledge of a prelinguistic, preconceptual reality is even possible. If there is no center or no accessible center, no "God, the Idea, the World Spirit, the Self, substance, matter and so on," then everything is language and the free play of signifiers and their interpretation. Nothing exists outside the "text." "Reading . . . cannot legitimately transgress the text toward something other than it, toward the referent (a reality that is metaphysical, historical, psychobiographical, etc.) or toward a signifier outside the text whose content could take place, could have taken place outside of language, that is to say, in the sense that we give to that word, outside of writing in general. . . . There is nothing outside of the text."[64]

If language is incapable of the mimetic representation of a final truth or reality but exists only as a self-referential system, then it is arbitrary. The meaning of terms is a function of the place they assume in a linguistic system. There is a free play of possibilities on such a linguistic field where few if any boundaries delimit the kinds of meanings or interpretations readers may find in or attribute to texts. Words are slippery objects, endlessly ambiguous and virtually impossible to define. According to Derrida, since words lack fixed or concrete

---

62. J. Richard Middleton and Brian J. Walsh, *Truth Is Stranger Than It Used to Be: Biblical Faith in a Postmodern Age* (Downers Grove, Ill.: InterVarsity, 1995), p. 33.

63. Jacques Derrida, *Writing and Difference*, trans. Alan Bass (Chicago: University of Chicago Press, 1976), p. 158.

64. Jacques Derrida, *Of Grammatology*, trans. Gayatri Chakravorty Spivak (Baltimore: Johns Hopkins University Press, 1976), p. 158.

definitions such that "meaning" only surfaces in the way that words *differ* from one another in the dynamics of the language system, then the possibility of any final signification or interpretation must be endlessly *deferred*.[65]

Now the upshot of all this is that what Western thinkers thought to be metaphysically *present*, namely, primordial reality accessed via language, is in fact metaphysically *absent*. Belief systems, which purportedly put their adherents in touch with the real world, are nothing but fictions of purely human construction. If no "transcendental signified" as the ultimate metaphysical reference point is available, then only the endless manipulation of alleged "transcendental signifiers" is possible. In addition to extending "the play of significations infinitely,"[66] deconstruction leads to the overturning and displacement of conceptual schemes as well as the "nondiscursive forces" and "nonconceptual orders" in which they are devised and sustained.

> Deconstruction cannot limit itself or proceed immediately to a neutralization: it must . . . practice an overturning of the classical opposition and a general displacement of the system. It is only on this condition that deconstruction will provide itself the means with which to intervene in the field of oppositions that it criticizes, which is also a field of nondiscursive forces. Each concept, moreover, belongs to a systematic chain, and itself constitutes a system of predicates. There is no metaphysical concept in and of itself. There is a work — metaphysical or not — on conceptual systems. Deconstruction does not consist in passing from one concept to another, but in overturning and displacing a conceptual order, as well as the nonconceptual order with which the conceptual order is articulated.[67]

This means nothing short of the exposure of the entire Western intellectual and cultural heritage for what it really is (at least according to Derrida), namely, a hoax. If we should ask, What kind of epistemic and metaphysical value do the diverse conceptual schemes possess? What is the status of the worldviews and cultural systems that have animated Western thought for two millennia? the answer would have to be: the process of deconstruction has revealed to us that they are nothing but the constructions of our own making, even though we have attributed them to the natural order of things and forgotten that we ourselves have manufactured them. We are the architects of our world, the craftsmen of our own reality. Thus deconstruction is explicitly de-

---

65. Derrida, *Of Grammatology,* p. 52. See also his *Margins of Philosophy,* trans. Alan Bass (Chicago: University of Chicago Press, 1982), pp. 1-27.

66. Derrida, *Writing and Difference,* p. 280.

67. Derrida, *Of Grammatology,* pp. 329-30.

signed to disabuse us of these "reifications,"[68] a concept central to postmodern discourse which Peter Berger and Thomas Luckmann have carefully examined and brought to prominence.

Peter Berger and Thomas Luckmann's Concept of "Reification"

In their discussion of "society as an objective reality," and on the basis of their observation of the historical variability of institutionalization, Berger and Luckmann raise the important question regarding the manner in which the institutional order is objectified: "To what extent is an institutional order, or any part of it, apprehended as a non-human facticity?"[69] This is the question about the "reification of social reality," which they define in the following manner:

> Reification is the apprehension of human phenomena as if they were things, that is, in non-human or possibly superhuman terms. Another way of saying this is that reification is the apprehension of the products of human activity as if they were something else than human products — such as facts of nature, results of cosmic laws, or manifestations of divine will. Reification implies that man is capable of forgetting his own authorship of the human world, and further, that the dialectic between man, the producer, and his products is lost to consciousness. The reified world is, by definition, a dehumanized world. It is experienced by man as a strange facticity, an *opus alienum* over which he has no control rather than as the *opus proprium* of his own productive activity.[70]

As a modality of consciousness, or way of thinking about things, reification is the objectification of the human world *in extremis*, such that "the objectivated world loses its comprehensibility as a human enterprise and becomes fixated as a non-human, non-humanizable, inert facticity." Human meanings are no longer recognized as things that make or create worlds, but are seen as embedded in the nature of things. The irony is that people are capable of creating cultural and social realities that in turn deny them and their authorship. Can the fact of this authorship or fabrication of a world be remembered and even reversed? "The decisive question," say Berger and Luckmann, "is

68. Middleton and Walsh, p. 33.
69. Peter L. Berger and Thomas Luckmann, *The Social Construction of Reality: A Treatise in the Sociology of Knowledge* (New York: Doubleday, 1966; Anchor Books, 1967), p. 88.
70. Berger and Luckmann, p. 89.

whether [one] still retains the awareness that, however objectivated, the social world was made by men — and, therefore, can be remade by them."[71] The following line from George Bernard Shaw's *Caesar and Cleopatra* speaks poignantly of one who has unfortunately lost this awareness: "Pardon him, Theodotus: He is a barbarian, and thinks that the customs of his tribe and island are the laws of nature."[72] This pitiful barbarian, however, is representative of the universal human tendency toward reification, which itself betrays a deep aspiration for security and a longing for truth.

Berger and Luckmann point out that both an institutional order as a whole and segments of it (e.g., marriage) can be understood in reified terms. Social roles are also prime candidates for reification (e.g., husband, father, general, archbishop, chairman of the board, gangster, hangman, Jew). Of particular importance for present purposes is the fact that Berger and Luckmann assert that reification is common in regard to both pretheoretical and theoretical constructs. Pretheoretical reification transpires primarily in the mind of the person on the street in whom the original apprehension of the social order is highly reified both ontologically and historically. "That's just the way things are and how they happened." Complex theoretical systems are also reified as absolute even though they may have their source in pretheoretical reifications well ensconced in this or that social situation.[73] Thus there is something that people characteristically do after they have created institutions, customs, social roles, mythologies, laws, and belief systems: they forget they created them, and live in a world they never knew they made.[74]

 Much of postmodernism — Derridean deconstruction in particular — is geared to the task of enabling individuals and societies to realize that they have created their own worlds, and that there is nothing transcendent, permanent, natural, or supernatural about them. It is an iconoclasm of the first order. "By uncovering our reifications[,] deconstruction attempts not to destroy in any nihilistic sense but to play a positive therapeutic role in the culture of late (and decomposing) modernity. We are to face up to our constructions and to own them as such."[75] According to Berger and Luckmann, this de-reification of consciousness external to oneself is a function of a partial de-reification of consciousness internal to oneself, an event that typically occurs only late in both

71. Berger and Luckmann, p. 89.

72. Quoted as an epigram in Anderson, *Reality*, p. vi.

73. Berger and Luckmann, pp. 89-90.

74. Walter Truett Anderson, ed., *The Truth about the Truth: De-Confusing and Re-Constructing the Postmodern World* (New York: Putnam, a Jeremy P. Tarcher/Putnam Book, 1995), p. 36.

75. Middleton and Walsh, p. 34.

cultural history and personal biography.[76] No wonder, then, that whole cultures and individual people fail to recognize the fact and fallacy of their reifications until later on in history and personal experience.

To the extent, then, that worldviews are associated with confidence in the ability of language to communicate truth about a reality that is really there, Derrida's program of the deconstruction of logocentrism and his critique of the metaphysics of presence would seem to put such worldviews out of business. None of them mirror reality. Therefore, in a postmodern context, all intellectual constructs, including worldviews, must be recognized, according to Berger and Luckmann, for what they truly are, namely, the creations of human beings suffering from severe cases of intellectual amnesia, ever forgetful of their own cultural handiwork. All worldviews, therefore, must be recognized as reifications, that is, as humanly fabricated, self-contained conceptual systems that in the final analysis are untethered to any external reality or objective truth. And not only that, but as pseudoknowledge constructs with a deep history, they also serve as instruments of power and social oppression.

Michel Foucault, Episteme, Genealogy, and Power

Michel Foucault (1926-84), rightly understood as "the greatest of Nietzsche's modern disciples," was an historian, philosopher, literary critic and even more, but certainly not in the modern sense.[77] The objective of his exhaustive investigations, stated in his own words, was "to create a history of the different modes by which, in our culture, human beings are made subjects."[78] The plethora of cultural forces at play in shaping a human life seem to be his primary object of investigation. As Edward Said explains, "he researched and revealed technologies of knowledge and self which beset society, made it governable, controllable, normal, even as these technologies developed their own uncontrollable drives, without limit or rationale." Additionally, on the critical level as the "philosopher of the death of man," Foucault "dissolved the [modern] anthropological models of identity and subjecthood underlying research in the humanistic and social sciences."[79] Foucault made

---

76. Berger and Luckmann, p. 90.

77. Edward W. Said, "Michel Foucault, 1926-1984," in *After Foucault: Humanistic Knowledge, Postmodern Challenges*, ed. Jonathan Arac (New Brunswick, N.J.: Rutgers University Press, 1988), p. 1.

78. Michel Foucault, afterword to *Michel Foucault: Beyond Structuralism and Hermeneutics*, by Hubert L. Dreyfus and Paul Rabinow (Chicago: University of Chicago Press, 1982), p. 208.

79. Said, pp. 10-11.

it clear that the way people functioned in society was not because they were free and independent Cartesian egos, solitary artists, gifted individuals, or trained professionals, but because of the power of ideologies, disciplines, discourses, and *epistemes* that specified the a priori rules that ordered the thought, speech, and behavior of all people. Foucault devised rules about such rules and exposed them for the power mechanisms they were. About these knowledge regimes, especially as they were embodied in such institutions as the clinic, the asylum, and the history of sexuality, Foucault brooked no illusions.[80] What role did the concept of worldview play in his analysis?

The notion of *episteme* is crucial to Foucault's thought, and it seems at least initially to bear a family resemblance to worldview. Pamela Major-Poetzl suggests as much when she writes that "The terms *discourse* and *episteme* are frequently regarded as idiosyncratic expressions for the more common terms *discipline* and *world view*."[81] There seems to be textual support for this contention, especially in *The Order of Things,* where the exposition of the classical *episteme* has been interpreted by many readers as a basic and fundamental category underlying the intellectual productions of the seventeenth and eighteenth centuries. For example, Foucault writes: "In any given culture and at any given moment, there is always only one *episteme* that defines the conditions of possibility of all knowledge, whether expressed in a theory or silently in a practice."[82] For Foucault the edifice of knowledge is a complex structure, and an *episteme,* which is analogous to a worldview, is a part of that deep complexity. In *The Archaeology of Knowledge* Foucault affirms that an "episteme may be suspected of being something like a world-view, a slice of history common to all branches of knowledge, which imposes on each one the same norms and postulates, a general stage of reason, a certain structure of thought that the men of a particular period cannot escape — a great body of legislation written once and for all by some anonymous hand."[83] This sentence is interesting, for it contains Foucault's own description of both an *episteme* and a worldview, given their close association. Both entail an inescapable set of rules and regulations, a way of

---

80. Said, p. 10.

81. Pamela Major-Poetzl, *Michel Foucault's Archaeology of Western Culture* (Chapel Hill: University of North Carolina Press, 1983), p. 23. David Carr, *Interpreting Husserl: Critical and Comparative Studies* (Dordrecht: Martinus Nijhoff, 1987), pp. 220-21, believes *epistemes* are equivalent to conceptual schemes or worldviews, though he recognizes that Foucault himself denies their isomorphism to worldviews or a cultural zeitgeist.

82. Michel Foucault, *The Order of Things: An Archaeology of the Human Sciences,* World of Man (New York: Random House, 1970; Vintage Books, 1973), p. 168.

83. Michel Foucault, *The Archaeology of Knowledge,* trans. A. M. Sheridan Smith (New York: Random House, Pantheon Books, 1972), p. 15.

reasoning, a pattern of thinking, a body of laws that generate and govern all aspects of formal knowing.

At the same time, Foucault confuses matters to some extent when he says that an *episteme* as a significant cognitive layer should not be identified with a worldview. In his introduction to *The Archaeology of Knowledge,* he admits that the absence of methodological sophistication in *The Order of Things* may have given the impression that his "analyses were conducted in terms of cultural totality."[84] This would be a mistake, however. In the subsequent English edition of *The Order of Things,* Foucault states that the original purpose of the book was not to be "an analysis of Classicism in general, nor a search for a *Weltanschauung,* but a strictly 'regional' study."[85] Corroboratively, in *The Archaeology of Knowledge* — which he deems in part to be a corrective to previous works, including *The Order of Things* — Foucault is clear in stating that his "aim is most decidedly not to use the categories of cultural totalities (whether world-views, ideal types, the particular spirit of an age) in order to impose on history, despite itself, the forms of structural analysis."[86] Thus Foucault distances *episteme* from *Weltanschauung* as an aspect of his historical methodology. His quest to identify the former as localized subterranean layers of belief must not be confused with comprehensive explanations of reality.

Despite this lexical ambiguity, it is this primordial and determinative field of the *episteme* that Foucault is most anxious to bring to light, and to do so not by means of typical historical study, but rather by means of his famed methods of "archaeology" and "genealogy." "Rather than focusing on *what* was known (history) or *why* knowledge is possible (epistemology), he investigated *how* fields of knowledge are structured (archaeology)."[87] He not only wanted to know the structures of knowledge, but also their ancestry (genealogy). Inspired by Friedrich Nietzsche's *Genealogy of Morals,* Foucault tentatively defined the notion as "the union of erudite knowledge and local memories which allows us to establish a historical knowledge of struggles and to make use of this knowledge tactically today." By means of this genealogical investigation, subjected knowledges would be identified, released, and brought into play.[88] Though in due course Foucault's deployment of archaeological description was eventually

---

84. Foucault, *The Archaeology of Knowledge,* p. 16.

85. Foucault, *The Order of Things,* p. x.

86. Foucault, *The Archaeology of Knowledge,* p. 15.

87. Major-Poetzl, p. 21.

88. Michel Foucault, *Power/Knowledge: Selected Interviews and Other Writings, 1972-1977,* ed. Colin Gordon, trans. Colin Gordon, Leo Marshall, John Mepham, and Kate Soper (New York: Pantheon Books, 1980), pp. 83, 85.

surpassed by genealogy, nonetheless he sought to keep them functioning in tandem.[89]

The archaeological and genealogical investigation of *epistemes* is intimately bound up with Foucault's reflections on the subject of power. He sets before his readers a view of the world in which human beings are trapped within language structures and knowledge regimes with no possibility of escape. Every human discourse is a power play, every social arrangement oppressive, and every cultural setting tyrannical. In this Foucaultian universe, there are no privileged or transcendent discourses unencumbered by the relativities of history or the dynamics of domination. The world is suffused with the will to power, and no social relationships are uncorrupted by it.[90] All discursive practices imply a specific power politics and epistemic despotism, for as Foucault explains, "truth is not outside of power or itself lacking in power."

> Truth is a thing of this world: it is produced only by virtue of multiple forms of constraint. And it induces the effects of power. Each society has its régime of truth, its "general politics" of truth: that is, the types of discourse which it accepts and makes function as true; the mechanisms and instances which enable one to distinguish true and false statements, the means by which each is sanctioned; the techniques and procedures accorded value in the acquisition of truth; the status of those who are charged with saying what counts as true.[91]

Knowledge is also linked to power because of its connection with discourse that creates a world. The world which is created by discourse is a world of institutions, knowledge, and practices that the present system of power finds advantageous. Knowledge is indeed power for the powerful. Foucault therefore recommends dropping the idea that knowledge is somehow independent of some stratagem and serves the common good. Rather, he make this alternative confession:

> We should admit rather that power produces knowledge . . . ; that power and knowledge directly imply one another; that there is no power relation without the correlative constitution of a field of knowledge, nor any knowledge that does not presuppose and constitute the same power relations. These "power-knowledge relations" are to be analysed, therefore, not on the basis of a subject of knowledge who is or is not free in relation

---

89. Foucault, *The Archaeology of Knowledge*, p. 234.
90. Sheldon S. Wolin, "On the Theory and Practice of Power," in *After Foucault*, p. 186.
91. Foucault, *Power/Knowledge*, p. 131.

to the power system, but, on the contrary the subject who knows, the objects to be known and the modalities of knowledge must be regarded as so many effects of these fundamental implications of power-knowledge and their historical transformations. In short, it is not the activity of the subject of knowledge, useful or resistant to power, but power-knowledge, the processes and struggles that traverse it and of which it is made up, that determines the forms and possible domains of knowledge.[92]

Worldviews as epistemic constructs must also be implicated in the power-knowledge relation. As visions of life and reality and determinative of ideas, values, and actions, they are not to be merely understood as neutral conceptual frameworks, but exist in service to some sociopolitical agenda and bastion of power (say, theism for the church, naturalism for Marxism and Darwinism, etc.). In skeptical Foucaultian terms, worldviews are merely the linguistic constructions of a power elite. They are the facades of an absentee reality, and function as effective means of social oppression.

As intimidating hypotheses about reality that serve as effective instruments of coercion, all worldviews, however they may fit into Foucault's overall reckoning of the epistemological order, must be associated with "the total set of relations that unite, at a given period, the discursive practices that give rise to . . . formalized systems."[93] As such they, too, must be submitted to archaeological and genealogical investigation, thereby exposing their intellectual structure and epistemic source. Such an investigation would manifest "whose justice and which rationality" worldviews do indeed serve. In a reincarnation of the spirit of Gorgias and Protagoras, Foucault is essentially saying something like this: nothing exists; if anything exists, it cannot be thought about or apprehended by humanity; even if it can be apprehended, it cannot be communicated; even if it can be communicated (and it can), it is communicated in discursive practices that are always in the interest of the stronger party! In the final analysis, the conclusion of a Foucauldian postmodernist must be this: worldviews are nothing but pseudointerpretations of an ultimate reality all dressed up in a linguistic power suit.

Thus, in the context of postmodernity, worldviews have been subject to considerable reconfiguration. According to Jacques Derrida, as logocentric systems of thought and belief, they must be deconstructed in order to expose them as self-referential symbol systems that fail to connect with external reality. Despite the time-honored Western tradition of an objective reference point for

92. Michel Foucault, *Discipline and Punish: The Birth of the Prison*, trans. Alan Sheridan (New York: Random House, Vintage Books, 1995), pp. 27-28.
93. Foucault, *The Archaeology of Knowledge*, p. 191.

philosophical assertions, there is really nothing outside worldview "texts" which conceptualize the cosmos except a gaping metaphysical absence. Worldviews, therefore, are actually sophisticated reifications — which in Berger and Luckmann's terms may be understood as ordained conceptual systems allegedly grounded in some recognized objectivity, but whose human origins have been perilously forgotten. In describing worldview as an associated product of a cognitive layer of the first order called *epistemes,* Michel Foucault has provided a basis to understand how worldviews are a part of the knowledge/power relationship that serves the interest of the stronger party, or the party seeking strength. A thorough archaeological analysis and genealogical investigation of the origin and content of such systems will reveal their true nature, and how they have functioned and are functioning socially in the shaping of the self, and in the fundamental categories of human experience. Thus the transition from the modern to the postmodern epochs has resulted in a remarkable change in understanding the nature and character of the concept of *Weltanschauung.*

Concluding Implications

What kinds of questions and issues do Ludwig Wittgenstein, Donald Davidson, and the postmodernists raise for Christian consideration regarding the matter of worldview? Contrary to Husserl and Heidegger, Wittgenstein rejected all positivistic approaches to describing the nature of things (despite his earlier view of language), and argued that all pictures of the world consisted of unverifiable language games rooted in various forms of life. While no living paradigm and its associated way of speaking is true, his approach still promoted conscious awareness of various social worlds and enhanced self-understanding. Wittgenstein's notion of *Weltbild,* therefore, sparks several questions for Christians to consider: (1) What are the distinctive traits of a Christian form of life, and is there a unique vocabulary or way of speaking, perhaps biblically based, associated with it? (2) How might various Christian forms of life and language games differ one from another, and why? (3) Is the Christian world picture cognitively defensible, and if so, how; or is it purely a faith commitment commensurate with a plethora of other religions and philosophies? In other words, how might Christianity escape the snare of Wittgensteinian fideism? (4) And finally, what worldview in fact underlies Wittgenstein's own philosophical reflections?

Donald Davidson debunked the very idea of alternative conceptual schemes on the basis of the intertranslatability of languages. In the process he attempted to thwart the modernist subject/object dualism he perceived as the third dogma of empiricism, and much like Heidegger, sought to reconnect the knower with the known. Questions to consider include these: (1) What aspect of Christian teaching might actually establish the basis for the existence of alternative conceptual schemes? How might the doctrine of the religious constitution and content of the human heart be the basis for various interpretations of reality? (2) Is there not a bona fide, substantial difference between alternative conceptual frameworks, between Christianity and, say, naturalism or pantheism? What is distinctive about the overall content of a Christian conceptual scheme and that of its competitors? (3) Is not human history in many ways the dynamic outworking of alternative conceptual schemes in a contest with each other for cultural hegemony? Cannot the spiritual battle at the heart of history and in the human heart be defined as a conflict between true and false conceptions of the world and between alternative interpretations of the meaning of the cosmos?

Finally, the postmodernists have attacked the traditional Western confidence in language as bearing the freight of reality, and in the process have denied the accessibility to an extralinguistic domain of truth. All worldviews are reifications, the products of human construction, and in human relations serve the interest of the stronger party in political ways. Postmodernity brings several inquiries to mind: (1) Does not postmodernism assume a naturalistic worldview as the basis of its assertions? (2) Is not the postmodern denial of the cogency of any worldview itself a worldview, and therefore self-defeating? (3) What implications does the Christian *Weltanschauung* have upon understanding the nature of language and the accessibility of a transtextual reality, especially with the aid of revelation? (4) On the basis of this revelation, does not Christianity have a much better story to tell than postmodernism, indeed a true one, especially in announcing the good news of the existence of God, the sacramental nature and meaning of the cosmos, the dignity of human persons as *imago Dei,* and the hope of a comprehensive redemption in the work of Jesus Christ through the power of the Holy Spirit?

Chapter Seven

A Disciplinary History of "Worldview" I:
The Natural Sciences

O ur discussion of the history of the concept of worldview continues, but now in a different context. We move from the philological and philosophical history of the term, covered in the last four chapters, to a disciplinary investigation. For indeed, the concept has migrated from its philosophical home to take up residence in a wide variety of enterprises, especially in the natural and social sciences. To the extent that basic ways of conceiving of the world and the place of human beings within it affect how one understands the natural and social domains, the importance of worldview in these disciplines is hard to overestimate. Hence, in this chapter we want to discover what impact the notion of worldview has had directly or indirectly on understanding the nature and methods of the natural sciences. Our investigation will begin by examining the revolutionary thought of two extraordinary thinkers. The first is the scientist-turned-philosopher Michael Polanyi, who argues in a way contrary to the modern scientific tradition that all knowledge is shaped and guided by gestaltlike frameworks and is both tacit and personal. And then we will move on to a discussion of Thomas Kuhn's understanding of the role worldview-like paradigms play in the normal operation and extraordinary revolutions in the natural sciences. In the next chapter we will turn our attention to the social sciences and focus on prominent thinkers in psychology, sociology, and anthropology for whom worldview has served as both a methodological tool and object of research. These explorations into the history of worldview in the disciplines of the natural and social sciences will enhance our recognition of the pervasive influence and extraordinary role of this salient notion.

Michael Polanyi's Tacit Dimension and Personal Knowledge in the Natural Sciences

It was an era characterized by a "logic of destruction"[1] (if destruction can indeed be termed "logical") that prompted the Jewish Hungarian scientist Michael Polanyi (1891-1976) to turn his attention away from his acclaimed research in chemistry to the study of epistemology and the philosophy of science. Having lived through the destruction of European civilization, which included countless unspeakable atrocities perpetrated on her own citizens, he could not help but ask himself this question: "why did we destroy Europe?"[2] A significant shift in the spiritual and intellectual climate of opinion had resulted in the crumbling of the moral foundations upon which Europe had been established for millennia. This sea change in perspective unleashed tidal waves of destructive nihilism which Friedrich Nietzsche, in moments of philosophical lucidity, had prophesied as a result of living in an "unsponsored"[3] universe. For Polanyi the specific problem resided in nothing less than a particular way of viewing the world, one that was rooted in an objectivist conception of science divorced from a human and moral base. As he put it, "the main [destructive] influence of science on modern man has not been through the advancement of technology, but through the effect of science on our world view."[4] Clearly, Polanyi did not blame science and technology per se for the European disaster; rather, it was the modern scientific image of the world, the specific kind of scientific outlook that shaped the Western mind-set that was the most pernicious problem. Consequently, he turned his considerable intellectual powers away from the laboratory to epistemological considerations, especially to questions regarding the nature and justification of scientific knowledge. As he explains in the preface to his most significant work, *Personal Knowledge,* his investigation involves a critique of "the [modern] ideal of scientific detachment" because it "falsifies our whole outlook far beyond the domain of science," and in its place he seeks to offer "an alternative ideal of knowledge" quite broad in scope and application.[5] Indeed, it is the

1. Richard Gelwick, *The Way of Discovery: An Introduction to the Thought of Michael Polanyi* (New York: Oxford University Press, 1977), p. 137.

2. Michael Polanyi, "Why Did We Destroy Europe?" *Studium Generale* 23 (1970): 909-16, cited in Gelwick, p. 160 n. 1.

3. Gelwick, p. 3.

4. Michael Polanyi, "Works of Art" (unpublished lectures at the University of Texas and the University of Chicago, February-May 1969), p. 30, quoted in Gelwick, pp. 5-6.

5. Michael Polanyi, *Personal Knowledge: Towards a Post-Critical Philosophy* (Chicago: University of Chicago Press, 1958, 1962), p. vii. This book is based on Polanyi's Gifford Lectures delivered at the University of Aberdeen in 1951-52.

general ideal of "personal knowledge" which Polanyi promulgates, and according to him it means "that into every act of knowing there enters a passionate contribution of the person knowing what is being known, and that this coefficient is no mere imperfection but a vital component of his knowledge."[6] He also adds this observation to his central thesis: "For, as human beings, we must inevitably see the universe from a centre lying within ourselves and speak about it in terms of a human language shaped by the exigencies of human intercourse. Any attempt rigorously to eliminate our human perspective from our picture of the world must lead to absurdity."[7]

This was a Copernican revolution of a radical kind. From a modern perspective, of course, it was entirely unorthodox and constituted a fundamental contradiction, "for true knowledge is deemed impersonal, universally established, objective."[8] However, with the help of the findings of Gestalt psychology, which Polanyi embraced wholeheartedly, he is able to demonstrate the cogency of his revolutionary doctrine, which neither abandons the scientific enterprise, though it does reshape it, nor gives way to subjectivism, though it does entail the human dimension, nor sacrifices reality, though it is encountered in a new way. Around his central commitment to a rehumanized epistemology Polanyi constructs a battery of "correlative beliefs" that flesh it out. For what he intended was nothing less than a fresh prescription for the European worldview which he hoped would spring forth from a comprehensive redefinition of the process of human knowing. I will discuss several of its features that are relevant to our present concern with worldview.

First of all, Polanyi argues that all knowledge is personal knowledge in the sense that it is tacit or is rooted in the tacit dimension. To employ the analogy of an iceberg, typical accounts of knowledge focus exclusively on what lies above the waterline. From Polanyi's perspective, however, the greater part of knowledge is hidden from view. It lies, so to speak, below the waterline. And yet it is enormously influential in shaping the knowing process.[9] There is an unobserved background structure of thought, and consequently *"we know more than we can tell."*[10] This notion challenges modern objectivism and also points out its potential dangers. "The declared aim of modern science is to establish a strictly detached, objective knowledge. Any falling short of this ideal is accepted

---

6. Polanyi, *Personal Knowledge*, p. viii.

7. Polanyi, *Personal Knowledge*, p. 3. Polanyi's conception of knowledge seems closely related to the biblical idea that the human heart is the unifying center and seat of the intellect, emotion, and will and consequently determines the very issues of life (Prov. 4:23).

8. Polanyi, *Personal Knowledge*, p. vii.

9. Gelwick, pp. 65-66.

10. Michael Polanyi, *The Tacit Dimension* (Garden City, N.Y.: Doubleday, 1966), p. 4.

only as a temporary imperfection, which we must aim at eliminating. But suppose that tacit thought forms an indispensable part of all knowledge, then the ideal of eliminating all personal elements of knowledge would, in effect, aim at the destruction of all knowledge. The ideal of exact science would turn out to be fundamentally misleading and possibly a source of devastating fallacies."[11]

Obviously, from Polanyi's point of view much is at stake if the thesis of the tacit dimension holds true. It would mean that a true model of knowledge, including the tacit aspect, would be under attack and potentially destroyed by the regnant objectivist paradigm. And it would mean that this regnant objectivist paradigm devoid of the tacit component would in fact be deceptive and the potential source of multiple misconceptions. Consequently, Polanyi offers a complex model of the knowing process grounded in the tacit dimension and points out the limitations in the reigning model. There is no way to do justice to its intricacies in a short space. But a brief sketch is possible.

In Polanyi's estimation, knowing is a humanly active, skillful comprehension of the things known. It operates at two levels. First, there is what he calls "focal awareness." It is the task, problem, or meaning to which a knower is attending directly, and because it can appear to be at a distance from the knower, he also calls it the "distal term." Second, there is what he calls "subsidiary awareness" or the "proximal term" in which a particular set of clues or tools are subordinated in the task of achieving a practical or theoretical insight. These clues and tools are things employed in the knowing process but are not in themselves observed. The knower relies on them but does not focus upon them, else there be a drastic change in the knower's awareness and performance (as any pianist, golfer, or carpenter knows). They are substructural, tacit in nature, a set of assumptions in which the knower dwells as he does his own body. In fact, they function as an extension of the body as the instrument by which the world is known, and consequently involve a change in the knower's very being. On account of these clues and tools, that is, because of the operation of subsidiary awareness, acts of understanding are noncritical in that they proceed on an assumptive basis, and are irreversible in that they can never be looked at in the same way again. In any case, people are able to know by relying on subsidiary awareness and by attending to the focal awareness. Polanyi's alternative epistemological vision, therefore, blends objective and subjective factors as the best way of accessing reality, as he explains in these words:

> Such is the *personal participation* of the knower in all acts of understanding. But this does not make our understanding *subjective*. Comprehension

11. Polanyi, *The Tacit Dimension*, p. x.

is neither an arbitrary act nor a passive experience, but a responsible act claiming universal validity. Such knowing is indeed *objective* in the sense of establishing contact with a hidden reality; a contact that is defined as the condition for anticipating an indeterminate range of yet unknown (and perhaps yet inconceivable) true implications. It seems reasonable to describe this fusion of the personal and the objective as Personal Knowledge.[12]

Since all knowledge is personal and possesses a hidden or "tacit" dimension, such characteristics must be taken into consideration when attempting to grasp the nature of knowledge itself. Polanyi hoped that his new model would offset the devastating effects of a scientific objectivism that severed the connection between knowing and being, that eliminated a sense of responsibility for truth, and that entailed the valueless manipulation of the world and its objects, including its human inhabitants.

Second, Polanyi argues that all knowledge is personal knowledge in that it is fiduciary in character rooted in the ancient Augustinian model in which faith establishes the basis for knowledge. The venerable Church Father was responsible for the first postcritical philosophy, and Polanyi calls upon him to establish yet a second. "Modern man is unprecedented; yet we must now go back to St. Augustine to restore the balance of our cognitive powers. In the fourth century A.D., St. Augustine brought the history of Greek philosophy to a close by inaugurating for the first time a post-critical philosophy. He taught that all knowledge was a gift of grace, for which we must strive under the guidance of antecedent belief: *nisi credideritis, non intelligitis* [Unless ye believe, ye shall not understand]."

This Augustinian approach ruled Europe for a thousand years. But with the advent of the Enlightenment, the doctrine of faith as a cognitive source declined and was replaced by a growing confidence in the rational and empirical powers of the human mind, giving birth to modern critical philosophy. Polanyi cites John Locke as the exemplar of this new perspective and quotes from his *Third Letter on Toleration:* "How well-grounded and great soever the assurance of faith may be wherewith it is received; but faith it is still and not knowledge; persuasion and not certainty. This is the highest the nature of things will permit us to go in matters of revealed religion, which are therefore called matters of faith; a persuasion of our own minds, short of knowledge, is the result that determines us in such truths" (p. 266).

---

12. Polanyi, *Personal Knowledge,* pp. vii-viii; the page references in the following paragraphs of text are from Polanyi's *Personal Knowledge.*

As a result of this increasingly majority opinion in the seventeenth and eighteenth centuries, "Belief was so thoroughly discredited that . . . modern man lost his capacity to accept any explicit statement as his own belief. All belief was reduced to the status of subjectivity: to that of an imperfection by which knowledge fell short of universality" (p. 266). But the Polanyian project is nothing other than the rehabilitation of the fiduciary mode as a humanly inescapable source for the knowing process. "We must now recognize belief once more as the source of all knowledge. Tacit assent and intellectual passions, the sharing of an idiom and of a cultural heritage, affiliation to a like-minded community: such are the impulses which shape our vision of the nature of things on which we rely for our mastery of things. No intelligence, however critical or original, can operate outside such a fiduciary framework."

To be sure, this framework of faith is not self-evident, and the certainty it possesses is derived solely by believing in it robustly. Still, as the centerpiece of a human being, it provides the exodus from a thoroughgoing objectivism and consists of a set of convictions that precede and govern any assertion and any form of knowledge. It is faith, therefore, which seeks understanding, and in seeking understanding the faith itself is also challenged in a kind of critical dialogue. By invoking this Augustinian formula, Polanyi writes: "It says . . . that the process of examining any topic is both an exploration of the topic, and an exegesis of our fundamental beliefs in the light of which we approach it; a dialectical combination of exploration and exegesis. Our fundamental beliefs are continuously reconsidered in the course of such a process, but only within the scope of their own basic premises" (p. 267). In other words, faith is always the basis of knowing, but in seeking knowledge the faith is always put to a test, but only within the boundaries that the faith itself provides. Hence, in drawing upon this thesis, Polanyi asserts that unless one first believes one will neither know or understand. Belief is the key to knowledge and is a critical component of the tacit dimension. Faith is the unifying center of every person, and as a consequence the personal component is inextricably linked to every act of knowing.

Third, because of the tacit dimension and fiduciary nature of personal knowledge, the task of truth seeking is always carried out in a circle, thereby entailing risk and inducing humility. This does not mean, however, being swallowed up in subjectivism. Polanyi firmly believes that there is an independently existing reference point for all knowledge enterprises. "The effort of knowing," he says, "is guided by a sense of obligation towards the truth: by an effort to submit to reality" (p. 63). In fact, the real problem comes when thinkers try to approach this objective reality with pure objectivity. Those who embrace the scientific outlook and its corollary of personal detachment face what Polanyi calls "the objectivist dilemma," namely, the requirement to abandon commitment in order to reach a commitment! "The reflecting person is then caught in an insoluble conflict between a demand for an impersonality which would discredit all commitment and an urge to make up his mind which drives him to recommit himself" (p. 304). Some, in trying to keep this requirement, end up dividing their lives into public/professional and personal/private spheres. The former realm is characterized by an attempted detachment, and the latter gives free rein to the human personality. The alternative to such a destructive personal dichotomy and the ultimately vain attempt at public/professional self-dispossession is to recognize the inescapable omnipresence of human beliefs and to acknowledge the circular character of the reasoning process. There is a danger in this, but what other alternative is left to human knowers? *"I believe that in spite of the hazards involved,"* says Polanyi, *"I am called upon to search for the truth and state my feelings. . . .* Any enquiry into our ultimate beliefs can be consistent only if it presupposes its own conclusion. It must be intentionally circular" (p. 299, emphasis Polanyi's). This is not far removed from Polanyi's recognition that people uncritically accept and identify themselves with their presuppositions as their inarticulate context for life. "When we accept a certain set of pre-suppositions and use them as our interpretative framework, we may be said to dwell in them as we do in our own body" (p. 60). Since an inevitable, commitment-based circularity attends every act and field of human knowing, every act of knowing presupposes a measure of risk. Things cannot be known either exhaustively or objectively because of human limitations and prejudices. And human limitations and prejudices mean that human knowers will know only in accordance with their constraints and commitments. Consequently, Polanyi's system calls for and he himself exhibits a unique epistemic humility. Even regarding his entire project, he explicitly denies any illusion of objectivity and recognizes that its roots and warrants are grounded in his own convictions. "Personal Knowledge is an intellectual commitment, and as such [is] inherently hazardous. Only affirmations that could be false can be said to convey objective knowledge of this kind. All affirmations published in the book are my own personal commitments; they claim this, and no more than this, for themselves" (p. viii).

Thus Polanyi seems to suggest that while it may be true that we know more than we can tell at the subsidiary level, at the same time we must be careful not to tell more than we actually know at the focal level. Personal knowledge is inherently circular, hazardous, and humble.

Fourth and finally, because of the tacit dimension, fiduciary character, and circular nature of personal knowledge — in short, because personal knowledge has such a different form and function — it must be communicated by means of alternative pedagogies. Knowledge that is objective can presumably be passed on to others by traditional objective methods. However, personal knowledge, especially in the form of an art, is different, involving a genuinely human dimension. "An art which cannot be specified in detail," according to Polanyi, "cannot be transmitted by prescription, since no prescription for it exists. It can be passed on only by example from master to apprentice." Here is his fuller description of the process of learning personal knowledge by means of personal example:

> To learn by example is to submit to authority. You follow your master because you trust his manner of doing things even when you cannot analyse and account in detail for its effectiveness. By watching the master and emulating his efforts in the presence of his example, the apprentice unconsciously picks up the rules of the art, including those which are not explicitly known to the master himself. These hidden rules can be assimilated only by a person who surrenders himself to that extent uncritically to the imitation of another. A society which wants to preserve a fund of personal knowledge must submit to tradition. (p. 53)

In due course, such an apprenticeship develops into the expertise of a "connoisseurship" which, "like skill, can be communicated only by example, not by precept. . . . you must go through a long course of experience under the guidance of a master" (p. 54). Furthermore, this whole process can only be sustained by "the civic coefficients of our intellectual passions," that is, by the support and nurture of a society that respects and promotes the intellectual passions which, in turn, provide a rich cultural life for that society. In Polanyi's term, it is the involvement of human knowers in the "conviviality" of a like-minded community that is crucial. As he puts it, "our adherence to the truth can be seen to imply our adherence to a society which respects the truth, and which we trust to respect it. Love of truth and of intellectual values in general will now reappear as the love of the kind of society which fosters these values" (p. 203). Consequently, then, over against the impersonal pedagogy and radical individualism bred by the epistemology of objectivism, there is a strong sense of commitment to learning by personal example and to the importance of an intellectually supportive community of conviviality fostered by the epistemology of personal knowledge.

Michael Polanyi certainly walked to the beat of a different drummer, and did so courageously. Ever so briefly we have seen that for him personal knowledge is tacit, fiduciary, circular, and requires unique pedagogical methods by which it may be transmitted to others. Gelwick thinks his unique contributions consist in the following: he forged a creative relationship between tradition and innovation, he emphasized the knower's unity with the world, he creatively joined science to the other human arts, he tightened the bonds between the world and humankind, and he fostered a view of history as a drama of high moral purpose.[13] Overall, however, his purpose was iconoclastic, yet with a constructive goal in mind. Truly he sought to smash the images which had smashed European civilization at the hands of a ruthlessly objectivist science. Yet at the same time, he labored assiduously to grind the lenses of a new *Weltanschauung* by which Western civilization, and indeed, the whole human race, could know itself and the world around it in accordance with the civilizing themes of personal knowledge. As Harry Prosch puts it, "Polanyi therefore attempted to show us what the consequences of his prescription are when we apply his new and more correct understanding of epistemology and of the philosophy of science to our views of life, of human beings, and of their activities."[14]

Polanyi's significant contribution was not lost on subsequent generations of thinkers. In fact, there is a remarkable confluence between Polanyi's understanding of the tacit character of the scientific enterprise and Thomas Kuhn's revolutionary concept of the "paradigm." In fact, Kuhn credits Polanyi with leading him to his notion, as he explains in an address at a 1961 symposium entitled "The Structure of Scientific Change" at Oxford University: "Mr. Polanyi himself has provided the most extensive and developed discussion I know of the aspect of science which led me to my apparently strange usage [of paradigms]. Mr. Polanyi repeatedly emphasizes the indispensable role played in research by what he calls the 'tacit component' of scientific knowledge. This is the inarticulate and perhaps inarticulable part of what the scientist brings to his research problem: it is the part learned not by precept but principally by example and practice."[15]

Hence we proceed to consider how Kuhn capitalized on Polanyi's insights as we investigate what amounts to a worldview revolution in understanding both the ongoing, normal operation as well as the structure of major cognitive changes in the natural sciences.

13. Gelwick, pp. 139-41.

14. Harry Prosch, *Michael Polanyi: A Critical Exposition* (Albany: State University of New York Press, 1986), p. 124.

15. Thomas Kuhn, *Scientific Change,* ed. A. Crombie (New York: Basic Books, 1963), p. 392, quoted in Gelwick, p. 128.

Thomas Kuhn's Paradigm Revolution in the Philosophy of Science

Thomas Kuhn's (1922-96) book *The Structure of Scientific Revolutions* fell like a bombshell on the field of science and the philosophy thereof.[16] The damage reports or victory pronouncements, depending upon your perspective, are still coming in. Kuhn's concept of scientific revolutions as paradigm shifts has been remarkably influential (as well as controversial), being nothing less than a frontal attack on the traditional understanding of the authority, rationality, and indeed, very nature of modern science. This is no small matter when we remember that science is (or was) the supreme cognitive and cultural authority in contemporary society.[17] The blast of Kuhn's bombshell has been most destructive to the theories of modern science associated with logical positivism developed and promulgated by such notables as Carl Hempel, Rudolf Carnap, and Karl Popper, a point of view dominant until the early 1960s.[18] The essential tenets of this traditional branch of the philosophy of science, which emphasizes such themes as epistemic realism, a universal scientific language, and the correspondence theory of truth, have been summarized in a helpful way by Mary Hesse.

> There is an external world which can in principle be exhaustively described in scientific language. The scientist, as both observer and language-user, can capture the external facts of the world in propositions that are true if they correspond to the facts and false if they do not. Science is ideally a linguistic system in which true propositions are in one-to-one relation to facts, including facts that are not directly observed because they involve hidden entities or properties, or past events or far distant events.

---

16. Thomas S. Kuhn, *The Structure of Scientific Revolutions*, 2nd enlarged ed., International Encyclopedia of Unified Science, vol. 2, no. 2 (Chicago: University of Chicago Press, 1970). Sales of this book, one of the most important academic works published in the last half of the twentieth century, had approximated some 750,000 copies in English by mid-1990, and by this time had been translated into nineteen different languages. For the bibliography of these translations, see Paul Hoyningen-Huene, *Reconstructing Scientific Revolutions: Thomas S. Kuhn's Philosophy of Science*, trans. Alexander T. Levine, foreword by Thomas S. Kuhn (Chicago: University of Chicago Press, 1993), p. xv n. 2.

17. Gary Gutting, "Introduction," in *Paradigms and Revolutions: Appraisals and Applications of Thomas Kuhn's Philosophy of Science*, ed. Gary Gutting (Notre Dame, Ind.: University of Notre Dame Press, 1980), pp. v, 1.

18. See Carl Hempel, *Aspects of Scientific Explanation* (New York: Free Press, 1965); Rudolf Carnap, *Logical Foundations of Probability* (Chicago: University of Chicago Press, 1950); Karl Popper, *The Logic of Scientific Discovery* (London: Hutchison, 1959).

These hidden events are described in theories, and theories can be inferred from observation, that is, the hidden explanatory mechanism of the world can be discovered from what is open to observation. Man as scientist is regarded as standing apart from the world and able to experiment and theorize about it objectively and dispassionately.[19]

From this description (which would send Polanyi over the edge), positivist science emphasizes a detached, external world the physical constitution of which can be ascertained by objective, rational human observers who can express their scientific theories and propositions by means of a logically formal linguistic system concerned with epistemic precision and verification. Obviously, this approach to the scientific enterprise is thoroughly ahistorical and oblivious to any psychosocial dimension. Kuhn and company balk at this elimination of history from the scientific domain, and seek to reconstitute the discipline with the insights from the annals of science.[20] As he states in the opening sentence of *The Structure of Scientific Revolutions,* "History, if viewed as a repository for more than anecdote or chronology, could produce a decisive transformation in the image of science by which we are now possessed."[21] In other words, if trustworthy, valid examples in scientific history demonstrate that the formal theories and methods imposed on science by the positivists are rarely followed or patently violated, then a better course would be to revise or replace

---

19. Mary Hesse, *Revolutions and Reconstructions in the Philosophy of Science* (Bloomington: Indiana University Press, 1980), p. vii.

20. Those who espouse Kuhn's approach and promote his agenda for a new philosophy of science in their own way and idiom include the following: N. R. Hanson, *Patterns of Discovery: An Inquiry into the Conceptual Foundations of Science* (Cambridge: Cambridge University Press, 1958); Paul Feyerabend, *Against Method* (London: New Left Books, 1975); Stephen Toulmin, *Foresight and Understanding* (Bloomington: Indiana University Press, 1961); Imre Lakatos, "Falsification and the Methodology of Scientific Research Programmes," in *Criticism and the Growth of Knowledge,* ed. I. Lakatos and A. Musgrave (Cambridge: Cambridge University Press, 1970), pp. 91-195. Foreshadowings of these developments in the philosophy of science include thinkers in the nineteenth and early twentieth centuries such as William Whewell, *The Philosophy of the Inductive Sciences* (London: Parker, [1847], 1945), chap. 2, who argued that what scientists take to be facts are a function of the theory they hold. Ludwick Fleck, *Genesis and Development of a Scientific Fact,* trans. F. Bradley and T. J. Trenn (Chicago: University of Chicago Press, [1921], 1979), argued for the existence of what he called "thought-styles" or "thought-collectives" which were not just ways of thinking, but also constituted the context in which science was conducted. Finally, R. G. Collingwood, *Essay on Metaphysics* (Oxford: Clarendon, 1940), developed the notion that all intellectual endeavors, science included, were based on a sequence of questions and answers, each pair presupposing another, and the entire construct was based on the foundation of absolute presuppositions.

21. Kuhn, *Structure,* p. 1.

the reigning, though traditional, conceptions of positivist science than to reject the value and contribution of the bona fide historical examples.[22] Positivist orthodoxy, Kuhn asserts, must be challenged by and adjusted to the dictates of the history of science. This approach creates a more complex and yet increasingly human picture of scientific rationality that affects both the ordinary operations and extraordinary transformations of the enterprise. This newly humanized and historicized version of the philosophy of science will not be as logically neat and epistemically clean as the old "Spockian" version, but it will be truer to the way scientists as human beings really are.

An emphasis on the relevance of history for the philosophy of science was originally bequeathed to Kuhn by James Conant.[23] And as we have seen already, Michael Polanyi's ideas of "personal knowledge" and the "tacit dimension"[24] led Kuhn to develop his celebrated doctrine of the paradigm, thereby inaugurating what Edwin Hung has called the "Weltanschauung Revolution."[25] Scientific research, indeed the very nature of scientific reason, is revolutionized by the recognition that it is always conducted within the jurisdiction of a paradigm or worldview, for "to accept a paradigm is to accept a comprehensive scientific, metaphysical, and methodological worldview."[26] Hung explains how in Kuhn's perspective, paradigmatic worldviews determine the very essence of the scientific enterprise. "According to Kuhn, paradigms play a decisive role in the practice of science. They determine the relevance of data, the content of observations, the significance of problems, and the acceptance of solutions. No, much more than just these. Paradigms supply values, standards, and methodol-

22. Carl G. Hempel, "Thomas Kuhn, Colleague and Friend," in *World Changes: Thomas Kuhn and the Nature of Science,* ed. Paul Horwich (Cambridge: MIT Press, 1993), pp. 7-8.

23. See James Conant, *Science and Common Sense* (New Haven: Yale University Press, 1951). For a helpful account of Conant's pioneering work that prepared the way for Kuhn, see Robert D'Amico, *Historicism and Knowledge* (New York: Routledge, 1989), pp. 32-51. Kuhn acknowledges his debt to Conant in the preface to *Structure,* p. xi.

24. Kuhn acknowledges his debt to Polanyi in *Structure,* p. 44 n. 1. For a helpful discussion connecting Polanyi's personal and tacit knowledge with *Weltanschauung* and the scientific enterprise, see Vladimir A. Zviglyanich, *Scientific Knowledge as a Cultural and Historical Process,* ed. Andrew Blasko and Hilary H. Brandt (Lewiston, N.Y.: Edwin Mellen Press, 1993), pp. 233-44. The third chapter, titled "Scientific Knowledge in the Context of Human Activity and Culture," contains a discussion on "Weltanschauung Assumptions and Their Influence as 'Tacit Knowledge.'"

25. Edwin Hung, *The Nature of Science: Problems and Perspectives* (Belmont, Calif.: Wadsworth, 1997), pp. 340, 355, 368, 370. Floyd Merrell, *A Semiotic Theory of Texts* (New York: Mouton de Gruyter, 1985), p. 42, similarly calls Kuhn's proposal the "*Weltanschauung* hypothesis," which he explains in the following statement: "Scientific activity, according to this hypothesis, is governed by holistic all-or-nothing world-views, or to use Kuhn's term, 'paradigms.'"

26. Gutting, p. 12.

ogies. In brief, each paradigm determines the way science should be practiced; it is a *Weltanschauung*."[27]

Thus Thomas Kuhn — as a kind of neo-Kantian constructivist in which the mind, senses, or concepts are the active agents in making the world — deposits a worldview-like paradigm at the heart of the scientific enterprise, thereby fathering the new postpositivist philosophy of science. This discovery of the centrality of paradigms has radically revolutionized the philosophy of science, and several essential features of this revolution must be mentioned.[28]

First of all, paradigms dominate normal science. What, however, is a paradigm? The name of Thomas Kuhn and the term "paradigm" are virtually synonymous, and this concept, for which he is justly famous, is (or was) not only trendy but also notoriously slippery, an idea he has revised considerably since he made it prominent.[29] Originally Kuhn took paradigms to be "universally recognized scientific achievements that for a time provide model problems and solutions to a community of practitioners."[30] In identifying paradigms with scientific achievements, he perhaps meant that scientific achievements serve as governing models in two ways, first in terms of a body of *content* associated with the achievement (laws, methods, metaphysics) — a very general scientific worldview — and second in terms of the *function* of the achievement in the scientific community (exemplary rules and regulations constituting the consensus for the operation of normal science).[31] Paradigms, then, as scientific achievements, consist of a certain content which functions as the basic assumptions and boundaries of daily scientific practice. Later on, in the postscript to the 1970 edition of *Structure*, Kuhn clarified his doctrine of the paradigm by calling it a "disciplinary matrix": "'disciplinary' because it refers to the common possession of the practitioners of a particular discipline; 'matrix' because it is composed of ordered elements of various sorts, each requiring further specification."[32] Kuhn mentions at least four components of a disciplinary matrix, including symbolic generalizations, shared commitments to various metaphys-

---

27. Hung, p. 368.

28. These features are found in Ian Barbour, "Paradigms in Science and Religion," in *Paradigms and Revolutions*, pp. 223-26.

29. Margaret Masterson, "The Nature of a Paradigm," in *Criticism and the Growth of Knowledge*, pp. 59-89, has allegedly discovered up to twenty-one nuances of paradigm in *Structure*. In responding to his critics regarding his notion of paradigm, Kuhn himself stated: "No aspect of my viewpoint has evolved more since the book [*Structure*] was written." See his "Reflections on My Critics," in *Criticism and the Growth of Knowledge*, p. 234.

30. Kuhn, *Structure*, p. viii.

31. Gutting, pp. 1-2.

32. Kuhn, *Structure*, p. 182.

ical models (e.g., heat and perceptible phenomena), scientific values (e.g., accuracy, simplicity, consistency, plausibility, etc.), and exemplary problem solutions. Like paradigms themselves, disciplinary matrices provide a lexicon of empirical concepts, specify the choice of research projects, and determine the acceptability of scientific solutions. Buttressed with historical examples and on the basis of observed laboratory activity, Kuhn concludes that "normal science" is conducted paradigmatically.

> Closely examined, whether historically or in the contemporary laboratory, that enterprise [of normal science] seems an attempt to force nature into the preformed and relatively inflexible box that the paradigm supplies. No part of the aim of normal science is to call forth new sorts of phenomena; indeed those that will not fit the box are often not seen at all. Nor do scientists normally aim to invent new theories, and they are often intolerant of those invented by others. Instead, normal-scientific research is directed to the articulation of those phenomena and theories that the paradigm already supplies.[33]

In the tradition of the great Procrustes, then, normal science forces nature to fit the dimensions of the reigning scientific paradigm. Like a pair of tinted glasses, paradigms color everything scientists see. To change the image again, paradigms are like the umpires at a baseball game: they control all the action on the (scientific) field, but no one pays much attention to them. As Hung says: "Paradigms provide *Weltanschauungen*, worldviews and conceptual frameworks, which, according to Kuhn, are necessary for the pursuit of science — that is, normal science."[34]

Interestingly, however, scientific revolutions themselves grow out of the practice of paradigm-dominated normal science. In Hoyningen-Huene's words, "For normal science produces the significant anomalies which serve as the concrete focal point of departure for revolutions. Significant anomalies may lead to the relatively isolated, unexpected discovery of new phenomena or entities, or they may trigger a great revolution of the kind in which theories aren't just modified but replaced."[35] That is to say, there are times when the scientific umpires (paradigms) are unable to call the action on the field; occasions when glasses seem distorted; situations when nature refuses to conform to the Procrustean bed. Such events are harbingers of a forthcoming transformation, and thus the second essential Kuhnian theme is this: scientific revolutions are

33. Kuhn, *Structure*, p. 24.
34. Hung, p. 370.
35. Hoyningen-Huene, p. 223.

paradigm shifts. The great scientific revolutions in the West are of course associated with names such as Copernicus, Newton, Lavoisier, Darwin, Bohr, and Einstein. However, the positivist and postpositivist interpretations of what each of these men accomplished are considerably different. The former school of thought maintains that scientific transformations consist of the displacement of less suitable descriptions of reality for more accurate ones. This is indicative of scientific progress. The latter, Kuhnian perspective insists that the presence of numerous anomalies engenders a crisis in the regnant scientific paradigm, thus inaugurating the search for a new model which, when confirmed, replaces the older one. Progress in science, then, is a function of a paradigmatic revolution and not the result of linear scientific achievement. Kuhn describes the salient traits of scientific revolutions in a number of key passages in *Structure*, including this rather comprehensive one:

> Each of them [scientific revolutions] necessitated the community's rejection of one time-honored scientific theory in favor of another incompatible with it. Each produced a consequent shift in the problems available for scientific scrutiny, and in the standards by which the profession determined what should count as an admissible problem or as a legitimate problem-solution. And each transformed the scientific imagination in ways that we shall need to describe as a transformation of the world within which scientific work was done. Such changes, together with the controversies that almost always accompany them, are the defining characteristics of scientific revolutions.[36]

Indeed, scientific revolutions bring significant modifications, including the discarding of the old paradigm, the adoption of new guidelines for isolating scientific problems, and the establishment of innovative standards for evaluating proposed solutions. Equally important is the imaginative creation of a transformed world of scientific work. Furthermore, the new paradigm possesses enhanced explanatory power and problem-solving capacity. Despite these advances, and Kuhn is clear about this, a scientific revolution does not bring its adherents closer to the truth. As he states it, "There is, I think, no theory-independent way to reconstruct phrases like 'really there'; the notion of a match between the ontology of a theory and its 'real' counterpart in nature now seems to me illusive in principle" (p. 206).

Not only is truth paradigm-dependent, but so also are all scientific criteria and observational languages. Regarding criteria, Kuhn alleges that when para-

---

36. Kuhn, *Structure*, p. 6. See also pp. 57, 94, 150, 151, 199. The page references in the text following are from *Structure*.

digms shift, "there are usually significant shifts in the criteria determining the legitimacy both of problems and of proposed solutions" (p. 109). Regarding observational languages, he is equally firm: "No language thus restricted to reporting a world fully known in advance can produce neutral and objective reports on 'the given'" (p. 127). As airtight, self-reflexive constellations of "truth," "criteria," and "meaning," scientific paradigms — whether before, during, or after revolutions — are incommensurable. This thesis is demonstrated in at least three ways, according to Kuhn. First of all, the proponents of competing paradigms will disagree about the kinds of problems their respective paradigms ought to solve. Second, despite the fact that new paradigms incorporate the vocabulary and apparatus of the old one, the meaning of this language and use of these tools is not the same. Third and most importantly for present purposes, Kuhn believes that "the proponents of competing paradigms practice their trades in *different worlds*" (p. 150, emphasis added). This is a very important idea for Kuhn, and he argues in the entirety of chapter 10 that scientific revolutions culminate in "changes of world view" (pp. 111-35). At the outset of this chapter he states that on the basis of evidence culled from contemporary scientific historiography, he can argue "that when paradigms change, the world itself changes with them." Furthermore, he states that "after a revolution scientists are responding to a different world" and that a "scientist with a new paradigm sees differently from the way he had seen before" (pp. 111, 115). For example, he mentions that subsequent to the Copernican revolution, "astronomers lived in a different world" (p. 117), and that after his discovery of oxygen, "Lavoisier worked in a different world" (p. 118). Kuhn somewhat clarifies what he means by these assertions when he notes that "though the world [itself] does not change with the change of a paradigm, the scientist afterward works in a different world" (p. 121). What does Kuhn mean by these and similar statements (pp. 6, 53, 102, 116-20, 122, 124, 144)?

These assertions might be explained in Kantian terms. There are two "worlds." The first is the world as it is in itself, the noumenal world, the *ding an sich*. The second world is the world as it appears to an observer, the phenomenal world. What appears to an observer as the phenomenal world, of course, is the product of the a priori forms of sensation and the categories of understanding. These forms and categories make knowledge of the world possible, not as it is in itself *(noumena),* but as it is structured by the human mind *(phenomena)*. Similarly for Kuhn, there is a world as it is in itself, but it can never be known as such but only as the construction, not of Kantian categories, but of Kuhnian paradigms. Hence, when a scientist's paradigm changes, the noumenal world technically does not change, but only the scientist's grid through which he sees the world changes. The change is in the subject, not the object, or more precisely, in the paradigmatic apparatus of the subject through which the world itself is constituted. Hoyningen-Huene explains what he thinks Kuhn means in this comment: "The way is thus opened for the possibility of a change in the phenomenal world, despite the consistency of the world-in-itself; such change occurs precisely when those world-constitutive moments located in the epistemic subject, together called the paradigm, change — not in such a way as to lose their world-constituting function, but rather in such a way as to give rise to a different phenomenal world."[37]

Thus for Kuhn, paradigms are constitutive of the world. Nowhere is this clearer than when he says: "As a result of the paradigm-embodied experience of the race, the culture, and, finally, the profession, the world of the scientist has come to be populated with planets and pendulums, condensers and compound ores, and other such bodies besides."[38] Those very things which exist for the scientist, indeed for the entire race, are not there in realist terms with natures or essences awaiting discovery and articulate expression. Rather "The idea, roughly speaking," says John Searle in critical language, "is that Kuhn is supposed to have shown that science does not give us an account of an independently existing reality; rather scientists are an irrational bunch who run from one paradigm to another for reasons that have no real connection with finding objective truths."[39] Thus Kuhn's thesis is not directed at rationality per se, but rather at the very root of realism.[40] Since Kuhn's incommensurate paradigms do seem unconnected to any metaphysical cornerstone, Hesse's description of the radical relativist implications of his thought seems apropos: "In extreme forms of relativism theories are regarded only as internally connected propositional systems, or 'language games'; they are world-views to be given significance in their own right. 'Truth' is defined as coherence with the theoretical system, and 'knowledge' becomes socially institutionalized belief. The view is 'relativist' in the sense that there are no cross-theory criteria for belief, nor progressive approximations to universally shared valid knowledge in the theoretical domain."[41]

37. Hoyningen-Huene, p. 36. See also the helpful analysis of this theme by Ian Hacking, "Working in a New World: The Taxonomic Solution," in World Changes, pp. 275-310.

38. Kuhn, Structure, p. 128.

39. John Searle, "Is There a Crisis in American Higher Education?" Bulletin of the American Academy of Arts and Sciences 46 (n.d.): 24-47, quoted in Phillip E. Johnson, Reason in the Balance: The Case against Naturalism in Science, Law, and Education (Downers Grove, Ill.: InterVarsity, 1995), p. 116.

40. Ernan McMullin, "Rationality and Paradigm Change in Science," in World Changes, p. 71.

41. Hesse, p. xiv. The association of language games with a relativism born of Kuhnian paradigms is also discussed by A. Maudgil, "World Pictures and Paradigms: Wittgenstein and

Kuhn, of course, resists and has responded to such accusations.[42] Some have extended the implications of his thought in the area of the sociology of science, and others have pursued it into a thoroughgoing antirealist constructivism.[43] Some have opposed him forthrightly, and sought to reestablish science on rational grounds.[44] Still others have been inspired by his notion of paradigm and reconfigured it. Lakatos, for one, has tried to reconcile Kuhn and Popper in what he called the "methodology of scientific research programs." Attempting to improve upon both Kuhn's paradigms and Lakatos's research programs, Larry Laudan devised what he called "research traditions."[45] These attempts indicated that philosophy of science after Kuhn has been forced to recognize that while science is certainly a rational endeavor, it is also a human one, and it has a history. This historical narrative manifests how human beings as scientists and scientists as human beings have undertaken their work under the influence of paradigms and disciplinary matrices. Furthermore, scientific work has not escaped the impact of sociopsychological and even political factors. Science as knowledge may even be said to serve the power interests of the ruling party (so Foucault). Be that as it may, to a lesser or greater extent all knowledge enterprises — the natural sciences included — are affected by the tincture of history. Knowledge is born and raised, consciously or unconsciously, in a context, and articulated from a particular point of view. There are no perfect reasoners. There is no pure human logic. There is no god's-eye point of view. Some kind of worldview, however narrowly or broadly conceived, underlies the practice of science (and life) simply because science (and life) is a human endeavor.

Whether one speaks of paradigms, research programs, or research traditions, one fact remains: Thomas Kuhn's *Weltanschauung* revolution in the philosophy of science has left an indelible mark. Several important contributions and consequences of Kuhn's thought regarding paradigms and worldviews should be mentioned by way of summary. First of all, Thomas Kuhn, perhaps

---

Kuhn," in *Reports of the Thirteenth International Wittgenstein-Symposium,* ed. P. Weingartner and G. Schurz (Vienna: Hölder-Pichler-Tempsky, 1988), pp. 285-90.

42. His postscript to the 1970 edition of *Structure* is one response. See also his essay "Objectivity, Value Judgment, and Theory Choice," in his *The Essential Tension: Selected Studies in Scientific Tradition and Change* (Chicago: University of Chicago Press, 1977), pp. 320-39.

43. See Hung, pp. 434-38, 440-52.

44. Israel Scheffler, *Science and Subjectivity,* 2nd ed. (Indianapolis: Hackett, 1982); Paul Thagard, *Conceptual Revolutions* (Princeton: Princeton University Press, 1992); Paul R. Gross and Norman Levitt, *Higher Superstition: The Academic Left and Its Quarrels with Science* (Baltimore: Johns Hopkins University Press, 1994).

45. Lakatos, pp. 91-195; Larry Laudan, *Progress and Its Problems* (Berkeley: University of California Press, 1977).

more than anyone else in the last half of the twentieth century, has highlighted how all of human life and thought, including the natural sciences, transpires in the context and under the dominion of paradigms or worldviews. Kuhn was certainly preceded in this awareness by a number of earlier worldviewish think-ers, including Kierkegaard (existentialism), Dilthey (historicism), Nietzsche (perspectivism), Wittgenstein (language games and forms of life), and Polanyi (tacit and personal knowledge). Nonetheless, Kuhn is *the* contemporary thinker who has brought paradigms into prominence, and by implication worldviews. Thereby he has contributed in a significant way to the history of *Weltanschauung* in the context of the natural sciences. Second, Kuhn has not only emphasized how paradigms govern the scientific enterprise, but he has also brought the issue of their incommensurability to the forefront. To what ex-tent is communication and mutual understanding across paradigms possible? How distinct and untranslatable are these disparate universes of discourse? How might cross-paradigmatic communication take place, if at all? Are worldviews, in the final analysis, windowless monads with only the appearance of interaction? Third, Kuhn's doctrine of paradigms has raised the specter of relativism by suggesting that the canons of rationality are not transcendent, but are rooted in and an expression of the worldview context in which reasoners think, live, and do their reasoning. All logic and argumentation is paradigm-dependent and caught in a circular pattern. Paradigmatic faith is tacit to every act of reason, whether employed intramurally within the system or in its apolo-getic defense. Kuhn's ideas seem to put people in a paradigm prison from which there is no apparent escape (try though they may through some kind of reha-bilitated Cartesian project). This matter leads directly toward a fourth consid-eration, and that is the nature of knowledge in a Kuhnian context. What are the epistemological implications of paradigms and worldviews? According to Kuhn, each scientist/person sees the world differently depending upon his or her paradigmatic orientation. Kuhn as a Kantian bids adieu to the things in themselves. Thus realism, at least in its naive variety, seems to be excluded. Kuhn's arguments entail a potential form of perspectivism, constructivism, and antirealism. Is knowledge, then, nothing but socially institutionalized beliefs? Is a mediating position between the extremes of naive realism and antirealism possible? From these four factors, it is evident that Kuhnian paradigms are in-commensurable, relative, arational, and antirealist. Whether one agrees with these extremist conclusions or not, the fact of the matter is that the weight of historical examples and the presence of human factors produced anomalies too great for the modern concept of objectivist science to bear. The structure of Thomas Kuhn's own *Weltanschauung* revolution has demonstrated the powerful role of paradigms in the scientific enterprise and engendered a shift in the philosophy of science of the greatest magnitude.[46]

Concluding Implications

The role of "worldview" in the natural sciences is noteworthy, and this brief overview raises questions and points of interest for Christians who care to think deeply about the theme of worldview from the vantage point of biblical faith. I will conclude this chapter with a look at these various implications.

Michael Polanyi was certainly a pioneering, postmodern kind of thinker in the area of contemporary epistemology and the philosophy of science.[47] Out of the resources of his own experience as a scientist and perhaps under the *tacit* influence of his own Jewish heritage, he crafted a perspective that challenged the established ways of understanding the process of human knowing, one that injected a distinctively human component into the equation. Is Polanyism *tacitly* Judeo-Christian? There seem to be elements of a biblical anthropology and epistemology that have influenced and been expressed in his reflections on personal knowledge. If this is indeed the case, it suggests the radical contrast that exists between modern epistemology and its biblical counterpart. Is not Polanyi's notion of tacit knowledge commensurate with a common understanding of the function of a worldview as a set of presuppositions lying just below the "waterline" of conscious awareness that govern an individual's way of knowing and being in the world? His distinction between subsidiary and focal awareness seems to parallel the typical distinctions made between a pretheoretical *Weltanschauung* and the activity of theory-making itself as a conscious attempt at explaining and knowing the world. Furthermore, is it not true, as Polanyi suggests, that faith and belief are the inescapable starting points of the knowing process? This seems to be one of the preeminently biblical aspects of Polanyi's system. He has brought the biblical and ancient Augustinian and Reformational traditions of faith to the attention of the modern world as an historic, cogent alternative to its objectivist, and ultimately amoral and dehumanizing, ways of conceptualizing the cosmos. Along these lines, what similarities exist between Polanyi's system and contemporary Christian or biblical presuppositionalism as a way of knowing and defending one's faith commitment? Does not his thinking about the circular nature of the reasoning process

---

46. I will deal with several of the questions listed in this summary in chap. 10.

47. For a consideration of Polanyi as a postmodern thinker, see Jerry H. Gill, *The Tacit Mode: Michael Polanyi's Postmodern Philosophy* (Albany: SUNY Press, 2000).

have historical and contemporary support among both non-Christian and Christian thinkers? Finally, how might Polanyi's reflections on the master-apprentice relationship and the importance of a supportive, convivial community by which traditions are preserved and passed along again be a biblically oriented thesis with significant applications for the Christian community in terms of the preservation and continuation of the Christian tradition itself? These and countless other questions and issues display the wide-ranging application of Polanyi's thought on contemporary Christian thinking about *Weltanschauung* and other related matters.

Thomas Kuhn made intellectual history and changed the course of modern thought by his paradigm revolution in the philosophy of science. He argued that all scientific activity (and by implication, all theoretical thought and academic endeavor) is conditioned by various scholarly traditions and a host of more or less intangible historical and human factors. This recognition has led many to conclude that the modern vision of a pure, scientific objectivity is chimerical. Christians sympathetic to worldview thinking, perhaps especially those steeped in the theological tradition stemming from Augustine, Calvin, and Kuyper, would likely agree: the scientific and scholarly enterprise is always pursued on the basis of an influential set of theory-guiding assumptions. Moreover, they may find themselves responding to Kuhn's thinking about worldview-like paradigms as Nicholas Wolterstorff did. "When I first read . . . *The Structure of Scientific Revolutions*," he says, "my main reaction was, 'Well, of course.'"[48] Since a faith always precedes and governs understanding (Augustine), since original sin has noetic implications (Calvin), and since spiritual regeneration, or the lack thereof, affects the total constitution of a person (Kuyper), this theological tradition would deny theoretical autonomy and affirm its "worldview" dependency. Though Kuhn's paradigms and philosophical worldviews may be different species technically, still they are of the same genus and bear a family resemblance. Consequently, Kuhn's revolutionary philosophy of science offers a kind of validation and/or confirmation to this school of Christian thought that recognizes the role of various worldviews in shaping human consciousness and affecting theoretical activity, the natural sciences included. If this is true, then scholarly disagreements, or at least some of them, may be traced in part to different paradigms or competing worldviews superintending the theorizing process and swaying its conclusions. A believing scientist or scholar, therefore, ought to be fully cognizant of the basic presupposi-

48. Nicholas Wolterstorff, "The Grace That Shaped My Life," in *Philosophers Who Believe: The Spiritual Journeys of Eleven Leading Thinkers*, ed. Kelly James Clark (Downers Grove, Ill.: InterVarsity, 1993), p. 270.

tions of the biblical *Weltanschauung,* and grant them their proper, wide-ranging role in all forms of theoretical thought.

However, we must ask: Do paradigms and worldviews really explain *everything?* Paradigms are powerful, but are they scientifically omnipotent? Worldviews are authoritative, but are they tyrannical in cognitive influence? To avoid the pitfalls associated with "romanticist expressivism," where all theoretic activity is an expression of inner dispositions; to avoid the pitfalls associated with "religious totalism," where all academic endeavor is spiritually determined (Wolterstorff has warned of these dangers); and to avoid the Kuhnian problem of paradigm incommensurability, perhaps it is fair to ask the following question: Is it not possible that scientists and thinkers, though they may work within various matrices and embrace different philosophical visions, might still share some kind of common ground and find some points of contact in their methods and conclusions? Worldviews are undoubtedly academically determinative, but the role they play may fluctuate along a continuum, depending upon the dynamic relations entailed in the character of the scientist, the substance of his or her *Weltanschauung,* and the nature of the object under investigation.

Chapter Eight

A Disciplinary History of "Worldview" II:
The Social Sciences

The social sciences, as the name implies, have always been concerned with things human. The ambiguities associated with human subjects studying human subjects have made it difficult to impute as much authority to the discoveries and laws of the social scientists when compared with the outcomes of their counterparts in the natural sciences. Indeed, those in the softer, hermeneutic disciplines have always suffered from a kind of "science" envy, worried and concerned about the validity of their findings and the value of their work. In this regard, recall the efforts of Wilhelm Dilthey, who sought to achieve epistemologically for the *Geisteswissenschaften* what Immanuel Kant had already achieved on behalf of the *Naturwissenschaften*. The thought of Michael Polanyi and especially Thomas Kuhn, of course, has changed all this. Kuhn's suggestion, as we have just seen, is that paradigms, worldviews, and other human and historical factors play a significant role in the conduct of normal science and also in scientific revolutions. As we might well expect, the same is true in the social sciences.[1] While their subject matters certainly differ, namely, the physical and social worlds respectively, still, from the vantage point of their practitioners, both kinds of sciences are constituted and controlled in part by human factors, worldviews included. Along these lines at least, a kind of parity has been created between these two previously conflicting intellectual cultures, and thus the field on which they play appears to be more level.[2]

1. For example, see Barry Barnes, *T. S. Kuhn and Social Science* (New York: Columbia University Press, 1982).

2. Drawing on Jurgen Habermas's *Knowledge and Human Interests*, Mary Hesse, *Revolutions and Reconstructions in the Philosophy of Science* (Bloomington: Indiana University Press, 1980), pp. 169-73, compares the doctrines of pre- and postpositivist science, and profiles the rapprochement that has resulted between the natural and social sciences. A similar analysis is

There is a difference, however. While the practice of natural science might be paradigmatically governed, such intellectual models are never the object or concern of the scientist's investigation (philosophers of science being the exception). Natural scientists investigate the physical, but not the human, world. On the other hand, social scientists are vitally concerned about analyzing and understanding powerful cognitive forces like worldviews that not only undergird the practice of their own disciplines, but radically affect and are a critical component of the human soul (psychology), society (sociology), and culture (anthropology). Hence, whereas worldviews and paradigms may at best be an *indirect* concern or influence in the natural sciences, they are an overt preoccupation and target of study in the social ones.[3]

As evidence of this fact, consider a conference held in July 1985 at Calvin College in Grand Rapids, Michigan, where the theme addressed was "Worldviews and Social Science." The explicit purpose of the meeting was to investigate the "problematics of worldviews in the social sciences."[4] Recognizing the complications imparted by a pervasive pluralism, the conveners of this symposium turned to the entity of worldview as a tool of analysis to help them navigate the surging waters of contemporary social and scientific diversity. In light of a bit of historical background, the editors of the conference proceedings explain the role of *Weltanschauung* in understanding life and its sciences.

> A study of worldviews can be expected to provide clues to how social theory seeks to come to grips with pluralism. In the first decade of this century, Wilhelm Dilthey described the plight of modernity as a *Streit der*

---

made by Charles Taylor, "Interpretation and the Sciences of Man," *Review of Metaphysics* 25 (1971): 3-51.

3. Along these lines, note the following comment from Karl Mannheim, "On the Interpretation of Weltanschauung," in *From Karl Mannheim,* edited and introduction by Kurt H. Wolff (New York: Oxford University Press, 1971), p. 12: "This emerging set of questions [concerning *Weltanschauung* in the social sciences] cannot be treated on its merits unless one is ready to emancipate oneself from the methodological principles of natural science; for in the natural sciences, where problems of this kind are necessarily lacking, we encounter nothing even faintly analogous to the thought patterns with which we have to deal at every step of the way in the cultural sciences."

4. Paul A. Marshall, Sander Griffioen, and Richard J. Mouw, eds., introduction to *Stained Glass: Worldviews and Social Science,* Christian Studies Today (Lanham, Md.: University Press of America, 1989), p. 12. In this vein, the interface between geography and worldview was explored at a conference in August 1996 at the Calvin [College] Center for Christian Scholarship. For the conference proceedings, see Henk Aay and Sander Griffioen, eds., *Geography and Worldview: A Christian Reconnaissance* (Lanham, Md.: Calvin Center Series and University Press of America, 1998). See especially the essay "Perspectives, Worldviews, Structures" by Sander Griffioen examining the benefits and hazards of worldview for the social sciences, pp. 125-43.

Weltanschauung (a clashing of worldviews). Again, Thomas S. Kuhn gave the notion of worldview a special place in his account of the *impondera-bilia* of scientific revolutions. In the wake of the Kuhnian revolution there seems to be remarkably widespread acknowledgment of the formative influence of worldviews. James Olthuis sums it up in these words: "Conflicts in life and science, we are discovering, come down to differences in underlying worldviews."[5]

As an underlying foundation, method of analysis, and object of study, worldviews are enmeshed deeply in the philosophy, theories, and investigations of the social sciences.[6] This will become increasingly clear as our examination unfolds, beginning with psychology.

"Worldview" in Psychology

Apart from the influence worldviews may have in trauma management, identity development, marital satisfaction, as well as the search for the purpose of life,[7] our primary concern here will be to examine the substance of two essays on *Weltanschauung* by the two most notable psychoanalysts in the twentieth century, Sigmund Freud and Carl Jung. Both considered this conception of crucial importance, and devoted entire essays to the subject with distinct concerns in mind. Whereas Jung occupied himself with the relationship between psychotherapy and worldview, Freud investigated the question of a *Weltanschauung* in an attempt to determine whether or not psychoanalysis constituted an independent worldview. I will "analyze" Freud's contribution first.

---

5. Marshall, Griffioen, and Mouw, p. 11.

6. For material supplementary to what I present here on this overall topic, see Sander Griffioen, "The Worldview Approach to Social Theory: Hazards and Benefits," in *Stained Glass*, pp. 81-118.

7. For example, Devora Carmil and Shlomo Brenznitz, "Personal Trauma and World View — Are Extremely Stressful Experiences Related to Political Attitudes, Religious Beliefs, and Future Orientation?" *Journal of Traumatic Stress* 4 (July 1991): 393-406; Anne V. Sutherland, "Worldframes and God-Talk in Trauma and Suffering," *Journal of Pastoral Care* 49 (1995): 280-92; L. J. Myers, "Identity Development and Worldview — toward an Optimal Conceptualization," *Journal of Counseling and Development* 70 (1991): 54-63; Bryce Bernell Augsberger, "World View, Marital Satisfaction and Stability" (Ph.D. diss., University of Denver, 1986); Carol C. Molcar, "Effects of World View on Purpose in Life," *Journal of Psychology* 122 (July 1988): 365-71.

Sigmund Freud: "The Question of a Weltanschauung"

In a fascinating essay, Sigmund Freud (1856-1939) noted that his followers had displayed a tendency to take his ideas and form them "into a cornerstone of a psycho-analytic Weltanschauung."[8] Surprisingly, Freud resisted the proposal, and he explains why in this remarkable statement:

> I must confess that I am not at all partial to the fabrication of a *Weltanschauung*. Such activities may be left to philosophers, who avowedly find it impossible to make their journey through life without a Baedeker [German publisher of guidebooks] of that kind to give them information on every subject. Let us humbly accept the contempt with which they look down on us from the vantage-ground of their superior needs. But since we cannot forgo our narcissistic pride either, we will draw comfort from the reflection that such "Handbooks to Life" soon grow out of date and that it is precisely our short-sighted, narrow and finicky work which obliges them to appear in new editions, and that even the most up-to-date of them are nothing but attempts to find a substitute for the ancient, useful and all-sufficient Church Catechism. We know well enough how little light science has so far been able to throw on the problems that surround us. But however much ado the philosophers may make, they cannot alter the situation. Only patient, persevering research, in which everything is subordinated to the one requirement of certainty, can gradually bring about a change. The benighted traveler may sing aloud in the dark to deny his own fears; but, for all that, he will not see an inch further beyond his nose.[9]

In rather derogatory tones, Freud asserts that the formation of worldviews is essentially a futile task, suitable for weak-minded philosophers who need a "guidebook" to provide information about the totality of life supplanting the didactic role of the church. However, such worldviews as guidance systems must be revised frequently due to scientific advances, especially those stemming from the psychoanalysts themselves. Only certain scientific knowledge is worthy of sustained endeavor, not worldview development which only provides false, existential comfort but no genuine insight. Scientism must reign in the kingdom of ideas.

8. Sigmund Freud, "Inhibitions, Symptoms and Anxiety," in *"An Autobiographical Study," "Inhibitions, Symptoms and Anxiety," "The Question of Lay Analysis," and Other Works,* vol. 20 in *The Standard Edition of the Complete Psychological Works of Sigmund Freud,* trans. James Strachey (London: Hogarth Press and the Institute of Psycho-Analysis, 1962), p. 95.

9. Freud, "Inhibitions, Symptoms and Anxiety," p. 96.

In another lecture titled "The Question of a Weltanschauung,"[10] delivered when he was seventy-six years old, Freud elaborates on his reasons for rejecting the proposal of a psychoanalytic worldview. He begins with this question: "Does psychoanalysis lead to a particular *Weltanschauung* and, if so, to which?" (p. 158). In order to respond to this inquiry, he begins by offering a definition of this "specifically German concept":

> A *Weltanschauung* is an intellectual construction which solves all the problems of our existence uniformly on the basis of one overriding hypothesis, which, accordingly, leaves no question unanswered and in which everything that interests us has its fixed place. It will easily be understood that the possession of a *Weltanschauung* of this kind is among the ideal wishes of human beings. Believing in it one can feel secure in life, one can know what to strive for, and how one can deal most expediently with one's emotions and interests.

A world "hypothesis," according to Freud, should be able to solve all problems, satisfy all interrogation, and put everything in its place. As an ultimate human ideal, a *Weltanschauung* in which one trusts should provide peace of mind or security by specifying the *summum bonum* and designating how to deal with life in practical ways. Can psychoanalysis satisfy these criteria? No, says Freud adamantly, only science can. "If that is the nature of a *Weltanschauung*," opines Freud, "the answer as regards psycho-analysis is made easy. As a specialist science, a branch of psychology — a depth-psychology or psychology of the unconscious — it is quite unfit to construct a *Weltanschauung* of its own: it must accept the scientific one" (p. 158). At the conclusion of his treatise, Freud reiterates this conviction about the relation of psychoanalysis to the question of worldview in similar words: "Psycho-analysis, in my opinion, is incapable of creating a *Weltanschauung* of its own. It does not need one; it is a part of science and can adhere to the scientific *Weltanschauung*" (p. 181). Science is humankind's last, best hope for knowledge, and psychoanalysis assumes its place as a subset of science. Psychoanalysis is no pseudoscience, but is a card-carrying member in the broader scientific community which attains salvific status in Freud's reckoning.

In the rest of the essay Freud makes two basic claims. First of all, not even science itself, given its own peculiar set of limitations, is capable of providing the kind of ideal, broad-based worldview as Freud has defined it. Furthermore,

10. Sigmund Freud, "The Question of a Weltanschauung," in *New Introductory Lectures on Psycho-Analysis and Other Works*, vol. 22 in *The Standard Edition of the Complete Psychological Works of Sigmund Freud*, pp. 158-82. The page references in the following text are to this work.

and second, no other intellectual resource is adequate to the task, either. Religion, art, philosophy, intellectual nihilism, or Marxism, which are the chief competitors to science as potential depositories for holistic worldview construction, cannot do the job. Indeed, what Freud suggests is that there is *no cognitive system available to humanity, science included,* that is capable of producing the kind of comprehensive worldview as a chief desideratum of the human race. Still, modern science, despite its limitations, is the very best, even the only option available. It exceeds the alternatives handily. Hence Freud offers an apologetic for the superiority of the scientific approach to life over against all other options, especially religion.[11] Science and science alone is humanity's only authentic epistemic hope. Psychoanalysis, as a branch of science, makes its contribution in this larger context. It is not a worldview *sui generis.*

How, then, does Freud describe the scientific worldview of which psychoanalysis is a part? Three basic features will be discussed. First of all, modern science is based on a metaphysical or at least a methodological naturalism. The

---

11. It will be helpful to present an outline of Freud's arguments by which he attempts to establish the triumph of the scientific over the religious worldviews from his "The Question," pp. 161-75. In Freud's estimation, religion and religion alone is the serious enemy of science. Religion has the strongest human emotions at its service. Because it is a consistent and self-contained worldview, it persists to the present day. Hence Freud felt he must respond to it. He argues that the religious *Weltanschauung* fulfills three functions. First, it satisfies the human thirst for knowledge. Second, it soothes the fear of the dangers and vicissitudes of life. Third, it issues precepts and lays down prohibitions and restrictions. Despite these important functions, science rooted in naturalism has demonstrated that religion is a human affair and has not been able to withstand critical examination, especially in regard to the issues of miracles, the origin of the universe, and the problem of evil. Furthermore, psychoanalysis itself has shown how the religious worldview originated from the helplessness of children, imposing the need for paternal protection upon the entire universe. Though some may object that it is inappropriate for science to criticize something as sublime and significant as religion, Freud responds by saying that religion has no right to restrict thought and to exclude itself from critical examination. The religious restriction on thought has produced massive damage, as individual biographies have shown. In response, religionists point out the limitations of science: What has and will it accomplish? It cannot bring consolation and exaltation. It cannot present a coherent view of the universe — its past, present, or future. Its fragmented discoveries are internally inconsistent, its laws and interpretations only provisionally true and frequently revised. Freud's response is to point to the recent history of scientific achievement and to highlight its youthfulness. Given time, any obstacles in the way of science will be surmounted. His conclusion is: "Things are not looking so bad in the business of science" (p. 174). In light of these arguments, Freud declares science to be the exclusive cognitive and cultural authority. The only recourse for religion is to admit that it proclaims "truth" in a higher, unverifiable sense. To opt, however, for an arational or irrational epistemology is to forfeit all its influence on the mass of humanity, for it would carry no true epistemic weight. Hence, on the basis of these arguments, Freud proclaims the victory of the scientific over the religious worldview. Of course, Freud's most elaborate critique of religion is found in his *The Future of an Illusion.*

"attitude of science" will not permit any contribution from supernatural, revelatory, or intuitive sources, else it forfeit the name of true science. As Freud states, science is characterized by "its sharp rejection of certain elements alien to it. It asserts that there are no sources of knowledge of the universe other than the intellectual working-over of carefully scrutinized observations — in other words, what we call research — and alongside of it no knowledge derived from revelation, intuition or divination" (p. 159). These elements are illusory, an expression of wishful impulses, and based on emotion. There is no reason to regard them as justified. However, the fact that they exist, Freud says, serves as a warning "to separate from [scientific] knowledge everything that is illusion and an outcome of emotional demands like these." Thus, for science to be science, it must be thoroughly grounded in naturalism.

Second, though a scientific naturalism like this may appear to be cheerless in its negation of the claims and the needs of the human intellect, Freud asserts that in psychoanalysis the mental aspects of human life are objects of scientific research in just the same way as nonhuman or physical things are. Psychoanalysis saves science from a serious omission, and presumably reenchants it. In Freud's words, "Psycho-analysis has a special right to speak for the scientific *Weltanschauung* at this point, since it cannot be reproached with having neglected what is mental in the picture of the universe. Its contribution to science lies precisely in having extended research to the mental field. And, incidentally, without such a psychology science would be very incomplete" (p. 159). Many would wish to demur at the suggestion that the "mind" can be studied in the same way as molecules. Psychoanalysis, they would say, is a pseudoscience and belongs in a different category. Freud, interestingly enough, is convinced that it belongs in fellowship with disciplines such as physics, chemistry, and biology, and thereby renders the hard sciences complete.

Third, and perhaps most interesting of all, Freud's scientific *Weltanschauung* is positivist and purely modern. Science is humanity's best hope for the future. His description of the scientific enterprise, which is worth quoting at length, entails all the familiar, modern themes of an independent world, human objectivity, rigorous experimentation, and the correspondence theory of truth.

> Scientific thinking does not differ in its nature from the normal activity of thought, which all of us . . . employ in looking after our affairs in ordinary life. It has only developed certain features: it takes an interest in things even if they have no immediate, tangible use; it is concerned carefully to avoid individual factors and affective influences; it examines more strictly the trustworthiness of the sense-perceptions which cannot be obtained by everyday means and it isolates the determinants of these new experiences

in experiments which are deliberately varied. Its endeavor is to arrive at correspondence with reality — that is to say, with what exists outside us and independently of us and, as experience has taught us, is decisive for the fulfillment or disappointment of our wishes. This correspondence with the real external world we call "truth." It remains the aim of the scientific work even if we leave the practical value out of account. (p. 170)

This statement about science is clearly pre-Polanyian and pre-Kuhnian — no individual or affective influences are to stain the enterprise. Furthermore, an exact knowledge of the external world is the goal of science, a knowledge that will provide the capacity to manipulate a reality that, as Freud says, is decisive for the fulfillment or disappointment of human wishes. No wonder, then, that for Freud the eschatological hope of humanity is rooted in the triumph of the rational spirit of the scientific worldview. "Our best hope for the future is that intellect — the scientific spirit, reason — may in process of time establish a dictatorship in the mental life of man. The nature of reason is a guarantee that afterwards it will not fail to give man's emotional impulses and what is determined by them the position they deserve. But the common compulsion exercised by such a dominance of reason will prove to be the strongest uniting bond among men and lead the way to further unions" (p. 171).

Freud's anxious longing and hope is that a scientific rationality will reign supreme among human beings. The rule of reason, he believes, will guarantee nonetheless a proper place for the affective dimensions of human life, and will serve as the rallying point for the unity of the race.

For Freud, then, psychoanalysis need not aspire to become a worldview because it is part and parcel of the emerging scientific *Weltanschauung*. This scientific worldview is based upon a thoroughgoing metaphysical and/or methodological naturalism. Thanks to psychoanalysis itself, science is completed by including within its ranks the rigorous study of the human mind and intellect. Finally, science in Freud's perspective is conceived entirely in positivist and modernist terms. He is optimistic that this scientific worldview, of which his own discipline was a vital part, would bring humanity together in a rational bond that would insure the future progress of the race.

Certainly there is reason for us to pause here and ask a question or two. Despite Freud's own protestations, does not psychoanalysis indeed lead to an independent worldview and, ironically, even to a kind of religion, as several theorists have recently argued?[12] D. H. Lawrence, with a touch of irony, thought so.

12. See, for example, S. A. Figueira, "Common (Under)Ground in Psychoanalysis — the Question of a *Weltanschauung* Revisited," *International Journal of Psycho-Analysis* 71 (1990): 65-75; P. L. Rudnysky, "A Psychoanalytic *Weltanschauung*," *Psychoanalytic Review* 79 (summer

"Psychoanalysts know what the end will be," he wrote. "They have crept in among us as healers and physicians; growing bolder, they have asserted their authority as scientists; two more minutes and they will appear as apostles. Have we not seen and heard the *ex cathedra* Jung? And does it need a prophet to discern that Freud is on the brink of a Weltanschauung?"[13]

Indeed, it does not take a rocket scientist or a prophet to realize, as the analysis above has made clear, that "as a profession of faith, Freud's *Weltanschauung* is simply an adherence to the acknowledged principles of nineteenth-century scientific methodology."[14] That is to say, "Philosophically speaking, psychoanalysis reflects the influence of classical empiricism as well as the Enlightenment tradition. . . . Freud adopted a materialistic, or naturalistic, world view as the backdrop for his model."[15] Even more than that, as Albert Levi believes, the anthropological content of Freud's project by necessity engendered a worldview.

> Freud's early disavowal of a *Weltanschauung* other than that of the methodology of empirical science was perhaps premature (if not disingenuous). . . . Certainly Freud had no conscious metaphysical ambitions, no intention of constructing a *Weltbild* in the classical model of Hegel or Spinoza. But in a sense he could not avoid it. For psychoanalysis is founded upon a theory of man, *a logic of the soul* in the strictest sense of that phrase, and whenever there arises in any age a new image of man, the theory which presents it becomes a part of the philosophical tradition.[16]

Freud's worldview entailed, then, a metaphysical naturalism, a scientific empiricism or positivism, and a distinctively psychoanalytic anthropology. These are not neutral positions derived in an objective manner. Instead they are chosen commitments, even a creed or statement of faith. While Freud may not have aspired to produce an independent worldview through psychoanalysis, it is certainly based on one, and to that extent transmits essential commitments embodied in its fundamental teachings.

1992): 289-305; B. Wood, "The Religion of Psychoanalysis," *American Journal of Psychoanalysis* 40 (1980): 13-26.

13. Quoted in Albert William Levi, *Philosophy and the Modern World* (Bloomington: Indiana University Press, 1959), p. 151.

14. Levi, p. 153.

15. Stanton L. Jones and Richard E. Butman, *Modern Psycho-Therapies: A Comprehensive Christian Appraisal* (Downers Grove, Ill.: InterVarsity, 1991), p. 67.

16. Levi, p. 160.

C. G. Jung: "Psychotherapy and a Philosophy of Life"

In 1942 Carl G. Jung (1875-1961) delivered an address analyzing the relationship between psychotherapy and worldview, "Psychotherapie und Weltanschauung," translated in English as "Psychotherapy and a Philosophy of Life."[17] Like his system as a whole, which has been described as "complex, esoteric, and obscure,"[18] this lecture is difficult to understand. Perhaps this is partially attributable to the fact that, unlike Freud, who claimed strict scientificity for his theories, Jung is much more receptive to the intangibles of psychotherapeutic practice. Jones and Butman explain as follows: "The analytic approach of Jung is certainly more open to the ineffable and mysterious than any other major approach to people-helping. Although it embraces aspects of the scientific approach, Jungian thought refuses to embrace the spirit of scientific objectification or reductionism. It repeatedly reminds us of mysteries beyond our current comprehension and understanding."[19]

The very fact that Jung's concern in this essay is to trace out psychotherapy's "own intellectual foundations" is testimony to his recognition of the role of the nonquantifiable aspects of human science and related enterprises (p. 76). Jung not only acknowledges that analytic psychology rests on essential intellectual assumptions, but he is acutely aware of the dynamics of *Weltanschauung* affecting both therapist and patient in the psychotherapeutic process. These dynamics are the primary focus of Jung's reflections in this essay. Despite its convoluted content in places, I will present several key themes that are at the heart of his discussion.

First of all, Jung realizes that in a psychotherapeutic relationship, an effective treatment aimed at the care of the soul *(cura animarum)* must take into consideration the deeper issues and questions about the meaning of persons and the world as a whole. Both therapist and patient are grounded in larger visions of life and reality that must be carefully heeded. In order to avoid any form of reductionism, one cannot afford to neglect the broader convictions af-

17. This was originally an address given at the Conference for Psychology, in Zürich, 26 September 1942. It was published as "Psychotherapie und Weltanschauung," *Schweizerische Zeitschrift für Psychologie und ihre Anwendungen* 1 (1943): 3, 157-64. This discussion is based on C. G. Jung, "Psychotherapy and a Philosophy of Life," in *The Practice of Psychotherapy: Essays on the Psychology of the Transference and Other Subjects,* trans. R. F. C. Hull, Bollingen Series 20, 2nd ed. (New York: Pantheon Books, 1966), pp. 76-83. The page references in the following text are to this work.

18. Richard M. Ryckman, *Theories of Personality,* 3rd ed. (Monterey, Calif.: Brooks/Cole, 1985), p. 62.

19. Jones and Butman, p. 121.

fecting the overall psychotherapeutic process. Ideally, patients must be treated as whole persons, taking into account their philosophies of life. Jung explains in these words: "[F]or sooner or later it was bound to become clear that one cannot treat the psyche without touching on man and life as a whole, including the ultimate and deepest issues, any more than one can treat the sick body without regard to the totality of its functions — or rather, as a few representatives of modern medicine maintain, the totality of the sick man himself" (p. 76).

Wholeness, therefore, is critical for Jung. As in medicine, so also in psychotherapy: the total person, including philosophies of life, must be considered in treatment. As he puts it, "The more 'psychological' a condition is, the greater its complexity and the more it relates to the whole of life."

To make sure the totality is covered, Jung makes a second important point by suggesting that in his model of therapy the overall condition of the soul is affected not just by one but by two factors, the physical and the mental. "There is not the slightest doubt," Jung affirms, "that the physiological factor forms at least one pole of the psychic cosmos." Even more important than the physical are certain mental phenomena — rational, ethical, aesthetic, religious, or other traditional ideas — that cannot be scientifically shown to have a physical grounding. As Jung says, "These extremely complex dominants form the other pole of the psyche," and as experience suggests, this pole is far more powerful in its effects on the soul than its physiological counterpart (p. 77). To this extent, then, philosophies of life, or worldviews, are an important part of the therapeutic process.

Thirdly, Jung suggests that the psychotherapist can expect revelations and discussions about one's philosophy of life to arise out of the "problem of opposites," that is, the dialectical or contrapuntal structure of the soul. For example, in the case of a repressed instinct, when the repression is lifted the instinct is set free. Then the question surfaces regarding the control of the newly liberated instinct that wishes to go its own way. How should the instinct be modified or sublimated? Reason is unable to solve the problem because human beings are not necessarily rational creatures; reason will be insufficient to modify the instinct or make it conform to the rational order. Hence, in this dilemma, all kinds of moral, philosophical, and religious issues emerge, and in order to respond to the problem of the instinct the therapist, according to Jung, "will be driven to a discussion of his philosophy of life, both with himself and his partner." Worldviews, therefore, play an important role in regulating liberated impulses and are germane to other dynamics in the therapeutic process.

This is not the only way philosophic discussion originates in the therapist/patient relationship. The fourth point that Jung makes is that "philosophic discussion is a task [to] which psychotherapy necessarily sets itself," especially when a patient demands an explanation of first principles. Though not all clients will make such a request, a therapist must be prepared to explain the philosophical foundations that are determinative for his recommendations and counsel. "The question of the measuring rod," as Jung calls it, "with which to measure, of the ethical criteria which are to determine our actions, must be answered somehow, for the patient may quite possibly expect us to account for our judgments and decisions." Hence Jung affirms that the therapist must have formulated a set of trustworthy beliefs and proven them in his own experience. As he puts it, "the art of psychotherapy requires that the therapist be in possession of avowable, credible, and defensible convictions which have proved their viability either by having resolved any neurotic dissociations of his own or by preventing them from arising" (p. 78). Philosophies of life, then, are necessary to explain to patients the very foundations for the therapy that is being administered.

With this, Jung explains the immense significance of worldview in human life and therapeutic practice. In making this fifth major point, Jung offers a description of a *Weltanschauung* in terms of its various characteristics, functions, and vicissitudes.

> As the most complex of psychic structures, a man's philosophy of life [*Weltanschauung*] forms the counterpole to the physiologically conditioned psyche, and, as the highest psychic dominant, it ultimately determines the latter's fate. It guides the life of the therapist and shapes the spirit of his therapy. Since it is an essentially subjective system despite the most rigorous objectivity, it may and very likely will be shattered time after time on colliding with the truth of the patient, but it rises again, rejuvenated by the experience. Conviction easily turns into self-defence and is seduced into rigidity, and this is inimical to life. The test of a firm conviction is its elasticity and flexibility; like every other exalted truth it thrives best on the admission of its errors.

In this rather amazing statement, Jung mentions a number of important features of worldviews. One, a worldview determines its holder's destiny in life. Two, it guides the life of the therapist. Three, it forms the contours of therapy itself. Four, it strives for objectivity but is essentially a subjective system of thought. Five, it may be shattered in confrontation with a patient, but will survive and even thrive as a result of the experience. Six, it can harden into a death-like rigidity. Seven, it must develop the ability to bend. Eight, it must admit its mistakes and learn from them. At the center, then, of life and therapeutic practice is an all-determinative *Weltanschauung*.

Given the centrality of worldview in the psychotherapeutic process, Jung sets forth a final suggestion that dissolves the contrast between psychotherapy, philosophy, and religion. The therapist, he suggests, ought to function as a philosopher and recognize the similarity of philosophy and religion at the deepest levels of life. I will let Jung speak for himself. "I can hardly draw a veil over the fact that we psychotherapists ought really to be philosophers or philosophic doctors — or rather that we already are so, though we are unwilling to admit it because of the glaring contrast between our work and what passes for philosophy in the universities. We could also call it religion *in statu nascendi,* for in the vast confusion that reigns at the roots of life there is no line of division between philosophy and religion" (p. 79).

Patients suffering from "cosmopathy" (worldview or philosophical disorders) would need the service of psychotherapists as "cosmophthalmologists," deploying their philosophic and religious insights in the formulation of new mental vision that is more consistent with reality.[20] In other words, images associated with a worldview may be seriously at variance with reality and thus maladaptive. Such a patient would require significant cognitive reorientation. In so treating a patient afflicted with various neuroses, philosophical or otherwise, the therapist must guard against being infected with the same psychic diseases, and depending upon the patient's response to treatment, it may be necessary to assist him in the search for religious and philosophical principles that best meet the patient's emotional needs.

To conclude, Freud and Jung are obviously concerned about separate matters when it comes to the notion of *Weltanschauung.* Freud is anxious to squelch the notion that psychoanalysis is an autonomous worldview. Rather, he wishes to show how his discipline proudly participates in the only viable kind of worldview suitable for the modern age, and that is the scientific one. There is considerable reason to question whether or not Freud was successful in his disavowal of a worldview, however, because he was committed to, and his theories embody, perspectives on reality that go far beyond the purview of a neutral, scientific objectivity. Jung, on the other hand, was concerned to point out the important connection between analytic psychology and fundamental philosophies of life. Worldviews must be considered and will emerge in the context of a therapeutic relationship, and the therapist must not only recognize their important role but also be capable of expressing her own beliefs and helping her client discover fundamental philosophical principles that will assist in the healing process. Through the writings of Freud and Jung, then, the concept of

20. The idea of "cosmophthalmology" is from William Rowe, "Society after the Subject, Philosophy after the Worldview," in *Stained Glass,* p. 159.

worldview has received significant attention in psychology. From their reflections, a couple things seem clear: any program of psychotherapy — Freudian,
Jungian, or otherwise — is established upon fundamental worldview assumptions, and philosophical underpinnings as such are extremely influential factors
in the overall psychotherapeutic process.[21]

"Worldview" in Sociology

We turn our attention to the contributions of several leading sociologists to this
present disciplinary history of worldview. Karl Mannheim, Peter Berger,
Thomas Luckmann, Karl Marx, and Friedrich Engels have each had significant
things to say about this vital theme. Mannheim's reflections focus on a methodology for determining the global outlook of a period. How can worldviews be
identified and communicated by sociologists in an objective, scientific manner?
Berger and Luckmann have been pioneers in formulating the conception of the
sociology of knowledge, which attempts to demonstrate how social dynamics
are at work in the construction of cognition, with clear implications on the formulation of worldviews. Finally, we will look briefly at the use of "worldview"
and "ideology" in the writings of Karl Marx and Friedrich Engels within the
framework of socialist thought. We begin with Karl Mannheim.[22]

Karl Mannheim: "On the Interpretation of Weltanschauung"

What is the place of *Weltanschauung* in the social sciences, and what appropriate methodology can be devised to analyze this concept in this field of inquiry?
These are the questions that Karl Mannheim (1893-1947) seeks to answer in his
lengthy essay titled "On the Interpretation of Weltanschauung."[23] He is not so

21. See, for example, Orlo Strunk, "The World View Factor in Psychotherapy," *Journal of
Religion and Health* 18 (July 1979): 192-97; Armand M. Nicholi, "How Does the World View of
the Scientist and the Clinician Influence Their Work?" *Perspectives on Science and the Christian
Faith* 41 (1989): 214-20.

22. For further discussion of the role of worldviews in sociology, see Jan Verhoogt, "Sociology and Progress: Worldview Analysis of Modern Sociology," in *Stained Glass,* pp. 119-39. In
particular he investigates a Kuhnian question: "Do the worldviews of sociologists — their personal values and interests — penetrate their scientific thinking?" (p. 119). For an evaluation of
the worldview concept itself from a sociological point of view, see Jerome Ashmore, "Three Aspects of *Weltanschauung,*" *Sociological Quarterly* 7 (spring 1966): 215-33.

23. Karl Mannheim, "On the Interpretation of Weltanschauung," in *From Karl Mannheim,*
pp. 8-58. The page references in the following text are to this work.

much concerned with providing a philosophical definition of "worldview," though his argument necessarily entails one, but rather with the following methodological issues that could help social scientists and others in identifying a worldview underlying a particular epoch or culture. "What kind of task is a student of a cultural and historical discipline (a historian of art, of religion, possibly also a sociologist) faced with when he seeks to determine the global outlook *(Weltanschauung)* of an epoch, or to trace partial manifestations back to this all-embracing entity? Is the entity designated by the concept of *Weltanschauung* given to us at all, and if so — how is it given? How does its givenness compare with that of other data in the cultural and historical disciplines?" (p. 8).

Assuming for the moment that there is such a thing as a global outlook or worldview, and it has indeed been grasped as the substructure of a given culture, the question remains: "Is there a way to transpose it into scientific and theoretical terms? Can such a 'given' ever become the object of valid, verifiable scientific knowledge? . . . Is it possible to determine the global outlook of an epoch in an objective, scientific fashion? Or are all characterizations of such a global outlook necessarily empty, gratuitous speculations?" (pp. 8, 9). In other words, how can that which lies at the most basic level of human cognition and culture be comprehended scientifically and communicated theoretically? Can a worldview become the object of scientific investigation? According to John Harms, Mannheim sought to answer these questions, and undertook this and other studies with the hope that education in social theory would foster "communication between different *Weltanschauungen* and . . . promote a greater understanding and awareness of the totality of society."[24]

To begin with, Mannheim notes how the social sciences, in patterning themselves after the natural sciences, concentrated their efforts almost entirely on atomistic research projects. However, by focusing on the parts — namely, the study of discrete, individual things — the human sciences neglected concrete experiential wholes and cultural totalities. Thereby they forfeited one of their fundamental research obligations. Nonetheless, because of the recent recognition that even a specialized discipline within cultural studies cannot abandon the "pre-scientific totality of its object," there has been a recent turn toward "synthesis" and a "synoptic approach" (pp. 9-11). "And the present trend toward synthesis," as Mannheim makes clear, "is evidenced above all by the awakening

---

24. John B. Harms, "Mannheim's Sociology of Knowledge and the Interpretation of *Weltanschauungen*," *Social Science Journal* 21 (April 1984): 44. According to Harms, Mannheim later abandoned this hope. This article contains a substantive exposition of Mannheim's essay on *Weltanschauung*.

interest in the problem of *Weltanschauung,* a problem that marks the most advanced point reached by efforts at historical synthesis" (pp. 11-12). Hence the synoptic mood is propitious for an investigation of this significant concept and its synthesizing capacities. Yet to do so, the social sciences have to abandon the dominant paradigm of the natural sciences which prohibits such concerns. Mannheim attempts to provide a credible method for a project such as this.

According to Mannheim, the chief problem associated with the study of *Weltanschauung* as a synthetic concept is that it stands outside, and is indeed prior to, the domain of theoretical reflection. That is to say that a worldview is not a theoretical but a pretheoretical phenomenon: it precedes and conditions abstract thought. Contrariwise, there is a strong tradition that equates worldview with a culture's rational constructions, whether they be philosophical, scientific, or religious. The collective pronouncements of these disciplines constituted a culture's essential philosophy, i.e., *Weltanschauung.* Though Mannheim originally embraced this perspective, Wilhelm Dilthey was the first to demonstrate that worldviews are not synonymous with theoretical systems, but stand in an antecedent relationship to them as their a priori foundation. Mannheim cites Dilthey's remark that "*Weltanschauungen* are not produced by thinking," that is, theoretically. If this is the case, then there is some intellectual distance between the "atheoretical" and "irrational" *Weltanschauung,* as Mannheim calls it, and the theoretical networks emanating from it. Mannheim explains this relationship in these terms: "If this totality we call *Weltanschauung* is understood in this sense to be something a-theoretical, and at the same time to be the foundation for all cultural objectifications, such as religion, *mores,* art, philosophy, and if, further, we admit that these objectifications can be ordered in a hierarchy according to their respective distance from this irrational, then the theoretical will appear to be precisely one of the most remote manifestations of this fundamental entity" (p. 13).

When a worldview is understood as the foundational entity which fosters cultural objectifications, then cultural studies are enhanced for several reasons. First, the search for a synthesis will encompass every single cultural field, each of which is reflective of the underlying perceptive framework. Second, acknowledging worldview as the presuppositional basis of things will put social researchers much "closer to the spontaneous, unintentional, basic impulse of a culture" (p. 14). This is certainly a great advantage for researchers who formerly were trying to ascertain a worldview from the overt theoretical pronouncements lodged within various disciplines. The primary point of Mannheim's analysis is that *Weltanschauung* belongs to the primordial realm in the most radical kind of way:

Not only that it [*Weltanschauung*] is in no way to be conceived of as a matter of logic and theory; not only that it cannot be integrally expressed through philosophical theses or, indeed, theoretical communications of any kind — in fact, compared to it, even all non-theoretical realizations, such as works of art, codes of ethics, systems of religion, are still in a way endowed with rationality, with explicitly interpretable meaning, whereas *Weltanschauung* as a global unit is something deeper, a still unformed and wholly germinal entity. (p. 16)

Therefore, for Mannheim, worldviews are virtually unconscious phenomena, having arisen spontaneously and unintentionally. As deep, unformed, and germinal entities, they are taken for granted by those who embrace them, and yet they are the prime movers in thought and action. They are the silent, speechless assumptions undergirding social life and cultural artifacts.

Now, it should be remembered that Mannheim's primary purpose in this essay is to elucidate the methodological principles for determining the global outlook of a specific era. Given the above description of worldviews as the primary cultural layer, then the original questions posed at the beginning resurface: Is it possible that they can be legitimate candidates for scientific research and discovery? Can these inchoate depth domains be scientifically studied and theoretically articulated?

Mannheim answers these questions affirmatively and proceeds to a lengthy discussion on the manner and method in which *Weltanschauung* can indeed be scientifically investigated and theoretically understood. Here I will only trace the broad brush strokes of his argument. He begins by examining the three possible kinds of meanings that cultural products may possess — the objective, the expressive, and the documentary or evidential. The objective is based *immediately* on the object as it is; the expressive is based *mediately* on what was meant by the subject; and the documentary or evidential is also based *mediately* on the essential character, synoptic appraisal, and global orientation of the subject (pp. 18-22). For Mannheim, a scientific knowledge of worldview is possible through the last of these three modes of meaning. He writes: "And the totality we call the 'genius' or 'spirit' (of an epoch) is given to us in this mode of 'documentary' meaning; this is the perspective in which we grasp the elements that go to make up the global outlook of a creative individual or of an epoch" (p. 23). What Mannheim then does is show that cultural products do in fact possess documentary meaning (pp. 24-28). His next step is to describe the way in which this documentary meaning of cultural artifacts is grasped in the direct experience of the pretheoretical (pp. 38-45). Finally, he shows that in every cultural product a documentary meaning, reflecting a global outlook, is given. To the extent that this is indeed the case, Mannheim is able to demonstrate that *Weltanschauung* and documentary meaning are capable of scientific investigation and theoretical articulation (pp. 45-57).

"The crucial question" that Mannheim wrestles with in this methodological section of his treatise "is how the totality we call the spirit, *Weltanschauung*, of an epoch, can be distilled from the various [cultural] objectifications of that epoch — and how we can give a theoretical account of it" (p. 48). To put it in another way, he asks: "How can we describe the [worldview] unity we sense in all works that belong to the same period in scientific terms capable of control and verification?" One particularly infamous problem plaguing his attempt to provide a scientifically sound methodology for the verification of an epochal worldview is the problem of the hermeneutic circle. Here is how Mannheim states the problem for his system: "We derive the 'spirit of the epoch' from its individual documentary manifestations — and we interpret the individual documentary manifestations on the basis of what we know about the spirit of the epoch. All of which goes to substantiate the assertion . . . that in the cultural sciences the part and the whole are given simultaneously" (p. 49).

Though he does not (and probably cannot) resolve this problem, he nonetheless attempts to show how his documentary method is capable of ascertaining the very spirit of an age with scientific credibility. As he puts it, "All such attempts at documentary interpretation gather the scattered items of documentary meaning together in overarching general concepts which are variously designated as the 'art motive,' . . . 'economic ethos,' . . . 'Weltanschauung,' . . . or 'spirit' . . . depending on the cultural fields explored" (p. 33). His ambition, as he states in his conclusion, is "to draw the meaning and form of pre-theoretical data within the orbit of science" and thereby provide social scientists in quest of a *Weltanschauung* the experience of an emancipation from a methodology derived entirely from the natural sciences (p. 57).

By way of summary, Mannheim seems to be a latter-day reincarnation of the spirit of Wilhelm Dilthey in at least two ways. First is his concern with methodology. As Dilthey sought to establish a firm scientific foundation for the social sciences, so here we see Mannheim attempting to do a similar thing by designing a method for grasping the very spirit of an age *(Zeitgeist)*. Motivated by the recent trend toward synthesis, and basing his method on a recognition that cultural artifacts cannot be properly understood in isolation or atomistically, Mannheim was in pursuit of an approach that could lead to valid, verifiable scientific knowledge of worldviews. Whether or not he was successful is another matter. Second, Mannheim is also reminiscent of Dilthey in placing *Weltanschauung* at the pretheoretical level. Dilthey was clear that the three fundamental worldviews which he categorized (naturalism, the idealism of freedom, and objective idealism) were ground zero for formal theoretical enterprises. A primordial layer of consciousness (or unconsciousness), a fundamental attitude about the world, animated public endeavors. Mannheim situates worldviews in the same epistemic location: as foundational to the construction of straightforward theoretical and cultural structures. Though Dilthey related worldviews to the cosmos, and Mannheim with the "social totality," still for both, worldviews constituted the *Urstoff*, or primary substance of thought. This, of course, is what gave rise to the methodological problem for Mannheim in the first place. And as a final aside, this Diltheyan and Mannheimian understanding of *Weltanschauung* as presuppositional to knowledge enterprises and cultural phenomena seems to be the position on worldview adopted by James Orr, Abraham Kuyper, the Dutch neo-Calvinists, and various North American evangelical thinkers.

Peter Berger and Thomas Luckmann: The Sociology of Knowledge and Sacred Canopy

The essential problematic addressed by the discipline of the sociology of knowledge is manifested clearly in this famous thought of Pascal's: "we see neither justice nor injustice which does not change its nature with change in climate. Three degrees of latitude reverse all jurisprudence; a meridian decides the truth. Fundamental laws change after a few years of possession; right has its epochs; the entry of Saturn into the Lion marks to us the origin of such and such a crime. A strange justice that is bounded by a river! Truth on this side of the Pyrenees, error on the other side."[25]

Why is it that conceptions of justice, jurisprudence, right, truth, and error change with changes in geography, epoch, and social setting? What, really, are the ultimate determinants of "truth" and "reality"? Must not these determinants be intimately related to social and existential factors? Are not the differences in spiritual and cognitive structures to be attributed to the diversity of social and historical contexts? How are worldviews, whether as pretheoretical entities or as more formal conceptual matrices, generated, distributed, and maintained by a social group and embraced by individuals within it? Why does culture differ from culture so markedly in knowledge, consciousness, and cos-

---

25. Blaise Pascal, *Pensées*, trans. W. F. Trotter, in *The Great Books of the Western World*, vol. 33 (Chicago: William Benton and Encyclopaedia Britannica, 1952), p. 225 (§5.294). Pascal's thought summarizes the issues addressed in the sociology of knowledge for Peter L. Berger and Thomas L. Luckmann. See their *The Social Construction of Reality: A Treatise in the Sociology of Knowledge* (New York: Doubleday, Anchor Books, 1966), p. 5.

mic outlook? These are the kinds of questions investigated in the sociology of knowledge. This subdiscipline within sociology may be roughly defined as an "analysis of the regularities of those social processes and structures that pertain to intellectual life and to modes of knowing (Scheler), and as a theory of the existential connectedness of thought (Mannheim)."[26] To be sure, if "worldview" conceptions are to be found in sociology, they are most likely to appear in the context of this enterprise (though it has considerable competition from other themes such as ideology, social frameworks, background assumptions, paradigms, etc.). Still, worldview has a natural home in this academic setting.[27] As Charles Smith suggests, a guiding principle of the sociology of knowledge is that the way people view the world is influenced if not determined by their social location. He states that "the sociologist of knowledge is out to understand 'the inherent biases of particular worldviews in terms of social conditions which gave rise to that particular worldview.'"[28] No less a figure than Karl Mannheim would seem to agree, for, according to Peter Hamilton, the sociology of knowledge is to him "the inquiry into the social conditions under which certain *Weltanschauungen* appear."[29] Max Scheler confirms this perspective by asserting that one of the chief purposes of the sociology of knowledge is to discover the laws governing the establishment of what he calls the "relatively natural Weltanschauung." As he states, the discovery of this species of worldview as an unjustified and unjustifiable mind-set which is accepted by a community or culture is one of the chief contributions of the sociology of knowledge.

> One of the most reliable insights with which the sociology of knowledge provides us with respect to so-called primitives, the biomorphic worldview of the child, and the whole Western civilization until the beginning of modern times, and which also is provided by comparing the relative . . . natural views of the world in the largest cultural units, is the following: there is *no one constant* natural view of the world belonging to "the" human being *at all;* rather, the various images of the world reach down into the categorical *structures of the given itself.*[30]

26. *The Blackwell Dictionary of Twentieth-Century Social Thought* (1993), s.v. "sociology of knowledge."

27. Griffioen, "Worldview Approach," p. 88.

28. Charles W. Smith, *A Critique of Sociological Reasoning: An Essay in Philosophical Sociology* (Oxford: Basil Blackwell, 1979), p. 110, quoted in Griffioen, "Worldview Approach," p. 88.

29. Peter Hamilton, *Knowledge and Social Structure: An Introduction to the Classical Argument in the Sociology of Knowledge* (London: Routledge and Kegan Paul, 1974), p. 121, quoted in Griffioen, "Worldview Approach," p. 88.

30. Max Scheler, *Problems of a Sociology of Knowledge,* trans. Manfred S. Frings, edited and introduction by Kenneth W. Stikkers (Boston: Routledge and Kegan Paul, 1980), pp. 74-75.

From these comments there seems to be little doubt about the connection between worldview and the discipline of the sociology of knowledge, the genealogy of which is rather fascinating. Examples demonstrating the relationship between social setting and the intellectual consciousness of the human mind may be traced all the way back to antiquity.[31] Plato's concept of *doxa,* for example, is the view that the opinions, and indeed the very souls, of people (nonphilosophers and the lower classes) are shaped by their encounter with the empirical world of becoming, and by their mechanical crafts. The fact that the fixed patterns of life and ideas in the Middle Ages were eventually acknowledged as socially affected is revealed in Machiavelli's quip that thought in the palace is one thing, but in the marketplace it is quite another. The doctrines of both the rationalists and the empiricists in the modern period also contribute to this heritage. The rationalists' belief that truth, like the algorithms of mathematics, must be one led them to explain the abundance of error as something rooted in sociocultural life. Despite the attempt of empiricists to give a realistic account of knowledge, their belief that nothing is in the mind unless it is first in the senses was a virtual guarantee that different experiences and sensory input would lead to different conceptions of reality, even to the point of skepticism. Francis Bacon's thesis of the "idols of the mind" as the sources of deception shows how much of human knowledge is generated by the tribe, the marketplace, the theater, and the cave. Even Immanuel Kant's attempt to establish knowledge in the a priori categories of the human mind has been "socially" questioned, especially in the observation that "Kant's table of categories is just a table of the categories of the European mind."[32] All these features of Western thought prepared the way for the analysis of knowledge sociologically.

The "root proposition" of the sociology of knowledge was conceived by Karl Marx. In his preface to *A Contribution to the Critique of Political Economy,* he wrote these often quoted words: "The mode of production of material life conditions the social, political and intellectual life process in general. It is not the consciousness of men that determines their being, but, on the contrary, their social being that determines their consciousness."[33] Obviously for Marx there are two fundamental cultural layers, the "substructure" *(Unterbau),* consisting of a set of economic relationships, which is determinative for the "superstructure" *(Überbau)* of consciousness and intellect. Knowledge does not

31. *The Encyclopedia of Philosophy* (1967), s.v. "sociology of knowledge."

32. Max Scheler, "The Sociology of Knowledge: Formal Problems," in *The Sociology of Knowledge: A Reader,* ed. James E. Curtis and John W. Petras (New York: Praeger, 1970), p. 178.

33. Karl Marx, "Preface to *A Contribution to the Critique of Political Economy,*" in *The Marx-Engels Reader,* ed. Robert C. Tucker, 2nd ed. (New York: Norton, 1978), p. 4. The expression "root proposition" applied to Marx is from Berger and Luckmann, p. 5.

spring eternal out of the sky (as those who believe in revelation might say) or purely out of the human mind (as rationalists and idealists would be inclined to think). Rather, it is the result of the socioeconomic conditions of life, as the materialists assert. This root proposition became the starting point for the modern discipline of the sociology of knowledge: What are the underlying, social determinants for knowledge, worldviews included?

Peter Berger and Thomas Luckmann present a theory of the sociology of knowledge which distinguishes them from their colleagues. They bracket the epistemological and methodological problems that are typically associated with this academic discipline, and place it entirely within the scope of general empirical, or "man on the street," sociology. This leads to a redefinition of the field itself. The sociology of knowledge has been concerned primarily with the social stimuli of intellectual history, theoretical thought, systems of ideas, and so on. While Berger and Luckmann allow that this is a legitimate *part* of the discipline, it should not be the *whole* of it. Whereas classic methods and models have emphasized intellectual history in its concern for the social genealogy of theories, ideas, and ideologies, they submit that the sociology of knowledge should cast a much wider net. *"The sociology of knowledge,"* they argue, *"must concern itself with everything that passes for 'knowledge' in society."*[34] The consequence, for our purposes, is that Berger and Luckmann reduce the importance of worldview as a central concern and object of investigation in this discipline because of its allegedly strong theoretical orientation. Instead they emphasize, under the influence of Alfred Schutz, the significance of the historical, sociocultural "lifeworld" *(Lebenswelt)* of common people as the primary source of cognitive awareness. Here is how they state their case: "Theoretical thought, 'ideas,' *Weltanschauungen* are not that important in society. Although every society contains these phenomena, they are only part of the sum of what passes for 'knowledge.' Only a very limited group of people in any society engages in theorizing, in the business of 'ideas,' and the construction of *Weltanschauungen*. But everyone in society participates in its 'knowledge' in one way or another."[35]

Since few people in any given society are theoretically sophisticated, and since all people in society occupy some kind of symbolic "world," to focus the sociology of knowledge on the minority rather than the majority is inappropriately restrictive. Naturally theorizers, like sociologists of knowledge, would tend to emphasize the importance of theory, but this is an "intellectualistic misapprehension." Rarefied cognitive systems, whether they be religious, scientific,

---

34. Berger and Luckmann, pp. 14-15, emphasis Berger and Luckmann's.
35. Berger and Luckmann, p. 15.

or philosophical, do not constitute the entirety of a society's knowledge supply. Therefore Berger and Luckmann draw this conclusion: "Since this is so, the sociology of knowledge must first of all concern itself with what people 'know' as 'reality' in their everyday, non- or pre-theoretical lives. In other words, commonsense 'knowledge' rather than 'ideas' must be the central focus for the sociology of knowledge. It is precisely this 'knowledge' that constitutes the fabric of meanings without which no society could exist."[36]

While Berger and Luckmann are clear that theoretical articulations like worldviews are still a part of their concern, they will not be their primary one. Rather, their major concern is with that level of knowing that is antecedent to all theorizing and taken for granted. They are concerned with that preconscious, epistemic substructure that is productive of worldviews as formal, theoretical constructs. Of course, some like Dilthey and Mannheim understand worldviews to reside precisely at that level, and when defined in this way, no doubt worldviews would be candidates for sociological scrutiny along the lines Berger and Luckmann have prescribed. In other words, worldviews, whether they realize it or not, would be "what people 'know' as 'reality' in their everyday, non- or pre-theoretical lives." Berger and Luckmann, however, do not define worldview in this way, and this is the reason for their lack of concern about it. In short, they are seeking to transform the sociology of knowledge from an elitist discipline to an egalitarian one. Here is how they summarize their position:

It is our contention, then, that the sociology of knowledge must concern itself with whatever passes for "knowledge" in a society, regardless of the ultimate validity or invalidity . . . of such "knowledge." And insofar as all human "knowledge" is developed, transmitted and maintained in social situations, the sociology of knowledge must seek to understand the process by which this is done in such a way that a taken-for-granted "reality" congeals for the man in the street. In other words, we contend that *the sociology of knowledge is concerned with the analysis of the social construction of reality.*[37]

The three parts of Berger and Luckmann's book — *The Social Construction of Reality* — are devoted to developing this thesis. After a prolegomenon in part 1, they turn their attention in the second section to an analysis entitled "Society as an Objective Reality." Here they consider how "reality" has congealed or become reified for the average person, especially in terms of institutionalization and legitimation. In the third part they discuss "Society as Subjective Reality," in which they analyze the internalization of "reality" through the socialization pro-

36. Berger and Luckmann, p. 15.
37. Berger and Luckmann, p. 3.

cess. This world that is socially created possesses both objective and subjective validity, and functions as if it were the law *(nomos)* that governs all reality. It is an intelligent, coherent, normative perspective that makes sense of things as they are encountered in daily life. Now, though they are unwilling to call such a perspective a "worldview," nonetheless, what they are describing certainly sounds like one. Defined more generally in this way, a "worldview" becomes precisely what Berger and Luckmann target for sociological understanding.

In Berger's estimation there are both biological and psychological imperatives ingrained into the human psyche necessitating the creation of such a symbolic, law-abiding world. Human beings must fabricate a conceptual shield to protect themselves from what would otherwise be an alienating and meaningless cosmos. It functions, as he puts it, as a "sacred canopy" which protects whole cultures and individuals from the ever present threat of chaos. In a separate book titled *The Sacred Canopy*, Berger as the lone author explains what he means by this concept, focusing on the idea of *nomos* which structures or orders the world: "Seen in the perspective of society, every nomos is an area of meaning carved out of a vast mass of meaninglessness, a small clearing of lucidity in a formless, dark, always ominous jungle. Seen in the perspective of the individual, every nomos represents the bright 'dayside' of life, tenuously held onto against the sinister shadows of the 'night.' In both perspectives, every nomos is an edifice erected in the face of potent and alien forces of chaos. This chaos must be kept at bay at all costs."[38]

A comprehensive system of law and order, then, is fabricated to shield its creators from catastrophe. A thin, cognitive line separates individuals and societies from a direct encounter with nihilism. Should that line be erased or the canopy collapse, a crisis of the highest magnitude would result in the exposure of absolute nothingness.

Long ago, the writer of the book of Ecclesiastes, with great bluntness, described the unvarnished character of human existence "under the sun" as vain and futile, a hopeless endeavor of chasing after the wind. Better, he said pessimistically, is the day of one's death than the day of one's birth (Eccles. 7:1). More recently, existential philosophers have depicted life in the cosmos in similarly alarming terms as a "plague" (Camus), or as the experience of unmitigated "nausea" (Sartre). Despair, anxiety, and boredom are the emotional companions of life. Though separated by several thousand years, these two points of view, one biblical and one extrabiblical, are poignant reminders of the essential nihilism that seemingly pervades the cosmos, at least in its fallen state. Human

38. Peter L. Berger, *The Sacred Canopy: Elements of a Sociological Theory of Religion* (New York: Doubleday, Anchor Books, 1967), pp. 23-24.

beings cannot survive, much less thrive, in such a chaotic environment without some kind of prophylactic apparatus that mercifully shields them from the hard, cold, cruel facts of reality. In this regard, we are reminded of Karl Jaspers's concept of the "ultimate situations" in life that consist of conflict, suffering, guilt, and death. These "limit" or "boundary" conditions, as he also calls them, spawn the production of various cognitive and fiduciary "shells" as necessary ways of coping with the virtually omnipresent pain and madness. As Jaspers himself noted, human beings cannot live without their "shells" any more than mussels can live without theirs.

For these reasons, we also have the production of what Berger calls "sacred canopies." Nihilism is, indeed, unlivable, and as a preventative measure to keep chaos at bay, the human race makes every effort to manufacture a stable, symbolic universe that shields it from the ultimate terrors of an unconceptualized world. Some kind of "truth" about the nature of things is a fundamental human and social necessity to offset cognitive and existential homelessness. Postponing for now the question about their truthfulness, it would seem that this is precisely the function worldviews play in human experience: not necessarily as well-developed conceptual systems (though they may be), but at least as general impressions about the nature of the universe and life within it, a law or framework or paradigm that generates some kind of order amidst plentiful chaos. A worldview is indeed a kind of "sacred canopy," "sacred" in its supreme value to adherents, and "canopy" in its service as a protective shield against the ever present threat of nihilism. Though Berger and Luckmann substantially removed worldviews as intellectual systems from epistemic consideration, to redefine them in less academic terms as presuppositional constructs and to connect them with the concept of the sacred canopy would make them suitable candidates for sociological analysis. Indeed, if worldviews have something significant to say about an individual's or society's understanding about the nature of reality, then it seems eminently plausible to suggest that a key to unlocking a comprehension of their production, distribution, and influence is to be found in the sociology of knowledge.

Karl Marx and Friedrich Engels: Worldview and Ideology

Because of the high stakes associated with this essential human activity of world making, socially constructed realities can sometimes harden into "ideologies" in which ideas are used as "weapons for social interest."[39] "Sacred cano-

---

39. Berger and Luckmann, p. 6.

pies" can solidify and quickly be used as a club. Karl Marx and Friedrich Engels were prescient in their understanding of this reality and its use by the bourgeois class for their own advantage. Though references abound to the "Marxist worldview," or the "Marxist-Leninist" *Weltanschauung*,[40] technically speaking it was Friedrich Engels (1820-95), more so than Karl Marx (1818-83), who was concerned about worldview, the materialist version in particular. In his reflections on the metaphysic of the "revolution," Engels argues that its basic philosophical hypothesis concerns the relationship of mind and matter. Mind is a function of matter in both ontological and epistemic ways. Nature, in other words, is the "whole show" (to use a "Lewisism"). This "general" and "simple" worldview of dialectical materialism, as Engels calls it, is the truly scientific philosophy. It is characterized by science's traditional claims to objectivity, rationality, universality, and certainty. Because of the influence of Engels in the Communist world, most of those occupying this geopolitical sphere accept his declaration that scientific, dialectical materialism is the normative way of conceiving reality.[41] This view of the communist *Weltanschauung* is more than apparent in the following description from the *Great Soviet Encyclopedia* which contains more than just a little propaganda.

> In contrast to the bourgeois world view, the communist world view, which summarizes advances in science and social practice, is consistently scientific, internationalist, and humanistic. Its origin coincided with the appearance of the workers' revolutionary movement. Marxist-Leninist philosophy — dialectical and historical materialism — forms the core of the communist world view. The Marxist-Leninist world view is a powerful tool for the revolutionary transformation of the world. It is one of the decisive forces that organizes people in the struggle for socialism and communism. In the contemporary world there is an acute struggle between two opposing world views — the communist and the bourgeois. The influence of Marxism-Leninism, which triumphs through the strength of truth and the validity of its consistently scientific premises, is growing during this struggle.[42]

The Marxist-Leninist worldview became the dominant ideology in socialist society, providing the context for meaning in life and supplying the grid for

---

40. For example, see John McMurtry, *The Structure of Marx's World-View* (Princeton: Princeton University Press, 1978); see the references to the "Marxist-Leninist" worldview in the *Great Soviet Encyclopedia*, 3rd ed. (1977), s.v. "world view."

41. Griffioen, "Worldview Approach," pp. 86-87.

42. *Great Soviet Encyclopedia*, 3rd ed., s.v. "world view."

shaping and interpreting the sum total of human events. "The formation of the communist worldview among broad masses of working people is the heart of all the party's work in ideological upbringing."[43] The implications of this *Weltanschauung* are total, affecting every area of thought, life, and culture. "The Communist Party strives to make every person see the meaning of his life in the struggle for the practical embodiment of the ideals of communism, understand clearly the course of and prospects for the development of world events, analyze sociopolitical events correctly, and consciously build the new society. A very important task of the party is the upbringing of people in the communist [worldview] attitude toward work, in communist morality, and in true humanism, patriotism, and internationalism."[44]

Engels believed that Marxism best embodied the implications of the materialist worldview for all the important fields of knowledge. Whereas Marx never showed much interest in the transformation of the sciences from the perspective of his own system, Engels did. The latter recognized that the masses of the working people — the proletariat — aspired to understand the totality of life and its mysteries within the framework of Marxist scientific materialism. Hence he proceeded to work out the details of this *intellectus* in a comprehensive way, extending its implications across the sciences and forming a vision of life that would serve as the cognitive center for the party.[45]

Now, whereas Marx may have been relatively complacent about the broader disciplinary implications of his own *Weltanschauung*, he was certainly concerned about its close relative in the notion of ideology.[46] According to the *Great Soviet Encyclopedia*, "The concept of world view is related to that of ideology but does not coincide with it. World view is a broader concept than ideology, which encompasses only those aspects of a world view that are oriented toward social phenomena and class relations. World view, in contrast, applies to all objective reality."[47] Marx explored how an ideology, as a subset or species of *Weltanschauung*, can be deployed as cognitive weaponry in service to class interests, whether they be revolutionary or reactionary, progressive or conservative, liberal or radical, internationalist or nationalist.

The Marxist notion of ideology may be understood in relation to a question that occupied the French philosophes but which they had not been able to answer

---

43. *Great Soviet Encyclopedia*, 3rd ed., s.v. "world view."
44. *Great Soviet Encyclopedia*, 3rd ed., s.v. "world view."
45. Griffioen, "Worldview Approach," p. 87.
46. For book-length treatments of this topic, see Martin Seliger, *The Marxist Conception of Ideology: A Critical Essay* (Cambridge: Cambridge University Press, 1977); Bhikhu Parekh, *Marx's Theory of Ideology* (Baltimore: Johns Hopkins University Press, 1982).
47. *Great Soviet Encyclopedia*, 3rd ed., s.v. "world view."

satisfactorily: "Why have there been so many false beliefs about society and human nature?"[48] Intellectual limitations and the rhetoric of propagandists were the reasons, said the Enlightenment theorists, but for Marx these factors were insufficient to account for such differences. Marx proposed an alternative explanation highlighting the theme of ideology: "As far as societies divided into classes are concerned, Marx's main answer is that much ideology is inevitable in a class society, because the economically dominant class requires the existence of false beliefs for its continued dominance and has resources for perpetuating beliefs that are in its interests."[49] In a society consisting of the bourgeoisie and proletariat, plus a division of labor of the mental and manual kinds, there is every likelihood that the members of the majority working class will experience a kind of alienation from their work, thereby creating a sense of dehumanization and unrest. However, those who own the means of production cannot afford to lose control of their profitable situation. In order to preserve their estate of preeminence and privilege, the dominant class must construct systems of belief about ultimate concerns (God, the universe, humanity, morality, etc.), and communicate them persuasively to the masses to keep them subdued. Stupefied by these reifications, the working class develops a false consciousness, convinced that the present socioeconomic order is sanctioned by the natural or eternal orders. In the ongoing class warfare, bourgeois capitalists devise an ideological superstructure that keeps the proletariat in check. Marx describes this process in his work *The German Ideology,* where many of his reflections on the subject are found. "The ideas of the ruling class are in every epoch the ruling ideas: i.e. the class, which is the ruling material force of society, is at the same time its ruling intellectual force. The class which has the means of material production at its disposal, has control at the same time over the means of mental production, so that thereby, generally speaking, the ideas of those who lack the means of mental production are subject to it."[50]

Marx believes that human beings are the architects of their own ideas and conceptions, especially as these are generated out of the material and social conditions of life. He is clear in his central proposition regarding the origin of human consciousness: "Life is not determined by consciousness, but consciousness by life."[51] The reigning intellectual paradigm is nothing other than an expression of the consciousness of the ruling class as it has been spawned by the existing material conditions. These governing ideas are received as timeless,

48. Richard W. Miller, "Social and Political Theory: Class, State, Revolution," in *The Cambridge Companion to Marx,* ed. Terrell Carver (Cambridge: Cambridge University Press, 1991), p. 73.

49. Miller, p. 74.

50. Karl Marx and Friedrich Engels, *The German Ideology,* Parts I and II, edited and introduction by R. Pascal (New York: International Publishers, 1947), p. 39.

51. Marx and Engels, p. 15.

universal laws, wrought into the very constitution of the universe. Hence the notions of the ruling class determine the intellectual contours of the epochs they dominate. "In so far, therefore, as they rule as a class and determine the extent and compass of an epoch, it is self-evident that they do this in their whole range, hence among other things rule also as thinkers, as producers of ideas, and regulate the production and distribution of the ideas of their age: thus their ideas are the ruling ideas of the epoch."[52]

Marx and Engels's ambition is to purge the working classes of their false consciousness so as to liberate them for the revolution against their oppressors. In the past, "philosophers have only *interpreted* the world differently." Marx, however, is quite clear: "the point is to *change* it."[53] This transformation must begin with a deliverance from ideological bondage. Consequently, Marx and Engels set their agenda forthrightly: "Let us liberate them from the chimeras, the ideas, dogmas, imaginary beings under the yoke of which they are pining away. Let us revolt against the rule of thoughts."[54]

Of course, Marx and Engels do not regard their own system of thought as either a reification or ideology. It does not seem to be caught in the quicksands of time or relativism either. How do they pull off this epistemological escape act? The answer is rather simple. They view their own system as the true philosophy and the only genuinely scientific *Weltanschauung*. All ideologies and competitive worldviews lack the distinguishing scientific and metaphysical credentials of Marxism. Its scientificity, grounded in dialectical materialism, provides it with the necessary criteria to critique oppressive socioeconomic structures and their self-serving ideologies. Marx and Engels, obviously quintessential modernists, shared the Enlightenment's confidence in reason and science. As an incarnation of this era's epistemology, they apparently saw their own system as a touchstone of truth, the coveted Archimedean point from which to judge and move the world. For Marx and Engels, then, the polar opposite of all ideologies was the truth and objectivity of their own scientific worldview.[55]

---

52. Marx and Engels, p. 39.

53. Marx and Engels, p. 199. This is number eleven of Marx's famous "Theses on Feuerbach."

54. Marx and Engels, p. 1. In line with this vision, Paulo Freire, in his *Pedagogy of the Oppressed*, trans. Myra B. Ramos, new revised twentieth anniversary edition (New York: Continuum, 1994), has formulated a radical philosophy of education that is aimed at overcoming the dominant "culture of silence" among the oppressed through the process of *"conscientização."* This pedagogy entails learning dialogically "to perceive social, political, and economic contradictions, and to take action against the oppressive elements of reality" (p. 17).

55. Job L. Dittberner, *The End of Ideology and American Social Thought: 1930-1960*, Studies in American History and Culture, no. 1 (UMI Research Press, 1979), p. 4.

To sum up, Marx and Engels made important contributions to ideas about ideology and worldview respectively. Marx did not trace out the theoretical implications of his own philosophical framework, but he did derive from its central propositions a powerful conception of ideology by which he explained the dynamics of cultural deception and domination. Ideologies are the offspring of material productivity and social relations, and are always ruling-class supportive. They are instruments of power serving the interests of the stronger party as mystifying interpretations of the order of things. Engels took the metaphysic of dialectical materialism, wed it to Marxism, and extended its application to all the relevant disciplines. In his hands Marxism became an all-encompassing *Weltanschauung* affecting the sum total of human existence. While they may be technically distinguishable in Marxist thought, worldviews and ideologies are fundamental ways of conceiving of the nature of things, and the latter can certainly be pressed into service to insure the hegemony of the dominant economic class.

"Worldview" in Cultural Anthropology

In this section we will undertake an inquiry into what might be called the "worldview tradition" in cultural anthropology, especially as it has developed in the United States.[56] The "ethos" of this worldview tradition has been captured nicely in a personal statement from Bronislaw Malinowski in which he expresses his anthropological passion in terms of worldview.

> What interests me really in the study of the native is his outlook on things, his *Weltanschauung*, the breath of life and reality which he breathes and by which he lives. Every human culture gives its members a definite vision of the world, a definite zest of life. In the roamings over human history, and over the surface of the earth, it is the possibility of seeing life and the

56. For surveys of anthropologists in the United States and elsewhere who contribute to this tradition, see *Dictionary of Concepts in Cultural Anthropology* (1991), s.v. "world view"; *International Encyclopedia of the Social Sciences* (1968), s.v. "world view." Two additional sources ought also to be consulted: Clifford Geertz, "Ethos, World-view and the Analysis of Sacred Symbols," *Antioch Review* 17 (1957): 421-37, reprinted in *The Interpretation of Cultures* (New York: Basic Books, 1973), pp. 193-233. In this work Geertz distinguishes between ethos and worldview, asserting that the former refers to the normative and evaluative aspects of culture and the latter to cognitive, existential aspects of the way the world is structured. See also W. T. Jones's report on a conference held in August 1968 at Burg Wartenstein under the sponsorship of the Wenner-Gren Foundation on the topic: "World Views: Their Nature and Their Function," *Current Anthropology* 13 (1972): 79-109.

world from the various angles, peculiar to each culture, that has always charmed me most, and inspired me with real desire to penetrate other cultures, to understand other types of life.[57]

Despite the importance of worldview, there is an unfortunate dearth of theoretical reflection on this topic. As Michael Kearney states, "Although world view is one of the central subjects of American cultural anthropology, there is surprisingly little theoretical literature concerning it."[58] Undeniably, the popularity of the worldview concept in contemporary anthropology has declined precipitously. This is largely due to the "linguistic turn" in social theory in which semiotics and other branches of language study now provide the paradigms for thinking about and interpreting cultural phenomena. Though they are roughly synonymous, references to the "symbolic order" or "cultural code" have replaced "worldview," and clearly are in ascendancy today.[59] Despite this recent trend, the concept of worldview has a marked place in anthropological theory and history, as we will see. We will begin with a look at Michael Kearney's book-length treatment of worldview in which he theorizes about the concept from a distinctively Marxist point of view.

Michael Kearney: Worldview

At the outset of his volume, Michael Kearney affirms what this present study has already demonstrated; namely, that "world view is a subject of immense importance in the social sciences and philosophy." His regret is that "a coherent theory of world view is nonexistent," and so one of the primary purposes of his book is "to advance the study of world view" both theoretically and practically.[60] His approach is scientific in nature and informed by a variety of Marxist assumptions (pp. 1, 53, and passim). First of all, Kearney believes that worldview "is a potentially powerful tool for exploring the recesses of socially constructed

57. Bronislaw Malinowski, *Argonauts of the Western Pacific* (London: Routledge and Kegan Paul, 1922), p. 517.

58. Michael Kearney, *Worldview* (Novato, Calif.: Chandler and Sharp, 1984), p. 1. Kearney's observation is confirmed by a survey of two prominent textbooks on anthropological theory in which the theme is nowhere addressed. See Marvin Harris, *The Rise of Anthropological Theory: A History of Theories of Culture* (New York: Harper Collins, 1968); Paul Bohannan and Mark Glazer, eds., *High Points in Anthropology* (New York: McGraw-Hill, 1988).

59. Griffioen, "Worldview Approach," p. 90.

60. Kearney, *Worldview*, p. 9; the page references in the following text are to this work. For additional insight on Kearney's project, see also his "World View Theory and Study," *Annual Review of Anthropology* 4 (1975): 247-70.

human consciousness, and thus has the potential — as largely yet unrealized — for liberation in all senses of the word" (p. ix). In other words, an understanding of worldviews as either the cause or effect of a socially constructed reality could contribute significantly to the de-reification of various belief or meaning systems, and facilitate the exodus of those held captive by them. This is certainly a Marxist concern.

Second, Kearney sees a deep connection between worldviews and ideology.[61] Not only do worldviews (plural) serve class interests, but even thinking or theorizing about "worldview" itself as a concept is ideologically grounded (especially in either the traditions of cultural idealism or historical materialism). As Kearney puts it, "The assumption here is that a world-view theory as well as any general world view is more often than not an outlook of a group or class, defined as such in opposition to others, hence it tends to be ideological in nature. That is, it serves to advance or perpetuate the social position of those who held [sic] the view, depending on how they sit in relation to their antagonists" (p. 2). Indeed, Kearney believes the ideological source of contemporary worldview theory is that of "American liberal bourgeois culture in general," and specifically the "tacit assumptions of liberal anthropology" (p. x). His goal is to craft an alternative model — a "progressive, truly liberating model of world view" that is sympathetic to Marxist dispositions (p. x). Kearney is obviously aware of the "sociological relativity of world-view theory" itself (p. 2). He recognizes that there is no neutral, value-free ground on which to stand in constructing, promoting, or critiquing worldview theory itself. Even positivism, besides being poor philosophy and bad science, is an ideological prejudice. Every theorist addressing worldview is doing so from this or that particular perspective. The results of such theorizing will naturally express the ideological point of view of the theorist. A worldview, in other words, underlies any and every theory of "worldview"!

This leads to one of the most important contributions of Kearney's book, namely, his call for a recognition of the ideological biases informing worldview

---

61. In a more recent publication, Kearney relates worldview not only to ideology but also to "hegemony." Ideology and hegemony as worldview (especially pertaining to race, class, or gender) are somewhere on a sliding scale or continuum. On the one hand, class-supportive ideologies are largely the direct work of intellectuals (teachers, politicians, writers, priests, etc.) who are busy explaining and interpreting the world in a certain way for class purposes. For example, propaganda created by specialists in the management of public opinion about a variety of social and political issues is a pure form of ideology. On the other hand, ideas that are hegemonic tend to be "nonagentive" and are conceived commonsensically as the way things are. Hegemonic ideas are embedded in folklore, figures of speech, ethnicity, values, and of course, worldview. Successful ideological endeavors in due course will become hegemonic. See Kearney's article in *Encyclopedia of Cultural Anthropology* (1996), s.v. "worldview."

theory itself. What is needed is a "reflexive anthropology of worldview," or a "meta-worldview theory," exposing the ideological backgrounds that generate a particular perspective on worldview and worldviews (pp. x, 2). Worldview models and theories are not the product of presuppositionless thinking.

To develop this important contribution just a bit more, Kearney declares that the two most prominent ideological orientations driving worldview theory are cultural idealism and historical materialism. The former point of view has dominated American cultural anthropology and is conservative, and the latter is Marxist in orientation and progressive. The question being debated by both camps is a familiar one: Do ideas in consciousness cause social conditions, or do social conditions cause ideas in consciousness? Cultural idealism, believing that ideas are the preeminent reality, "assumes that material conditions are shaped by some immaterial force that operates essentially independent of matter and is responsible for material phenomena" (p. 11). According to this model in anthropology, culture consists of shared knowledge, acquired tacitly, and the goal of the anthropologist is to study the culture which is the product of ideas lodged in the minds of members of a community. On this score, worldviews would be conceived largely out of the thin air of thought, or by the independent operation of the mind creating its concepts or symbols which in due course shape the material conditions of life. Kearney argues that one primary reason why this idealist approach has dominated cultural anthropology in America is that most influential anthropologists have been relatively affluent and associated with the upper classes in Europe and America (including the tradition stemming from Franz Boas).[62] He makes this interesting and provocative comment: "And even today most anthropologists have not personally experienced hunger and poverty associated with life lived at a survival level. Consequently, living in a world of ideas, they tend to let this preoccupation with mental phenomena shape their anthropological theory and assume that ideas have the same importance in the lives of the people they study" (p. 16).

Contrary to this existential indifference is the school of historical materialism. This perspective, which embraces materiality as the final reality, "does give prime importance to material and social conditions as the origin of any particular self-consciousness and of knowledge in general. . . . In this view, the issue of human knowledge is inseparable from human practical affairs and human history" (p. 14). The label "historical materialism" is accurate, for the content of human thinking is the product of the flow of a history vitally connected to the material world. To draw on Kearney's colorful metaphor, the historical-

---

62. Kearney also places Edward Sapir, Ruth Benedict, Margaret Mead, Morris Opler, and Alfred Kroeber, among others, in the cultural idealist camp.

materialist substructure is the dog that wags the superstructural tail of consciousness (cultural idealists put this in reverse). If human consciousness is the fruit of absorption in historical and material life, then it is no wonder that advocates of this point of view criticize their idealist counterparts for wandering "in the superstructures of society without grounding their analyses in the base that is a major — usually the main — condition which shapes the social or cultural phenomena they are interested in" (p. 16). Whether theoreticians interested in worldview are materialists or idealists makes a big difference on the way they approach the subject, and on the outcome of their thinking. They cannot remain neutral, but must commit to one school of thought or the other. Given Kearney's own predilection, his main goal in this essay is "to rescue worldview from the idealist camp and take it to its proper home — which is . . . historical materialism" (p. 16).

Thus he proceeds to formulate a theory of "worldview" that is guided at every stage of its development by his commitment to this fundamental orientation. This includes Kearney's definition of "worldview," which he says "is a set of images and assumptions about the world" (p. 10). He elaborates on this cameo description with this enhanced statement: "The world view of a people is their way of looking at reality. It consists of basic assumptions and images that provide a more or less coherent, though not necessarily accurate way of thinking about the world. A world view comprises images of Self and of all that is recognized as not-Self, plus ideas about relationships between them, as well as other ideas . . ." (p. 41).

On the basis of this working definition of "worldview," Kearney cites three main problems that must be addressed in order to develop a coherent worldview theory (pp. 10, 65, 109, 207).[63] The first problem has to do with the necessary and universal types of images and assumptions which are part of any worldview. What universal, cognitive categories as products of the evolutionary process are constitutive of the human mind and necessary for worldview formation anywhere on the globe? What themes or images are intrinsic to every worldview, making comparisons and cross-cultural communication possible? This is an important feature to Kearney's model, and it is something of a Kantian one. He argues that just as there are universal characteristics to human anatomy and physiology that allow a doctor anywhere anytime to make a diagnosis and treat a patient medically, so also there is a "universal set of diagnostic categories to describe world views" (p. 65). Though the *substance* or content of these universals may and does differ, nonetheless they exist as independent categories in their own right. They are the universal worldview a prioris. Kearney

63. The content of these three problems has been summarized from the page numbers cited.

lists five of them: the self and other, relationship, classification, causality, space and time.[64] These dimensions of the mind are determinative for human thinking about life and reality, though the content of them shifts from time to time, context to context, culture to culture. These categories are integrated into a "logico-structural linkage" that comprises the skeleton upon which the flesh of any worldview must hang (pp. 65-107).

The second problem for Kearney's model has to do with the formation of these universals and categories. What connection or relationship do they sustain with the world they supposedly represent? What kinds of forces determine or shape the content of these various categories? What are the reasons for the differences in worldviews? Kearney mentions two basic factors. First are "external causes," by which he means noncognitive, environmental forces and conditions, including the natural environment, material living conditions, social organization, technology, and historical events that influence and shape thought. Second are "internal causes," which Kearney says have to do with the inner dynamics or the "jostling" of worldview assumptions in an attempt to achieve "logico-structural integration." Some kind of inner coherence and existential harmony must be created among the cognitive categories shaped by ideas and the material conditions of life. "For example," as Kearney states elsewhere, "ideas about causality are related to the classification of things in such a way that ideas about magical causality are consistent with the assumed presence of beings that can transform their identity, such as a witch that can take the form of an animal."[65] Kearney also illustrates this aspect of worldview formation by looking at the internal dynamics of Greek cosmology, and the intellectual structure of the scientific and biblical worldviews (pp. 109-45). Kearney also mentions that worldviews are frequently *projected* onto the universe and *reified*. As he explains, this comes about because "Humans seem to be uncomfortable not having answers to basic concerns such as life, death, illness, cosmology, and their own destinies in general. Consequently humans tend unconsciously to supply satisfying answers that often have little direct bearing on the things they purport to explain" (p. 117). These two features of Kearney's model — external and internal causes — are his attempt to explain how the universal worldview categories are formed and integrated into a comprehensive perspective on reality. This process is Kearney's explanation for worldview diversity and serves as the basis for their comparison, as well as communication between paradigms.

---

64. Kearney states in the conclusion of his book that these five universals are "artifacts of the Western intellectual tradition" and a reflection of a "pre-Einsteinian physics." They have obviously been generated sociologically and are therefore only provisional (p. 208).

65. *Encyclopedia of Cultural Anthropology*, s.v. "worldview."

This leads to the third and most important problem: the issue of a worldview's practical impact on daily life and behavior. What relationship exists between the content of worldview categories and sociocultural behavior? What kind of influence does a worldview have on life? To answer these questions, Kearney turns to two ethnographic examples. First is his study of the Indians of California (before their contact with Europeans) that illustrates the integration of one entire worldview. Secondly, he shows how the universals of the worldview of Mexican peasants, especially in Ixtepeji, have been formed through history by the experience of poverty, and how this worldview in turn affects their sociocultural-cultural behavior.[66] His main argument here is that the peasant worldview "can be understood only in an historic perspective that includes economic, political, and demographic relationships with the greater world of which the peasant community is a part" (p. 7). The essential ingredients of Kearney's model, then, are fleshed out in these two examples which include a demonstration of the impact of worldview on human behavior.

To review, Michael Kearney makes a fine effort to fill up what is lacking in worldview theory, especially in the context of cultural anthropology. He recognizes how the worldview concept can assist in understanding the nature of the socially constructed human consciousness and assist in its liberation. He also outlines the relationship of worldview to ideology in what is a most important contribution of his book. Kearney demonstrates not only how worldviews may serve as ideologies, but how certain ideological underpinnings affect theories about the nature, content, and function of worldviews themselves. Kearney's model consists of three basic components. First is the structuralist or Kantian identification of worldview universals. Second is formation and development of these universals through external and internal causes. The third aspect has to do with the impact of worldview categories, shaped by external and internal causes, on daily life and sociocultural-cultural behavior. Kearney's Marxist model of worldview is rich and fertile, spawning further thought and insight. As it stands, it is one of the most complete worldview models available today in any discipline.

66. For a book-length treatment of the worldview and social organization in Ixtepeji in the state of Oaxaca, Mexico, see Kearney's *The Winds of Ixtepeji: World View and Society in a Zapotec Town,* Case Studies in Cultural Anthropology, ed. George Spindler and Louise Spindler (New York: Holt, Rinehart and Winston, 1972).

Robert Redfield: The Primitive and Modern Worldview

For Robert Redfield (1897-1958), worldviews are as old as humankind. As he put it, "World view, of some sort, is as old as the other things that are equally human and that developed along with world view: culture, human nature, and personality."[67] Perhaps because he saw worldview as something intrinsically and venerably "anthropological," he made this theme one of the foci of his research program. Redfield was the leader of a larger group of scholars headquartered at the University of Chicago in the 1950s that made "worldview" a main topic of their work. Redfield showed initial interest in the subject in one of his earlier publications titled *The Folk Culture of Yucatan* (1941).[68] As his thinking progressed, he produced several important works on this topic. The first was a paper titled "The Primitive World View," published in 1952, followed by a chapter of similar substance called "The Primitive World View and Civilization"[69] that appeared in his book *The Primitive World and Its Transformations* (1953). Two additional monographs published in 1955 and 1956 present only modest advancements over his previous statements.[70] For present purposes, I will survey Redfield's 1953 installment "The Primitive World View and Civilization" that presents his essential thinking on the notion itself, and describes what he calls "the great world view transformation" as he explains the shift from the primitive to the modern view of life.[71]

Redfield believes that "worldview" identifies one of those things that are most general and persistent about people. It takes its place among a constellation of other humanistic concepts such as culture, ethos, national character, and personality type. According to Redfield, "worldview" should be defined as "the way a people characteristically look outward upon the universe" (p. 85). Culture, for example, designates the way a people appears to an anthropologist, but "'world view' suggests how everything looks to a people, 'the designation of the existent as a whole.'" "Worldview" is frequently associated with a variety of

---

67. Robert Redfield, *The Primitive World and Its Transformations* (Ithaca, N.Y.: Cornell University Press, Cornell Paperbacks, 1953), p. 103.

68. Robert Redfield, *The Folk Culture of Yucatan* (Chicago: University of Chicago Press, 1941).

69. Robert Redfield, "The Primitive World View," *American Philosophical Society Proceedings* 96 (1952): 30-36.

70. Robert Redfield, *The Little Community: Viewpoints for the Study of a Human Whole* (Chicago: University of Chicago Press, 1955); *Peasant Society and Culture: An Anthropological Approach to Civilization* (Chicago: University of Chicago Press, 1956).

71. The page numbers in the following text are from *The Primitive World and Its Transformations*.

issues: what is and ought to be, patterns and forms of thought, attitudes, time, emotions, and so on. However, for Redfield the term has a specific nuance, referring to "the structure of things as man is aware of them. It is in the way we see ourselves in relation to all else" (p. 86). A worldview is like a stage set on which each human being is a character seeing himself, speaking his lines, and viewing everything else. It encompasses many things — nature, unseen things (beings, principles, trends, destinies), history, and more. What is most important, according to Redfield, is the fact that all these things are organized and structured by a worldview. As he explains it, "The thing about world view that is different from culture, ethos, or national character, is that it is an arrangement of things looked out upon, things in first instance conceived of as existing. It is the way the limits or 'illimits,' the things to be lived with, in, or on, are characteristically known" (p. 87). Worldviews, then, parse the cosmos and all things in it paradigmatically, making knowledge of reality possible.

Does everyone in the same society have the same worldview? Redfield does not think so. There may be a very general way to classify a given people. All Americans, for example, could be described in very general terms as believing in liberty, equality, and the sovereignty of the people. At the same time, the more reflective, theoretical types in a culture see the world differently from their less philosophical neighbors. Even in primitive societies there are worldview differences between active and contemplative types, and this is even more the case in advanced, scientific societies. Worldviews, it seems, do differ *within* cultures (pp. 87-89).

Redfield wants to know what is true of all human beings, and what, if anything, is true of all worldviews. He believes the concept of worldview is one way to ascertain what is universal in human nature. One thing seems certain: all people look out upon and share the very same world. There is only one world, no matter how many ways it may be interpreted. Also, the concept of worldview itself seems universal. Everyone has a worldview, no exceptions. If this is so, as Redfield believes, it is possible to identify the common themes and categories with which all worldviews are concerned. In a manner similar to Kearney, he proceeds to identify several "worldview universals." First, there is the "self" and the "other." The self can be split between the "I" and the "me." The "other" than self can be subdivided into two categories, the "human" and the "nonhuman." The "human other" can be classified into groups of the "young" and the "old," the "male" and the "female," the "us" and the "them." The "nonhuman other" is also divisible into two domains, "God" and "nature." Finally, "everyman's world view," as Redfield calls it, includes both space and time as well as birth and death.

Every worldview addresses these universal categories, though they are filled in radically different ways in each cultural context. To highlight the "brilliance of each unique world view," Redfield articulates four sets of questions based on these ubiquitous worldview themes: What is confronted? What is the nature of the not-man? What is man called upon to do? What is the source of the orderliness of things? He compares the responses of several cultural groups to these questions, including the Mountain Arapesh, the Zuni, and the ancient Mesopotamians, thereby demonstrating sharp differences despite their shared concerns. In the matter of worldviews, then, there is a remarkable unity of universals and a great diversity in substance.

This discussion segues into the issue of the transformation of the primitive worldview by its encounter with modern civilization dominated by science. Redfield says three basic things may be said about the primitive, precivilized worldview. The first characteristic is the unitary character of the cosmos in which humanity, nature, and God were one. In this unity the cosmos was conceived as sacred and personal. The second attribute is the sense of mutuality and cooperation that existed between man and not-man. God, nature, and humanity coexisted in a coherent system of interdependence and shared support. The third trait of the primitive worldview is the fact that man and not-man are bound together in one moral order. Life in the universe is governed by an established system of right and wrong, and is held in check by a mechanism of consequences.

Now Redfield says that if a comparison is made between this primitive worldview and the "civilized" one, we will observe one of the greatest transformations ever in the architecture of the human mind. The three traits of the primitive mind have all been weakened if not overthrown by the rise of civilization and cities. The change began when humanity separated itself from the unified order of the interdependent and moral universe, and stood over against it as something to be known and mastered. In this new environment the cosmos was conceived as a system of objective, physical properties and lost its sacral character, and the moral order of the universe vanished. The world began to be perceived as an uncaring, virtually hostile order uniquely indifferent to the welfare of human beings. The great transformation consists in changes in worldview, in the way the West understood the relation of man, God, and nature. Here is how Redfield articulates the initial shifts in point of view: "[In the primitive worldview], man was part of nature and god and acted out of this sense of participation. But gradually man comes to stand aside and look first at God-Nature, then, in the case of the Hebrews, God-without-Nature, and then, beginning with the Ionian philosophers . . . at nature without God" (p. 109).

Hence the transition from the primitive to the modern worldview entails several stages. In stage one, humanity, god, and nature are consolidated (primitivism). In stage two, man is separated off and views God and nature in tandem. In stage three, man views God alone independent from nature (monotheism).

In stage four, man views nature alone independent from God (materialism). In later development when both man and God are separated from nature, "the exploitation of material nature comes to be a prime attitude" (pp. 109-10). As Redfield points out, quoting Sol Tax, this radical departure from the primitive worldview is the West's unique "cultural invention." Redfield's implication seems to be that nowhere else in the world has this kind of radical shift in perspective taken place. It is the description of the loss of a unified, sacred, and moral cosmos, and its replacement by a thoroughly fragmented, disenchanted, and amoral one. Redfield tells how the story of this great paradigm shift was completed.

> By the seventeenth century in European philosophy, God was outside the system as its mere clockmaker. To the early American, nature was God's provision for man's exploitation. . . . it is Descartes who enunciated the principle that the fullest exploitation of matter to *any* use is the whole duty of man. The contemporary Western world, now imitated by the Orient, tends to regard the relation of man to nature as a relation of man to physical matter in which application of physical science to man's material comfort is man's paramount assignment on earth. (p. 110)

Of course, the view of God as the cosmic clockmaker is called deism, which entails an attitude toward nature as the resource for scientific exploitation in service to human needs. Essentially this was Descartes's (or at least his disciples') grand philosophic and scientific vision for the Western world. It entails a specific understanding of the human vocation. The highest calling and most noble pursuit is the scientific subjection of a recalcitrant earth to the end of human fulfillment and consolation. The great worldview transformation, in other words, culminates in secularized modernity.

The distance traveled in this fascinating journey from the primitive worldview to modern civilization is great. Redfield valorized primitive cultures, stressing their positive aspects, and viewed any departure from such an outlook as negative and disruptive. "In approaching modern urban culture via the peasant culture which is its rural counterpart, Redfield sought to rediscover the purity of folk culture and, indeed, to reimpose it by a concern with the good life and by an interest in the cause of peace and understanding among nations."[72] Thus Redfield's doctrine of "worldview" was put in service to sociopolitical causes and became a reforming agenda. Modernity had corrupted our conception of the cosmos and life within it, and was in serious need of redemption. As if it were a kind of gospel, the primitive worldview, from which the West had

---

72. *International Encyclopedia of the Social Sciences*, s.v. "world view."

fallen, provided positive cultural alternatives and needed to be reintroduced into this thoroughly secularized context. Redfield was thus a kind of incipient postmodernist who issued a call for a cultural antidote to the modern metaphysical, epistemic, and moral catastrophes rooted ironically in the primitive worldview derived from his anthropological research.

To review Redfield's contribution, he sees the formation of worldviews as an innate human characteristic. Everyone shares the same world and everyone has a view of it, though these views are indeed different. For him the term "worldview" meant something specific; namely, how people at the center of things look out upon and see the universe, especially in terms of totals. With human observers at the center, a worldview organizes things in the cosmos and makes knowledge of them possible. It is also the way a person orients himself or herself to everything else. Redfield desired to know what is true of all human beings and their worldviews — the common categories by which all people analyze the cosmos. So he developed a universal typology consisting of the self, others (human and nonhuman), space and time, life and death. Since each of these domains can be construed differently, worldviews can be markedly divergent. One startling contrast is between the primitive and civilized worldviews. Redfield offers a provocative description of the primitive outlook as unified, interdependent, and moral. This perspective has been eclipsed by modernity with its fragmented, amoral vision of the cosmos from which God, humanity, and nature are alienated. Redfield uses his knowledge of the primitive worldview as the basis for a critique, and proposes it as a constructive, "postmodern" alternative to the tragedies of modern life.

Concluding Implications

In psychology, Freud's reflections concerned the worldview status of psychoanalysis. For him it did not constitute an independent *Weltanschauung* since it fit snugly under the umbrella of modern naturalism and scientism. For Freud, this was humanity's only philosophical option and cognitive alternative. From a Christian perspective, however, this position constitutes a serious reductionism metaphysically (nature is the whole show) and epistemologically (there are only scientific facts, no final values). Contrariwise, Christian theism offers a comprehensive alternative rooted in the transcendent God who is the Creator of the universe and consequently the ultimate source of all facts and values, or even better, of all valued facts and all factual values. This outlook on reality is nonreductionistic or holistic in scope, integrating the visible and invisible and embracing both reason and faith. A Christian *Weltanschauung* is compelling because of its capacity to explain in rich and satisfying ways the remarkable diversity of created existence and the full range of human experience in a unified, coherent manner.

Jung certainly takes the discussion in a different direction. He is concerned about worldview dynamics in relationships, especially therapeutic ones. Basic philosophical assumptions animate both therapist and client, must be brought out into the open, will serve as the basis of diagnosis and treatment, and must be challenged and reformed as the occasion dictates. Specifically, we might wonder how a Christian worldview of either a therapist or a patient or both might affect their relationship, or the quality of the therapy itself. How might a biblically based view of life affect mental health in positive ways, especially if it rightly relates the doctor and patient to the objective order of reality? Surely relationships in any employment are strongly affected by the various points of view represented by professionals and their clients. Certainly in the context of the church, a shared commitment to the Christian vision of reality ("unity in a lifeview," as Kierkegaard called it) is the foundation for Christian friendship, and supplies the basis for the fellowship, or koinonia, of the community of believers in search of an authentic "life together."[73] Jung's reflections on the role of Weltanschauung in psychotherapy generate multiple possibilities for considering the implications of the Christian worldview in this context, in other professional settings, and in the Christian community.

In sociology, Mannheim sought to devise a scientific method by which to identify objectively various worldviews as pretheoretical cognitive layers in diverse cultural and historical contexts. While his methodological reflections are interesting, what is more important is his definition of "worldview" as an underlying phenomenon which can be perceived through its evident "documentary meaning." As a structure that resides in the tacit dimension (to use a Polanyism), this view of "worldview" has been taken up by many Christian thinkers, especially those in the neo-Calvinist tradition. But what is the rationale for identifying a worldview with this underlying, tacit dimension of human cognition? Is there a biblical warrant for such an understanding? Might worldview in a Christian context be looked at differently, perhaps as nothing other than a popular term, even as a way of referring to the basic essence of Christian teaching and theology? Mannheim's reflections prompt reflection on the role of worldview in human cognition.

Berger and Luckmann's articulation of the critical notions of the sociology of knowledge and the sacred canopy also raises important points for consideration. That the bulk of human knowledge is indeed sociologically generated may

---

73. As Dietrich Bonhoeffer demonstrated in his Life Together, translated and introduction by John W. Doberstein (San Francisco: Harper and Row, 1954).

actually provide insight into understanding the divine plan along these lines. That is, perhaps God intended people to acquire their view of things through the influence of their associates in daily life. Cultural immersion and peer pressure, for better or worse, are the source of what most people believe. The reception of the Christian view of life is no exception: though it does not originate sociologically (it is derived from revelation), certainly it is communicated sociologically. Since social groups are epistemically significant, the church should never lose sight of the power of the Christian community in shaping Christian consciousness. If this is so, is not and should not the cultivation of a Christian view of life be the deliberate fruit of such social dynamics and historical experience? What content and conditions must exist in homes, communities, churches, cultures, and so on for a Christian perspective on reality to be effectively communicated and absorbed? What role should the church and her liturgy play in this process? As socially assimilated sacred canopies, worldviews serve as human constructs to provide order, protect from terror, supply purpose, and guide activity in life. While Christianity is certainly to be numbered among them, it distinguishes itself from competing "canopies" by its claim to final religious and philosophical veracity.

Marx and Engels identified dialectical materialism as the true scientific *Weltanschauung,* and pointed out the role of ideology in class warfare and cultural combat. From Engels, who extended the implications of dialectical materialism into every aspect of communist thought and life, Christian thinkers must recognize the total implications of the biblical vision under the all-encompassing sovereignty of God. Christianity is more than a church polity, theological system, or pietistic program, but is in fact a view of the entire cosmos with something significant to say about everything. From Marx, who recognized the deceptive and coercive powers of ideologies in service to the ruling class, Christians must guard against ideologizing the Christian faith. Recognizing when this has happened in the past (crusades, inquisitions, fundamentalisms, etc.), the church must advance the kingdom and its worldview through the exercise of godly power with reliance upon appropriate spiritual weaponry. Otherwise, how could unbelievers be expected to respond to the faith if its adherents wield it as a club in politically oppressive and/or in socially or economically self-serving ways?

In anthropology, Michael Kearney makes a most remarkable contribution to thinking about the meaning of "worldview." His approach echoes themes present in the previous discussion on worldview and ideology in Marx and Engels. He offers three important ideas that ought to assist Christians in their own reflections on our topic. First, he is quite aware of the sociological relativity of worldview theory itself: a thinker's view of "worldview" is determined by his or her own social location and basic worldview assumptions. For Christians the implication should be obvious: What bearing does or should the content of Christianity (or a Christian worldview) have upon the formulation of a theory of *Weltanschauung* itself? Just as Kearney's Marxism directly impinges upon his theoretical speculations, so also a believer's doctrinal commitments ought to have a conceptual impact in devising a model of worldview as well.[74] Second, Kearney identifies five universal worldview categories present in every depiction of the universe, though they are filled with different content in different times and contexts. Might these categories be grounded in the created order established by God, and to what extent might the enterprise of natural theology shed light on these and other possible worldview motifs? Once the basic themes are ascertained, how might they be filled with distinctively Christian content derived from revelation both natural and special? Third, Kearney traces the necessary and important relationship between worldview and behavior: How are conceptual frameworks lodged in consciousness worked out in practice? How do the social and cultural conditions out of which the worldview arises affect behavior? Specifically for believers, how ought Christian worldview belief and behavior be related properly? To what extent does the social, cultural, and political situation in life in which a biblically based outlook on the world is acquired affect the choices of believers and move them toward faithfulness or disobedience? Kearney's reflections on worldview theories, categories, and behaviors are catalytic to important insights about the nature of *Weltanschauung* from a Christian perspective.

Finally, Robert Redfield not only highlights worldview as an inescapable human pursuit, but like Kearney, he also sets forth his version of the essential categories with which every interpretation on life is concerned. Particularly significant, however, is his project to rehabilitate the primitive worldview for contemporary life. Redfield's anthropological research led him to conclude that the worldview content of "uncivilized" people supplied antidotes to the fragmentation and amoral character of modern life. But what about and why not the Christian worldview? With its unified vision of the cosmos; its coherent system of divine, human, and natural interdependence; and its firm moral order — the traits Redfield valorized in primitivism — does not Christianity trump any pagan option as a fresh religious and philosophical alternative for today? A whole host of recent Christian thinkers such as James Orr, Abraham Kuyper, Carl Henry, and Francis Schaeffer have certainly thought so. With cultural awareness and spiritual sensitivity, the Christian church must promote her own glorious vision of the cosmos with prophetic passion and apostolic authority to meet the needs of a world in crisis.

74. This will be the thrust of the reflections on "worldview" from a Christian perspective in the next chapter.

Chapter Nine

Theological Reflections on "Worldview"

I n the first eight chapters of this book, we have examined the distinguished intellectual history of the concept of worldview in religious, philosophical, and disciplinary contexts. In this chapter and the next, however, we will turn our attention from historical to theoretical concerns. Presently I will show how any theory or definition of "worldview" is itself a ·function of the actual worldview of the theorist or the definer. Since the use of this concept has been of serious concern to the evangelical Christian community for a variety of reasons, especially its connotation of relativism, I will reflect theologically on the implications of a Christian worldview on a theory of worldview. What nuances, in other words, does Christian theism as a *Weltanschauung* impart to the notion of *Weltanschauung* itself? Then, in light of this discussion, in the following chapter I will offer some philosophical reflections in an attempt to show that a worldview is a semiotic system of narrative signs that has a significant influence on the fundamental human activities of reasoning, interpreting, and knowing. I begin here with a look at how any view of "worldview" is itself worldview-dependent.

Worldviews and "Worldview"

In the halcyon days of the Enlightenment, the prejudice against prejudice reigned supreme.[1] The promoters of this project were concerned about epistemological infection stemming from the germs of personal biases and cul-

1. Hans-Georg Gadamer, *Truth and Method,* 2nd rev. ed., translation revised by Joel Weinsheimer and Donald G. Marshall (New York: Continuum, 1993), pp. 269-77.

tural presuppositions. Thus they sought to apply the antibiotic of objective, scientific rationality to all serious theoretical enterprises in order to produce an
uncontaminated form of knowledge characterized by mathematical precision.
Despite the herculean efforts of those who promoted this dehumanized epistemological program, the dogma of value-free ways of knowing has recently
fallen on hard times. The prejudice against prejudice has been recognized as a
prejudice, and the self-defeating nature of this aspect of the Enlightenment
project has been exposed. In these "postmodern" times, many thinkers have
perceived that it is virtually impossible, and indeed not even healthy, to attempt
to quarantine thought, and to rid all conceptual endeavors of the encroachment of personal and cultural contingencies. Theories are not unaffected, but
are influenced from the beginning by the various traditions, values, and attitudes of the theoreticians themselves. This recent rehumanization of the intellectual process means it is infeasible for anyone to approach any topic apart
from the conditioning presence of the thinker's worldview.

This includes all theories about that "mysterious entity German philosophers have termed *Weltanschauung*."[2] There simply is no impartial ground
upon which to stand when attempting to develop, promote, or criticize a thesis
about this concept. Definitions, meanings, and models about "worldview" are
definitely *not* the result of presuppositionless thinking, but reflect the perspectives and interests of their originators. From the last chapter you may recall that
anthropologist Michael Kearney spoke about the "sociological relativity of
worldview theory" and pointed out that every thinker addressing the question
does so from a particular ideological vantage point.[3] So, as we mentioned, one's
view of "worldview" depends upon one's worldview! Two examples illustrate
this point.

Historian of philosophy W. T. Jones was given the assignment of summarizing the proceedings of an anthropology conference held in August 1968 in
Europe on the nature of worldviews and their role in culture. One major goal of
this gathering was to discuss and define the term "worldview" itself. The conveners' perspectives were plentiful, their agreements few, their negotiations
mostly unsuccessful. There was a simple reason, however, for their patented
lack of progress on this front. As Jones tells the story in his report, as the confer-
ees were *openly discussing* "worldview," they were *tacitly revealing* their own.
The conflicts over "worldview" which surfaced at the table reflected a variety of

2. Jacob Klapwijk, "On Worldviews and Philosophy," in *Stained Glass: Worldviews and Social Science*, ed. Paul A. Marshall, Sander Griffioen, and Richard J. Mouw, Christian Studies Today (Lanham, Md.: University Press of America, 1989), p. 47.

3. Michael Kearney, *Worldview* (Novato, Calif.: Chandler and Sharp, 1984), p. 2.

latent worldviews held by the participants. Jones states the matter succinctly in this way: "these differences of opinion about worldview reflect differences in our own worldviews."[4] For Jones, then, the best way to explain the impasse at this conference was to locate the problem in the various ideological frameworks of the participants informing their respective opinions about *Weltanschauung*.[5]

A second example comes from the third edition of James Sire's book *The Universe Next Door: A Basic Worldview Catalog*. His volume is structured around the answers of eight different worldviews to seven big philosophical questions. The questions begin with a metaphysical or ontological query about the nature of ultimate reality or being; move on to interrogations about the cosmos, humanity, death, knowledge, and ethics; and conclude with an inquiry about history.[6] These questions, however, given their particular order, reveal something about Sire's view of worldview. Critics pointed out that the way he presented the issues to be investigated at the outset of his volume determined the scope of his analysis. Stimulated by Anthony Giddens's comment that the contemporary period is self-reflexive in character, Sire sensed the need to step back and identify the preconceptions upon which his seven questions and perspective of "worldview" were based. His "metanalysis" revealed that the order of his interrogatives was premodern and theistic, commencing with metaphysics or ontology as the primary and all-determinative category to which the other concerns about humanity, knowledge, history, and so on were subordinated. Worldviews, from Sire's perspective, stem from a view of a being or reality that is ultimate, and on this basis all other questions are answered and all other worldviews are evaluated. To put it succinctly, Sire's ontology, specifically his commitment to Christian theism, served as the basis for his understanding

---

4. W. T. Jones, "World Views: Their Nature and Their Function," *Current Anthropology* 13 (Feb. 1972): 79. For another work on worldview by Jones, see his "Worldviews — West and East," *Journal of the Blaisdell Institute* 7 (1971): 9-24.

5. In an earlier article titled "Philosophical Disagreements and World Views," in *Proceedings and Addresses of the American Philosophical Association* 43 (1971), Jones contends that the typical plethora of perspectives on various philosophical issues could also be explained worldviewishly. His argument is "that the wealth of proposed solutions generated for any particular philosophical problem, be it in ethics, epistemology, or metaphysics, can be accounted for at least in part, by differences in the world views of philosophers" (p. 24). He also states that worldview differences also explain why philosophical disagreements typically remain unresolved, if not unresolvable, stating that "underlying such inconclusive disagreements, are profound differences in world view, profound differences in what may be called a pre-cognitive vision of the world" (p. 41). For Jones, then, philosophical differences, including those about "worldview," may be explained at least partially by differences in *Weltanschauung*.

6. James W. Sire, *The Universe Next Door: A Basic Worldview Catalog*, 3rd ed. (Downers Grover, Ill.: InterVarsity, 1997), pp. 17-18.

of *Weltanschauung*. As a Christian and "premodernist," he began with being; but had he been a modernist, his analysis would have likely begun with epistemology; and had he been a postmodernist, it would have probably commenced with language and/or meaning. But as he is, so is his theory of worldview. Sire's Christianity determined his view of *Weltanschauung*.[7]

Sire is certainly not alone in this particular matter. In fact, in light of our historical survey, there is little doubt that Hegel's idealism, Kierkegaard's theism, Dilthey's historicism, Nietzsche's atheism, Husserl's phenomenology, Jaspers's existentialism, Heidegger's ontologism, Wittgenstein's linguisticism, and the postmodernists' skepticism affected their hypotheses on "worldview" deeply. All this leads to an important point for our purposes. If it is indeed true that particular worldviews set the framework for a worldview theory, then we must inquire about the implications of a *Christian* worldview based on the Bible on the nature of this concept as well.

This is an important task. Several Christian thinkers, especially in the Reformed tradition, have been concerned about possible menacing connotations associated with "worldview" when it comes to its use in the church. In a colorful metaphor that highlights this danger, William Rowe has suggested that "worldview" was loaded with conceptual baggage when it migrated from its native cultural context into the Christian commonwealth. To make it suitable for Christian service, that baggage, he says, must be seized and replaced with appropriate biblical content.

> We have been reminded, or warned, that the concept of worldview is not a native but rather an immigrant into Christian intellectual territory. And, like all immigrants, it has crossed our borders with its baggage in hand. It is possible . . . to conduct a kind of border search, opening the linguistic suitcases of the worldview idea in order to examine the contents for semantic contraband. To be consistent in their thinking, Christians need to confiscate such contraband and bring it captive to Christ. But I do not think merely impounding certain aspects of the worldview idea will suffice; we must also replace its illicit content with, biblically speaking, licit content, if we wish the idea to settle and prosper in the Kingdom of God.[8]

By the time James Orr and Abraham Kuyper appropriated *Weltanschauung* in the later part of the nineteenth century and began to employ it for evangelical purposes, it had already become drenched with modern implications.

---

7. Sire, pp. 175-76, 226 n. 7.

8. William V. Rowe, "Society after the Subject, Philosophy after the Worldview," in *Stained Glass*, p. 156.

Within the framework of European idealism and romanticism, it had taken on its characteristic signification of a thoroughgoing subjectivism, and a person-relative or culture-relative perspective on reality. For example, Jan Verhoogt suggests, "In Romanticism, the concept of worldview arose in order to legitimize the rich variety of cultures within human history against the leveling impact of classic rationalistic philosophy represented by Descartes and Kant."[9] Not only was "worldview" part of a romantic revolt against rationalist attempts at cultural streamlining, but its concern for the concrete particulars of life and the flow of historical experience distanced it from the classical view of philosophy as a rational, scientific discipline concerned with universal essences.[10] This is why Husserl rejected it in favor of a stance on philosophy as a "strong science." As a result, the term has carried the connotations of historicism, subjectivism, perspectivism, and relativism. In modernity, then, worldviews have not been considered "facts" but "values," and thus have been consigned to the domain of private life.

As the personal, dated constructs of myopic selves or cultures, the status of "worldview" becomes even more questionable in the context of postmodernity. Worldviews slump to the status of a personal story in an age characterized by an "incredulity toward metanarratives."[11] A "hermeneutics of suspicion" places all final interpretations of the world in doubt. The "death of the self" eliminates confidence in any human subject to form a coherent view of life. A "metaphysics of absence" denies access to reality and asserts that all systems of "truth" are merely socially constructed and epistemically reified. A "metaphysics of violence" implies that any view of reality aspiring to cultural dominance contains the seeds of oppression that should not germinate. "Tolerance" is the highest value in this age of radical pluralism in which all outlooks on life are to be accepted, most are even interesting, but none of them are true. As competing metanarratives, worldviews are thoroughly "deconstructed," and now they are regarded as privatized micronarratives possessing little if any public authority.[12]

9. Jan Verhoogt, "Sociology and Progress: Worldview Analysis of Modern Sociology," in *Stained Glass*, p. 120.

10. Albert M. Wolters, "On the Idea of Worldview and Its Relation to Philosophy," in *Stained Glass*, pp. 18-19.

11. Jean-François Lyotard, *The Postmodern Condition: A Report on Knowledge*, trans. Geoff Bennington and Brian Massumi, foreword by Fredric Jameson, Theory and History of Literature, vol. 10 (Minneapolis: University of Minnesota Press, 1984), p. xxiv.

12. See Rowe, pp. 156-83; also see Howard Snyder, "Postmodernism: The Death of Worldviews?" in his *EarthCurrents: The Struggle for the World's Soul* (Nashville: Abingdon, 1994), pp. 213-30.

Given this background, evangelicals who employ the term "worldview" regularly would be irresponsible to neglect or negate the historical development of this term and the significations it has acquired in modern and postmodern parlance. Consequently, the Christian community must come to grips with several important questions. First, are believers aware of the relativistic and privatized connotations that "worldview" has acquired over time? Probably not. Second, do these implications render it unacceptable for Christian use? Not necessarily. Third, can the term "worldview" be regenerated and baptized in biblical waters, cleansing it of the modern and postmodern toxins and making it useful for Christian service?[13] I believe that it can.

As a matter of fact, plucking the concept of *Weltanschauung* out of recent cultural discourse and using it for Christian purposes can be compared admirably to Saint Augustine's ancient strategy of appropriating pagan notions and employing them suitably in the church. He believed firmly that all truth was God's truth, and in his famous "Egyptian gold" analogy in *De doctrina Christiana,* he explains on the basis of a story found in Exodus 11–12 how that truth can be recovered and utilized in superior ways by believers.

> If those, however, who are called philosophers happen to have said anything that is true, and agreeable to our faith, the Platonists above all, not only should we not be afraid of them, but we should even claim back for our own use what they have said, as from its unjust possessors. It is like the Egyptians, who not only had idols and heavy burdens, which the people of Israel abominated and fled from, but also vessels and ornaments of gold and silver, and fine raiment, which the people secretly appropriated for their own, and indeed better, use as they went forth from Egypt; and this not on their own initiative, but on God's instructions, with the Egyptians unwittingly lending them things they were not themselves making good use of.

13. Paul A. Marshall, Sander Griffioen, and Richard J. Mouw, introduction to *Stained Glass,* pp. 8, 10. Wolters, "Idea of Worldview," pp. 23-24, has asked and sketched an answer to questions like these. First, he points out that for Christian use the term needs to be redefined or reformed in light of the biblical ideas of creation and revelation (as Abraham Kuyper attempted to do). Second, he invokes the Reformed principle that "grace restores nature," suggesting that concepts and categories supplied by human intellectual traditions can be received and renewed for Christian employment on this basis. As he explains, "It is always a matter of spiritual judgment whether, in a given historical situation, the secular connotations of a term require that it be rejected altogether or whether the term can be explicitly redefined in the context of a Christian categorical framework." In his judgment, as well as my own, redefinition in a Christian context is the preferred option. Indeed, "worldview" is a good word, expressing a fundamental human aspiration to cultivate a perspective on life. It does, however, need to be redirected along Christian lines.

Augustine elaborates on this comparison, first offering words of caution, then advocating the bold and confident appropriation of intellectual concepts from non-Christians who have obtained them by common grace.

> In the same way, while the heathen certainly have counterfeit and superstitious fictions in all their teachings, and the heavy burdens of entirely unnecessary labor, which everyone of us must abominate and shun as we go forth from the company of the heathen under the leadership of Christ, their teachings also contain liberal disciplines which are more suited to the service of the truth, as well as a number of most useful ethical principles, and some true things are to be found among them about worshiping only the one God. All this is like their gold and silver, and not something they instituted themselves, but something which they mined, so to say, from the ore of divine providence, veins of which are everywhere to be found. As they for their part make perverse and unjust use of it in the service of demons, so Christians for theirs ought, when they separate themselves in spirit from their hapless company, to take these things away from them for proper use of preaching the gospel. Their fine raiment too, meaning, that is, what are indeed their human institutions, but still ones that are suitable for human society, which we cannot do without in this life, are things that it will be lawful to take over and convert to Christian use.[14]

Now I would submit that the notion of worldview is a valuable piece of "Egyptian gold." If we follow Augustine's reasoning, we can propose that believers need to claim it for their own and convert it to Christian use. In doing so, however, we must cleanse it of its pagan associations, reform it biblically, and make it a concept submissive to Christ. As Saint Paul says in 2 Corinthians 10:5b, "We are taking every thought captive to the obedience of Christ."[15] This we will seek to do in the rest of the chapter.

Christian Worldview and "Worldview"

What is *not* at stake in this present discussion, even for the church, is the ordinary "dictionary" definition of "worldview." In fact, the meaning of the term —

14. Augustine, *Teaching Christianity — De Doctrina Christiana*, introduction, translation, and notes by Edmund Hill, O.P., in *The Works of St. Augustine for the Twenty-first Century*, vol. 11 (Hyde Park, N.Y.: New City Press, 1996), pp. 159-60 (§2.60).

15. This and other biblical quotations in this chapter are taken from the New American Standard Bible (NASB).

what it actually *denotes* — is reasonably straightforward and relatively noncontroversial for *all* concerned. Roughly speaking, it refers to a person's interpretation of reality and a basic view of life. The controversies arise, along with various ecclesiastical concerns, when its *implications* or various *nuances* are considered — what it in fact *connotes* — and when its relationship to theoretical or scientific thought is explored. I will postpone discussion on this latter topic until the next chapter. Here I will attempt to shed some light on what inferences are built into "worldview" when it is examined from a biblical standpoint. In this investigation I will treat (1) issues of objectivity, (2) issues of subjectivity, (3) issues of sin and spiritual warfare, and (4) issues of grace and redemption. In comparison to its secular significance, biblical Christianity flavors the term much differently. For it suggests that "worldview" entails God's gracious redemption that delivers the hearts of men and women from idolatry and false views of life engendered by satanic deception and the blindness of sin, and enables them through faith in Jesus Christ to come to a knowledge of God and the truth about his creation and all aspects of reality.

Issues of Objectivity

> *"Worldview" in Christian perspective implies the objective existence of the trinitarian God whose essential character establishes the moral order of the universe and whose word, wisdom, and law define and govern all aspects of created existence.*

To the extent that the term "worldview" has been tinted (or tainted) for over two centuries with the hues of relativism — that is, the idea "that there are no universal truths about the world: [that] the world has no intrinsic characteristics, [and that] there are just different ways of interpreting it"[16] — this affirmation of objectivity rooted in God is the antidote. The existence and nature of God is the independent source and the transcendent standard for everything. After all, the basic premise of the Bible is that the eternal God exists. And ac-

---

16. *The Cambridge Dictionary of Philosophy*, 2nd ed., (1999), s.v. "relativism." In addition to this definition of "cognitive relativism," this article also describes "ethical relativism" as "the theory that there are no universally valid moral principles: all moral principles are valid relative to culture or individual choice." It also adds that according to relativism, in whatever way truth and/or morality may be conceived, they can be given no greater status than the *conventions* of a particular culture or society. All cognitive judgments and all moral principles are traceable to and no deeper than the *subjective* choices of individual human beings. As we have said, relativistic notions such as these have been associated with "worldview" since its inception.

cording to the central doctrine of Christian theology, he exists as one divine substance who subsists as three coequal and coeternal persons — the Father, Son, and Holy Spirit. While models of this mystery of the Trinity differ east and west, ancient and modern, it is hard to improve on this classic formulation from Saint Augustine's *De Trinitate:* "As regards this question, then, let us believe that the Father, and the Son, and the Holy Spirit, is one God, the Creator and Ruler of the whole creature; and that the Father is not the Son, nor the Holy Spirit either the Father or the Son, but a trinity of persons mutually interrelated, and a unity of an equal essence."[17]

Regarding his nature, God is indeed unity in diversity and diversity in unity, one God in three persons, three persons in one God — trinitarian, monotheistic, and personal. Thus he accounts for the unity and diversity in the universe and its ultimately personal character, revealing his nature and glory in everything, "for from Him and through Him and to Him are all things" (Rom. 11:36). He is the transcendent majesty, and in character is thrice holy (Isa. 6:3), perfect in justice (Deut. 32:4), and perfect in love (1 John 4:8). He is unalloyed in his superlative kindness and severity (Rom. 11:22). He is truly that "than which nothing greater can be thought."[18] Regarding his works, they are faultless in creation (Gen. 1:31), in judgment (Ps. 51:4), and in redemption (Rev. 5:9). His providence is comprehensive, for "The LORD has established His throne in the heavens; / and His sovereignty rules over all" (Ps. 103:19). He does all things well (Mark 7:37). Overall, "He . . . is the blessed and only Sovereign, the King of kings and Lord of lords; who alone possesses immortality and dwells in unapproachable light; whom no man has seen or can see. To Him be honor and eternal dominion! Amen" (1 Tim. 6:15-16).

God, therefore, is that ultimate reality whose trinitarian nature, personal character, moral excellence, wonderful works, and sovereign rule constitute the objective reference point for all reality. From a biblical perspective the universe is not neutral, but it comes with an intrinsic meaning rooted in God. He is the reason why something is here rather than nothing at all. He is also the reason why things are the way they are (excluding evil) and not different. Because reality is theistically grounded, human beings do not have the freedom of, the justification for, or even the capability of creating and ascribing an independent meaning to the universe. They are not free to do so because God already has

---

17. Augustine, *On the Holy Trinity,* trans. Arthur W. Haddan, revised and introduction by William G. T. Shedd, Nicene and Post-Nicene Fathers, vol. 3 (Peabody, Mass.: Hendrickson, 1994), p. 125 (§9.1.1).

18. Anselm, *Proslogion,* in *Anselm of Canterbury: The Major Works,* edited and introduction by Brian Davies and G. R. Evans, Oxford World's Classics (New York: Oxford University Press, 1998), p. 87 (§2).

done it. They are not justified in doing so because it is a violation of their subordinate, creaturely status. And they are not capable of doing so simply because of their formidable limitations. Only the rebellious, the proud, and the deceived, that is, only a human nature that is corrupt, would attempt such a ridiculous feat. The meaning of the universe and the authority to determine it are not open questions since both are fixed in the existence and character of God. Relativism and subjectivism are thereby excluded. The doctrine of God in Christian theism, therefore, establishes the basis for a robust *theological objectivity* rooted in him.

Furthermore, God's holiness, justice, and love constitute the transcendent, authoritative standard in which the moral order of the universe is anchored. This divinely grounded moral architecture — external to all human thinking, believing, or acting — consists of a prescription of virtue for human character and a set of laws governing human conduct. The fact that human existence is ordered by transcendent virtues and laws fixed in a theistic source means that certain dispositions and forms of behavior are intrinsically right or wrong, good or bad. There is also a divinely instituted system of appropriate consequences for wise and foolish behavior. The divine design of moral experience makes it certain that people will reap that which they sow, both in life and on the Day of Judgment (Gal. 6:7; Rom. 2:5-10).

God graciously provides insight into the ethical patterns of human existence through both natural and special revelation. As Paul makes plain in his epistle to the Romans, all people, regardless of their spiritual condition, are innately aware of God's basic moral expectations which are inscribed upon their hearts and reinforced by their consciences. "For when Gentiles who do not have the Law do instinctively the things of the Law, these, not having the Law, are a law to themselves, in that they show the work of the Law written in their hearts, their conscience bearing witness, and their thoughts alternately accusing or else defending them, on the day when, according to my gospel, God will judge the secrets of men through Christ Jesus" (Rom. 2:14-16).

Furthermore, the company of the redeemed are not only cognizant of God's general law written on the heart as natural revelation, but are also aware of his specific commandments written in Scripture as special revelation. The divine mandates in the Mosaic Law, the ethical teachings of Jesus in the Gospels, and the hortatory pericopes of the New Testament epistles express God's moral will within the framework of the covenant of redemption. Through the media of natural and special revelation, then, God's casuistic expectations, anchored in his own holy character, are revealed to all human beings.

Perhaps more than any other twentieth-century thinker, C. S. Lewis was acutely aware of the forces at play that were undermining the objective, moral tradition of the West. In his classic work *The Abolition of Man,* he discusses the sources of moral relativism that were inimical to this tradition. For example, acceptance of an educational system based upon this ethical posture, according to Lewis, meant not only the production of moral reprobates (which he color-fully designated "trousered apes," "urban blockheads," and "men without chests"), but also the eventual "destruction of the society which accepts it."[19] However, his own analysis of the major intellectual and religious traditions in the West *and* East — Platonic, Aristotelian, Stoic, Christian, and Oriental — convinced him of the validity of the cosmic moral order, which for him had a theistic foundation. Lewis's shorthand for this order was the "Tao" which he de-scribes in these words: "It is the doctrine of objective value, the belief that cer-tain attitudes are really true, and others really false, to the kind of thing the uni-verse is, and the kind of thing we are."[20] Indeed, in a related essay titled "The Poison of Subjectivism," Lewis asserts that until modernity, no prominent thinker ever doubted the *objectivity* of moral values or the *rationality* of moral judgments about them. In modern times, however, moral "judgments" are not considered judgments at all; instead, they are nothing but "sentiments, or com-plexes, or attitudes" that are emotive in nature, socially conditioned, culturally diverse, and infinitely malleable.[21] Lewis, however, is adamant in his condem-nation of this perspective, calling it "the disease that will certainly end our spe-cies (and, in . . . [his] view, damn our souls) if it is not crushed; the fatal super-stition that men can create values, that a community can choose its 'ideology' as men choose their clothes."[22] The peril posed by this perspective prompted Lewis to call for a revival of the objectivist moral tradition as the only effective way to dam the polluted waters of relativism that were inundating the West and threatening to destroy it. Thus the ethical vision of the Scriptures, buttressed by Lewis's apology for absolute values, confirms the component of *moral objectiv-ity* in the Christian tradition.

Christianity is not only characterized by theological and moral verities, but is also marked by objective, cosmological structures based on the biblical doctrine of creation. An independent "givenness" characterizes the universe. All aspects of reality manifest an intrinsic integrity and inner coherence which may be traced to three theological or biblical sources. First, Scripture insists that we understand the existence of God's creation "cosmo*logically*" as a prod-

19. C. S. Lewis, *The Abolition of Man* (New York: Macmillan, 1944, 1947; New York: Simon and Schuster, Touchstone, 1996), pp. 25, 41.

20. Lewis, *The Abolition of Man,* p. 31.

21. C. S. Lewis, "The Poison of Subjectivism," in *Christian Reflections,* ed. Walter Hooper (Grand Rapids: Eerdmans, 1967), p. 73.

22. Lewis, "The Poison of Subjectivism," p. 73.

uct of his Word *(logos)*. God not only created the universe out of nothing *(ex nihilo)*, but did so by means of his divine voice *(per verbum)*. In the presence of an unformed and empty earth God spoke, and in six "days," through eight creative acts (Gen. 1:3, 6, 9, 11, 14, 20, 24, 26), the chaos gave way to order and the cosmic void was filled. God uttered his divine fiats, a very good world emerged, and his creative will was done. As the psalmist says,

> By the word of the Lord the heavens were made,
> And by the breath of His mouth all their host. . . .
> For He spoke, and it was done;
> He commanded, and it stood fast.
>
> (Ps. 33:6, 9; cf. Ps. 148:1-6)

Creation, of course, is a christological theme in the New Testament. In the prologue to the Fourth Gospel, John identifies Jesus Christ as the Word of God (John 1:1) and agent of creation. "All things came into being by Him," he writes, "and apart from Him nothing came into being that has come into being" (John 1:3). The thinking of the apostle Paul is identical. He depicts Jesus in Colossians as the cosmic creator, the one who "is before all things" (Col. 1:17a), and the one by whom "all things were created, both in the heavens and on earth, visible and invisible, whether thrones or dominions or rulers or authorities — all things have been created by Him and for Him" (Col. 1:16). The author of Hebrews agrees, affirming that God, through his Son, made the world (Heb. 1:2). Jesus as the Word of God is not only the creator of the universe, but its sustainer and preserver as well. In him, says Saint Paul, "all things hold together" (Col. 1:17b), and in Hebrews we learn that he "upholds all things by the word of His power" (Heb. 1:3). The entire cosmos, then, in its very existence, nature, and maintenance, is the work of Jesus Christ as the Word of God and agent of creation.

Second, Scripture also requires that we understand the design of God's creation "cosmo*sophically*" as an achievement of his wisdom *(sophia)*. The cosmos was not only created through God's utterances, but also well designed by that essential divine skillfulness which "governs the world down to the leaves that tremble on the trees."[23] According to Proverbs 3:19-20,

> The Lord by wisdom founded the earth;
> By understanding He established the heavens.
> By His knowledge the deeps were broken up,
> And the skies drip with dew.

23. Augustine, *Confessions,* translated, introduction, and notes by Henry Chadwick, Oxford World's Classics (New York: Oxford University Press, 1991), p. 117 (§7.6).

Jeremiah 10:12 also states that

> It is He who made the earth by His power,
> Who established the world by His wisdom;
> And by His understanding He has stretched out the heavens.
>
> (see also Job 28:23-28)

Correspondingly, the song of praise to wisdom in Proverbs 8:22-31, a passage which the early church interpreted christologically, suggests in the words of one interpreter that "Not a speck of matter . . . , not a trace of order . . . came into existence but by wisdom. . . . God Himself has made and done nothing without it."[24] The words of the psalmist, therefore, come as no surprise. Having surveyed the wonder of creation and its amazing diversity, he declares exuberantly:

> O LORD, how many are Thy works!
> In wisdom Thou hast made them all;
> The earth is full of Thy possessions.
>
> (Ps. 104:24)

Third, Scripture also proposes that we apprehend the providential administration of God's creation "cosmo*nomically*" as a consequence of his law.[25] As the Old and New Testaments demonstrate, divine legislation is total in its application to the physical universe, to religious and moral life, and to the basic domains of human existence. God rules all things through the instrumentality of his law. Psalm 148 indicates that the heavens and the earth have been created by God's commands, are governed by his decrees, and are called upon to praise him comprehensively. Psalm 19 offers a meditation on the all-encompassing jurisdiction of God's law in the skies and the scriptures, focusing on natural revelation through creation and presenting the spiritual and intellectual value of the law for the worshiper of God. In Psalm 119 David declares his love for God's all-encompassing law, revels in his contemplation of it, proclaims his obedience to it, and affirms his abhorrence of those who forsake it. Of course, Mosaic legislation governed every aspect of Jewish life, and new covenant law in Christ written in Scripture and on the tablets of human hearts has complete moral authority in the lives of believers. In addition to laws regulating the physical universe and religious life are divine principles that govern the total life of human-

24. Derek Kidner, *The Proverbs: An Introduction and Commentary,* Tyndale Old Testament Commentaries, ed. D. J. Wiseman (Downers Grove, Ill.: InterVarsity, 1977), pp. 78-79.

25. This notion, of course, is Herman Dooyeweerd's. For a discussion of his "philosophy of the cosmonomic idea," see Brian Walsh and Jon Chaplin, "Dooyeweerd's Contribution to a Christian Philosophical Paradigm," *Crux* 19 (1993): 14-18.

kind. The Bible explicitly teaches that such diverse areas as art (Exod. 35:30-35), farming (Isa. 28:23-29), marriage (Matt. 19:1-12), work (Col. 3:22–4:1), and government (Rom. 13:1-7) are ordered by God's precepts. By simple extension, other domains such as education, politics, family life, business, diplomacy, sports, and so on would be as well. God's principles honeycomb creation, and by careful study and spiritual illumination they can be known and understood in their regulatory function. While they operate automatically in the order of nature, they are subject to obedience or disobedience in all things human. Depending upon the kind of response given to them, the whole of life can either be rightly or wrongly directed, honored or violated, blessed or cursed.[26] What accounts, therefore, for the givenness of creation and its own inherent excellence is its "cosmologic," "cosmosophic," and "cosmonomic" character. At the heart of the Christian tradition, therefore, is a *creational objectivity* which is the product of God's word, wisdom, and law.

Consequently, a biblically based worldview distinguished by a *theological, moral, and creational objectivity* has significant implications for a Christian portrayal of *Weltanschauung*. The trinitarian God exists, there is a theistically based moral order to the universe, and all created reality reflects the divine workmanship. Thus, within the framework of the Bible, "worldview" must shed its relativist and subjectivist clothing and assume new objectivist attire. God's existence and character constitute the absolute value in the universe. He establishes and imparts meaning to everything. In Christian perspective, *Weltanschauung* takes these truths into consideration and they are implied in its meaning. To put it differently, the objectivist implications associated with "Christian" and "biblical" make a tremendous difference when they are used as adjectives before the noun "worldview." The expression "Christian or biblical worldview," therefore, does not imply a mere religious possibility or philosophical option, but suggests an absolutist perspective on life that is real, true, and good. For God indeed is responsible for the whole scheme of things, and no one has expressed this more eloquently than Saint Augustine.

> Thus God is the supreme reality, with his Word and the Holy Spirit — three who are one. He is the God omnipotent, creator and maker of every soul and every body. . . . From him derives every mode of being, every species, every order, all measure, number, and weight. He is the source of all that exists in nature, whatever its kinds, whatsoever its value, and of the seeds of forms, and the forms of seeds, and the motions of seeds and forms. He has given to

26. For an in-depth discussion of "law" in the sense summarized here, see Albert Wolters, *Creation Regained: Biblical Basics for a Reformational Worldview* (Grand Rapids: Eerdmans, 1985), chap. 2.

flesh its origin, beauty, health, fertility in propagation, the arrangement of the bodily organs, and the health that comes from their harmony. He has endowed even the soul of irrational creatures with memory, sense, and appetite, but above all this, he has given to the rational soul thought, intelligence, and will. He has not abandoned even the inner parts of the smallest and lowliest creature, or the bird's feather (to say nothing of the heavens and the earth, the angels and mankind) — he has not left them without a harmony of their constituent parts, a kind of peace. It is beyond anything incredible that he should have willed the kingdoms of men, their dominations and their servitudes, to be outside the range of the laws of his providence.[27]

God is truly great in himself, in the way he has created all creatures and creation, and in his magisterial governance of humankind. But we must balance this objectivist component of a Christian approach to "worldview" by also considering its subjectivist counterpart. For God, who does all things well, has not only made the universe in a certain way, but has also created people as conscious creatures who possess the capacity to think about and respond to the world one way or another out of the faculty of the human heart.

Issues of Subjectivity

"Worldview" in Christian perspective implies that human beings as God's image and likeness are anchored and integrated in the heart as the subjective sphere of consciousness which is decisive for shaping a vision of life and fulfilling the function typically ascribed to the notion of Weltanschauung.

As the image and likeness of God, people are animated subjectively from the core and throughout their being by that primary faculty of thought, affection, and will which the Bible calls the "heart." As Gordon Spykman states, "the *imago Dei* embraces our entire selfhood in all its variegated functions, centered and unified in the heart."[28] Similarly, Karl Barth affirms that "the heart is not merely *a* but *the* reality of man, both wholly of soul and wholly of body."[29] Un-

27. Augustine, *City of God,* trans. Henry Bettenson, introduction by John O'Meara (New York: Penguin Books, 1972, 1984), p. 196 (§5.11).

28. Gordon J. Spykman, *Reformational Theology: A New Paradigm for Doing Dogmatics* (Grand Rapids: Eerdmans, 1992), p. 227.

29. Karl Barth, *Church Dogmatics,* III/2, trans. Harold Knight, J. K. S. Reid, and R. H. Fuller (Edinburgh: T. & T. Clark, 1960), p. 436.

questionably, of all the words that are crucial to biblical anthropology, the word "heart" is by far the most important. The term possesses the nuance of "central-ity" since it is used in the Scriptures to refer literally to the innermost part of things, including that of a tree (2 Sam. 18:14), the sea (Exod. 15:8; Ps. 46:2; Jon. 2:3), the heavens (Deut. 4:11), and the earth (Matt. 12:40). In a few texts "heart" contains physiological meaning and designates the actual organ which pumps blood (2 Sam. 18:14; 2 Kings 9:24; Ps. 37:15; Jer. 4:19) and can be strengthened by food and drink (Gen. 18:5; Judg. 19:5, 8; 1 Kings 21:7; Ps. 104:15; Acts 14:17; James 5:5). The preponderance of biblical passages, however, speak of the "heart" as the central, defining element of the human person. In Hebrew, "heart" *(leb, lebab)* may have been derived from an ancient Semitic root meaning "throb" which suggests an original pathematic meaning. It occurs approximately 855 times in the Old Testament, where it stands for "all the aspects of a person."[30] In Hebraic thought the heart is comprehensive in its operations as the seat of the intellectual (e.g., Prov. 2:10a; 14:33; Dan. 10:12), affective (e.g., Exod. 4:14; Ps. 13:2; Jer. 15:16), volitional (e.g., Judg. 5:15; 1 Chron. 29:18; Prov. 16:1), and religious life of a human being (e.g., Deut. 6:5; 2 Chron. 16:9; Ezek. 6:9; 14:3). Because of this ultimate and vital role, to know a person's heart is to know the actual person. It is the mirror image of a man or woman. As Proverbs 27:19 puts it,

> As in water face reflects face,
> So the heart of man reflects man.

Since the heart holds the key to one's essential makeup, its content and condi-tion must be regularly examined. "Watch over your heart with all diligence," ad-monishes the sage in Proverbs 4:23, "for from it flow the springs of life." Thus, while others may take pride in appearance or look outwardly upon the bodily frame, God knows what constitutes a person's essential self and casts his pene-trating gaze upon the heart (1 Sam. 16:7; cf. John 7:24; 8:15; 2 Cor. 5:12).

The New Testament and the teaching of Jesus advance this perspective. The 150 or so uses of "heart" *(kardia)* from Matthew to Revelation demonstrate that it is "the main organ of psychic and spiritual life, the place in man at which God bears witness to himself, . . . the whole of the inner being of man in con-trast to his external side, . . . the one center in man to which God turns, in which the religious life is rooted, which determines moral conduct."[31] Indeed, accord-ing to various New Testament authors, the heart is the psychic center of human affections (Matt. 22:37-39; John 14:1, 27; 2 Cor. 2:4), the source of the spiritual life (Acts 8:21; Rom. 2:29; 2 Cor. 3:3), and the seat of the intellect and the will

---

30. *Theological Dictionary of the Old Testament,* s.v. "leb, lebab."
31. *Theological Dictionary of the New Testament,* s.v. "kardia."

(Rom. 1:21; 2 Cor. 9:7; Heb. 4:12). Jesus shares this point of view, teaching that the heart is the spiritual nucleus of the person about which life orbits. He affirms this anthropological reality in the Sermon on the Mount. There Jesus offers a warning about earthly and heavenly treasures as contrasting options for a person's basic pursuit in life, the choice of a *summum bonum* if you will. Terrestrial treasures, he says, are subject to corruption and theft, whereas celestial treasures possess eternal durability. The choice of either is all-determinative, and for this reason Jesus associates it with that unifying faculty and hub of life, stating, "for where your treasure is, there will your heart be also" (Matt. 6:19-21; cf. Luke 12:33-34). Once one's treasure is identified, the heart will not be far behind. Neither will a particular way of life. Jesus knew that the kind of treasure occupying one's heart will manifest itself in practical ways through patterns of speech and conduct. He also employed a dendrological metaphor to communicate this point. In fact, he uses both "trees" and "treasures" in several Gospel texts, including the following one, to illustrate that out of the heart are the issues of life. "For there is no good tree which produces bad fruit; nor, on the other hand, a bad tree which produces good fruit. For each tree is known by its own fruit. For men do not gather figs from thorns, nor do they pick grapes from a briar bush. The good man out of the good treasure of his heart brings forth what is good; and the evil man out of the evil treasure brings forth what is evil; for his mouth speaks from that which fills his heart" (Luke 6:43-45; cf. Matt. 7:17-20; 12:33-35; 15:18-20; Mark 7:21-23).

For Jesus, then, in the heart a treasure resides, out of it fruit is produced, and from it words and deeds emerge. Regardless of the metaphor he uses (trees or treasures), he was obviously convinced that the cornerstone of a human being, the very foundation of a human life, is to be found in the heart.

On the basis of this anthropological perspective presented in the teachings of Jesus as well as the Old and New Testaments, I would like to offer three suggestions regarding a biblical approach to "worldview." The first is that the phenomenon of worldview itself must be comprehended in terms of the biblical doctrine of the heart. In other words, the heart of the matter of worldview is that worldview is a matter of the heart. Of course, this notion of worldview as a life-determining vision of reality was conceived and promoted extrabiblically out of the Western philosophical tradition, and intuitively it seems to express something very real and profoundly human. Assuming its legitimacy and value as a concept, its essence must be explained from a biblical vantage point. What did the originators of "worldview" accidentally stumble upon, what were they unintentionally identifying about humankind when they invented this notion? I propose that they were putting their finger, in an adequate though incomplete way, on the biblical understanding of the pivotal nature and function of the heart in human experience. What the heart is and does in a biblical way is what the philosophers were getting at unconsciously in coining the term "world-view." Without knowing it, they were mining an insight from the ore of divine providence, to use Augustine's language from his Egyptian gold illustration. Having been excavated by the labor and resourcefulness of the philosophers, the true origin, the fuller meaning, and the proper use of this valuable nugget of truth can now be identified biblically. As a precious stone, it needs to undergo the process of Christian refinement, transforming it into a vessel useful for the smith (cf. Prov. 25:4). Thus, when "worldview" is reinterpreted in light of the doctrine of the heart, not only is its true source located, but it becomes a richer concept than its philosophical counterpart, being more than just a reference to an abstract thesis about reality, but an Hebraic expression of the existential condition of the whole person.[32] It is even conceivable that a perceptive interpreter apart from philosophical stimulation could have (and perhaps should have) invented the notion of worldview, albeit in its fuller sense, on the basis of a careful, inductive study of the term "heart" as it appears in Scripture. For what he or she would discover there is what we have already seen in our previous study; namely, that the heart is the religious, intellectual, affective, and volitional center of a person. Believing, thinking, feeling, and doing all transpire within it. It is concerned with a particular treasure as an ultimate good. It is the source of how one speaks and lives. It is a reflection of the entire man or woman. It constitutes the springs of life. Consequently, human existence proceeds "kardioptically" on the basis of a vision of the heart, for according to its specific disposition, it grinds its own lenses through which it sees the world. According to the Bible, therefore, I propose that the heart and its content as the center of human consciousness creates and constitutes what we commonly refer to as a *Weltanschauung*.

Second, *into* the heart go the issues of life.[33] Before the springs of life flow *out of* the heart, something must first and even continue to flow *into it*. The heart not only expresses the life within it, but also receives it from without. Things are internalized *before* they are externalized. For indeed, the life-shaping content of the heart is determined not only by nature or organic predisposi-

---

32. Actually, Wilhelm Dilthey approximates what I am suggesting here. He argued that worldviews are formed according the dictates of character and possess a structure that reflects the inherent psychic order of human beings, namely, intellect, emotion, and will. These are functions that the Bible associates with the heart. Refer back to pp. 86-88 for my exposition of Dilthey's thinking along these lines.

33. This phrase is from Nicholas Wolterstorff, "On Christian Learning," in *Stained Glass*, p. 73. I have taken his suggestion of an *interactive* relationship of the heart to life and the world as a corrective to Kuyperian expressivism in this paragraph.

tions, but very much by nurture. Certainly one's natural genetic inheritance, basic personality, and inborn insights are critical components of the heart's composition. But it is also deeply influenced by what enters it from the outside through the manifold experiences of life. This is why, for example, both Plato and Augustine were very concerned about the narrative education of the young. The latter was very anxious for children who were receiving great drafts of Virgil's poetry into their unformed minds, quoting on one occasion Horace, who observed that "new vessels will for long retain the taste of what is first poured into them."[34] Certainly from childhood on a torrential amount of content is poured into the reservoir of the heart from seemingly unlimited sources of varying quality, some of it pure, some of it polluted. Various heart-shaping influences include religious, philosophical, and cultural traditions; socioeconomic conditions; various institutions such as marriage, the family, and education; human relations and friendships; vocational choice and work experience; psychological and physical health; sexual experiences; warfare; and so on. Because the consequences of these factors in due course will be retained and form the wellsprings of life, the wisdom teacher in Proverbs admonishes his hearers to watch over the heart most diligently (Prov. 4:23). Hence the sum and substance of the heart — its essential religious posture, patterns of thought, basic affections, and volitional activity — in short, what I am calling a "worldview," sustains an *interactive or reciprocal* relationship with the external world. As an individual passes through the various stages of human development, the heart obtains a vision of reality, even though it cannot explain exactly how.[35] Over time this outlook is probably discovered, followed, confirmed, challenged, put in crisis, reaffirmed or replaced, and solidified as the individual clings to a first, second, or even more "naïvetés" until death. There are periods of stability as well as tumult and change as new input makes its way into the heart, where it is filtered, accepted or rejected. Worldviews, in one way or another, are always works in progress. Throughout life, therefore, the heart not only gives but receives, and what flows into the heart from the external world eventually determines what flows out of it in the course of life.

Third, *out of* the heart go the issues of life. Once the heart of an individual is formed by the powerful forces of both nature and nurture, it constitutes the presuppositional basis of life. Presuppositions are those first principles that most people take for granted. They are multifaceted in character, and, knit together, they make up the most basic psychic layer of life. They constitute the background logic for all thinking and doing. They do not rest upon other prin-

---

34. Augustine, *City of God*, p. 8 (§1.3).
35. William James, *A Pluralistic Universe* (New York: Longmans, Green, and Co., 1925), p. 13.

ciples but are rested upon; they are not argued *to* but argued *from*. They are responsible for how the world appears and life is conducted. "They refer us," says Ted Peters, "to our fundamental vision of reality and the self-evident truths which are tacitly acknowledged in everything we comprehend and assert."[36] They are the work of the heart, which establishes the foundation for all human expression and experience. Though mostly hidden, and often ignored, these most basic intuitions guide and direct most, if not all, of life. They are compasslike in effect, a Polaris in the night sky. They are gyroscopic amid many imbalances, a thread in the labyrinth of life. These baseline beliefs are so humanly significant, they are like a nest to a bird or a web to a spider. As Michael Polanyi states, when we acknowledge a set of presuppositions as an interpretative framework for life, "we may be said to dwell in them as we do in our own body."[37] Therefore, examine a person carefully (perhaps even yourself): listen to him speak, watch him act, observe his attitudes, detect his beliefs, and in a short while you will be led back to the taproot of his life in the presuppositions of his heart which supply him with his conception of life.

From a scriptural point of view, therefore, the heart is responsible for how a man or woman sees the world. Indeed, what goes into the heart from the outside world eventually shapes its fundamental dispositions and determines what comes out of it as the springs of life. Consequently, the heart establishes the basic presuppositions of life and, because of its life-determining influence, must always be carefully guarded.

There is a strong tradition in Western thought and theology which affirms the thesis that the heart and its content, or what I am calling a "worldview," is decisive for human existence. The Bible itself asserts that the inner life must be rightly aligned with God and have the appropriate attitude of reverence if it is to receive insight into the divine wisdom which orders the cosmos (Prov. 1:7; 9:10; 15:33; Job 28:28; Ps. 111:10; Col. 2:2-3). Plato argued in his seventh letter that an ability to understand virtue is contingent upon virtuous character, regardless of intelligence quotient.[38] Saint Augustine recognized that comprehending the truth of Christianity was no mere intellectual exercise, but rather an act of the heart that must *first* be reconditioned by faith.[39] John Calvin affirmed Au-

---

36. Ted Peters, "The Nature and Role of Presupposition: An Inquiry into Contemporary Hermeneutics," *International Philosophical Quarterly* 14 (June 1974): 210.

37. Michael Polanyi, *Personal Knowledge: Towards a Post-Critical Philosophy* (Chicago: University of Chicago Press, 1958), p. 60.

38. *Plato's Epistles*, translated, essays, and notes by Glenn R. Morrow, Library of Liberal Arts (Indianapolis: Bobbs-Merrill, 1962), pp. 240-41 (§344). The same principle is found in the *Republic* 486d, 487a, 494d, 501d.

39. Augustine, *On the Holy Trinity*, p. 200 (§15.2).

gustine's order of knowing in reissuing the principle that piety, which is "reverence joined with love of God," is a prerequisite for a knowledge of him. People do not have the eyes to see, he said, "unless they be illuminated by the inner revelation of God through faith."[40] Blaise Pascal believed that the truth is known "not only by means of the reason but also by means of the heart." In perhaps his most well known aphorism, he states that "It is the heart that feels God, not reason: that is what faith is. God felt by the heart, not by reason. The heart has its reasons which reason itself does not know."[41] Jonathan Edwards believed that life, and especially religion, is a function of the "affections" of the heart, which, as one commentator puts it, "express the whole man and give insight into the basic orientation of his life."[42] And finally, the melancholy Dane, Søren Kierkegaard, emphasized, perhaps overly so, the role of subjectivity and inwardness as the source of truth.[43] Whether as biblical fear, Platonic character, Augustinian faith, Calvinistic piety, the Pascalian heart, Edwardean affections, or Kierkegaardian subjectivity, each of these contributions to this grand tradition testifies to the hegemony of the heart in human affairs. As the American pragmatist philosopher William James states, the heart is "our deepest organ of communication with the nature of things."[44]

When it comes, therefore, to considering the subjective component to a Christian understanding of worldview, the thesis to remember is that human beings as God's image and likeness are anchored and integrated in the heart as

40. John Calvin, *Institutes of the Christian Religion,* ed. John T. McNeill, translated and indexed by Ford Lewis Battles, Library of Christian Classics, vol. 20 (Philadelphia: Westminster, 1960), pp. 41 (§1.2.1), 68 (§1.5.14). For an in-depth discussion of Calvin's Christian "epistemology," see Edward A. Dowey, Jr., *The Knowledge of God in Calvin's Theology* (Grand Rapids: Eerdmans, 1994).

41. Blaise Pascal, *Pensées and Other Writings,* trans. Honor Levi, Oxford World's Classics (New York: Oxford University Press, 1995), pp. 35, 157-58 (§§142, 680).

42. John E. Smith, introduction to *Religious Affections,* by Jonathan Edwards, in The Works of Jonathan Edwards, vol. 2 (New Haven: Yale University Press, 1959), p. 14.

43. Søren Kierkegaard, *Concluding Unscientific Postscript to Philosophical Fragments,* translated, edited, introduction, and notes by Howard V. Hong and Edna H. Hong, vol. 1 (Princeton: Princeton University Press, 1992), p. 203. For a balanced treatment of Kierkegaard's views on objectivity and subjectivity, faith and reason, see C. Stephen Evans, *Passionate Reason: Making Sense of Kierkegaard's Philosophical Fragments* (Bloomington: Indiana University Press, 1992).

44. William James, "Is Life Worth Living?" in *The Will to Believe and Other Essays in Popular Philosophy* (New York, ca. 1896; reprint, New York: Dover, 1956), p. 62, quoted in William J. Wainwright, *Reason and the Heart: A Prolegomena to Passional Reason* (Ithaca, N.Y.: Cornell University Press, 1995), p. 97. Wainwright exposits a heart-based approach to the verification of religious knowledge in the work of Jonathan Edwards, John Henry Newman, and William James in chaps. 1–3 of his book.

the subjective sphere of consciousness which, according to its basic orientation, is decisive for shaping a vision of life. It fulfills the function the philosophers have ascribed historically to *Weltanschauung*. Unfortunately, however, something disastrous has happened, for the heart's perspective on reality has been altered radically by sin, and its view of the world is a principal target of Satan's strategy in the spiritual battle between the forces of good and evil.

Issues of Sin and Spiritual Warfare

"Worldview" in Christian perspective implies the catastrophic effects of sin on the human heart and mind, resulting in the fabrication of idolatrous belief systems in place of God and the engagement of the human race in cosmic spiritual warfare in which the truth about reality and the meaning of life is at stake.

There is no better passage in all of Scripture that describes the noetic effects of sin than Romans 1:18-32, and it contains direct implications for a Christian theory of "worldview." The text asserts that there is a natural knowledge of God available to all people, but that this revelation is summarily rejected — suppressed, to be exact — in humanity's titanic pride and rebellion. Given the resulting spiritual vacuum, the text charts the path of the human mind in its futility and darkness to construct idolatrous belief systems (essentially worldviews) in the place of God. It concludes by showing how those who have replaced divine truth with substitute deities and the foolish ratiocinations of their own hearts are handed over to moral degradation as a form of judgment. For matters relating to sin and the notion of worldview, then, Romans 1:18-32 is indeed the *locus classicus,* a passage Karl Barth has aptly designated as "The Night."[45]

The apostle begins by pointing out that the anger of God is manifested in the world because of those who beat down the truth about him through their idolatrous worship and immoral behavior. The knowledge of God is readily available to all people, providing insight into both his power and deity. Yet this revelation is unrighteously suppressed, incurring his wrath. "They have trimmed it," Barth says, "to their own measure, and thereby robbed it both of its earnestness and significance."[46] The result is spiritual excuselessness, as Saint

45. Karl Barth, *The Epistle to the Romans,* trans. Edwyn C. Hoskyns (London: Oxford University Press, 1968), pp. 42-54.
46. Barth, *Romans,* p. 45.

Paul explains: "For the wrath of God is revealed from heaven against all ungod-liness and unrighteousness of men, who suppress the truth in unrighteousness, because that which is known about God is evident within them; for God made it evident to them. For since the creation of the world His invisible attributes, His eternal power and divine nature, have been clearly seen, being understood through what has been made, so that they are without excuse" (Rom. 1:18-20).

Human beings are inescapably religious beings, even though they have turned away from the true God. On biblical grounds it is not hard to fathom why people possess this essential religious disposition and are naturally in-clined toward orienting their lives around some ultimate concern. They are the image and likeness of God (Gen. 1:26-27), and even after their defacement due to sin, they still seem to carry about in their consciousness the memory of their essential constitution. This is probably the basis for Calvin's argument that God has not only imparted an "awareness of divinity" *(Divinitatis sensum)* but also implanted the "seed of religion" *(semen religionis)* in the human heart.[47] Or, as Alexander Schmemann has said, "'*Homo sapiens,*' '*homo faber,*' . . . yes, but, first of all '*homo adorans.*'"[48] People are thinkers and makers, to be sure, but before they are these things or anything else they are worshipers whose essential na-ture is to adore. Thus there are no truly *non*-religious or *un*-believing people, personal protestations to the contrary notwithstanding. The human heart, given its divine design, abhors a vacuum just as nature does. Its emptiness must be filled, its longings satisfied, its questions answered, its restlessness calmed. It is in a constant search for peace, truth, contentment, and completion.

The question, therefore, is not whether someone is religious or a believer, but rather how and in what. In Langdon Gilkey's words, "Whether he wishes it or not, man as a free creature must pattern his life according to some chosen ul-timate end, must center his life on some chosen ultimate loyalty, and must commit his security to some trusted power. Man is thus essentially, not acciden-tally, religious, because his basic structure, as dependent and yet free, inevitably roots his life in something ultimate."[49] How this fundamental religious instinct is directed is the most important fact about a man or a woman individually, and collectively about a culture. The options at the end of the day are only two-fold: either the human heart will worship God or an idol, and will cultivate a perspective on life that flows out of the power and illumination of either com-mitment. The god of one's heart determines the light and direction of one's life.

47. Calvin, pp. 43-44 (§1.3.1).

48. Alexander Schmemann, *For the Life of the World: Sacraments and Orthodoxy* (Crest-wood, N.Y.: St. Vladimir's Seminary Press, 1973), p. 15.

49. Langdon Gilkey, *Maker of Heaven and Earth: A Study of the Christian Doctrine of Cre-ation,* Christian Faith Series (Garden City, N.Y.: Doubleday, 1959), p. 193.

As Henry Zylstra puts it, "No man is religiously neutral in his knowledge of and his appropriation of reality."[50]

This is precisely the logic of Romans 1. Because people *are* sinful, they are religiously hostile toward God, have replaced the knowledge of him with false deities, and consequently have concocted erroneous explanations of reality. The diversity and relativity of worldviews, therefore, must be traced to the idolatry and the noetic effects of sin upon the human heart. Since people are sinful, they have spurned God, for sin consists of rebellion against him; and since people have spurned God, they have replaced him with an idol, for religious humanity cannot live apart from an object of devotion; and since they have replaced God with an idol, they have reinterpreted reality, for idolatry imparts a different meaning to the universe; and since they have replaced God and reconstructed reality, they have sought to live autonomously, for the only law they follow is their own; and since they have sought to live autonomously from God and his truth, then divine judgment will overtake them as he gives them over to themselves in their sin. In short, an *exchange* of worship means an *exchange* of truth which means an *exchange* of life which means a divine judgment. Saint Paul describes this tragic human condition in these words:

> For even though they knew God, they did not honor Him as God, or give thanks; but they became futile in their speculations, and their foolish heart was darkened. Professing to be wise, they became fools, and exchanged the glory of the incorruptible God for an image in the form of corruptible man and of birds and four-footed animals and crawling creatures. Therefore God gave them over in the lusts of their hearts to impurity, that their bodies would be dishonored among them. For they exchanged the truth of God for a lie, and worshiped and served the creature rather than the Creator, who is blessed forever. Amen. (Rom. 1:21-25)

According to this passage, the fallen human heart does not rest in its rejection of God, but manufactures a multitude of new deities and ideas in accordance with its own desires. In this regard, Calvin points out that "each one of us forges his own particular error," and in doing so we "forsake the one true God for idols." In a remarkable passage, the Reformer describes the human mind in its spiritual blindness as an error and idol factory. It produces a multitude of superstitions and falsehoods by which the earth is flooded and led astray.

> Hence arises that boundless filthy mire of error wherewith the whole earth was filled and covered. For each man's mind is like a labyrinth, so that it is

---

50. Henry Zylstra, *Testament of Vision* (Grand Rapids: Eerdmans, 1958), pp. 145-46.

no wonder that individual nations were drawn aside into various falsehoods; and not only this — but individual men, almost, had their own
gods. For as rashness and superficiality are joined to ignorance and darkness, scarcely a single person has ever been found who did not fashion for
himself an idol or specter in place of God. Surely, just as waters boil up
from a vast, full spring, so does an immense crowd of gods flow forth from
the human mind, while each one, in wandering about with too much li-
cense, wrongly invents this or that about God himself. However, it is not
necessary here to draw up a list of the superstitions with which the world
has been entangled, because there would be no end to it, and so without a
word of them it is sufficiently clear from so many corruptions how horrible is the blindness of the human mind.[51]

Though he forgoes a list of the world's superstitions here, in a nearby passage Calvin illustrates what he means by the work of the horrible blindness of
the human mind in a discussion about "naturalism" and "pantheism" (though
not by these labels). He notes that some thinkers like the Epicureans substitute
"nature" for God, and by crediting it as the source of all things they seek to suppress God's name as far as they can. Quoting Virgil, Calvin describes ancient
"pantheism" as a view in which "an inner spirit feeds . . . and mind pervades" the
entire universe. In Calvin's critique, however, this secret inspiration or universal
mind that allegedly animates the universe is nothing but the construction of a
"shadow deity to drive away the true God whom we should fear and adore."[52]
For Calvin, therefore, naturalism and pantheism are just two examples among
many that demonstrate how the heart is prone to replace God with alternative
religious outlooks and systems of belief. Either by replacing God with nature or
by trying to identify him with it, naturalists and pantheists respectively make an
idol of the creation in either a totally nonreligious or religious way. In either case
the idolatrous heart conceives of the universe differently in spiritual and intellectual terms. In generating these new worldviews, the hearts of unbelievers find
a way to deflect the truth about God and his creation in their unrighteousness.

51. Calvin, pp. 64-65 (§1.5.12). For additional discussion on the noetic consequences of sin,
see Merold Westphal, "Taking St. Paul Seriously: Sin as an Epistemological Category," in *Christian Philosophy*, ed. Thomas P. Flint, University of Notre Dame Studies in the Philosophy of Religion, no. 6 (Notre Dame, Ind.: University of Notre Dame Press, 1990), pp. 200-226. Westphal
cites not only Pauline evidence for the noetic effects of sin, but also points to Augustine, Luther,
Calvin, and Kierkegaard as proponents of a view of sin with epistemic consequences. Ellen T.
Charry includes an excellent discussion of Calvin's view of the mind in sin and grace in her *By
the Renewing of Your Minds: The Pastoral Function of Christian Doctrine* (New York: Oxford
University Press, 1997), chap. 9.
52. Calvin, pp. 56-58 (§1.5.5-6).

But fiddling around with God and the truth is extremely serious business. If we return to the text of Romans 1, we find that Paul offers a fourfold evaluation of this process of swapping the biblical God and his truth for a false god and a lie. No doubt the background for his criticisms is classic Old Testament maledictions against the foolishness of idolatry and idol worshipers found in passages like Psalm 115, Psalm 135, and Jeremiah 10. First, Paul says that belief systems that replace God and the truth amount to *futile speculations* (v. 21b). Second, he asserts that those who promote these new idolatrous perspectives become *darkened in their foolish hearts* (v. 21c; cf. Eph. 4:18). Third, he states that devotees of these new religions and philosophies are deceived, since they *profess to be wise but are in fact fools* (v. 22). Fourth, Paul states that those who are guilty of the "Great Exchange" are *given over by God* in judgment to moral reprobation, specifically in the forms of impurity (v. 24), degrading passions (vv. 26-27), and a depraved mind (vv. 28-32). These four facts about false gods and fictitious beliefs make Paul's warning to the Corinthians seem most apropos: "Let no man deceive himself. If any man among you thinks that he is wise in this age, let him become foolish that he may become wise. For the wisdom of this world is foolishness before God. For it is written, 'He is the one who catches the wise in their craftiness'; and again, 'The LORD knows the reasonings of the wise, that they are useless'" (1 Cor. 3:18-20).[53]

Romans 1 paints a disturbing picture, yet it seems true to life. From Paul's perspective the human heart is intuitively aware of God and the manifestation of his power and glory in his handiwork. But because of sin-induced corruption, it disregards this intuitive awareness. Yet its native religious impulses prompt it nonetheless to manufacture alternative faiths and philosophies in place of God and the truth. It reconceives religion and reinvents reality industriously, and is responsible for the existence of a multitude of fallacious worldviews in any culture at any time. But these bogus visions of the heart are subject to a forthright apostolic critique. They are an exercise in speculative futility. They cast men and women into profound spiritual ignorance. They are confused with wisdom (and vice versa). They terminate in moral reprobation as divine judgment. These idolatrously based belief systems, in their futility, darkness, foolishness, and depravity, make up what the New Testament calls "worldliness." As Craig Gay asks, could it not be true that "worldliness" rests not so much in personal temptations to debauchery, but instead lies in "an in-

---

53. See these other New Testament warnings about false teaching, alternative philosophies, and the foolishness of the world's wisdom: 2 Cor. 11:3-4; Gal. 4:8-11; Eph. 4:14; Phil. 3:2; Col. 2:4, 8, 20-23; 1 Tim. 1:3-7; 4:1-5, 7; 6:3-5; 2 Tim. 2:16-18, 23; 4:3-4; Titus 1:1, 14; Heb. 13:9; James 3:15-16; 2 Pet. 2:1-3; 1 John 2:18-19; 4:1-6; Jude 3-4.

terpretation of reality that essentially excludes the reality of God from the business of life"?[54] In other words, worldly behavior is the eventual outcome of worldly views that dot the cultural landscape. Therefore, the origin and multiplicity of relativistic worldviews are rooted in the depravity of the human heart as explained by the theology of Romans 1.

This picture of the human condition is intensified by the fact that the Bible reveals that the entire creation and its human stewards are caught up in the midst of a spiritual war of cosmic proportions. It pits God and the forces of good against Satan and the powers of evil. These finite powers that insanely oppose the infinite God were originally made by him and had to be good, even as he is good. Romans 8:38-39 indicates that angels, principalities, and powers are among the divinely "created things." Colossians 1:16 teaches that Christ as the agent of creation is responsible for the existence of the entire cosmos, including "thrones or dominions or rulers or authorities." In short, God through Christ created the whole realm of reality, including the company of the angels. Though they received their being, purpose, and power from God, these spiritual creatures turned against him in a mysterious and monstrous act of pride and rebellion (e.g., Isa. 14:12-14; Ezek. 28:11-19; 2 Pet. 2:4; Jude 6). Motivated by fierce animosity, they became his resolute enemies, intent upon subverting his divine authority and destroying all his works. They are good creatures gone bad, and now in an attempt to certify their autonomy they engage God and the angels of light in a fierce fight for universal domination. As the pinnacle of God's creative work, the human family is directly implicated in this battle of the ages. Not only are all people affected by it — caught in its cross fire, so to speak — but they are also participants in it, aligning themselves consciously or unconsciously with and fighting for one side or the other, depending upon their spiritual orientation. Thus humankind has to struggle not only with an inherited internal depravity, but also with temptations and assaults from without that reinforce their fallen condition. How difficult it is, therefore, to know God and view the world aright![55]

---

54. Craig Gay, *The Way of the (Modern) World; or, Why It's Tempting to Live As If God Doesn't Exist*, foreword by J. I. Packer (Grand Rapids: Eerdmans, 1998), p. 4.

55. A number of classic and contemporary works examine angelology and its subdisciplines along with the theme of spiritual warfare, establishing both as essential to biblical theology. For example, see Clinton E. Arnold, *Powers of Darkness: Principalities and Powers in Paul's Letters* (Downers Grove, Ill.: InterVarsity, 1992); Hendrikus Berkhof, *Christ and the Powers*, trans. John Howard Yoder (Scottdale, Pa.: Herald, 1977); Gregory A. Boyd, *God at War: The Bible and Spiritual Conflict* (Downers Grove, Ill.: InterVarsity, 1997); George Caird, *Principalities and Powers: A Study in Pauline Theology* (Oxford: Clarendon, 1956); Anthony Lane, ed., *The Unseen World: Christian Reflections on Angels, Demons, and the Heavenly Realm* (Grand

Under the vice grip of the disenchanted worldview of modern naturalism and scientism, many have relegated this scriptural depiction of angels, Satan, the demons, and spiritual warfare to "the dustbin of superstition."[56] There is no doubt, however, that what Gregory Boyd aptly calls "a warfare worldview" permeates biblical revelation, is foundational to its message, and has been essential to Christian theology throughout the history of the church. Marshaling impressive evidence from cultures worldwide, Boyd demonstrates that Western secularism is perilously unique in its elimination of the "warfare worldview" from its cultural consciousness, especially its biblical version, which he describes in these terms: "God's good creation has in fact been seized by hostile, evil, cosmic forces that are seeking to destroy God's beneficent plan for the cosmos. God wages war against these forces, however, and through the person of Jesus Christ has now secured the overthrow of this evil cosmic army. The church as the body of Christ has been called to be a decisive means by which this final overthrow is to be carried out."[57]

"The world is a battle zone," Boyd says, and that "is why it looks that way!"[58] Now assuming the veracity of this perspective, I submit that central to the "warfare worldview" of the Bible is a "worldview warfare." A worldview warfare is a warfare *over* worldviews; that is, a megabattle between the forces of light and darkness over the identity or definition of the universe. A key stratagem of the devil, who is the father of lies (John 8:44), is to conceal the true nature of things through the proliferation of multiple cosmic falsehoods in order to secure the blindness of the human heart and its ultimate spiritual perdition (2 Cor. 4:3-4). In the conflagration that has engulfed the universe, the truth about reality is satanically enshrouded in darkness, and a multitude of idolatries and fallacious conceptions of life, counterfeiting as wisdom and enlightenment, are put in its place. The truths about God, creation, fall, and redemption must forever be banished from human consciousness. What better way for Sa-

---

Rapids: Baker, 1996); Tremper Longman III and Daniel G. Reid, *God Is a Warrior*, Studies in Old Testament Biblical Theology (Grand Rapids: Zondervan, 1995); Stephen F. Noll, *Angels of Light, Powers of Darkness: Thinking Biblically about Angels, Satan, and Principalities* (Downers Grove, Ill.: InterVarsity, 1998); Peter T. O'Brien, "Principalities and Powers: Opponents of the Church," in *Biblical Interpretation and the Church*, ed. D. A. Carson (Nashville: Nelson, 1984), pp. 110-50; Heinrich Schlier, *Principalities and Powers in the New Testament* (New York: Herder and Herder, 1961). Walter Wink has authored a trilogy of books on this theme, *Naming the Powers: The Language of Power in the New Testament* (Philadelphia: Fortress, 1984); *Unmasking the Powers: The Invisible Forces That Determine Human Existence* (Philadelphia: Fortress, 1986); *Engaging the Powers: Discernment and Resistance in a World of Domination* (Minneapolis: Fortress, 1992).

56. Wink, *Engaging the Powers*, p. 3.
57. Boyd, p. 19.
58. Boyd, p. 17.

tan to deflect the light of truth than by corrupting it and replacing it with false visions of reality that dominate the cultural landscape? The control of the zeitgeist, or the intellectual and spiritual climate of the age, is a most effective means of controlling what goes into the hearts of men and women, shaping their interests and ruling their lives. Worldviews are the basis for a zeitgeist and are at the center of this process. If this big-picture strategy succeeds, then there is only an occasional need for personal temptation to sin. How people get their jollies is of little interest to Satan if he has already captured and misdirected their hearts.

This proposal that a "worldview warfare" is a critical component of the "warfare worldview" of the Bible has been supported in an influential way by Heinrich Schlier. On the basis of Ephesians 2:2, he proposes that a worldview, or what he calls the "spiritual atmosphere" of a culture, is the "principal source of his [Satan's] domination." In this text, he believes the meaning of the word "air" in the expression "the prince of the power of the air" is best interpreted appositively by the phrase following it, "of the spirit that is now working in the sons of disobedience." Thus he suggests the "air" is not only the literal realm in which Satan exercises his powers (in accordance with Jewish understanding), but it also refers in context to the universal spirit which fosters rebellion in unbelievers. Therefore Schlier thinks it has significant sociocultural meaning. "It is the general spiritual climate which influences mankind, in which men live, which they breathe, which dominates their thoughts, aspirations and deeds. He exercises his 'influence' over men by means of the spiritual atmosphere which he dominates and uses as the medium of his power. He gains power over men and penetrates them by means of this atmosphere, which is his realm, the realm of his power. If men expose themselves to this atmosphere, they become its carriers, and thereby contribute to its extension."[59]

Ephesians 6:12 would seem to reinforce this interpretation with its reference to the struggle "against the world forces of this darkness, against the spiritual forces of wickedness in the heavenly places." Also, in 1 Corinthians 2:6 Paul implies that there is a wisdom of this age and of the rulers of this age which stands in sharp contrast to the divine wisdom in Christ which he proclaims. Schlier notes, however, that this is not the devil's exclusive method of control, for he attacks natural life at every level and can even inflict physical harm quite apart from such socio-spiritual concerns. Still he is convinced, based on the authority of the apostle, that the "spiritual atmosphere" is Satan's principal source of domination, a concept which functions very much like a *Weltanschauung*.

59. Schlier, p. 31.

At any rate, St. Paul regards it as the chief means by which the principalities exercise their domination. This domination usually begins in the general spirit of the world, or in the spirit of a particular period, attitude, nation or locality. This spirit, in which the course of this world rules, is not just floating about freely. Men inhale it and thus pass it on into their institutions and various conditions. In certain situations it becomes concentrated. Indeed, it is so intense and powerful that no individual can escape it. It serves as a norm and is taken for granted. To act, think or speak against this spirit is regarded as non-sensical or even wrong and criminal. It is "in" this spirit that men encounter the world and affairs, which means that they accept the world as this spirit presents it to them, with all its ideas and values, in the form in which he wants them to find it. The domination which the prince of this world exercises over the atmosphere, gives to the world with its affairs, relationships and situations, and even to existence itself, the appearance of belonging to him; it imposes his valuation on everything.[60]

Schlier believes these efforts at remodeling reality lead to an individual's misunderstanding of himself and the world, and thus result in his utter ruin. After all, the goal of Satan and the powers is to create a culture of falsehood and death aimed at "the distortion, thwarting, ruin, annihilation, and undoing of creation."[61] The individual's immersion in such an environment can only contribute to his demise.

---

60. Schlier, pp. 31-32. Schlier's interpretation of Eph. 2:2 is controversial. Marcus Barth, *Ephesians: Introduction, Translation, and Commentary on Chapters 1–3*, Anchor Bible (Garden City, N.Y.: Doubleday, 1984), p. 215 n. 31, speaks against it, as does Arnold, pp. 196-97. The latter argues that Schlier's view is in effect too modern, and "would have been unintelligible to a first-century reader." Instead he suggests that "Paul is using *spirit* here in the sense of a personal being." Other commentators at least allow for Schlier's viewpoint as a grammatical option, as Andrew T. Lincoln does in his *Ephesians*, Word Biblical Commentary, vol. 42 (Dallas: Word, 1990), p. 96. Others embrace it wholeheartedly, including Caird, p. 51; Klyne Snodgrass, *Ephesians*, NIV Application Commentary (Grand Rapids: Zondervan, 1996), p. 96, and F. F. Bruce, *The Epistle to the Ephesians* (London: Pickering and Inglis, 1961), p. 48. E. K. Simpson (and F. F. Bruce), *Epistles to the Ephesians and Colossians* (Grand Rapids: Eerdmans, 1957), is enthusiastic about Schlier's viewpoint. He cites Beck, Candlish, and Findlay as supporters of this perspective, describing it as follows: "The air may indicate a specific locality, but it is also an appropriate emblem of the prevailing influence or surroundings amid which an individual or community breathes or moves. In that sense it answers to the German compound *Zeitgeist* and to our *spirit of the age*" (p. 48). Wink, *Naming the Powers*, p. 84, also adopts Schlier's interpretation: "He [Paul] uses the figure of the 'power of the air' to specify not the locale of demons but the world-atmosphere, which Satan exploits for our destruction." Even if Schlier's specific exegesis proves wrong, the overall biblical presentation of the names, character, and activities of Satan and the powers would seem to justify it.

61. Schlier, p. 33.

C. S. Lewis's character Screwtape would seem to agree. The seasoned satanic mastermind, in a speech to young devils at the annual dinner of the Tempters' Training College, suggests a strategy of domination and destruction through cultural atmospherics. This is easily accomplished, says Screwtape, because the human "vermin" are "so muddled in mind, so passively responsive to environment," and because "their consciousness hardly exists apart from the social atmosphere that surrounds them." By this process the tempters are able to induce an individual "to enthrone at the centre of his life a good solid, resounding lie." These are their means, and their ultimate end is sinister. It is "the destruction of individuals. For only individuals can be saved or damned, can become sons of the Enemy [God] or food for us [devils]. The ultimate value, for us [devils], of any revolution, war, or famine lies in the individual anguish, treachery, hatred, rage, and despair which it may produce."[62]

Since Satan and the demons can manipulate men and women only to the extent that they are deceived, what better way to achieve this than by the promulgation of fallacious conceptions of reality through the conduit of the spirit of the age from which no one can escape? To top off this scheme, the principalities and powers under devilish management cleverly cover their tracks and operate in such a clandestine fashion so as to suggest their nonexistence. "They withdraw from sight into the men, elements, and institutions through which they make their power felt. To seem not to appear is part of their essence."[63]

Thus Satan is an expert in the spiritual and intellectual murder of his subjects through his demons, who delight in the deception of countless numbers of people taken in by the ideas, traditions, and customs in which they live, move, and have their being. "Woe to you, torrent of human custom! 'Who can stand against you?' (Ps. 75:8)," bemoaned Saint Augustine, who recognized the power of custom to shape the young. "When will you run dry? How long will your flowing current carry the sons [and daughters] of Eve into the great and fearful ocean which can be crossed, with difficulty, only by those who have embarked on the Wood of the cross (Wisd. 14:7)?"[64] In recent memory, the torrents of human custom have been based in the worldview waters of naturalism such as Darwinism, Marxism, Freudianism, secular humanism, existentialism, nihilism, and postmodernism. These mighty rivers have flowed together into a "great and fearful ocean" of deception in which many in the West, and elsewhere, have drowned. Even more recently, a flood of pantheistic and panen-

---

62. C. S. Lewis, *The Screwtape Letters and Screwtape Proposes a Toast* (New York: Macmillan, 1961), pp. 156, 162, 170.

63. Schlier, p. 29.

64. Augustine, *Confessions*, p. 18 (§1.16.25).

theistic thought has also capsized many. At the outset of a new millennium, who can forecast with any certainty what the "atmospheric" pressures will be in days ahead?

What is certain, however, is that the human heart in its fallen condition will continue to suppress the truth in unrighteousness and to manufacture surrogate gods and errant perspectives on the world. For the human heart in its religious restlessness must have something in which to believe and by which to make sense of life. What is also certain is that spiritual warfare will continue, and it will continue to revolve around worldviews. The kingdom of Satan will capitalize on human pride and self-sufficiency as the source of idolatries and errors to insure the fact that the world's religious and philosophical environments are dominated by false notions that sustain deception and keep people from God and the truth. The doctrines of sin and spiritual warfare, therefore, play a vital role in understanding the notion of worldview from a Christian vantage point. They are products of the noetic effects of sin and are indispensable satanic weaponry in spiritual warfare against God. There is no way out from this spiritual, intellectual, and moral destitution apart from the grace of God.

Issues of Grace and Redemption

> "Worldview" in Christian perspective implies the gracious inbreaking of the kingdom of God into human history in the person and work of Jesus Christ, who atones for sin, defeats the principalities and powers, and enables those who believe in him to obtain a knowledge of the true God and a proper understanding of the world as his creation.

Few would expect the eleemosynary character of God and/or an historical work of salvation achieved by an incarnate God to show up in a theory of *Weltanschauung*. Certainly nothing of the kind appeared in the philosophic or disciplinary history of worldview we surveyed earlier in this book. From a biblical perspective, however, it makes perfect sense. A few remarks about the doctrine of soteriology and some insights from Calvin and Edwards will establish a basis for understanding the influence of grace and redemption on a Christian view of "worldview."

The salvaging of a sin-wrecked creation is what the Bible is all about.[65] The first two chapters of Genesis tell the story of creation, the third recounts

---

65. Wolters, *Creation Regained*, p. 11.

the episode of the fall, and the rest of the Bible covers the story of redemption. Salvation history is its central theme. Now what God promised in the Old Testament to his people about the anticipated offspring of the woman who would crush the serpent and destroy evil is fulfilled and consummated in the person of Jesus Christ in the New Testament. In him and through his ministry, death, resurrection, and ascension to the right hand of God, the kingdom of God has broken into human history and redeemed the entire cosmos from the powers of evil — from sin, Satan, and death. He has accomplished an atonement for sin and reconciled all things in heaven and on earth to God through the blood of his cross (Matt. 1:21; John 1:29; Acts 10:43; Eph. 1:7-10; Col. 1:14, 20; Heb. 9:26). He has bound and judged Satan, and defeated the principalities and powers (Matt. 12:28-29 and par.; John 12:31; 16:11; Col. 2:15; Heb. 2:14-15; 1 John 3:8; 1 Pet. 3:22). He has vanquished death through the triumph of his resurrection (Matt. 28:6 and par.; Acts 2:22-32; 1 Cor. 15). As the ascended Lord, he sits on the right hand of God, who has given to him all rule, authority, and power in heaven and on earth (Ps. 110; Matt. 28:16-20; 1 Cor. 15:20-28; Eph. 1:20-23; 3:10; Phil. 2:9-11; Col. 2:10; Heb. 1:3-4, 13; 10:12-13; Rev. 1:5, 17-18; 20:6). From his heavenly throne he poured forth the Holy Spirit he had promised upon his church (John 14:16-18, 26; 15:26-27; 16:7-14; Acts 2:1-21). One day he will return to earth in apocalyptic power and glory to consummate his redemptive work and to assume his rightful place as King of kings and Lord of lords over his people and all creation (Matt. 24–25 and par.; John 14:1-3; Acts 1:6-11; 1 Cor. 15:20-28, 50-58; 1 Thess. 4:13-18; 2 Thess. 2:1-12; Titus 2:11-14; Heb. 12:26-29; 2 Pet. 3:10-13; Rev. 19–22). Until that time, however, men and women everywhere are urged to repent (Mark 1:14-15; Luke 24:46-47; Acts 17:30; 26:20; 2 Pet. 3:9), to trust in Jesus Christ as Lord and Savior (John 3:16; Acts 16:31; Rom. 3:21–5:1; 10:8-15; Gal. 3:5-14; Eph. 2:8-10; Heb. 11) and receive the comprehensive blessings provided by the redemptive reign of God in time and for eternity (Matt. 5:3-12 and par.; Eph. 1:3). This salvation is obtained, not by human works, but by God's perfect grace which both saves and sustains (John 1:14-18; Acts 15:11; Rom. 3:24; 4:16; 2 Cor. 12:7-10; Eph. 2:5, 8-9; 2 Tim. 1:9; Titus 2:11; 3:7). What God has achieved in Jesus Christ through the Holy Spirit is wholly eschatological in nature. New Testament theology is defined by the tension between the present and future aspects of the kingdom of God, the already and the not yet. No one has expressed this more clearly than the late George E. Ladd in these often quoted words: "Our central thesis is that the Kingdom of God is the redemptive reign of God dynamically active to establish his rule among human beings, and that this Kingdom which will appear as an apocalyptic act at the end of the age, has already come into human history in the person and mission of Jesus to overcome evil, to deliver people from its power, and to bring them into the blessings of God's reign. The Kingdom of God involves two great moments: fulfillment within history, and consummation at the end of history."[66]

As the one who has overcome evil, Christ is designated appropriately as *Christus Victor*.[67] His triumph changes everything. For those who are related to him by faith, the evils of idolatry, the noetic effects of sin, and satanic deception have been broken. For the first time things become clear. This is as it should be, for as Christ said, "I am the light of the world; he who follows Me shall not walk in the darkness, but shall have the light of life" (John 8:12). In turning "from idols to serve a living and true God" (1 Thess. 1:9), Christian believers come to know him (or be known by him, Gal. 4:9) as he truly is in his excellent greatness and according to his mighty deeds (Ps. 150:2; 2 Cor. 4:6; Gal. 4:9; Eph. 1:17; Col. 1:10; 2 Pet. 1:2). The darkness of their hearts has been replaced by the mind of Christ (1 Cor. 2:16). The satanically induced blindness has been penetrated by God, who in creation said, "Light shall shine out of darkness," and who in new creation has shined his light into the heart "to give the light of the knowledge of the glory of God in the face of Christ" (2 Cor. 4:6).

As a result, a whole new world and worldview is open to behold. Everything can now be seen and interpreted clearly in the light of God himself: that true happiness is found in total love, obedience, and service to him; that the world is his creation, that he made it by his wisdom, ordered it by his law, and reveals himself in it as a manifestation of his glory; that human beings are finite, dependent creatures made as the image and likeness of God, possessing inherent dignity and value, and deserving of the love with which one loves oneself; that the callings of human beings consist in familial responsibilities and cultural tasks that are to be carried out in ways that bring blessing to humanity and honor to God; that sin is exceedingly sinful and that the moral law rooted in God's nature ought to be honored and obeyed in shaping human character, conduct, and culture; that the church is the body and bride of Christ, the temple of the Holy Spirit wherein God is to be worshiped, the sacraments administered, the word preached, believers discipled, community established, and the warfare with the satanic forces in their residual power waged in the armor and strength of God; that there is a soteriological and doxological purpose to human history, that God is glorifying himself in the redemption of his people and the cosmos, terminating in a final judgment and the creation of a new heaven and a new earth in which righteousness dwells. In coming into the knowledge

66. George Eldon Ladd, *A Theology of the New Testament*, ed. Donald A. Hagner, rev. ed. (Grand Rapids: Eerdmans, 1993), pp. 89-90.

67. For one of the best treatments of this theme, see Gustaf Aulén, *Christus Victor: An Historical Study of the Three Main Types of the Idea of the Atonement*, trans. A. G. Hebert, foreword by Jaroslav Pelikan (New York: Macmillan, 1969).

of these and other truths, in seeing God and the world anew, not only is the mind informed but the heart is transformed. Indeed, Christ's true followers, as Augustine says, "have passed from the night of blasphemy and perdition into the daylight of salvation and true godliness."[68]

But what is involved theologically in developing this kind of Christian mind on God and world? Calvin and Edwards recognized that a proper comprehension of the whole of things — God, the universe, humankind — was a deeply spiritual matter, and offer pertinent insights on this whole issue with which I find it hard to disagree. As we have seen, for Calvin a right understanding of God the creator, that is, knowing God and his creation aright, is blocked by the rampant superstitions and utter blindness of the human heart. As repositories of idolatry and falsehood, the unregenerate live in the context of a total spiritual eclipse. What can penetrate this darkness and open their minds to vistas of truth never before imagined? For Calvin the process of plowing up lies and planting in the truth can only be achieved by a sincere openness to and faith in the Scriptures. In a famous illustration he compares the Bible to "spectacles" through which a proper understanding of God, though previously blurred and out of focus, is elucidated and clarified. "Just as old or bleary-eyed men and those with weak vision, if you thrust before them a most beautiful volume, even if they recognize it to be some sort of writing, yet can scarcely construe two words, but with the aid of spectacles will begin to read distinctly; so Scripture, gathering up the otherwise confused knowledge of God in our minds, having dispersed our dullness, clearly shows us the true God."[69]

In this context Calvin also says God has provided in his Word a dependable revelation about himself which serves as a "thread" to lead people through the labyrinth of bewilderment to theological perspicuity.[70] Therefore, with the aid of the corrective lenses of Scripture and the guidance of biblical twine, men and women whose hearts are prepared properly by faith attain to a knowledge of God the creator for the very first time. This new theological revelation has immediate cosmological implications in the recognition of the universe as the expression and arena of God's mighty works. Believers make the amazing discovery of the sacramental character of creation and see it as the dazzling theater of the divine glory. The truth about God and his handiwork, formerly suppressed and smudged, is finally revealed in crispness and light! The eyes of the heart are changed and things are seen as they really are. The results of this great redemption are transfiguring. According to Calvin, believers become fully con-

---

68. Augustine, *City of God,* p. 85 (§2.28).
69. Calvin, p. 70 (§1.6.1).
70. Calvin, p. 73 (§1.6.3).

scious that they hold in their hearts "the unassailable truth." They are so deeply affected by this word which penetrates to the heart of their hearts and to the marrow of their bones that, by its divine power and majesty, they "are drawn and inflamed, knowingly and willingly, to obey him [God]."[71] What a change this means for the Christian believer in heart, in faith, in knowledge, in affections, and in action! Based on God's Word, it is the birth of an entirely new, biblical worldview through God's grace and redemption.

Jonathan Edwards would agree. He was convinced that the true Christian, that is, one who is possessed of holy affections, is given a new spiritual sense or capacity of taste implanted in the heart by which to understand God and relish his holiness. This involves a metamorphosis at the center of one's being. He explains that this new capacity of spiritual insight "consists in a sense of the heart, of the supreme beauty and sweetness of the holiness or moral perfection of divine things, together with all that discerning and knowledge of things of religion, that depends upon, and flows from such a sense."[72] Thus the original cognitive faculties of the regenerated believer are freshly empowered and redirected by a new foundational principle infused within them, resulting in a complete spiritual overhaul of human perception.

> Hence the work of the Spirit of God in regeneration is often in Scripture compared to the giving [of] a new sense, giving eyes to see and ears to hear, unstopping the ears of the deaf, and opening the eyes of them that were born blind, and turning from darkness unto light. And because this spiritual sense is immensely the most noble and excellent, and that without which all other principles of perception, and all our faculties are useless and vain; therefore, the giving of this new sense, with the blessed fruits and effects of it in the soul, is compared to a raising [of] the dead, and to a new creation.[73]

A new sense, new eyes, new ears, new light, new life, new creation! For Edwards these are the results of the renewal of this powerful and authoritative spiritual capacity in the heart. No wonder he said that in regard to divine things, it "opens a new world to its view"[74] and "makes a great change in a man," even greater than had he been born physically blind and all at once received the gift of sight. "For though sight be more noble than any of the other

71. Calvin, pp. 78-82 (§§1.7.4–1.8.1).
72. Jonathan Edwards, *Religious Affections*, ed. John E. Smith, The Works of Jonathan Edwards, vol. 2 (New Haven: Yale University Press, 1959), p. 272.
73. Edwards, p. 206.
74. Edwards, p. 273.

external senses; yet this spiritual sense . . . is infinitely more noble than that, or any other principle of discerning that a man naturally has, and the object of this sense [God] infinitely greater and more important."[75] For Edwards, therefore, it is hard to overestimate the importance of this gift of a new spiritual sense. It so enlightens the "eyes of [the] heart" (Eph. 1:18) that the believer's perception of God and all things related to him is utterly transformed through God's grace and redemption.

How, then, is a worldview formed? From a Christian perspective, there is a source that is not subordinate to either nature or nurture, and in fact can overcome the impact of both if they have been detrimental in the shaping of a person's life. No matter who one is, or how one has been raised, or what one has experienced, and no matter how deeply a person has been entangled in sin, or been blinded by satanic deception, God can break into an individual's life, establish a beachhead in the heart, soften it to the truth of his Word, and save him or her by the power of the gospel of Jesus Christ through faith in him. There is a Savior in the three-personed God who in sheer grace can deliver men and women from the deleterious effects of their own character and background and redeem them from the prison house of idolatry and falsehood. The results of a transaction of this kind are wholly transformative in converting them to the worship of the true God and renewing their hearts and minds with truth. From a biblical perspective, therefore, the formation of a Christian worldview is ultimately a function of God's grace and redemption.

Summary and Conclusion

The evangelical Christian community, especially the Reformed tradition, has expressed serious concern about whether or not the notion of worldview is a suitable concept for Christian service. Because it has been associated since its inception with the unacceptable nuance of relativism, the question has arisen whether the expressions "Christian worldview" or "biblical worldview" are infelicitous and compromise the veracity of historic Christianity. You may recall that William Rowe asserted that "worldview" immigrated from the realm of philosophic discourse into Christian territory and brought lexical contraband with it in its suitcases. His recommendation, which I have taken seriously in this chapter, was that its illicit content must be confiscated and replaced with licit content, biblically speaking. It was necessary to bring *Weltanschauung* captive to the obedience of Christ (2 Cor. 10:5). Only in this way can the idea *legiti-*

---

75. Edwards, p. 275.

mately settle down and prosper, even as it already has, in the colonies of the kingdom of God.[76]

In order to accomplish this task of the Christian naturalization of "worldview," my goal has been to demonstrate how to think about this notion biblically in four particular ways. First, we have seen that it possesses robust objectivist connotations based upon the existence and nature of God and his order for the moral life and the structures of creation. Second, in considering subjectivist issues, we have argued that the notion of worldview must be conceived in terms of the biblical doctrine of the heart as that essential faculty of human consciousness consisting of an essential spiritual orientation and view of reality that determines one's way in the world. Third, we have recognized that sin and a satanic strategy in spiritual warfare account for the multitude of idolatrous interpretations of reality and the blindness of the human heart to the truth about God and his creation. Fourth, we have concluded that the only hope of knowing God aright and having a proper conception of the universe is found in divine grace and redemption through Jesus Christ. Within this biblical framework the term *Weltanschauung*, or "worldview," assumes appropriate Christian meanings, and any harmful implications associated with the word historically are muted. Through this process of Christian naturalization, the concept as a valuable piece of "Egyptian gold" receives a new identity and is made useful for service in the church and acceptable to her Lord.

76. Rowe, p. 156.

Chapter Ten

Philosophical Reflections on "Worldview"

Now, if a worldview is primarily the work of the human heart in its essential operations, thereby defining the person, and if it supplies the fundamental assumptions upon which a life is based, then we must take another step forward and ask a few more questions that prompt philosophical reflection on the nature of this concept. What kind of thing is a worldview in its essence or character? Of what does a worldview consist in terms of basic makeup? It is one thing to suggest that a worldview is "kardioptical," that is, a vision of the heart; it is another thing to suggest in what manner it so exists, of what kinds of materials it consists, and what kind of influence it has on specific areas of human practice. Thus in this chapter I will propose that a worldview might best be understood as a *semiotic phenomenon*. Since people are the kinds of creatures who make and manage signs, especially in the form of words spoken or written, and since most if not all aspects of human thought and culture are semiotically constituted, it seems plausible to include the notion of *Weltanschauung* in this category and construe it as a system of signs generating a symbolic world. In particular I will also propose that a worldview as a semiotic structure consists primarily of a network of *narrative signs* that offers an interpretation of reality and establishes an overarching framework for life. Since people are storytelling creatures who define themselves and the cosmos in a narrative fashion, the content of a worldview seems best associated with this most relevant activity of human nature. Finally, I will propose that a worldview as a semiotic system of world-interpreting stories also provides a foundation or governing platform upon or by which people think, interpret, and know. Since the shape of the human condition is largely a product of the various rational, hermeneutic, and epistemic activities, I will sketch how a heart-inhabiting *Weltanschauung* of this kind exerts an influential relationship upon these salient areas of daily, human praxis. Thus, against the background of the previous chapter with its affirmations of an objective reality rooted in God, the central significance of the human heart, the dynamics of sin and spiritual warfare, and the hope of Christian grace and redemption, we undertake these philosophical reflections in an attempt to deepen our understanding of the nature of a worldview and its influence on all things human.

Worldview and Semiotics

In his book *A Theory of Semiotics,* Umberto Eco subsumes the entire edifice of human culture under the discipline of semiotics. His two propositions are that "(i) the whole of culture *must* be studied as a semiotic phenomenon; (ii) all aspects of culture *can* be studied as the contents of semiotic activity." Stating it a bit differently, he suggests that "the whole of culture *should* be studied as a communicative phenomenon based on signification systems" and that "only by studying it in this way can certain of its fundamental mechanisms be clarified."[1] In other words, semiotics is best conceived as a general theory of culture, and all cultural realities can best be explained and understood under the rubric of semiotics. This would include the cultural reality and the fundamental mechanism of *Weltanschauung.* As a foundational component to human culture, then, it is entirely appropriate to examine the nature and function of worldviews *sub specie semiotica.*

Consequently, we must connect semiotics as the science of signs with human subjects who use them so profusely. What is the nature of this apparently natural activity of making and managing signs — some in the form of a dominant *Weltanschauung?* An answer may be found in the essential semiotic nature of human persons. A defining trait of persons as persons who possess *logos* is the ability to use one thing to stand for another thing *(aliquid stans pro aliquo),* to section off one part of reality and employ it to refer to, mean, or stand for another part of reality. Most characteristically, human beings deploy sound in the form of speech to signify thoughts, feelings, and ideas as well as people, places, and things in the world. In turn they have developed a symbol system of letters, words, and written discourse to represent the same. By these primary semiotic activities, people have been able to parse the cosmos and to create maps of reality.[2] Theo-

1. Umberto Eco, *A Theory of Semiotics,* Advances in Semiotics (Bloomington: Indiana University Press, 1976), p. 22.
2. For more, see Everett M. Stowe, *Communicating Reality through Symbols* (Philadelphia: Westminster, 1966).

logically speaking, an explanation for this human production of signs and symbol systems may be found in the cognitive structure of human beings as the *imago Dei*. They themselves are signs or images of a trinitarian God whose own personal nature and relations may be conceived semiotically: the ingenerate, unimaginable Father is known only to himself by beholding his own image in his Son, who is eternally begotten or created (2 Cor. 4:4; Col. 1:15; Heb. 1:3), and who with the Father is revealed in power by the Holy Spirit, who eternally proceeds forth from the Father and the Son in a coequal and coeternal relation (John 15:26).[3] The communicative acts of human beings consisting of the assertion of meanings with power through signs and symbols testify to their creation as the image of trinitarian God whose personal relations may be construed semiotically. Thus the source of human semiosis itself is possibly a *vestigium trinitatis*.

To this I must add that not only do human beings manifest the ontosemiotic Trinity in their speech and writing as the *imago Dei*, but that according to sacramental theology, the entire universe should be conceived pansemiotically and interpreted as the sign of God and his glory and power. "The heavens are telling of the glory of God," the psalmist affirms, "and their expanse is declaring the work of His hands" (Ps. 19:1). "The whole earth is full of His glory," declares Isaiah the prophet (Isa. 6:3). "For since the creation of the world," says the apostle Paul, "His invisible attributes, His eternal power and divine nature, have been clearly seen, being understood through what has been made, so that they are without excuse" (Rom. 1:20). The world as God's creation is nothing less than "an epiphany of God, a means of His revelation, presence, and power."[4] As the *codex Dei*, all natural objects in the universe possess spiritual meaning (as exemplified in medieval lapidaries and bestiaries). As the *speculum Dei*, the totality of creation is divine iconography. Everything in this enchanted, sacramental, symbol-friendly universe is drenched with *sacred* signs.

Saint Augustine certainly recognized the semiotic character of the cosmos and of human life. In his book *De doctrina Christiana*, the tireless bishop

---

3. Derived from Dorothy L. Sayers, "Toward a Christian Esthetic," in *The Whimsical Christian: Eighteen Essays by Dorothy L. Sayers* (New York: Macmillan, Collier Books, 1987), p. 84. John Milbank has attempted to offer an account of the nature of human communication in terms of the divine Trinity. He argues that the Spirit is the audience that judges the testimony of the Son, whose character or *êthos* is an essential part of the communication. In his "The Second Difference: For a Trinitarianism without Reserve," *Modern Theology* 2 (April 1986): 230, he writes: "The Spirit which proceeds from the paternal-filial difference is genuinely a 'second difference' whose situation is that of a listener to a rhetorical plea of one upon behalf of the other. As the Father is not immediately available, the Spirit must listen to, judge and interpret the testimony of the Son — a testimony in which 'personal integrity' *is* the content of witness to reality."

4. Alexander Schmemann, *For the Life of the World: Sacraments and Orthodoxy* (Crestwood, N.Y.: St. Vladimir's Seminary Press, 1973), p. 120.

of Hippo demonstrates most profoundly the role and power of signs in the process of communication and the acquisition of knowledge. As he states forthrightly, "things are learned about through signs,"[5] and the primary "thing" he is concerned to learn about is God through the signs or words of Scripture which tell of him and all his works. For Augustine God is the greatest human good, and knowing him in a relationship of rightly ordered love is the exclusive source of genuine happiness and determinative for the course of history. Everything is at stake in the momentous semiotic process of interpreting and proclaiming the sign-words of the Scriptures as God's self-revelation. Since the Bible presents the ultimate symbolic world, those who handle its truth regularly must be well trained in hermeneutics and homiletics. And training in these areas is the primary reason why Augustine wrote this book. "There are two things," he states, "which all treatment of the scriptures is aiming at: a way to discover what needs to be understood, and a way to put across to others what has been understood."[6] Thus, in the first three books of *De doctrina Christiana*, Augustine proceeds to offer instruction on the issue of biblical interpretation. In book 1 he distinguishes between things and signs, arguing that among things, some are to be used and others loved. God as trinity is that thing that is to be loved for his own sake, and all else is to be loved for God's sake, that is, in him. As such, he is the primary object of teaching and learning through biblical signs. Hence Augustine proceeds in books 2 and 3 to a discussion of the interpretation of unknown and ambiguous biblical signs, and he also delineates an educational curriculum in other kinds of signs (especially the liberal arts) that are necessary for understanding Scripture with care and accuracy. Once the Bible is correctly interpreted, it must also be skillfully communicated. Thus the Church Father proceeds in the fourth book to a discussion on homiletics, that is, to the matter of proclaiming the truth of scriptural signs effectively. He asks rhetorically if anyone would dare maintain "that those speakers . . . who are trying to convince their hearers of what is untrue, should know how to get them on their side . . . while these who are clearly defending the truth should not?"[7] His essentially Ciceronian treatment of biblical preaching in this final book is his own eloquent answer to this question. Now the telos, or end, of biblical interpretation and proclamation is *caritas* — the love of God for his own sake and the love of humanity for God's sake in

---

5. Augustine, *Teaching Christianity* — *"De Doctrina Christiana,"* introduction, translation, and notes by Edmund Hill, O.P., in *The Works of Saint Augustine: A Translation for the Twenty-first Century*, ed. John E. Rotelle, O.S.A., vol. 11 (Hyde Park, N.Y.: New City Press, 1996), p. 106 (§1.1).

6. Augustine, *Teaching Christianity*, p. 106 (§1.1).

7. Augustine, *Teaching Christianity*, p. 201 (§4.3).

fulfillment of the first and second greatest commandments (cf. Matt. 22:37-39). To be done well, all hermeneutic and homiletic activity must therefore be led "right through to the kingdom of charity."[8]

Nestled, then, in this Augustinian treatise is a cogent recognition that semiotic systems and symbolic worlds are at the heart of the human drama. They are the basic instruments of meaning and have the power of controlling life. Words as signs in themselves are "choice and precious vessels," and into them is poured either the wine of truth or error. Quaffing down large drafts of one or the other intoxicates the heart with either light and liberty or darkness and servitude.[9] For Augustine, therefore, how important it is to drink deeply from the sign vessels of the Scriptures which must be well prepared and properly served.

Against this ancient background, more recent thinkers have also emphasized the semiotic quality of human existence. For example, Charles Sanders Peirce (1839-1914), recognized by many as the founder of modern semiology, established his theory of signs on the notion that all thought and cognition, and indeed human beings themselves, are thoroughly semiotic in their basic nature. In his words, "the fact that every thought is a sign, taken in conjunction with the fact that life is a train of thought, proves that man is a sign."[10] Furthermore, Peirce adopted what we might call a "semiotic worldview," that is, a pan-semiotic view of the universe in which signs are not merely regarded as one class of things among many nonsemiotic objects, but where "the entire universe is perfused with signs, if it is not composed exclusively of signs."[11] Hence, for Peirce, semiotics characterizes not only the universe but also human beings as essentially sign-begetting and sign-bound creatures.

Ernst Cassirer (1874-1945), in a similar manner, posits in his *Philosophy of Symbolic Forms* that human beings are primarily symbol-creating animals *(animal symbolicum)*, and that the comprehension of reality is possible only by semiotic means.[12] Cassirer thus promoted a pan-semiotic epistemology, arguing that everything that has meaning is composed of "symbolic forms." This included such things as language, myth, art, religion, science, and history, each of which is based on its own set of symbolic laws and is independent of nature.

8. Augustine, *Teaching Christianity,* p. 179 (§3.23).

9. A gloss on Augustine, *Confessions,* trans. F. J. Sheed, introduction by Peter Brown (Indianapolis: Hackett, 1992), p. 16 (§1.17).

10. Charles Sanders Peirce, *Collected Papers,* ed. Charles Hartshorne and Paul Weiss, vol. 5 (Cambridge: Harvard University Press, 1931-58), §314, quoted in Winfried Nöth, *Handbook of Semiotics,* Advances in Semiotics (Bloomington: Indiana University Press, 1990), p. 41.

11. Peirce, §448 n, quoted in Nöth, p. 41.

12. Nöth, p. 35.

According to Cassirer, then, sign systems are the only possible road to knowledge, even though for him they do not in any way copy or imitate reality but instead create it.[13]

Behold, then, the power of signs and symbols across the whole spectrum of reality and human existence. They permeate the physical universe; they are germane to all aspects of culture; they are essential to human thought, cognition, and communication; they are efficacious instruments of either truth or falsehood; they create symbolic worlds in which people live, move, and have their being. Indeed, a certain string of symbols possesses unique cultural power and determines the meaning of life. Those symbols I would designate a worldview. As an individual's or culture's foundation and system of denotative signs, they are promulgated through countless communicative avenues and mysteriously find their way to the innermost regions of the heart. There they provide a foundation and interpretation of life. They inform the categories of consciousness. They are the putative object of faith and the basis for hope, however it may be conceived. They are embraced as true and offer a way of life. They are the essential source of individual and sociocultural security. They are personal and cultural structures that define human existence. Thus, when they are in crisis or are challenged, people respond anxiously, and even with hostility. For example, in Plato's cave analogy the resistance of the released prisoner to having his sign system altered through the discovery of new realms of reality, and the hostility he encountered when he returned to the cave and sought to reshape the symbolic world of his former cave dwellers, manifests the power residing in a semiotically constituted *Weltanschauung*.[14] Similarly, it is quite likely that the hostility aimed at Jesus and a primary reason for his crucifixion was that during his ministry he directly and indirectly attacked the sacred symbols of the Second Temple Jewish worldview. Indeed, the semiotic system of his own ministry was extraordinarily provocative, and he virtually reorganized the entire Jewish theological tradition through his proclamation of the mysteries of the kingdom of God. No wonder, then, that such wrath was directed toward him, even to the point of death.[15] Whether as an illustration in Platonic philosophy or as an historical event in first-century Palestine, or even as a present-day construct that determines the meaning of life, worldviews are tenacious systems of semiosis that occupy the interior spaces of the human heart, determine the thoughts and acts of men and women, and set the course of local cultures

13. Nöth, p. 36. Cassirer's antirealism is obviously anti-Christian in its denial of an objective reality that has its source in God and his law-defining work of creation.

14. See Plato's *Republic* 514a-517c.

15. N. T. Wright, *Jesus and the Victory of God*, Christian Origins and the Question of God, vol. 2 (Minneapolis: Fortress, 1996), p. 369.

and entire civilizations for either good or ill. If all cultural phenomena can and perhaps should be explained semiotically, then worldviews should be no exception. One reason why these signs making up a worldview are so powerful individually and culturally is because of the particular shape they assume: they have been formulated and received internally as a set of narratives or stories that establish a particular perspective on life.

Worldview and Narrative

Semiotically constituted human beings in want of a solution to the riddles of the universe primarily fulfill this need in their trademark activity of telling stories that form a symbolic world for which people are inclined to live and even die. Indeed, the power of stories to establish a context for life has been recognized since time immemorial. No one in antiquity saw this more clearly than Socrates and Plato.[16] They knew well that the kinds of stories the future rulers of their ideal republic would encounter, especially in childhood, would be particularly influential both cognitively and morally, with ultimate public and political implications. Therefore Socrates and Plato, and later on even Aristotle, recognized the importance of the narrative education of the young, as fairy-tale expert Bruno Bettelheim explains: "Plato — who may have understood better what forms the mind of man than do some of our contemporaries who want their children exposed only to 'real' people and everyday events — knew what intellectual experiences make for true humanity. He suggested that the future citizens of his ideal republic begin their literary education with the telling of myths, rather than with mere facts or so-called rational teachings. Even Aristotle, master of pure reason, said: 'The friend of wisdom is also a friend of myth.'"[17]

Thus the wisdom of the ages, going all the way back to Socrates, Plato, and Aristotle, would suggest that the development of the human mind and consciousness is a function of the weightiness of stories and their plots, their characters, their denouements, and their overall explanations of things. As a proponent of this perspective, Bettelheim has argued that fairy tales and myths are the basic means by which children fashion and refashion their worlds. This is largely true because, in his estimation, such tales and myths are concerned with

---

16. For Socrates' and Plato's views on the role and power of stories, see especially bks. 2, 3, and 10 in the *Republic*. For Aristotle's reflections on the same, consult his *Poetics*.

17. Bruno Bettelheim, *The Uses of Enchantment: The Meaning and Importance of Fairy Tales* (New York: Random House, Vintage Books, 1977), p. 35.

basic questions of life: "Who am I? Where did I come from? How did the world come into being? Who created man and all the animals? What is the purpose of life?" He is convinced, however, that children ponder these issues, not philosophically, but in a childlike way as they pertain to a specific boy or girl and his or her individual well-being. "He [the child] worries not whether there is justice for individual man, but whether *he* will be treated justly. He wonders who or what projects him into adversity, and what can prevent this from happening to him. Are there benevolent powers in addition to his parents? Are his parents benevolent powers? How should he form himself, and why? Is there hope for him, though he may have done wrong? Why has all this happened to him? What will it mean for his future?"[18]

For Bettelheim, myths and fairy tales provide the answers to these pressing questions which children become aware of only as they are exposed to these stories and follow their plots all the way through. The answers given by myths are definite, says Bettelheim, while the responses of fairy tales are suggestive. The content of fairy tales, in particular, fit the nature of children and their childlike outlook on the world, and this is why they are so convincing to and comforting for them. They reflect and order their world.[19]

Rollo May has affirmed something similar, but with application also to adults. He believes that myth, which may be compared to the hidden framework of a house, is the very structure that imparts meaning to life and thereby holds it together. "A myth is a way of making sense in a senseless world. Myths are narrative patterns that give significance to our existence. Whether the meaning of existence is only what we put into life by our own individual fortitude . . . or whether there is a meaning we need to discover . . . , the result is the same: myths are our way of finding this meaning and significance. Myths are like the beams in a house: not exposed to outside view, they are the structure which holds the house together so people can live in it."[20]

Another place where worldview and narrative intersect is in the context of the folktale. Linda Dégh notes that although the term "worldview" is rather vague, and though it seldom appears as a major research goal in folk narrative study, "one way or another it is addressed in all descriptive and analytical studies of stories and their tellers."[21] When folklorists speak about *Weltanschauung*, she says they mean the subjective, individual interpretations of the totality of reality according to the way it is perceived and experienced. She believes that all

18. Bettelheim, p. 47.
19. Bettelheim, p. 45.
20. Rollo May, *The Cry for Myth* (New York: Bantam Doubleday Dell, Delta, 1991), p. 15.
21. Linda Dégh, "The Approach to Worldview in Folk Narrative Study," *Western Folklore* 53 (July 1994): 246.

human thought and action are affected by worldview perception and interpretation. Consequently, she asserts that worldview "permeates all cultural performances, including folklore." "Narratives, in particular, are loaded with worldview expressions: they reveal inherited communal and personal views of human conduct — this is their generic goal. Bearers of narrative tradition, as much as seasoned researchers, know and anticipate how a joke, an exemplum, or a ballad to be performed is going to characterize the world, yet we cannot single out one type of worldview or deal with all that is expressed in one narrative or one telling."[22]

Dégh contends that worldview motivates and defines all human attitudes and behaviors, and that human action is unintelligible without it. Hence her argument is that the study of the folktale "as a human product and its specific versions as personal acts of creation can show how the world is featured by this genre: what is the genre specific image of the world?"[23]

Thus, from Plato to the present, the human relevance of the narrative genre with life-defining power seems self-evident. Yet despite this all-times, all-places recognition of stories as the bearers of a symbolic world in which human beings might find a secure, cognitive home — what Stephen Crites has called the "narrative quality of experience"[24] — the architects of the modern project did their best to rid *homo narrator* of their troublesome tales and banish them from cultural significance. Because the presence and influence of competing mythologies engendered enormous sociocultural conflict, and even warfare, especially of the religious variety, their solution was to exterminate the narrative-infested polis and fill it with ratio-scientific objectifications. Relegating the category of narrative to private life and the domain of values, their goal was to provide an allegedly neutral and hostility-free way of ordering public life. Human existence established upon a new, scientific foundation betokened modern man come of age, who no longer had need for the primitive mythologies of bygone religious or metaphysical eras.

But Enlightenment denarrativization came at a high human cost, and nobody has understood that cost better than Friedrich Nietzsche. In *The Birth of Tragedy* he writes, "But without myth every culture loses the healthy natural power of its creativity: only a horizon defined by myths completes and unifies a

---

22. Dégh, p. 247.

23. Dégh, p. 250. See also the follow-up comments to Dégh's study by Alan Dundes, "Worldview in Folk Narrative: An Addendum," *Western Folklore* 54 (July 1995): 229-32.

24. Stephen Crites, "The Narrative Quality of Experience," in *Why Narrative? Readings in Narrative Theology,* ed. Stanley Hauerwas and L. Gregory Jones (Grand Rapids: Eerdmans, 1989), pp. 65-88. Crites argues that "experience is molded, root and branch, by narrative forms, that its narrative quality is altogether primitive" (p. 84).

whole cultural movement."[25] Nietzsche knew, however, that the Western world had been drifting slowly toward the destruction of its narrative resources — a kind of "mythoclasm"[26] — by its intoxication with scientific rationalism. Consequently, modern humanity, "untutored by myth," is famished and in search for any narrative morsel on which to feed itself, as the frenzied activities and compulsions of contemporary life indicate. "And now the mythless man stands eternally hungry, surrounded by all past ages, and digs and grubs for roots, even if he has to dig for them among the remotest antiquities. The tremendous historical need of our unsatisfied modern culture, the assembling around one of countless other cultures, the consuming desire for knowledge — what does all this point to, if not to the loss of myth, the loss of the mythical home, the mythical maternal womb?"

Nietzsche perceives that the "feverish and uncanny excitement" of modern culture — its incessant pace, its quest for exotic traditions, its passion for knowledge — must be interpreted as nothing other than a hunger for myth, "the greedy seizing and snatching at food of a hungry man."[27] No matter how much it devours materialistically or otherwise, a storyless world and mythless culture cannot and will never be satiated. The only solution to narrative starvation is the preparation and consumption of primordial, explanatory tales that nourish and satisfy the mythological cravings of human beings.

Because of this inescapable narrative need built into the human soul, recent cultural history has proven that the modern attempt at extirpating narratives was muddleheaded and vain. Indeed, a deep irony has characterized this crusade against narratives, for it has been based on an unconscious Cartesian story featuring heroic human reason as the protagonist of a master plot to take possession of the world by scientific prowess. As Richard Middleton and Brian Walsh point out, "[T]he very notion that in modern times we have outgrown the childish, prescientific stage of mythical thinking and progressed to the maturity of scientific reason and technological mastery is itself a *story*. It is, therefore, only by telling its own 'tall tale' that modernity can claim to have surpassed the need for stories."[28] In other words, the antinarrativity of Enlightenment modernism is self-referentially incoherent.

Perhaps more than any other contemporary thinker, Alasdair MacIntyre

25. Friedrich Nietzsche, *The Birth of Tragedy and the Case of Wagner*, translated and commentary by Walter Kaufmann (New York: Random House, Vintage Books, 1967), p. 135 (§23).

26. Jerome S. Bruner, "Myth and Identity," in *Myth and Mythmaking*, ed. Henry A. Murray (New York: George Braziller, 1960), p. 285, quoted in May, p. 16.

27. Nietzsche, p. 136 (§23).

28. J. Richard Middleton and Brian J. Walsh, *Truth Is Stranger Than It Used to Be: Biblical Faith in a Postmodern Age* (Downers Grove, Ill.: InterVarsity, 1995), p. 67.

has argued most persuasively for a recovery of the narrative foundations of human existence. In his celebrated *After Virtue,* he notes that because of social and philosophical forces, the narrative unity of life, or of an individual life, was destroyed in the context of modernity.[29] A human self, nonnarratively conceived, cannot be the bearer of Aristotelian virtues, which is MacIntyre's primary concern. On the contrary, a virtuous life is possible only to the extent that it is conceived, unified, and evaluated as a whole. Hence MacIntyre seeks to recover a concept of an integrated human existence grounded in the integrity of a narrative which links birth, life, and death, or beginning, middle, and end, into a singular, coherent story embraced communally. MacIntyre argues that it is natural to think of the self in the narrative mode, and that all human conversations and actions are best understood as "enacted narratives" (p. 211). Narrative, not free-floating, independent selves, is the most basic category. Stories are necessary to make sense of one's own life and the lives of others. MacIntyre focuses on the stories of a lived tradition, but he also recognizes that the wellspring of these narratives is located at a deeper, mythological level. "Hence," MacIntyre writes, "there is no way to give us an understanding of any society, including our own, except through the stock of stories which constitute its initial dramatic resources. Mythology, in its original sense, is at the heart of things" (p. 216). In other words, the narrative stories which are lived out in the world of human experience are a product of bedrock, first-order myths that essentially constitute a worldview. MacIntyre's fundamental proposal essential to his revival of the Aristotelian tradition of virtue ethics is this: "A central thesis then begins to emerge: man is in his actions and practice, as well as in his fictions, essentially a story-telling animal. He is not essentially, but becomes through his history, a teller of stories that aspire to truth. But the key question for men is not about their own authorship; I can only answer the question 'What am I to do' if I can answer the prior question 'Of what story or stories do I find myself a part?'" (p. 216).

For MacIntyre, then, human life is governed by story. The roles which people play, how they understand themselves and others, how the world itself is structured and operates are a function of the narrative plots that reign in a human community. While MacIntyre applies these arguments to rehabilitate a tradition-based virtue ethics, for our purposes his ideas highlight the role and importance of stories that human beings employ to make sense of life in the cosmos.

29. Alasdair MacIntyre, *After Virtue: A Study in Moral Theory,* 2nd ed. (Notre Dame, Ind.: University of Notre Dame Press, 1984), pp. 204-25. Page references in this paragraph are to this work.

In light of the preceding reflections, therefore, it is safe to say that worldviews contain an unmistakable and irreducible narrative component.[30] As Plato once pointed out, people are concerned about "the heavens and the whole story of existence, divine and human."[31] Thus human beings, as semiotic creatures and inherent storytellers, come to grips with themselves and the nature of life in the cosmos through the formation of worldviews as systems of narrative signs that form a basic outlook on life. They provide narrative answers to the fundamental questions about the realm of the divine, the nature of the cosmos, the identity of human beings, the solution to the problems of suffering and pain, and so on. Even the seemingly nonnarratival aspects of a *Weltanschauung* — its doctrinal, ethical, or ritual dimensions — can be explained by a fundamental narrative content. Middleton and Walsh support this contention in their recognition of the virtual omnipresence of narrative in faiths and philosophies worldwide.

> Both Judaism and Islam . . . articulate their worldview in narrative form, appealing to the destiny of history as revelatory of God's intent. Even Eastern religions, such as Hinduism and Buddhism, which are often portrayed as suspicious of history . . . have passed on a rich heritage of myths in storied form, including an epic narrative, the Mahabrata (of which the Bhagavad-Gita is a part). Myths and folktales of good, evil and redemption are also the stock-in-trade of the contemporary indigenous religions of Africa, North and South America, and Australia, as well as the classical religions of Greece, Rome, Egypt, and Mesopotamia. In each case, ultimate truths about the world, humanity, evil and salvation are communicated in terms of stories which give guidance and set the parameters for ethical action.[32]

These stories that establish a symbolic world do indeed guide all forms of human activity. Worldview narratives create a particular kind of "mind," and serve in a normative fashion as "controlling stories."[33] The most fundamental

---

30. N. T. Wright, *The New Testament and the People of God*, Christian Origins and the Question of God, vol. 1 (Minneapolis: Fortress, 1992), p. 38. Part II of this volume contains helpful reflections on the relation of stories to worldview, and on the relation of worldview to New Testament theology and biblical studies.

31. Plato, *Phaedrus*, translated and introduction by Walter Hamilton (New York: Penguin Books, 1973), p. 70.

32. Middleton and Walsh, pp. 64-65.

33. Wright, *The New Testament*, pp. 41-42. Wright acknowledges that the idea of "controlling stories" is derived from Nicholas Wolterstorff's concept of "control beliefs," which he discusses in his *Reason within the Bounds of Religion*, 2nd ed. (Grand Rapids: Eerdmans, 1984), p. 67.

stories associated with a *Weltanschauung* — those closest to its metaphysical, epistemological, and ethical epicenter — possess a kind of finality as the ultimate interpretation of reality in all its multifaceted aspects. Such stories are considered sacred, and they provide the adhesive that unites those who believe in them into a society characterized by shared perspectives and a common way of life. They also provide a tenacious grid by which competing narratives and alternative claims to truth are judged. Controlling stories, therefore, function in a regulatory fashion both positively and negatively, and are able to bind those who accept them into an intellectual or spiritual commonwealth. Thus the bulk of human praxis does seem to be under the jurisdiction of a worldview, including the significant activities of reasoning, interpreting, and knowing.

Worldview and Reason

The faculty of human reason has had a distinguished career in the history of Western thought. It is that capacity by which men and women have been typically distinguished from the brutes. It is an endowment in which people as thinking beings *(homo sapiens)* have trusted to provide a knowledge of themselves, their surroundings, and beyond. As Pascal said in the *Pensées,* "Man is a thinking reed. . . . It is by means of thought that . . . [one] can comprehend the universe."[34] But what is the nature of rational thought, and how does reason itself function? Specifically for our purposes, what is the relationship between a particular conception of the universe — a *Weltanschauung* — and the exercise and content of rationality? What influence, if any, does a worldview have upon the way reason works and what it says? Is rationality dependent upon or free from a semiotic or narrative context? Is there an "arch" or "Olympian" kind of rationality transcending worldviews that is homogeneous and the same for all?[35] Perhaps three examples will illustrate the precise thrust of this inquiry regarding the relation of worldview and rationality.

First, are the beliefs of primitive, prescientific cultures less "rational" than those of the modern West? According to Peter Winch in his celebrated article "Understanding a Primitive Society" (1964), the answer must be a resounding

34. *The Mind on Fire: An Anthology of the Writings of Blaise Pascal,* ed. James M. Houston, introduction by Os Guinness (Portland, Oreg.: Multnomah, 1989), pp. 82-83 (4.347-48).

35. The idea of an "arch-rationalism" as an absolutist style of reason is from Ian Hacking, "Language, Truth and Reason," in *Rationality and Relativism,* ed. Martin Hollis and Steven Lukes (Cambridge: MIT Press, 1982), pp. 51-53; the notion of "Olympian reason" as a reasoning process from a "god's-eye point of view" is from Herbert A. Simon, *Reason in Human Affairs* (Stanford: Stanford University Press, 1983), pp. 34-35.

NO. Taking as his example the African Azande, he notes that they "believe that certain of their members are witches, exercising a malignant occult influence on the lives of their fellows. They engage in rites to counteract witchcraft; they consult oracles and use magic medicines to protect themselves from harm."[36] In an anthropological context, Winch argues against Lucien Lévy-Bruhl, who asserts that primitive people have a prelogical if not irrational mentality, and sides with E. E. Evans-Pritchard, who maintains that the Western scientific understanding of cause and effect which leads Westerners to jettison magical ideas is no proof of any rational superiority on their part.[37] In essence Winch is suggesting that what counts as "rational" does indeed seem to shift from culture to culture, and that any one culture must beware of imposing its canons of rationality on another as if they were superior or fixed.

Second, in the agon between Jews, Gentiles, and Christians regarding the credibility of the New Testament gospel, with which party does rationality side? Does it make any sense to believe that Jesus of Nazareth was the incarnation of God and the fulfillment of the messianic hopes of Israel? Is it cogent to think that the death of Jesus on a Roman cross and his resurrection from the dead constitute an atonement for sin and are the spiritual hope of the world? The New Testament indicates that for both the Jews and Gentiles, the *kerygma* constituted an undiminished *sacrificium intellectum* as a stumbling block and foolishness respectively. On the other hand, for the believing Christian it is the consummate rationality or wisdom of God, just as the world's supposed wisdom or form of rationality is in fact pure foolishness. Saint Paul explains in 1 Corinthians 1:20-25:

> Where is the wise man? Where is the scribe? Where is the debater of this age? Has not God made foolish the wisdom of the world? For since in the wisdom of God the world through its wisdom did not come to know God, God was well-pleased through the foolishness of the message preached to save those who believe. For indeed Jews ask for signs and Greeks search for wisdom; but we preach Christ crucified, to Jews a stumbling block, and to

36. Peter Winch, "Understanding a Primitive Society," in *Rationality*, ed. Bryan R. Wilson (New York: Harper and Row, First Torchbook Library Edition, 1970), p. 78. This article was originally published in the *American Philosophical Quarterly* 1 (1964): 307-24.

37. Winch, p. 79. See Lucien Lévy-Bruhl, *Primitive Mentality*, trans. Lilian A. Clare (London: George Allen and Unwin, 1923); E. E. Evans-Pritchard, *Witchcraft, Oracles, and Magic among the Azandi*, foreword by G. C. Seligman (Oxford: Clarendon, 1937). Sir James Frazer, who offers an exhaustive account of the beliefs, activities, and institutions of humankind in his famed work *The Golden Bough* (1890-1915), makes the argument that man progresses from irrational magical and religious stages ultimately to the level of scientific thought.

Gentiles foolishness, but to those who are the called, both Jews and Greeks, Christ the power of God and the wisdom of God. Because the foolishness of God is wiser than men, and the weakness of God is stronger than men.

The singular evangelistic message is obviously capable of generating significantly different judgments regarding the sanity of its essential content. One person's foolishness or stumbling block is indeed another person's wisdom, and vice versa.

Third, do human beings manifest the utmost in rational virtue when they insist that for a proposition to be true, it must either be a part of or rightly rest upon an epistemological foundation that consists of one or more statements that are indubitably known to be either self-evident, evident to the senses, or incorrigible? Does the house of reason consist of epistemic planks that are securely nailed together and established upon an unshakable foundation of solid cognitive concrete? Perhaps the edifice of knowledge is constructed only when human knowers willfully set aside all pernicious prejudices and presuppositions, jettison all encumbering narratives and traditions, and purge themselves of the subjective influences that arise from various allegiances and their historical and social locations. Perhaps a purely objective way of knowing submits all propositions to the bar of dispassionate reason, demands that all claims to truth pass empirical muster, apportions all epistemic judgments according to the evidence, and requires that all possible knowledge conform to the highest possible scientific standards. This, of course, is the modernist model of rationality, the distinctive product of the Enlightenment. As Alasdair MacIntyre explains it, "So, it was hoped, reason would displace authority and tradition. Rational justification was to appeal to principles undeniable by any rational person and therefore independent of all those social and cultural particularities which the Enlightenment thinkers took to be the mere accidental clothing of reason in particular times and places."[38] But is the modern version of rationality truly rational?

Critics point out at least two major problems with this foundationalist account of reason that render it suspect. The first is that it seems to be the idiosyncratic product of a limited number of western European thinkers in a specific historical period. Indeed, it seems that their ideas about rationality are curiously out of step with the overwhelming majority of the human race whose ways of knowing are neither devoid of tradition, nor as scientifically and philo-

---

38. Alasdair MacIntyre, *Whose Justice? Which Rationality?* (Notre Dame, Ind.: University of Notre Dame Press, 1988), p. 6.

sophically rigorous, nor as secular or nonreligious in substance.[39] The second is that Enlightenment epistemology has faltered in its inability to agree upon what propositions constitute an indubitable foundation, in excluding from cogency forms of knowledge that seem to be universally accepted (for example, memory beliefs and other minds), and in its inability to establish cultural epistemic consensus (hence, social fragmentation). Perhaps the greatest irony of the modernist model of rationality is that, despite its attempt to extirpate narrative traditions from the knowing process, its own epistemic methods and outlook have been accepted by most of the post-Enlightenment intelligentsia, and itself has been "transformed into a tradition whose continuities are partly defined by the interminability of the debate over such principles [of shared rationality]."[40] Thus the Enlightenment's very prejudice against prejudice as well as its antitraditionalism has become (at least until recently) the predominate modern prejudice and the new cultural and intellectual tradition!

Now, regarding these three examples, there are intense disputes among anthropologists about what constitutes cultural rationality; among Jews, Gentiles, and Christians concerning soteriological rationality; and among modern and postmodern philosophers over the question of epistemic rationality. These very differences over the African Azande, the gospel, and foundationalism make one thing seem patently clear: rationality is context- and commitment-dependent. What a person deems to be rational or irrational appears to be a function of the reasoner's worldview. The system of narrative signs that comprises one's conception of reality rooted in the human heart also governs one's way of thinking and determines the canons of rational thought. Reason is embarrassed by nakedness and always seeks to be clothed in a narrative-based worldview tradition.[41]

---

39. For example, Seyyed Hossein Nasr, the first Muslim ever to deliver the Gifford Lectures (1981), has addressed this latter issue in his *Knowledge and the Sacred* (New York: State University of New York Press, 1989). His line of argument is this: Knowledge has become nearly completely externalized and desacralized, especially for those segments of the human race which have been transformed by the process of modernization. Because of the influence of modernity, he says that knowledge of the sacred "has become well-nigh unattainable and beyond the grasp of the vast majority of those who walk upon the earth" (p. 1). Nevertheless, drawing on the full range of the great religious traditions (Hindu, Buddhist, Jewish, Christian, and Islamic), he affirms that the root and essence of genuine knowledge is inseparable from the sacred because the substance of genuine knowledge itself is, as he put it, knowledge of "the Supreme Substance, the Sacred as such . . ." (p. 1). Hence, contrary to the thoroughgoing secularism of the Enlightenment, there is a global epistemological tradition that makes room for the divine.

40. MacIntyre, *Whose Justice? Which Rationality?* p. 335.

41. This is not to suggest that the very laws of logic are altered by cultural context or philosophical orientation. Quite the contrary. The principles of reason itself — noncontradiction, identity, and excluded middle — are universal. For example, there is no way to deny the law of

Two thinkers who contribute to the idea of rationality rooted in commitment are R. G. Collingwood and Alasdair MacIntyre. Collingwood has crafted a point of view in which rationality inheres in a "logic of question and answer" which is related to a series of relative and absolute presuppositions. Relative presuppositions consist of the answer to a previous question which in turn becomes the basis for the next question. And the whole system of question and answer arises from and is dependent upon a set of absolute presuppositions that fosters the system of thought in the first place. Collingwood has set forth most of what he teaches about absolute presuppositions in his *Essay on Metaphysics* (1940). In these pages he makes a number of fundamental points, but one is particularly important here. Absolute presuppositions, according to Collingwood, whether in a "consupponible" constellation or by themselves, are not subject to proof or disproof. Since they are not propositions (for only propositions are capable of verification or falsification in Collingwood's view), then it follows that presuppositions are not capable of being true or false. After all, "it is proof which depends on them," he says, "not they on proof."[42] In other words, people argue *from* but not *to* presuppositions. Also, if an absolute presupposition could be proven by something else, then it would not be absolute, but that from which it is proven would be. Thus the logical efficacy of absolute presuppositions does not depend on their epistemological veracity, or even on their being believed to be true, but only on their being supposed absolutely. From the bedrock beginning of these unassailable assumptions the rationality of a particular system of thought — a logic of question and answer — is derived. Collingwood's doctrine of absolute presuppositions, which approximates the function of a *Weltanschauung*, supports the argument that rationality does not function abstractly, but by commitment, and in this case, to a set of absolute presuppositions.[43]

---

noncontradiction in any setting without using and thereby affirming it. The content, however, on the basis of which and with which these laws of logic function, is markedly different. In Aristotelian terms, the formal cause of rationality is the same, but its material cause may vary considerably. For a series of articles that demonstrate the material influence of Calvinism on the reasoning process, see Hendrik Hart, Johan Van Der Hoeven, and Nicholas Wolterstorff, eds., *Rationality in the Calvinian Tradition*, Christian Studies Today (Lanham, Md.: University Press of America, 1983).

42. R. G. Collingwood, *Essay on Metaphysics* (Oxford: Clarendon, 1940), p. 173.

43. Similarly, Kenneth Pike, *Talk, Thought, Thing: The Emic Road toward Conscious Knowledge* (Dallas: Summer Institute of Linguistics, 1993), p. 44, has stated: "Logic, by itself, can never determine that anything is ultimately true, since logic requires starting presuppositions which are accepted as true by persons — and eventually some of those propositions are unprovable by that person. He starts by believing them." For further discussion on presuppositions, see Ted Peters, "The Nature and Role of Presupposition: An Inquiry into Contemporary Hermeneutics,"

Alasdair MacIntyre, whose work we have already drawn upon in helpful ways, offers a proposal that is developed quite differently, but in the final analysis amounts to just about the same thing as Collingwood's. His concern in his *Whose Justice? Which Rationality?* is of course moral matters, in particular the conception of justice. In his investigation he soon recognized that rival conceptions of justice presupposed rival conceptions of rationality. As he puts it, "To know what justice is . . . we must first learn what rationality in practice requires of us. Yet someone who tries to learn this at once encounters the fact that disputes about the nature of rationality in general and about practical rationality in particular are apparently as manifold and as intractable as disputes about justice."[44] MacIntyre thus commences to investigate the nature and character of reason as crafted by champions of modernity and finds it wanting. Among other things, Enlightenment rationality as expressed in epistemological foundationalism, as he puts it, "ignores the inescapably historically and socially context-bound character which any substantive set of principles of rationality, whether theoretical or practical, is bound to have" (p. 4). Because of this negation, debates over particular issues — moral or otherwise — were detached from the background contexts of incompatible assumptions out of which disagreements arose in the first place. Because Enlightenment thinking located rationality at the upper, theoretical level, it prevented discussion from penetrating to the fundamental worldview presuppositions. Consequently, MacIntyre notes, "the legacy of the Enlightenment has been the provision of an ideal of rational justification which it has proved impossible to attain" (p. 6). He himself wants to take the discussion to a deeper level, all the way back to ground zero, and so he argues for a conception of rational inquiry that is embodied in a tradition. As he puts it, "from the standpoint of tradition-constituted and tradition-constitutive enquiry, what a particular doctrine claims [i.e., its rationality] is always a matter of how precisely it was in fact advanced, of the linguistic particularities of its formulation, of what in that time and place had to be denied, if it was to be asserted, of what was at that time and place presupposed by its assertion, and so on." The rationality of doctrines, in other words, has to be understood in terms of historical context, and for that reason, MacIntyre argues, there are "rationalities rather than [a] rationality" (p. 9). For all practical purposes, then, MacIntyre seems to be saying that the deep questions about "whose

---

International Philosophical Quarterly 14 (June 1974): 209-22; Nicholas Rescher, "On the Logic of Presuppositions," *Philosophy and Phenomenological Research* 21 (1961): 521-27; Eugene F. Bertoldi, "Absolute Presuppositions and Irrationalism," *Southern Journal of Philosophy* 27 (1989): 157-72.

44. MacIntyre, *Whose Justice? Which Rationality?* p. 2. The page references in the following text are to this work.

justice" and "which rationality" are a matter intimately related to worldview. This is indicated by one of his final declarations on the matter, located toward the very end of his book.

> The enquiry into justice and practical rationality was from the outset informed by a conviction that each particular conception of justice requires as its counterpart some particular conception of practical rationality and vice versa. Not only has that conviction been reinforced by the outcome of the enquiry so far, *but it has become evident that conceptions of justice and of practical rationality generally and characteristically confront us as closely related aspects of some larger, more or less well-articulated, overall view of human life and of its place in nature.* Such overall views, insofar as they make claims upon our rational allegiance, give expression to traditions of enquiry which are at one and the same time traditions embodied in particular types of social relationship. (p. 389, emphasis added)

Whether one posits the much more abstract notion of "absolute presuppositions," as Collingwood has, to elucidate the structure of rational thought, or whether the more inviting notion of "historical traditions" is invoked, as MacIntyre has done, the general conclusion once again is established: the character and content of rationality are *Weltanschauung*-dependent. As Thomas Kuhn argued that scientific reasoning is carried out in the framework of "paradigms" or disciplinary matrices, so also Alasdair MacIntyre has defended the notion that to make sense of virtue, it too must be contextualized in a narrative-historical tradition.

When a person discovers his set of absolute presuppositions or the narrative-historical worldview tradition he inhabits, several consequences follow. He grows not only in self-knowledge, but also in an understanding of the traditions and contexts that animate others around him. He also recognizes that he must either speak and live out his particular understanding of reason and justice or else fall silent (pp. 394-95, 401). Martin Luther is a good example in this regard. In the context of his new Reformational view of justification and his conception of theological rationality, he encountered hostile ecclesiastical authorities who did not accept his dissident outlook. When called upon to explain his new positions, he refused to remain silent, and made this famous declaration before the assembled dignitaries of the Roman Church at the Diet of Worms in 1521:

> Your Imperial Majesty and your lordships demand a simple answer. Here it is, plain and unvarnished. Unless I am convicted of error by the testi-

mony of Scripture or . . . *by manifest reasoning* . . . I can not and will not recant anything. For to act against our conscience is neither safe for us, nor appropriate for us. On this I take my stand. I can do no other. God help me. Amen.[45]

What Luther understood by "manifest reasoning" was surely associated with his interpretation of the Scriptures and the Protestant religious outlook that would one day bear his name. His course of action, his sense of justice, his rational processes were bound up in a new, revolutionary narrative tradition that had so captured his moral imagination that he could do nothing but take his stand, even at the prospect of great personal cost. The pattern of reasoning shared by Luther's inquisitors was obviously bound up in an opposing horizon of belief. The rational trajectories of these two parties, rooted in their respective worldviews, put them on a collision course. A powerful way to explain such historical encounters which have the potential to redirect the course of history is by recognizing that rationality is not a formal, atemporal process, but a way of thinking that is grounded in a commitment to a system of narrative signs associated with an historical tradition. That is, reason is grounded in worldview. And so are acts of interpretation.[46]

Worldview and Hermeneutics

A virtually insuperable quandary seems to have plagued seekers after knowledge and interpreters of texts since time immemorial. The attempt to discover what one does not already know, and the endeavor to interpret what one does not already understand, places inquirers and expositors in the confines of an apparently inescapable "learners" paradox. This dilemma has been aptly captured in a brief exchange between Meno and Socrates in one of the Platonic dialogues, the title of which bears the name of the former as the latter's interlocutor.

> *Meno:* And how will you enquire, Socrates, into that which you do not know? What will you put forth as the subject of enquiry? And if you find what you want, how will you ever know that this is the thing which you

---

45. From Henry Bettenson, ed., *Documents of the Christian Church* (New York: Oxford University Press, 1947), p. 285, emphasis added.

46. These assertions should not be taken to mean that there is no such thing as truth or final meaning. Far from it. It is only to suggest that our reasoning and interpreting processes are influenced in significant ways by worldview considerations, as we seek to think well and interpret rightly.

did not know? *Socrates:* . . . You argue that a man cannot enquire either about that which he knows, or about that which he does not know; for if he knows, he has no need to enquire; and if not, he cannot; for he does not know the very subject about which he is to enquire.[47]

Aristotle also addressed this perplexity in the first chapter of his *Posterior Analytics,* citing the above exchange and stating in the opening line that "All instruction given or received by way of argument proceeds from pre-existent knowledge."[48] In the task of interpretation, a similar law seemingly prevails: the explication of texts always proceeds on the basis of various preunderstandings and governing commitments. The implications of this apparent fact, and the difficulties associated with it, are twofold. One, the meaning of a text is determined in advance on the basis of the interpreter's preexisting knowledge. Two, because of the influence of the expositor's assumptions, interpretations are substantially subjective and forever debarred from the domain of pure science. Responses to the predetermined, subjective nature of all interpretative activity are typically twofold: (1) accept it as the inescapable condition of exegesis and recognize the inevitable bias accompanying all interpretive acts, or (2) try to design a scientific method of explication that circumvents the problem and guarantees objective interpretive results. The former position roughly describes the approach taken in the premodern and postmodern periods (with differences); the latter is the brainchild of modernity.

In many ways the intellectual archers of the Enlightenment were aiming their arrows at one essential target: the problem of circular reasoning. In relation to hermeneutics, Martin Heidegger articulates the predicament in these words: "But if interpretation must in any case already operate in that which is understood, and if it must draw its nurture from this, how is it to bring any scientific results to maturity without moving in a circle, especially if, moreover, the understanding which is presupposed still operates within our common information about man and the world [that is, worldview]?"[49]

In the estimation of the modernists, the chaos of Western culture was created by commitments to religious traditions and philosophies that were adhered to tenaciously and invoked, *petitio principii,* as the basis for understand-

---

47. Plato, *Meno,* trans. Benjamin Jowett, in *The Great Books of the Western World,* ed. Robert Maynard Hutchins, vol. 7 (Chicago: Encyclopaedia Britannica, 1952), p. 179 (§80).

48. Aristotle, *Posterior Analytics,* trans. G. R. G. Mure, in *The Great Books of the Western World,* ed. Robert Maynard Hutchins, vol. 8 (Chicago: Encyclopaedia Britannica, 1952), p. 97 (§1.1).

49. Martin Heidegger, *Being and Time,* trans. John Macquarrie and Edward Robinson (New York: Harper and Row, 1962), p. 194.

ing and responding to every important issue in their time. Question-begging thought and life, proceeding on the basis of personal prejudices (especially religious ones), was tearing the fabric of European civilization apart at the seams. Again, the way to resolve this problem and stop the bloodshed, so it appeared, was to create a purely rational method for knowing the truth that would bypass various belief traditions and be accepted by all thinking people with a particle of intelligence. Presumably this approach eluded the problem of *circulus vitiosus* and guaranteed objective epistemological results. In terms of hermeneutics, this either meant that all acts of interpretation would be equally objective or that there would be no need for interpretation at all. Invoking Platonic categories, Tom Rockmore explains that scientific knowledge *(episteme)* based on an unshakable, self-evident foundation was to be sharply distinguished from interpretation based on prejudice and opinion *(doxa)*. "The [Enlightenment] view of knowledge as a function of the distinction between *episteme* and *doxa*, knowledge and opinion, truth and belief, excludes interpretation, which is restricted to the level of conviction only. To put the same point in other words: on this view when we know, interpretation is unnecessary; and when we interpret, we do not know. It follows that knowledge and interpretation are mutually exclusive categories."[50]

This separation of categories, however, seems naive, unrealistic, and self-referentially incoherent: naive in its view of the complexities of human nature, unrealistic in its expectation of a self-dispossessed objectivity, and incoherent in its establishment of a prejudice against prejudice. As Gadamer has pointed out famously, "There is one prejudice of the Enlightenment that defines its essence: the fundamental prejudice of the Enlightenment is the prejudice against prejudice itself, which denies tradition its power."[51] Despite the Enlightenment's agenda to deny prejudice and tradition their epistemic and hermeneutic role, it ironically ended up demonstrating that both are unavoidable. The effort at stamping out all question-begging traditions became the new question-begging tradition of modernity. Given the belief and value orientation of human beings, indeed their essential religious nature rooted in the heart, the elimination of presupposed commitments is impossible. Enlightenment thinkers, who proved to be not immune to these definitive human traits, immediately found themselves presupposing their newly emerging intellectual tradition which they were trying to prove. The intention to escape the subjectivity of the

50. Tom Rockmore, "Epistemology as Hermeneutics: Antifoundationalist Relativism," *Monist* 73 (1990): 116.

51. Hans-Georg Gadamer, *Truth and Method,* 2nd rev. ed., translation revised by Joel Weinsheimer and Donald G. Marshall (New York: Continuum, 1993), p. 270.

circle by means of the objectivity of science failed. In the contest, then, between Enlightenment and circular reasoning, the latter, as postmodern critics have gleefully pointed out, triumphed over the former. The process of interpretation, like reason, is guided by prejudices and is tradition-bound. It rests ultimately, according to the present argument, on worldview.[52]

Indeed, this is the primary point defining the relationship between *Weltanschauung* and hermeneutics. As the New Testament theologian Rudolf Bultmann (1884-1976) affirmed, "there cannot be any such thing as exegesis without presuppositions."[53] A *Weltanschauung* — as the primary system of narrative signs that articulate a vision of reality and lie at the base of individual and collective life — is the most significant set of presuppositions on the basis of which interpretation operates. One set of privileged signs — the worldview — provides the foundation and framework by which another set of signs — speech acts, texts, or artifacts — is understood. Hermeneutics is, therefore, a matter of signs interpreting other signs, a context-specific and tradition-bound operation rooted in a fundamental outlook and form of life. Every explanation of the social and natural world is always conditioned by *Weltanschauung*, the presence of which relativizes the desideratum of unaffected, noncircular scientific knowledge championed by the architects of the Enlightenment.

Both Martin Heidegger and Hans-Georg Gadamer have critiqued this Enlightenment position by reconnecting humanity to being, history, and the world. This reimmersion into the stream of human experience effectively eliminated the possibility of a "God's-eye point of view" in all attempts to explain objectively the nature of things. Interpretation, therefore, is an inescapable component to human existence. Hence Heidegger's and Gadamer's reconfiguration of the human condition led them both to make the discipline of hermeneutics central to their respective purposes. Heidegger's insights on the forestructure of understanding and Gadamer's reflections on the role of prejudice and horizon in interpretation contribute to the argument being developed here in proposing the influence of *Weltanschauung* on hermeneutics.

---

52. This is the primary point made by Wilhelm Dilthey in his noted *Weltanschauunglehre*. Spellbound by the dictates of Enlightenment reason, Dilthey was in search of a hermeneutic that would provide the human sciences with the kind of QED knowledge yielded by the natural sciences. His project was virtually derailed in his recognition of the interpretative influence of pretheoretical worldviews on all knowledge enterprises, leaving them bobbing about in the seas of relativism. On this issue, see Thomas J. Young, "The Hermeneutical Significance of Dilthey's Theory of World Views," *International Philosophical Quarterly* 23 (June 1983): 125-40.

53. Rudolf Bultmann, "Is Exegesis without Presuppositions Possible?" in *New Testament and Mythology and Other Basic Writings*, selected, edited, and translated by Schubert M. Ogden (Philadelphia: Fortress, 1984), p. 146.

For Heidegger, scientific objectification led to depersonalization, and most importantly to a forgetfulness of Being. Thus he set himself to the recovery of the meaning of Being. In order to do so, he developed a "phenomenological analysis" of humanity or Dasein since Dasein (the being there) is the only being among all beings for whom Being is the primary issue. Dasein is the only entity that asks questions about Being itself, and is the only being in and through which the meaning of Being is disclosed. Hence Heidegger's task is thoroughly hermeneutic: to understand Being through a preliminary phenomenological understanding of the "being there" (Dasein).

> Our investigation itself will show that the meaning of phenomenological description as a method lies in *interpretation*. The λόγος of the phenomenology of Dasein has the character of a ἑρμηνεύειν through which the authentic meaning of Being, and also those basic structures of Being which Dasein itself possesses, are *made known* to Dasein's understanding of Being. The phenomenology of Dasein is a *hermeneutic* in the primordial signification of the word, where it designates this business of interpreting.[54]

Heidegger's discussion of the hermeneutic experience, which is the basic way in which Dasein exists in the world, is rich, and it is impossible to do justice to it here. However, one aspect of it is particularly germane to our purposes: the forestructure of understanding. Heidegger argues that interpretation is always an attempt to understand "something as something," that is, it is always by means of what he calls a "fore-having," a "fore-sight," and a "fore-conception." In words anticipating Bultmann's own hermeneutic principle cited above, Heidegger states his point thusly: "An interpretation is never a presuppositionless apprehending of something presented to us" (pp. 191-92). This is true of all types of interpretation, including the exegesis of texts.

> If, when one is engaged in a particular concrete kind of interpretation, in the sense of exact textual Interpretation, one likes to appeal [*beruft*] to what "stands there," then one finds that what "stands there" in the first instance is nothing other than the obvious undiscussed assumption [*Vormeinung*] of the person who does the interpreting. In an interpretative approach there lies such an assumption, as that which has been "taken for granted" [*gesetzt*] with the interpretation as such — that is to say, as that which has been presented in our fore-having, our fore-sight, and our fore-conception. (p. 192)

---

54. Heidegger, pp. 61-62. The page references in the following text are to Heidegger's *Being and Time*.

Heidegger explains that by "fore-having," he means that all acts of interpretation are conducted on the basis of a "totality of involvements" which are presupposed, and by means of a prepossessed "point of view" which governs and guides the act of understanding (p. 191). Furthermore, he argues that not only is interpretation established upon "something we have in advance," but also on the basis of "something we see in advance," a "fore-sight," which is the initial insight gleaned on the basis of the "fore-having." In Heidegger's words, "In every case interpretation is grounded in *something we see in advance* — in a *fore-sight*. This fore-sight 'takes the first cut' out of what has been taken into our fore-having, and it does so with a view to a definite way in which this can be interpreted." Objects become conceptualized in acts of interpretation as well, but an interpretation leading to conceptualization can either be congruent with or contrary to the object's own nature. The understanding of things is either an exegesis if derived from the object, or an eisegesis if the interpretation is imposed on it. In either case, however, the result is predetermined by a set of concepts grasped in advance, what Heidegger calls a "fore-conception" (p. 191).

Consequently for Heidegger, this threefold forestructure of understanding is responsible for the dilemma of the hermeneutical circle: "All interpretation, moreover, operates in the fore-structure," Heidegger states. "Any interpretation which is to contribute to understanding, must already have understood what is to be interpreted" (p. 194). He is quick to point out, however, that the circle is not just an orbit in which any kind of knowledge may move. Rather, it is the expression of the existential forestructure of Dasein itself, and is essential to it. "The 'circle' in understanding belongs to the structure of meaning, and the latter phenomenon is rooted in the existential constitution of Dasein — that is, in the understanding which interprets" (p. 195). Hence the circle must not be considered vicious, or something just to be tolerated, or even eliminated if possible. If this is one's mind-set, then for Heidegger the very nature of Dasein and the act of interpretation have been thoroughly misconstrued. Rather, the circle itself creates for Dasein the "positive possibility of the most primordial kind of knowing" (p. 195). What is important is that one understand the value of the circle and approach it appropriately.

> But if we see this circle as a vicious one and look out for ways of avoiding it, even if we just "sense" it as an inevitable imperfection, then the act of understanding has been misunderstood from the ground up. The assimilation of understanding and interpretation to a definite ideal of knowledge is not the issue here. Such an ideal is itself only a subspecies of understanding — a subspecies which has strayed into the legitimate task of grasping the present-at-hand in its essential unintelligibility [*Unverständlichkeit*]. If the

basic conditions which make interpretation possible are to be fulfilled, this must rather be done by not failing to recognize beforehand the essential conditions under which it can be performed. What is decisive is not to get out of the circle but to come into it in the right way. (pp. 194-95)

For Heidegger, the Enlightenment attempt to avoid the hermeneutical circle was a major mistake, rooted in a profound misunderstanding of Dasein, that is, the being that is there. Dasein or humanity is not a detached observer of the cosmos seeking to analyze and control it; rather, humanity is thoroughly grounded in being and time, and these existential involvements establish a forestructure of understanding by which the world is interpreted. This is similar to how a *Weltanschauung* works in the hermeneutic process. It establishes a set of assumptions by which interpretative acts are guided. Indeed, a worldview is responsible for the hermeneutic circle itself, for all things are ultimately understood in terms of its fundamental signs and categories. As such, they constitute those particular cognitive positions that serve as keys to the doors of knowledge and truth. Without them no entry would be available, and human beings would be ostracized from the circle of understanding.[55] Perhaps this is what Heidegger means when he says that interpreters must come to the circle in the right way, recognizing both its opportunities and yet its limitations. In any case, Heidegger's description of the hermeneutical circle correlates well with the notion that interpretation is worldview-dependent.

Hans-Georg Gadamer (1900-2002), in his justly recognized work *Truth and Method,* develops his own interpretive program in which he also rejects the Enlightenment aversion to hermeneutics inspired by the Cartesian vision of objectivity. He crafts his own ontologically based hermeneutics in the light of the phenomenological research of Edmund Husserl and especially Martin Heidegger in order to do justice to history. He focuses on the concepts of prejudice and horizon, two items that reinstate the hermeneutic circle and suggest the role of *Weltanschauung* in the task of interpretation. The Heidelberg philosopher explains his program in these words: "Heidegger entered into the problems of historical hermeneutics and critique only in order to explicate the fore-structure of

---

55. Even Jesus himself, as a person connected to space and time, made his approach to things through the instrumentality of a particular cultural and linguistic context. Though he is Creator and Lord and possesses all authority in heaven and on earth, still "as a man among men, He is bound to the land of Israel by all the fibers of His being. [His] . . . is a message of universal salvation which He comes to reveal to men, but He does so with the language of a particular country and civilization. The landscapes and the customs of Palestine have in some way shaped the imagination of Him who created them." See *Dictionary of Biblical Theology,* rev. ed. (1973), s.v. "earth."

understanding for the purposes of ontology. Our question, by contrast, is how hermeneutics, once freed from the ontological obstructions of the scientific concept of objectivity, can do justice to the historicity of understanding."[56]

For Gadamer, hermeneutics is an original characteristic and mode of human life, and the essence of interpretative experience rests in the dialectical encounter between the prejudices of the interpreter and the text to be interpreted. The task becomes a questioning of things, of the preunderstandings brought to the text, and of the meanings of the text brought to the interpreter. This interplay is brought out quite nicely in these words in which Gadamer is the most explicit about the dynamics created by the hermeneutical circle:

> [A] person trying to understand a text is prepared for it to tell him something. That is why a hermeneutically trained consciousness must be, from the start, sensitive to the text's alterity. But this kind of sensitivity involves neither neutrality with respect to content nor the extinction of one's self, but the foregrounding and appropriation of one's own fore-meanings and prejudices. The important thing is to be aware of one's own bias, so that the text can present itself in all its otherness and thus assert its own truth against one's own fore-meanings. (p. 269; cf. p. 293)

This is Gadamer's version of "coming to the circle in the right way." He asserts that texts are understood not *in spite of* tradition and prejudice, but rather *because of* their proper fore-projection in their interaction with the passage. The Enlightenment's self-contradictory prejudice against prejudice is quite detrimental to the entire hermeneutic enterprise, for it seeks to deny tradition its central power and role. Conversely, as Gadamer remonstrates, prejudice and tradition give the hermeneutical problem its real thrust. For this reason he found it not only necessary to rehabilitate the prejudices of authority and tradition, but also to make them the centerpiece of his hermeneutic reflections.

For Gadamer, then, the methodological demands of the Enlightenment were not only contradictory but also entailed unrealistic expectations of historically embedded, tradition-laden, finite human beings. History always is prior to the person, and has radical impact on the development of human consciousness and the formation of these prejudices which are central to the hermeneutic process. "In fact history does not belong to us; we belong to it. Long before we understand ourselves through the process of self-examination, we understand ourselves in a self-evident way in the family, society, and state in which we live. The focus of subjectivity is a distorting mirror. The self-awareness of the indi-

---

56. Gadamer, p. 265. The references in the following text are to Gadamer's *Truth and Method*.

vidual is only a flickering in the closed circuits of historical life. *That is why the prejudices of the individual, far more than his judgments, constitute the historical reality of his being"* (pp. 276-77).

This is a very important statement, especially for relating Gadamer's notion of prejudice to worldview and hermeneutics. What he seems to suggest is that prejudices as pretheoretical notions, more so than theoretical judgments, constitute the historical reality of human beings and make them what they are. History has shaped people in tacit ways, filling their minds with a content that constitutes their prejudices, which in turn play a central role in the interpretative process. On this basis Gadamer approaches what he calls "the point of departure for the hermeneutical problem," and so he writes: "What appears to be a limiting prejudice from the viewpoint of the absolute self-construction of reason in fact belongs to historical reality itself. If we want to do justice to man's finite, historical mode of being, it is necessary to fundamentally rehabilitate the concept of prejudice and acknowledge the fact that there are legitimate prejudices" (p. 277). What tradition or authority — religious or philosophical — could be the source of "legitimate prejudices," of course, remains unspecified; but what is important is the fact of these prejudices, their historical genesis, their legitimacy, and their interpretative influence.

This is seen in the intimate connection Gadamer makes between the notion of prejudice and his concept of "horizon" which is also crucial to his hermeneutic model. It seems that the notion of prejudice sets the contours and establishes the substance of the latter idea of horizon. As Gadamer explains, "[A] hermeneutical situation is determined by the prejudices that we bring with us. They constitute, then, the horizon of a particular present" (p. 306). From the fact that a horizon constitutes a vantage point in which an interpreter is located, and insofar as this vantage point is defined by the interpreter's prejudices, it may be surmised that horizon, so understood, serves as a helpful metaphor for a structure similar to a worldview. Interpretation, in other words, is guided by worldview-like prejudices or horizons.

The key question, of course, for Gadamer and his *Horizontlehre* is the precise role horizons play in the interpretive process. One thing is for sure: there should be no attempt to seek to escape one's own horizon and leap empathetically, subjectively, or psychologically to the horizon of the object to be interpreted. This is the Enlightenment/romantic version of hermeneutics, and it violates Gadamer's first-order law of always being grounded in a singular historico-ontological situation. Working out the hermeneutical situation, then, means seeking to achieve the "fusion of these horizons supposedly existing by themselves" (p. 306). This terminology could be easily misinterpreted. What happens is the coming together of a shared understanding of truth that is resident in the one great historical horizon, the experience of which enriches and enlarges the interpreter's own horizon. In the fusion of horizons, prejudices are risked, tested, confirmed, or discarded. Learning from other forms of life thereby expands one's own self-understanding. It is in this dynamic process that understanding occurs. Thus Gadamer's notions of prejudice and horizon, like Heidegger's concepts of the forestructure of understanding and the hermeneutic circle, support the contention that interpretation is never an independent, objective procedure, but one that is grounded in the historical experiences and precommitments of the interpreter. In short, Gadamer's reflections suggest that hermeneutics is vitally connected to and affected by the interpreter's *Weltanschauung*.

Therefore, no one is an interpretative island existing independently as a purely rational hermeneutic entity. The radically individualistic hermeneutic model of modernity, which was based on methodological scientific reason and submitted everything to a "hermeneutic of doubt," stands in sharp contrast to the communitarian ideals of the premodern and postmodern periods. In both of these other eras, the power of a narrative tradition to shape historical consciousness is recognized, along with its hermeneutic implications, but with significant differences nonetheless.[57]

The premodern Christian community, for example, shared a set of stories that was regarded as the final explanation of reality. Their overall *Weltanschauung* consisted of a system of definitive signs that represented the cosmos and were validated by the divine Logos himself. As an interpretative community, their doctrinal beliefs and practices, sustained by the liturgy and communal memory, constituted a tradition that served as a "hermeneutic of trust" which set the interpretative parameters for the faithful. It was to be securely guarded, even to the point of death.

In the postmodern world after Marx, Nietzsche, and Freud, human communities are considerably different. They are self-reflexive social and linguistic constructions consisting of conventions to be suspected, interests to be unmasked, myths to be exploded, power relations to be short-circuited, and meanings to be deconstructed. The semiotic systems that define the world in such contexts are unattached to any "transcendent signifier," and are endlessly fluid. Consequently, they provide no definitive interpretative boundaries, and are not sustained by any substantive communal traditions or memory. They destroy trust, and their essential interpretative principle consists in a "hermeneutics of suspicion."

57. Anthony C. Thiselton, *New Horizons in Hermeneutics: The Theory and Practice of Transforming Biblical Reading* (Grand Rapids: Zondervan, 1992), p. 143.

Perhaps in light of these examples, it could be suggested that in the matter of knowledge and interpretation there should be a healthy mixture of a hermeneutics of trust with an adequate amount of doubt or suspicion in relation to the tradition in which one stands. Too much trust can lead to blind obedience; too much doubt and suspicion can lead to nihilism. It is possible to err in both directions, but a balance of both confidence and criticism will create the possibility of communal belongingness, but not naively so. One must originally believe in order to understand (trust), but then as one grows in understanding and encounters criticisms of the original belief (doubt), one must continue to seek new understandings in order to continue to believe (trust), else suspicion overtakes trust.

Perhaps the most important question, however, in the matter of relating hermeneutics and worldview is whether or not any final meaning is possible. Is there an interpretative master code which forms a final horizon of all textual interpretation? Is there a final system of signs that determines the meaning of all other signs with adequate certainty? Is there a metanarrative, an ultimate *Weltanschauung* that explains all other worldviews? Does hermeneutics result in nothing other than an endless exchange of signs and symbols that eventually and effectively banishes meaning from the universe? The answer, so it seems, depends on one's worldview! Two quotations presenting the two basic different worldview responses to the above questions, from Stanley Rosen and George Steiner, will provide the conclusion to this discussion on *Weltanschauung* and hermeneutics. First, Stanley Rosen:

> We may conclude this history of hermeneutics with the following remark. The initial purpose of hermeneutics was to explain the word of God. This purpose was eventually expanded into the attempt to regulate the process of explaining the word of man. In the nineteenth century we learned, first from Hegel and then more effectively from Nietzsche, that God is dead. In the twentieth century, Kojève and his students, like Foucault, have informed us that man is dead, thereby as it were opening the gates into the abyss of postanthropological deconstruction. As the scope of hermeneutics has expanded, then, the two original sources of hermeneutical meaning, God and man, have vanished, taking with them the cosmos or world and leaving us with nothing but our own garrulity, which we choose to call the philosophy of language, linguistic philosophy, or one of their synonyms. If nothing is real, the real is nothing; there is no difference between the written lines of a text and the blank spaces between them.[58]

58. Stanley Rosen, *Hermeneutics as Politics*, Odéon (New York: Oxford University Press, 1987), p. 161.

Now George Steiner, who is responding to the claim of Nietzsche (and others like him) that "Where God clings to our culture, to our routines of discourse, He is a phantom of grammar, a fossil embedded in the childhood of rational speech." In the introduction to his essay on language and the possibility of meaning, especially the aesthetic kind, Steiner argues in reverse.

> It proposes that any coherent understanding of what language is and how language performs, that any coherent account of the capacity of human speech to communicate meanings and feeling is, in the final analysis, underwritten by the assumption of God's presence. I will put forward the argument that the experience of aesthetic meaning in particular, that of literature, of the arts, of musical form, infers the necessary possibility of this "real presence." The seeming paradox of a "necessary possibility" is, very precisely, that which the poem, the painting, the musical composition are at liberty to explore and enact. This study will contend that the wager on the meaning of meaning . . . is a wager on transcendence.[59]

Thus, not only is the art or science of interpretation affected by a worldview, but the question about the very possibility of meaning itself is also worldview-dependent. In the West the question hinges on the decision between the antithetical worldviews of atheism or theism. For if there is no God, there is no final meaning, but if there is, it makes all the difference in the world.

Worldview and Epistemology

If the presence of the power of a worldview affects reasoning and interpreting in significant ways, what kind of impact does it have on the process of knowing? When it comes to a *Weltanschauung*, are its adherents connected with the world itself or just their view of it? Or is it perhaps a little bit of both? This matter has been articulated well by John Peifer in these words:

> Do we in knowing, by means of what is in thought, attain to things, to realities which enjoy an independence in physical existence outside of thought, or do we by knowing attain only to what is in thought? . . . The question then concerns the object of human thought and principally of intellectual thought. Is that object reality or thought? Does thinking terminate in things, or in thought? Obviously the whole problem of human knowledge is involved. It matters immensely whether one is considering in

---

59. George Steiner, *Real Presences* (Chicago: University of Chicago Press, 1989), pp. 3-4.

knowledge a transcendent, objective reality, or an immanent, subjective thought.[60]

Alternative positions regarding access to the brute facts about reality have been aptly illustrated by the following joke about three baseball umpires comparing their umpiring philosophy after a game: "They are sitting around over a beer, and one says, 'There's balls and there's strikes, and I call 'em the way they are.' Another says, 'There's balls and there's strikes, and I call 'em the way I see 'em.' The third says, 'There's balls and there's strikes, and they ain't *nothin'* until I call 'em.'"[61] Each of these reflects a position on how we know: the first umpire represents a naive, direct, or commonsense realism; the second personifies critical realism; and the third stands for antirealism. As a mediating element in cognition, a worldview plays no role in the first alternative, a conditioning role in the second, and the total role in the third. The first model exhibits a thoroughgoing objectivism where everything is black and white; the second a combination of objectivism and subjectivism consisting of shades of gray; and the third a thoroughgoing subjectivism in which true knowledge is shrouded in darkness. I will present a cameo description of these three positions that articulates the relationship of *Weltanschauung* to the knowing process. For comparative purposes I will examine commonsense realism and antirealism before taking a look at critical realism.[62]

The first position, roughly labeled *naive, direct, or commonsense realism,* argues that comprehension of the cosmos is direct and accurate, unaffected by worldview presuppositions or any other subjective influences. This position is established on at least four basic premises: (1) an objective, independent reality exists; (2) the character of this reality is fixed and independent of any observer; (3) human knowers have trustworthy cognitive capacities by which to apprehend this fixed reality unencumbered by personal prejudices or traditions; and (4) truth and knowledge about the world are discovered and certain, not invented and relative. In short, a realist of this type denies the interposition of any kind of mental entity between the perceiver and a physical object. At a layman's

---

60. John Peifer, *The Mystery of Knowledge* (Albany, N.Y.: Magi Books, 1964), p. 11.

61. Walter Truett Anderson, *Reality Isn't What It Used to Be: Theatrical Politics, Ready-to-Wear Religion, Global Myths, Primitive Chic, and Other Wonders of the Postmodern World* (San Francisco: Harper and Row, 1990), p. 75. Thanks to Middleton and Walsh, p. 31, for pointing out this illustration.

62. For more on versions of realism and antirealism, see Gerald Vision, *Modern Anti-Realism and Manufactured Truth,* International Library of Philosophy, ed. Ted Honderich (New York: Routledge, 1988); Peter A. Finch, Theodore E. Uehling, Jr., and Howard K. Wettstein, eds., *Realism and Antirealism,* Midwest Studies in Philosophy, vol. 12 (Minneapolis: University of Minnesota Press, 1988).

level, this position is rightly called *naive realism,* the pedestrian view of the man and woman on the street who place implicit trust in their cognitive powers to inform them about what the real world is like in an objective and direct way. There is a sophisticated version of commonsense realism in the work of the eighteenth-century Scottish philosopher Thomas Reid, and the position has been rehabilitated in light of difficulties with other positions by several con-temporary epistemologists as well.[63] In any case, to put a spin on an expression of Richard Rorty's, the net effect of this epistemological outlook is a world "well found."[64]

The second position is that of *creative antirealism,* a view positing a radical disjunction between what is there and the multiple views of it. Worldviews in this context are all there are, belief systems that are reified and sustain no real connection to the cosmos. Reality is indeed absent. This position may be sum-marized in four theses: (1) while an external world may and probably does exist, its objective character remains forever obscure; (2) human knowers lack epistemic access to apprehend the world as it is in itself; (3) what poses as reality is linguistically constructed, an idealistic product of the human mind; and (4) consequently, truth and knowledge about the world are not discovered and certain, but invented and relative. The speciousness of the so-called "given," the creative power of the mind, the variety and formative function of sign systems, and the multiplicity of symbolic worlds are the chief characteristics of this point of view.[65] This doctrine has roots in Protagoras, who is reported in Plato's *Theaetetus* to have claimed that "man is the measure of all things" *(homo mensura),* and that "things are to you such as they appear to you, and to me such as they appear to me."[66] Moreover, Plato's Socrates later in that same dia-logue asserts that Protagorean relativism consists in the view that "What seems to a man, is [true] to him."[67] More recently, creative antirealism received its ini-tial impetus in the transcendental idealism of Immanuel Kant, whose over-throw of classic objectivist epistemology was carried through to completion by those who followed in his philosophical wake. In contemporary, postmodern thought, Kant's Copernican revolt has evolved into a radical perspectivism in which signs and symbols are the whole show: the world truly "ain't" anything

---

63. For example, D. M. Armstrong, John Searle, and William Alston.

64. Richard Rorty, "The World Well Lost," in *Consequences of Pragmatism: Essays: 1972-1980* (Minneapolis: University of Minnesota Press, 1982), pp. 649-65.

65. Nelson Goodman, "Words, Works, Worlds," in *Starmaking: Realism, Anti-Realism, and Irrealism,* ed. Peter J. McCormick (Cambridge: MIT Press, Bradford, 1996), p. 61.

66. Plato, *Theaetetus,* trans. Benjamin Jowett, in *The Great Books of the Western World,* ed. Robert Maynard Hutchins, vol. 7 (Chicago: Encyclopædia Britannica, 1952), p. 517 (§152).

67. Plato, *Theaetetus,* p. 527 (§170).

until it is made into something by language. Antirealism lacks confidence in human reason to plumb the contours of reality. Instead it promotes "useful fictions" or "sacred canopies" that shield humanity from the abyss of meaninglessness. Indeed, there are only perspectives and points of views, for the world itself, to quote Rorty verbatim this time, is "well lost." Human beings have no other alternative than to live by presumptive faith in the various language games associated with their particular forms of life.

The third and final view is that of *critical realism*. It posits an objectively existing world and the possibility of trustworthy knowledge of it, but also recognizes the prejudice that inevitably accompanies human knowing and demands an ongoing critical conversation about the essentials of one's outlook. This viewpoint may also be summarized in four basic propositions: (1) an objective, independent reality exists; (2) the character of this reality is fixed and independent of any observer; (3) human knowers have trustworthy cognitive capacities by which to apprehend this fixed reality, but the influence of personal prejudices and worldview traditions conditions or relativizes the knowing process; and (4) truth and knowledge about the world, therefore, are partially discovered and certain and partially invented and relative. This position has been aptly summarized by N. T. Wright.

> This [critical realism] is a way of describing the process of "knowing" that acknowledges *the reality of the thing known, as something other than the knower* (hence, "realism"), while also fully acknowledging that the only access we have to this reality lies along the spiraling path of *appropriate dialogue or conversation between the knower and the thing known* (hence, "critical"). This path leads to critical reflection on the products of our enquiry into "reality," so that our assertions about "reality" acknowledge their own provisionality. Knowledge, in other words, although in principle concerning realities independent of the knower, is never itself independent of the knower.[68]

From this description, it is clear that this point of view is something of a golden mean epistemology which seeks to avoid the extremes of commonsense realism and creative antirealism. It is a blend of objectivism and subjectivism, acknowledging both a real world and yet real human beings in all their particularities attempting to know it. It places neither too much nor too little confidence in human reason, but recognizes what human cognitive powers can and cannot do. This position avoids the arrogance of modernity and the despair of postmodernity, but instead enjoys a rather modest, chastened view of knowl-

68. Wright, *The New Testament*, p. 35.

edge marked by epistemic humility. Critical realism refrains from saying, "I call things like they are." It refuses to assert, "Things are what I call them." Instead, this approach declares: "I call them as I see them." With Saint Paul, it would carefully state: "I see, but in a glass darkly" (1 Cor. 13:12, paraphrase). The consequence of critical realism is neither dogmatism nor skepticism, and its mood is neither excessively optimistic nor cynical. In each category it maintains a balanced realism. According to this model, to invoke Rorty one last time, the world is neither completely found nor completely lost, but to some extent both lost and found. A worldview partially gets it wrong and partially gets it right. As a semiotic construct, its signs and symbols both obfuscate and clarify, articulating both error and truth. There is the persistent need, therefore, for interaction with others and other perspectives to challenge or certify an individual's knowledge of the nature of things.

There is, therefore, no view from nowhere! All things are known from somewhere! Where one stands will determine whether things are obscured or clarified.[69] An image from C. S. Lewis which he used for a bit different purpose may be helpful. As he says in his brief but masterful essay "Meditation in a Toolshed," it is one thing to stand and look *at* a beam of bright sunlight that breaks into the darkness from a crack in the door. It is another thing entirely to stand *in* the beam of light and see other things by it. As he puts it, "Looking along the beam, and looking at the beam are very different experiences."[70] In the toolshed one can never know about the darkness except from the vantage point of the light or about the light except from the vantage point of the darkness. As Lewis points out, "[Y]ou can step outside one experience only by stepping inside another." What we know is always from the inside of one experience or another, and the content of that experience will indeed affect what and how we know. Lewis then adds this sobering, antirealist thought to his analysis: "Therefore, if all inside experiences [which is all there is] are misleading, we are always misled."[71]

But are we always misled? Is there any basis for affirming the possibility of a true experience? With Lewis I propose that there is, and it is to be found in the experience of the living God. Just as a wager on the meaning of meaning is a wager on transcendence (Steiner), so also is a wager on the possibility of knowledge. If God exists and is the maker of heaven and earth; if he has created all things by his word and designed all things by his wisdom and law; if he is the

69. Notwithstanding the view of Thomas Nagel, *The View from Nowhere* (New York: Oxford University Press, 1986).

70. C. S. Lewis, "Meditation in a Toolshed," in *God in the Dock: Essays on Theology and Ethics,* ed. Walter Hooper (Grand Rapids: Eerdmans, 1970), p. 212.

71. Lewis, "Meditation in a Toolshed," p. 215.

architect of the human mind and its cognitive powers; and if he has so made people that their lives and perspectives consist of the belief content of the human heart (the system of semiosis or narrative framework embraced in faith that dominates it), then it is reasonable to assume that knowledge of the cosmos is possible, though it is always conditioned by human finitude, sinfulness, and the experience of redemption. There are always epistemic limitations and the need for criticism and improvement. Still, the real world can be known because God has made it possible, but such knowledge must always be tempered by criticism.

Along these lines, Russian literary theorist Mikhail Bakhtin has championed a viewpoint that emphasizes "the dialogical imagination" as central to the knowing process. Rather than trying to understand others by empathetic means, he proposes what he calls "creative understanding" in which all of the parties in the great, critical conversation retain their distinctive identities but learn from others what they are helpless to teach themselves.

> *Creative understanding* does not renounce itself, its own place in time, its own culture; and it forgets nothing. In order to understand, it is immensely important for the person who understands to be *located outside* of the object of his or her creative understanding — in time, in space, in culture [outsiders must remain outsiders in order to understand insiders inside their own culture]. For one cannot even really see one's own exterior and comprehend it as a whole, and no mirrors or photographs can help [insiders cannot help insiders to see themselves]; our real exterior can be seen and understood only by other people, because they are located outside us in space and because they are *others*.[72]

This process that Bakhtin has articulated has four critical trajectories. Each person in the dialogue has something to contribute individually and to the other: I see things in my framework that you do not see; you see things in your framework that I do not see. I see and point out shortcomings of your

---

72. Mikhail M. Bakhtin, *Speech Genres and Other Late Essays*, ed. Caryl Emerson and Michael Holquist, trans. Vern W. McGee (Austin: University of Texas Press, 1986), p. 7. Michael Holquist, *Dialogism: Bakhtin and His World* (New York: Routledge, 1990), pp. 36-37, draws out the implications of Bakhtin's words in this helpful commentary: "You can see things behind my back I cannot see, and I can see things behind your back that are denied to your vision.... The fact that I cannot see [certain] things does not mean that they do not exist; we are arranged that I simply cannot see them. But it is equally the case that I see things that you are unable to see, such as your forehead and the wall behind your back.... The aspect of the situation that you see, but that I do not, is what Bakhtin calls your 'surplus of seeing'; those things that I see but that you cannot constitute my 'surplus of seeing.'"

framework which you cannot see; you see and point out shortcomings in my framework that I cannot see. Through these respective contributions and mutual criticisms, through the exercise of this "dialogical imagination," the desideratum is that an ever increasing understanding of reality will be achieved. Hence, to invoke Lewis's conclusion to his toolshed meditation, "One must look both *along* and *at* everything."[73]

In looking along or at worldviews, it seems reasonable to conclude that some are indeed epistemically superior to others. How might this be determined? What is the best way to examine the intellectual and practical validity of alternative paradigms? Responses to these questions should be a central part of the great conversation in critical realism.

Whether adherents are examining their own perspective or the perspectives of others, three "tests" may be suggested in a procedural fashion in order to isolate the strengths and weaknesses of the various conceptual frameworks. These three criteria for evaluating worldviews roughly correspond to the coherence, correspondence, and pragmatic theories of truth. In brief, worldviews ought to be submitted to rational, empirical, and existential inspections.

The rational test is the coherence test: Do the propositions that make up a *Weltanschauung* agree with each other? Are they rationally coherent and non-contradictory? Do the sentences constituting the system fit together as a whole in a consistent manner? While statements that agree with each other do not necessarily demonstrate the truthfulness of a worldview perspective, propositions that are patently contrary to one another would falsify the worldview, or at least certain claims within it. Hence a valid worldview must possess rational coherence.

The empirical test is the correspondence test: Does the worldview fit with reality, and is it capable of offering cogent explanations or interpretations of the totality of things? Does the worldview adequately cover and explain all the data? Is the worldview, to put it in slightly different terms, true to the way things are? Does it cover the whole of life in an adequate way? If large chunks of human experience are neglected or negated by the worldview, if it seems incapable of opening up and elucidating important domains of the human experience and the cosmos, then the worldview, or aspects of it, is rendered suspect. A cogent *Weltanschauung* ought to be empirically comprehensive in its coverage and strong in its explanations.

The third and final test is existential or pragmatic: Does the worldview work? Is it livable? Does it have "cash value"? Can it be applied helpfully to the most important areas of human life and experience? Does it have something

---

73. Lewis, "Meditation in a Toolshed," p. 215.

meaningful to say about fundamental human concerns and issues? A worldview worthy of the name ought to be not only practical but also personally satisfactory. It ought to meet the internal needs of human beings and provide a sense of peace and well-being. A sound worldview, then, ought to be useful and existentially satisfying. Superior worldviews, then, are those that pass muster rationally, empirically, and pragmatically. Only those paradigms that satisfy these qualifications possess adequate philosophic integrity in order to be embraced.[74]

There is yet a final matter to be addressed in highlighting the salient features of critical realism, and it is this: the fact is that in some areas of human knowledge the realist element will seemingly prevail, whereas in other areas the need for criticism will dominate. The system of narrative signs constituting a *Weltanschauung* penetrates all knowledge enterprises, but it seems obvious that some disciplinary areas are more directly impacted by worldview than others. In other words, the epistemic implications of worldview vary per discipline. Worldviews seem to be least influential (which is not to say noninfluential) in the so-called exact and formal sciences, but are much more telling in the humanities, the social sciences, and the fine arts. For example, the impact of worldview assumptions seems to be much less in the practice of chemistry than in history, far less pervasive in mathematics than in philosophy. This seems intuitive, unless one is talking about the philosophy of chemistry or mathematics, for then one has slipped away from the practice of these disciplines into a discussion of their first principles. When this occurs, worldview factors become quite significant. To the extent, then, that worldviews impinge on the "softer sciences," the need for critical dialogue about the methods and findings of these disciplines increases proportionately. To the extent that worldviews have a lesser degree of impact on the "harder sciences," the realist element increases and the need for critical dialogue decreases proportionately. Disagreement among practitioners of the latter category of disciplines is likely to be less *despite* worldview differences, and disagreement among practitioners of the former category of disciplines is likely to be more *because* of worldview differences.

---

74. William J. Wainwright, *Philosophy of Religion*, Wadsworth Basic Issues in Philosophy Series, ed. James P. Sterba (Belmont, Calif.: Wadsworth, 1988), chap. 7, offers twelve exhaustive criteria for assessing worldviews. They are succinct and worth reduplication: (1) the facts that the system explains must actually exist; (2) a good metaphysical system should be compatible with well-established facts and theories; (3) it must be logically consistent; (4) it shouldn't be self-stultifying; (5) it should be coherent; (6) simpler systems are preferable to complex ones; (7) it should avoid ad hoc hypotheses; (8) it should be precise; (9) it should be of adequate scope; (10) it should be adequately fruitful; (11) it should provide illuminating explanations of the phenomena within their explanatory range; and (12) it should be judged by efficacy in human life.

Why might this be the case? Perhaps the answer is this: because world-views have to do with such fundamental realities and the most basic questions about the meaning of the universe, the closer any discipline is to these realities and questions of meaning, the greater the likelihood that a worldview will affect theorizing in that disciplinary area. Emil Brunner has called this (in a theological context) "the law of closeness of relation."[75] The idea is that the closer a discipline stands to the center of existence, viz., the divine, the greater the impact ultimate commitments will have on that area of life. Hence theology is primary (at least for theists), then philosophy, followed by the humanities, the arts, and the social sciences, after which come the natural sciences, and finally the basic, symbolic studies of mathematics, grammar, and logic. If this analysis be somewhat cogent, then it can perhaps be seen why the conditioning effect of worldview is indeed greater in some disciplinary areas than others. The need for a critical evaluation of its impact varies accordingly.

Summary and Conclusion

A creative way of thinking about this wildly influential entity known as a worldview is to look upon it semiotically. Every human life and all human cultures are under the jurisdiction of a particular sign or set of signs that holds sway over individual and collective consciousness. This internalized, semiotic structure may assume the form of doctrines or propositions, but ultimately it consists of and is traceable to a series of world-interpreting narratives that provide the individual's "bottom line" as well as the primary cultural "given." These stories, consciously or unconsciously, form "the well worn grooves of thought"[76] carved deeply into the human heart. Consequently, they have about them "a breathless air of unquestionable truth."[77] A worldview, then, is a

---

75. Emil Brunner, *Revelation and Reason,* trans. Olive Wyon (Philadelphia: Westminster, 1946), p. 383. In his *The Christian Doctrine of Creation and Redemption,* trans. Olive Wyon (Philadelphia: Westminster, 1952), p. 27, he writes: "Hence mathematics and the natural sciences are much less affected by this negative element [the noetic effect of sin] than the humanities, and the latter less than ethics and theology. In the sphere of natural science, for instance — as opposed to natural philosophy — it makes practically no difference whether a scholar is a Christian or not." For criticisms of Brunner and the articulation of a more complete model on the relation of sin to the mind and its scholarly and religious functions, see Stephen K. Moroney, "How Sin Affects Scholarship: A New Model," *Christian Scholars Review* 28 (spring 1999): 432-51.

76. C. S. Lewis, "In Praise of Solid People," in *Poems,* ed. Walter Hooper (London: Harper Collins, Fount Paperbacks, 1994), p. 199.

77. Ninian Smart, *Worldviews: Crosscultural Explorations of Human Beliefs,* 2nd ed. (Englewood Cliffs, N.J.: Prentice-Hall, 1995), p. 78.

semiotic system of narrative signs that creates the definitive symbolic universe which is responsible in the main for the shape of a variety of life-determining, human practices. It creates the channels in which the waters of reason flow. It establishes the horizons of an interpreter's point of view by which texts of all types are understood. It is that mental medium by which the world is known. The human heart is its home, and it provides a home for the human heart. At the end of the day it is hard to conceive of a more important human or cultural reality, theoretically or practically, than the semiotic system of narrative signs that makes up a worldview.

Chapter Eleven

Concluding Reflections

There is a tradition of criticism built into the philosophical and disciplinary history of "worldview," aspects of which we have already touched upon in our previous survey in chapters 4 through 8. Furthermore, the totality of chapter 9 was devoted to a biblical and theological response to concerns raised by various Reformed thinkers about the relativist connotations associated with "worldview," prompting my attempt to reconceptualize the notion in distinctively Christian terms. And yet there are just a few more things to say about the concept of worldview, both negatively and positively, as we bring this volume to a close. These reflections have the Christian community and a reformational worldview specifically in mind, as I examine the philosophical, theological, and spiritual dangers and benefits associated with the use of the concept. I will then offer a final conclusion.

Dangers of Worldview

To what extent does worldview as a modernist concept not only carry the connotation of relativism, but paradoxically also convey a thoroughgoing objectivism which is equally antithetical to an historic, Christian understanding of creation and humankind and the relationship between them? Furthermore, could the formation of a worldview, even a Christian one, potentially distort the process of hearing and responding to the Word of God as divine revelation? And finally, might the intellectual project of constructing a coherent, biblically based worldview along with a concomitant vision for cultural transformation inappropriately supplant the final end of all Christian activity rooted in the love of God and neighbor? These three questions surface the philosophical, theological, and spiritual hazards associated with the language of *Weltanschauung* as a means of apprehending the Christian faith. I will flesh out each one briefly.

A Philosophical Danger

In the context of modernity, the term "worldview" not only assumed the nuance of a person or culture relativism, but some thinkers also believed it implied (and perhaps continues to imply) *the radical objectification of reality.* Martin Heidegger, for example, believed that on the basis of the Cartesian project and the rise of modern science, human beings were seen as knowing subjects who were placed at the center of the universe, and who stood over against the world as an entity to be conceived and grasped objectively as a picture. For him the Enlightenment was the age of a pictured world, and thus the notion of worldview was distinctively modern. In this framework nature itself was something to be known, represented, used, and discarded as needed. Certainly the modern de-divinization of the cosmos and the rise of a secular anthropocentrism meant a significant reconceptualization of humankind and the cosmos. In its apotheosis, humanity sought a position from and by which it can be "that particular being who gives measure and draws up the guidelines for everything that is."[1] As the apex of reality, Western denizens aspired to interpret the world and manipulate it as they would, especially scientifically. It was the birth of a thoroughgoing objectivism, and *Weltanschauung* was its token expression.

As a result of this modern mind-set, "worldview," as the term itself suggests, has emphasized a visual approach to reality. Like Heidegger, Walter Ong thinks the notion is likely a culture-bound concept, the peculiar product of a technological society that looks upon the cosmos as a thing to be viewed. Thus for him it may be excessively dependent upon the sense of "sight" to the neglect of other sensory and cognitive faculties which are employed more prominently in non-Western settings.

> As a concept and term, "world view" is useful but can at times be misleading. It reflects the marked tendency of technological man to think of actuality as something essentially picturable and to think of knowledge itself by analogy with visual activity to the exclusion, more or less, of the other senses. Oral or nonwriting cultures tend much more to cast up actuality in

1. Martin Heidegger, "The Age of the World Picture," in *The Question concerning Technology and Other Essays,* translated and introduction by William Lovitt (New York: Harper and Row, Harper Torchbooks, 1977), p. 134.

comprehensive auditory terms, such as voice and harmony. Their "world" is not so much markedly something spread out before the eyes as a "view," but something dynamic and relatively unpredictable, an event-world rather than an object-world, highly personal, overtly polemic, fostering sound-oriented, traditionalist personality structures less interiorized and solipsistic than those of technologized man. The concept of world view may not only interfere with the empathy necessary for understanding such cultures but may even be outmoded for our own, since modern techno-logical man has entered into a new electronic compact with sound.[2]

If Heidegger's reflections and Ong's criticisms are cogent, Christians who have been enchanted by the ethos of the Enlightenment and who employ the worldview concept often must be aware of the possible lingering connotation of its alienating objectivism, as well as its widely recognized, and often criti-cized, panoptic emphasis. Undoubtedly, the objectivism of high modernity is contrary to the historic Christian conception of the universe in which human beings as God's creatures living in his creation conceive of the universe in sacra-mentalist tones and sustain a more unified, even sacred connection to the na-ture of things. "What made Augustine, Aquinas, and the other medieval think-ers so fundamentally alike," says W. T. Jones, "was this [sacramental] outlook they shared. What distinguishes the modern mind so sharply from the medi-eval mind is that modern men have largely lost that outlook and now share the basically secular point of view of the Greeks. Thus, whereas for us (and for the Greeks) the world by and large means just what it seems to be, for men of the Middle Ages it meant something beyond itself and immeasurably better."[3] This something better and something beyond must be kept in mind when interpret-ing the universe and humanity's relationship to it from the perspective of an historic Christian *Weltanschauung*. The human-to-human and human-to-creation connection is one of solidarity and community theistically conceived in which the excellence of each reality is recognized and respected for its place in a doxological cosmos. A kind of biblically based sacramental and personalist realism must be reinserted into the consciousness of the church in place of the objectivist habit of mind that has not only wreaked ecological havoc but has also resulted in the rise of authoritarian personalities, political totalitarianisms, and a profound dehumanization at the hands of modern science so characteris-tic of the twentieth century.[4] An authentic Christian view of reality as a net-

2. Walter Ong, "World as View and World as Event," *American Anthropologist* 71 (1969): 634.

3. W. T. Jones, *A History of Western Philosophy*, vol. 2, *The Medieval Mind*, 2nd ed. (New York: Harcourt, Brace and World, 1969), p. xix.

work of interconnecting relationships characterized by love can reverse these extraordinarily undesirable trends.

Furthermore, ways of knowing the world complementing the capacities of sight and mind should also be embraced by believers in order to do justice to their complete God-given natures and allow them to comprehend the totality of reality in its rich multiplicity and fullness. To this end spiritual writer Parker Palmer has advocated what he calls "wholesight," which fuses sensation and rationality into a union with other, yet often neglected ways of knowing such as imagination, intuition, empathy, emotion, and most certainly faith.[5] In God's epistemic grace, he has provided a variety of cognitive capacities which are adequate for and to be employed in grasping the diverse modes of created reality, an ancient concept known as the *adaequatio*. All capacities ought to be well employed when it comes to apprehending the truth about God, humankind, and the cosmos, else one suffers from metaphysical indigence, as E. F. Schumacher explains:

> The answer to the question "What are man's instruments by which he knows the world outside him?" is . . . quite inescapably this: "Everything he has got" — his living body, his mind, his self-aware Spirit. . . . It may even be misleading to say that man has many instruments of cognition, since, in fact, the *whole man* is one instrument. . . . The Great Truth of *adaequatio* teaches us that restriction in the use of instruments of cognition has the inevitable effect of narrowing and impoverishing reality.[6]

Thus, at the heart of any Christian worldview worthy of the name ought to be the lodestar of wholeness which offsets any form of epistemic myopia and reconnects human subjects and created objects into a sympathetic relation which appropriately honors the diversity, unity, and sacred character of all aspects of reality.

---

4. Parker J. Palmer, *To Know as We Are Known: A Spirituality of Education* (San Francisco: Harper San Francisco, 1983), p. 66. Concerns such as these fueled C. S. Lewis's reflections in his monumental *The Abolition of Man*, and also prompted Michael Polanyi's critiques of modern epistemology in his *Personal Knowledge*.

5. Palmer, pp. xi-xii.

6. E. F. Schumacher, *A Guide for the Perplexed* (New York: Harper and Row, 1977), 51, quoted in Palmer, pp. 52-53.

A Theological Danger

Karl Barth's antagonism toward the notion of worldview, and of a Christian worldview in particular, is well known. For a variety of reasons, including his basic rejection of philosophy and his commitment to the primacy of revelation, he was more than reluctant to recommend the *Weltanschauung* approach to the Christian faith. As he put it, "The true God and His activity can never be pereceived [*sic*] within the framework of a general philosophy."[7] Though he recognized that it belonged to the very nature of human beings to form conceptions about the cosmic process, a worldview was nonetheless rooted in the subjectivity of human consciousness and could be granted no greater status than that of "an opinion, postulate and hypothesis even when it pretends to be Christian."[8] In his mind, the theoretic orientation, programmatic nature, and alleged infallibility of worldviews were also points in their disfavor. In brief, he wanted no *Weltanschauung* as an expression of human faith and thought to interfere with or be a substitute for genuine faith in the pure Word of God as the divine self-disclosure and exclusive source of an encounter with the living Lord. In his words, "It is thus the case that when and as a man accepts the Word of God he does not have to interpret the cosmic process of himself, or according to the patterns given him by others, on the basis of his own assertions and judgments of right, value or taste, but that even while he does this he may also hear the infallible voice of his Lord, and cleave to it."[9]

Despite the aspersions he casts upon philosophy itself and upon the project of formulating a worldview, even a Christian one, ironically Barth engages in philosophic dialogue in support of his dogmatics, and "he himself secretly — and sometimes not so secretly — cherishes a world view all his own," especially one drawn from the wells of existential thought.[10] Nonetheless, he still has a point: namely, the dangers inherent in non-Christian modes of thought and the attempt to understand the Scriptures by means of them. Given the plethora of philosophical perspectives by which people have lived and by which the Bible has been interpreted (and corrupted) throughout church history —

7. Karl Barth, *Church Dogmatics* III/3, ed. G. W. Bromiley and T. F. Torrance, trans. G. W. Bromiley and R. J. Ehrlich (Edinburgh: T. & T. Clark, 1960), p. 140 (§49.2).

8. Barth, p. 18 (§48.2).

9. Barth, p. 24 (§48.2).

10. Carl F. H. Henry, "Fortunes of the Christian World View," *Trinity Journal*, n.s., 19 (1998): 167. Henry continues: "But scholars who deplore the notion of a Christian world view are not immune to sponsoring covertly or promoting an alternative world view while professing to purge Christianity of supposed non-Christian commitments. While Barth dismisses every world view as intellectual barbarism, he has a world view of his own, inconsistent though it may be" (p. 168).

including the perspectives of Platonism, Aristotelianism, rationalism, empiricism, scientism, deism, commonsense realism, evolutionism, idealism, historicism, existentialism, romanticism, phenomenologism, logical positivism, Marxism, Freudianism, psychologism, New Age pantheism, postmodernism, pop culturism, and so on — Barth's concern is well taken. For him, hearing the pure Word of God in or by the text of Scripture was absolutely primary.

Though what he means by this is framed by his neo-orthodoxy and theology of crisis, he reminds evangelical believers of the importance of the Bible as the Word of God and its centrality in Christian thought and experience. It is the alpha and omega of divine revelation. The church, therefore, must get her view of life from the Scriptures. As Martin Luther noted, perhaps with the notion of *sola Scriptura* in mind, "[T]here is great danger in speaking of things of God in a different manner and in different terms than God himself employs."[11] Since the Bible contains its own unique vision of God, humanity, and the sum total of reality, "authentic evangelical theism resists such imposition of preformulated philosophical conceptions on the content of divine revelation."[12] While philosophy may assist in the worldview process, and in fact does, it must never usurp it. While there will never be a perfect agreement between the Bible and a biblical worldview, every effort must still be made to shape a Christian perspective of the universe by the teachings of the Scriptures. In brief, a genuine Christian *Weltanschauung* must always be formed and reformed by the Bible as the Word of God.

Barth's warning, then, should prompt believers to see if they are living by a foreign frame of reference and squeezing the Scriptures into its mold. To what extent are Christian worldviews truly biblical? Might one's conception of the faith be philosophically tainted? Has a believer's *Weltanschauung* been co-opted by cultural forces classic or contemporary, high-, medium-, or lowbrow? For indeed, many have been deceived by failing to recognize how the purity of faith and the Scriptures can be polluted subtly by an alien worldview.

A Spiritual Danger

About halfway through his intriguing tale *The Great Divorce*, C. S. Lewis — who had placed himself into the story as one who was enjoying a visit to heaven on a "holiday from hell" (the *refrigerium*, as it was called) — meets his childhood literary inspiration George MacDonald. MacDonald is able to explain to

11. Martin Luther, "To the Councilmen of All Cities in Germany That They Establish and Maintain Christian Schools," trans. A. T. W. Steinhauser, rev. W. I. Brandt, in *Luther's Works*, vol. 45 (Philadelphia: Muhlenberg, n.d.), p. 366.

12. Henry, p. 168.

Lewis why none of the ghosts who were free to visit the celestial paradise ever chose to remain there. The reason, he says, is because they would have to admit error and give up what they had selected as the absolute good in life — things such as patriotism, art, self-respect, mother love, and so on. Their pride, however, prevented them from making these admissions and sacrifices. In truth, the things for which they lived were relative goods, but in every case the human ghosts, while still alive, had transformed them into gods and sacrificed everything else for them. And now they even sacrificed the possibility of heaven after death. Sir Archibald, for example, was one who had made "survival" the absolute end of his life. But then he died, and discovered, on his own *refrigerium,* that no one in heaven was interested in this matter anymore. The overriding theme of his life proved to be misplaced and futile. "Of course," as MacDonald explains, "if he would only have admitted that *he'd mistaken the means for the end* and had a good laugh at himself he could have begun all over again like a little child and entered into joy. But he would not do that. He cared nothing about joy. In the end he went away."[13] He had placed his priority on the wrong thing, and yet his pride kept him from admitting it. His superciliousness blocked him from heaven and kept him in hell.

Unfortunately, Sir Archibald's confusion of the means of life for its ultimate end, not to mention his hellish pride, is not an unusual thing. Many people, including the deeply devout, are capable of the same mistake, even within the Christian tradition. People do get sidetracked regarding the final goal of their actions. The narrative of *The Great Divorce* continues with this convicting observation by MacDonald:

> There have been men before now who got so interested in proving the existence of God that they came to care nothing for God Himself . . . as if the good Lord had nothing to do but *exist!* There have been some who were so occupied in spreading Christianity that they never gave a thought to Christ. Man! Ye see it in smaller matters. Did ye never know a lover of books that with all his first editions and signed copies had lost the power to read them? Or an organiser of charities that had lost all love for the poor? It is the subtlest of all the snares.[14]

This kind of inverted emphasis — the swapping of means for ends — is at the heart of the spiritual danger associated with the notion of a Christian worldview. Just as it is quite possible for philosophers of religion and evangelists to become more excited about their proofs and preaching than about God or Je-

13. C. S. Lewis, *The Great Divorce* (New York: Macmillan, 1946), p. 71.
14. C. S. Lewis, *The Great Divorce,* pp. 71-72.

sus; and just as there is also the potential for bibliophiles and the eleemosynary to become more ardent about their collections and causes than about their reading or the poor; so also, I suggest, it is also possible for Christian worldview advocates to cultivate an immoderate enthusiasm for their biblical systems with their cultural and apologetic potential and to become forgetful of the God who stands behind them. It is a grave mistake to confuse or substitute a proper relationship with the trinitarian God for the crafting and promulgation of a Christian *Weltanschauung*. Now hopefully the two are fruitfully combined such that one's relationship with God fosters the appropriate worldview, and vice versa. But it is still relatively easy to absolutize the process of worldview formation as a means of Christian ministry and transform it into an intellectual or spiritual idol as an end in itself. Like all human endeavor, however, the endeavor to develop and apply a biblical worldview in relevant ways ought to be considered another avenue by which the church is able to achieve the ultimate goal of loving God and neighbor more effectively (cf. Matt. 22:37-40; 1 Tim. 1:5). A rightly ordered love both divine and human ought to be the ultimate outcome of all our action, including that of biblical worldview development. At the end of the day, therefore, growing in the knowledge and wisdom of a Christian *Weltanschauung* is another important means to authentic spirituality and genuine holiness. As Augustine's young, precocious son Adeodatus put it in *The Teacher:* "With His help, I shall love Him the more ardently the more I advance in learning."[15]

Along these lines, Gregory Clark believes that the evangelical emphasis on the modern idea of worldview is an unfortunate displacement of more essential commitments. In his essay "The Nature of Conversion: How the Rhetoric of Worldview Philosophy Can Betray Evangelicals," Clark questions whether the use of this concept as an extrabiblical and foreign frame of reference will distort the essentials of Christian faith and substitute for them an alternative form of spirituality. Its deployment may be laudatory, he says, in leading to the demise of naive dogmatism and obscurantist fideism by showing Christianity's rational superiority among worldview options. However, with its roots in German idealism, *Weltanschauung* might severely deform the faith, especially when it comes to understanding the nature of Christian conversion. The canonical Gospels, for example, demonstrate clearly how the person of Jesus Christ is at the center of the salvific process. In his estimation, however, worldview philosophy usurps the place of Jesus in this matter, and replaces him with the activity of examining and choosing an adequate system of belief. In other words, worldview substitutes a normative set of coherent propositions for a personal Savior.

---

15. Augustine, *"Against the Academicians" and "The Teacher,"* translated, introduction, and notes by Peter King (Indianapolis: Hackett, 1995), p. 146 (§13.46).

Worldview philosophy brings its practitioners out of fideism and naiveté, while Scripture points us to One who can bring us out of death, darkness, unbelief and falsity. Followers of Christ oppose these spiritual powers rather than other worldviews. At the center of the conversion to Christianity stands the encounter with the crucified and resurrected Jesus, the One with whom we die and who is the guarantee of our resurrection. Conversion in worldview philosophy culminates in gaining admission to a theatre of worldviews. When one converts to Jesus, one has the sense that nothing is more real than this One who wrecked the gates of hell, whereas in worldview philosophy one is keenly aware of the distance between one's worldview and reality. Coming into contact with Jesus inspires worship, gives us access to the very mind of God and provides enough confidence to endure martyrdom, while worldview philosophy brings us out of dogmatism but has tendencies toward skepticism. Conversion within Christianity, then, is quite different from conversion in worldview philosophy.[16]

While Clark's case may be somewhat overstated, and though he may be guilty of an either/or fallacy, he does make a good point nonetheless. He suggests that the spirituality associated with forming a coherent pattern of biblical propositions in the form of a worldview is no valid substitute for the kind of spirituality associated with the person and work of Jesus Christ, who himself is the truth (John 14:6). Truth is personal, and there are the biblical propositions which reveal him. It would be a mistake, however, to so focus on the coherent organization of such propositions as to neglect the personal God they present. No systematic, biblical *Weltanschauung* ought to usurp the primacy of Truth and the ultimate end of agapic love.

Benefits of Worldview

In addition to these dangers, three questions prompt reflection on the philosophical, theological, and spiritual benefits of clothing the content of Christian faith in the garment of a worldview. First, how might the three standard criteria used to test the value of any belief system demonstrate the philosophic integrity and superior credibility of a worldview grounded in the Bible? Next, in what way does the notion of worldview provide the conceptual space that is helpful in

16. Gregory A. Clark, "The Nature of Conversion: How the Rhetoric of Worldview Philosophy Can Betray Evangelicals," in *The Nature of Confession: Evangelicals and Postliberals in Conversation*, ed. Timothy R. Phillips and Dennis L. Okholm (Downers Grove, Ill.: InterVarsity, 1996), pp. 201-18; quote on p. 217.

grasping the all-encompassing scope of the fundamental doctrines at the heart of a biblical interpretation of life? And finally, how is it that Christianity conceived in terms of a worldview seems uniquely effective in fostering personal and cultural transformation? I will address each of these matters succinctly.

A Philosophical Benefit

A perennial concern of a number of worldview thinkers from the very beginning has been to show how Christianity is uniquely capable of satisfying the standard tests for truth that philosophers have devised and applied to any network of beliefs — religious, philosophic, or political. There has been a desire to manifest in superlative ways the intellectual coherence, the empirical and transempirical comprehensiveness, and the practical viability of the Christian faith. Especially since the Enlightenment, great non-Christian systems of thought, making claims to truth and seeking cultural dominance, have offered perspectives on the totality of human existence that boasted of being an organized whole. How was the church to have confidence in her own view of things and avoid succumbing to a crippling sense of inferiority if she was unable to match her spiritual and intellectual competitors with an equally impressive conception of life? How was she to have any hope of success in the culture and apologetic war raging about her if she merely resorted to the defense of particular doctrines and was not able to present Christianity as a consistent, all-encompassing, and pragmatic life system?

Any attempt to set forth an interpretation of Christianity on the grand scale would certainly not be without historical precedent. After all, Augustine's *City of God*, Thomas's *Summa Theologica*, and Calvin's *Institutes of the Christian Religion* are more than harbingers of this enterprise. They are masterworks of master minds that demonstrate the magnitude and splendor of the Christian faith in every conceivable respect. James Orr was standing on solid ground, therefore, when he argued in the late nineteenth century that since the attacks against Christianity stemmed from the strength of total worldviews, it must be explained and defended by means of a comprehensive method setting it forth as a coherent whole.[17] Likewise, Abraham Kuyper knew that in modernism Christianity was being assaulted by "the vast energy of an all-embracing life-system," and that the church of Jesus Christ must take its stand against it "in a life-system of equally comprehensive and far-

---

17. James Orr, *The Christian View of God and the World*, foreword by Vernon C. Grounds (Grand Rapids: Kregel, 1989), pp. 3-4.

reaching power."[18] Since the very definition of reality was at stake in this battle, he admonished Christians to set in opposition to the comprehensive belief systems of the day *"a life- and world-view of your own, founded as firmly on the base of your own principle, wrought out with the same clearness and glittering in an equally logical consistency."*[19]

Therefore, when Christianity is conceived as a total *Weltanschauung* according to the recommendation by Orr, Kuyper, and others, the three philosophical tests mentioned above demonstrate it to be of superlative quality intellectually, empirically, and existentially. It shows itself to hang together with an amazing internal consistency, including the transrational matters of the Trinity, the hypostatic union, and the mystery of sovereignty and human responsibility. It is also able to provide cogent explanations of the sum total of existing realities, including the divine, angelic, human, animalic, and natural realms. And it offers a way of life that is subjectively satisfying and preeminently fruitful privately and publicly when faithfully obeyed. As a result, a philosophically sophisticated, God-centered conception of a Christian worldview spares believers from a naive fideism, a scandalous anti-intellectualism, and a cultural obscurantism. In turn, it imparts to them a cognitive confidence, an apologetic strategy, a cultural relevance, and a sound, spiritual basis for life in the coherent picture of God's larger story.[20]

A Theological Benefit

For a variety of reasons — perhaps a bits-and-pieces mentality, or an inability to make the theological connection between the Old and New Testaments, or a pernicious dualism that divides life into the airtight compartments of the sacred and secular — contemporary biblical understanding among average, everyday Christians is subject to extreme forms of reductionism. A comprehension of the overall

18. Abraham Kuyper, *Lectures on Calvinism: Six Lectures Delivered at Princeton University under Auspices of the L. P. Stone Foundation* (1931; reprint, Grand Rapids: Eerdmans, 1994), p. 11.

19. Kuyper, p. 190, emphasis Kuyper's.

20. Along these lines, Alister McGrath has sought to demonstrate the intellectual coherence of the evangelical theological vision through an exposition of the uniqueness of Jesus Christ and the authority of Scripture, at the same time disclosing the limitations and inner tensions of its closest competitors (postliberalism, postmodernism, religious pluralism). See his *A Passion for Truth: The Intellectual Coherence of Evangelicalism* (Leicester, England: Inter-Varsity, Apollos, 1996). As he says, his "work is best understood as a prolegomenon to the formation of an evangelical mind" (p. 23). Others who have used a combination of tests to establish the credibility of Christianity are E. J. Carnell, *An Introduction to Christian Apologetics: A Philosophic Defense of the Trinitarian Christian Faith* (Grand Rapids: Eerdmans, 1948); Gordon R. Lewis, *Testing Christianity's Truth Claims: Approaches to Christian Apologetics* (Chicago: Moody, 1976). Lewis favors Carnell's approach.

biblical story and its constituent components is lost upon the minds of far too many evangelical believers. There is precious little understanding of the broader horizons of the Scriptures. For example, creation is merely a doctrine to be defended against evolution, sin only affects people, and redemption has exclusive application to the human soul. When it comes to the faith, many well-intended saints understand it in limited terms as a church view, or a Bible view, or a doctrine view, or a ministry view, or a spirituality view, or a religious view, or a God view, but not as a comprehensive, all-embracing, wholistic world and life view.[21]

But the notion of worldview has a mysterious way of opening up the parameters of the Bible so that believers might be delivered from a fishbowl-sized Christianity into an oceanic perspective on the faith. Somehow it removes the cognitive blinders and breaks the spiritual chains that have bound believers and thwarted the ministry of the church and sets them free. Perhaps the magic is found in the word "worldview" itself, with an emphasis placed on the first word of this two-part compound term. It places the familiar doctrines of the faith in a new, cosmic context and opens them up so that their comprehensive scope, deeper meaning, and spiritual power is unleashed. This scope, meaning, and power, of course, is resident in these biblical doctrines themselves, but the framework provided by worldview enables them to be seen more clearly in their true light. Thus, when believers can understand the all-encompassing significance of the doctrine of creation, when they recognize radical consequences of sin across the whole spectrum of created existence, and when they understand the Lord Jesus Christ in his larger roles as the cosmic creator and redeemer of all things — then perhaps the doctrinal bits and pieces can be fit together into a totality, the narrative connections can be made between the Old and New Testaments, and the danger of dualism can be destroyed once for all. Worldview serves as a catalyst to an interpretation of biblical Christianity that focuses on the big picture — unified, coherent, and whole. Conceiving of the faith in this manner opens up fresh vistas and exciting possibilities rooted in the true nature of historic biblical faith. Christianity does indeed come into its own as a profound theological vision of the total cosmos with the help of the notion of worldview.

A Spiritual Benefit

Perhaps it results from a combination of several factors — its biblical wholeness, its intellectual coherence, its empirical and transempirical comprehensiveness,

---

21. Albert M. Wolters, *Creation Regained: Biblical Basics for a Reformational Worldview* (Grand Rapids: Eerdmans, 1985), p. 7.

its interpretive power, and its practical nature — but it seems that Christianity conceived in terms of a worldview possesses remarkable power to foster personal transformation and positive spiritual change in the lives of believers. And through these transformed Christians, it possesses remarkable potential to foster transformation and change in the church and in the broader culture as well. That is its chief spiritual benefit. Certainly whatever transformation and change may occur is a gracious work of God produced by the power of the Holy Spirit working in the lives of redeemed men and women. Though particularly weighty and difficult to describe, in general it has to do with the comprehensive restoration of human beings as the *imago Dei* whose hearts are being reshaped in substantial ways by the truth and perspectives of the Scriptures. It begins with an enlarged understanding of God the Trinity, whose existence, nature, and sovereignty constitute the explanatory and unifying principle of the universe. It involves the recognition of the overall narrative pattern of the Scriptures, consisting of the unmitigated goodness of creation, God's original purposes for humanity, the catastrophe of the fall, and the history of redemption culminating in the person and work of the Lord Jesus Christ as the agent of new creation. This larger biblical story connects the Old and New Testaments, unifies biblical theology, furnishes the background for the particulars of Christian doctrine and practice, and provides a narrative context by which believers can establish their own identities, make sense of their lives, and discover their place in the world. It entails a profound Christian humanism based on an understanding of the dignity of men and women created as the image and likeness of God who possess a fundamental spirituality, a unique set of cognitive powers, and a distinctive cultural calling to be the stewards of creation, which is to be developed for human blessing and God's glory. It shatters a multitude of malicious dualisms and reductionisms and replaces them with a biblically based wholeness that appropriately unifies time and eternity, body and soul, faith and reason, sacred and secular, earth and heaven, resulting in an inner psychological coherence, spiritual freedom, and the ability to delight in creation and enjoy the totality of life. It generates the awareness that there is a presuppositional basis of life based on a tacit or explicit faith commitment rooted in the human heart. Such assumptions serve as the starting point for all forms of human life individually and corporately, giving rise to the ways people think, speak, and act in this world. These themes are at the heart of a biblical worldview and constitute the basis for significant personal, ecclesiastical, and cultural transformation.

No wonder that many Christians, especially students I have known, testify to the difference that an encounter with a biblical worldview has made in their lives. For Crystal it provided an understanding of authentic Christian freedom, supplying the liberty to be a human being fully alive. For Angie it constituted her most significant discovery at the university. For Kendra it was the development of a holistic perspective on life. For Matt it meant a deeper love for God and others in all things, provided a recognition of the value of all God-honoring vocations, and issued a challenge to be involved in society Christianly. For Rachel it was a grid of truth by which to renew culture, share her faith, and live in the fullness of her humanity. For Dayspring it supplied a reference point for all reality and a clarity of vision about the world. For Kevin it meant a fresh recognition of the incredible scope of redemption. For Jennifer it resulted in the breakdown of dualism and the cultivation of deep love for learning. In short, these individuals have undergone a significant, spiritual transformation through their encounter with a biblical worldview involving the revitalization of their hearts and the formation of a new kind of Christian mind.

In evaluating, then, the concept of worldview, there are dangers and benefits associated with approaching the Christian faith in this manner. The objectification of reality, the obfuscation of the voice of God in the Scriptures, and a misplaced affection for worldview formation over the love for God and neighbor constitute the dangers associated with the idea of a Christian *Weltanschauung*. Contrariwise, the philosophical competencies, the theological breadth, and the spiritual power associated with the worldview concept commend it as a helpful device in articulating the essentials of biblical religion. Each believer and the church as a whole must be cognizant of these dangers and benefits and pursue the task of Christian worldview formation with insight and wisdom.

Final Conclusion

This examination of the role of worldview in Protestant evangelicalism, Roman Catholicism, and Eastern Orthodoxy; the massive philological and philosophical history of the concept; its prominent use in the natural and social sciences; its theological utility; and its impact as a semiotic system of narrative signs on reason, hermeneutics, and epistemology all lead to three simple conclusions. The first is that worldview has played an extraordinary role in modern and Christian thought. The second is that it is one of the central intellectual conceptions in recent times. The third is that it is a notion of utmost, if not final, human, cultural, and Christian significance. In fact, it is this third conclusion that explains the previous two. As G. K. Chesterton once wrote, "the most practical and important thing about a man is still his view of the universe." Indeed, as he continued, "We think the question is not whether the theory of the cosmos affects matters, but whether, in the long run, anything else affects them."[22] After all, what could be more important or influential than the way an individual, a family, a community, a nation, or an entire culture conceptualizes reality? Is there anything more profound or powerful than the shape and content of human consciousness and its primary interpretation of the nature of things? When it comes to the deepest questions about human life and existence, does anything surpass the final implications of the answers supplied by one's essential *Weltanschauung?* Because of the divine design of human nature, each person in a native religious quest possesses an insatiable desire to understand the secret of life. A hunger and thirst, indeed, a burning fire rages to solve the riddle of the universe. There is a yearning in the very core of the heart to rest in some understanding of the alpha and omega of the human condition. Nowhere has this search been more effectively expressed than in these intense lines taken from Matthew Arnold's poem "The Buried Life":

> But often, in the world's most crowded streets,
> But often, in the din of strife,
> There rises an unspeakable desire
> After the knowledge of our buried life;
> A thirst to spend our fire and restless force
> In tracking out our true, original course;
> A longing to inquire
> Into the mystery of this heart which beats
> So wild, so deep in us — to know Whence our lives come
>   and where they go.[23]

The mystery of a heart is the mystery of its *Weltanschauung.* The mystery of a *Weltanschauung* is the mystery of a heart. A heart-bound worldview and a worldview-bound heart is the root of that embedded force that determines how lives come and go. It is decisive for time and eternity. It was for good reason, therefore, that Solomon offered this sound piece of advice:

> Watch over your heart with all diligence,
> For from it flow the springs of life.

(Prov. 4:23)

22. G. K. Chesterton, *Heretics,* in *The Complete Works of G. K. Chesterton,* ed. David Dooley, vol. 1 (San Francisco: Ignatius, 1986), p. 41. In the same context, Chesterton makes this clever point: "We think that for a landlady considering a lodger, it is important to know his income, but still more important to know his philosophy" (p. 41).

23. Matthew Arnold, "The Buried Life," in *The Norton Anthology of English Literature,* rev. ed., M. H. Abrams, gen. ed., vol. 2 (New York: Norton, 1968), p. 1021, lines 45-54.

Epilogue

Eustace in C. S. Lewis's
The Voyage of the "Dawn Treader"[1]

O ne of the most memorable episodes in *The Voyage of the "Dawn Treader"* illustrates in vivid terms how the human heart directs the course of life and how it needs to be transformed. In this story we are introduced to Eustace Clarence Scrubb, Edmund and Lucy's disagreeable nine-year-old cousin. He was educated in progressive schools and by forward-thinking parents, but unfortunately had "read none of the right books" (p. 69). The three of them were whisked into Narnia through a picture of a Viking-like ship that hung in Lucy's bedroom. They found themselves on board the *Dawn Treader* with King Caspian, who was on a mission to find the seven Narnian lords whom the usurper Miraz had sent to explore the lands beyond Narnia's eastern shore. The courageous little mouse Reepicheep, who was also on board, hoped to find Aslan's own country by this deep journey into the land of the sunrise. But Eustace found the whole experience unpleasant, and was unable to get along with his companions, especially the intrepid rodent. Overall Eustace was an "unmitigated nuisance" (p. 85), even an "ass" (p. 91).

On one island an independent and incorrigible Eustace separated himself from the group, and while on his solo adventure unexpectedly witnessed the demise of a fire-breathing dragon. In a torrential rain he entered its empty lair in order to find shelter. Once inside he discovered what any literate person would expect to find in a dragon's cave: treasure! "There were crowns . . . coins, rings, bracelets, ingots, cups, plates and gems" (p. 71). He was quickly overtaken by greed, for with this treasure he could become rich in this new world he was just discovering. After slipping a golden bracelet on his upper left arm, he fell

1. The page numbers in parentheses are from C. S. Lewis, *The Voyage of the "Dawn Treader"* (New York: Macmillan, Collier Books, 1952, 1970).

into a deep sleep, for he was quite tired from his journey. What awoke him was a severe pain where the bracelet was, and he soon discovered that "he had turned into a dragon while he was asleep. Sleeping on a dragon's hoard with greedy, dragonish thoughts in his heart, he had become a dragon himself" (p. 75). Outwardly he had become what he was in his heart. At first he thought he would use his new monster powers to get even with his peers, but then he realized just how lonely he was as a dragon. "But the moment he thought this he realised he didn't want to. He wanted to be friends. He wanted to get back among humans and talk and laugh and share things. He realised that he was a monster cut off from the whole human race. An appalling loneliness came over him. He began to see the others had not really been fiends at all. He began to wonder if he himself had been such a nice person as he had always supposed. He longed for their voices. He would have been grateful for a kind word even from Reepicheep" (pp. 75-76).

Eventually Edmund, Lucy, and the others discovered that a dragon hanging about their camp was Eustace incarnate. And they learned that his character had changed considerably for the better as a result of his being endragoned. He was anxious to help out, and he did so in ways only a dragon could. He kept himself from despair by savoring the new pleasure of not only being liked by his friends, but of liking them as well. As a result, how Eustace-as-dreary-dragon wanted to be changed back into a real little boy again! Yet it seemed utterly impossible. But it did happen, and here's how.

Out of nowhere a Lion appeared to Eustace and escorted him to a mountaintop garden where there was a well of clear water which he thought would ease the pain in his foreleg where the gold bracelet was. But the Lion said he must undress first, presumably by removing his scaly dragon skin. After three futile attempts at removing his own scaly dragon skin, the Lion informed him that he would have to do the undressing. Though fearful of his huge claws, Eustace lay flat on his back and let him proceed. Here is how he described his metamorphosis: "The very first tear he made was so deep that I thought it had gone right into my heart. And when he began pulling the skin off, it hurt worse than anything I've ever felt. . . . Well, he peeled the beastly stuff right off — just as I thought I'd done it myself the other three times, only they hadn't hurt — and there it was lying on the grass: only ever so much thicker, and darker, and more knobbly looking than the others had been. And there I was as smooth and soft as a peeled switch and smaller than I had been" (p. 90).

After his undressing, the Lion threw Eustace in the water and all the pain vanished from his arm. Then he dressed him in brand-new clothes. Eustace had been "un-dragoned" (p. 91) and was turned into a boy again! He felt constrained to apologize for his former behavior. And when the restored Eustace returned to his companions at their camp, "great was the rejoicing" (p. 92) over his return. And though he lost the treasure which had gotten him into trouble in the first place, he had no desire to go back and try to get more. He had been transformed. "'From that time forth Eustace was a different boy.' To be strictly accurate, he began to be a different boy. He had relapses. There were still many days when he could be very tiresome. But most of those I shall not notice. The cure had begun" (p. 93).

Edmund's explanation to Eustace of what happened to him is the best: "I think you have seen Aslan" (p. 91). Indeed he had, for it was the swipe of the Lion's redemptive claws that did go right into his heart that resulted in such a change. Eustace had tried but could not renew himself. He needed the Lion in his grace and power to do it, and he did, an act for which he deserves unmitigated praise!

Appendix A

Synopses of Additional
Evangelical Worldview Contributions

James Olthuis, "On Worldviews," *Christian Scholars Review* 14 (1985): 153-64.
This essay is also published under the same title in *Stained Glass: Worldviews
and Social Science,* ed. Paul A. Marshall, Sander Griffioen, and Richard J. Mouw,
Christian Studies Today (Lanham, Md.: University Press of America, 1989), pp.
26-40. Citations are from this latter installment.

In this essay Olthuis surveys the sources, structure, and function of worldviews,
and defines the concept in a manner reminiscent of Abraham Kuyper and his
followers.

> A worldview (or vision of life) is a framework or set of fundamental be-
> liefs through which we view the world and our calling and future in it.
> This vision need not be fully articulated: it may be so internalized that it
> goes largely unquestioned; it may not be explicitly developed into a sys-
> tematic conception of life; it may not be theoretically deepened into a phi-
> losophy; it may not even be codified into a creedal form; it may be greatly
> refined through cultural-historical development. Nevertheless, this vision
> is a channel for the ultimate beliefs which give direction and meaning to
> life. It is the integrative and interpretative framework by which order and
> disorder are judged; it is the standard by which reality is managed and
> pursued; it is the set of hinges on which all our everyday thinking and do-
> ing turns. (p. 29)

Olthuis asserts that worldviews so defined serve both descriptive and pre-
scriptive functions, and that they arise out of faith and are shaped by experience. He argues that emotional health and social status deeply influence the

kind of worldview adopted for good or for ill. He analyzes what he calls "worldview crises" which arise when the gap between worldview beliefs and reality as it is experienced widens to the breaking point. He notes how a worldview is always a work in progress, and must ever be open to revision and development. Finally, he points out the connection between worldview and praxis, and asserts that as an integrator between faith and life, a worldview fulfills the following tasks:

- grounds life in the confessed ultimate certainty;
- relates life to the universal order of existence;
- serves as the interpretative and integrative framework for all of life;
- acts as the cohesive, motivating, and pervasive "mind" binding adherents into a community;
- is expressed in symbol;
- is crucial in shaping personal identity;
- evokes and occasions deeply held emotional attitudes and moods of deep satisfaction, inner joy, and peace;
- induces intellectual assent and deepened conceptual reflection;
- sanctions sacrifice on its behalf;
- once shaken, shakes its adherents to the very core;
- induces and invites incarnation in a way of life. (p. 38)

From this overview two basic things can be observed. One, Olthuis defines "worldview" at the tacit level primarily, while at the same time allowing for the possibility that worldviews may congeal theoretically and become overt. Two, worldviews seem to be omnipotent in human experience. If indeed they accomplish all the things Olthuis attributes to them, then their influence and power would seem to be unmatched by other competing influences.

Brian Walsh and J. Richard Middleton, *The Transforming Vision: Shaping a Christian Worldview*, foreword by Nicholas Wolterstorff (Downers Grove, Ill.: InterVarsity, 1984).

This popular volume, in print since 1984, is divided into four main sections. The first is an attempt to describe the nature of worldviews and their cultural incarnation. The second section is an exposition of the Christian worldview, which the authors believe consists in the articulation of three fundamental biblical themes: the doctrine of creation, the fall of humanity into sin, and transformation through Christian redemption. These three biblical motifs answer the four fundamental worldview questions that are at the heart of every worldview: "(1) *Who am I?* Or, what is the nature, task and purpose of human beings? (2) *Where am I?* Or, what is the nature of the world and universe I live in? (3) *What's wrong?* Or, what is the basic problem or obstacle that keeps me from attaining fulfillment? In other words, how do I understand evil? And (4) *What is the remedy?* Or, how is it possible to overcome this hindrance to my fulfillment? In other words, how do I find salvation?" (p. 35).

The biblical worldview, say the authors, provides coherent, comprehensive, and livable answers to these fundamental questions regarding identity, location, evil, and salvation. In answering these four questions, every worldview, Christian or not, must be understood as a faith commitment.

Walsh and Middleton proceed to the third part of their book and a discussion of "the modern worldview" which has emerged as the chief competitor to the Christian outlook. They connect the rise of modernity with the problem and development of an unbiblical "dualism" which divides reality into the airtight categories of the sacred and the secular. Because of this unfortunate distinction (for which the church itself is partially to blame), they argue that in the course of Western history the secular mind-set overcame the sacred aspects of life, and the modern worldview, featuring human autonomy and scientific reason, was born. The long-term fruits of this modern worldview, however, have been horrific. They proceed to describe the "gods of our age" which they believe are incarnate in the idols of science, technology, and the economy. With modernity on the verge of collapse, they offer the alternative of "the Christian worldview in action." Their approach is no mere call for a revival, but a sophisticated one, concentrating on a Christian cultural response, sketching the relationship between worldview and scholarship, and finally presenting a philosophical framework for thinking deeply about the structure of the created order from a Christian vantage point. This work is firmly grounded in the neo-Calvinist tradition, and the influence of Kuyper, and especially Dooyeweerd, is everywhere present.

Middleton and Walsh have written a follow-up volume in which they examine the relationship of the Christian worldview to postmodernity through a careful and creative reading of the biblical text in light of postmodern sensitivities. See *Truth Is Stranger Than It Used to Be: Biblical Faith in a Postmodern Age* (Downers Grove, Ill.: InterVarsity, 1995).

APPENDIX A

Albert Wolters, *Creation Regained: Biblical Basics for a Reformational Worldview*
(Grand Rapids: Eerdmans, 1985).

Like the preceding volume, Wolters's book is consciously written in the
Kuyperian tradition. He begins with a discussion of what a worldview is, defining it very simply as "the comprehensive framework of one's basic beliefs about
things" (p. 2). According to the author, the distinctives of the reformational
worldview, in contrast to other Christian worldviews, are its cosmic scope, its
eschewing of the dualistic categories of the sacred and the secular, and its idea
that Christian salvation is concerned with the comprehensive restoration of the
entire created order ("grace restores nature" is the expression frequently used).
Wolters proceeds in the next three chapters to an in-depth discussion of the
three basic biblical themes of creation, fall, and redemption. In a fifth and final
chapter he applies the "creation-fall-redemption schema" to the important areas of social and personal renewal. In the latter category he offers helpful comments on issues ranging from aggression to spiritual gifts, sexuality, and finally
to the place of dance in Christian life. He speaks of the necessity of discerning
between "structure and direction." In the Reformed worldview, everything created by God is *structurally* good and ought to be received as a gift and enjoyed.
Human sin, however, has taken each of these gifts in the wrong *direction* spiritually. The goal of Christian salvation is not the rejection of fundamental areas
of human life and culture, but the restoration of these areas to their true purpose as originally intended by God. The net result of this process, as the title of
the volume indicates, is *Creation Regained,* that is, the recovery of all aspects of
life, thought, and culture in service to God. This volume demonstrates that Calvinist Christianity, contrary to popular perception, is a life-affirming faith that
is concerned about the renewal of the totality of life for the sake of human
flourishing and the glory of God.

Arthur F. Holmes, *Contours of a World View,* Studies in a Christian World View,
ed. Carl F. H. Henry (Grand Rapids: Eerdmans, 1983).

Holmes begins this volume on an existential note, speaking about the fourfold
human need for a worldview: "the need to unify thought and life; the need to
define the good life and find hope and meaning in life; the need to guide
thought; the need to guide action" (p. 5). He contends that a valid *Weltanschauung,* a Christian one in particular, is desperately needed today not only at the
individual level, but also at the cultural level, especially in a post-Christian age
that is subject to a contemporary humanism and the secularization of values.

Holmes proceeds to investigate the "anatomy" or nature of a worldview as a concept, with assistance from Wilhelm Dilthey and Herman Dooyeweerd. He notes that according to Dilthey, worldviews commence at the pretheoretical level, observing that he "called the pretheoretical beginning a world picture *(Weltbild)*, claiming that it arises from one's life world *(Lebenswelt)*, and in time gives rise to a formulated world view *(Weltanschauung)*" (p. 32). Holmes indicates that Dooyeweerd was in search of the unifying element in the human personality, and determined that the religious factor is preeminent and provides the needed centripetal force. Regardless of the specific content of worldviews, they are religiously generated and able "to effectively unify all aspects of life and thought in a meaning-giving way" (p. 34).

Holmes scrutinizes the sources of worldview content, focusing on the contributions of theology, philosophy, science, and other influences. Theology's contribution to the development of an initial *Weltbild* into a formulated Christian *Weltanschauung* potentially involves the whole range of systematic theology, particularly a conception of God and his relation to the cosmos. Theology also contributes in a practical way through what Holmes calls "worldviewish theology." The fact of theological pluralism, especially in the articulation of the relationship between Christianity and culture, contributes extensively to the diverse formulations of Christian worldviews themselves which are also pluralistic.

Philosophy has its impact on worldview in terms of the discipline's activity and history. The activity of philosophical inquiry focuses on the analysis of concepts and arguments, and examines foundational issues underlying all the sciences. The history of philosophic inquiry provides a fund of concepts and arguments about almost any subject and every worldview type, theistic, naturalistic, or otherwise. Philosophy also contributes in a practical way through what Holmes calls "worldviewish philosophy."

Finally, science, particularly the history of science viewed in a Kuhnian perspective, makes its contribution to worldview formation, especially by showing how the Pythagorean, Aristotelian, Newtonian, and Einsteinian models of the cosmos have affected the content of worldviews. As Holmes puts it, "Scientific conceptions of nature affect our thinking about every natural process and human activity and are frequently extended by way of analogy to God" (p. 43). Indeed, science has its impact on worldviews, but, as Holmes points out, the reverse is true as well: worldviews also influence science paradigmatically (Kuhn) and personally (Polanyi).

The problem of subjectivism, worldview pluralism, and the question of truth arise and must be addressed. Holmes examines three "strategies" for this process, focusing on fideism, foundationalism, and coherentism. Holmes prefers the third of these options on the basis of the "*unity of truth* which is to say that truth *in toto* is itself an interrelated and coherent whole" (p. 51). Any system that displays this epistemic unity must be favored over its competitors, but at the same time its internal coherence must maintain contact with metaphysical objectivity.

From this point Holmes develops the contours of the Christian *Weltan-schauung* in an extensive way. He examines five fundamental components — God, persons, truth, values, and society and history — drawing on theological, philosophical, and scientific resources in the articulation of each. Then in light of these considerations, he applies this basic framework to four areas of practical activity, including human creativity, science and technology, work, and play, expressing a Christian point of view in each. Holmes believes that the overall result of his study is a recognition of the coherence, vitality, and relevance of a Christian worldview in all aspects of human life and experience.

James W. Sire, *The Universe Next Door: A Basic Worldview Catalog,* 3rd ed. (Downers Grove, Ill.: InterVarsity, 1997).

In its third edition, this book, according to its cover, has sold over one hundred thousand copies. Sire specifies four basic purposes for his volume: (1) to outline the fundamental worldviews that lie at the base of the way people in the West cognize reality; (2) to trace how these worldviews have unfolded historically; (3) to show how postmodernism has put a new "twist" on all worldviews; (4) to encourage his readers to learn to think worldviewishly, that is, "with a consciousness of not only our own way of thought but also that of other people, so that we can first understand and then genuinely communicate with others in our pluralistic society" (p. 15).

Sire defines worldviews as conceptual "universes fashioned by words and concepts that work together to provide a more or less coherent frame of reference for all thought and action." He also describes a worldview as "a set of presuppositions (assumptions which may be true, partially true or entirely false) which we hold (consciously or subconsciously, consistently or inconsistently) about the basic makeup of our world" (p. 16). And finally he takes a question-and-answer approach, proposing that worldviews are a person's essential, "rock bottom" answers to these seven questions, taken verbatim from his work (p. 18).

1. What is prime reality — the really real?
2. What is the nature of external reality, that is, the world around us?
3. What is a human being?

4. What happens to a person at death?
5. Why is it possible to know anything at all?
6. How do we know what is right and wrong?
7. What is the meaning of history?

According to Sire, people cannot avoid answering these questions somehow, some way. For him, to discover one's worldview is a most "significant step toward self-awareness, self-knowledge, and self-understanding" (p. 16).

In the balance of the book, Sire examines the answers given by eight different worldviews to the seven fundamental questions itemized above. He does so in historical sequence, moving from Christian theism, to deism, to naturalism, to nihilism, to existentialism, to Eastern pantheistic monism, to New Age consciousness, to postmodernism. In a concluding chapter he discusses the "examined life" and encourages his readers to make the monumental choice of a worldview on the basis of four essential criteria. A credible worldview ought to: (1) possess "inner intellectual coherence," (2) "comprehend the data of reality," (3) be able to "explain what it claims to explain," and finally (4) be "subjectively satisfactory" (pp. 195-98). Sire himself recommends Christian theism, arguing that it leads to "an examined life that is well worth living" (p. 200).

Charles Colson and Nancy Pearcey, *How Now Shall We Live?* (Wheaton, Ill.: Tyndale House, 1999).

This popular yet substantive volume is filled with interesting stories, but it comes with a serious purpose which the coauthors explain in these terms: "Our goal is to equip believers to present Christianity as a total worldview and life system, and to seize the opportunity of the new millennium to be nothing less than God's agents in building a new Christian culture" (pp. xii-xiii). To forfeit this agenda would be to deny the doctrine of God's sovereignty over all reality, and to miss a window of cultural opportunity which is ripe for a breakthrough of historic Christianity. They want Christians to acknowledge not only God's saving grace which redeems believers, but also his common grace which renews and preserves the culture. But for this to happen, believers must not interpret Christianity pietistically, but as an all-encompassing worldview. Consequently, part 1 of their book examines the notion of worldview and why it is important. In parts 2 through 4 they posit the familiar themes of creation, fall, and redemption as the basic answers to the questions about our location and identity, and explain what has gone wrong with the world and what can be done to fix it. The focus of the book in many ways is on the fourth section on restoration, which answers the question given in the title of the book itself: How now shall we live? Here they show the relevance of Christianity to just about every important aspect of life. As Colson and Pearcy say, "Only Christianity offers a comprehensive worldview that covers all areas of life and thought, every aspect of creation. Only Christianity offers a way to live in line with the real world" (p. xi). This generous understanding of the faith has remarkable personal, evangelistic, cultural, and apologetic value. But as the authors point out, their goal is not to be original, but rather, as C. S. Lewis once said, to present ancient truth in a form that the current generation can comprehend. It is an excellent volume that will introduce this topic to the wider Christian public who would not be inclined to investigate it otherwise.

Appendix B

A Bibliography of Books on the Christian Worldview Not Addressed in This Volume

Baldwin, J. F. *The Deadliest Monster: A Christian Introduction to Worldviews.* Eagle Creek, Oreg.: Coffee House Ink, 1998.

Barcus, Nancy. *Developing a Christian Mind.* Downers Grove, Ill.: InterVarsity, 1977.

Blamires, Harry. *The Christian Mind: How Should a Christian Think?* Ann Arbor: Servant, 1978.

———. *The Post Christian Mind: Exposing Its Destructive Agenda.* Foreword by J. I. Packer. Ann Arbor: Servant, Vine Books, 1999.

———. *Recovering the Christian Mind: Meeting the Challenge of Secularism.* Downers Grove, Ill.: InterVarsity, 1988.

Borthwick, Paul. *Six Dangerous Questions to Transform Your View of the World.* Downers Grove, Ill.: InterVarsity, 1996.

Cook, Stuart. *Universe Lost: Reclaiming a Christian World View.* Joplin, Mo.: College Press, 1992.

Doran, Robert. *Birth of a Worldview: Early Christianity in Its Jewish and Pagan Context.* Boulder, Colo.: Westview Press, 1995.

Frey, Bradshaw, et al. *All of Life Redeemed: Biblical Insight for Daily Obedience.* Jordan Station, Ont.: Paideia Press, 1983.

———. *At Work and Play: Biblical Insight for Daily Obedience.* Foreword by Anthony Campolo. Jordan Station, Ont.: Paideia Press, 1986.

Garber, Steven. *The Fabric of Faithfulness: Weaving Together Belief and Behavior during the University Years.* Downers Grove, Ill.: InterVarsity, 1996.

Geisler, Norman L., and William D. Watkins. *Worlds Apart: A Handbook on World Views.* 2nd ed. Grand Rapids: Baker, 1989.

Gill, David W. *The Opening of the Christian Mind: Taking Every Thought Captive to Christ.* Downers Grove, Ill.: InterVarsity, 1989.

Gnuse, Robert. *Heilsgeschichte as a Model for Biblical Theology: The Debate concerning the Uniqueness and Significance of Israel's Worldview.* Lanham, Md.: University Press of America, 1989.

Hart, Hendrik. *Understanding Our World: An Integral Ontology.* Christian Studies Today. Lanham, Md.: University Press of America, 1984.

Hesselgrave, David J. *Communicating Christ Cross-Culturally.* Grand Rapids: Zondervan, 1978. See especially pp. 190-285.

Hiebert, Paul G. *Anthropological Insights for Missionaries.* Grand Rapids: Baker, 1985. See especially chap. 5.

Hoffecker, W. Andrew, ed., and Gary Scott Smith, assoc. ed. *Building a Christian Worldview: God, Man, and Knowledge,* vol. 1. *The Universe, Society, and Ethics,* vol. 2. Phillipsburg, N.J.: Presbyterian and Reformed, 1986 and 1988.

Holmes, Arthur F. *All Truth Is God's Truth.* Grand Rapids: Eerdmans, 1977.

————. *Faith Seeks Understanding.* Grand Rapids: Eerdmans, 1971.

Jordon, James B. *Through New Eyes: Developing a Biblical View of the World.* Brentwood, Tenn.: Wolgemuth and Hyatt, 1988.

Kraft, Charles H. *Christianity in Culture: A Study in Dynamic Biblical Theologizing in Cross-Cultural Perspective.* Maryknoll, N.Y.: Orbis, 1979.

————. *Christianity with Power: Your Worldview and Your Experience of the Supernatural.* Ann Arbor: Servant, Vine Books, 1989.

Kraft, Marguerite G. *Understanding Spiritual Power: A Forgotten Dimension of Cross-Cultural Mission and Ministry.* American Society of Missiology, no. 22. Maryknoll, N.Y.: Orbis, 1995. Saturated with worldview content.

Lugo, Luis E. *Religion, Pluralism, and Public Life: Abraham Kuyper's Legacy for the Twenty-first Century.* Grand Rapids: Eerdmans, 2000.

Marshall, Paul, with Lela Gilbert. *Heaven Is Not My Home: Living in the Now of God's Creation.* Nashville: Word, 1998.

Nash, Ronald H. *Worldviews in Conflict: Choosing Christianity in a World of Ideas.* Grand Rapids: Zondervan, 1992.

Newport, John P. *Life's Ultimate Questions: A Contemporary Philosophy of Religion.* Dallas: Word, 1989.

————. *The New Age Movement and the Biblical Worldview: Conflict and Dialogue.* Grand Rapids: Eerdmans, 1998.

Niebuhr, H. Richard. *Christ and Culture.* New York: Harper and Row, 1951.

Noebel, David A. *Understanding the Times: The Story of the Biblical Christian, Marxist/Leninist, and Secular Humanist Worldviews.* Manitou Springs, Colo.: Summit Press, 1991.

Olasky, Marvin. *Whirled Views: Tracking Today's Culture Storms.* Wheaton, Ill.: Crossway, 1997.

Palmer, Michael D., comp. and ed. *Elements of a Christian Worldview.* Foreword by Russell P. Spittler. Springfield, Mo.: Logion Press, 1998.

Richardson, Alan. *Genesis 1–11: The Creation Stories and the Modern Worldview.* London: SCM Press, 1953.

Schlossberg, Herbert, and Marvin Olasky. *Turning Point: A Christian Worldview Declaration.* Turning Point Christian Worldview Series, edited by Marvin Olasky. Wheaton, Ill.: Goodnews Publishers, Crossway, 1987. See the other volumes in this series on the media, the poor and oppressed, politics, economics, film, popular culture, international politics, population, childbearing, literature, the arts, Christian education, and postmodernism.

Schweiker, William, and Per M. Anderson, eds. *Worldviews and Warrants: Plurality and Authority in Theology.* Lanham, Md.: University Press of America, 1987.

Senn, Frank C. *New Creation: A Liturgical Worldview.* Minneapolis: Fortress, 2000.

Simkins, Ronald A. *Creator and Creation: Nature in the Worldview of Ancient Israel.* Peabody, Mass.: Hendrickson, 1994.

Snyder, Howard A. *EarthCurrents: The Struggle for the World's Soul.* Nashville: Abingdon, 1995.

Sproul, R. C. *Lifeviews: Making a Christian Impact on Culture and Society.* Old Tappan, N.J.: Revell, Power Books, 1986.

Tracy, David. *Blessed Rage for Order.* New York: Seabury Press, 1975.

Van Til, Henry R. *The Calvinistic Concept of Culture.* Grand Rapids: Baker, 1959.

Veith, Gene E. *Modern Fascism: Liquidating the Judeo-Christian Worldview.* St. Louis: Concordia, 1993.

Weerstra, Hans M. "Worldview, Missions and Theology." *International Journal of Frontier Missions* 14, nos. 1 and 2 (1997). Both editions of this journal contain numerous articles relating worldview to various aspects of missionary endeavor.

Wolterstorff, Nicholas. *Reason within the Bounds of Religion.* 2nd ed. Grand Rapids: Eerdmans, 1984.

Works Cited

Anderson, Walter Truett. *Reality Isn't What It Used to Be: Theatrical Politics, Ready-to-Wear Religion, Global Myths, Primitive Chic, and Other Wonders of the Postmodern World.* San Francisco: Harper and Row, 1990.

————, ed. *The Truth about the Truth: De-Confusing and Re-Constructing the Postmodern World.* New York: Putnam, a Jeremy P. Tarcher/Putnam Book, 1995.

Anselm. *Proslogion.* In *Anselm of Canterbury: The Major Works,* edited and introduction by Brian Davies and G. R. Evans. Oxford World's Classics. New York: Oxford University Press, 1998.

Aristotle. *Posterior Analytics.* Translated by G. R. G. Mure. In *The Great Books of the Western World,* edited by Robert Maynard Hutchins, vol. 8. Chicago: Encyclopaedia Britannica, 1952.

Arnold, Matthew. "The Buried Life." In *The Norton Anthology of English Literature,* 2:1021. Rev. ed. M. H. Abrams, general editor. New York: Norton, 1968.

Augustine. *"Against the Academicians" and "The Teacher."* Translated, introduction, and notes by Peter King. Indianapolis: Hackett, 1995.

————. *City of God.* Translated by Henry Bettenson. Introduction by John O'Meara. Penguin Classics, advisory editor Betty Radice. New York: Penguin Books, 1984.

————. *Confessions.* Translated, introduction, and notes by Henry Chadwick. Oxford World's Classics. New York: Oxford University Press, 1991.

————. *Confessions.* Translated by F. J. Sheed. Introduction by Peter Brown. Indianapolis: Hackett, 1992.

————. *On the Holy Trinity.* Translated by Arthur W. Haddan. In *Nicene and Post-Nicene Fathers,* edited by Philip Schaff, vol. 3. Peabody, Mass.: Hendrickson, 1994.

————. *Teaching Christianity — "De Doctrina Christiana."* Introduction, translation, and notes by Edmund Hill, O.P. In *The Works of Saint Augustine: A Translation for the Twenty-first Century,* edited by John E. Rotelle, O.S.A., vol. 11. Hyde Park, N.Y.: New City Press, 1996.

Bakhtin, Mikhail M. *Speech Genres and Other Late Essays.* Edited by Caryl Emerson and

Michael Holquist. Translated by Vern W. McGee. Austin: University of Texas Press, 1986.

Barbour, Ian. "Paradigms in Science and Religion." In *Paradigms and Revolutions: Appraisals and Applications of Thomas Kuhn's Philosophy of Science,* edited by Gary Gutting, pp. 223-45. Notre Dame, Ind.: University of Notre Dame Press, 1980.

Barth, Karl. *Church Dogmatics,* III/2, *The Doctrine of Creation,* Part 2. Edited by G. W. Bromiley and T. F. Torrance. Translated by Harold Knight, J. K. S. Reid, and R. H. Fuller. Edinburgh: T. & T. Clark, 1960.

―――. *Church Dogmatics,* III/3, *The Doctrine of Creation,* Part 3. Edited by G. W. Bromiley and T. F. Torrance. Translated by G. W. Bromiley and R. J. Ehrlich. Edinburgh: T. & T. Clark, 1960.

―――. *The Epistle to the Romans.* Translated by Edwyn C. Hoskyns. London: Oxford University Press, 1968.

Berger, Peter L. *The Sacred Canopy: Elements of a Sociological Theory of Religion.* New York: Doubleday, Anchor Books, 1967.

Berger, Peter L., and Thomas Luckmann. *The Social Construction of Reality: A Treatise in the Sociology of Knowledge.* New York: Doubleday, 1966; Anchor Books, 1967.

Betanzos, Ramon J. Introduction to *Introduction to the Human Sciences: An Attempt to Lay a Foundation for the Study of Society and History,* by Wilhelm Dilthey. Translated by Ramon J. Betanzos. Detroit: Wayne State University Press, 1988.

Bettelheim, Bruno. *The Uses of Enchantment: The Meaning and Importance of Fairy Tales.* New York: Random House, Vintage Books, 1977.

Bettenson, Henry, ed. *Documents of the Christian Church.* New York: Oxford University Press, 1947.

Betz, Werner. "Zur Geschichte des Wortes 'Weltanschauung.'" In *Kursbuch der Weltanschauungen,* Schriften der Carl Friedrich von Siemens Stiftung, pp. 18-28. Frankfurt: Verlag Ullstein, 1980.

Biemel, Walter. "Introduction to the Dilthey-Husserl Correspondence." Translated by Jeffner Allen. In *Husserl: Shorter Works,* edited by Peter McCormick and Frederick A. Elliston, translated by Jeffner Allen, pp. 198-202. Notre Dame, Ind.: University of Notre Dame Press; Brighton, England: Harvester Press, 1981.

Boyd, Gregory A. *God at War: The Bible and Spiritual Conflict.* Downers Grove, Ill.: InterVarsity, 1997.

Bratt, James D., ed. *Abraham Kuyper: A Centennial Reader.* Grand Rapids: Eerdmans, 1998.

Bruner, Jerome S. "Myth and Identity." In *Myth and Mythmaking,* edited by Henry A. Murray, pp. 276-87. New York: George Braziller, 1960.

Brunner, Emil. *Revelation and Reason.* Translated by Olive Wyon. Philadelphia: Westminster, 1946.

Bulhof, Ilse N. *Wilhelm Dilthey: A Hermeneutic Approach to the Study of History and Culture.* Martinus Nijhoff Philosophy Library, vol. 2. Boston: Martinus Nijhoff, 1980.

Bultmann, Rudolf. "Is Exegesis without Presuppositions Possible?" In *New Testament and Mythology and Other Basic Writings,* selected, edited, and translated by Schubert M. Ogden, pp. 145-53. Philadelphia: Fortress, 1984.

Buttiglione, Rocco. *Karol Wojtyla: The Thought of the Man Who Became Pope John Paul II.* Grand Rapids: Eerdmans, 1997.

Calvin, John. *Institutes of the Christian Religion.* Edited by John T. McNeill. Translated and indexed by Ford Lewis Battles. Library of Christian Classics, edited by John Baillie, John T. McNeill, and Henry P. Van Dusen, vol. 20. Philadelphia: Westminster, 1960.

Carr, David. "Husserl's Problematic Concept of the Life-World." In *Husserl: Expositions and Appraisals,* edited and introduction by Frederick A. Elliston and Peter McCormick, pp. 202-12. Notre Dame, Ind.: University of Notre Dame Press, 1977.

———. *Interpreting Husserl: Critical and Comparative Studies.* Boston/Dordrecht: Martinus Nijhoff, 1987.

———. *Phenomenology and the Problem of History: A Study of Husserl's Transcendental Philosophy.* Evanston, Ill.: Northwestern University Press, 1974.

Catechism of the Catholic Church. Liguori, Mo.: Liguori Publications, 1994.

Chesterton, G. K. *Heretics.* In *The Complete Works of G. K. Chesterton,* edited by David Dooley, vol. 1. San Francisco: Ignatius, 1986.

Clark, Gordon H. *A Christian Philosophy of Education.* Grand Rapids: Eerdmans, 1946.

———. *A Christian View of Men and Things: An Introduction to Philosophy.* Grand Rapids: Eerdmans, 1951. Reprint, Grand Rapids: Baker, 1981.

Clark, Gregory A. "The Nature of Conversion: How the Rhetoric of Worldview Philosophy Can Betray Evangelicals." In *The Nature of Confession: Evangelicals and Postliberals in Conversation,* edited by Timothy R. Phillips and Dennis L. Okholm, pp. 201-18. Downers Grove, Ill.: InterVarsity, 1996.

Clendenin, Daniel B., ed. *Eastern Orthodox Theology: A Contemporary Reader.* Grand Rapids: Baker, 1995.

Collingwood, R. G. *Essay on Metaphysics.* Oxford: Clarendon, 1940.

Colson, Charles. "The Common Cultural Task: The Culture War from a Protestant Perspective." In *Evangelicals and Catholics Together: Toward a Common Mission,* edited by Charles Colson and Richard John Neuhaus, pp. 1-44. Dallas: Word, 1995.

Conway, Gertrude D. *Wittgenstein on Foundations.* Atlantic Highlands, N.J.: Humanities Press, 1989.

Copleston, Frederick, S.J. *A History of Philosophy.* Vol. 7, *Modern Philosophy from the Post-Kantian Idealists to Marx, Kierkegaard, and Nietzsche.* New York: Doubleday, Image Books, 1994.

Counelis, James Steve. "Relevance and the Orthodox Christian Theological Enterprise: A Symbolic Paradigm on Weltanschauung." *Greek Orthodox Theological Review* 18 (spring-fall 1973): 35-46.

Crites, Stephen. "The Narrative Quality of Experience." In *Why Narrative? Readings in Narrative Theology,* edited by Stanley Hauerwas and L. Gregory Jones, pp. 65-88. Grand Rapids: Eerdmans, 1989.

Cunningham, Lawrence S. *The Catholic Faith: An Introduction.* New York: Paulist, 1987.

Works Cited

Danto, Arthur C. *Nietzsche as Philosopher.* New York: Macmillan, 1965.

Davidson, Donald. "The Myth of the Subjective." In *Relativism: Interpretation and Confrontation,* edited and introduction by Michael Krausz, pp. 159-72. Notre Dame, Ind.: University of Notre Dame Press, 1989.

————. "On the Very Idea of a Conceptual Scheme." In *Inquiries into Truth and Interpretation,* pp. 183-98. Oxford: Clarendon, 1984.

Dégh, Linda. "The Approach to Worldview in Folk Narrative Study." *Western Folklore* 53 (July 1994): 243-52.

Derrida, Jacques. *Margins of Philosophy.* Translated by Alan Bass. Chicago: University of Chicago Press, 1982.

————. *Of Grammatology.* Translated by Gayatri Chakravorty Spivak. Baltimore: Johns Hopkins University Press, 1976.

————. *Writing and Difference.* Translated by Alan Bass. Chicago: University of Chicago Press, 1976.

Deutsches Wörterbuch von Jacob Grimm und Wilhelm Grimm. Vierzehnter Band, I. Abreilung. 1 Teil. Bearbeitet von Alfred Götze und der Arbeitsstelle des Deutschen Wörterbuches zu Berlin. Leipzig: Verlag von S. Hirzel, 1955.

De Vries, John Hendrick. Biographical note to *Lectures on Calvinism,* by Abraham Kuyper. 1931. Reprint, Grand Rapids: Eerdmans, 1994.

Dilthey, Wilhelm. *Dilthey's Philosophy of Existence: Introduction to Weltanschauunglehre.* Translated and introduction by William Kluback and Martin Weinbaum. New York: Bookman Associates, 1957. Reprint, Westport, Conn.: Greenwood Press, 1978.

Dittberner, Job L. *The End of Ideology and American Social Thought: 1930-1960.* Studies in American History and Culture, no. 1. Ann Arbor: UMI Research Press, 1979.

Dooyeweerd, Herman. *A New Critique of Theoretical Thought.* Translated by David H. Freeman, William S. Young, and H. De Jongste. 4 vols. Jordan Station, Ont.: Paideia Press, 1984.

Dornseiff, Franz. "Weltanschauung. Kurzgefasste Wortgeschichte." *Die Wandlung: Eine Monatsschrift* 1 (1945-46): 1086-88.

Dulles, Avery, S.J. "The Unity for Which We Hope." In *Evangelicals and Catholics Together: Toward a Common Mission,* edited by Charles Colson and Richard John Neuhaus, pp. 115-46. Dallas: Word, 1995.

Eagleton, Terry. *Literary Theory.* Minneapolis: University of Minnesota Press, 1983.

Eco, Umberto. *A Theory of Semiotics.* Advances in Semiotics, edited by Thomas A. Sebeok. Bloomington: Indiana University Press, 1976.

Edwards, James C. *Ethics without Philosophy: Wittgenstein and the Moral Life.* Tampa: University Presses of Florida, 1982.

Edwards, Jonathan. *Religious Affections.* Edited by John E. Smith. The Works of Jonathan Edwards, vol. 2. New Haven: Yale University Press, 1959.

Edwards, Steven D. *Relativism, Conceptual Schemes, and Categorical Frameworks.* Avebury Series in Philosophy of Science. Brookfield, Vt.: Gower, 1990.

Emerson, Ralph Waldo. *Selected Essays*. Illustrated by Walter S. Oschman. Chicago: People's Book Club, 1949.

Ermath, Michael. *Wilhelm Dilthey: The Critique of Historical Reason*. Chicago: University of Chicago Press, 1978.

Farrell, Frank B. *Subjectivity, Realism, and Postmodernism — the Recovery of the World*. Cambridge: Cambridge University Press, 1994.

Fichte, Johann Gottlieb. *Attempt at a Critique of All Revelation*. Translated and introduction by Garrett Green. Cambridge: Cambridge University Press, 1978.

Finch, Henry LeRoy. *Wittgenstein: The Later Philosophy — an Exposition of the "Philosophical Investigations."* Atlantic Highlands, N.J.: Humanities Press, 1977.

Flannery, Austin P., ed. *Documents of Vatican II*. Rev. ed. Grand Rapids: Eerdmans, 1984.

Foucault, Michel. Afterword to *Michel Foucault: Beyond Structuralism and Hermeneutics*, by Hubert L. Dreyfus and Paul Rabinow, pp. 208-26. Chicago: University of Chicago Press, 1982.

———. *The Archaeology of Knowledge*. Translated by A. M. Sheridan Smith. New York: Random House, Pantheon Books, 1972.

———. *Discipline and Punish: The Birth of the Prison*. Translated by Alan Sheridan. New York: Random House, Vintage Books, 1995.

———. *The Order of Things: An Archaeology of the Human Sciences*. New York: Random House, 1970; Vintage Books, 1973.

———. *Power/Knowledge: Selected Interviews and Other Writings, 1972-1977*. Edited by Colin Gordon. Translated by Colin Gordon, Leo Marshall, John Mepham, and Kate Soper. New York: Pantheon Books, 1980.

Freud, Sigmund. "Inhibitions, Symptoms and Anxiety." In *"An Autobiographical Study," "Inhibitions, Symptoms and Anxiety," "The Question of Lay Analysis," and Other Works*. Vol. 20 of *The Standard Edition of the Complete Psychological Works of Sigmund Freud*, translated by James Strachey. London: Hogarth Press and the Institute of Psycho-Analysis, 1962.

———. "The Question of a Weltanschauung." In *New Introductory Lectures on Psycho-Analysis and Other Works*. Vol. 22 of *The Standard Edition of the Complete Psychological Works of Sigmund Freud*, translated by James Strachey. London: Hogarth Press and the Institute of Psycho-Analysis, 1964.

Gadamer, Hans-Georg. *Truth and Method*. 2nd rev. ed. Translation revised by Joel Weinsheimer and Donald G. Marshall. New York: Continuum, 1993.

Gay, Craig. *The Way of the (Modern) World; or, Why It's Tempting to Live As If God Doesn't Exist*. Foreword by J. I. Packer. Grand Rapids: Eerdmans, 1998.

Geehan, E. R., ed. *Jerusalem and Athens: Critical Discussions on the Philosophy and Apologetics of Cornelius Van Til*. Phillipsburg, N.J.: Presbyterian and Reformed, 1980.

Gelwick, Richard. *The Way of Discovery: An Introduction to the Thought of Michael Polanyi*. New York: Oxford University Press, 1977.

Genova, Judith. *Wittgenstein: A Way of Seeing*. New York: Routledge, 1995.

Gier, Nicholas F. *Wittgenstein and Phenomenology: A Comparative Study of the Later*

Works Cited

Wittgenstein, Husserl, Heidegger, and Merleau-Ponty. SUNY Series in Philosophy, edited by Robert C. Neville. Albany: State University of New York Press, 1981.

Gilkey, Langdon. *Maker of Heaven and Earth: A Study of the Christian Doctrine of Creation.* Christian Faith Series, consulting editor Reinhold Niebuhr. Garden City, N.Y.: Doubleday, 1959.

Gombert, Albert. "Besprechungen von R. M. Meyer's 'Vierhundert Schlagworte.'" *Zeitschrift für deutsche Wortforschung* 3 (1902): 144-58.

——. "Kleine Bemerkungen zur Wortgeschichte." *Zeitschrift für deutsche Wortforschung* 8 (1907): 121-40.

Goodman, Nelson. *Ways of Worldmaking.* Indianapolis: Hackett, 1978.

——. "Words, Works, Worlds." In *Starmaking: Realism, Anti-Realism, and Irrealism,* edited by Peter J. McCormick, pp. 61-77. Cambridge: MIT Press, Bradford, 1996.

Götze, Alfred. "Weltanschauung." *Euphorion: Zeitschrift für Literaturgeschichte* 25 (1924): 42-51.

Granier, Jean. "Perspectivism and Interpretation." In *The New Nietzsche,* edited by David B. Allison, pp. 190-200. Cambridge: MIT Press, 1985.

Griffioen, Sander. "The Worldview Approach to Social Theory: Hazards and Benefits." In *Stained Glass: Worldviews and Social Science,* edited by Paul A. Marshall, Sander Griffioen, and Richard J. Mouw, pp. 81-118. Lanham, Md.: University Press of America, 1989.

Gutting, Gary. Introduction to *The Cambridge Companion to Foucault,* edited by Gary Gutting, pp. 1-27. Cambridge: Cambridge University Press, 1994.

——. Introduction to *Paradigms and Revolutions: Appraisals and Applications of Thomas Kuhn's Philosophy of Science,* edited by Gary Gutting. Notre Dame, Ind.: University of Notre Dame Press, 1980.

Habermas, Jürgen. "Work and Weltanschauung: The Heidegger Controversy from a German Perspective." In *Heidegger: A Critical Reader,* edited by Hubert L. Dreyfus and Harrison Hall, pp. 186-208. Oxford/Cambridge, Mass.: Basil Blackwell, 1992.

Hacking, Ian. "Language, Truth and Reason." In *Rationality and Relativism,* edited by Martin Hollis and Steven Lukes, pp. 48-66. Cambridge: MIT Press, 1982.

Hamilton, Peter. *Knowledge and Social Structure: An Introduction to the Classical Argument in the Sociology of Knowledge.* London: Routledge and Kegan Paul, 1974.

Harms, John B. "Mannheim's Sociology of Knowledge and the Interpretation of Weltanschauungen." *Social Science Journal* 21 (April 1984): 33-48.

Hegel, G. W. F. *Aesthetics: Lectures on Fine Art.* Translated by T. M. Knox. 2 vols. Oxford: At the Clarendon Press, 1975.

——. *The Difference between Fichte's and Schelling's System of Philosophy.* Translated by H. S. Harris and Walter Cerf. Albany: State University of New York Press, 1977.

——. *Lectures on the History of Philosophy.* Translated by E. S. Haldane and Frances H. Simson. 3 vols. Lincoln: University of Nebraska Press, 1995.

——. *Lectures on the Philosophy of Religion Together with a Work on the Proofs of the Existence of God.* Translated by Rev. E. B. Speirs and J. Burdon Sanderson. Vol. 1. New York: Humanities Press, 1962.

————. *The Phenomenology of Mind*. Translated with introduction and notes by J. B. Baillie. 2nd ed. London: George Allen and Unwin, 1961.

————. *The Philosophy of History*. Translated by J. Sibree. In *The Great Books of the Western World*, edited by Robert Maynard Hutchins, vol. 46. Chicago: Encyclopaedia Britannica, 1952.

Heidegger, Martin. "The Age of the World Picture." In *The Question concerning Technology and Other Essays*, translated and introduction by William Lovitt, pp. 115-54. New York: Harper and Row, Harper Torchbooks, 1977.

————. "Anmerkungen zu Karl Jaspers' *Psychologie der Weltanschauungen*." In *Karl Jaspers in der Diskussion*, edited by Hans Saner, pp. 70-100. Munich: R. Piper, 1973.

————. *The Basic Problems of Phenomenology*. Translation, introduction, and lexicon by Albert Hofstadter. Studies in Phenomenology and Existential Philosophy. Bloomington: Indiana University Press, 1982.

————. *Being and Time*. Translated by John Macquarrie and Edward Robinson. New York: Harper and Row, 1962.

————. *Being and Time: A Translation of "Sein und Zeit."* Translated by Joan Stambaugh. SUNY Series in Contemporary Continental Philosophy, edited by Dennis J. Schmidt. Albany: State University of New York Press, 1996.

————. *Die Grundproblem der Phänomenologie*. In *Gesamtausgabe*, edited by F.-W. von Herrmann, vol. 24. Frankfurt: Klostermann, 1975, 1989.

————. "Die Idee der Philosophie und das Weltanschauungs problem." In *Zur Bestimmung der Philosophie*, in *Gesamtausgabe*, edited by Bernd Heimbüchel, vol. 56/57, pp. 3-117. Frankfurt: Klostermann, 1987.

————. *The Metaphysical Foundations of Logic*. Translated by Michael Heim. Bloomington: Indiana University Press, 1984.

————. *Metaphysische Anfangsgründe der Logik im Ausgang von Leibniz*. In *Gesamtausgabe*, edited by Klaus Held, vol. 26. Frankfurt: Klostermann, 1978.

————. "'Only a God Can Save Us': The Spiegel Interview (1966)." In *Heidegger: The Man and the Thinker*, edited by Thomas Sheehan, pp. 45-72. Chicago: Precedent Publishing, n.d.

————. *Wegmarken*. In *Gesamtausgabe*, edited by F.-W. von Herrmann, 9:1-44. Frankfurt: Klostermann, 1976.

————. "Die Zeit des Weltbildes." In *Holzwege*, in *Gesamtausgabe*, edited by F.-W. von Herrmann, 5:75-113. Frankfurt: Klostermann, 1977.

Hempel, Carl G. "Thomas Kuhn, Colleague and Friend." In *World Changes: Thomas Kuhn and the Nature of Science*, edited by Paul Horwich, pp. 7-8. Cambridge: MIT Press, 1993.

Henderson, R. D. "How Abraham Kuyper Became a Kuyperian." *Christian Scholars Review* 22 (1992): 22-35.

Henry, Carl F. H. *Confessions of a Theologian: An Autobiography*. Waco, Tex.: Word, 1986.

————. "Fortunes of the Christian World View." *Trinity Journal*, n.s., 19 (1998): 163-76.

Heslam, Peter S. *Creating a Christian Worldview: Abraham Kuyper's Lectures on Calvinism*. Grand Rapids: Eerdmans, 1998.

Hesse, Mary. *Revolutions and Reconstructions in the Philosophy of Science.* Bloomington: Indiana University Press, 1980.

Hodges, H. A. *Wilhelm Dilthey: An Introduction.* New York: Howard Fertig, 1969.

Holmes, Arthur. "Phenomenology and the Relativity of World-Views." *Personalist* 48 (summer 1967): 328-44.

Hoyningen-Huene, Paul. *Reconstructing Scientific Revolutions: Thomas S. Kuhn's Philosophy of Science.* Translated by Alexander T. Levine. Foreword by Thomas S. Kuhn. Chicago: University of Chicago Press, 1993.

Hung, Edwin. *The Nature of Science: Problems and Perspectives.* Belmont, Calif.: Wadsworth, 1997.

Hunnings, Gordon. *The World and Language in Wittgenstein's Philosophy.* Albany: State University of New York Press, 1988.

Husserl, Edmund. *The Crisis of European Sciences and Transcendental Phenomenology: An Introduction to Phenomenological Philosophy.* Translated and introduction by David Carr. Northwestern University Studies in Phenomenology and Existential Philosophy, general editor John Wild. Evanston, Ill.: Northwestern University Press, 1970.

―――. "Philosophie als strenge Wissenschaften." *Logos* 1 (1910-11): 289-341.

―――. "Philosophy as Rigorous Science." In *Husserl: Shorter Works,* edited by Peter McCormick and Frederick A. Elliston, pp. 185-97. Notre Dame, Ind.: University of Notre Dame Press; Brighton, England: Harvester Press, 1981.

Husserl, Edmund, and Wilhelm Dilthey. "The Dilthey-Husserl Correspondence." Edited by Walter Biemel. Translated by Jeffner Allen. In *Husserl: Shorter Works,* edited by Peter McCormick and Frederick A. Elliston, pp. 203-9. Notre Dame, Ind.: University of Notre Dame Press; Brighton, England: Harvester Press, 1981.

Hyppolite, Jean. *Genesis and Structure of Hegel's Phenomenology of Spirit.* Translated by Samuel Cherniak and John Heckman. Northwestern University Studies in Phenomenology and Existential Philosophy, edited by James M. Edie. Evanston, Ill.: Northwestern University Press, 1974.

James, William. "Is Life Worth Living?" In *The Will to Believe and Other Essays in Popular Philosophy,* pp. 32-62. New York, ca. 1896. Reprint, New York: Dover, 1956.

―――. *A Pluralistic Universe.* New York: Longmans, Green, and Co., 1925.

Jaspers, Karl. *Basic Philosophical Writings.* Edited, translated, and introduction by Edith Ehrlich, Leonard H. Ehrlich, and George B. Pepper. Atlantic Highlands, N.J.: Humanities Press, 1986.

―――. "Philosophical Autobiography." In *The Philosophy of Karl Jaspers,* edited by Paul Arthur Schlipp, pp. 5-94. Augmented edition. Library of Living Philosophers. La Salle, Ill.: Open Court, 1981.

―――. *Psychologie der Weltanschauungen.* Berlin: Verlag von Julius Springer, 1919.

John Paul II, Pope (see Wojtyla, Karol)

Jones, Stanton L., and Richard E. Butman. *Modern Psycho-Therapies: A Comprehensive Christian Appraisal.* Downers Grove, Ill.: InterVarsity, 1991.

Jones, W. T. *A History of Western Philosophy.* Vol. 2, *The Medieval Mind.* 2nd ed. New York: Harcourt, Brace and World, 1969.

———. "World Views: Their Nature and Their Function." *Current Anthropology* 13 (February 1972): 79-109.

Jung, C. G. "Psychotherapy and a Philosophy of Life." In *The Practice of Psychotherapy: Essays on the Psychology of the Transference and Other Subjects,* translated by R. F. C. Hull, pp. 76-83. Bollingen Series, vol. 20. 2nd ed. New York: Pantheon Books, 1966.

Kant, Immanuel. *Critique of Judgment: Including the First Introduction.* Translated and introduction by Werner S. Pluhar. Foreword by Mary J. Gregor. Indianapolis: Hackett, 1987.

Kantzer, Kenneth S. "Carl Ferdinand Howard Henry: An Appreciation." In *God and Culture: Essays in Honor of Carl F. H. Henry,* edited by D. A. Carson and John D. Woodbridge, pp. 369-77. Grand Rapids: Eerdmans, 1993.

Kaufmann, Walter. "Jaspers' Relation to Nietzsche." In *The Philosophy of Karl Jaspers,* pp. 407-36. Library of Living Philosophers, edited by Paul Arthur Schlipp. Augmented edition. La Salle, Ill.: Open Court, 1981.

Kearney, Michael. *Worldview.* Novato, Calif.: Chandler and Sharp, 1984.

Kidner, Derek. *The Proverbs: An Introduction and Commentary.* Tyndale Old Testament Commentaries, edited by D. J. Wiseman. Downers Grove, Ill.: InterVarsity, 1977.

Kierkegaard, Søren. *Attack upon "Christendom."* Translated, introduction, and notes by Walter Lowrie. New introduction by Howard A. Johnson. Princeton: Princeton University Press, 1968.

———. *Concluding Unscientific Postscript.* Translated by David F. Swenson. Completed, with introduction and notes by Walter Lowrie. Princeton: Princeton University Press, 1941.

———. *Either/Or.* Edited and translated with introduction and notes by Howard V. Hong and Edna H. Hong. 2 vols. Princeton: Princeton University Press, 1987.

———. *Journals and Papers.* Edited and translated by Howard V. Hong and Edna H. Hong. Assisted by Gregor Malantschuk. Vol. 3, L-R. Bloomington: Indiana University Press, 1975.

———. *The Journals of Kierkegaard, 1834-1854.* Translated and edited by Alexander Dru. London: Oxford University Press, 1938.

———. *On Authority and Revelation.* Translated with an introduction and notes by Walter Lowrie. Introduction by Frederick Sontag. New York: Harper and Row, Harper Torchbooks, 1966.

———. *Stages on Life's Way: Studies by Various Persons.* Edited and translated with introduction and notes by Howard V. Hong and Edna H. Hong. Princeton: Princeton University Press, 1988.

Kisiel, Theodore. *The Genesis of Heidegger's "Being and Time."* Berkeley: University of California Press, 1993.

Klapwijk, Jacob. "On Worldviews and Philosophy." In *Stained Glass: Worldviews and So-*

cial Science, edited by Paul A. Marshall, Sander Griffioen, and Richard J. Mouw, pp. 41-55. Christian Studies Today. Lanham, Md.: University Press of America, 1989.

Kovacs, George. "Philosophy as Primordial Science in Heidegger's Courses of 1919." In *Reading Heidegger from the Start: Essays in His Earliest Thought,* edited by Theodore Kisiel and John van Buren, pp. 91-110. SUNY Series in Contemporary Continental Philosophy, edited by Dennis J. Schmidt. Albany: State University of New York Press, 1994.

Kraut, Robert. "The Third Dogma." In *Truth and Interpretation: Perspectives on the Philosophy of Donald Davidson,* edited by Ernest LePore, pp. 398-416. Cambridge, Mass.: Basil Blackwell, 1986.

Kreeft, Peter. *Three Philosophies of Life.* San Francisco: Ignatius, 1989.

Krell, David Farrell. *Intimations of Mortality: Time, Truth, and Finitude in Heidegger's Thinking of Being.* University Park: Pennsylvania State University Press, 1986.

Kuhn, Thomas S. *The Essential Tension: Selected Studies in Scientific Tradition and Change.* Chicago: University of Chicago Press, 1977.

———. "Reflections on My Critics." In *Criticism and the Growth of Knowledge,* edited by I. Lakatos and A. Musgrave, pp. 231-78. Cambridge: Cambridge University Press, 1970.

———. *The Structure of Scientific Revolutions.* International Encyclopedia of Unified Science, edited by Otto Neurath. 2nd enlarged edition. Vol. 2. Chicago: University of Chicago Press, 1970.

Kuyper, Abraham. *Lectures on Calvinism: Six Lectures Delivered at Princeton University under Auspices of the L. P. Stone Foundation.* 1931. Reprint, Grand Rapids: Eerdmans, 1994.

———. *Principles of Sacred Theology.* Translated by J. Hendrik De Vries. Introduction by Benjamin B. Warfield. Grand Rapids: Baker, 1980.

———. "Sphere Sovereignty." In *Abraham Kuyper: A Centennial Reader,* edited by James D. Bratt. Grand Rapids: Eerdmans, 1998.

Ladd, George Eldon. *A Theology of the New Testament.* Edited by Donald A. Hagner. Rev. ed. Grand Rapids: Eerdmans, 1993.

Lakoff, George, and Mark Johnson. *Metaphors We Live By.* Chicago: University of Chicago Press, 1980.

Latzel, Edwin. "The Concept of 'Ultimate Situation' in Jaspers' Philosophy." In *The Philosophy of Karl Jaspers,* pp. 177-208. Library of Living Philosophers, edited by Paul Arthur Schlipp. Augmented edition. La Salle, Ill.: Open Court, 1981.

Lefebre, Ludwig B. "The Psychology of Karl Jaspers." In *The Philosophy of Karl Jaspers,* pp. 467-97. Library of Living Philosophers, edited by Paul Arthur Schlipp. Augmented edition. La Salle, Ill.: Open Court, 1981.

Levi, Albert William. *Philosophy and the Modern World.* Bloomington: Indiana University Press, 1959.

Levine, Peter. *Nietzsche and the Modern Crisis of the Humanities.* Albany: State University of New York Press, 1995.

Lewis, C. I. *Mind and the World Order.* New York: Scribner, 1929.

Lewis, C. S. *The Abolition of Man*. New York: Macmillan, 1944; New York: Simon and Schuster, Touchstone, 1996.

———. "De Descriptione Temporum." In *Selected Literary Essays*, edited by Walter Hooper, pp. 1-14. Cambridge: At the University Press, 1969.

———. *The Great Divorce*. New York: Macmillan, 1946.

———. "In Praise of Solid People." In *Poems*, edited by Walter Hooper, pp. 199-200. London: Harper Collins, Fount Paperbacks, 1994.

———. "Meditation in a Toolshed." In *God in the Dock: Essays on Theology and Ethics*, edited by Walter Hooper, pp. 212-15. Grand Rapids: Eerdmans, 1970.

———. "The Poison of Subjectivism." In *Christian Reflections*, edited by Walter Hooper, pp. 72-81. Grand Rapids: Eerdmans, 1967.

———. *The Screwtape Letters and Screwtape Proposes a Toast*. New York: Macmillan, 1961.

Loewenberg, Jacob, ed. Introduction to *Hegel: Selections*, by G. W. F. Hegel. New York: Scribner, 1929.

Lubac, Henri de. *At the Service of the Church*. San Francisco: Ignatius, 1993.

Luther, Martin. "To the Councilmen of All Cities in Germany That They Establish and Maintain Christian Schools." In *The Christian in Society II*, edited by Walther I. Brandt, translated by A. T. W. Steinhauser and revised by W. I. Brandt, pp. 347-78. Vol. 45 of Luther's Works, general editor Helmut T. Lehmann. Philadelphia: Muhlenberg, n.d.

Lyotard, Jean-François. *The Postmodern Condition: A Report on Knowledge*. Translated by Geoff Bennington and Brian Massumi. Foreword by Fredric Jameson. Theory and History of Literature, edited by Wlad Godzich and JochenSchulte-Sasse, vol. 10. Minneapolis: University of Minnesota Press, 1984.

MacIntyre, Alasdair. *After Virtue: A Study in Moral Theory*. 2nd ed. Notre Dame, Ind.: University of Notre Dame Press, 1984.

———. "Epistemological Crises, Dramatic Narrative, and the Philosophy of Science." In *Why Narrative? Readings in Narrative Theology*, edited by Stanley Hauerwas and L. Gregory Jones, pp. 138-57. Grand Rapids: Eerdmans, 1989.

———. *Whose Justice? Which Rationality?* Notre Dame, Ind.: University of Notre Dame Press, 1988.

Major-Poetzl, Pamela. *Michel Foucault's Archaeology of Western Culture*. Chapel Hill: University of North Carolina Press, 1983.

Malcomb, Norman. "Wittgenstein's *Philosophical Investigations*." In *Wittgenstein: The Philosophical Investigations*, edited by George Pitcher, pp. 65-103. Garden City, N.Y.: Anchor Books, 1966.

Malinowski, Bronislaw. *Argonauts of the Western Pacific*. London: Routledge and Kegan Paul, 1922.

Malpas, J. E. *Donald Davidson and the Mirror of Meaning: Holism, Truth, Interpretation*. Cambridge: Cambridge University Press, 1992.

Mannheim, Karl. "On the Interpretation of Weltanschauung." In *From Karl Mannheim,* edited and introduction by Kurt H. Wolff, pp. 8-58. New York: Oxford University Press, 1971.

Marsden, George M. "The State of Evangelical Christian Scholarship." *Reformed Journal* 37 (1987): 12-16.

Marshall, Paul A., Sander Griffioen, and Richard J. Mouw, eds. Introduction to *Stained Glass: Worldviews and Social Science,* pp. 8-13. Christian Studies Today. Lanham, Md.: University Press of America, 1989.

Marx, Karl. "Preface to *A Contribution to the Critique of Political Economy.*" In *The Marx-Engels Reader,* edited by Robert C. Tucker, pp. 3-6. 2nd ed. New York: Norton, 1978.

Marx, Karl, and Friedrich Engels. *The German Ideology.* Edited and introduction by R. Pascal. New York: International Publishers, 1947.

Masterson, Margaret. "The Nature of a Paradigm." In *Criticism and the Growth of Knowledge,* edited by I. Lakatos and A. Musgrave, pp. 59-89. Cambridge: Cambridge University Press, 1970.

May, Rollo. *The Cry for Myth.* New York: Bantam Doubleday Dell, Delta, 1991.

McBrien, Richard P. *Catholicism.* 2 vols. Minneapolis: Winston Press, 1980.

McCarthy, Vincent A. *The Phenomenology of Moods in Kierkegaard.* The Hague and Boston: Martinus Nijhoff, 1978.

McDermott, John M., S.J., ed. *The Thought of Pope John Paul II: A Collection of Essays and Studies.* Rome: Editrice Pontifica Università Gregoriana, 1993.

McMullin, Ernan. "Rationality and Paradigm Change in Science." In *World Changes: Thomas Kuhn and the Nature of Science,* edited by Paul Horwich, pp. 55-78. Cambridge: MIT Press, 1993.

Meier, Andreas. "Die Geburt der 'Weltanschauung' im 19. Jahrhundert." *Theologische Rundschau* 62 (1997): 414-20.

Meier, Helmut G. "'Weltanschauung': Studien zu einer Geschichte und Theorie des Begriffs." Ph.D. diss., Westfälischen Wilhelms-Universität zu Münster, 1967.

Middleton, J. Richard, and Brian J. Walsh. *Truth Is Stranger Than It Used to Be: Biblical Faith in a Postmodern Age.* Downers Grove, Ill.: InterVarsity, 1995.

Miller, Richard W. "Social and Political Theory: Class, State, Revolution." In *The Cambridge Companion to Marx,* edited by Terrell Carver, pp. 55-105. Cambridge: Cambridge University Press, 1991.

Mouw, Richard J. "Dutch Calvinist Philosophical Influences in North America." *Calvin Theological Journal* 24 (April 1989): 93-120.

Nash, Ronald H. "The Life of the Mind and the Way of Life." In *Francis A. Schaeffer: Portraits of the Man and His Work,* edited by Lane T. Dennis, pp. 53-69. Westchester, Ill.: Crossway, 1986.

————. Preface to *The Philosophy of Gordon H. Clark: A Festschrift.* Edited by Ronald H. Nash. Philadelphia: Presbyterian and Reformed, 1968.

Nassif, Bradley. "New Dimensions in Eastern Orthodox Theology." In *New Dimensions in Evangelical Thought: Essays in Honor of Millard J. Erickson,* edited by David S. Dockery, pp. 92-117. Downers Grove, Ill.: InterVarsity, 1998.

Neuhaus, Richard John. Foreword to *Springtime of Evangelization: The Complete Texts of the Holy Father's 1998 ad Limina Addresses to the Bishops of the United States*, by Pope John Paul II. Edited and introduction by Rev. Thomas D. Williams, L.C. Preface by Francis Cardinal George, O.M.I. San Francisco: Ignatius, 1999.

Niebuhr, H. Richard. *Christ and Culture*. New York: Harper and Row, 1951.

Nietzsche, Friedrich. *Basic Writings of Friedrich Nietzsche*. Translated, edited, and commentaries by Walter Kaufmann. New York: Modern Library, 1968.

———. *Beyond Good and Evil*. In *Basic Writings of Friedrich Nietzsche*, translated, edited, and commentaries by Walter Kaufmann. New York: Modern Library, 1968.

———. *The Birth of Tragedy and the Case of Wagner*. Translated and commentary by Walter Kaufmann. New York: Random House, Vintage Books, 1967.

———. *The Complete Works of Friedrich Nietzsche*. Edited by Dr. Oscar Levy. 16 vols. New York: Russell and Russell, 1964.

———. *The Gay Science, with a Prelude in Rhymes and an Appendix of Songs*. Translated with commentary by Walter Kaufmann. New York: Random House, Vintage Books, 1974.

———. *The Genealogy of Morals*. Translated by Horace B. Samuel. In *The Complete Works of Friedrich Nietzsche*, edited by Oscar Levy, vol. 13. New York: Russell and Russell, 1964.

———. *Human, All Too Human: A Book for Free Spirits*. Translated by R. J. Hollingdale. Introduction by Erich Heller. Texts in German Philosophy, general editor Charles Taylor. New York: Cambridge University Press, 1986.

———. *The Joyful Wisdom*. Translated by Thomas Common. In *The Complete Works of Friedrich Nietzsche*, edited by Oscar Levy, vol. 10. New York: Russell and Russell, 1964.

———. *On the Advantage and Disadvantage of History for Life*. Translated and introduction by Peter Preuss. Indianapolis: Hackett, 1980.

———. *On the Genealogy of Morals*. Translated, edited, and commentaries by Walter Kaufmann. New York: Modern Library, 1968.

———. "On Truth and Lie in an Extra-Moral Sense." In *The Portable Nietzsche*, edited and translated by Walter Kaufmann, pp. 42-47. New York: Penguin Books, 1982.

———. *Thus Spoke Zarathustra*. In *The Portable Nietzsche*, edited and translated by Walter Kaufmann. New York: Penguin Books, 1982.

———. *Twilight of the Idols*. In *The Portable Nietzsche*, edited and translated by Walter Kaufmann. New York: Penguin Books, 1982.

———. *The Will to Power*. Translated by Anthony M. Ludovici. In *The Complete Works of Friedrich Nietzsche*, edited by Oscar Levy, vol. 15. New York: Russell and Russell, 1964.

Novak, Michael. Foreword to *Karol Wojtyla: The Thought of the Man Who Became Pope John Paul II*, by Rocco Buttiglione. Translated by Paolo Guietti and Francesca Murphy. Grand Rapids: Eerdmans, 1997.

Ong, Walter. "World as View and World as Event." *American Anthropologist* 71 (August 1969): 634-47.

Works Cited

Orr, James. *The Christian View of God and the World as Centering in the Incarnation.* New York: Scribner, 1887. Reprint, with a foreword by Vernon C. Grounds, Grand Rapids: Kregel, 1989.

Ortega y Gassett, José. *Concord and Liberty.* Translated by Helene Weyl. New York: Norton, Norton Library, 1946.

Paci, Enzo. *The Function of the Sciences and the Meaning of Man.* Translated with an introduction by Paul Piccone and James E. Hansen. Northwestern University Studies in Phenomenology and Existential Philosophy, general editor John Wild. Evanston, Ill.: Northwestern University Press, 1972.

Packer, J. I. "On from Orr: Cultural Crisis, Rational Realism and Incarnational Ontology." In *Reclaiming the Great Tradition: Evangelicals, Catholics, and Orthodox in Dialogue,* edited by James S. Cutsinger, pp. 155-76. Downers Grove, Ill.: Inter-Varsity, 1997.

Palmer, Parker J. *To Know as We Are Known: A Spirituality of Education.* San Francisco: Harper San Francisco, 1983.

Pascal, Blaise. *The Mind on Fire: An Anthology of the Writings of Blaise Pascal.* Edited by James M. Houston. Introduction by Os Guinness. Portland, Oreg.: Multnomah, 1989.

———. *Pensées.* Translated by W. F. Trotter. In *The Great Books of the Western World,* edited by Robert Maynard Hutchins, vol. 33. Chicago: William Benton and Encyclopaedia Britannica, 1952.

———. *Pensées and Other Writings.* Translated by Honor Levi. Oxford World's Classics. New York: Oxford University Press, 1995.

Peifer, John. *The Mystery of Knowledge.* Albany, N.Y.: Magi Books, 1964.

Peirce, Charles Sanders. *Collected Papers.* Edited by Charles Hartshorne and Paul Weiss. Vol. 5. Cambridge: Harvard University Press, 1931-58.

Peters, Ted. "The Nature and Role of Presupposition: An Inquiry into Contemporary Hermeneutics." *International Philosophical Quarterly* 14 (June 1974): 209-22.

Plantinga, Theodore. *Historical Understanding in the Thought of Wilhelm Dilthey.* Toronto: University of Toronto Press, 1980.

Plato. *Meno.* Translated by Benjamin Jowett. In *The Great Books of the Western World,* edited by Robert Maynard Hutchins, vol. 7. Chicago: Encyclopædia Britannica, 1952.

———. *Phaedrus.* Translated and introduction by Walter Hamilton. New York: Penguin Books, 1973.

———. *Plato's Epistles.* Translated, essays, and notes by Glenn R. Morrow. Library of Liberal Arts. Indianapolis: Bobbs-Merrill, 1962.

———. *Theaetetus.* Translated by Benjamin Jowett. In *The Great Books of the Western World,* edited by Robert Maynard Hutchins, vol. 7. Chicago: Encyclopaedia Britannica, 1952.

Polanyi, Michael. *Personal Knowledge: Towards a Post-Critical Philosophy.* Chicago: University of Chicago Press, 1958.

———. *The Tacit Dimension.* Garden City, N.Y.: Doubleday, 1966.

————. "Why Did We Destroy Europe?" *Studium Generale* 23 (1970): 909-16.

————. "Works of Art." From unpublished lectures at the University of Texas and the University of Chicago, February-May 1969, p. 30.

Prosch, Harry. *Michael Polanyi: A Critical Exposition*. Albany: State University of New York Press, 1986.

Quine, W. V. O. "Two Dogmas of Empiricism." In *From a Logical Point of View*, pp. 20-46. Cambridge: Harvard University Press, 1953.

Redfield, Robert. *The Primitive World and Its Transformations*. Ithaca, N.Y.: Cornell University Press, Cornell Paperbacks, 1953.

Rescher, Nicholas. "Conceptual Schemes." In *Midwest Studies in Philosophy*, vol. 5, edited by Peter A. French, Theodore E. Uehling, Jr., and Howard K. Wettstein, pp. 323-45. Minneapolis: University of Minnesota Press, 1980.

Rockmore, Tom. "Epistemology as Hermeneutics: Antifoundationalist Relativism." *Monist* 73 (1990): 115-33.

Rorty, Richard. *Consequences of Pragmatism: Essays: 1972-1980*. Minneapolis: University of Minnesota Press, 1982.

Rosen, Stanley. *Hermeneutics as Politics*. Odéon, edited by Josué V. Harari and Vincent Descombes. New York: Oxford University Press, 1987.

Rowe, William V. "Society after the Subject, Philosophy after the Worldview." In *Stained Glass: Worldviews and Social Science*, edited by Paul A. Marshall, Sander Griffioen, and Richard Mouw, pp. 156-83. Christian Studies Today. Lanham, Md.: University Press of America, 1989.

Runzo, Joseph. *World Views and Perceiving God*. New York: St. Martin's Press, 1993.

Ryckman. Richard M. *Theories of Personality*. 3rd ed. Monterey, Calif.: Brooks/Cole, 1985.

Said, Edward W. "Michael Foucault: 1926-1984." In *After Foucault: Humanistic Knowledge, Postmodern Challenges*, edited by Jonathan Arac, pp. 1-11. New Brunswick, N.J.: Rutgers University Press, 1988.

Sarna, Jan W. "On Some Presuppositions of Husserl's 'Presuppositionless' Philosophy." *Analecta Husserliana* 27 (1989): 239-50.

Sayers, Dorothy L. *The Letters of Dorothy L. Sayers*. Vol. 2, *1937-1943: From Novelist to Playwright*. Edited by Barbara Reynolds. New York: St. Martin's Press, 1998.

————. "Toward a Christian Esthetic." In *The Whimsical Christian: Eighteen Essays by Dorothy L. Sayers*, pp. 73-91. New York: Macmillan, Collier Books, 1987.

Scanlon, John. "The Manifold Meanings of 'Life World' in Husserl's *Crisis*." *American Catholic Philosophical Quarterly* 66 (spring 1992): 229-39.

Schaeffer, Francis A. *Art and the Bible*. L'Abri Pamphlets. Downers Grove, Ill.: InterVarsity, 1973.

————. *The Complete Works of Francis A. Schaeffer: A Christian Worldview*. 2nd ed. 5 vols. Wheaton, Ill.: Crossway, 1982.

Scheler, Max. *Problems of a Sociology of Knowledge*. Translated by Manfred S. Frings. Edited and introduction by Kenneth W. Stikkers. Boston: Routledge and Kegan Paul, 1980.

―――. "The Sociology of Knowledge: Formal Problems." In *The Sociology of Knowledge: A Reader,* edited by James E. Curtis and John W. Petras, pp. 170-86. New York: Praeger, 1970.

Schlier, Heinrich. *Principalities and Powers in the New Testament.* New York: Herder and Herder, 1961.

Schmemann, Alexander. *Church, World, Mission.* Crestwood, N.Y.: St. Vladimir's Seminary Press, 1979.

―――. *For the Life of the World: Sacraments and Orthodoxy.* Crestwood, N.Y.: St. Vladimir's Seminary Press, 1973.

Schrag, Oswald O. *An Introduction to Existence, Existenz, and Transcendence: The Philosophy of Karl Jaspers.* Pittsburgh: Duquesne University Press, 1971.

Schumacher, E. F. *A Guide for the Perplexed.* New York: Harper and Row, 1977.

Scorgie, Glen G. *A Call for Continuity: The Theological Contribution of James Orr.* Macon, Ga.: Mercer University Press, 1988.

―――. "James Orr." In *Handbook of Evangelical Theologians,* edited by Walter A. Elwell, pp. 12-25. Grand Rapids: Baker, 1993.

Searle, John. "Is There a Crisis in American Higher Education?" *Bulletin of the American Academy of Arts and Sciences* 46 (n.d.): 24-47.

Simon, Herbert A. *Reason in Human Affairs.* Stanford: Stanford University Press, 1983.

Sire, James W. *The Universe Next Door: A Basic Worldview Catalog.* 3rd ed. Downers Grove, Ill.: InterVarsity, 1997.

Small, Robin. "Nietzsche and a Platonist Idea of the Cosmos: Center Everywhere and Circumference Nowhere." *Journal of the History of Ideas* 44 (January-March 1983): 89-104.

Smart, Ninian. *Worldviews: Crosscultural Explorations of Human Beliefs.* 2nd ed. Englewood Cliffs, N.J.: Prentice-Hall, 1995.

Smith, Charles W. *A Critique of Sociological Reasoning: An Essay in Philosophical Sociology.* Oxford: Basil Blackwell, 1979.

Smith, John E. Introduction to *Religious Affections,* by Jonathan Edwards. The Works of Jonathan Edwards, vol. 2. New Haven: Yale University Press, 1959.

Solomon, Robert C.. *Continental Philosophy Since 1750: The Rise and Fall of the Self.* A History of Western Philosophy, vol. 7. Oxford: Oxford University Press, 1988.

Spykman, Gordon J. *Reformational Theology: A New Paradigm for Doing Dogmatics.* Grand Rapids: Eerdmans, 1992.

Stack, George J. *Nietzsche: Man, Knowledge, and Will to Power.* Durango, Colo.: Hollowbrook Publishing, 1994.

Steiner, George. *Real Presences.* Chicago: University of Chicago Press, 1989.

Strawser, Michael. *Both/And: Reading Kierkegaard from Irony to Edification.* New York: Fordham University Press, 1997.

Thiselton, Anthony C. *New Horizons in Hermeneutics: The Theory and Practice of Transforming Biblical Reading.* Grand Rapids: Zondervan, 1992.

Thompson, Josiah. *The Lonely Labyrinth: Kierkegaard's Pseudonymous Works.* Foreword by George Kimball Plochman. Carbondale: Southern Illinois University Press, 1967.

Van Til, Henry R. *The Calvinistic Concept of Culture.* Grand Rapids: Baker, 1959.

Verhoogt, Jan. "Sociology and Progress: Worldview Analysis of Modern Sociology." In *Stained Glass: Worldviews and Social Science,* edited by Paul A. Marshall, Sander Griffioen, and Richard J. Mouw, pp. 119-39. Lanham, Md.: University Press of America, 1989.

Wallraff, Charles F. *Karl Jaspers: An Introduction to His Philosophy.* Princeton: Princeton University Press, 1970.

Ware, Timothy (Bishop Kallistos of Diokleia). *The Orthodox Church.* New York: Penguin Books, 1963, 1964.

Warnock, Mary. "Nietzsche's Conception of Truth." In *Nietzsche's Imagery and Thought: A Collection of Essays,* edited by Malcolm Pasley, pp. 33-63. Berkeley: University of California Press, 1978.

Weigel, George. *Witness to Hope: The Biography of Pope John Paul II.* New York: Harper Collins, Cliff Street Books, 1999.

Winch, Peter. "Understanding a Primitive Society." In *Rationality,* edited by Bryan R. Wilson, pp. 78-111. New York: Harper and Row, First Torchbook Library Edition, 1970.

Windelband, Wilhelm. *A History of Philosophy.* Edited and translated by James H. Tufts. 2nd ed. New York: Macmillan, 1901.

Wink, Walter. *Engaging the Powers: Discernment and Resistance in a World of Domination.* Power Series. Minneapolis: Fortress, 1992.

Wittgenstein, Ludwig. *Culture and Value.* Edited by G. H. von Wright in collaboration with Heikki Nyman. Translated by Peter Winch. Chicago: University of Chicago Press; Oxford: Basil Blackwell, 1980.

———. *Notebooks, 1914-1916.* Edited by G. H. von Wright and G. E. M. Anscombe. Translated by G. E. M. Anscombe. New York: Harper and Row, Harper Torchbooks, 1969.

———. *On Certainty.* Edited by G. E. M. Anscombe and G. H. von Wright. Translated by Denis Paul and G. E. M. Anscombe. New York: Harper and Row, Harper Torchbooks, 1972.

———. *Philosophical Investigations.* Translated by G. E. M. Anscombe. New York: Macmillan, 1953, 1966, 1968.

———. *Remarks on Frazer's "Golden Bough."* Edited by Rush Rhees. Translated by A. C. Miles and revised by Rush Rhees. Atlantic Highlands, N.J.: Humanities Press, 1979.

———. *Tractatus Logico-Philosophicus.* Translated by D. F. Pears and B. F. McGuinness. Introduction by Bertrand Russell. London: Routledge and Kegan Paul, 1961.

———. *Zettel.* Edited by G. E. M. Anscombe and G. H. von Wright. Translated by G. E. M. Anscombe. Los Angeles: University of California Press, 1970.

Wojtyla, Karol (Pope John Paul II). *Crossing the Threshold of Hope.* Edited by Vittorio Messori. Translated by Jenny McPhee and Martha McPhee. New York: Knopf, 1994.

———. *Fides et Ratio: On the Relationship between Faith and Reason.* Encyclical letter. Boston: Pauline Books and Media, 1998.

———. *The Redeemer of Man: Redemptor Hominis.* Encyclical letter. Boston: Pauline Books and Media, 1979.

———. *Sources of Renewal: The Implementation of the Second Vatican Council.* Translated by P. S. Falla. San Francisco: Harper and Row, 1980.

———. *Springtime of Evangelization: The Complete Texts of the Holy Father's 1998 ad Limina Addresses to the Bishops of the United States.* Edited and introduction by Rev. Thomas D. Williams, L.C. Preface by Francis Cardinal George, O.M.I. Foreword by Rev. Richard John Neuhaus. San Francisco: Ignatius, 1999.

Wolin, Richard. *The Politics of Being: The Political Thought of Martin Heidegger.* New York: Columbia University Press, 1990.

Wolin, Sheldon S. "On the Theory and Practice of Power." In *After Foucault: Humanistic Knowledge, Postmodern Challenges,* edited by Jonathan Arac, pp. 179-201. New Brunswick, N.J.: Rutgers University Press, 1988.

Wolters, Albert M. *Creation Regained: Biblical Basics for a Reformational Worldview.* Grand Rapids: Eerdmans, 1985.

———. "Dutch Neo-Calvinism: Worldview, Philosophy and Rationality." In *Rationality in the Calvinian Tradition,* edited by Hendrik Hart, Johan Van Der Hoeven, and Nicholas Wolterstorff, pp. 113-31. Christian Studies Today. Lanham, Md.: University Press of America, 1983.

———. "The Intellectual Milieu of Herman Dooyeweerd." In *The Legacy of Herman Dooyeweerd: Reflections on Critical Philosophy in the Christian Tradition,* edited by C. T. McIntire, pp. 4-10. Lanham, Md.: University Press of America, 1985.

———. "On the Idea of Worldview and Its Relation to Philosophy." In *Stained Glass: Worldviews and Social Science,* edited by Paul A. Marshall, Sander Griffioen, and Richard J. Mouw, pp. 14-25. Christian Studies Today. Lanham, Md.: University Press of America, 1989.

———. "'Weltanschauung' in the History of Ideas: Preliminary Notes." N.d. Photocopy.

Wolterstorff, Nicholas. "The Grace That Shaped My Life." In *Philosophers Who Believe: The Spiritual Journeys of Eleven Leading Thinkers,* edited by Kelly James Clark, pp. 259-75. Downers Grove, Ill.: InterVarsity, 1993.

———. "On Christian Learning." In *Stained Glass: Worldviews and Social Science,* edited by Paul A. Marshall, Sander Griffioen, and Richard J. Mouw, pp. 56-80. Christian Studies Today. Lanham, Md.: University Press of America, 1989.

Wright, N. T. *The New Testament and the People of God.* Christian Origins and the Question of God, vol. 1. Minneapolis: Fortress, 1992.

———. *Jesus and the Victory of God.* Vol. 2 of *Christian Origins and the Question of God.* Minneapolis: Fortress, 1996.

Young-Bruehl, Elisabeth. *Freedom and Karl Jaspers' Philosophy.* New Haven: Yale University Press, 1981.

Zylstra, Henry. *Testament of Vision.* Grand Rapids: Eerdmans, 1958.

Index

249-50; in G. W. F. Hegel, 68-73, 104; in Martin Heidegger, 128-46, 147; and hermeneutics, 310-21; in Edmund Husserl, 108-21, 146; in Karl Jaspers, 121-28, 147; in C. G. Jung, 218-21, 250; in Immanuel Kant, 58-59; in Michael Kearney, 239-44, 251-52; in Søren Kierkegaard, 73-82, 104-5; in Thomas Kuhn, 196-206, 207-8; in Thomas Luckmann, 227-32, 250-51; in Karl Mannheim, 222-27, 250; in Karl Marx, 233-38, 251; and narrative, 297-303; and natural sciences, 187-208; in Friedrich Nietzsche, 98-103, 106-7; and Orthodoxy, 44-46; in Michael Polanyi, 188-95, 206-7; and postmodernism, 173-85, 186; and problem of relativism, 256-

58; and psychology, 211-22; and reason, 303-10; in Robert Redfield, 245-49, 252; and semiotics, 292-97; and social sciences, 209-52; and sociology, 222-38; theoretical relativity of, 253-56; in Ludwig Wittgenstein, 148-62, 185. *See also* Christian worldview; *Weltanschauung;* Worldviews

Worldviews: impact on academic disciplines, 328-29; tests of, 327-28; and worldview theorizing, 253-59. *See also* Christian worldview; *Weltanschauung;* Worldview

Wright, N. T., 324

Zylstra, Henry, 276